FUNDAMENTALS OF COMPUTERS

ABOUT THE AUTHOR

E Balagurusamy, former Vice Chancellor, Anna University, Chennai, is currently Member, Union Public Service Commission, New Delhi. He is a teacher, trainer, and consultant in the fields of Information Technology and Management. He holds an ME (Hons) in Electrical Engineering and PhD in Systems Engineering from the Indian Institute of Technology, Roorkee. His areas of interest include Object-Oriented Software Engineering, Electronic Business, Technology Management, Business Process Re-engineering, and Total Quality Management.

A prolific writer, he has authored a large number of research papers and several books. His best selling books, among others, include:

- Programming in C#, 2e
- Programming in Java, 3e
- Programming in ANSI C, 4e
- Object-Oriented Programming with C++, 4e
- Programming in BASIC, 3e
- Numerical Methods
- Reliability Engineering

A recipient of numerous honours and awards, he has been listed in the Directory of Who's Who of Intellectuals and in the Directory of Distinguished Leaders in Education.

FUNDAMENTALS OF COMPUTERS

E Balagurusamy
Member
Union Public Service Commission

McGraw Hill Education (India) Private Limited

Published by McGraw Hill Education (India) Private Limited,
Anjana Complex No.: 5/90 A, Butt Road, St. Thomas Mount, Chennai – 600016, Tamil Nadu, India.

FUNDAMENTALS OF COMPUTERS

24th reprint 2021
RZCRRDRJRQADX

ISBN (13 digits): 978-0-07-014160-5
ISBN (10 digits): 0-07-014160-6

25 26 27 28 29 APO 25 24 23 22 21

Managing Director: *Lalit Singh*
Assistant Manager—Production Services: *Atul Gupta*
General Manager—Production: *Rajender P Ghansela*
Manager—Production: *Reji Kumar*

Typeset at BukPrint India, B 180A, Guru Nanak Pura, Laxmi Nagar, New Delhi 110092, and,
Printed and Bound in India at A.P Offset Pvt. Ltd., Zulfe Bengal, Dilshad Garden, New Delhi 110095.

Visit us at: www.mheducation.co.in
Toll free in India: **1800 103 5875**
Write to us at: info.india@mheducation.com
CIN: U80302TN2010PTC111532

PREFACE

We live in a technology-driven world, where almost everything is automated. The last two decades have seen a renaissance in the world of innovations. We have seen doctors perform surgery by sitting miles away from their patients. The fashion industry is soon to replace supermodels with robots (one such, the HRP-4C, was recently unveiled in Tokyo). There are similar advances being made in every field, all of whose foundations are based on computers.

It can often be perplexing for a beginner to keep pace with such developments. To be lost in the world of codes and bytes can be nerve-racking. And this is where a text book of this nature comes in. Written assuming absolutely no prior knowledge of computers, this book carries the reader through the world of Computers in a simple and structured manner.

There are certain things that this book achieves and some it doesn't. If you are looking for an exhaustive discussion on topics like DBMS and Computer Networks, this book is not meant for you. I would rather have you pick up books written by a Forouzan or a Gehrke. This book will not make you go through miles of C programming codes. So, if you want a good discussion on C implementation, I would rather have you pick my ANSI C book.

What this book does aim to achieve is to give you an eye opener, a mild introduction, to the fascinating world of Computers. It will show you the basic building blocks of a computer, how they interact among each other, what are the various input and output devices and how a computer interprets and understands your language. It also gives an introduction to the various software that are popularly used on desktop computers. Seeing the importance of programming in today's world, I have also provided a chapter on C programming, which serves as an introduction to this amazingly powerful language.

There indeed are several books that flood local book shops on this subject. So why should you use this one? The answer is simple; I haven't written this book keeping a specific audience in mind. Whether you are a school student, a budding engineer pursuing technical education, or simply an inquisitive being in search of an appropriate introduction to computers, chances are I have kept all your requirements in mind while writing. I have kept the language at a level that can be accessed by one and all, and yet kept the discussions thorough and focused.

More specifically, it can be used by the following:

- Students pursuing DCA, BSc (IT), BCA, MCA, MSc (IT), DOEACC 'O' Level courses
- Students pursuing first-year engineering course in computers
- Students pursuing BBA, MBA and MCM courses
- Students pursuing short-term courses in various IT training institutes
- Self-learners for acquiring knowledge on various computer components, be it software or hardware.

Finally, this book is for everyone who is either excited about computers or interested in knowing more about computers.

This book is impregnated with several salient features:

- A complete self-study material for obtaining basic knowledge and understanding of various hardware and software components of computers.
- Covers Microsoft Office suite of software such as MS Word and MS Excel in great detail.
- Concepts are explained using ample number of illustrations and screen shots for visualisation of the commands.

- A chapter dedicated for further reading on Programming concepts.
- Appendices on Multimedia and Computer Graphics.

The chapter organisation makes way for an easy graduation of topics from the very basic to seemingly complicated aspects of Computers. The first nine chapters elaborate the fundamentals of a computer system by delving on topics like Organisation, Architecture, Storage Systems, Computer Arithmetic, and Boolean Algebra. The next six chapters cover Software that we often use in our everyday life through chapters on Operating Systems, Database Management Systems, Computer Networks and Programming Languages. The concluding chapter on C Programming readies the reader to develop and implement C programs.

ONLINE LEARNING CENTRE

The accompanying web supplement to this book provides an additional resource for students and instructors. This domain is filled with entities like chapter wise PowerPoint slides, additional solved programming examples, and few case studies on C programming.

ACKNOWLEDGEMENTS

My sincere thanks are also due to the editorial and publishing professionals at Tata McGraw Hill for their keen interest and support in bringing out this book in record time. The readers of the book are encouraged to send their comments, queries and suggestions at the following email id—tmh.csefeedback@gmail.com (*kindly mention the title and author name in the subject line*).

E Balagurusamy

CONTENTS

WALKTHROUGH

CHAPTER 11

OPERATING SYSTEMS

Chapter Objectives

In this chapter, we will learn:

- The concept of operating systems.
- Various functions of operating systems.
- Different types of operating systems.
- How user interfaces are provided in an operating system.
- Highlights of some important operating systems.

Chapter Outline

Chapter Objectives

The objectives enable students to set tangible goals before they begin each chapter.

CHAPTER 8

BOOLEAN ALGEBRA OF SWITCHING CIRCUITS

Chapter Outline

Chapter Objectives

In this chapter, we will learn:

- The concept of Boolean algebra.
- Use of Boolean algebra in designing switching circuits.
- Different elements of Boolean algebra.
- Basic postulates and laws of Boolean algebra.
- Different operations used in Boolean algebra.
- The two different types of Boolean expressions.
- Importance of Venn diagrams.

8.1 INTRODUCTION

We face many situations where there are only two possible decisions 'YES' or 'NO' or two possible outcomes 'TRUE' or 'FALSE'. For instance, consider the following situations:

- A student can get admission in an engineering college *if and only if* he has studied mathematics in school and has secured an average of more than 60% of marks.
- A cheque is valid only if it is signed by the accounts officer and the director.
- The fire alarm in the office will sound if it senses heat or smoke.

Each of these statements contains three parts known as *propositions*. In the first one, the

Chapter Outline

A listing of topic headings is provided for each chapter, to help students organise the material in their own minds.

284 Fundamentals of Computers

Editing the document Editing a document generally involves the operations, such as selecting the text, moving and copying the text and deleting either the selected text or the entire text in the document window. For selecting the text, say "This is my word", in the mydoc document, we need to perform the following steps:

1. Open the mydoc — Microsoft Word window.
2. Set the insertion point before the word "This" in the document window, as shown in Fig. 12.9.

Fig. 12.9 Placing the insertion point

3. Press the left mouse button and drag the mouse pointer up to the desired level of the selection.
4. Release the left mouse button to complete the selection, as shown in Fig. 12.10.

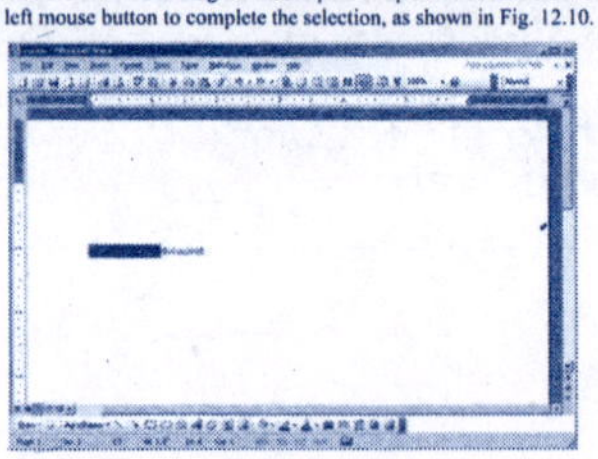

Fig. 12.10 Selecting the desired text in the document window

Note: *We can select the entire content of the document by either selecting Edit → Select All option or by pressing the Ctrl and A keys simultaneously.*

66 Fundamentals of Computers

- **Optical mouse** An optical mouse is a pointing input device in which the reflected light determines the movement of the cursor on the displayed screen. The upper portion of the optical mouse is similar to that of the mechanical mouse. The lower portion of the optical mouse consists of a ball having Light Emitting Diodes (LEDs), an optical sensor and a Digital Signal Processor (DSP). Figure 4.3 shows the lower portion of the optical mouse.

Fig. 4.3 The lower portion of the optical mouse

4.3.2 Trackball

Trackball is a pointing device that basically consists of a socket containing the ball, which can be rolled manually to move the cursor on the screen. The socket also contains sensors, which detect the movement of the ball. With the help of the trackball, we can change the position of the cursor on the screen by simply rotating the ball with our fingers or thumb. On the basis of size, the trackballs are classified into two types, small trackball and large trackball. The small trackballs are commonly used in portable computers, whereas the large trackballs find their use in the desktop computer systems, which are used for computer-aided designing. One of the most important advantages of the trackball is that it can be placed on different surfaces, such as desk, mouse pad and even user's hand. The trackball finds its use as a game controller in games like Centipede, Golden Tee and Marble Madness. Figure 4.4 shows the trackball placed on a desk.

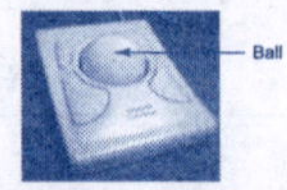

Fig. 4.4 The trackball on the desk

4.3.3 Light Pen

Light pen is an electro-optical pointing device that is used for selecting the objects on the display screen with the help of a light sensitive pen. It is generally connected to the Visual Display Unit (VDU) of the computer system. The pen contains a light-sensitive diode, which helps in pointing the objects displayed on the screen. Using a light pen, we can directly draw the objects on the screen by holding it in our hand. When the tip of the light pen is brought in contact with the screen, the light coming from the screen causes a pulse to be generated in the pen which in turn causes the processor to identify the position pointed to by the pen.

Light pens provide all the capabilities of a mouse. They do not require any pad or horizontal surface and therefore, are useful when desk space is limited. Figure 4.5 shows the light pen attached to a computer system.

Fig. 4.5 The light pen

Clear Illustrations

Figures and Tables interspersed throughout the text, illustrate key concepts.

Programming Languages 335

important high-level programming languages of this era are **Java, VB** and **C#**. Most of the programming languages of this era employed object-oriented programming paradigm for designing and developing robust and reliable software applications.

Table 13.1 summarises the history of development of programming languages:

Table 13.1 The evolution of programming languages

Period of employment	Programming language	Characteristics
1940s	Machine language	• Machine dependent • Faster execution • Difficult to use and understand • More prone to errors
1950s	Assembly language	• Machine dependent • Faster execution • More prone to errors • Relatively simple to use
1950–1970	FORTRAN, LISP, COBOL, ALGOL 60, BASIC, APL	• High-level languages • Easy to develop and understand programs • Less prone to errors
1970–1990	C, C++, Forth, Prolog, Smalltalk, Ada, Perl, SQL	• Very high-level languages • Easier to learn • Highly portable
1990s	Java, HTML, VB, PHP, XML, C #	• Internet-based languages • Object-oriented languages • More efficient • Reliable and robust

13.3 GENERATIONS OF PROGRAMMING LANGUAGES

Programming languages have been developed over the years in a phased manner. Each phase of development has made the programming languages more user-friendly, easier to use and more powerful. Each phase of improvement made in the development of the programming languages can be referred as a *generation*. The programming languages, in terms of their performance, reliability and robustness can be grouped into five different generations.

- First generation languages (1GL)
- Second generation languages (2GL)
- Third generation languages (3GL)
- Fourth generation languages (4GL)
- Fifth generation languages (5GL)

2.1 INTRODUCTION

Computer organisation and computer architecture are two different but related, important concepts that are required to describe a computer system. *Computer architecture* refers to the definition of basic attributes of hardware components and their interconnections, in order to achieve certain specified goals in terms of functions and performance. The attributes may include, for example the instruction set, data representation, I/O mechanisms, etc. The architecture basically defines the logical structure of a computer system.

Computer organisation refers to the design and physical arrangement of various hardware units to work in tandem, in an orderly manner, in order to achieve the goals specified in the architecture. For a given architecture, there could be many

Introduction

Each chapter opening section contains an introduction providing the students with an overview of the topics to be presented within the chapter.

Chapter Summary

Summary serves as an ideal mini-study guide, for reviewing the major concepts in the chapter prior to examinations.

Chapter Summary

A collection of networks in which a large number of computers are connected to each other is known as the Internet. The Internet marked its beginning with a network known as ARPAnet which was developed at Advanced Research Projects Agency (ARPA) of the U S in 1969. The first protocol used on the ARPAnet was TCP/IP. From 1975 to 1982, different scientists developed many new networks, such as Telnet, Usenet and Eunet. All these continuous developments led to the eventual development of the Internet.

The Internet can be used to gather information on a wide variety of topics. Today the Internet is used in many fields such as business, education and entertainment. In business, the most popular use of the Internet is e-business through which an organisation and a consumer can communicate with each other and perform business transactions. In education field, the students use discussion forums and newsgroups on the Internet to gain specific information. The internet also extends its application in communication field by providing services such as e-mail and instant messaging through which a person at one location can communicate to another person located at a remote place. The Internet also provides entertainment through games, music and movies.

To access the Internet and the WWW, the user requires a software known as web browser. Some commonly used web browsers are IE, Netscape Navigator and Mozilla Firefox. To gather information from the Internet, a user has to search for the information on the Internet. This is done with the help of search engines provided on the Internet. The most commonly used search engines are www.google.com, www.altavista.com and www.askjeeves.com.

Key Terms to Remember

- **Data communication**: It is the process of transmission of data from the source computer to the destination computer.
- **Modem**: It is a device that converts outgoing digital signal into analog signal for onward transmission and converts incoming analog signal into digital signal suitable for the computer.
- **LAN**: It is a group of interconnected computers covering a small area such as a building.
- **WAN**: It usually connects the computers in a large area such as country, continents etc.
- **MAN**: It is the regional area network that typically connects the computers within a city, campus etc.
- **Internet**: It is the global network, which comprises of various networks spread over globally.
- **Intranet**: It is the private network of computers, usually contained within an organisation.
- **CSN**: CSN consists of two computers, client computer and server computer, where the server computer simply receives the request from the client computer and processes these requests.
- **PPN**: In PPN, every computer communicates directly with other computers by sending and receiving the requests.
- **Network topology**: The network topology is the physical arrangement of the computers connected with each other in a network such as ring, star, bus, hierarchical and hybrid.
- **Network protocol**: The network protocol is the standard according to which different computers over the network communicate with each other.
- **Network media**: It is the physical media used to connect the computer nodes together.
- **Network software**: It is a computer program that aids the computers to communicate with each other effectively.

Key Terms to Remember

Key terms give a list of the important words discussed in the chapter.

Review Questions

Fill in the Blanks

1. A computer system consists of two types of components, ____________ components and ____________ components.
2. Computer software is classified into two categories, namely, ____________ and ____________.
3. System software consists of two groups of programs: ____________ and ____________.
4. ____________ is responsible for managing the allocation of devices and resources to the various processes.
5. Device driver acts as a translator between the ____________ and the ____________.
6. A computer system requires special software called ____________ in order to interact with the I/O devices.
7. Language translator converts the high-level language program into the low-level program called ____________.
8. Application software includes two types programs: ____________ and ____________.
9. ____________ enables you to enter text in the document in a particular format.
10. Spreadsheet is generally used to calculate the values stored in a cell by applying ____________ on the values of other cells.
11. Database refers to a set of records, which are stored in a ____________ in the computer system.
12. In the hierarchical model, records are arranged in form of a ____________ in which each record is attached with one parent node and one or more children node.
13. Desktop publishing system is also known as ____________.
14. Pseudocode is not written using any specific ____________ of a programming language.
15. ____________ is a pictorial representation of a process, which describes the sequence and flow of the control and information in a process
16. In the ____________ structure, multiple statements are written in a simple sequence in the program.

Multiple Choice Questions

1. Which of the following is a hardware device?
   A. Device driver B. Barcode reader C. Interpreter D. Linker
2. A device driver acts as an interface between:
   A. End-user and I/O device B. Application software and I/O device
   C. Application software and operating system D. Operating system and I/O device
3. Which of the following software components enables a user to store data in the form of tables?
   A. Spreadsheet B. Editor C. DBMS D. Word processor
4. Which of the following is not a system software?
   A. Linkers B. Device drivers C. Operating system D. Word processor
5. Which of the following software helps the users to detect the errors while executing a program?
   A. Language Translator B. Debugger C. Loader D. Linker
6. Which of the following software runs at the basic level of computer system?
   A. Application software B. System software C. User software D. All of the above

Review Questions

Readers can assess their knowledge by answering Fill in the Blanks and Multiple Choice Questions, provided under the heading 'Review Questions'

Output Devices 93

Discussion Questions

1. What is an output device? Why is it a vital part of computer hardware?
2. Name some of the output devices, which are commonly used with the computer system.
3. Define a display monitor.
4. Name the different types of monitors available in the market.
5. Explain the use of a printer in a computer system.
6. Differentiate between an impact printer and a non-impact printer. Give one example of each.
7. Briefly explain the different types of impact printers.
8. Explain the different types of non-impact printers.
9. What are the advantages and disadvantages of a daisy wheel printer?
10. What are the characteristics of a laser printer?
11. What is the use of plotters?
12. Define a plotter. Explain at least two types of plotters.
13. What are the advantages and disadvantages of a CRT monitor?
14. Which is a better monitor—a CRT or a TFT? State the reasons as well.
15. Explain the term voice response system and list different types used today.
16. What is a projector? Why is it needed?
17. What are the different types of projector?
18. State the characteristics on the basis of which the efficiency of a printer can be measured.
19. Distinguish between a printer and a plotter.
20. Define a terminal.
21. Explain the different types of terminals.
22. What do you mean by speech synthesis?
23. Draw a diagram to show the internal components of a CRT.
24. What are the special purpose printers? What are their applications?
25. State some applications where dumb terminals may be used.

Discussion Questions

Discussion questions, at the end of each chapter, allow a student to review the key concepts and assess his or her understanding.

Example 7.59 *Multiply the number 0.350000 E40 by 0.500000 E70.*

Solution

E_z = 110
f_y = 0.175000
z = 0.175000 E110

Example 7.60 *Divide the number 0.875000 E–18 by 0.200000 E95.*

Solution

E_z = – 18 – 95 = – 113
f_z = 0.875000 ÷ 0.200000
= 4.375000
z = 4.375000 E–113
= 0.437500 E–114

Example 7.61 *Subtract 0.499998 from 0.500000.*

Solution

f_x = 0.500000
f_y = 0.499998
$f_x - f_y$ = 0.000002
E_z = 0
Thus, z = 0.000002×10^0
= 0.200000×10^{-5}

Example 7.62 *Associative law for addition.*

Solution

Let $x = 0.456732 \times 10^{-2}$,
$y = 0.243451$,
$z = -0.248000$
$(x + y) = 0.004567 + 0.243451 = 0.248018$
$(x + y) + z = 0.248018 - 0.248000 = 0.000018 = 0.180000 \times 10^{-4}$
$(y + z) = 0.243451 - 0.248000 = -0.004549 = -0.4549 \times 10^{-2}$
$x + (y + z) = (0.456732 - 0.454900)\ 10^{-2} = 0.183200 \times 10^{-2}$

Thus,

$(x + y) + z \neq x + (y + z)$

7.13 LAWS OF ARITHMETIC

The different arithmetic laws hold true for addition as well multiplication operations. The arithmetic laws can be divided into the following four major categories:

Solved Examples

Provided at appropriate locations, solved examples aid in learning the technique of applying concepts to practical problems.

Example 16.3 *Write a program to determine whether the year entered by the user is a leap year or not.*

Solution: The following program determines whether the year is a leap year or not:

```
#include<stdio.h>
#include<conio.h>
void main()
{
int yr;
clrscr();
printf("Enter the year");
scanf("%d",&yr);
if(yr%100==0)
{
      if(yr%400==0)
            printf("\n Year is leap year");
      else
            printf("\n Year is not leap year");
}
else
{
      if(yr%4==0)
            printf("\n Leap year");
      else
            printf("\n Not a leap year");
}
getch();
}
```

In the above code, variable *yr* is taken as an integer data type that stores the value of the year entered by the user. The nested **if else** statements are used to determine whether the year entered by the user is a leap year or not and the result is displayed on the screen by using the **printf** statement.

Figure 16.11 shows the output of the above program.

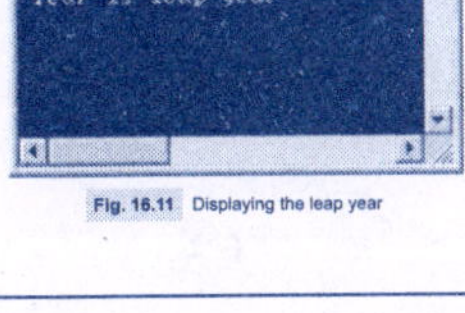

Fig. 16.11 Displaying the leap year

Sample Programs

Chapter 16 on Introduction to C Programming depicts implementation of C programming concepts.

APPENDIX A

MULTIMEDIA

A.1 INTRODUCTION

Multimedia is one of the most commonly used terms in the entertainment industry, which produces various entertainment products such as movies and video games. It is defined as a system, which represents information through various media components, such as music, video, sound, text and images.

Multimedia is of two types, *interactive multimedia* and *non-interactive multimedia*. Interactive multimedia refers to the multimedia, which runs on the basis of the instructions provided by the end user. It consists of the various user interfaces such as command buttons and audio commands that enable an end user to interact with the multimedia application. The interactive multimedia is also kno: n as *non-linear multimedia*. E-learning applications, which include text images and audio, are good examples of interactive multimedia. The non-interactive multimedia does not contain any user interface and runs on the basis of instructions and information stored in the storage medium of computer system. The non-interactive multimedia is generally known as *linear multimedia*. Cartoon films are a very good example of non-interactive multimedia system.

Figure A.1 shows the interactive and the non-interactive multimedia systems.

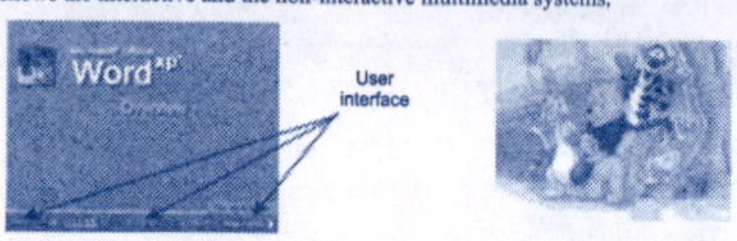

Interactive Multimedia   Non-interactive Multimedia

Fig. A.1 Interactive and non-interactive multimedia

A.2 IMPORTANT MULTIMEDIA ISSUES

Whenever we need to develop a multimedia product, which consists of multiple media components, we must take care of the different issues pertaining to these media components, such as text, audio, graphics and video. The issues could be related to the ownership and publication of the multimedia product. The various issues are:

- **Copyright issue** Copyright issue is related to the protection of the ownership of a publishing product. Copyright can be defined as a collection of rights that permits or prohibits the use of the

APPENDIX B

COMPUTER GRAPHICS

B.1 INTRODUCTION

Computer graphics is a branch of computer science that deals with the creation and manipulation of visual information on a computer system. It involves the creation of both 2-dimensional (2D) and 3-dimensional (3D) graphics. Graphics can be created on a computer system with the help of special graphics software, such as Macromedia Flash and Corel draw. Computer graphics involves the use of various techniques that are used develop a good quality image of an object. Computer graphics created on the computers can be used to represent surfaces of different shapes and represent the motion in bodies. The images created can also be edited using the same computer programs in which they were created.

The various application areas of computer graphics are:

- **Illustrations** Illustration is used to visually represent a subject or a particular situation in the form of line drawing or painting. There are several graphics software available that allow the users to create illustrations. The simplest of all these software is MS Paint that comes bundled in Microsoft operating systems as a utility software.
- **Designs** Computer-aided Design (CAD) and Computer-aided Modeling (CAM) have revolutionized the way engineering drawings are created these days. Special CAD / CAM software are available that provide a robust user-interface for creating engineering drawings. Some of these software also provide a simulated environment for the user to test their designs.
- **Simulations** Computer graphics are being increasingly used for education and training purposes where the trainees are taught using a simulated environment The simulated environment is rich with graphics and moving pictures that recreate a real-life situation in the best possible manner. One of most common examples of using simulation is a flight simulator, which aids the pilots in running an aircraft in a simulated environment.
- **Animations** Computer graphics are also used for creating animations and cartoon characters that are represented in the form of an animated picture.

B.2 DISPLAY DEVICES

Display device refers to an electronic device, which is used to display the videos and images created using computer programs. In a computer system, the most common display device is a computer monitor. The computer monitor has a specific size, which is determined according to the distance between the two opposite corners of the screen. A display device could be based on different hardware technologies like

Useful Appendices

Appendix A and B provide useful information on Multimedia and Computer Graphics.

CHAPTER 1

UNDERSTANDING THE COMPUTER

Chapter Outline

Chapter Objectives

In this chapter, we will learn:

- How computers receive, store and process data to generate useful information.
- The improvements in functioning of computers in the last few decades.
- The five generations of computers.
- How to classify computers on the basis of operating principles, applications and size.
- The computer system as a combination of hardware, software, data and people.
- The use of computers in different fields.

1.1 INTRODUCTION

A computer is an *electronic machine* that takes input from the user, processes the given input and generates output in the form of useful information. A computer accepts input in different forms such as data, programs and user reply. *Data* refer to the raw details that need to be processed to generate some useful *information*. Programs refer to the set of instructions that can be executed by the computer in sequential or non-sequential manner. User reply is the input provided by the user in response to a question asked by the computer. The main task of a computer system is to process the given input of any type in an efficient manner. Therefore, computer is also known by various other names such as data processing unit, data processor and data processing system.

A computer includes various devices that function as an integrated system to perform several tasks described above. These devices are:

Central Processing Unit (CPU) It is the processor of the computer that is responsible for controlling and executing instructions in the computer. It is considered as the most significant component of the computer. It is the "brain" of the computer.

Monitor It is a screen, which displays information in visual form, after receiving the video signals from the computer.

Keyboard and Mouse These are the devices, which are used by the computer, for receiving input from the user.

Figure 1.1 shows the various components of a computer.

The unique capabilities and characteristics of a computer have made it very popular among its various users, including engineers, managers, accountants, teachers, students, etc. The characteristics and capabilities of a modern digital computer include, among others:

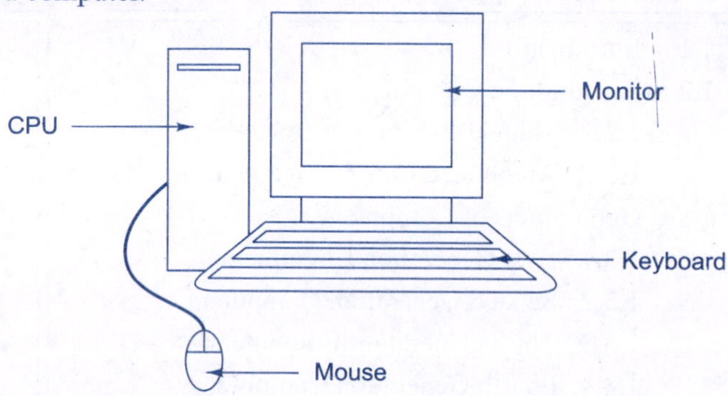

Fig. 1.1 The components of computer

Speed A computer is a fast electronic device that can solve large and complex problems in few seconds. The speed of a computer generally depends upon its hardware configuration.

Storage capacity A computer can store huge amount of data in its different storage components in many different formats. The storage area of a computer system is generally divided into two categories, main memory and secondary storage.

Accuracy A computer carries out calculations with great accuracy. The accuracy achieved by a computer depends upon its hardware configuration and the instructions.

Reliability A computer produces results with no error. Most of the errors generated in the computer are human errors that are created by the user itself. Therefore, they are very trustworthy machines.

Versatility Computers are versatile machines. They can perform many different tasks and can be used for many different purposes.

Diligence Computers can perform repetitive calculations any number of times with the same accuracy. Computers do not suffer from human traits, such as tiredness, fatigue, lack of concentration, etc.

Although computers are highly reliable and versatile machines, they do possess certain limitations. Since computers are capable of doing only what they are instructed to do, any wrong instruction (or faulty logic) or any wrong data may result in erroneous output. This is popularly known as "Garbage-In, Garbage-Out" (GIGO).

Computer is a dumb machine and therefore lacks "common sense". Anything it does is a result of human instructions. It carries out instructions as long as it can understand them, no matter whether they are right or wrong.

Although computers can be instructed to make certain decisions based on mathematical or logical equations, they cannot make decisions in situations where qualitative considerations are involved.

1.2 EVOLUTION OF COMPUTERS

In ancient times, people used different devices and methods for performing the computing operations. However, these devices and methods used for calculations were not very fast and accurate. This fact had led to the invention of computer. The computer was developed to produce accurate results at a very fast speed.

The computer has gone through several phases of technological development. We can understand these developments by just looking at the history of computers. Before the invention of any type of calculating device, people carried out simple arithmetic calculations, such as addition and subtraction on their fingers. This method of counting is still quite preferred in schools as it teaches the children about how to count. In ancient times, people also started using stones for representing numbers and carrying out simple calculations. These stones were then kept at a place suitable for adding and subtracting more stones. In that way, people performed simple arithmetic calculations. However, the use of stones did not constitute the only method of performing calculation at that time. People also used other devices—such as notches in a stick, knots in a rope, etc.—for carrying out simple calculations. However, the purpose of each device was to represent numbers. Some of the early computing devices were manually operated, while the later computing devices were completely automated.

1.2.1 Manual Computing Devices

The idea of using stones for representing numbers and putting them at a place for performing simple calculations invented the device called *sand table*. A sand table was a device that arranged stones in three channels in the sand. Each channel could have a maximum of 10 stones. The addition operation was performed on this device by incrementing the count of right hand channel by one and by adding one stone in it. As soon as the right hand channel reached its maximum capacity, the stones were removed from that channel and one stone was added to the left hand channel. Figure 1.2 shows the idea of sand table used for the purpose of calculations.

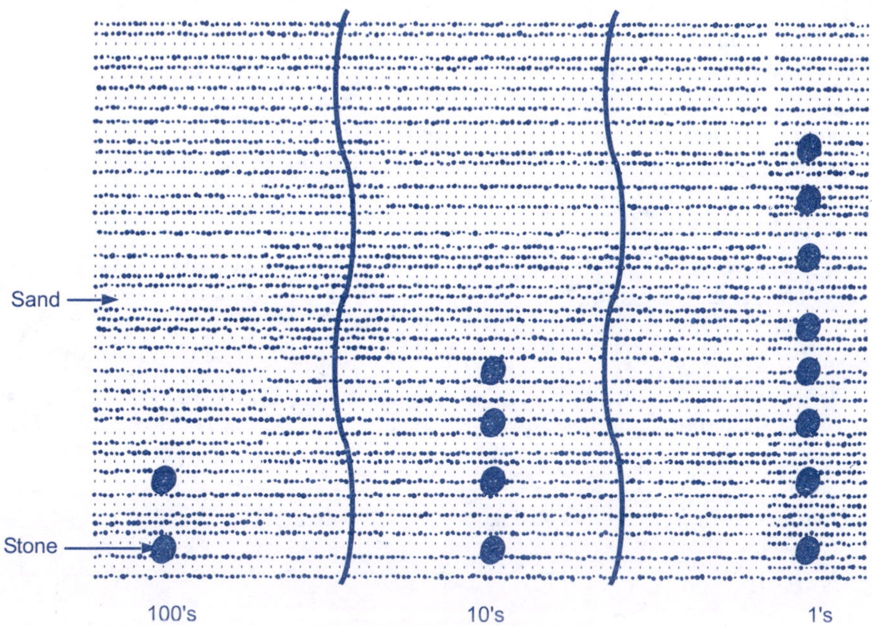

Fig. 1.2 A sand table

The idea of sand table led to the development of a fast calculating device of that time, which was known as *abacus*. Unlike the sand table, abacus replaced the sand frame with a wooden frame, the grooves with wires and the stones with beads. An abacus was also known as a *counting frame* and became popular among the people in Asia Minor around 5000 years back. This device is still in use in many parts of the world. In this device, the wooden frame consists of many wires, with beads sliding on them. The user of an abacus can perform arithmetic operations by sliding the beads on the wires by hand. Figure 1.3 shows an abacus consisting of beads on different wires of a wooden frame.

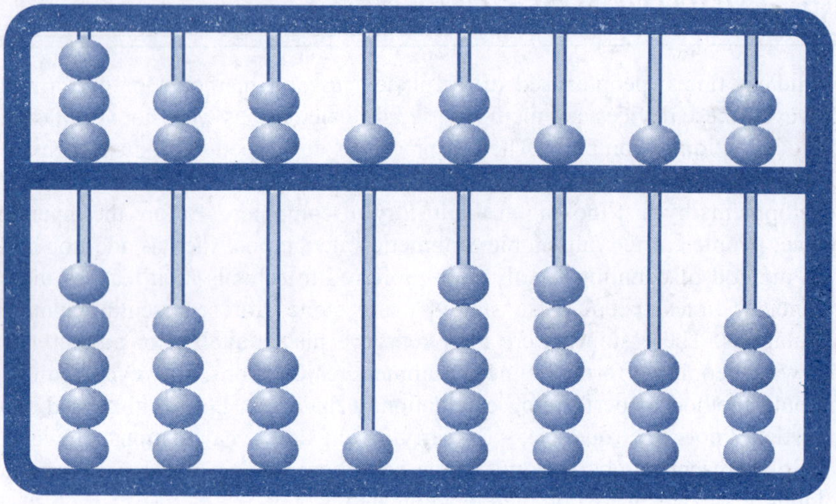

Fig. 1.3 An abacus

Another complicated manual computing device called *napier bones* was developed by **John Napier** in the year 1614. This device was specially designed for the multiplication and quotient of numbers. Napier bones consisted of a board whose left edge was divided into 9 squares. These 9 squares were used to hold the numbers from 1 to 9. It also consisted of 10 rods, which were made up of the strips of ivory bones. The multiplication of two numbers with Napier bones could be performed in a faster manner, if one of the numbers involved in multiplication was of a single digit only. Figure 1.4 shows the arrangement of bones for the multiplication of two numbers; one is of four digits and the other of one digit.

1	5	4	3	7
2	1/0	0/8	/6	1/4
3	1/5	1/2	0/9	2/1
4	2/0	1/6	1/2	2/8
5	2/5	2/0	1/5	3/5
6	3/0	2/4	1/8	4/2
7	3/5	2/8	2/1	4/9
8	4/0	3/2	2/4	5/6
9	4/5	3/6	2/7	6/3

Fig. 1.4 The napier bones

Figure 1.4 shows the process of multiplying the number 5437 with any other number of single digit. For instance, suppose we want to multiply 5437 with 6. The computation process with this device starts with the rightmost bone and proceeds towards the left bones. The last digit in the 6th row of the 7-bone is 2, so the rightmost digit of the multiplication output is 2. After this, add the two adjacent numbers in the same row forming the parallelogram, which are 8 and 4. The addition of these two numbers is 12, so the next rightmost digit of the multiplication output is 2. Now, we have obtained 22 with a carry 1. Similarly, add the next two adjacent numbers and the carry to obtain the digit 6. At this stage, we have obtained 622 with no carry. We can proceed like this to obtain the final answer as 32622.

The idea of using bones to carry out the multiplication of numbers was modified by **Edmund Gunter** in 1620 to produce a device known as *slide rule*. This device consisted of two sets of graduated scales, which could slide over each other. The slide rule was developed not only for performing multiplication and division of numbers, but also for various scientific functions, such as logarithms, trigonometry, roots, etc.

Apart from these manual computing devices, many other devices were also developed for computation purposes. Some of these devices were *pascaline*, *stepped reckoner*, *punch card system* etc. Pascaline was a calculator developed by **Blaise Pascal** in 1642. It was also known as a numerical wheel calculator. This device contained a set of toothed wheels that could be operated by hand. Pascaline was designed to handle numbers up to 999,999.999. Pascaline was further improved by German mathematician **Gottfried Wilhem Von Leibriz** to produce a device, called stepped reckoner. *Stepped reckoner* was able to perform the multiplication and division of numbers as well as calculation of the square root of a number.

1.2.2 Automated Computing Devices

Charles Babbage, a professor of mathematics at the Cambridge University, made some worthwhile efforts towards automatic computing. He is also considered to be the *father of modern computer*. In 1812, Charles Babbage decided to automate the repeated series of steps needed in tabulating various functions, such as polynomial, logarithmic and trigonometric. In 1822, he presented a working model of his concept with the help of an automatic mechanical computing machine. He named the automatic mechanical computing machine as *difference engine*. In 1823, Babbage made it more automatic by providing the feature of printing the tabulated results. Babbage did not stop here and started working on developing the *analytical engine*.

The analytical engine was considered as the completely automatic general-purpose programmable digital computer. The analytical engine was the first device that used all the features of a modern digital computer, which include an input unit, an output unit, a storage unit, a processor and a control unit. This engine was designed to perform various mathematical operations by getting two sets of inputs from the user. The first set of input is a program that contains a set of instructions to operate on the data. The other set of input contains the list of variables used in the program or data. The analytical engine built by Babbage in 1833 was digital, programmable and automatic. However, it was a slow engine that took almost 3 minutes to multiply two numbers of twenty figures each.

In 1937, an American mathematician, **Howard Aiken** designed *MARK I* and completed it in the year 1944. MARK I was one of the well-known early computers that could perform the multiplication of two numbers of twenty figures in just 6 seconds. Hence, as compared to the analytical engine, MARK I performed calculations at a much faster speed. However, this computer was also not considered very fast from the user's point of view because it printed the results of calculations at the rate of one result per 5 seconds. Also, MARK I computer was noisy and large in size.

In the year 1944, a British mathematician, **Alan Mathison** developed the first pure electronic digital programmable computer. This computer was known as *Colossus*. Colossus was a special purpose electronic device that used the vacuum tube technology in performing different operations. It was designed to perform only some specific functions.

The Electronic Numerical Integrator And Calculator (*ENIAC*) was another general-purpose electronic digital computer developed at the Moore School of Engineering of the University of Pennsylvania by **John Ecker**, **John Mauchly** and their team in the year 1946. This computer also used the vacuum tube technology in constructing the basic circuits. It was a general purpose computer that was capable of solving all types of computing problems. It included all the features and components of a modern digital computer. The internal hardware structure of ENIAC included 17,468 vacuum tubes, 1,500 relays, 70,000 registers, 7,200 crystal diodes and 10,000 capacitors. It was a bulky computer and operated at 1000 times more speed than that of MARK I computer. ENIAC was designed to perform simple arithmetic operations as well as some advanced operations, such as separating the sign of a number and comparing different numbers to check whether they are equal or not. The computer used the decimal number system for representing and processing values.

In 1949, another electronic computer that used the binary number system for representing and processing values was introduced. This computer was known as Electronic Discrete Variable Automatic Computer (*EDVAC*). EDVAC was also invented by John Eckert and John Mauchly and was considered as the successor of ENIAC. EDVAC was the first computer that worked on the principle of stored program. The stored program computer considers the programs and data stored in the memory as the string of binary numbers. Therefore, programs and data stored in the memory are indistinguishable inputs for the computer. The different hardware components of EDVAC were magnetic tape, control unit, dispatcher unit, processor, timer, dual memory and three temporary tanks to hold a single word.

Electronic Delay Storage Automatic Calculator (*EDSAC*) was another early British electronic computer developed by **Maurice Wilkes** and his team at the University of Cambridge Mathematical Laboratory in 1949. It also used the vacuum tube technology in constructing the basic logic circuits and mercury delay lines for constructing the memory of a computer. The typical input and output unit of this computer system was punch card and teleprinter respectively. These computer systems were only able to carry out 650 instructions per second. Therefore, these computers were not considered as fast computing devices.

During 1950s, Eckert-Mauchly Computer Corporation, a company of John Eckert and John Mauchly, made some serious efforts in the field of automated computing. In 1951, the company invented the first commercial computer that was known as Universal Automatic Computer (*UNIVAC*). This computer was a bulky computer that used 5200 vacuum tubes for constructing the basic logic circuits. The mercury data lines were used to construct the memory for storing data and programs. UNIVAC was able to process numbers as well as alphabetic characters in an efficient manner. The important feature of UNIVAC—that made it unique among other well-known early computers—was that it provided separate processes for handling input/output and processing functions.

1.3 GENERATIONS OF COMPUTERS

Over the years, various computing devices were invented that enabled the people to solve different types of problems. All these computing devices can be classified into several generations. These generations refer to the phases of improvement made to different computing devices. The different phases of improvement made to computing devices resulted in a small, cheap, fast, reliable and productive computer. The technological development in the field of computers not only refers to the improvements made to the hardware technologies, but also the improvements made to the software technologies. The history of computer development is often discussed in terms of different generation of computers, as listed below.

- First generation computers
- Second generation computers

- Third generation computers
- Fourth generation computers
- Fifth generation computers

1.3.1 First Generation Computers

The first generation computers were employed during the period 1940–1956. These computers used the *vacuum tubes* technology for calculation as well as for storage and control purposes. Therefore, these computers were also known as vacuum tubes or thermionic valves based machines. Figure 1.5 shows the vacuum tube used in first generation computers. A vacuum tube is made up of glass and contains filaments inside it. The filaments when heated generate electrons, which eventually help in the amplification and deamplification of electronic signals. The input and output medium for first generation computers was the punched card and printout respectively. Some examples of first generation computers are ENIAC, EDVAC, EDSAC and UNIVAC.

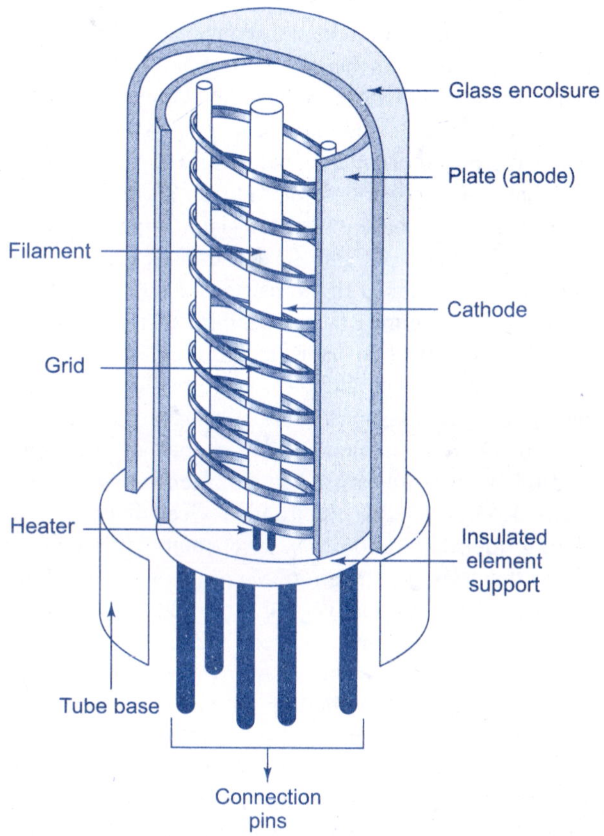

Fig. 1.5 A vacuum tube

The following are the two major advantages of first generation computer systems:

- These computers were the fastest computing devices of their time.
- These computers were able to execute complex mathematical problems in an efficient manner.

The above two advantages of first generation computers were not sufficient enough to make these computers popular among its users. The first generation computers had many disadvantages associated with them. The following are some of the disadvantages of first generation computers:

- The functioning of these computers depended on the machine language. A machine language is a language in which all the values are represented in the form of 0s and 1s. Therefore, these computers were not very easy to program.
- They were generally designed as special-purpose computers. Therefore, they were not very flexible in running different types of applications.
- The use of vacuum tube technology made these computers very large and bulky. Due to their large size, it was not an easy task to install them properly.
- They were not easily transferable from one place to another due to their huge size and also required to be placed in cool places.

- They were single tasking because they could execute only one program at a time and hence, were not very productive.
- They generated huge amount of heat and hence were prone to hardware faults. Hence, they were not considered as reliable and required proper maintenance at regular intervals.

1.3.2 Second Generation Computers

The second generation computers were employed during the period 1956–1963. The main characteristic of these computers was the use of *transistors* in place of vacuum tubes in building the basic logic circuits. The transistor was invented by Shockley, Brattain and Bardeen in 1947 for which they won the Nobel Prize. A transistor is a semiconductor device that is used to increase the power of the incoming signals by preserving the shape of the original signal. It has three connections, which are emitter (E), base (B) and collector (C). The base of transistor is the gate through which the signal, needed to be amplified, is sent. The signal sent through the base of the transistor is generally a small flow of electrons. Therefore, the base terminal also acts as the input gate for the transistor. The collector of the transistor is used to collect the amplified signal. The emitter of the transistor acts as the output gate for emitting the amplified signal to the external environment. Figure 1.6 shows the transistor used to manufacture circuitry of second generation computers.

The use of transistor technology helped in improving the performance of computers to a large extent. Transistor was a superior technology over vacuum tubes. Transistors used in second generation computers were smaller, faster, cheaper and generated less heat than that of vacuum tubes used in first generation computers. Transistors were also light weight electronic devices that required very less power during their operation. These characteristic features of transistors made the second generation computers smaller, faster, cheaper, more efficient, more productive and more reliable, as compared to the first generation computers. Printers, secondary storage and operating system technology were also invented during this era. However, these computers still relied on punched card and printout for carrying out their input/output operations. Another major technological development made to these computers was the replacement of the machine language with the assembly language. Assembly language is a low-level language that allows the programmer to use simple English words—called mnemonics—to represent different instructions in a program. Some examples of second generation computers are PDP-8, IBM 1401 and IBM 7090.

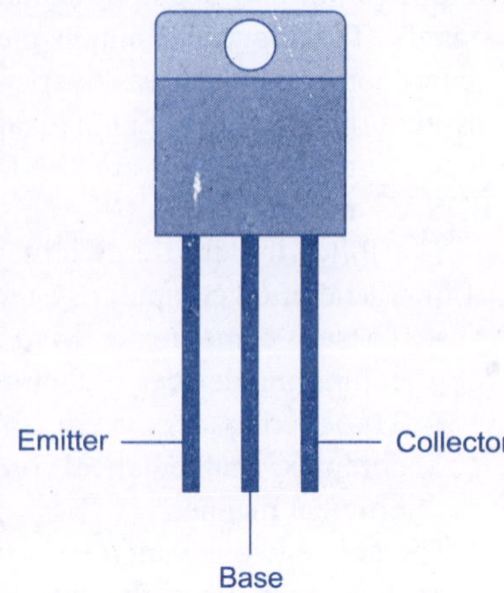

Fig. 1.6 A transistor

The following are the advantages of second generation computers:

- They were the fastest computing devices of their time.
- They were easy to program because of the use of assembly language.
- They could be transferred from one place to other very easily because they were small and light weight computing devices.
- They required very less power in carrying out their operations.
- They were more reliable as compared to first generation computers and hence, did not require maintenance at regular intervals of time.

The following are the limitations of first generation computers:

- The input and output media for these computers were not improved to a considerable extent.
- They were required to be placed in air-conditioned places.

- The cost of these computers was very high and they were beyond the reach of home users.
- They were special-purpose computers and could execute only specific applications.

1.3.3 Third Generation Computers

The third generation computers were employed during the period 1964–1975. The major characteristic feature of third generation computer systems was the use of *Integrated Circuits* (ICs). The IC technology was also known as microelectronics technology. ICs are the circuits that combine various electronic components, such as transistors, resistors, capacitors, etc. onto a single small silicon chip. The first IC was developed by **Jack Kilby** and **Robert Noyce** in the year 1958. Figure 1.7 shows a typical IC chip used for manufacturing third generation computers.

ICs were superior to vacuum tubes and transistors in terms of cost and performance. The cost of ICs was very low and the performance was very high because all the electronic components were arranged very close to each other. They also required very low power for performing their operations. Therefore, the use of ICs in third generation computers made them smaller, faster, more efficient and more reliable than the first and second generation of computers. Some examples of third generation computers are NCR 395, B6500, IBM 370, PDP 11 and CDC 7600.

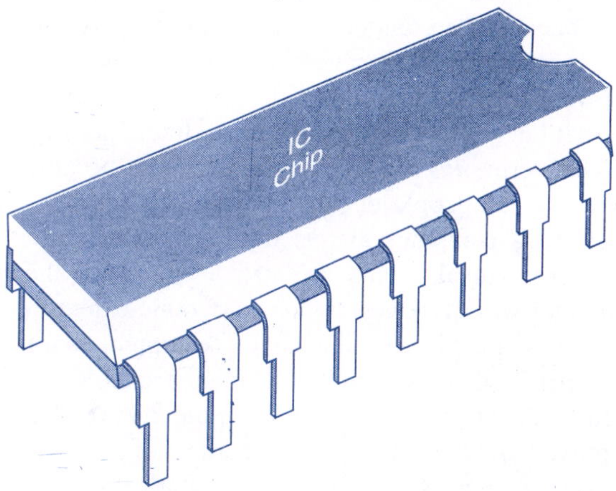

Fig. 1.7 An integrated circuit

The following are the merits of the third generation computers:

- They were the fastest computing devices as compared with first and second generation of computers. The computational time for these computers was also reduced to great extent. The computational time for these computers was usually measured in nanoseconds.
- They were very productive because of their small computational time.
- They were easily transportable from one place to another because of their small size.
- They used high-level languages. A high-level language is a computer programming language that is independent of the machine details. Hence, the programmer finds it very easy to use them and the programs written in these languages on one computer can be easily executed on some other computer.
- They could be installed very easily and required less space for their installation.
- They were able to execute any type of application, such as business and scientific applications. Hence, the third generation computers were also considered as general-purpose computers.
- They were more reliable and required less frequent maintenance schedules.

Some of the disadvantages of third generation computers are:

- The storage capacity of these computers was still very small.
- The performance of these computers degraded while executing large applications, involving complex computations because of the small storage capacity.
- The cost of these computers was very high.
- They were still required to be placed in air-conditioned places.

1.3.4 Fourth Generation Computers

The fourth generation computers were employed during 1975–1989. The invention of *Large Scale Integration* (LSI) technology and *Very Large Scale Integration* (VLSI) technology led to the development of fourth generation computers. However, these computers still used the IC technology to build the basic circuits. The LSI technology allowed thousands of transistors to be fitted onto one small silicon chip. On the other hand, the VLSI technology allowed hundreds of thousands of transistors to be fitted onto a single chip. As a result, the manufacturers were able to reduce the size of the computers and made them cheaper as compared to the other generation of computers.

The progress in LSI and VLSI technologies led to the development of *microprocessor*, which became the major characteristic feature of the fourth generation computers. A microprocessor incorporates various components of a computer—such as CPU, memory and Input/Output (I/O) controls—onto a single chip. The computers in this generation were designed to have a microprocessor, some additional storage chips and support circuitry. Figure 1.8 shows the Intel P4004 microprocessor chip developed in 1971. Some popular later microprocessors include Intel 386, Intel 486 and Pentium.

The term *Personal Computer* (PC) became known to the people during this era. The term PC refers to a computer that is designed to be used by an individual. Since the size and cost of the computer was decreased to a considerable extent in this period, people started using these computers for their personal work too. The storage technologies used in the fourth generation computers were also improved and they started using static and dynamic *Random Access Memory* (RAM). The advantage of using this type of memory was that it allowed the computers to access the stored information at a rapid pace and hence helped in increasing the productivity and performance of the computers. Some of the examples of fourth generation computers are IBM PC, IBM PC/AT, Apple and CRAY-1.

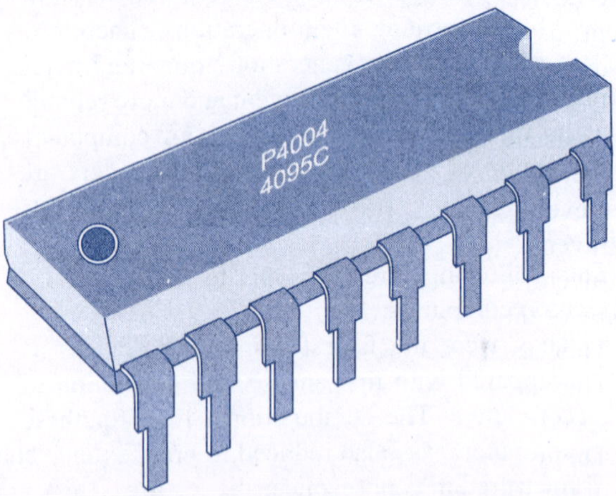

Fig. 1.8 The Intel P4004 microprocessor chip

The use of LSI and VLSI technologies made the fourth generation computers small, cheap, compact and powerful. Apart from these technologies, the fourth generation also include the following developments:

- Development of Graphical User Interfaces (GUIs)
- Development of new operating systems
- Invention of various secondary storage and I/O devices
- Development of Local Area Network (LAN)

Some of the advantages of fourth generation computers are as follows:

- The use of LSI, VLSI and semiconductor technologies made these computers very powerful in terms of their processing speed and access time.
- The storage capacity of these computers was very large and faster and hence they were very productive and highly optimised.
- They were highly reliable and required very less maintenance.
- They provided a user-friendly environment while working because of the development of GUIs and interactive I/O devices.

- The programs written on these computers were highly portable because of the use of high-level languages.
- They were very versatile and suitable for every type of applications.
- They required very less power to operate.

Some of the problems associated with fourth generation computers are as follows:

- The soldering of LSI and VLSI chips on the wiring board was not an easy task and required complicated technologies to bind these chips on the wiring board.
- The working of these computers is still dependent on the instructions given by the programmer.

1.3.5 Fifth Generation Computers

The different types of modern digital computers come under the categories of fifth generation computers. The fifth generation computers are based on the Ultra Large Scale Integration (ULSI) technology that allows almost ten million electronic components to be fabricated on one small chip. The ULSI technology helps in increasing the power and speed of the microprocessor chips and the capacity of primary and secondary storage devices to a great extent. As a result, the fifth generation computers are faster, cheaper and more efficient, as compared to the fourth generation computers. Some of the improvements or developments made during this generation of computers are as follows:

- Development of various portable computers such as laptop, pocket computer, Personal Digital Assistant (PDA), etc.
- Development of Parallel Processors.
- Development of centralised computers called servers.
- Invention of optical disk technology.
- Invention of the Internet and its different services.

Some of the advantages of fifth generation computers are as follows:

- They are the fastest and powerful computers till date.
- They are able to execute a large number of applications at the same time and that too at a very high speed.
- The use of ULSI technology helps in decreasing the size of these computers to a large extent. Some of the fifth generation computers are so small in size that they can be used while traveling.
- The users of these computers find it very comfortable to use them because of the several additional multimedia features.
- They are versatile for communications and resource sharing.

The fifth generation computers are really enjoyed by their users because of the several advantages offered by them. However, the major disadvantage of the fifth generation computers is that they are not provided with an intelligent program that could guide them in performing different operations. Nowadays, scientists are making some serious efforts in this field and artificial intelligence and expert system applications are the results of these efforts.

Figure 1.9 shows a tree of computer family that illustrates the area-wise developments during the last four decades and their contributions to the various generations of computers.

1.4 CLASSIFICATION OF COMPUTERS

There are different types of computers available these days. The function of each type of computer is to process the data and provide some output to the users. However, the methods or techniques used by these

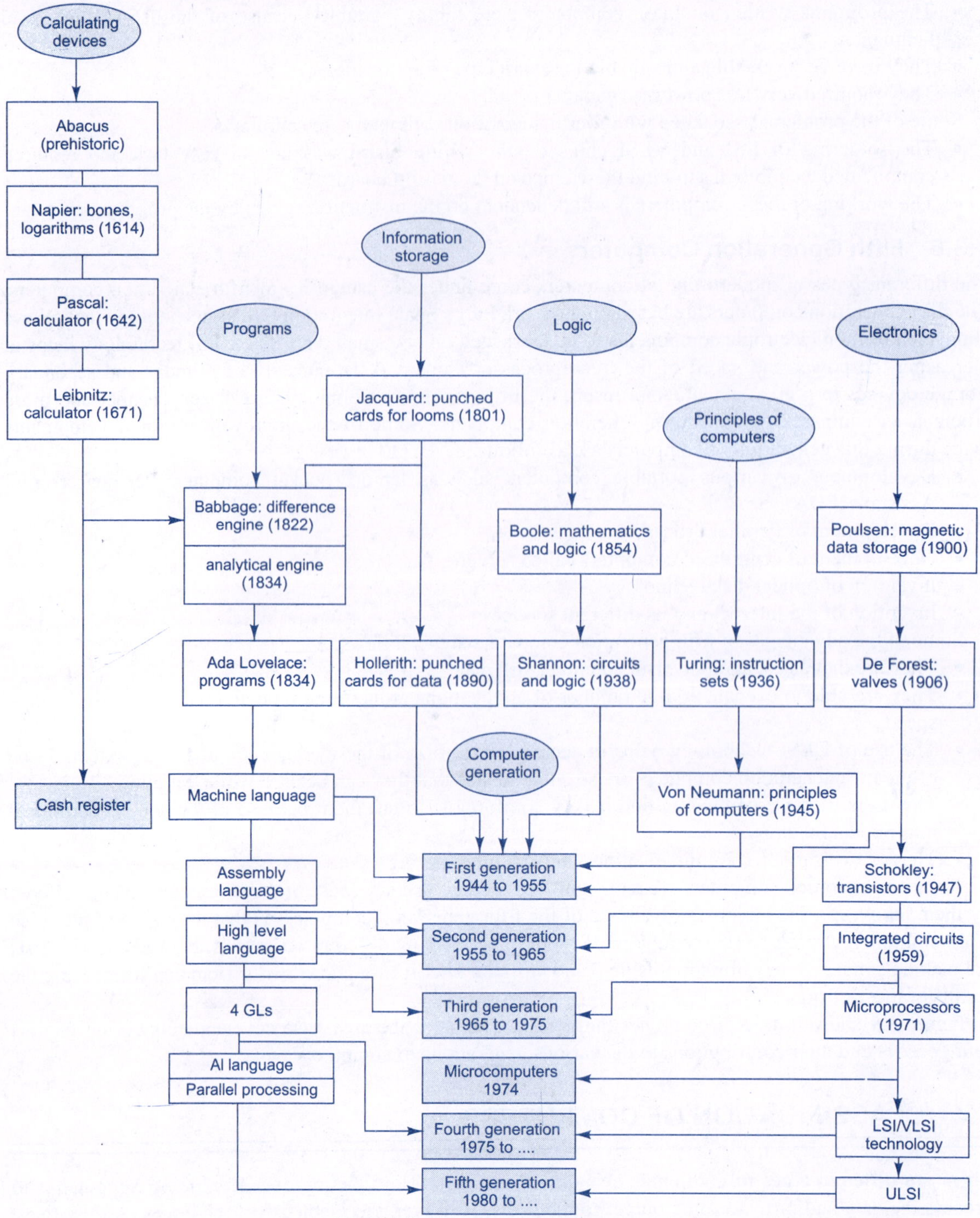

Fig. 1.9 Tree of computer family

computers to process and handle the data may be different. We can classify the computers according to the following three criteria:

1. Based on operating principles
2. Based on applications
3. Based on size and capability

1.4.1 Based on Operating Principles

On the basis of operations performed and methods used to store and process the data and information, computers can be classified into the following categories:

- Analog computers
- Digital computers
- Hybrid computers

Analog computers The analog computers represent data in the form of continuous electrical signals having a specific magnitude. These computers are very fast in their operation and allow several other operations to be carried out at the same time. However, the results produced by these computers are not very accurate. Therefore, the analog computers are widely used in applications in which the accuracy of results is not a major concern. They are powerful tools to solve differential equations.

The electronic circuit employed in modern analog computers is generally an *Operational Amplifier* (Op-Amp). It is made up of semiconductor integrated circuits. The three different characteristic features of Op-Amps are as follows:

- They have large voltage gain. The voltage gain of an amplifier is defined as the ratio of the output voltage to the input voltage.
- They have infinite input resistance. The input resistance is defined as the ratio of change in the input voltage to the change in input current.
- They have zero output resistance. The output resistance is the nominal resistance measured with no load.

Figure 1.10 shows the basic circuit used in analog computers.

In Fig. 1.10, the triangle represents an amplifier that is used to invert the incoming signal. If the incoming signal is a positive signal, then it will be inverted into a negative output signal. Similarly, if the incoming signal is a negative signal, then it will be inverted into a positive output signal. R_f and R_{in} are used to represent the feedback resistor and the input resistor respectively.

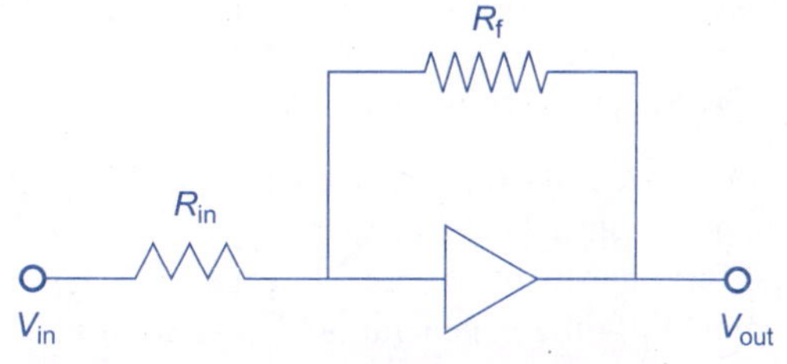

Fig. 1.10 Integrated circuit of an operational amplifier

Digital computers The digital computer, also known as the digital information processing system, is a type of computer that stores and processes data in the digital form. Therefore, each type of data is usually stored in these computers in terms of 0s and 1s. The output produced by these computers is also in the digital form. The digital computers are also capable of processing the analog data. However, the analog data should be first converted to the digital form, before being processed by these computers. Similarly, if we want the output in the analog form, then the digital information produced by these computers should be first converted to an analog form. These conversions are generally carried out by the in-built components of digital computers.

Digital computers are generally faster and more reliable than the analog computer systems and provide more accurate results. The computer used by a home user is a typical example of digital computer. The digital computers are also employed in colleges, universities and small and medium sized businesses.

The different hardware components of a digital computer are an Arithmetic-Logic Unit (ALU), a Control Unit (CU), a memory unit and I/O units. The ALU of a digital computer is used to perform various arithmetic operations, such as addition, subtraction, multiplication and division and various logic operations such as AND, OR, NOT, etc. CU helps in directing the operations of ALU. The memory unit is used to store the data on temporary or permanent basis. The input units are used to enter the data into the computer and the output units is used to display the information generated by the computer to the user.

Hybrid computers The hybrid computer is a combination of analog computer and digital computer because it encompasses the best features of both these computers. Therefore, the hardware components of hybrid computers are usually the mixture of analog and digital components. These features make the hybrid computers very fast, efficient and reliable. In these computers, data is generally measured and processed in the form of electrical signals and is stored with the help of digital components. However, these computers can also be used to perform various types of logical operations.

The input accepted by the hybrid computers is a continuously varying input signal. This input signal is then converted by them into a set of discrete values for performing different operations. These computers prove to be very cost-effective in performing complex simulations. The hybrid computers are also less expensive than the digital computers.

The computer used in hospitals to measure the heartbeat of the patient is a very good example of a hybrid computer. Apart from this, the hybrid computers are also used in scientific applications, various engineering fields and in controlling business processes.

1.4.2 Based on Applications

Different computers are designed for different purposes so that they can perform their tasks according to their capabilities. On the basis of different applications or purposes, computers can be classified into the following categories:

- General purpose computers
- Special purpose computers

General purpose computers They are designed in such a manner that they can work in all environments. The general purpose computers are versatile and can store a number of programs meant for performing distinct tasks. However, the general purpose computers are not efficient and consume a large amount of time in generating the result.

Special purpose computers They are designed in such a manner that they can perform only a specified task. The special purpose computers are not versatile and their speed and memory size depend on the task that is to be performed. These computers are less expensive as they do not contain any redundant information. The special purpose computers are efficient and consume less amount of time in generating the result.

1.4.3 Based on Size and Capability

Computers differ from each other in terms of their shape, size and weights. Each type of computer performs some unique functions and can be employed in the fields suited for them. These computers also differ in terms of processing speed. Some of them are of moderate speed, whereas some others operate at a very fast speed. On the basis of size and capability, computers can be classified into the following categories:

- Microcomputers
- Mini computers
- Mainframe computers
- Super computers

Microcomputers A microcomputer is a small and cheap digital computer that is designed to be used by individuals. It is built around a microprocessor, a storage unit and an I/O channel. Apart from these components, the other parts that a microcomputer includes are power supply, connecting cables, keyboard, mouse, printer and scanner. These computers also include several software programs such as operating system, system software and utility software. The micro computers are generally available in the form of PCs, workstations and notebook computers. Figure 1.11 shows the block diagram of a microcomputer.

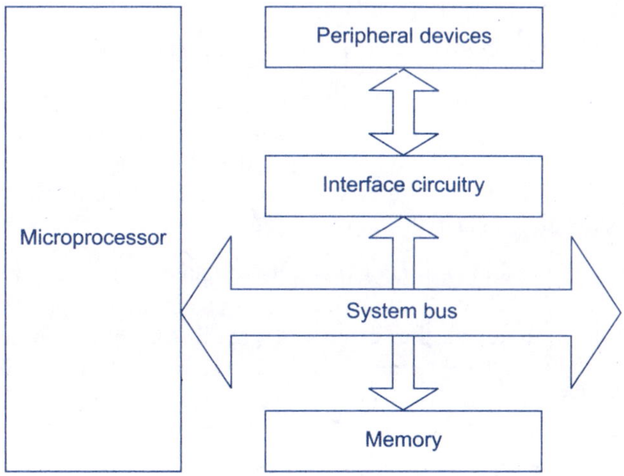

Fig. 1.11 The block diagram of a microcomputer

Microprocessor It is the heart of the microcomputer. It incorporates all the functions of a CPU onto a single IC in a microcomputer. The basic units of microprocessor are ALU, register unit and CU. ALU is used to perform various arithmetic and logic operations. The register unit is used to store the data and instructions temporarily needed by the ALU. The various registers used by a microcomputer are Accumulator (AC), program control register, I/O register, instruction register, Memory Address Register (MAR) and Memory Buffer Register (MBR). CU is used to manage and direct the operations performed by the microcomputer.

Memory It is used to store the data and instructions on temporary or permanent basis. A microcomputer generally employs two types of memories, i.e., primary memory and secondary memory. Primary memory, also called main memory, is used to store the data and instructions temporarily. It stores only those instructions and data that are needed by the microprocessor of the computer for processing. The secondary memory, also called auxiliary memory, is used to store the data and instructions permanently. Magnetic disks and magnetic tapes are some of the examples of secondary storage.

Peripheral devices They are generally the input and output devices attached to the computer. The various input devices—such as keyboard and mouse—are used to enter program and data into the computer before performing any kind of operation. They are used to transfer data and instructions from the external environment into the computer. The various output devices—such as monitor and printer—are used to display the results computed by the computer to the user. The major function performed by the output devices is to convert the binary result computed by the computer into a form that can be easily understood by the users.

System bus It is also referred to as the frontside bus, memory bus, local bus or host bus. The system bus in the micro computer is used to connect microprocessor, memory and peripheral devices into a single unit. The system bus is a collective name given to address, data and control bus. The address bus is a unidirectional bus that is used to identify a peripheral device or a memory location. The data bus is a bidirectional bus that is used to transfer data among microprocessor, memory and peripheral devices of the computer. The control bus is used by the microprocessor to send control signals to the various devices within the computer.

Depending on the size, the microcomputer can be further classified into the following types:

Desktop computer It is also known as PC. The desktop computer systems are designed to be used by an individual at a single location. The typical components of a desktop computer are keyboard, mouse, monitor, hard disk storage, peripheral devices and a system unit. These computers are very cheap and an individual can easily purchase them for home or business use. The different manufacturers of desktop computers are Apple, IBM, Dell and Hewlett-Packard (HP).

Laptop computer It is a portable computer that can be taken from one place to another at any time very easily. It is also known as notebook computer, notepad or mobile computer. The laptop computer is a small size computer that incorporates all the features of a typical desktop computer. These computers are provided with a rechargeable battery that removes the need of continuous external power supply. However, these computer systems are more expensive than desktop computers. The different manufacturers of laptop computers are Acer, Apple, Panasonic, Sony and HP.

Hand-held computer It is also known as Personal Digital Assistant (PDA), converged device, palmtop or mobile device. The hand-held computer is a very small size computer that can be kept in pocket. It generally has a very small display screen and the input device for these computers is a pen or an electronic stylus. The storage capacity of hand-held computers is not very large. They generally use small cards to store data and programs instead of disk drives. Therefore, they are less powerful as compared to the desktop and laptop computers. The different examples of hand-held computers are Apple Newton, Casio Cassiopeia, Franklin eBookMan, etc.

Mini computers A mini computer was first introduced in the year 1960 by Digital Equipment Corporation (DEC). They were called mini computers because of their smaller size than the other computers of those times. They can handle more data and more input and output than micro computers. Mini computers are less powerful than mainframe computers but more powerful than micro computers. Therefore, they are also referred to as the midrange computers. They are able to cater to the needs of multiple users at a single instant of time. The number of users supported by mini computers may range between 4 and 200. These computers are generally designed for small and medium sized business environments.

Mini computers are generally used in business environments as the centralized computer or the *network server*. After implementing the mini computer as the network server, hundreds of desktop computers can be connected to it. Mini computers can also be used as the web servers that can handle thousands of transactions in a day. These computers are less expensive than mainframe computers and hence suitable for those organizations that cannot afford high priced servers. The different examples of mini computers are PDP 11, IBM (8000 series), VAX 7500, etc.

Mainframe computers A mainframe computer is a very large computer that is employed by large business organisations for handling major applications, such as financial transaction processing, Enterprise Resource Planning (ERP), industry and consumer statistics, and census. They are capable of handling almost millions of records in a day. The mainframe computers can also be used as the centralised computers with several user terminals connected to it. The mainframe computers are actually considered as the predecessor of servers. These computers are bigger and more expensive than other computers. The implementation of mainframe computers also requires large space with a closely monitored humidity and temperature levels. These computers are termed as mainframe because all the hardware units are arranged into a frame. The different manufacturers of mainframe computers are IBM, Amdahl, Hitachi, etc. Examples of mainframe computers are IBM 3000, VAX 8000 and CDC 6600.

The mainframe computers can maintain large databases that can be accessed by remote users with a simple terminal. Therefore, the mainframe computers are also known as *super servers* or *database servers*. The processing speed of these computers is generally optimised by employing more than one microprocessor to execute millions of instructions per second. The mainframe computers also have large capacity of primary and secondary storage as compared with other types of computers.

Some of the characteristic features of mainframe computers are as follows:

- A typical mainframe computer generally has a maximum of 16 microprocessors. However, some modern mainframe computers can have more than 16 microprocessors.
- The RAM capacity of these computers lies between 128 MB and 8 GB.
- They are able to run multiple operating systems, and therefore, termed 'virtual machines'.
- They have different cabinets for primary storage, secondary storage and I/O units.
- They can handle huge amount of I/O operations at the same time.

Super computers A super computer is the fastest type of computer that can perform complex operations at a very high speed. The super computers were first presented in the year 1960 by Seymour Cray at Control Data Corporation (CDC). They are more expensive than the other categories of computers and are specially designed for the applications in which large number of complex calculations have to be carried out to get the desired output. The main reason behind the fast speed of super computers is that they are designed only to execute small number of programs at a time rather than many programs simultaneously. Some of the manufacturers of super computers are IBM, Silicon Graphics, Fujitsu, Intel, etc. Examples of Super Computers are CRAY 3, Cyber 205, NEC SX-3 and PARAM from India.

The various application areas of super computers are as follows:

- Weather forecasting
- Animated graphics
- Fluid mechanics
- Nuclear energy research
- Petroleum exploration

Super computers are manufactured with no special hardware. Like the typical computer, they have CPU and memory as their major components. However, the CPU of super computer operates at faster speed, as compared to the other categories of computers. Super computers are the fastest computers because they employ thousands of processors, hundreds of gigabytes of RAM and thousands of gigabytes of secondary storage.

The designers of super computers use two different methods for optimising their performance. These methods are *pipelining* and *parallelism*. Pipelining is a technique that allows the microprocessors to execute the second instruction before the execution of the first instruction is completed, whereas parallelism allows the microprocessors to execute several instructions at the same time. In this type of computing, a large and complex problem is first divided into smaller problems, that are solved concurrently by the microprocessor of the computer.

1.5 COMPUTING CONCEPTS

We can understand how a computer functions by analysing the fundamental computing concepts. The most elementary computing concepts include receiving input—known as *data*—from the user, manipulating the input according to the given set of instructions and delivering the output—known as *information*—to the user. Figure 1.12 shows the functioning of a computer based on these concepts.

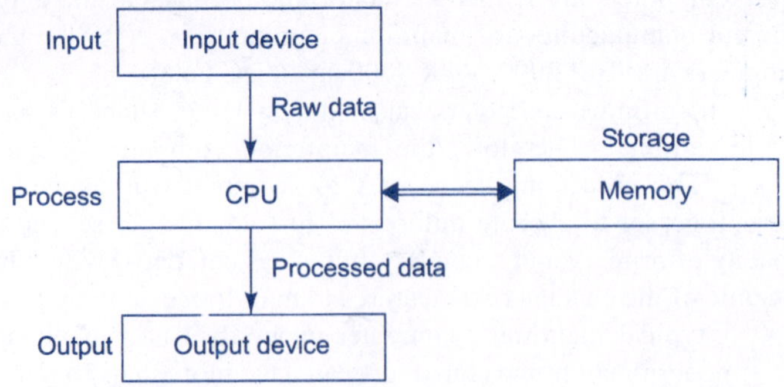

Fig. 1.12 The Input-Process-Output Cycle of a computer

The various functions performed by the computer are briefly described below:

Accepting the raw data The first task to be performed by a computer is to accept the data from the user, with the help of an input device, such as mouse and keyboard. Mouse is used to enter the data through point-and-click operation while keyboard is used to enter the character data by typing the various keys. We need to enter the data into the computer so as to obtain the required result as output.

Processing the data The data is processed with the help of specific instructions known as *programs* after taking the input from the user. The manipulation of data is handled by the CPU of the computer. CPU is considered as the *brain of the computer* because it controls the execution of various instructions. The raw data entered by the user through input devices is processed by the CPU to generate meaningful information.

Storing the data The data is stored in the main memory of a computer in its processed form. The various external storage devices—such as hard disk and magnetic disk—can also be used for storing the processed data so that it can again be fetched later.

Delivering the output The processed data is delivered as useful information to the user with the help of output devices, such as printer and monitor.

1.6 THE COMPUTER SYSTEM

A Computer System, small or big, in order to carry out its functions successfully, must essentially include the following four sub-systems:

- Hardware

- Software
- Data
- People

1.6.1 Hardware

The physical devices that make up the computer are called *Hardware*. The hardware units are responsible for entering, storing and processing the given data and then displaying the output to the users. The basic hardware units of a general purpose computer are keyboard, mouse, memory, CPU, monitor and printer. Among these hardware units, keyboard and mouse are used to input data into the computer, memory is used to store the entered data, CPU is used to process the entered data and monitor and printer are used to display the processed data to the users.

CPU is the main component inside the computer that is responsible for performing various operations and also for managing the input and output devices. It includes two components for its functioning, *Arithmetic Logic Unit* (ALU) and *Control Unit* (CU). ALU is used to perform the arithmetic operations, such as addition, subtraction, etc. and logic operations, such as AND, OR, etc. on the data obtained from the memory. CU is used to control the activities related to the input and output devices. It obtains the instructions from the memory, decodes them and then, executes them, so as to deliver output to the users.

1.6.2 Software

The term *software* refers to a set of *programs* and instructions that help the computers in carrying out their processing. Software is very necessary for the proper functioning of a computer. There are mainly two types of software, viz. *Application Software* and *System Software*:

Application software The programs, which are designed to perform a specific task for the user, are known as application software. Application software is also referred as end-user programs because its functions are used by the user for obtaining the desired results. Word processor, database programs, presentation programs and spreadsheets are the examples of application software.

System software The programs, which are designed to control the different operations of the computer, are known as system software. It mainly manages the activities of the computer hardware and interacts with the application software to perform a particular task. Operating systems, compilers, assemblers, interpreters and device drivers are the examples of system software.

1.6.3 Data

Data refer to the raw facts and pieces of information that is usually entered into the computer system by the user, so as to generate the desired output. The data are presented in the form understandable by the computer system and the result is delivered in the form understandable by the users. In a computer system, data are manipulated by the program consisting of different instructions. Depending on the requirement, data can be presented in two forms, viz. Quantitative and Qualititative.

Qualitative data The data, which are represented in words or text form, are known as qualitative data. This type of data can also include images, videos and audios used for the graphical presentation.

Quantitative data The data, which are represented in numerical form, are known as quantitative data. This type of data include different numbers and symbols used for representing a particular quantity.

The data entered by a user into the computer system can be in the form of numbers, text or images. The data—stored in the memory of the computer system—is in the form of bits and bytes. A bit is defined as the smallest unit of information used in the computer system and a byte equals to a group of eight bits.

1.6.4 People

Computer systems are designed by the people, for the people. People, therefore, include the people who design and build hardware and software (known as *systems people*) and the people who actually use computer systems for their applications (known as *users*).

Systems people include hardware engineers, software engineers, programmers, etc. Users might include a variety of people working in different areas of applications, such as education, business, entertainment, training, etc. Users may use the available standard software or develop their own software depending upon their requirements.

1.7 APPLICATIONS OF COMPUTERS

Today, computers are used in almost every sphere of life. The users from different locations can easily and quickly communicate with each other with the help of computers. The use of computers has reduced the paper work to a large extent. Thus, computers have become a basic need to perform various tasks in our day-to-day life. Some common applications of computers are discussed below.

Education Computers are used in schools and colleges to teach students in a better and easy way. The students can get more information about a specific topic or subject using the Internet. Computers help in easy learning by creating presentations on a specific topic. Today, students can fill their application forms and give their exams online that facilitates distance education. Computer-based learning and web-based learning are very popular amongst students.

Business Computers are used in different types of business to store a large amount of information in the form of databases. Using computers, business meetings can be held between people sitting at remote locations through web conferencing. Buyers and sellers can conduct business online through the use of computers and Internet.

Communication Computers that are connected with each other can be used to transfer data to and from other computers. In order to establish communication between two users, Internet is one of the most common mediums. E-mail is a popular system through which a user can send/receive text messages, graphic messages and file attachments.

Science Computers are used by various scientists for the purpose of research and development. They generally make use of computer for research and analysis of new theories. With the help of computers, scientists are moving towards the possibility of predicting natural disasters, such as earthquake and tsunami.

Engineering Computers are used by the engineers for the creation of complex drawings and designs while working in different fields, like automobiles and construction. Engineers use computers extensively for numerical computing.

Entertainment Computers are used in the entertainment industry for creating graphics and animations. There are various free as well as proprietary graphics softwares available for creating graphics and animations.

Banking Nowadays, computers are being increasingly used for online banking. Through online banking, the users or customers can transfer and receive money by using computers and Internet. Some banks also provide the facility of online bill payment through their websites.

Health Computers are used by doctors to diagnose various kinds of diseases and ailments. Several analog and digital devices are connected with computers enabling the doctors to monitor the condition of a patient and view the internal organs of the body. Hospitals use computers to maintain and manage patient records and billing systems. They also use the concept of 'tele-medicine' to serve the patients at remote locations.

Government Computers play a crucial role in almost all government departments. Revenue, industry, census, police, defense and many other departments use computers extensively to serve the people better. The concept of 'e-governance' is becoming popular among various government agencies.

Chapter Summary

Computer is a machine that accepts the data as input and stores and processes them, based on the instructions provided by the user. A computer basically consists of hardware and software. Along with these components, the data and users are also related to a computer as without them a computer cannot function. Hardware refers to the physical components of the computer, such as keyboard, mouse, CPU and printer. Software refers to the set of instructions provided to the computer by the user for performing a specific task. Data refers to the type of input given by the user to the computer; it can be in the form of numbers, words or images. Users refer to the persons who use the computer for getting the required result corresponding to the given input.

Computers are used for performing complex calculations at a very fast speed. Earlier, the manual computing devices, such as sand table, abacus and napier bones were used for performing different calculations. These devices consumed a large amount of time and were unable to handle large numbers in calculations. Due to the drawbacks of manual computing devices, the automated computing devices such as MARK I, ENIAC and EDVAC were developed for performing calculations automatically. These devices are much faster as compared to the manual computing devices.

There are five generations of computers associated with the development of computers. During these generations, the computers have seen tremendous shift in technology, size, and speed. Computers can be classified into three categories—analog computers, digital computer and hybrid computers—on the basis of their operating principles. Depending upon their application areas, computers are categorised into two types, general purpose computers and special purpose computers. On the basis of the size and capability, computers are categorised into four types, micro computers, mini computers, super computers and mainframe computers.

These days, computers are being used in almost every field because of their high processing speed and large storage capacity. Education, science, business and healthcare are some of the areas where computers are widely used.

Key Terms to Remember

- **Computer**: An electronic machine that takes input from the user and stores and processes it to generate the output in the form of useful information to the user.
- **Data**: The raw details that need to be processed to generate some useful information.
- **Program**: The set of instructions that can be executed by the computer in sequential or non-sequential manner.
- **Information**: Processed data useful for the user.
- **CPU**: The processor of the computer that is responsible for controlling and executing instructions.
- **Monitor**: A screen, which displays the information in the visual form, after receiving the video signals from the computer.
- **Transistor**: A semiconductor device that is used to increase the power of the incoming signals by preserving the shape of the original signal.

- **Microprocessor:** An integrated circuit that contains the entire central processing unit of a computer on a single chip.
- **Vacuum Tube:** An electron tube from which all or most of the gas has been removed, permitting electrons to move with low interaction with any remaining gas molecules.
- **LSI:** Large Scale Integration
- **VLSI:** Very large-scale integration (VLSI) refers to an IC or technology with many devices on one chip.
- **ULSI:** Ultra-large-scale integration
- **ICs**: The circuits that combine various electronic components, such as transistors, resistors, capacitors, etc. onto a single small silicon chip.
- **Analog Computer**: A type of computer which represents data in the form of continuous signals.
- **Digital computer**: A type of computer that stores and processes data in digital form and is also known as the digital information processing system.
- **Hybrid computer**: A combination of analog computer and digital computer because it encompasses the best features of both these computers.
- **Microcomputer**: A small digital computer that is designed to be used by individuals.
- **Super computer**: The fastest type of computer that can perform complex operations at a very high speed.
- **Mainframe computer**: A very large computer that is employed by large business organisations for handling major applications, such as financial transaction processing applications and ERP.
- **Hardware**: A group of electronic devices that make up a computer. They are used for performing tasks, such as entering the data, processing of data and then displaying the output to the users.
- **Software**: The programs and instructions that help the computer in carrying out their processing.
- **Application software**: The programs, which are designed to perform a specific task for the user.
- **System software**: The programs, which are designed to control the different operations of the computer system.

Review Questions

Fill in the Blanks

1. A __________ is an electronic machine that takes input from the user and stores and processes the given input to generate the output in the form of useful information to the user.
2. The raw details that need to be processed to generate some useful information is known as __________.
3. The set of instructions that can be executed by the computer is known as __________.
4. __________ is the processor of the computer that is responsible for controlling and executing the various instructions.
5. __________ is a screen, which displays the information in visual form, after receiving the video signals from the computer.
6. A __________ was a device that arranged stones in three channels in the sand.
7. In __________, the wooden frame consists of many wires with beads sliding on them and it was also known as a counting frame.
8. __________ computing device consists of a board whose left edge is divided into 9 squares and these 9 squares are used to hold the numbers from 1 to 9.

9. ___________ is considered to be the father of modern digital computers.
10. The ___________ was the first device that used all the features of a modern digital computer.
11. Colossus was a special purpose electronic device that used the ___________ technology to perform different operations.
12. ___________ computers were also known as vacuum tubes or thermionic valves based machines.
13. A ___________ is a semiconductor device that is used to increase the power of the incoming signals by preserving the shape of the original signal.
14. ___________ is a low-level language that allows the programmer to use simple English words, called mnemonics, to represent different instructions in a program.
15. The main characteristic feature of third generation computers was the use of ___________.
16. The invention of ___________ and ___________ technology led to the development of the fourth generation computers.
17. The fifth generation computers are based on the ___________ technology that allows almost ten million electronic components to be fabricated on one small chip.
18. ___________, also known as digital information processing system, is a type of computer that stores and processes data in digital form.
19. A ___________ is the fastest type of computer that can perform complex operations at a very high speed.
20. The term ___________ refers to the programs and instructions that help the computer in carrying out their processing.
21. The programs, which are designed to perform a specific task for the user, are known as ___________.
22. The programs, which are designed to control the different operations of the computer, are known as ___________.

Multiple Choice Questions

1. Which component of the computer is known as the brain of computer?

   A. Monitor B. CPU C. Memory D. None of the above

2. Which of the following is an input device?

   A. Printer B. Monitor C. Mouse D. None of the above

3. Which of the following is a characteristic of the modern digital computer?

   A. High speed B. Large storage capacity C. Greater accuracy D. All of the above

4. Which one of the following device used stones for performing calculations?

   A. Sand table B. Abacus C. Napier bones D. Pascaline

5. Who is known as the father of modern digital computers?

   A. Gottfried Wilhem Von Leibriz B. Charles Babbage

   C. Alan Mathison D. John Mauchly

6. Which of the following was the first pure electronic programmable computer developed in the year 1944?

   A. MARK I B. ENIAC C. Colossus D. EDVAC

7. Which of the following was the first commercial computer developed in the year 1951?

   A. ENIAC B. EDVAC C. EDSAC D. UNIVAC

8. What are the different number of computer generations?

   A. Four B. Five C. Six D. Seven

9. Which technology was used in the first generation computers?
   A. Transistors B. Vacuum tubes C. ICs D. None of the above
10. Which technology was used in the second generation computers?
   A. Transistors B. Vacuum tubes C. Microprocessors D. ICs
11. Which technology was used in the third generation computers?
   A. Transistors B. Vacuum tubes C. ICs D. All of the above
12. Which technology was used in the fourth generation computers?
   A. Microprocessors B. Vacuum tubes C. ICs D. Transistors
13. Which semiconductor device is used to increase the power of the incoming signals by preserving the shape of the original signal?
   A. Sand table B. Transistor C. Vacuum tubes D. None of the above
14. Which of the following can be termed as a connection present in a transistor?
   A. Emitter B. Base C. Collector D. All of the above
15. In which generation of computers, assembly language was introduced?
   A. First B. Second C. Third D. Fourth
16. Which of the following technologies is also known as microelectronics technology?
   A. Vacuum tubes B. ICs C. Microprocessors D. Transistors
17. Which generation uses the ULSI technology?
   A. Second B. Third C. Fourth D. Fifth
18. On what basis computers can be classified?
   A. Operating principles B. Applications C. Size and capability D. All of the above
19. Which of the following unit is a part of the CPU?
   A. ALU B. CU C. Memory unit D. All of the above
20. Which of the following is known as a midrange computer?
   A. Microcomputer B. Mini computer C. Mainframe computer D. Super computer
21. The programs and instructions that help the computer in carrying out their processing are known as?
   A. Hardware B. Software C. Data D. None of the above

Discussion Questions

1. What are the different components of a computer? Explain, each of them.
2. Discuss briefly the various characteristics of a computer.
3. Differentiate between manual computing devices and automated computing devices.
4. Explain the working of napier bones device for performing calculations.
5. What do you mean by UNIVAC? What are its features?
6. Explain the first generation computers?
7. What were the advantages and disadvantages of using the first generation computers?
8. Which technology was used in the second generation computers? How does it compare with the technology used in the first generation computers?
9. What are the advantages and disadvantages of the second generation computers?

10. Enumerate the advantages and disadvantages of third generation computers.
11. What are the software related developments that took place during the fourth generation period?
12. Explain how the fourth generation computer is superior to the earlier generations of computer.
13. Explain the unique features and advantages of fifth generation computers.
14. Distinguish between analog and digital computers.
15. How general purpose computers are different from special purpose computers?
16. Describe the various types of computers on the basis of size and capability.
17. Draw the block diagram of a microcomputer.
18. Differentiate between hardware and software of a computer?
19. Explain the importance of data and users in relation to computers.
20. List, with examples, five important application areas of computers today.

CHAPTER 2

COMPUTER ORGANISATION AND ARCHITECTURE

Chapter Outline

Chapter Objectives

In this chapter, we will learn:

- The role of Central Processing Unit (CPU) in a computer system.
- The working of various components of CPU.
- The concept of processor communication with memory and I/O devices.
- The concept of machine cycle for executing an instruction.
- Different types of bus, used in a computer system, and their purposes.
- Types of instructions set implemented in a computer system.

2.1 INTRODUCTION

Computer organisation and computer architecture are two different but related, important concepts that are required to describe a computer system. *Computer architecture* refers to the definition of basic attributes of hardware components and their interconnections, in order to achieve certain specified goals in terms of functions and performance. The attributes may include, for example the instruction set, data representation, I/O mechanisms, etc. The architecture basically defines the logical structure of a computer system.

Computer organisation refers to the design and physical arrangement of various hardware units to work in tandem, in an orderly manner, in order to achieve the goals specified in the architecture. For a given architecture, there could be many different models, each representing a different type of organisation, depending on the cost, physical size and technology used.

In this chapter, we shall discuss in detail the functioning of the central processor of a computer system, how the processor communicates with the memory and input/output devices, and the instruction sets used in the design of processors.

2.2 CENTRAL PROCESSING UNIT

The function of any computer system revolves around a central component known as *central processing unit* (CPU). The CPU, which is popularly referred to as the "brain" of the computer, is responsible for processing the data inside the computer system. It is also responsible for controlling all other components of the system. Figure 2.1 shows a typical block diagram of the computer system, illustrating the arrangement of CPU with the input and output units as well as the memory of the computer system.

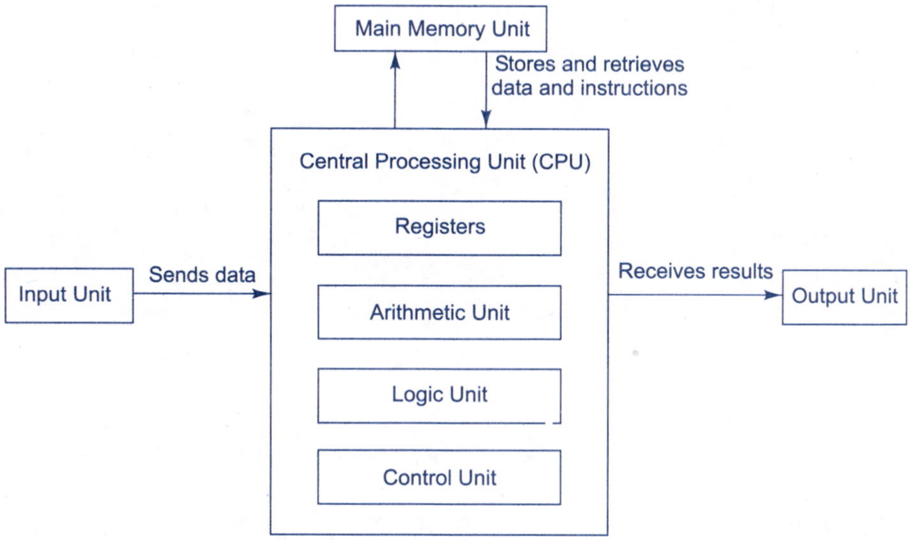

Fig. 2.1 The block diagram of a computer system

The main operations of the CPU include four phases:

- Fetching instructions from the memory.
- Decoding the instructions to decide what operations to be preformed.
- Executing the instructions.
- Storing the results back in the memory.

This four-phase process is known as the *CPU cycle*, which is illustrated in Fig. 2.2.

As shown in the Fig. 2.1, the central processing unit consists of the following subsystems:

- Arithmetic Unit (AU)
- Logic Unit (LU)
- Control Unit (CU)

The CPU makes use of the following memory subsystems for carrying out its processing operations:

- Main Memory Unit
- Cache Memory
- Registers

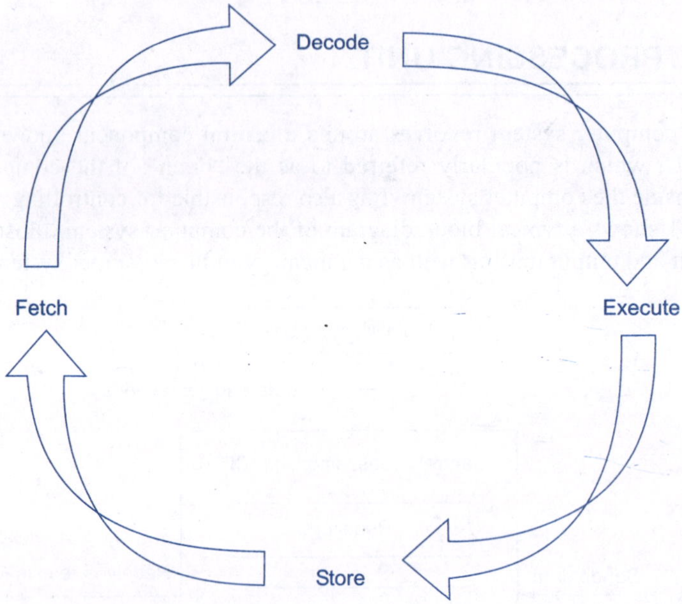

Fig. 2.2 The CPU cycle

2.2.1 Arithmetic Unit

Arithmetic Unit (AU) is a part of the CPU that performs arithmetic operations on the data. The arithmetic operations can be addition, subtraction, multiplication or division. The multiplication and division operations are usually implemented by the AU as the repetitive process of addition and subtraction operations respectively. Some CPUs contain separate AUs for integer or fixed-point operations (integers) and real or floating-point operations (real/decimal). AU takes the input in the form of an instruction that contains an opcode, operands and the format code. The opcode specifies the operation to be performed and the operands specify the data on which operation is to be performed. The format code suggests the format of the operands, such as fixed-point or floating-point. The output of AU contains the result of the operation and the status of the result, whether it is final or not. The output is stored in a storage register by the AU. Register is a small storage area inside the CPU from where data is retrieved faster than any other storage area.

2.2.2 Logic Unit

Logic Unit (LU) is a part of the CPU that performs logical operations on the data. It performs 16 different types of logical operations. The various logical operations include greater than (>), less than (<), equal to (=), not equal to (≠), shift left, shift right, etc. LU makes use of various logic gates, such as AND, OR, NOR, etc for performing the logical operations on the data.

2.2.3 Control Unit

Control Unit (CU) is an important component of CPU that controls the flow of data and information. It maintains the sequence of operations being performed by the CPU. It fetches an instruction from the storage area, decodes the instruction and transmits the corresponding signals to the AU or LU and the storage registers. CU guides the AU and LU about the operations that are to be performed and also suggests the I/O devices to which the data is to be communicated. CU uses a program counter register for retrieving the next instruction that is to be executed. It also uses a status register for handling conditions such as overflow of data.

2.2.4 Main Memory Unit

The *main memory* is referred to as the *internal memory* or *primary memory* of the computer. It is also known as Random Access Memory (RAM). It is a temporary storage medium that holds the data only for a short period of time. Once the computer is switched off, the data stored in the RAM gets erased. The memory space of RAM is limited and therefore all the files and instructions cannot be stored in it. These files and instructions are normally stored in a different location known as secondary storage and are copied from there to the RAM before execution. This technique is referred as *swapping*. The memory space available in RAM also affects the speed of a computer system. If the memory space is more, more number of instructions can be copied and executed at the same time. As a result, the computer system need not read the data from the secondary storage again and again, thus making the processing faster. The main memory is also responsible for holding intermediate data transferred between CPU and the I/O devices.

2.2.5 Cache Memory

Cache memory is a small, fast and expensive memory that stores the copies of data that needs to be accessed frequently from the main memory. The processor, before reading data from or writing data to the main memory, checks for the same data in the cache memory. If it finds the data in the cache memory the processor reads the data from or writes the data to the cache itself because its access time is much faster than the main memory. The cache memory is always placed between CPU and the main memory of the computer system, as shown in Fig. 2.3.

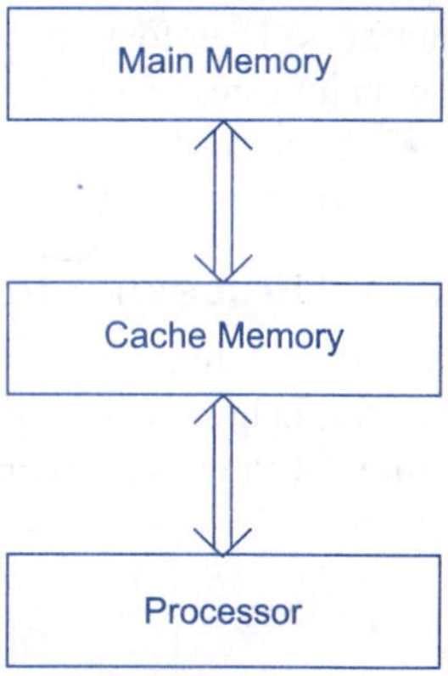

Fig. 2.3 The cache memory

Figure 2.3 shows that the transfer of data between the processor and the cache memory is bidirectional. The availability of data in the cache is known as *cache hit*. The capability of a cache memory is measured on the basis of cache hit.

There are usually two types of cache memory found in the computer system:

- **Primary cache** It is also known as Level 1 (L1) cache or internal cache. The primary cache is located inside the CPU. It is smaller but fastest type of cache that provides a quick access to the frequently accessed data by the microprocessor.
- **Secondary cache** It is also known as Level 2 (L2) cache or external cache. The secondary cache is located outside the CPU. It is normally positioned on the motherboard of a computer. The secondary cache is larger but slower than the primary cache.

2.2.6 Registers

Central processing unit contains a few special purpose, temporary storage units known as *registers*. They are high-speed memory locations used for holding instructions, data and intermediate results that are currently being processed. A processor can have different types of registers to hold different types of information. They include, among others:

- *Program Counter (PC)* to keep track of the next instruction to be executed.
- *Instruction Register (IR)* to hold instructions to be decoded by the control unit.
- *Memory Address Register (MAR)* to hold the address of the next location in the memory to be accessed.
- *Memory Buffer Register (MBR)* for storing data received from or sent to CPU.
- *Memory Data Register (MDR)* for storing operands and data.
- *Accumulator (ACC)* for storing the results produced by arithmetic and logic units.

Many computers employ additional registers for implementing various other requirements. The number and sizes of registers therefore vary from processor to processor. An effective implementation of registers can increase considerably the speed of the processor.

2.3 INTERNAL COMMUNICATIONS

CPU of the computer system communicates with the memory and the I/O devices in order to transfer data between them. However, the method of communication of the CPU with memory and I/O devices is different. The CPU may communicate with the memory either directly or through the cache memory. However, the communication between the CPU and I/O devices is usually implemented with the help of interfaces. Therefore, the internal communication of a processor in the computer system can be divided into two major categories:

- Processor to memory communication
- Processor to I/O devices communication

2.3.1 Processor to Memory Communication

The direct communication between the processor and memory of the computer system is implemented with the help of two registers, Memory Address Register (MAR) and Memory Buffer Register (MBR). Figure 2.4 shows the communication between the processor and the memory of the computer system.

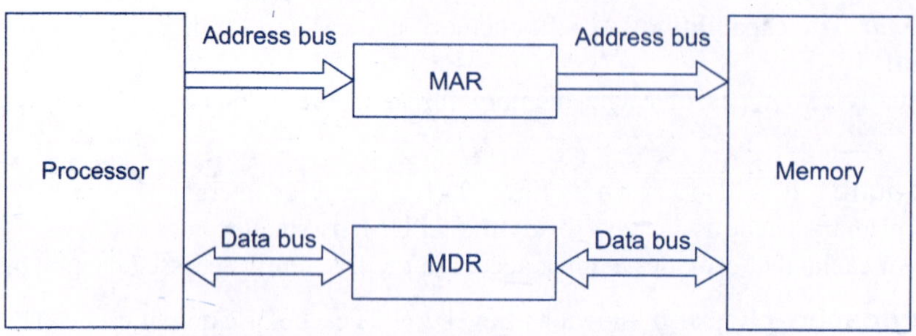

Fig. 2.4 Processor to memory communication

The processor can interact with the memory of the computer system for reading data from the memory as well as for writing data on to the memory. The MAR and MBR registers play a very important role in implementing this type of communication. These registers are the special-purpose registers of the processor. MAR is used by the processor to keep track of the memory location where it needs to perform the reading or writing operation. This register actually holds the address of the memory location. On the other hand, the Memory Data Register (MDR) is used by the processor to store the data that needs to be transferred from/to the memory of the computer system. The reading and writing operations performed by the processor are called *memory read* and *memory write* operations.

Figure 2.5 illustrates the memory read operation performed by the processor of the computer system. The processor performs the following steps to read the data from the desired memory location:

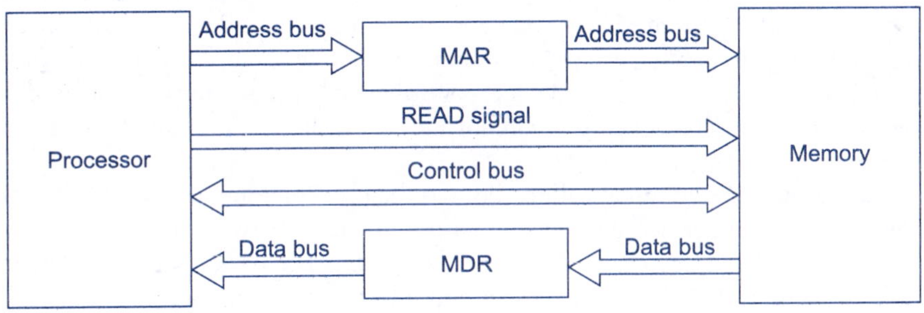

Fig. 2.5 Illustrating the memory read operation

1. First, the processor loads the address of the memory location from where data is to be read into the MAR register, using the address bus.
2. After loading the address of the memory location, the processor issues the READ control signal through the control bus. The control bus is used to carry the commands issued by the processor, and the status signals are generated by the various devices in response to these commands.
3. After receiving the READ control signal, the memory loads the data into the MDR register from the location specified in the MAR register, using the data bus.
4. Finally, the data is transferred to the processor.

The memory write operation helps the processor to write the data at the desired memory location. Figure 2.6 illustrates the memory write operation performed by the processor of the computer system.

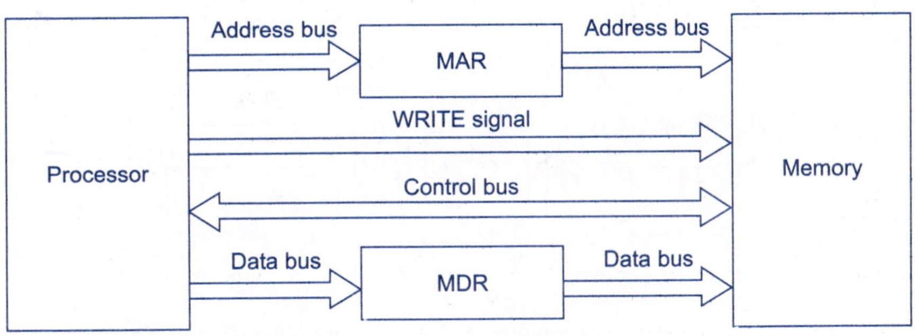

Fig. 2.6 Illustrating memory write operation

The processor performs the following steps for writing the data at the desired memory location in the computer system:

1. First, the processor loads the address of the memory location where data is to be written in the MAR register, using the address bus.
2. After loading the address of the memory location, the processor loads the desired data in the MDR register, using the data bus.
3. After this, the processor issues the WRITE control signal to the memory, using the control bus.
4. Finally, the memory stores the data loaded in the MDR register at the desired memory location.

2.3.2 Processor to I/O Devices Communication

The communication between I/O devices and processor of the computer system is implemented using an *interface unit*. In a computer system, data is transferred from an input device to the processor and from the processor to an output device. Each input and output device in the computer system is provided with a controller, called *device controller*. The device controller is used to manage the working of various peripheral devices. The processor actually communicates with the device controllers of the various I/O devices for performing the I/O operations.

Figure 2.7 illustrates how the communication between the processor and the I/O devices of the computer system is implemented. The interface unit acts as an intermediary between the processor and the device controllers of various peripheral devices in the computer system. The basic function of the interface unit is to accept the control commands from the processor and interpret the commands so that they can be easily understood by the device controllers for carrying out necessary operations. Therefore, we can say that the interface unit is responsible for controlling the input and output operations between the processor and the I/O devices. The interface unit contains data register and status register. The data register is used to store the data to be transferred, either to the processor or to an output device. The status register is used to indicate the status of the data register, i.e., whether it is currently holding the data or not. If the data register is holding the data to be transferred, the flag bit of the status register is set to one. The processor to I/O devices communication involves two important operations, i.e., I/O read and I/O write. The I/O read operation helps the processor to read the data from an input device.

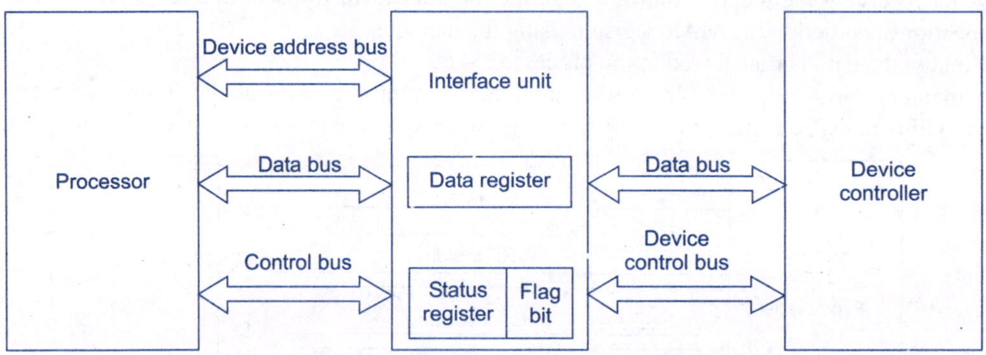

Fig. 2.7 Illustrating the communication process between the processor and I/O devices

Figure 2.8 illustrates how the data is transferred from an input device to the processor of the computer system. The steps performed while transferring the data from an input device to the processor are:

1. The data to be transferred is placed on the data bus by the input device, which transfers single byte of data at a time.

2. The input device then issues the data valid signal through the device control bus to the data register, indicating that the data is available on the data bus.
3. When the data register of the interface unit accepts the data, it issues a data accepted signal through the device control bus as an acknowledgement to the input device, indicating that the data has been received. The input device then disables the data valid signal.
4. As the data register now holds the data, the F or the flag bit of the status register is set to 1.
5. The processor now issues an I/O read signal to the data register in the interface unit.
6. The data register then places the data on the data bus connected to the processor of the computer system. After receiving the data, the processor sends an appropriate acknowledgement signal to the input device, indicating that the data has been received.

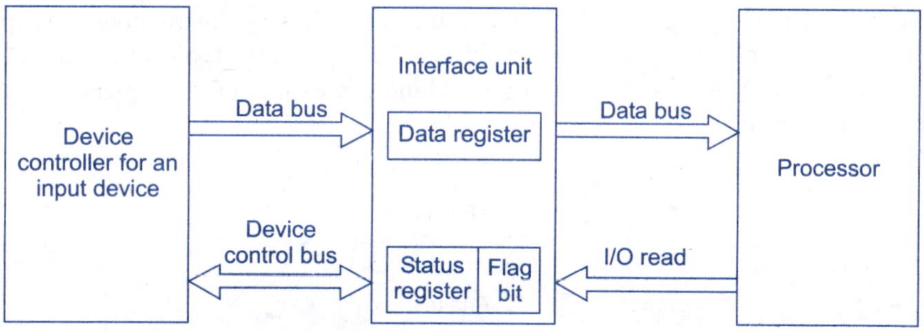

Fig. 2.8 Illustrating the I/O read operation

The I/O write operation helps the processor to write the data to an output device. Figure 2.9 illustrates how the data is transferred from the processor to an output device. The steps performed while transferring the data from the processor to the output device are:

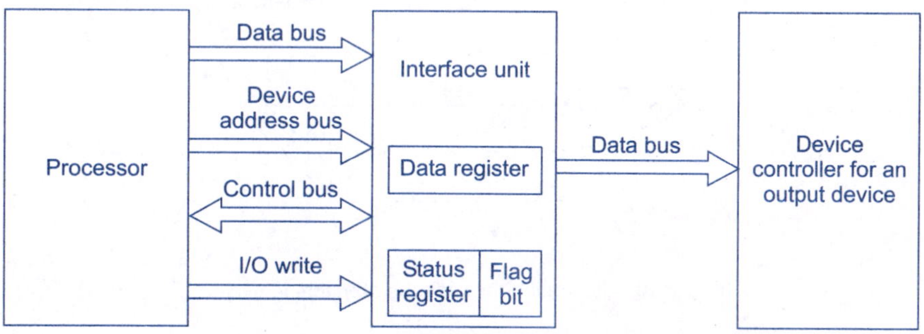

Fig. 2.9 Illustrating I/O write operation

1. The processor places the data that needs to be transferred on the data bus connected to the data register of the interface unit.
2. The CPU also places the address of the output device on the device address bus.
3. After placing the address and data on the appropriate buses, CPU issues the I/O write signal, which writes the data on the data register. The flag bit in the interface unit is set to 1, indicating that the data register now holds the data.

4. The data register of the interface unit issues a data accepted signal through the control bus to the processor, indicating that the data has been received.
5. The interface unit then places the data stored in the data register on to the data bus connected to the device controller of the output device.
6. The output device then receives the data and sends an acknowledgement signal to the processor of the computer system through the interface unit, indicating that the desired data has been received.

2.4 MACHINE CYCLE

The cycle during which a machine language instruction is executed by the processor of the computer system is known as *machine cycle*. If a program consists of 10 machine language instructions, 10 separate machine cycles would be executed for running the program. Figure 2.10 shows the typical machine cycle performed by the CPU of a computer system. As shown, the machine cycle contains four phases, namely, fetching, decoding, executing and storing.

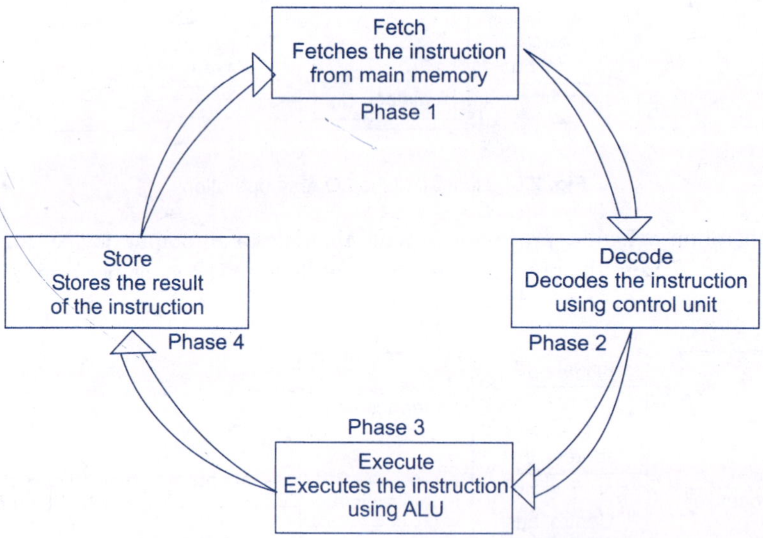

Fig. 2.10 Illustrating the process of machine cycle

The four phases of the machine cycle are usually grouped into two categories:

- Instruction cycle
- Execution cycle

2.4.1 Instruction Cycle

Instruction cycle includes the first two phases, fetching and decoding.

- **Fetching** In this phase, the CPU retrieves the instruction from the main memory of the computer system. The address of the instruction that needs to be executed is sent to the CPU through the address bus. The address of the instruction is then stored by the CPU in its internal register known as Program Counter (PC). After the address of the instruction is confirmed by the CPU, the actual instruction is retrieved by the CPU form the main memory and stored in the Instruction Register (IR).

- **Decoding** This phase of instruction cycle is responsible for breaking down the instruction into different parts, so that it can be easily understood before being processed by the CPU. The instruction is usually decoded by the instruction decoder, which is a vital component of the CPU. The decoding of an instruction is also known as interpreting. The instructions are interpreted to determine two key attributes of an instruction, the *opcode* and the *operands*. The opcode specifies the operation to be performed and the operands specify the data on which the operation is to be performed. The data is transferred to the Data Register (DR).

2.4.2 Execution Cycle

Execution cycle includes two phases, executing and storing. The execution cycle executes the instruction and stores the result back to the main memory or sends it to the output device of the computer system.

- **Executing** In this phase, the decoded instruction is executed by the ALU of the CPU. The execution time spent by the ALU for executing an instruction may vary, depending on the type of the instruction. The execution time also depends on the processor architecture.
- **Storing** In this phase, the result computed in the execution phase is either sent to the memory or to an output device of the computer system. The PC of the CPU is also updated in this phase to point to the next instruction that is to be executed.

After the execution cycle is completed, the next machine cycle begins.

2.5 THE BUS

A bus is a set of wires that is used to connect the different internal components of the computer system for the purpose of transferring data as well addresses amongst them. There may be several buses in a computer system. A bus can either be a serial bus or a parallel bus. In serial bus, only one bit of data is transferred at a time amongst the various hardware components. On the other hand, in parallel bus, several bits of data can be transferred at a time amongst the various hardware components. The speed of any type of bus is measured in terms of the number of bits transferred per second, between two components.

Figure 2.11 shows a bus system used in a computer system. The figure depicts the two different types of buses according to the type of operations performed by them. These buses are *data bus* and the *address bus*. Apart from data and address bus, a third type of bus—known as

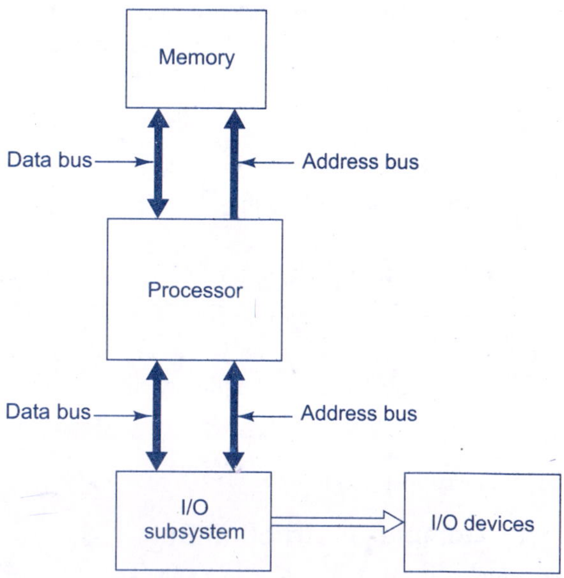

Fig. 2.11 Data and address buses

control bus—also exists in the computer system. The control bus manages the transfer of data and addresses among various components by transferring appropriate control signals.

2.5.1 Data Bus

As the name suggests, the data bus in a computer system is used to transfer data amongst the different internal components. The speed of the data bus also affects the overall processing power of a computer system. Modern computer systems use 32-bit data buses for data transfer. This means that these buses are capable of transferring 32 bits of data at a time. Figure 2.12 shows the data bus implemented between the main memory and the processor of a computer system.

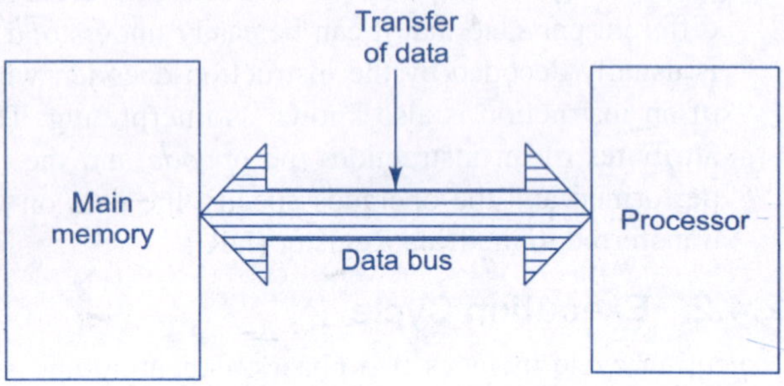

Fig. 2.12 The data bus

The figure shows that a bidirectional data bus is implemented between the main memory and the processor of the computer system. The bidirectional data bus allows the transfer of data in both the directions. The data bus is generally bidirectional in nature in most computer systems.

2.5.2 Address Bus

The address bus is also known as memory bus. It transfers the memory addresses for read and write memory operations. It contains a number of address lines that determine the range of memory addresses that can be referenced using the address bus. For example, a 32-bit address bus can be used to reference 2^{32} memory locations. Like data bus, the address bus can also be a serial or a parallel bus. Figure 2.13 shows the address bus, used for transferring memory locations between processor and memory.

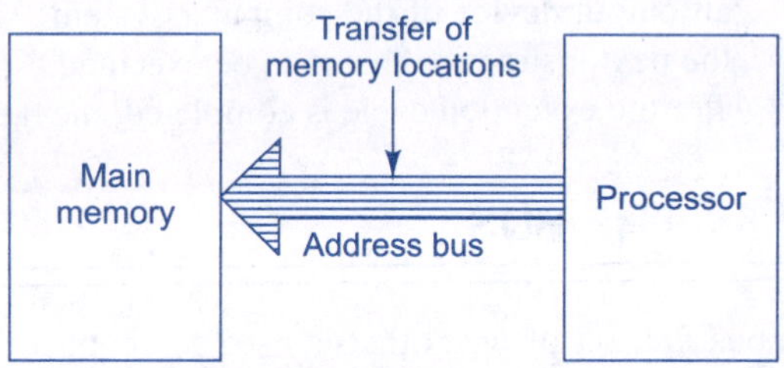

Fig. 2.13 An address bus

The figure shows that the address bus between the main memory and the processor of a computer system is unidirectional. However, an address bus may also be bidirectional. For example, the address bus between the processor and the I/O system is bidirectional.

2.6 INSTRUCTION SET

An instruction set can be defined as a group of instructions that a processor can execute to perform different operations. On the basis of complexity and the number of instructions used, the instruction set can be classified as:

- Complex instruction set
- Reduced instruction set

2.6.1 Complex Instruction Set

The complex instruction set refers to the set of instructions that includes very complex and large number of instructions. The number of instructions in this set varies from 100 to 250. The instructions in this set are mostly memory-based instructions, which involve frequent references to the memory. The complex instruction set makes use of a large number of addressing modes because of the frequent references to registers as well as memory. The instructions in this instruction set have variable length instruction format, which is not limited to only 32-bits. The execution of the instructions takes a lot of time because the instructions are memory-based and accessing the memory is a time consuming process as compared to accessing the registers.

The computer, which makes use of complex instruction set, is called Complex Instruction Set Computer (CISC). The instruction set of CISC has a large number of instructions and for each instruction type, the computer requires a separate circuitry, which makes the CPU design more complicated.

Some of the advantages of CISC are as follows:

- There is no need to invent an instruction set for each new design. A new processor can use the instruction set of its predecessor.
- A program written in CISC requires less memory space, as the code is confined to less number of instructions.
- CISC makes the job of a compiler easier by facilitating the implementation of high-level language constructs.

Some of the disadvantages of a CISC are as follows:

- The inheritance of old instructions into new processors increases the complexity.
- Many CISC instructions are not frequently used.
- CISC commands are translated into a large number of lines of microcode, which makes the CPU processing slower.
- CISC systems have a complex hardware, so they require more time for designing.

2.6.2 Reduced Instruction Set

The reduced instruction set refers to a set of instructions that contains very few instructions ranging from 0 to 100. It comprises of only those instructions, that are frequently used by the processor for the execution of a program. These instructions are generally very simple to execute. The instructions used in this set are mostly register-based, which means that the execution of the instruction involves frequent references to the registers. The memory-based instructions, which involve frequent references to the memory locations, are very few in this instruction set. The memory-based instructions include only load and store instructions. The instructions in this instruction set have fixed length instruction format of 32 bits. An instruction format divides the bits of instruction into small groups called fields. Generally, an instruction has the following fields:

- **Opcode field.** It represents the operation to be performed by the instruction.
- **Operand field.** It represents the data on which the operation is to be performed, or the memory location or register where the data is stored.
- **Mode field.** It represents the method of fetching the operands stored at specified memory location or registers.

The computer, which makes use of reduced instruction set, is called Reduced Instruction Set Computer (RISC). As the instruction set of RISC has very few instructions, the design of hardware circuitry becomes easier and also the speed of processing increases. The speed of RISC processors is measured in MIPS (Millions of Instructions Per Second).

The comparison of RISC and CISC processors indicates that the RISC processors are always preferred over the CISC processors because of their compact size and small instruction set. The other advantages of the RISC processors over the CISC processors are as follows:

- In RISC processors, the instructions are executed by decoding, whereas in CISC processors, the instructions are executed by first translating them into equivalent microcode instructions. The conversion of instructions into microcode consumes a lot of space in the memory, thereby reducing the speed of execution.

- The RISC processors execute instructions in a single clock cycle, while the CISC processors require multiple clock cycles for the execution of an instruction.
- The hardware of the RISC processors is very simple and can be designed easily, as compared to the hardware of the CISC processors that is very complex, difficult to design and large in size.

The only disadvantage of RISC, in comparison to CISC, is that the number of instructions required to perform an operation is comparatively large.

Chapter Summary

Computer organisation and architecture refers to the study of different functional components of the computer system and the manner in which these components interact with each other to perform a specific operation. The central and main component of a computer system is the CPU. CPU is the only component in the computer system that is responsible for carrying out different operations. The major internal components of CPU are AU, LU, and CU. The two major components of a computer system that communicate with the CPU to perform an operation are main memory unit and cache memory. AU is responsible for performing arithmetic operations while LU is responsible for performing logical operations. CU controls the functioning of the CPU.

The CPU also interacts with the memory unit for reading and writing the data in the computer system. Generally, the communication between the memory and the CPU is direct. However, a computer system can also be provided with a cache memory to speed up the process of CPU to memory communication. CPU can also interact with the I/O devices through an interface unit to perform various input and output operations.

An instruction is executed by the CPU in two different phases, known as instruction cycle and execution cycle. During the instruction cycle, the CPU fetches the instruction from the memory and decodes it. The execution cycle executes the instruction and stores the result back to the main memory or sends it to the output device of the computer system.

Key Terms to Remember

- **Computer architecture**: It refers to the definition of basic attributes of hardware components and their interconnections, in order to achieve certain specified goals in terms of functions and performance.
- **Computer organisation**: It refers to the design and physical arrangement of various hardware units to work in tandem, in an orderly manner, in order to achieve the goals specified in the architecture.
- **CPU**: It is referred to as the brain of the computer and is responsible for processing the data inside the computer system.
- **AU**: It is a part of the CPU that performs arithmetic operations on the data.
- **LU**: It is a part of the CPU that performs logical operations on the data.
- **CU**: It is an important component of CPU that controls the flow of data and information.
- **Opcode**: It specifies the operation to be performed on data.
- **Operand**: It is the data on which the operation is to be performed.
- **Main memory**: It is referred to as the internal memory or primary memory of the computer and is a temporary storage medium that holds the data only for a short period of time.
- **Cache memory**: It is a small, fast and expensive memory that stores the copies of the data that needs to be accessed frequently from the main memory.

- **Primary cache**: It is known as L1 cache or internal cache and is located inside the CPU.
- **Secondary cache**: It is also known as L2 cache or external cache and is located on the motherboard of a computer.
- **Registers**: They are high-speed memory locations used for holding instructions, data and intermediate results that are currently being processed.
- **PC**: This register is used to keep track of the next instruction to be executed.
- **IR**: This register is used to hold instructions to be decoded by the control unit.
- **MAR**: This register is used to hold the address of the next location in the memory to be accessed.
- **MBR**: This register is used to store data received from or sent to CPU.
- **MDR**: This register is used to store operands and data.
- **Accumulator**: This register is used to store the results produced by arithmetic and logic units.
- **Machine cycle**: It refers to a cycle during which a machine language instruction is executed by the processor of the computer system.
- **Bus**: It is a set of wires that is used to connect the different internal components oi the computer system for the purpose of transferring data as well addresses amongst them.
- **Data bus**: It is a bus used to transfer data among the different internal components.
- **Address bus**: It is a bus used to transfer the memory addresses for read and write memory operations.
- **Control bus**: It is a bus that manages the transfer of data and addresses among various components by transferring appropriate control signals.
- **Complex instruction set**: It refers to a set of instructions that includes very complex and large number of instructions.
- **Reduced instruction set**: It refers to a set of instructions that contains very few instructions ranging from 0 to 100.
- **CISC**: It refers to a computer that makes the use of complex instruction set.
- **RISC**: It refers to a computer that makes use of reduced instruction set.

Review Questions

Fill in the Blanks

1. The central processing unit of the computer system is popularly known as ________ of the computer system.
2. _________ unit is responsible for performing all the arithmetic operations in the computer system.
3. The _________ register keeps the track of the next instruction to be executed.
4. _____________ is called the main-memory of the computer.
5. The access time of _________ memory is faster as compared to that of main memory.
6. The group of wires used to connect the components of CPU to transfer the data is called ________________
7. The time taken by the CPU to fetch an instruction and execute it is called ________________.
8. The group of instructions that a processor can execute is called ________________.
9. _________ bus is used to transfer data from the memory.
10. The instruction set can be classified as ________________ and ________________.
11. The _______ field represents the operation to be performed by the instruction.

12. The instruction set of _________ has a few instructions compared to that of _________.
13. The direct communication between processor and memory of the computer system is implemented with the help of two registers, _________ and _________.
14. The two important operations performed while communicating with the memory of the computer system are _________ and _________.
15. The flag bit of the status registeı is ______, when the register holds the data.
16. The computer, which makes use of reduced instruction set, is called ________.
17. The speed of the RISC processors is measured in _________.
18. _________ bus transfers the memory addresses for reading or writing the data.

Multiple Choice Questions

1. The definition of basic attributes of hardware components and their interconnections, in order to achieve certain specific goals, in terms of functions and performance is known as:
   A. Computer organisation
   B. Computer architecture
   C. Computer management
   D. Computer arrangement
2. The design and physical arrangement of various hardware components to work in a tandem in an orderly manner, so as to archive the goals specified in the architecture is known as:
   A. Computer organisation
   B. Computer architecture
   C. Computer management
   D. Computer arrangement
3. What does CPU stand for?
   A. Center processing unit
   B. Central processing unit
   C. Central programming unit
   D. Computer processing unit
4. Which one of the following is not an internal component of CPU?
   A. Arithmetic unit
   B. Logic unit
   C. Interface unit
   D. Control unit
5. What is the main function of CPU in a computer system?
   A. Storing the data
   B. Programming the computer
   C. Transferring the data to an output device
   D. Processing the data
6. Which of the following memory locations are first referred by the CPU while searching for data?
   A. Main memory
   B. Cache Memory
   C. ROM
   D. Secondary memory
7. Cache memory is used to transfer data between:
   A. Main memory and secondary memory
   B. Processor and an input device
   C. Main memory and processor
   D. Processor and an output device
8. Which one of the following cache memory is also known as internal cache?
   A. L2 cache
   B. L1 cache
   C. L3 cache
   D. L4 cache
9. Which one of the following hardware components is normally used to accommodate secondary cache?
   A. Motherboard
   B. Processor
   C. RAM
   D. Any secondary storage device

10. Which one of the following statement is not true about L1 cache?
    A. L1 cache is a type of cache memory.
    B. L1 cache stores the data from the main memory.
    C. L1 cache is an expensive type of memory.
    D. L1 cache is usually slower than L2 cache.
11. Which one of the following register is not a CPU register?
    A. Memory control register B. Memory data register
    C. Memory buffer register D. Instruction register
12. What is the purpose of memory address register?
    A. Stores the address of the next location in the main memory
    B. Stores the address of the next location in the secondary memory
    C. Stores the address of the next location in the cache memory
    D. Stores the address of an output device to which the data is to be sent
13. Which of the following registers is used to indicate whether the data register holds the data to be transferred or not?
    A. Status register B. MAR C. MBR D. MDR
14. Which of the following two registers are used by the CPU to transfer the data between processor and memory?
    A. MDR and IR B. PC and IR C. IR and MAR D. MAR and MDR
15. Which of the following sequence of operations represents the machine cycle?
    A. Fetch-Execute-Decode-Store B. Store-Execute-Fetch-Decode
    C. Fetch-Decode-Execute-Store D. Store-Fetch-Decode-Execute
16. The decoding phase of the instruction cycle is also known as:
    A. Translating B. Interpreting C. Analysing D. Breaking
17. Which of the following is not a type of bus used in the computer system?
    A. Data bus B. Address bus C. Information bus D. Control bus
18. Which of the following is a characteristic of the CISC processor?
    A. Number of instructions varying between 100 and 250
    B. Large number of addressing modes
    C. Variable length instruction format
    D. All of the above
19. What is the fixed length of the instruction format used in RISC processors?
    A. 30-bits B. 16-bits C. 32-bits D. 24-bits

Discussion Questions

1. What do you understand by computer architecture? Is it same as computer organisation? If no, explain the difference between the two.
2. Draw the block diagram of a computer system and explain its main components.
3. How does the control unit assist the CPU in carrying out its operations?
4. What do you understand by CPU cycle? What are the main operations accomplished using the CPU cycle?

5. Explain the concept of cache memory with diagram. What are the different types of cache memory found in a computer system?
6. List the different types of CPU registers.
7. What do you understand by internal communications? List the major categories of internal communications.
8. Explain the importance of MAR and MDR in accomplishing processor to memory communication.
9. What is the difference between memory read and memory write operations? List the different steps involved in memory read and memory write operations.
10. Explain the concept of processor to I/O devices communication. What is the role of interface unit in implementing such type of communication in a computer system?
11. Explain how data is transferred from processor to an output device within a computer system.
12. What is the difference between instruction cycle and execution cycle?
13. What is the importance of decoding phase of machine cycle? Which component of CPU plays an important role in decoding phase?
14. Explain the importance of a bus in the computer system. What are the different types of buses usually found in the computer system?
15. What is the function of a control bus in a computer system?
16. Explain the concept of instruction set. Which component of a computer system is mostly associated with instruction set?
17. What are the different factors considered for classifying an instruction set?
18. Explain in detail the different categories of instruction sets.
19. What do you understand by CISC? List the advantages and disadvantages of CISC.
20. What do you understand by RISC? List the advantages of RISC processors.

CHAPTER 3

MEMORY AND STORAGE SYSTEMS

Chapter Outline

Chapter Objectives

In this chapter, we will learn:

- The concept of memory and its representation.
- How data is stored in Random Access Memory (RAM) and the various types of RAM.
- How data is stored in Read Only Memory (ROM) and the various types of ROM.
- The concept of storage systems and the various types of storage systems.
- The criteria for evaluating storage systems.

3.1 INTRODUCTION

Computers are used not only for processing of data for immediate use, but also for storing of large volume of data for future use. In order to meet these two specific requirements, computers use two types of storage locations—one, for storing the data that are being currently handled by the CPU and the other, for storing the results and the data for future use. The storage location where the data are held temporarily is referred to as the *primary memory* while the storage location where the programs and data are stored permanently for future use is referred to as the *secondary memory*. The primary memory is generally known as "memory" and the secondary memory as "storage".

The data and instructions stored in the primary memory can be directly accessed by the CPU using the data and address buses. However, the information stored in the secondary memory is not directly accessible to CPU. Firstly, the information has to be transferred to the primary memory using I/O channels and then, to the CPU.

Computers also use a third type of storage location known as the *internal process memory*. This memory is placed either inside the CPU or near the CPU (connected through special fast bus). Figure 3.1 illustrates all the three categories of computer memory and their relative speed, storage capacity and cost.

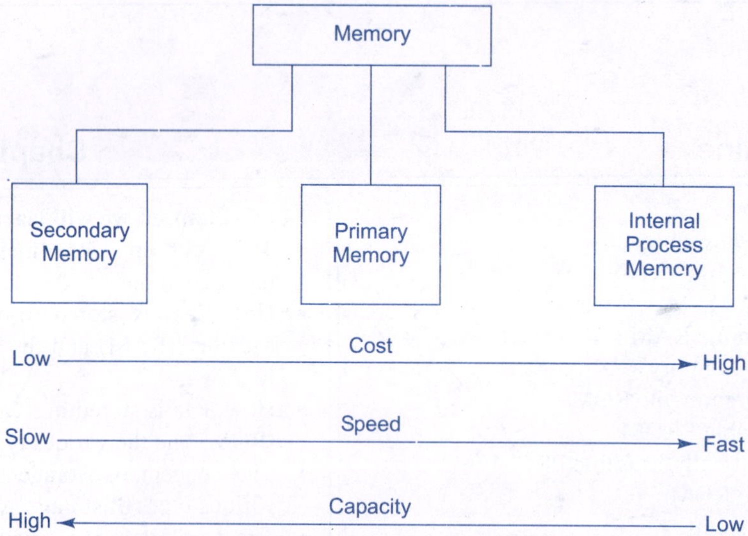

Fig. 3.1 Memory categories

Primary memory (also known as main memory) includes two types, namely, Random Access Memory (RAM) and Read Only Memory (ROM). The data stored in RAM are lost when the power is switched off and therefore, it is known as *volatile memory*. However, the data stored in ROM stay permanently even after the power is switched off and therefore ROM is a *non-volatile memory*.

Secondary memory (also known as auxiliary memory) includes primarily magnetic disks and magnetic tapes. These storage devices have much larger storage capacity than the primary memory. Information stored on such devices remains permanent (until we remove it).

Internal process memory usually includes cache memory and registers both of which store data temporarily and are accessible directly by the CPU. This memory is placed inside or near the CPU for the fast access of data.

We have discussed briefly cache memory and various registers used in Chapter 2. In this chapter, we shall discuss the various types of memory units, RAM and ROM and their functions. We shall also discuss the classification of storage devices such as magnetic disks, magnetic tapes and optical disks and their functions.

3.2 MEMORY REPRESENTATION

As we discussed earlier, data being worked on is stored in the computer memory. In the memory, values are represented by sequences of binary digits, known as *bits*. Most computers use a group of eight bits, known as a *byte*, to represent a character. How does the computer know what any particular sequence of bits represents? We can think of memory as a "bunch" of bytes or cells into which we can place data. Each cell, known as a data item, is assigned a unique number known as *address* (which is like the index in an array). The CPU can identify each cell by its address as shown in Fig. 3.2.

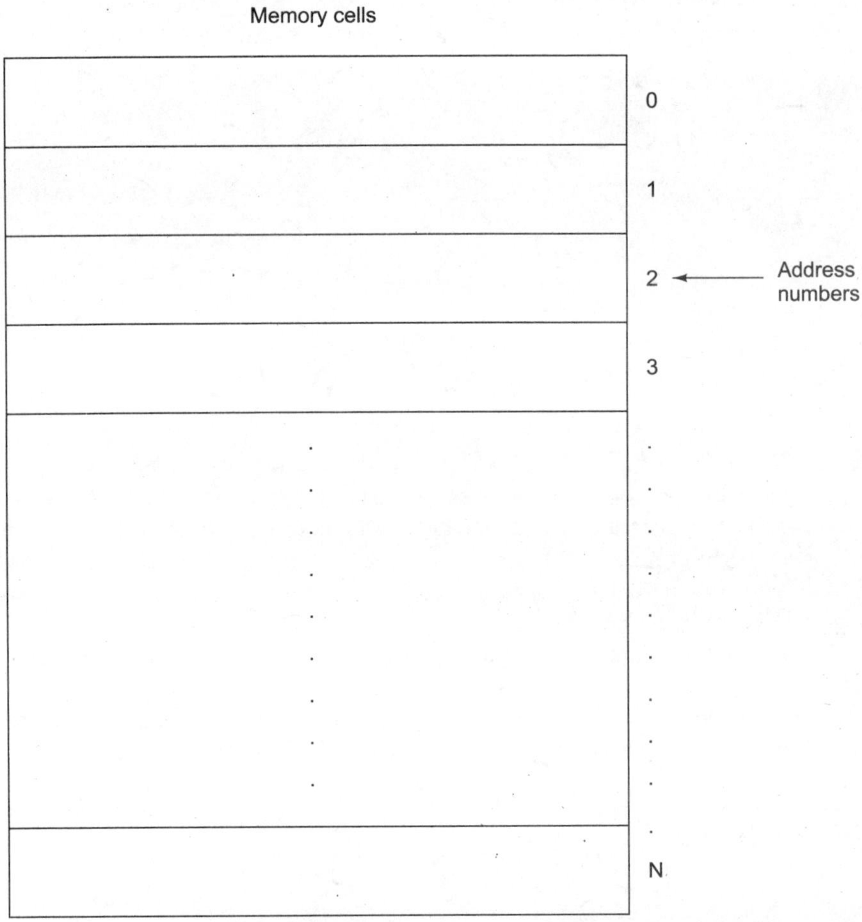

Fig. 3.2 Memory representation

The byte is defined as the "smallest addressable unit" of memory. Most computers use groups of bytes, usually 2 or 4, known as "words" to represent information.

Computer memories are often rated in terms of their capacity to store information. Typically, capacities are described using the unit of byte as follows:

1 KB (Kilobyte) = 1,024 bytes
1 MB (Megabyte) = 1,048,576 bytes
1 GB (Gigabyte) = 1,073,741,824 bytes
1 TB (Terabyte) = 1,099,511,627,776 bytes

3.3 RANDOM ACCESS MEMORY

Random Access Memory (RAM) is a volatile memory and loses all its data when the power is switched off. It is the main memory of the computer system that stores the data temporarily and allows the data to be accessed in any order. As compared to the secondary storage, the data can be accessed at a faster speed in RAM because it is the internal memory of the computer. Figure 3.3 shows RAM with ICs.

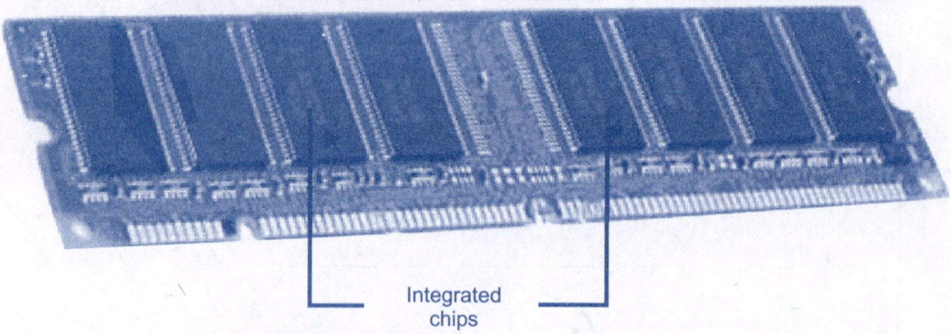

Fig. 3.3 Random access memory with ICs

RAM is made up of different ICs, which are mounted on a printed circuit board. RAM stores the application programs and the data on which the user is currently working so that the processor can easily access the required application program and data in a less amount of time. RAM is also known as read/write memory because it can perform both read as well as write operations. The speed of RAM is faster than the other memory devices, such as hard disk, floppy disk, etc.

The programs, which are being currently executed by the computer system, are stored in RAM. RAM is volatile and, therefore, the programs and the data stored in the RAM get lost when the power supply is switched off. The storage capacity of RAM is usually less than the secondary storage devices.

RAM can be categorised into two main types, namely, Static RAM (SRAM) and Dynamic RAM (DRAM), which can be further divided into various types for storing data. Figure 3.4 shows the hierarchy of RAM memory.

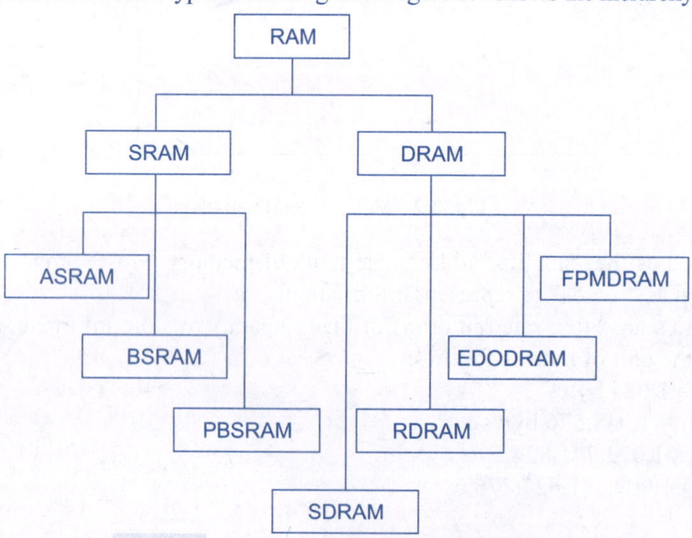

Fig. 3.4 Types of random access memory

3.3.1 Static RAM

Static RAM (SRAM) is a type of RAM in which data is stored till the power of the computer system is switched on. SRAM uses a number of transistors to store a single bit of digital information. Figure 3.5 shows the organisation of data in a cell of SRAM.

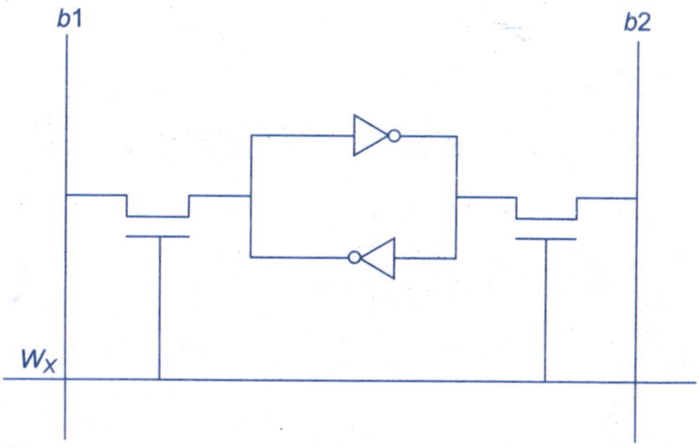

Fig. 3.5 Organisation of data in a cell of static random access memory

In the figure, $b1$ and $b2$ represent the two bit lines and W_x represents the word line. In the memory, the data is stored in the form of a two-dimensional array, containing rows and columns. The row can be accessed globally by a line (known as word line) and the column can be accessed individually by a line (known as bit line). Depending on the function performed by SRAM, it can be divided into the following three types:

- **Asynchronous SRAM (ASRAM)** ASRAM performs its operations without the use of system clock. It makes use of three signals for working, namely, Chip Select (CS), Write Enable (WE) and Output Enable (OE). The CS signal enables the processor to select the memory for performing read and write operations. If the value of CS signal equals zero, then the memory is enabled to perform the operations. On the other hand, if the value of the CS signal equals one, then the memory is disabled and operations—such as reading and writing in ASRAM—cannot be performed. The signal WE makes the decisions related to data, i.e., whether it should be read from or write to the memory. If the value of WE signal equals zero, then no data can be read from or written to the memory. The signal OE is an active low signal that enables the processor to give the output for the data. If the value of OE signal equals zero, then only it will output the data.

- **Burst SRAM (BSRAM)** BSRAM works in association with the system clock and is also known as synchronous SRAM. BSRAM is most commonly used with high-speed applications because the read and write cycles are synchronised with the clock cycles of the processor. The access-waiting time gets reduced after the read and write cycles are synchronised with the clock cycles. The speed and the cost of BSRAM increases or decreases simultaneously.

- **Pipeline Burst SRAM (PBSRAM)** PBSRAM makes use of the pipeline technology in which a large amount of data is broken up in the form of different packets containing data. These packets are arranged in a sequential manner in the pipeline and are sent to the memory simultaneously. PBSRAM can handle a large amount of data at a very high speed. It is the fastest type of SRAM because it can operate at bus rates as high as 66 MHz.

3.3.2 Dynamic RAM

DRAM is the RAM in which data is stored in a storage cell, consisting of a transistor and a capacitor. Unlike SRAM, the DRAM needs to be continuously refreshed with power supply because the capacitor has the tendency to get discharged. DRAM retains the data for a very short span of time, even after the power supply is switched off. Figure 3.6 shows the organisation of data in a cell of DRAM.

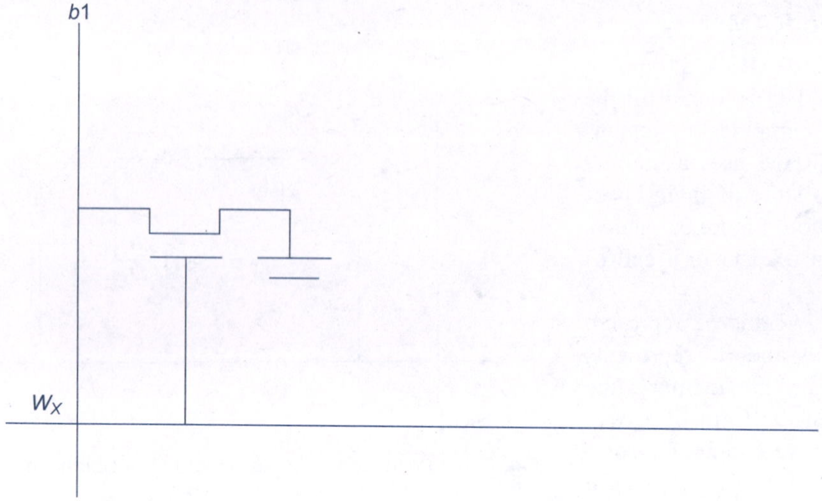

Fig. 3.6 Organisation of data in a cell of dynamic random access memory

In Fig. 3.6, *b*1 represents a bit line and W_x represents a word line. The DRAM can be divided into the following types:

- **Synchronous DRAM (SDRAM)** SDRAM performs its operations in the synchronous mode, i.e., in association with the clock cycle of the processor bus. It consists of two internal memory banks such that if the address lines are sent from the first bank, then the address can be read by using the second bank. The internal banks are used because the row and the column address lines need to be charged for reading an address. SDRAM provides a synchronous interface in which it waits for a clock signal before responding to a control input. Generally, it is used with the processors for storing the data in a continuous manner. The continuous form of data storage helps in processing more number of instructions per unit time that increases the speed of data access.
- **Rambus DRAM (RDRAM)** RDRAM designed by Rambus Inc. works at a faster speed, as compared to SDRRAM. It is compact in size and uses 16-bit address bus. It provides the facility to transfer data at a maximum speed of 800 MHz. It contains multiple address and data lines that help in increasing the speed of data access. These multiple address and data lines help in performing different read and write operations simultaneously. It is not popular among the users because of its high cost and low compatibility.
- **Extended Data Out DRAM (EDODRAM)** EDODRAM can access more than one bit of data at one time which helps in achieving faster data access rates. It provides the facility to perform various operations at one time such as reading, writing, etc. It starts accepting the next bit of data immediately after getting the first bit of data for performing read or write operation.
- **Fast Page Mode DRAM (FPMDRAM)** FPMDRAM makes use of paging in which read or write operation is performed by selecting the address of the data from the rows and the columns of a matrix. Once the data is read, the address of the particular column is incremented, so that the user can read the next part of the data. The use of paging concept in FPDRAM does not allow to work with the buses at the memory speed more than 66 MHz. As a result, a lot of time is consumed in reading and writing the data from the matrix.

3.4 READ ONLY MEMORY

ROM is the memory that stores the data permanently, i.e., it can retain the data even when the power of the computer system is switched off. The data can be easily read from this type of memory but cannot be changed. ROM is most commonly used in devices such as calculators, laser printers, etc.

ROM does not allow the random access of data rather it allows sequential access of data. It is less expensive as compared to RAM and other storage devices, such as magnetic disk, etc. ROM is divided into four types, which are as follows:

- Programmable ROM (PROM)
- Erasable PROM (EPROM)
- Electrically Erasable PROM (EEPROM)
- Flash ROM

3.4.1 Programmable ROM

Programmable ROM (PROM) is a memory chip on which the write operation of data can be performed only once. The data is stored on this chip permanently, i.e., once a program is written on the PROM, it cannot be erased or destroyed. To write the data on the PROM chip, a device known as PROM programmer or PROM burner is required. The method of writing data on the chip is known as burning the PROM. PROM is reliable and stores the data permanently without making any change in it. It is mostly used in video games and electronic dictionaries.

3.4.2 Erasable PROM

Erasable PROM (EPROM) is a type of ROM in which data can be erased or destroyed using Ultraviolet Light (UL). Erasable ROM provides the facility of changing the contents of the data, i.e., it can be reprogrammed. It contains the floating gate transistors, which have the capability to hold an electric charge, even when the power of the computer system is switched off. It also facilitates the storage of data for a longer period of time.

3.4.3 Electrically Erasable PROM

Electrically Erasable PROM (EEPROM) is a type of ROM in which data can be erased or destroyed by exposing it to an electric charge. It has the ability to retain the data stored in it, even if the power of the computer system is switched off. It stores the data permanently but allows us to make changes in the data by erasing it with the help of electric charges. In this type of memory, the data can be written or erased only one byte at a time because of which it works very slowly.

3.4.4 Flash ROM

Flash ROM is a type of EEPROM that stores the information using floating-gate transistors, which can store electric charge for a longer period of time as compared to the normal transistors. This memory is mainly used in the memory cards of mobile phones, digital cameras and ipods for storing data. The data stored in flash ROM memory can be easily transferred using transmission mediums such as data cable, bluetooth and infrared technology. For example, we can transfer the data stored in flash ROM memory of mobile phone to the memory of a computer using data cable. We can easily erase the data stored in flash ROM memory and reprogram this type of memory. Flash ROM has faster speed of reading data, as compared to any other type of ROM. It uses continuous memory cells for storing data.

The memory cells of flash ROM are made up of floating-gate transistors. A Single-level Cell (SLC) can store only one bit of data, whereas Multi-level Cell (MLC) provides the facility of storing more than one byte. The two types of flash ROM memory are as follows:

- **NAND flash** In NAND flash or NAND gate flash memory, each cell behaves like a Metal Oxide Semiconductor Field Effect Transistor (MOSFET), which has two gates for amplifying an electric signal.
- **NOR flash** NOR gate flash or NOR flash memory provides the facility to write data or information, with the help of tunnel injection. It can be defined as the process of inserting electrons to an electric conductor using a layer of electric insulator. It also provides the facility to erase the instructions using tunnel release.

3.5 STORAGE SYSTEMS

Storage systems are the devices—such as hard disks, optical disks and magnetic disks—used for data storage. The main objective of the storage system is to permanently store data—which can be of any type, such as images, videos and text—for future use. The storage systems provide the facility to use the data at any time.

Different storage systems have varying storage capacities. For example, the normal storage capacity of Compact Disk (CD) is 700 Megabytes (MB). The storage systems can be classified as shown in Fig. 3.7.

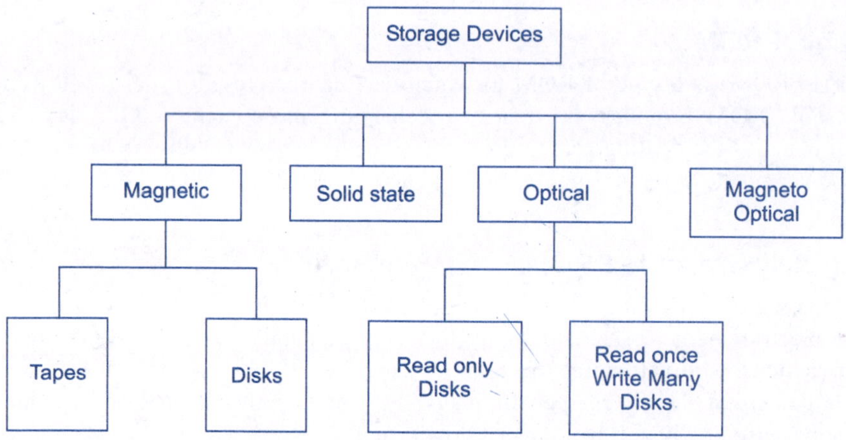

Fig. 3.7 Classification of storage systems

3.6 MAGNETIC STORAGE SYSTEMS

Magnetic storage systems can be defined as the storage systems that store the data on a magnetised medium, with the help of magnetised particles. Magnetic tapes, magnetic disks, hard disks, floppy disks are examples of magnetic storage systems. The magnetic storage systems are non-volatile and provide the facility to store any type of data, such as text, audio, video, image, etc. In case of magnetic storage systems, data can be accessed randomly as well as sequentially. For example, we can access data sequentially from a magnetic tape and randomly from a magnetic disk. When data is accessed sequentially, the access time is directly proportional to the searching point. In other words, if the searching point is near, then the access time is less, and if the searching point is far, then the access time is more. On the other hand, when data is accessed randomly, the access time is less.

3.6.1 Magnetic Tapes

Magnetic tapes are the plastic tapes with magnetic coating that are used for storing the data, such as text, audio or video. Magnetic tapes are similar to the normal recording tapes, which are used for audio and video recording. The data stored on the magnetic tapes can be accessed using the sequential access method. The magnetic tape could be compared with a cassette in which, in order to listen to the third song, we have to go pass the first two songs first. Similarly, in the magnetic tape, we cannot directly jump over to the third song. Therefore, magnetic tapes are used in the cases where a large amount of data needs to be stored, but performance is not a major issue. Magnetic tapes are best suited as the backup devices for storing a large amount of the data. Figure 3.8 shows a magnetic tape.

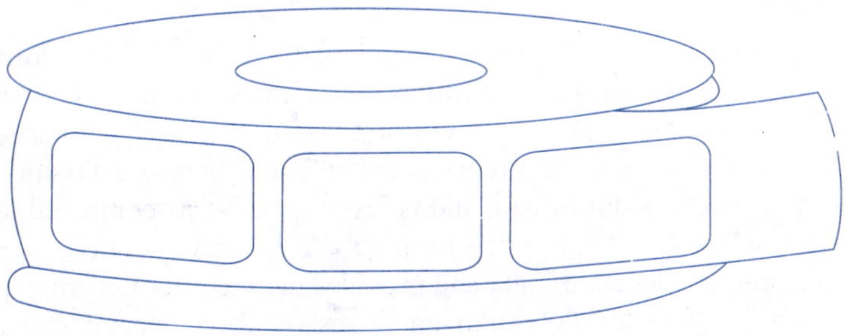

Fig. 3.8 Magnetic tape

A magnetic tape usually consists of a tape of 1/2 or 1/4 inch wide, 600 to 3,000 feet long and is wound on a spool in the form of a cartridge or a reel. A metal foil, called marker, is used to determine the Beginning of Tape (BOT). When a write command is given, a block of data is written on the tape. The next block is then written after a gap called Inter Block Gap (IBG). One block may contain one or more records that are again separated by blank spaces known as Inter Record Gaps (IRG). A series of blocks are written in this manner and the end-of-tape is described by the marker known as End of Tape (EOT). After the data is written, the tape is rewound and kept ready for reading. The data is stored in the form of tiny magnetised segments. A magnetised portion refers to the binary digit '1' while the non-magnetised portion refers to '0'.

Labelling can be done on a magnetic tape in order to retrieve any particular information when required. Magnetic tape is easy to store and is less prone to damage as compared to the other storage devices, such as hard disk, floppy disk, etc.

Generally 1/2 inch magnetic tape, consisting of either seven or nine tracks, is used for storing data. These tracks are mainly decided by the read/write heads of the tape unit that helps in reading or writing the data from or to the magnetic tape.

In magnetic tapes, the data is stored in the form of *records* and a set of different records is known as *file*. The data of any size can be recorded on a magnetic tape but the length and the storage capacity of the magnetic tape should be considered before storing the data. The speed of the magnetic tape should be predetermined for reading and writing data. When the magnetic tape moves at high speed, slows down or stops, the data cannot be read or written to the tape.

Major advantages of magnetic tapes are:

- Low cost
- Large storage capacity
- Easily transportable
- Easy to handle and store

Major disadvantages of using magnetic tapes are:

- Low data transmission speed due to sequential access.
- Not suitable for random access.
- Require protected environment for storage.
- Updating, such as insertion or deletion is difficult.
- Fast wear-out.

3.6.2 Magnetic Disks

Magnetic disk is a flat disk that is covered with magnetic coating for holding information. It is a type of secondary memory device that is used to store different programs and files. It is used to store digital information in the form of small and magnetised needles. These needles help in encoding a single bit of information by getting polarized in one direction represented by 1, and opposite direction represented by 0.

Magnetic disk can store a large amount of data and is less expensive as compared to RAM. As it takes more time to read the information from a specified location, its data access rate is slow compared to the main memory. It allows the random access of data and provides the facility of erasing and re-recording the data as many times as required. Figure 3.9 shows a magnetic disk with sectors and tracks.

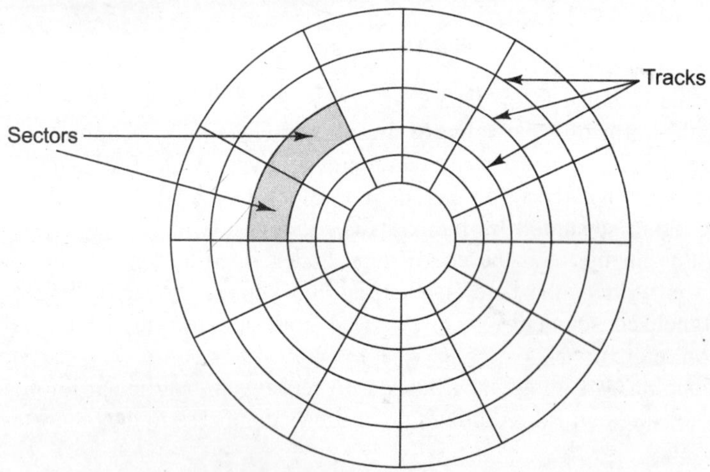

Fig. 3.9 Magnetic disk surface

Tracks are the concentric circles on the magnetic disk, having a common centre and containing a block of recorded data. The thickness between two tracks affects the storage capacity of a magnetic disk. If the thickness between the two tracks is less, then the magnetic disk can store a large amount of data. On the other hand, if the thickness between the two tracks is more then less amount of data can be stored in the magnetic disk. The data is stored in a magnetic disk in the form of tiny dots on the tracks, which are known as *spots*. The size of these spots should be small, in order to hold large amount of data and information.

The broken-up units of tracks are known as *sectors*. The data stored on the sectors is in the form of very small unit, which can be read or written. The size of a sector in a magnetic disk is 512 bytes.

There are two popular types of magnetic disks:

- Hard disks
- Floppy disks

A hard disk, also known as a fixed disk, can hold a large volume of data and is used with large computers. A floppy disk, a removable disk with relatively less storage capacity, is commonly used with personal computers.

Major advantages of magnetic disks are:

- High storage capacity
- Easy, direct access to data
- Easily moveable from one place to another
- Better data transfer rate as compared to magnetic tapes
- Low cost compared to RAM
- Less prone to corruption of data as compared to tapes

The disadvantages of magnetic disks are:

- More expensive as compared to magnetic tapes.
- When used on-line, they are more susceptible to data corruption and data theft.
- Not ideally suitable, when the data files are to be read sequentially.
- Require dust-free environment.

3.7 OPTICAL STORAGE SYSTEMS

The optical storage systems are used for the same purpose as the magnetic storage systems. However, like magnetic storage systems, the optical storage systems do not employ the magnetism medium to read and store data. The optical storage systems use the laser light as the optical medium to retrieve as well as record data. The following are some of the examples of optical storage systems:

- Compact Disk—Read Only Memory (CD-ROM)
- Digital Video Disc (DVD)
- Compact Disc—Recordable (CD- R)
- Compact Disc—Rewritable (CD-WR)
- Digital Video Disc—Recordable (DVD-R)
- Digital Video Disc—Rewritable (DVD-WR)

Note: *The DVD disks have much higher storage capacity than the CD disks.*

Like other storage systems, the optical storage systems are non-volatile in nature. Also, the optical storage systems are more reliable as compared to the magnetic storage systems because they are less prone to mechanical damage. Unlike magnetic storage systems, which are fully read and write-capable storage devices, the optical storage devices are either read-only or writable. Among the writable optical storage devices, those devices that can be used for writing data multiple times are termed as rewritable optical storage devices. Some examples of read-only optical storage devices are CD-ROM and DVD, while some examples of writable optical storage devices are CD-R, CD-RW and DVD-R.

The following are some of the significant properties of the optical storage devices:

- **Storage capacity** Storage capacity refers to the amount of data that can be stored in an optical storage system. It is directly proportional to the spot size and the geometrical dimensions of disk.
- **Data transfer rate** Data transfer rate refers to the speed at which data can be read from the optical storage system. It depends on the linear density and the rotational speed of the drive.
- **Access time** Access time defines the time taken to access the desired data from the optical storage systems. It is directly proportional to the weight of head and the rotation speed of the disk.

Major advantages of optical disks are:

- Large storage capacity
- Longer life span as compared to magnetic disks
- Lost cost per bit of storage
- Easily portable and stored

The disadvantages of optical disks include:

- Low data access speed as compared to magnetic disks.
- Drive mechanism is more complicated compared to that of magnetic disks.

3.7.1 Read-only Optical Disks

Read-only optical disk is a storage device that provides the facility of storing data, such as audio, video, and text. It stores the data permanently and allows it to be accessed randomly, whenever required. Read-only optical disks can store data in the range of 700 MB. The data is burnt into the read-only optical disks from a master disk. The end users can read the data by using a disk drive. Figure 3.10 shows an optical disk.

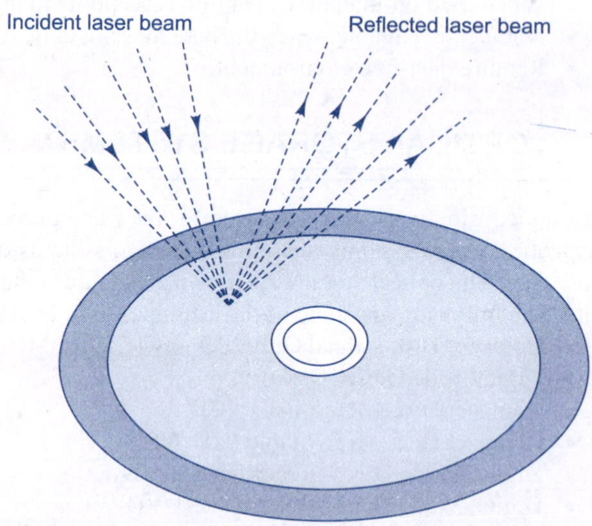

Fig. 3.10 Optical disk

3.7.2 Write Once, Read Many Disks

Write Once, Read Many (WORM) disks allow the end users to write the data onto the disk only once. The burnt data can later be read as many number of times. A WORM disk is also called blank disk, since initially it does not contain any data. To burn the data onto the WORM disk, a CD writer device is required. Together with the CD writer device and the appropriate burning software, data can be written on to the disk. The main objective of WORM optical disk is to store the data for backup use, i.e. these disks are used for writing the data once and storing it for a long period of time. WORM disks are much cheaper than the read-only optical disks, which contain the data already burnt by the manufacturer.

3.8 MAGNETO OPTICAL SYSTEMS

Magneto Optical (MO) storage systems include the features of both magnetic and optical disks. The main objective of the MO system is to store the data used in personal computers for a long period of time. It reads/writes data by making use of laser and optical technologies. It has a ferromagnetic material enclosed in the plastic coating. The laser beam used for reading data gets reflected due to the magnetic surface of the disk. The MO system is not popular among the users because its speed is slower and manufacturing cost is higher than other storage devices. These optical storage systems are available in two standard forms:

- 3.5 inch form factor
- 5.5 inch form factor

3.8.1 Principle used in Recording Data

The MO systems use Curie temperature for recording data. Curie temperature is the temperature at which the material loses its magnetic properties and above this temperature the material becomes paramagnetic. Paramagnetic is the form of magnetism at extreme magnetic field. The Curie temperature of the modern MO systems is 200°C. The coercivity of a material can be defined as the resistance of the material against magnetisation. Coercivity decreases at a higher temperature by applying magnetic field and provides the facility of recording data. When the temperature of a material becomes equal to the room temperature, its coercivity increases—that helps in preserving the magnetic data. Figure 3.11 shows the principle of recording data in MO systems.

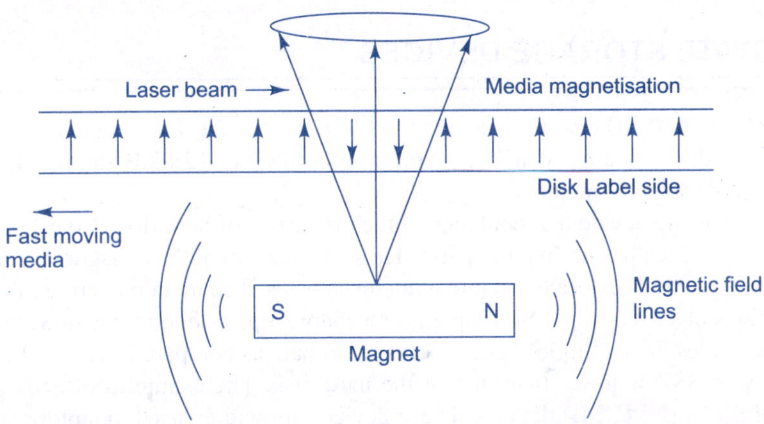

Fig. 3.11 Principle used in recording data

The basic requirements of a material used for recording in MO system are as follows:

- It should have low thermal conductivity that provides the facility to limit lateral heating.
- It should have a smooth surface and domain boundaries to decrease the system's noise.
- The coercivity of the material should be high at room temperature.
- The melting point of the material should be high enough to provide stability.

3.8.2 Architecture of Magneto Optical Disks

The architecture or the design of MO disks includes various layers of materials, protective coating and laser beam. The design of the MO disks defines the combination and the uses of anti-reflection layer, quadrilayers and amorphous metal. The anti-reflection layers are used to increase the light absorption. The quadrilayers are used to decrease the reflection of light that provides the facility to decrease the requirement of laser light. The amorphous metal is used as MO media. Figure 3.12 shows the design features of MO disks.

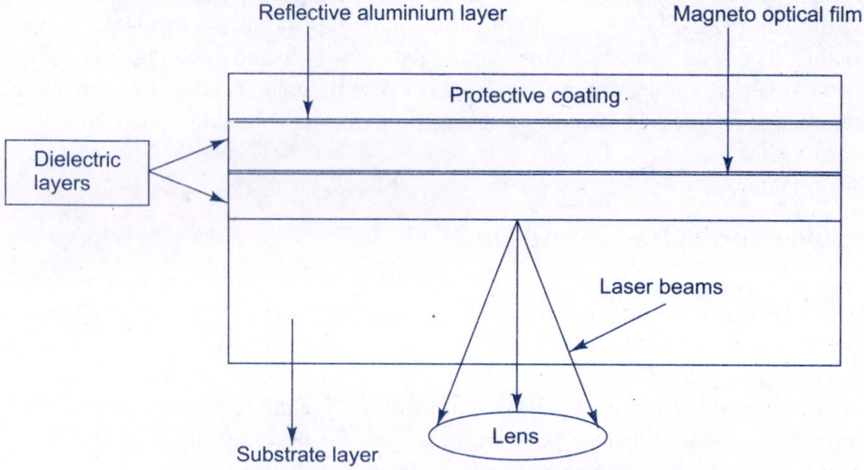

Fig. 3.12 Architecture of MO disks

3.9 SOLID-STATE STORAGE DEVICES

Solid-state Storage Devices (SSDs) were developed in 1978 by Storage Tek Company. In 1983, the Sharp-5000 laptop computers developed by Sharp Corporation used SSD of 128 KB storage. In 1995, M-System developed the SSD on flash based memory.

SSD can be defined as the device that contains all the properties of hard disk drives to store the data and use solid-state memory, which has no moving parts. These devices do not use magnetic and optical medium to store data. Rather, these devices use the semiconductor devices. The main objective of these devices is to process the instructions electronically. SSDs have no mechanical parts due to which access time in case of SSDs is less. This provides the facility of faster accessing of data as compared to any other storage devices. The storage capacity of SSD is lower than that of the hard disk. The examples of SSD are flash memory cards and Universal Serial Bus (USB) devices. These devices are widely used in laptops to store data. They also prove to be of great use in the critical applications used in defence industry.

3.9.1 Structure of SSD

The structure of SSD basically uses the advantages, such as non volatility, low consumption and high reliability of DRAM and NAND flash memory. These advantages of DRAM and NAND flash memory help in creating SSD. The SSD created using the advantages of flash memory is called flash memory based SSD. On the other hand, the SSD created using advantages of DRAM is called DRAM based SSD. The flash memory based SSD is slower, as compared to the DRAM volatile memory. DRAM based SSD provides the facility of accessing the data at a faster speed as compared to hard drive and flash memory. It secures data using the backup storage system and battery, which allows us to save data by copying all the data from the RAM to the backup storage, when the power is switched off due to any reason. It also works as a buffer memory. Nowadays, in case of power problem, lithium-iron batteries are being used as back-up.

3.9.2 Advantages of SSD

Solid-state storage devices possess many advantages. They include:

- **Better performance** Performance includes various factors like accessing speed, searching and spin-up function. SSDs provide random accessing of the stored data and their accessing speed is faster as compared to the hard drives. The searching process of the required data is faster than the hard disk drives. Moreover, they do not need any spin-up process to start-up.
- **Low power and heat** SSD provides the facility to decrease the power consumption due to low storage capacity. They provide the facility to decrease the heat reduction due to low storage capacity, except for the D-RAM based SSD.
- **High reliability** SSD provides constant and more reliable performance, as compared to hard disk drives because the seek time, which is the delay associated with the reading or writing data on computer's disk drives, is constant in SSDs. They provide the facility of high mechanical reliability, as they have no moving parts in their construction.
- **Small dimension** SSDs have low weight and small size, as compared to the weight and size of the hard disk drives. The reason behind the less weight and the small size is the low storage capacity of the SSD that also facilitates easy transportation.
- **Small form factor** Form factor defines the size and the dimensions of a physical device. SSD provides small form factor to Ultra Mobile Personal Computers (UMPC) that can be very useful in the market of Personal Computers (PC) for compact space.

3.9.3 Disadvantages of SSD

Apart from the various advantages, the solid-state storage devices possess some disadvantages too. These include:

- **High price** The prices of SSD are high as compared to the prices of hard disk drives. Generally, the price of SSD is 32 times more than the hard disk drives. However, their cost is decreasing these days.
- **Low capacity** The storage capacity of the SSD is lower, as compared to that of hard disk drives.
- **Low writing speed** The writing speed of flash memory based SSD is slower, as compared to the writing speed of hard disk drives, due to the presence of large erased blocks.
- **Low storage density** Storage density can be defined as data per unit volume. It is low in case of SSDs as compared to hard disk drives.
- **Vulnerable** SSD are affected by power loss, electrostatic discharge and magnetic fields, whereas the hard disk drives are not affected by these processes. The data in the SSD can get damaged due to electrical failures. The recovery of data damaged due to electrical failure is more difficult, as compared to the data recovery in case of hard disk drives.

3.10 STORAGE EVALUATON CRITERIA

Before selecting a memory device to store the data, we must evaluate critically the different characteristics of storage systems. They primarily include:

- **Access mode** Access mode is used for accessing some specific data from the memory. The different access modes include random access mode, sequential access mode and direct access mode. In the random access mode, the data can be accessed randomly, i.e., without considering the location of the required data. On the other hand, in the sequential access mode, the data and the information can be accessed in a sequential manner, i.e., by specifying the location of the required data. In the direct access mode, the data can be accessed by using both the random access mode and the sequential access mode. Cassette player is an example of a device using sequential access mode because data is accessed from it in a sequential manner only. On the other hand, CD player is an example of a device using random access mode as well as direct access mode because data can be accessed from it randomly as well as sequentially.
- **Access time** Access time refers to the time taken by the processor in completing the requests made by the user for performing the read and write operations. The access time depends on the type of storage device used and the access mode of the data. The access time of primary memory is faster than that of the secondary memory.
- **Storage capacity** It refers to the storage space available in the computer system for holding the data. In other words, storage capacity is defined as the size of the memory available for storing the data in the system. The storage capacity is measured in terms of bytes and usually a large storage capacity is desirable for storing the data. The storage capacity of the secondary memory devices is more than the primary memory devices.
- **Storage type** It refers to the type of memory used to store the data. The storage type includes the temporary and permanent memory. The temporary memory is also known as the volatile memory, which is able to store the data only when the power or computer system is switched on. The permanent memory is also known as the non-volatile memory, which is able to store the data, even when the power or computer system is turned off.
- **Cost** It refers to the cost of the storage device used in the computer system for holding the data. It is measured by determining the cost per bit of storage for a given storage capacity.

Chapter Summary

Computer systems use two types of memory, namely primary memory and secondary memory. Primary memory is used to store data that is used by the CPU during processing. It consists of two types, RAM and ROM. RAM is a volatile type of memory and stores data temporarily. On the other hand, ROM is a non-volatile memory and holds data permanently.

Secondary memory includes magnetic disks, magnetic tapes and optical disks. Magnetic disks store data in concentric circles known as tracks and these tracks are further divided into sectors. Magnetic tapes are used to store data sequentially. Optical disks use an optical medium to store data and a laser diode to read data.

A hybrid version of magnetic and optical technologies known as magneto-optical disk is also available. It employs a laser beam to read data and an electromagnetic head to write data. Storage systems developed using solid-state technology have no mechanical moving parts, thus providing better data access speed.

Key Terms to Remember

- **Primary memory:** It refers to the storage locations that are used to hold the programs and data temporarily in a computer system. The primary memory is usually known as memory.
- **Secondary memory:** It refers to the storage locations that are used to hold the data and programs permanently. The secondary memory of a computer system is popularly known as storage.
- **Internal process memory:** This type of memory is placed either inside or near the CPU. It is generally connected to the CPU through special fast bus. Internal process memory usually includes the cache memory and the registers.
- **RAM:** It is a volatile memory in which data can be accessed in random fashion. Since it is a volatile memory, the data and programs stored in it will be lost when the power is switched off.
- **ROM:** It is a non-volatile memory that is used to store data permanently.
- **Byte:** It is the smallest addressable unit of memory.
- **Static RAM:** It is a type of RAM in which data is stored till the power of the computer system is switched on. Static RAM uses a number of transistors to store a single bit of digital information.
- **Dynamic RAM:** It is the RAM in which data is stored in a storage cell consisting of a transistor and a capacitor. Unlike SRAM, the DRAM needs to be continuously refreshed with power supply because the capacitor has the tendency to get discharged. DRAM retains the data for a very short span of time even after the power supply is switched off.
- **Programmable ROM:** It is a memory chip on which the write operation of data can be performed only once.
- **Erasable PROM:** It is a type of ROM in which data can be erased or destroyed using ultraviolet light.
- **Electrically Erasable PROM:** It is a type of ROM in which data can be erased or destroyed by exposing it to an electric charge. It has the ability to retain the data stored in it, even if the power of the computer system is switched off.
- **Flash ROM:** It is a type of EEPROM that stores the information using floating-gate transistors.
- **Magnetic storage systems:** These are the storage systems that store the data on a magnetised medium with the help of magnetised particles.
- **Magnetic disk:** It is a flat disk that is covered with magnetic coating for holding information.
- **Magnetic tapes:** These are the magnetic-coated plastic tapes, which are used for storing data and audio or video files.
- **Optical storage systems:** It uses the laser light as the optical medium to retrieve as well as record data.
- **Magneto Optical (MO) storage systems:** These are the storage systems that include the features of both magnetic and optical storage systems.

Review Questions

Fill in the Blanks

1. The data to be stored in the memory is assigned a unique number known as _________.
2. The permanent memory is also called _______ while temporary memory is called ________.
3. _________ and ________ belong to the primary memory of the computer system.
4. The ________ memory is kept near the CPU.
5. The data is stored in the memory by considering the _________ of the memory.

6. The ________ includes the temporary and permanent memory.
7. ________ is the smallest unit of measurement in a computer system's memory.
8. ________ and ________ are the two main types of RAM.
9. ________ performs its operations without the use of system clock.
10. RDRAM is compact in size and uses ________ bit address bus.
11. The memory, which is used to store the data permanently, is known as ________.
12. A computer system stores the data on a hard disk by using ________ and ________ methods.
13. A ________ is defined as a circle within a circle on the magnetic disk.
14. The broken-up units of tracks are known as ________.
15. The ________ is used in the hard disk in order to read or write the data from or to the specific tracks on the disk.
16. ________ provides the facility of erasing and re-recording of data as many times as required.
17. ________ is also known as a diskette as it is flexible in nature.
18. An optical disk is the ________ memory storage device.
19. ________ reads/writes the data by making use of laser and optical technologies.
20. ________ are defined as the memory locations where the data and instructions are stored temporarily.

Multiple Choice Questions

1. Which one of the following memories is used to store data permanently?
   A. Primary memory B. Secondary memory C. Cache memory D. Registers
2. Which of the following memory is the fastest type of memory?
   A. Secondary memory B. Primary memory
   C. Cache memory D. ROM
3. Which of the following is the cheapest type of memory?
   A. Primary memory B. Registers C. Cache memory D. Secondary memory
4. Which one of the following memory is not a type of primary memory?
   A.. RAM B. ROM C. Cache D. SRAM
5. Which of the following statement is not true about RAM?
   A. It is usually faster, as compared to the internal processor memory.
   B. It is a volatile memory.
   C. It is the type of primary memory of a computer system.
   D. The data and information stored in the RAM is directly accessible by the CPU.
6. Which of the following is the auxiliary memory of the computer system?
   A. ROM B. SRAM C. Magnetic tape D. Cache memory
7. The amount of space available in the computer system for holding the data is called:
   A. Storage space B. Storage capacity C. Storage area D. Storage address
8. On which type of ROM, data can be written only once?
   A. PROM B. EPROM C. EEPROM D. EROM

9. In which memory, are the files and programs that are currently being used by a user, stored?
   A. ROM   B. RAM   C. Cache   D. Registers
10. Which of the following statement is not true about storage systems?
   A. They are used to store data permanently.
   B. They can store any type of data.
   C. The data stored in these systems can be accessed at any time.
   D. The data stored in these systems can be directly accessed by the CPU.
11. Which one of the following is not a type of magnetic storage system?
   A. Magnetic tape   B. Compact disk   C. Hard disk   D. Floppy disk
12. What does IBG stand for?
   A. Inter bit gaps   B. Intra byte gaps   C. Intra block gaps   D. Inter block gaps
13. Which of the following is a type of magnetic disk?
   A. Hard disk   B. Compact disk   C. Digital video disk   D. All the above
14. What is the medium used in optical storage systems for reading and recording data?
   A. Ultraviolet light   B. High-energy visible light
   C. Laser light   D. Black light
15. Which one of the following is not a type of optical disk?
   A. Write-only optical disk   B. Write once, read many optical disk
   C. Read-only optical disk   D. All of the above are optical disks
16. Which of the following temperature is used in MO systems as the recording medium?
   A. Curie temperature   B. Neel temperature
   C. Room temperature   D. Boiling point temperature
17. Which of the following is a solid-state memory?
   A. Parallel serial bus   B. Universal parallel bus   C. Universal computer bus   D. Universal serial bus

Discussion Questions

1. What do you understand by memory? List the two different categories of memory.
2. What is meant by internal processor memory? What is the advantage of having an internal process memory in a computer system?
3. What is a RAM and why it is called so?
4. What is the difference between volatile and non-volatile memory? Is RAM a volatile or non-volatile memory?
5. What is the difference between primary memory and secondary memory of a computer system? List two examples of secondary memory.
6. Differentiate between a bit, a byte and a word.
7. Describe the way of storing information in the memory of a computer system, with the help of a diagram.
8. What is the difference between static RAM and dynamic RAM? List different types of static and dynamic RAM.
9. Explain the concept of ROM by listing a few applications in which it is employed.
10. List different types of ROM with their key features.
11. What is meant by storage systems? What is the advantage of having storage systems in a computer system?

12. Describe the classification of storage systems with the help of a diagram.
13. What is the difference between a magnetic tape and a magnetic disk? List the advantages and disadvantages of both.
14. How do optical storage systems differ from magnetic storage systems? Give some examples of optical storage systems.
15. What do you understand by tracks and sectors on the surface of a magnetic disk?
16. Write some important properties of optical storage systems.
17. What do you understand by magneto-optical storage systems? Describe the principle used in magneto storage systems for recoding data.
18. What are solid-state devices? State the advantages and disadvantages of solid-state devices.
19. What characteristics should a user evaluate before employing a memory device?

CHAPTER 4

INPUT DEVICES

Chapter Outline

Chapter Objectives

In this chapter, we will learn:

- The input devices used for pointing the objects on the screen, such as mouse, trackball and joystick.
- The process of scanning documents with the help of different scanning devices, such as hand-held scanner and flat-bed scanner.
- The various optical recognition devices that are used for recognising characters in different application areas.
- The input devices, such as microphone and graphics tablet used in media.
- The data acquisition sensor, an advanced input device, used for inputting data.

4.1 INTRODUCTION

Input devices are electromechanical devices that are used to provide data to a computer for storing and further processing, if necessary. They act as an interface between the computer and the user. The basic task of an input device is to take the input from the user, translate it into the machine-readable form and then present it to the processing unit of the computer for execution. In effect, the input devices provide a means of communication between the computer and the outer world.

The input may be in different forms, such as numeric data, text commands, graphics, video and audio. We can provide the input to a computer in two ways, either manually through devices such as keyboard and mouse, or directly from documents using devices such as scanners. Depending upon the type or method of input, the input device may belong to one of the following categories:

- Keyboard
- Pointing devices
- Scanning devices
- Optical recognition devices
- Digital camera
- Voice recognition devices
- Media input devices

We shall discuss in this chapter briefly the operation and applications of these devices.

4.2 KEYBOARD

Keyboard is the most commonly used input device. We can use a keyboard to type data and text and execute commands. A standard keyboard, as shown in Fig. 4.1, consists of the following groups of keys:

- **Alphanumeric keys** The alphanumeric keys include the number keys and alphabet keys. These keys are arranged in the same style as in the normal typewriters, popularly known as QWERTY layout.
- **Function keys** The function keys are arranged in a row on the top of the keyboard. These keys help perform specific tasks, such as searching a file or refreshing a web page.
- **Central keys** The central keys are used for controlling the movement of cursor and screen display. These include arrow keys (for moving the cursor) and modifier keys such as SHIFT, ALT and CTRL (for modifying the input).
- **Numeric keypad** The numeric keypad is located on the right side of the keyboard. This looks like a calculator's keypad with its 10 digits and mathematical operators.
- **Special purpose keys** The special purpose keys help perform a certain kind of operation, like exiting a program or deleting some characters in a document. The various special purpose keys in a keyboard are Escape, Insert, Delete, Print Screen, Pause, Tab, Spacebar, etc.

A standard keyboard would include about 100 keys. However, many manufacturers add special buttons to perform some special tasks.

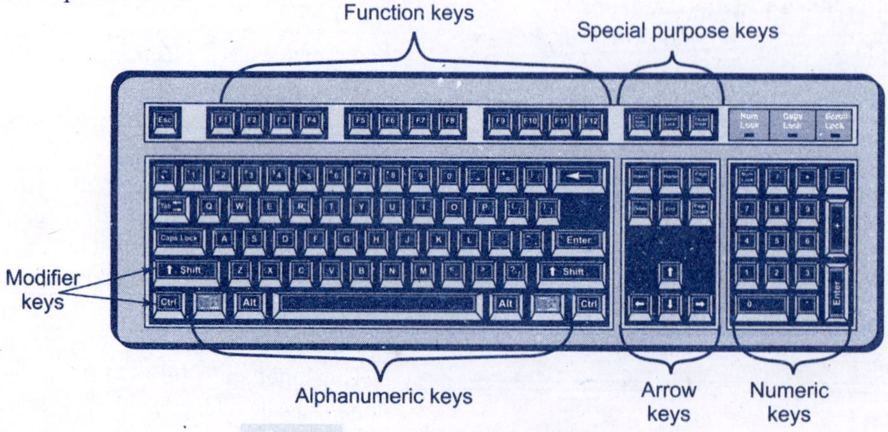

Fig. 4.1 The presently used keyboard

Keyboards are attached to the computer system with the help of a cable. Each key of the keyboard, when pressed, sends a different signal to the processor. However, today wireless keyboards are also available that work with the help of batteries. We can also classify the keyboards on the basis of additional keys present in them. For example, multimedia keyboard and gaming keyboard are the keyboards, which are classified on the basis of the additional keys present in them.

4.3 POINTING DEVICES

Pointing devices are the input devices that are generally used for moving the cursor to a particular location to point an object on the screen. With the help of pointing devices, we can easily select the icons, menus, windows, etc on the Graphical User Interface (GUI). Thus, the users can easily interact with a computer system by means of a pointing device. We can simply change the position of the objects displayed on the screen by first pointing at the object and then dragging it to the desired position. Some of the commonly used pointing devices are:

- Mouse
- Trackball
- Light pen
- Joystick
- Touchscreen

4.3.1 Mouse

Mouse is a small hand-held pointing device that basically controls the two-dimensional movement of the cursor on the displayed screen. It is an important part of the Graphical User Interface (GUI) based Operating Systems (OS) as it helps in selecting a portion of the screen and copying and pasting the text. The mouse, on moving, also moves the pointer appearing on the display device. The most commonly used types of mouse are as follows:

- **Mechanical mouse** A mechanical mouse consists of three buttons: left button, right button and scroll button. Inside the plastic coating of the mouse, there is a ball, which is rolled over a flat surface corresponding to which the cursor moves on the display screen. The left button on the mouse is the most frequently used button as it helps in selecting the icons, folders and text on the display screen. The right button on the mouse helps in displaying the short cut menu, whereas the scroll button helps in moving the cursor up and down on the screen by scrolling it. Figure 4.2 shows the upper and the lower portion of the mechanical mouse.

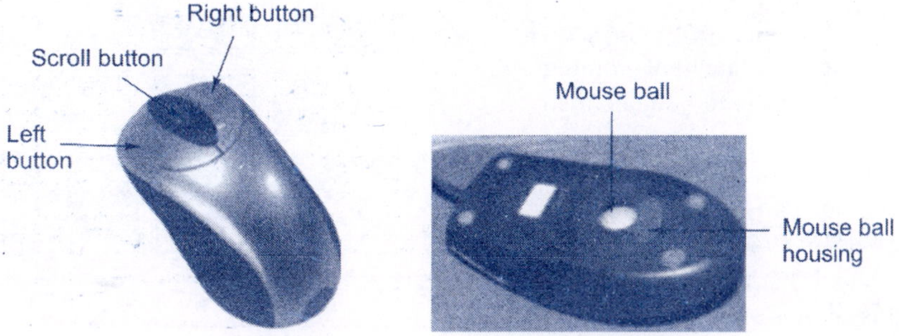

(a) *The upper portion* **(b)** *The lower portion*

Fig. 4.2 Mechanical mouse

- **Optical mouse** An optical mouse is a pointing input device in which the reflected light determines the movement of the cursor on the displayed screen. The upper portion of the optical mouse is similar to that of the mechanical mouse. The lower portion of the optical mouse consists of a ball having Light Emitting Diodes (LEDs), an optical sensor and a Digital Signal Processor (DSP). Figure 4.3 shows the lower portion of the optical mouse.

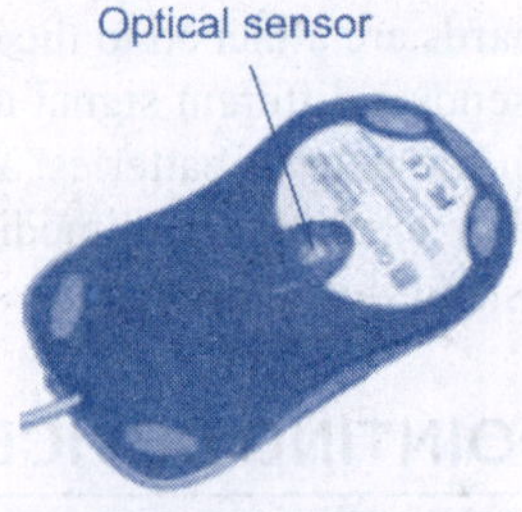

Fig. 4.3 The lower portion of the optical mouse

4.3.2 Trackball

Trackball is a pointing device that basically consists of a socket containing the ball, which can be rolled manually to move the cursor on the screen. The socket also contains sensors, which detect the movement of the ball. With the help of the trackball, we can change the position of the cursor on the screen by simply rotating the ball with our fingers or thumb. On the basis of size, the trackballs are classified into two types, small trackball and large trackball. The small trackballs are commonly used in portable computers, whereas the large trackballs find their use in the desktop computer systems, which are used for computer-aided designing. One of the most important advantages of the trackball is that it can be placed on different surfaces, such as desk, mouse pad and even user's hand. The trackball finds its use as a game controller in games like Centipede, Golden Tee and Marble Madness. Figure 4.4 shows the trackball placed on a desk.

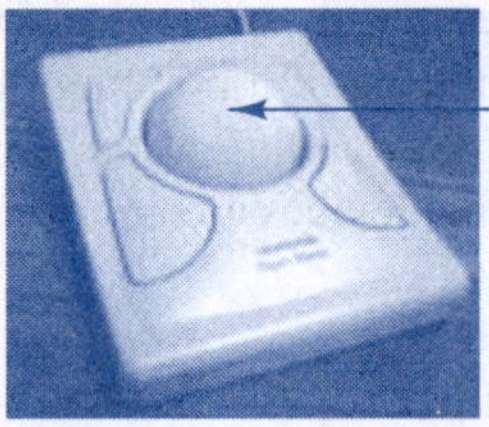

Fig. 4.4 The trackball on the desk

4.3.3 Light Pen

Light pen is an electro-optical pointing device that is used for selecting the objects on the display screen with the help of a light sensitive pen. It is generally connected to the Visual Display Unit (VDU) of the computer system. The pen contains a light-sensitive diode, which helps in pointing the objects displayed on the screen. Using a light pen, we can directly draw the objects on the screen by holding it in our hand. When the tip of the light pen is brought in contact with the screen, the light coming from the screen causes a pulse to be generated in the pen which in turn causes the processor to identify the position pointed to by the pen.

Light pens provide all the capabilities of a mouse. They do not require any pad or horizontal surface and therefore, are useful when desk space is limited. Figure 4.5 shows the light pen attached to a computer system.

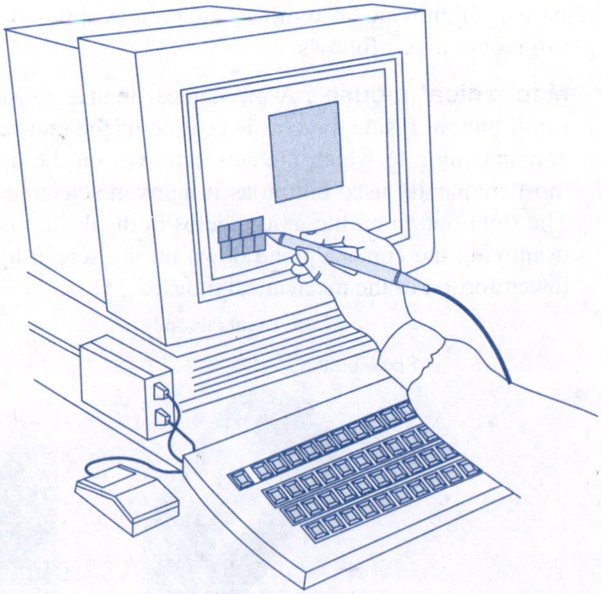

Fig. 4.5 The light pen

4.3.4 Joystick

Joystick is a pointing device that usually consists of one or more buttons and a stick, which controls the movement of the cursor on the screen by pointing in all directions. It continues to point in a particular direction until and unless it is brought back to the vertical position. The trigger button, which is used to trigger some kind of action like firing in game sequence, is made available on a joystick. The joystick facilitates three types of control: glide, direct and digital. The glide and the direct control allow the movement of the joystick in all possible directions, i.e., left, right, up and bottom. On the other hand, the digital control helps in the movement of the joystick in limited directions. Earlier, the joysticks could provide only 2D movements, but now, the joysticks are capable of providing 3D movements as well. The joystick is generally used in computer games, CAD systems, industrial applications, etc. Figure 4.6 shows a joystick.

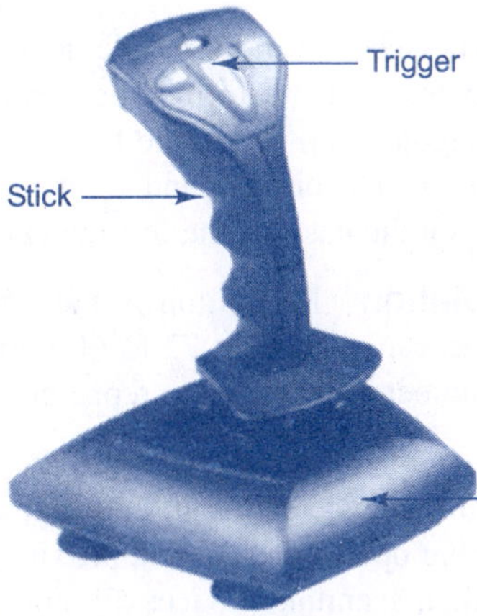

Fig. 4.6 Joystick

4.3.5 Touchscreen

Touchscreen is a pointing device that enables us to enter data such as text, pictures and images by directly touching the screen. The touchscreen is the display monitor with which the user can directly interact with the computer system by touching the screen. These devices do not make use of the keyboard and the mouse for inputting the data in the computer system. The touchscreen is used in a variety of applications, such as cell phones, ATM's, PDA's and games. Figure 4.7 shows a touchscreen.

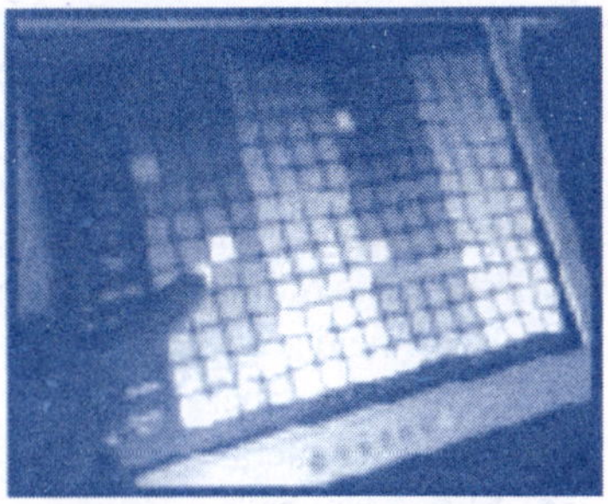

Fig. 4.7 Touchscreen

There are different types of touchscreen technologies used today. They include:

- **Surface wave technology** This technology generally makes use of ultrasonic waves, which are absorbed when they are passed through the touchscreen panel. These waves are generally absorbed, when a user touches a point on the touchscreen pad. Then, these absorbed waves are sent to the controller for further processing. This is greatly affected by elements such as dust and water.
- **Capacitive technology** This technology makes use of indium tin oxide material, which is coated on the touchscreen for providing continuous electric charge. In this, the touchscreen is provided with circuits at each corner. When the user touches the screen, a small amount of charge is absorbed at this point. This charge is then transferred by the circuits to the controller for further processing. The touchscreens based on capacitive technology do not get damaged by elements such as dust or liquids.
- **Resistive technology** In this technology, the touchscreen panel generally consists of different layers, which are coated with very thin electrically conductive metal and separated by some space. When the user touches the panel at any point, the change in the electric current occurs that is passed to the controller for further processing. The touchscreens based on resistive technology do not get damaged by elements like dust or water.

4.4 SCANNING DEVICES

Scanning devices are the input devices that can electronically capture text and images, and convert them into computer readable form. The basic task of a scanning device is to convert an image or the textual data into digital data, i.e., in the form of boxes, where each box represents either zero or one. The resultant matrix is known as bit map and is displayed on the screen. The scanning devices can be differentiated from each other on the basis of the following characteristics:

- **Resolution** Resolution is the closeness of the pixels in the bit map. The resolution of scanning devices can vary from 72 to 600 dots per inch (dpi), depending on the bit depth. Bit depth represents the number of bits used to represent each pixel of an image or a text.
- **Size** Some scanning devices are very small in size, whereas others are very big. The small sized scanning device can scan approximately two to five inches of the document, whereas the large sized scanning device can scan approximately up to forty inches of the document. Therefore, it follows that the small scanning devices are appropriate for scanning small documents, whereas the large scanning devices are appropriate for scanning large documents.
- **Scanning technology** Some scanning devices use Charged Coupled Device (CCD) arrays, whereas others use Photo Multiplier Tubes (PMT) technology. The CCD consists of a series of light receptors, which are sensitive to the variation in the light frequency. As the frequency of light changes, these scanning devices detect the change and the output obtained after scanning also gets accordingly changed. The PMT consists of a photocathode, which is a photosensitive surface used for generating the electrons. PMT is used for identifying the light emitted by the weak signals.

On the basis of these characteristics, the scanning devices can be categorised as follows:

- Hand-held scanners
- Flat-bed scanners
- Drum scanners
- Slide scanners

4.4.1 Hand-held Scanners

Hand-held scanners are the scanning devices that are generally used for digitising the images into bit map, which is a matrix of 0's and 1's.The size of these scanners is small and the price is relatively less as compared to the other three types of scanners. These scanners are also known as half page scanners, as they can scan maximum upto 5 inches at a time. The hand-held scanners are suitable for scanning small images rather than the whole page of text or pictures. Figure 4.8 shows a hand-held scanner.

Fig. 4.8 Hand-held scanner

The hand-held scanning devices are generally used for identifying the bar-code label of the products. They are divided into two categories, namely, contact scanning device and non-contact scanning device. The contact scanning device works by moving the tip of a light pen across the bar-code label to capture the bar-code. The bar-code is a code comprising vertical bars of different widths that can be read only electronically. The code captured by the scanning device is stored permanently in the memory. The non-contact scanning device operates by pointing the gun to the bar-code label so as to capture the code. These devices are comparatively more complex, heavier and costlier than the contact scanning device.

4.4.2 Flatbed Scanners

Flatbed scanners consist of a flat surface composing of glass pane on which the documents are kept for scanning. Under this glass pane, there is xenon light and a CCD, which consists of an array of red, green and blue filters. The object to be scanned is put upside down on the glass pane and the cover is lowered. The light reflected from the document surface helps in identifying the image or the text present in the document. The scanning is done from left to right horizontally, line by line and the procedure is repeated until all the lines are scanned. Nowadays the flatbed scanners are widely used in almost every organisation. Figure 4.9 shows a flat-bed scanner.

Fig. 4.9 A flat-bed scanner

The lid of flat-bed scanners is adjustable that makes the scanning of different objects such as documents and leaflets possible. The size of these scanners usually starts from 8.5"×11", which is the standard letter size. The flat-bed scanners are best suited for slides and photo scanning, as they provide the optical resolution of 5,500 dots per inch (dpi).

4.4.3 Drum Scanners

Drum scanners generally consist of a large drum, which is used for scanning the documents. These scanners make use of the Photo Multiplier Tubes (PMT) technology, instead of the CCD technology. The resolution image of these scanners is very high due to which they are very expensive. The disadvantage of these scanners is that they are slow in speed. Figure 4.10 shows a drum scanner.

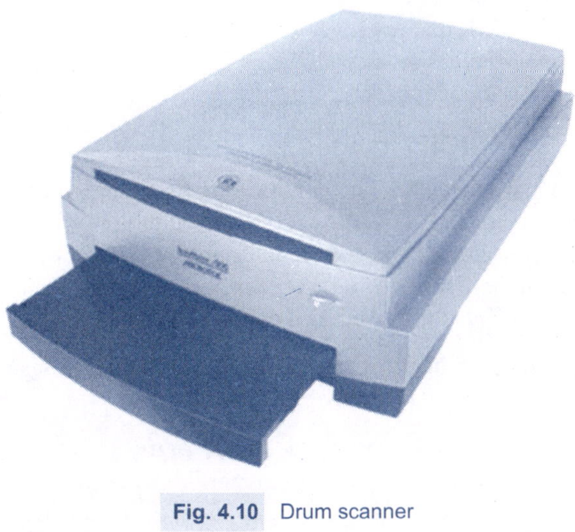

Fig. 4.10 Drum scanner

The drum scanners can usually scan the documents having the size up to 8"×10" but there are few drum scanners that can scan even up to 11"×24". The optical resolution of these scanners ranges from 8000 dpi to 11000 dpi. These scanners are suitable for scanning negatives. The aperture, which is the opening space through which light can pass and scan the document, is easily controlled by the drum scanners. In addition, the drum scanners can also control the sample area, which is the area of the individual pixel scanned by the scanner.

4.4.4 Slide Scanners

Slide scanners are used for scanning slides as well as film negatives. The slides are created on a transparent base using photochemical solution. The film negatives are the inversion of the positive images. In order to scan the slide, it is put into the tray, which is meant for scanning the objects. These scanners are also known as film scanners as they can easily scan the original image of the film. In the slides taken with this scanner, the dark areas appear light and the light areas appear dark. These scanners consist of a stepper motor and a CCD sensor, which helps in scanning the film. Figure 4.11 shows a slide scanner.

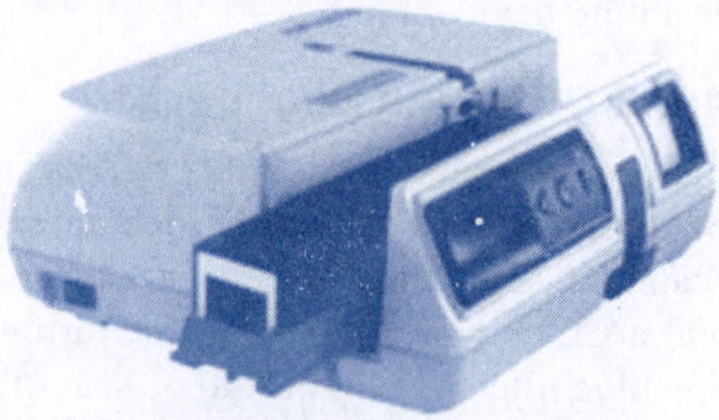

Fig. 4.11 A slide scanner

The slide scanners are capable of scanning up to 35 slides at a time and offer an optical resolution ranging from 4000 dpi to 4800 dpi. Slide scanners can efficiently scan negatives and black and white films. With the help of slide scanners, we can very easily scan the photos and send them to our friends via e-mail and the Internet.

4.5 OPTICAL RECOGNITION DEVICES

Optical recognition devices are used for recognising the characters optically. The optical recognition devices basically make use of optical scanner for inputting data. Unlike keyboards, the optical recognition devices do not enter the data by pressing the keys. Therefore, these devices help the user in saving a lot of time as entering data through a keyboard is a time consuming task. The following are some of the commonly used optical recognition devices:

- OCR devices
- OMR devices
- MICR devices
- Bar code reader

4.5.1 OCR Devices

Optical Character Recognition (OCR) devices scan a particular document by recognising its individual characters and converting it into the editable form. These devices distinguish the dark area on the document from the light areas for recognising the characters. The images scanned by the OCR device can be easily edited and formatted on a computer system. These devices generally consist of the following three components for the purpose of character recognition:

- **Image scanner** The basic task of the image scanner is to capture the text image, which is to be recognised optically.
- **OCR software and hardware** The OCR software and hardware processes the text images captured by the image scanner. In order to scan the document, firstly it is analysed so as to extract the character images. After analysing, the character images are recognised according to their shapes.
- **Output interface** The output interface helps in establishing communication between the OCR devices and the outside world.

Figure 4.12 illustrates the basic function of an OCR system. The paper document is fed into the optical scanner for scanning. The optical scanner typically scans the text and converts it into machine readable form using the OCR software. The document displayed on the user's computer is in the editable format.

The OCR devices basically make use of photoelectric cells for recording the patterns of the light reflected by the printed text. These patterns are recognised for the identification of the characters represented by them. The software program also recognises the character images and converts them into character code data, if any color change exists in the image. The OCR devices are popularly used in telebanking and in the processing of credit cards.

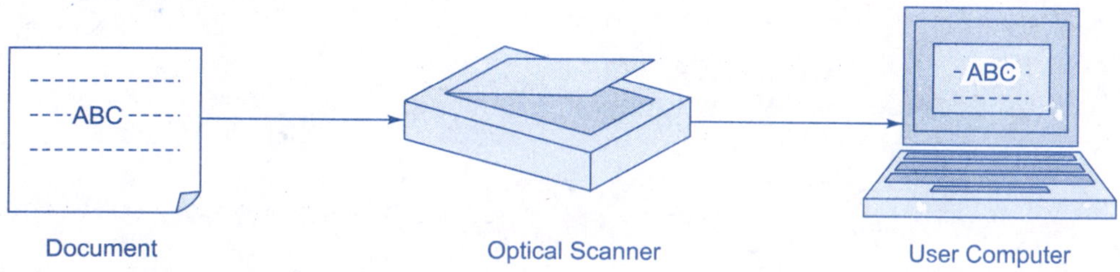

Fig. 4.12 Illustrating the basic functioning of an OCR device

4.5.2 OMR Devices

The Optical Mark Recognition (OMR) devices make use of OMR technology, which helps in obtaining the data from the marked fields. These devices prove to be of great use in recognising characters in question sheets, enrolment forms, registration forms, employee payroll, etc. Most popularly, the OMR devices are used for scanning the documents having multiple choices as in the question papers used in schools, colleges, etc. The correct answer is marked by the student in the boxes with the dark pencil or ink while answering. The OMR device consists of OMR reader, which is a special device that helps in recognising the marks on the predefined box areas. The OMR devices do not scan the entire document sheet. Instead, they analyse the darkened area only to check whether it is marked or not.

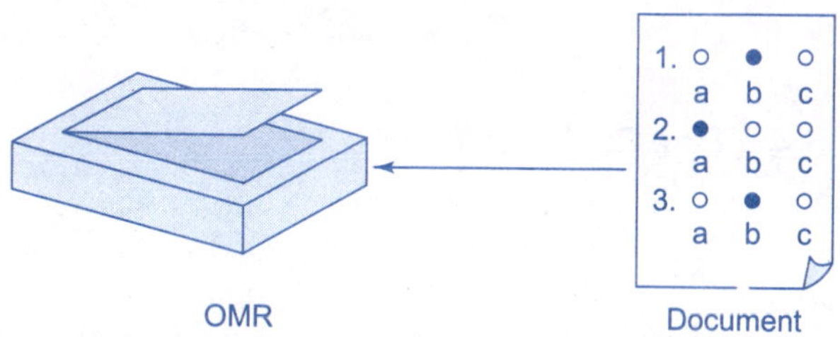

Fig. 4.13 Illustrating the functioning of the OMR device

Figure 4.13 illustrates the basic use of the OMR device. The document having marked and unmarked boxes is fed into the OMR device for scanning. The OMR device will scan only the box area and not the whole document. The OMR device generally scans the documents accurately and quickly. It can scan maximum 10000 documents per hour.

4.5.3 MICR Devices

Magnetic Ink Character Recognition (MICR) devices are the special devices used for recognising the characters written with magnetic ink consisting of iron oxide particles. These devices were specially developed for the banking operations. The details on the bank cheques, such as cheque number, bank and branch code are written with the magnetic ink. The MICR devices process the cheque, identify the numeric characters and store the data on the disk. The characters present at the bottom of the cheque are in human readable form and can be recognised, even if the cheque has become trampled or dirty. If a copy of the cheque is made with the help of coloured photocopy scanning machine, then the characters written with the magnetic ink will simply not respond. This provides an extra level of security in the banks for the protection of the cheques from illegal copying.

Figure 4.14 illustrates the basic functioning of an MICR device. The bank cheque containing the magnetic characters is fed into the MICR scanner for processing. The MICR scanner consists of MICR toner, which produces magnetic charge for reading the MICR line. The MICR scanner scans the cheques at a faster speed, and thus helps in saving a considerable amount of time while processing the cheques.

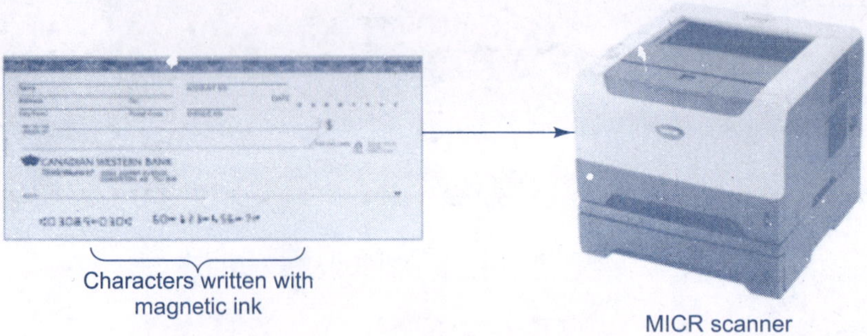

Fig. 4.14 Illustrating the basic functioning of the MICR device

4.5.4 Bar Code Reader

Bar code reader is the scanner that usually reads bar code, which is used to label the items in the super markets, retail stores, books numbering in library, etc. The bar code is the computer readable code representing vertical lines of different widths. The bar code reader basically consists of a scanner, decoder and cable. The scanner is used for scanning the bar code, which is later converted into numbers or letters using decoder. Finally, the decoded data is sent to the computer system via cable for processing.

Figure 4.15 illustrates the basic use of the bar code reader. The bar code is scanned with the help of the bar code reader, which directs the light beam over the bar code. A part of the beam is reflected back from the bar code by the sensor. Then, this light energy is converted into electrical energy by the bar code scanner. Finally, the electrical energy is transformed into data and forwarded to the computer system.

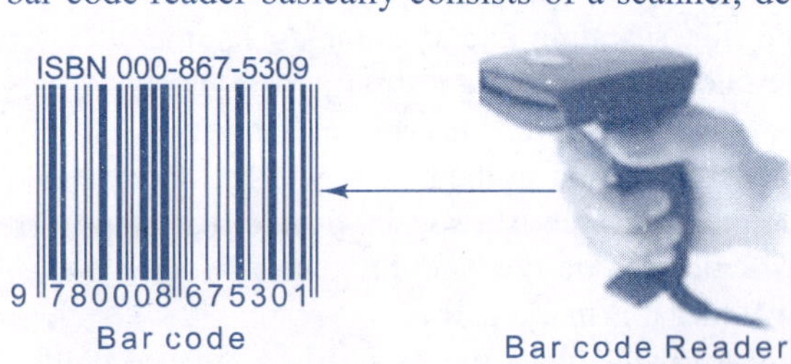

Fig. 4.15 Illustrating the basic functioning of the bar code reader

4.6 DIGITAL CAMERA

A digital camera is a handheld electronic device that is used to capture the image of an object electronically. The digital camera consists of a built-in computer, which helps in recording the images electronically. Whenever a user initiates the process of capturing an image by pressing the button available on the camera, the image light enters the camera through the lens. This light gets stored on a microchip consisting of an array of light sensitive sensors. The light sensitive sensors are the charge-coupled devices (CCD) that consist of a number of light sensitive diodes known as photosites. These diodes convert light into electric charges called electrons. These charges are in the analog form but are later converted into the digital form using the analog to digital converter. The following are the main features of the digital camera:

- It is capable of capturing and storing thousands of images on a single memory chip.
- It is capable of editing as well as deleting the images.
- It is capable of recording the video clip with sound.
- It is capable of showing the just recorded video clip on the camera screen.

Figure 4.16 shows the front and the rear view of a digital camera.

The digital cameras can be classified into the following types:

- **Video cameras** Video cameras are the digital cameras that capture an image by converting it into horizontal lines and then scanning each line from top to bottom. The two main types of video cameras include professional video cameras and camcorders. The professional video cameras are used for recording the moving images and are mostly used in film studios. On the other hand, the camcorders are not only used for capturing images but also help in recording audio. These video cameras consist of a Liquid Crystal Display (LCD) for displaying the captured picture and the built-in recorder for recording audio.

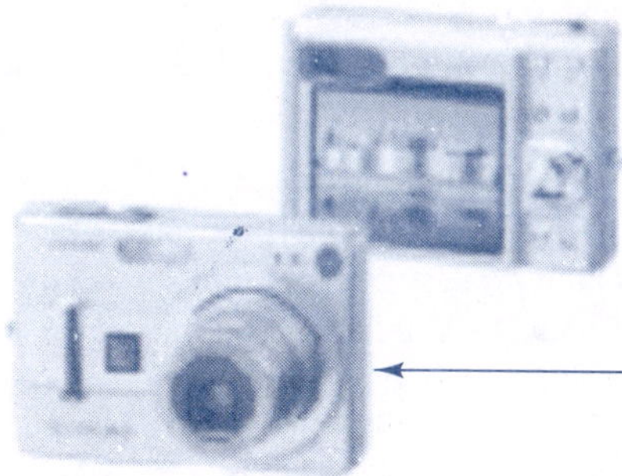

Fig. 4.16 The front and the rear view of the digital camera

- **Compact digital cameras** Compact digital cameras are very small in size, and hence can easily be carried by a person. These cameras do not contain advanced features for capturing an image. Therefore, the quality of the picture produced by the compact digital cameras is not as good as the pictures produced by the other cameras. The images are stored in these cameras in the Joint Photographic Experts Group (JPEG) format.
- **Digital single-lens reflex cameras** Digital single-lens reflex cameras consist of a mirror and a pentaprism that are used for capturing the image digitally. The light entering through the lens is reflected by the mirror attached with the lens. It then passes through the pentaprism to reach the eyepiece of the camera. These cameras have live preview feature, which helps in previewing the captured image before taking the final photograph.
- **Line-scan camera** Line-scan camera consists of an array of image sensors. These cameras capture the image in the form of lines and then scan the image line by line. These cameras capture the images very quickly and their image resolution is also very high.

The image captured by a digital camera is in the digital format and can be easily downloaded on a computer system. By using a digital camera, the photographs can be developed in a considerably less amount of time and that too, at a very low price. The quality of the pictures captured by a digital camera depends on the resolution factor. The more the resolution of a digital camera, the better is the image quality.

4.7 VOICE RECOGNITION SYSTEM

The voice recognition devices generally record the voice of a person and transform it into electrical signals. The electrical signals are then converted into the machine readable code. The voice recognition system only recognises the voice of the speaking person rather than what he speaks. The following are the two methods, which are used to identify the voice with the help of voice recognition system:

- **Template matching** This method of voice recognition is speaker dependent, i.e., this method matches the words spoken by the users to the predefined templates. In this method of voice recognition, a phrase or a word is spoken by the user into the microphone. This phrase or word is then converted into the machine readable code by the analog to digital converter (A/D converter). The output of the A/D converter is compared with the voice templates, which are the digitised entries stored in the database. This comparison is performed by the voice recognition software. The biggest limitation of this system is the availability of limited vocabulary that consists of only the words, which have been used in the training sessions.
- **Feature analysis** This method of voice recognition is speaker independent as it does not match the speaker's voice with the predefined templates, rather just processes the voice input by means of fourier analysis. It is the process of changing the frequency of the voice input. The output of the fourier analysis is matched with the stored voice input template for finding the featuristic similarities between the two. The major limitation of the feature analysis method is that it fails to match the accents, volume, pitch and inflection of different users.

The voice recognition devices are used for various purposes such as dictation, training air-traffic controllers, etc. These systems allow users to communicate with computers directly without using a keyboard or mouse. They are ideal for people who are visually impaired.

4.8 DATA ACQUISITION SENSORS

Sensors are the devices that are used for detecting and measuring the physical quantities, such as heat and temperature and converting them into electrical signals. The sensors are most commonly used in data acquisition systems. The data acquisition system collects the electrical signals from various devices and converts them into the digital signals for further assessment.

The data acquisition sensor is one of the most important components of the data acquisition system as it helps in detecting the electrical properties of different signals such as resistance. The data acquisition system simply accepts these signals and converts them into the digital format. The computer system, which is used for communicating with the data acquisition system, helps in gathering the signals. As per the requirements of the users, the data acquisition system can be constructed as a simple or a complex system. The data acquisition system is generally portable, battery operated and easy to use.

4.9 MEDIA INPUT DEVICES

The input devices, which are generally used in media for communicating with the mass audiences, are known as media input devices. The following are the most popularly used media input devices:

- **Microphone** It is an input device that basically converts the sound waves into electrical signals with the help of sensors. The sound wave pattern is converted into the electrical pattern, which is either in the form of voltage or current. The microphones are also called transducers as they transform one form of signal into another. The cable used for connecting the microphones should be less than 10 feet so that it helps in avoiding noise disturbances. A number of techniques—such as capacitance change, electromagnetic generation, magnetic change and resistance change—are used for the conversion of signals. The microphones are used in various applications, such as radios, tape recorders and telephones. Figure 4.17 shows a microphone.

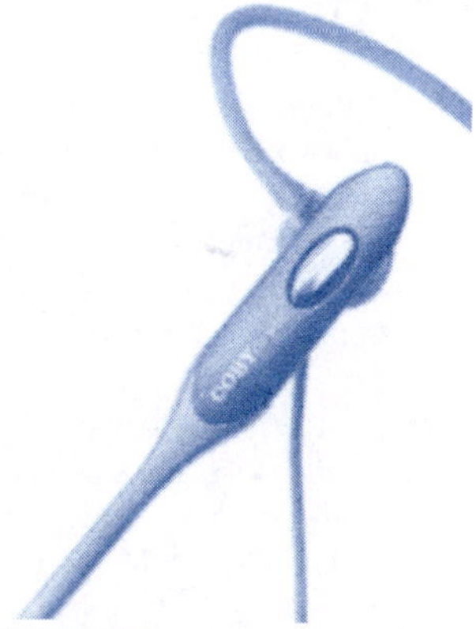

Fig. 4.17 A microphone

- **Webcam** It is an input device that is usually attached to the user's computer for recording videos as well as images. It functions like a video camera and can be used for displaying the images over the Internet. With the help of a webcam, the users can easily participate in video conferencing, which is the online video communication between two persons. The quality of the video taken through the webcam largely depends upon two factors—frame rate and resolution. The frame rate is defined as the frequency of the images captured per second by a webcam. On the other hand, the resolution is defined as the number of pixels appearing on the computer screen. For a video to be smooth and clear, the frame rate and the resolution should be maximum. Today, the webcams have become very popular and are widely used in a number of applications. Figure 4.18 shows the web cam.

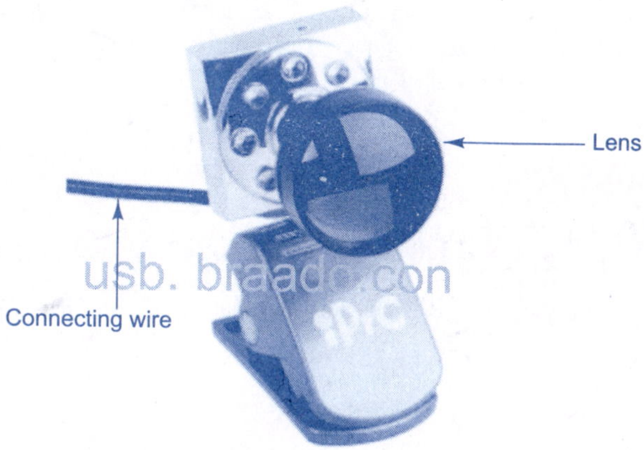

Fig. 4.18 The webcam

- **Graphics tablet** It is a media input device with the help of which a user can enter pictorial information into the computer system. The graphics tablet is a combination of a digitising pen and an electronic tablet. The digitising pen is similar to the ballpoint pen and has an electronic head for drawing the images. The digitising pen is also known as cursor or stylus. The electronic tablet refers to the flat surface, which is used for converting the movement of the pen into the digital signals. These digital signals are sent to the computer system and are represented on the display screen. The image drawn on the tablet is visible on the display screen rather than on the tablet itself. The graphics tablet helps in drawing more accurately as compared to the mouse. The graphics tablet is commonly used for technical drawings and Computer System Design (CAD) systems. Figure 4.19 shows the graphics tablet with a digitising pen.

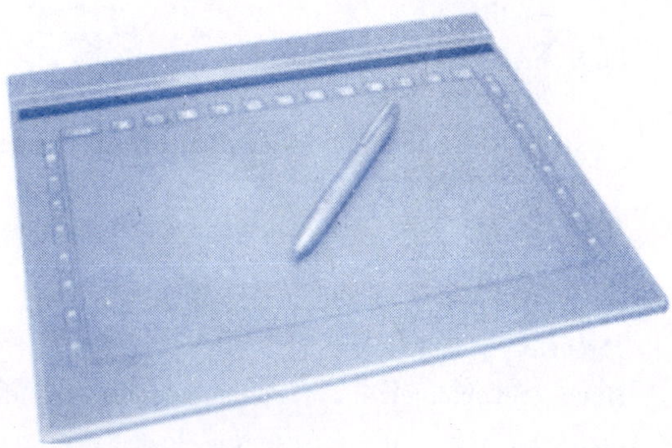

Fig. 4.19 The graphics tablet with a pen

Chapter Summary

Input devices are the hardware devices that help in inputting the data from any outside source into the computer system. There are various input devices, with the help of which a user can enter different types of data into the computer system. Keyboard is one of the most widely used input devices for providing alphanumeric information to the computer. A user simply presses these buttons for entering the data into the computer system. The user can also input data into a computer system with the help of pointing devices such as mouse, trackball, light pen joystick and touchscreen. The user can easily select the objects, menus and icons available on the screen using a pointing device. These devices basically control the movement of the pointer on the screen. Apart from the pointing devices, different scanning devices are also available, which are used for capturing the text and the images and converting them into the graphical image. A variety of scanning devices are available for scanning the documents, such as hand-held scanners, flatbed scanners, drum scanners and slide scanners.

Optical recognition devices are used for recognising the characters optically. These devices make use of optical scanner for scanning documents and images. OCR device, OMR device, MICR device and bar code reader are the various types of optical recognition devices. Voice recognition devices are used for recognising the voice of the user. These devices generally record the voice of a person and transform it into electrical signals. Devices—such as microphone, webcam and graphics tablet—generally used in media are known as media input devices. Apart from these commonly used input devices, there are certain advanced devices—such as data acquisition sensors—that are used for inputting the data.

Key Terms to Remember

- **Input device**: It is an electromechanical device that is generally used for entering information into a computer system.
- **Keyboard**: It is a computer input device consisting of keys or buttons arranged in the similar fashion as they are arranged in a typewriter.
- **Pointing devices**: These are the input devices used for moving the cursor to a particular location to point an object on the screen.
- **Mouse**: It is a pointing device that basically controls the two-dimensional movement of the cursor on the displayed screen.
- **Trackball**: It is a pointing device consisting of a socket containing the ball that can be rolled manually to move the cursor on the screen.
- **Light pen**: It is a pointing device containing the light-sensitive element, which is used for selecting the objects displayed on the screen.
- **Joystick**: It is a pointing device that consists of one or more buttons and a stick that controls the movement of the cursor on the screen.
- **Touchscreen**: It is a pointing device that enables the users to enter data such as text, pictures and images by directly touching the screen.
- **Scanning devices**: These are the input devices that electronically capture text and images and convert them into computer readable form.
- **Hand-held scanner**: It is a scanning device used for digitising the images into bit map.
- **Flatbed scanner**: It is a scanning device that consists of a flat surface composing of glass pane on which the documents are kept for scanning.

- **Drun scanner**: It is a scanning device consisting of a large drum that is used for scanning the documents.
- **Slide scanner**: It is a scanning device used for scanning slides as well as film negatives.
- **OCR devices**: These devices scan a document by recognising its individual characters optically and converting it into the editable form.
- **OMR devices**: These are input devices are used for electronically recognising the characters written in the marked fields only.
- **MICR devices**: These are input devices used for recognising the characters written with the help of magnetic ink.
- **Bar code reader**: It is a scanning device used to read bar codes labelled on different items.
- **Digital camera**: It is a handheld electronic device that is capable of capturing videos as well as graphical images electronically.
- **Video cameras**: These are the digital cameras that capture an image by converting it into horizontal lines and then scanning each line from top to bottom.
- **Compact digital cameras**: These are the small-sized digital cameras that lack some of the advanced image capturing features.
- **Digital single-lens reflex cameras**: These cameras consist of a mirror and a pentaprism used for capturing the image digitally.
- **Light-scan cameras**: These cameras consist of an array of image sensors and are used to capture an image in the form of lines. After capturing an image, it scans the image line by line.
- **Voice recognition system**: It is a system that recognises the voice of an individual and converts it into the machine readable code.
- **Data acquisition sensors**: These are the devices used for detecting and measuring the different physical quantities and converting them into electrical signals.
- **Media input devices**: These are the input devices used in media for communicating with the mass audiences.
- **Microphone**: It is a media input device that converts the sound waves into the electrical signals with the help of sensors.
- **Webcam**: It is a media input device that is attached with the computer for recording videos as well as images.
- **Graphics tablet**: It is a media input device that helps a user to enter pictorial information into the computer system.

Review Questions

Fill in the Blanks

1. An input device generally acts as an interface between __________ and __________.
2. The __________ layout was generally used in the traditional keyboards.
3. The arrow keys used for controlling the movement of __________ are known as __________ keys.
4. Keyboards are also classified as __________ and __________ keyboards, based on additional keys present on them.
5. __________ devices are used for changing the position of the cursor on the screen.
6. A mechanical mouse basically consists of __________, __________ and __________ buttons.
7. An optical mouse consists of __________, __________ and __________ for moving the position of the pointer on the screen.

8. In case of trackball, ___________ is used for effecting the movement of the cursor on the screen.
9. ___________ device consists of a light- sensitive diode, which is used for pointing the objects on the screen.
10. The ___________, ___________ and ___________ are the different types of controls provided by joystick.
11. __________ devices are used for inputting data into a computer system with the help of human touch.
12. _____________devices are used for converting the images into machine-readable form.
13. Hand-held scanners are also called ______________.
14. ________________ scanners use red, green and blue filters.
15. Drum scanners make use of ________________ technology for scanning a particular document.
16. Slide scanners also known as _________scanners.
17. The OCR devices make use of____________ for recognising the characters on the document.
18. _______________ devices are used for recognising the characters written only in the marked fields.
19. A MICR device basically recognises the numerals written with the ____________ ink.
20. ______________ is the computer readable code representing the vertical lines of different widths.
21. ___________ is the hand-held device used for capturing images and videos.
22. The methods used for recognising the voice of the users are ___________ and _____________.
23. ________________helps in detecting the electrical properties of different signals.
24. _____________ input device is used for converting the sound waves into the electrical waves.
25. Graphics tablet is the combination of ____________ and _________________.

Multiple Choice Questions

1. What is the main function of an input device in a computer?
   A. Receiving data from a computer
   B. Providing data to a computer
   C. Storing data for processing
   D. Processing the data
2. Which of the following devices is not an input device?
   A. Scanner
   B. Keyboard
   C. Disk
   D. Joystick
3. Which one of the following is a modifier key?
   A. Tab
   B. ALT
   C. Insert
   D. Pause
4. Which of the following belongs to the category of special purpose keys?
   A. Tab
   B. SHIFT
   C. ALT
   D. CTRL
5. Which of the following device is not a pointing device?
   A. Joystick
   B. Mouse
   C. Trackball
   D. Scanner
6. Which of the following statements is not true for a mouse?
   A. It controls the two-dimensional movement of the cursor on the displayed screen.
   B. It is usually of two different types: mechanical mouse and optical mouse.
   C. It can be used as an alternate to keyboard for all purposes.
   D. It is an input device.
7. Which pointing device exhibits the point, click and drag functions?
   A. Trackball
   B. Joystick
   C. Mouse
   D. Light pen

8. Which of the following technologies is not a part of an optical mouse?
   A. LED B. DSP C. Optical sensor D. CCD
9. Which of the following indicates the location on the computer screen?
   A. Scroll bar B. Light pen C. Cursor D. Track ball
10. Which of the following devices is used for pointing in all directions?
   A. Light pen B. Joystick C. Trackball D. Mouse
11. Which one of the following technologies is not a touch-screen technology?
   A. Surface wave technology B. Capacitive technology
   C. Resistive technology D. Inductive technology
12. What is the other name of a hand-held scanner?
   A. Drum scanner B. Slide scanner C. Half page scanner D. Full page scanner
13. Which scanning device consists of a stepper motor and a CCD sensor?
   A. Drum scanner B. Slide scanner C. Flatbed scanner D. None of the above
14. Which of the following device is not an optical recognition device?
   A. MICR B. OMR C. OCR D. Microphone
15. Which of the following devices makes use of photoelectric cells for character recognition?
   A. Hand-held scanner B. OCR C. OMR D. Bar code reader
16. What does MICR stand for?
   A. Magnetic Ink Character Recognition B. Magnetic Input Column Reader
   C. Magnetic Ink Column Recognition D. Magnetic Ink Character Reader
17. Which device is used for scanning the question sheet having multiple choices?
   A. Drum scanner B. OMR device C. OCR device D. Flatbed scanner
18. Which of the following devices are used for recognising the characters in the supermarkets?
   A. OCR device B. OMR device C. MICR device D. Bar code reader
19. Which device is used for reading the characters written on the cheques?
   A. Hand-held scanner B. Light pen C. MICR device D. OCR device
20. Which of the following devices help in viewing a video clip just after it has been recorded?
   A. Joystick B. Webcam C. Digital camera D. All of the above
21. Which of the following device is not a media input device?
   A. Microphone B. Webcam C. Digital camera D. Graphics tablet

Discussion Questions

1. What is meant by an input device? What is the importance of an input device in a computer system?
2. List different categories of input devices.
3. Explain all the categories of keys found on a typical keyboard with the help of a diagram.
4. What are pointing devices? List different types of pointing devices.
5. Explain the basic functioning of mechanical and optical mouses with the help of sketches.
6. How does light pen help in inputting data into a computer system?

7. Which input device is used for playing games? Explain it in detail with the help of a diagram.
8. Explain the different technologies used in the touchscreens.
9. What are scanning devices? Explain the basic characteristics of these devices.
10. Explain hand-held scanners and drum scanners in detail.
11. What is meant by optical recognition?
12. What are the basic components of the OCR devices? Explain each component briefly.
13. How are OMR devices used for recognising the characters in the document to be scanned?
14. Explain briefly the basic function of an MICR device.
15. How does bar code reader help in recognising the characters on the labels?
16. Define digital camera. Explain the basic features of a digital camera.
17. Briefly explain the different types of digital cameras.
18. What does voice recognition system mean?
19. Explain the different methods used for identifying the voice of the user in the voice recognition system.
20. What are data acquisition sensors?
21. What are media input devices? Explain any two media input devices briefly.
22. How can we enter data into a computer system with the help of graphics tablet?
23. Explain briefly any five pointing devices with the help of diagrams.
24. What are flatbed scanners?
25. Explain the basic function of a slide scanner.

CHAPTER 5

OUTPUT DEVICES

Chapter Outline

Chapter Objectives

In this chapter, we will learn:

- Different output devices used to present the processed data to the users.
- Different types of display mc.iitors.
- Working of printers and plotters.
- How printers and plotters are classified into various categories.
- Different types of voice output devices.
- How projectors and terminals function.

5.1 INTRODUCTION

Output devices are essential part of a computer system. They receive the processed data (information) from the CPU and present it to the user in a desired form. They act as an interface between the computer and the user. The main task of an output device is to convert the machine-readable information into human-readable form which may be in the form of text, graphics, audio or video. Depending upon the form of output required, the output device may belong to one of the following categories:

- Display monitors
- Printers
- Plotters
- Voice output systems
- Projectors

While the printers and plotters provide the physical form of output known as *hard copy*, the display monitors, voice output systems and projectors provide temporary output known as *soft copy*. Unlike hard copy, soft copy is not a permanent form of output.

In this chapter, the principle of operation and application of some of the popular output devices will be discussed briefly.

5.2 DISPLAY MONITORS

Display monitors are the most commonly used soft copy output devices. Earlier the display monitors were capable of displaying the characters only in a single font and in a single colour. These characters were arranged in a rectangular grid on the screen. The display screens, which are available today, support many fonts and colours. Different types of display monitors use different technology for displaying the data. On the basis of technology used display monitors may be classified into three categories:

1. Cathode Ray Tube Monitor
2. Liquid Crystal Display Monitor
3. Thin Film Transistor Monitor

5.2.1 Cathode Ray Tube (CRT) Monitor

A CRT monitor contains an empty glass tube with a phosphor coated fluorescent screen and a source of electrons known as *electron gun*. This glass tube containing screen and electron gun is known as a CRT. When the CRT gets heated due to the current flowing through it, the electron gun present inside the CRT emits a beam of electrons, which hits the screen comprising small dots known as pixels. The striking of electron beam on the phosphor coated pixels results in emission of light. The intensity of light emitted at a certain point varies with the force with which the electron beam strikes the screen. The electron beam scans across the screen due to the deflection caused to it by the electromagnetic coils present in the glass tube. This scanning of screen by the electron beam produces an image on the screen and the variation in the intensity of emitted light enables the human eyes to see the image thus produced. Figure 5.1(a) and (b) show a CRT monitor and the internal components of a CRT.

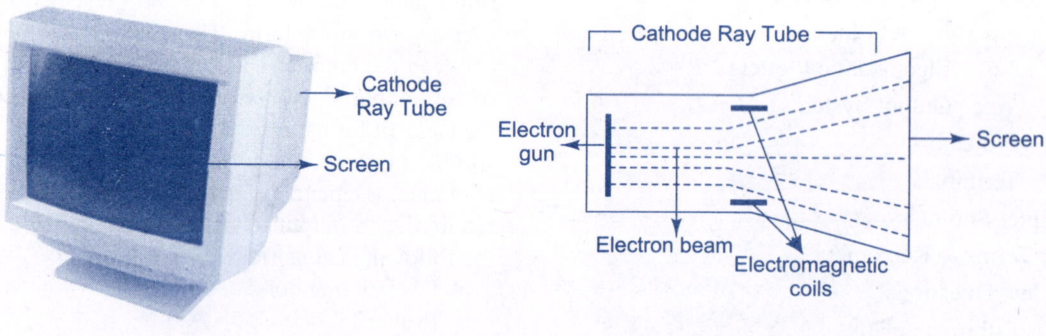

(a) CRT Monitor (b) Internal Components of CRT

Fig. 5.1 A CRT monitor and the internal components of a CRT

A CRT monitor has many advantages, such as a high contrast ratio and colour depth because of which many graphic designers prefer this type of display monitors. It also provides a change in the resolution without affecting the clarity of the picture. Though CRT monitor has many advantages, there are some disadvantages associated with it. It is very bulky and occupies a lot of space on the desk. It also consumes a lot of power and produces a large amount of heat.

5.2.2 Liquid Crystal Display (LCD) Monitor

An LCD monitor uses liquid crystals technology to display the images. The liquid crystals are actually the molecules of the liquid filled in the LCD. These molecules easily flow in different directions and have the capability to bend a beam of light. Each pixel on the LCD screen contains a number of liquid molecules layered between two transparent electrodes and crossed polarising filters. The liquid molecules uphold their directions and remain in the same position with respect to each other. As the light falls on the molecules, they bend the light and direct them towards a polarising filter. The polarising filter absorbs the light making the polariser appear dark for the display of images. Figure 5.2 shows an LCD monitor.

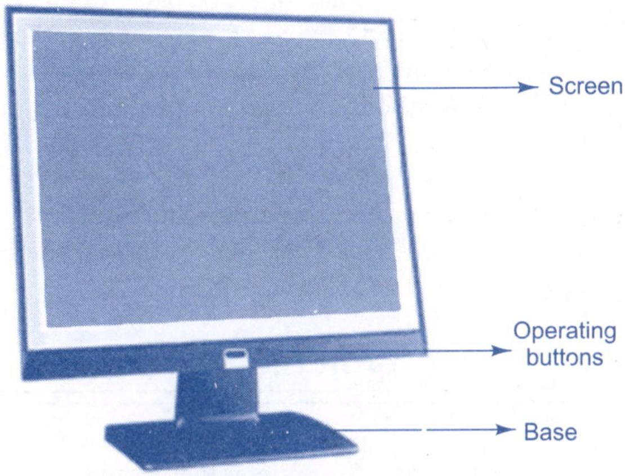

Fig. 5.2 An LCD monitor

An LCD monitor is small in size and light in weight so it occupies less space on the desk. Also, the power consumption by an LCD monitor is very less as liquid molecules need less power to bend light. There are a few disadvantages of using an LCD monitor. It has a fixed resolution due to which the images on an LCD monitor become blurred when the resolution is changed. The clarity of the images also gets reduced when the images on an LCD monitor move at a fast rate or, say, when the rate of change of images on the screen is high. Moreover, it has a weak colour quality as compared to a CRT monitor.

5.2.3 Thin Film Transistor (TFT) Monitor

A TFT monitor is similar to an LCD monitor except for one difference that it uses thin film transistor technology along with liquid crystal technology to improve the quality of the image (unlike LCD, which uses only the liquid crystal technology). For each pixel on the screen, a small transistor switch as well as a capacitor is used and each pixel is controlled separately. A row scan driver turns on the transistor switch to charge the capacitors of all the pixels in a particular row. The transistor is switched off as soon as the capacitors get charged. When the transistor is switched off, the capacitor maintains the same voltage of the pixels till the transistor is switched on again by the row scan driver. Figure 5.3 shows a TFT monitor.

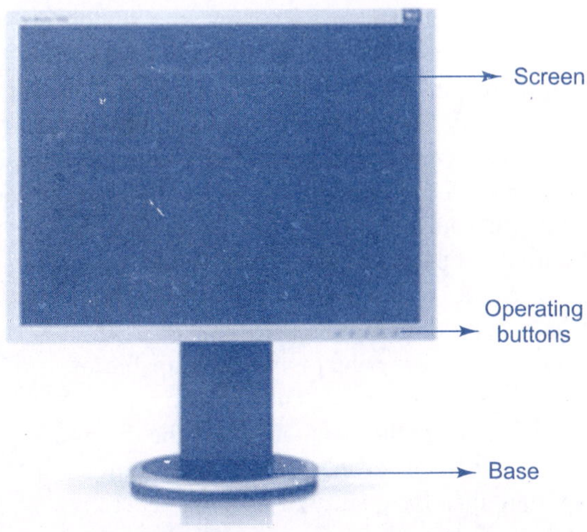

Fig. 5.3 A TFT monitor

5.3 PRINTERS

Printers are the most widely used output devices in real life applications. A printer is a computer hardware that generates the hard copy of the information processed by a computer system. The hard copy produced by the printer can be in the form of a paper or any other physical printing medium. To produce a hard copy, first the printer is connected to a computer with the help of a cable and then the print command is given by the user through the user interface of the computer. The output on the hard copy produced by a printer can be preserved for a long time as compared to the output displayed on the display monitors. Based on the features, such as colour, resolution, memory and speed possessed by the printers, they are classified into many types. Some printers have a very high printing speed, whereas others have a slow printing speed. Moreover, all computers cannot produce multicoloured printouts. Some of them produce single colour printouts only. On the basis of their working principles printers can be classified into two major categories, namely impact and non-impact printers.

5.4 IMPACT PRINTERS

Impact printers are those printers in which there exists a mechanical contact between print head and paper. Print head is the part of the printer that resembles a hammer and is responsible for transferring the ink to the paper in the form of required characters. Impact printer contains an individual print head for each character. The print head of a character strikes the ink ribbon, and the ink ribbon in turn strikes the paper, leaving an impression of that particular character on the paper. Some of the most popular impact printers are as follows:

- Dot matrix printers
- Daisy wheel printers
- Drum printers

5.4.1 Dot Matrix Printer

A dot matrix printer is an impact printer in which a character is printed on the paper by the back and forth movement of a print head against the ribbon drenched in ink. In dot matrix printer, the characters are formed out of a matrix containing dots as shown Fig. 5.4. Each dot is produced with the help of a metal pin brought forward by a small electromagnet. A small plate guides the pins to the ribbon and the pins strike the ribbon to form an impression of a dot on the paper.

Dot matrix printer is capable of printing a complete line of characters at a time. It is very durable as it does not wear out quickly; however, the circular channels on the guide plate get damaged due to frequent striking of pins. This damage in the shape of circular channels makes the guide plate less accurate because of which the printed characters become hazy.

The dot matrix printers are also capable of producing carbon copies. They ensure reliable printing and are best suitable for the fields where the content of the printed data is more important than the quality of printing. There is no need of providing individual single sheets to these printers again and again as they take continuous papers. Figure 5.5 shows a dot matrix printer.

Fig. 5.4 Matrix characters

Dot matrix printers are cheap to use as the cost of printing per page is very less. If the printer has not been in use for a long time, even then, the ink ribbon remains preserved for the future use and does not dry quickly. Besides advantages, these printers have some disadvantages. They produce a lot of noise while printing and have low printing speed as well as printing quality. These printers support limited colours and need a lot of maintenance as the damage to the pins may cause printing of improper text.

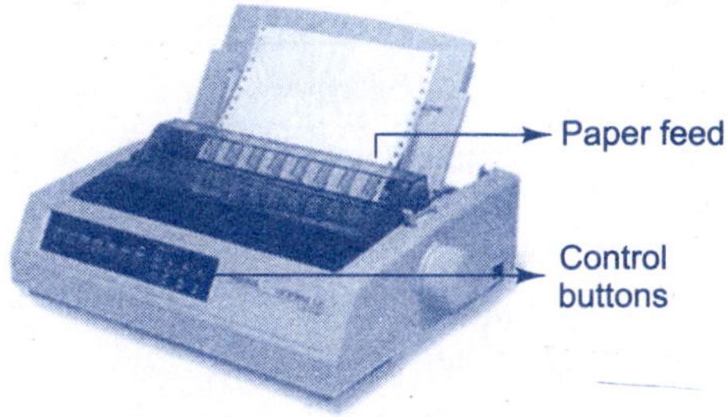

Fig. 5.5 A dot matrix printer

Although dot matrix printers are not commonly used at homes, they are still widely used in business and industries as they are cheap and can produce carbon copies.

5.4.2 Daisy Wheel Printer

A daisy wheel printer is an impact printer that produces printouts of good quality characters. It contains a metal or a plastic disk on which the characters reside on the outer edge of the petals. Figure 5.6 shows a daisy wheel printer.

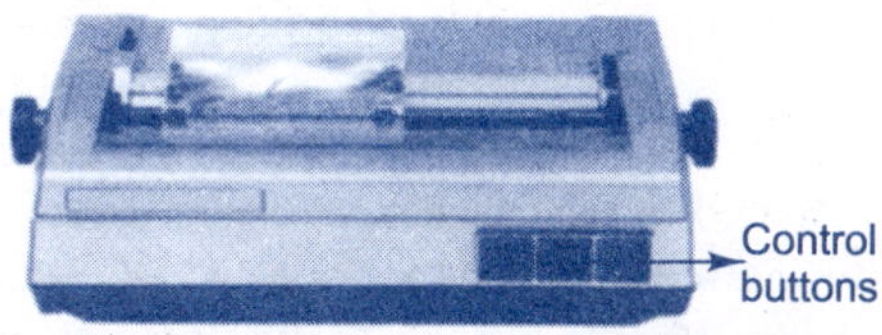

Fig. 5.6 A daisy wheel printer

The disk in the daisy wheel printer is rotated until the petal, containing the character to be printed, faces the paper. Once the required character is positioned towards the paper, the disk is struck by a hammer, which acts as print head. The striking of hammer on the disk forces the disk to hit the ink-soaked ribbon and the ribbon leaves an impression of the character on the paper. Figure 5.7 shows the disk of a daisy wheel printer.

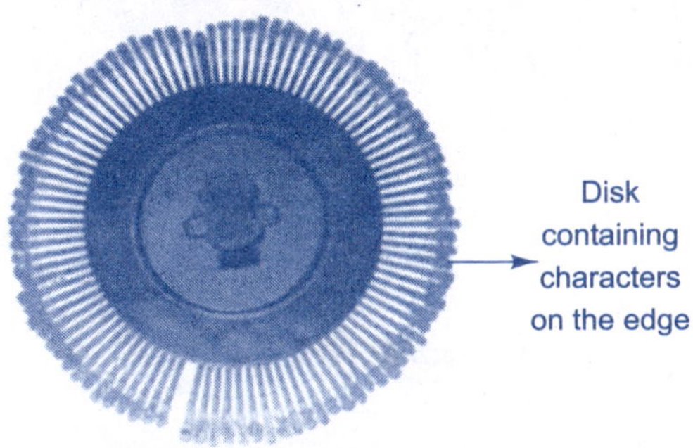

Fig. 5.7 Disk of a daisy wheel printer

The only advantage of daisy wheel printers is that they allow the printing of characters in different fonts. The daisy wheel printers are capable of printing text only and not graphics. They are very noisy as well as very slow and can print approximately 10 to 75 characters per second.

5.4.3 Drum Printer

Drum printers are the impact printers in which the characters are engraved on a cylindrical drum, which is rotated around print head hammer. The paper and the ink ribbon lie between the hammer and the drum. When a character is to be printed, the hammer strikes the paper and forces it to hit the ribbon. The ribbon in turn hits the character on the drum and the impression of the character is formed on the paper. The advantages of the drum printers are low cost, higher speed as compared to other impact printers; and it requires no feeding of paper again and again. The disadvantages of these printers include poor quality of printing and large noise production. Figure 5.8 shows the internal components of a drum printer.

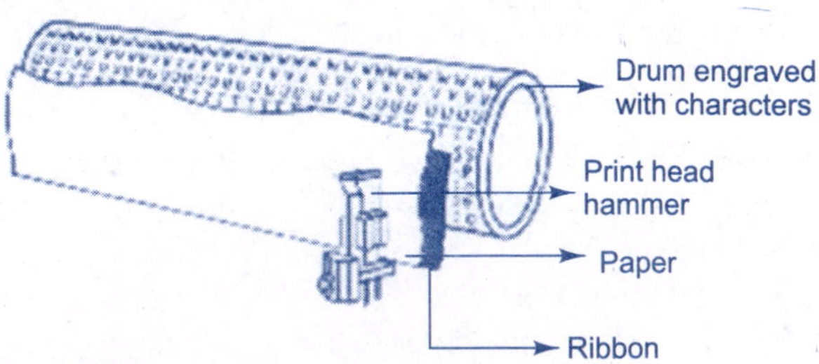

Fig. 5.8 Internal components of a drum printer

5.5 NON-IMPACT PRINTERS

Non-impact printers are the printers in which there exists no mechanical contact between the print head and paper. These printers spray ink on the paper with the help of a nozzle. Non-impact printers do not produce much noise and are fast as compared to impact printers. The reason for the production of less noise is the absence of mechanical moving parts in the printer. The most popular non-impact printers are:

1. Ink-jet printers
2. Laser printers

5.5.1 Ink-jet Printer

Ink-jet printers are the non-impact printers that produce an image by spraying small droplets of ink on the paper with the help of a nozzle. A magnetised plate guides the sprayed ink to form the particular shape of a character or a symbol on the paper. The ink-jet printers offer a resolution of 300 dots per inch and produce high quality printouts, such as graphics and images. They are cheaper and portable as compared to the other non-impact printers. The slow speed and the requirement of a special ink, which is suitable for the inexpensive papers, are the two drawbacks of the ink-jet printers. The printouts taken from an ink-jet printer also require some time to dry. Figure 5.9 shows an ink-jet printer.

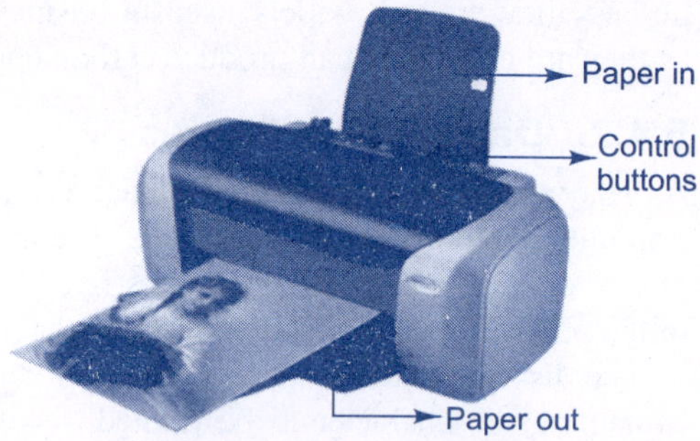

Fig. 5.9 An ink-jet printer

5.5.2 Laser Printers

Laser printers are the non-impact printers that produce images with the help of a laser beam. It works on the same technology as the one used in a copier machine. The laser beam electrically charges the drum coated with selenium and then transfers the entire document, which is to be printed to it. The charged drum is then allowed to roll into the dry powder ink known as toner. The toner sticks to the charged images on the drum and is then transferred to the paper with the help of heat and pressure. The electrical charges and the remaining toner automatically get removed from the drum after the printing of the document. Laser printers are capable of printing both black and coloured text but as colour laser printers are very costly so generally single colour laser printers are used. Laser printers have a high speed and resolution. They produce high quality printing in various fonts and that too, without producing any noise. Figure 5.10 shows a laser printer.

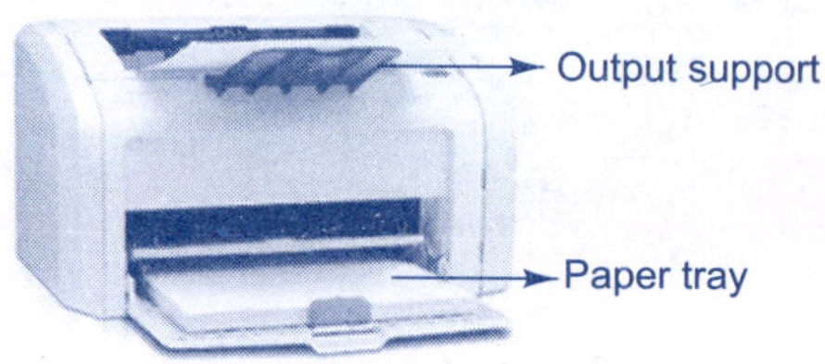

Fig. 5.10 A laser printer

5.5.3 Special Purpose Printers

Although most applications use ink-jet or laser printers, there are some high quality printers that are primarily used by publishers and print shops to create high quality colour images. These printers include:

- Photo printers
- Thermal-wax printers
- Dye-sublimation printers

These printers are very slow and expensive.

5.6 PLOTTERS

Plotter is a device used to print high quality graphics and images. It uses one or more pens to produce a high quality drawing. These pens change their positions and draw continuous lines to produce an image. The plotters were used as a substitute to the coloured printers when the printers were very expensive and were also not capable of drawing bigger images such as graphs. The plotters provided cheap and efficient drawing but required a separate pen for each colour. This affected the speed of plotters but later the plotters started using four basic colours only, i.e., cyan, magenta, yellow and black. These are the primary colours, which combine in different ratios to form other different colours. So, now the speed of plotters increased as there was no need of changing the pens frequently. The plotters are further divided into the following four categories on the basis of their working:

- Drum plotters
- Flat-bed plotters
- Ink-jet plotters
- Electrostatic plotters

5.6.1 Drum Plotter

Drum plotter is a plotter in which pen is moved vertically, i.e., along the Y axis and the paper wrapped on the drum is moved horizontally, i.e., along the X axis. The movement of pen in left or right direction and the movement of paper in backward or forward direction produce a graph or an image. Figure 5.11 shows a drum plotter.

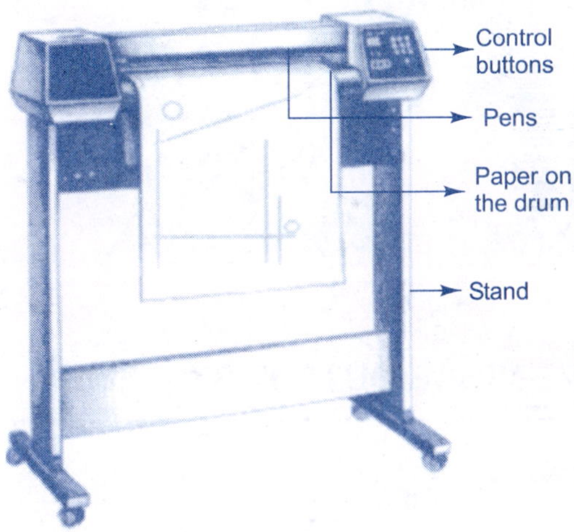

Fig. 5.11 A drum plotter

5.6.2 Flat-bed Plotter

Flat-bed plotter is the plotter in which the position of the paper is kept constant and the pens are moved around in various directions to draw graphs and images. The pens can be moved both along X and Y axis. The size of the drawing, which can be drawn using these plotters, depends on the size of the flat bed on which the paper is adjusted. Figure 5.12 shows a flat-bed plotter.

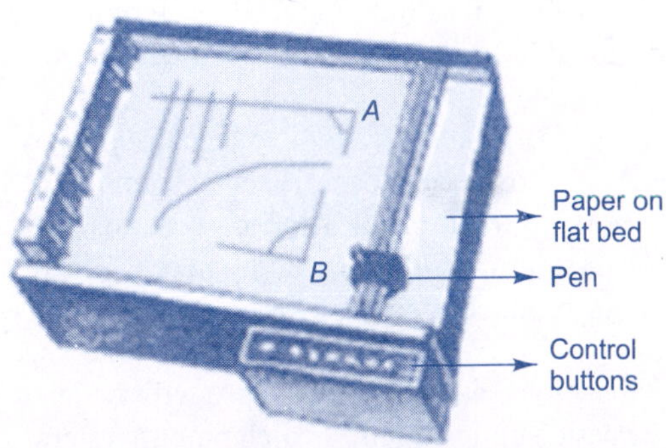

Fig. 5.12 A flat-bed plotter

5.6.3 Ink-jet Plotter

Ink-jet plotters are the plotters in which a line or a solid colour output is drawn with the help of spraying ink droplets on the paper. They have a high speed and produce higher quality output as compared to the other plotters. However, as the nozzles, which spray the ink can get blocked soon, they require more maintenance as compared to the other plotters. Figure 5.13 shows an ink-jet plotter.

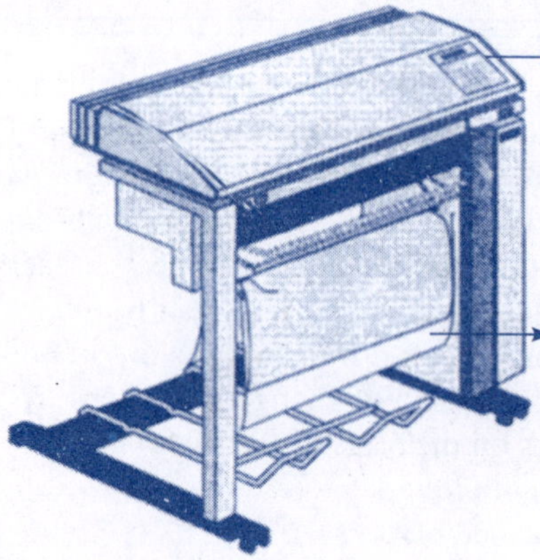

Fig. 5.13 An ink-jet plotter

5.6.4 Electrostatic Plotter

Electrostatic plotters are the plotters in which the electrostatic charges are used to draw images and graphs. These images and graphs are made of tiny dots on a special paper. The electrostatic plotters are the fastest plotters and produce an output of high quality and resolution. One of the disadvantages of using these plotters is that one becomes vulnerable to chemicals, which are used in the plotters to produce the electrostatic charge. Figure 5.14 shows an electrostatic plotter.

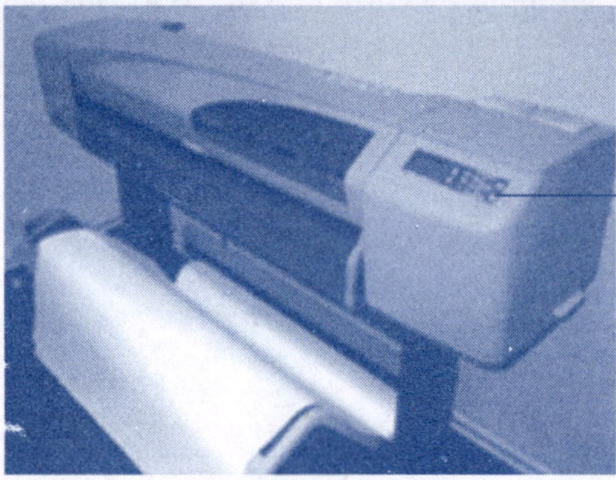

Fig. 5.14 An electrostatic plotter

5.7 VOICE OUTPUT SYSTEMS

Voice output systems are also known as voice response systems. These systems record the simple messages in human speech form and then combine all these simple messages to form a single message. The voice response system is of two types—one uses a reproduction of human voice and other sounds, and the other uses speech synthesis.

The voice response system, which uses a reproduction of human voice takes the sound input in the analog form and converts it into the digital form. It stores the converted data permanently on some storage device. The digital sound produced as an output may be in the form of words, phrases or music. The digital sound stored at the storage device is then sent to the speakers through which the output is made audible to the users.

The voice response system, which uses speech synthesis, takes the sound input in analog form and converts it into speech form. Besides sound expansion card and speech synthesiser, the written text to be converted into the form of a speech requires special software. The speech synthesiser is a device used for the conversion of written text into speech. The speech synthesiser combines approximately 50 to 60 basic sounds to produce a single word. The different words formed by the combination of basic sounds then combine to form a speech. The quality of the speech produced as an output depends on its resemblance to the human voice and also on the ease with which a user can understand it.

The basic application of a voice output system is in Interactive Voice Response (IVR) systems, which are used by the customer care or customer support departments of an organisation, such as telecommunication companies, etc.

5.8 PROJECTORS

A projector is a device that is connected to a computer or a video device for projecting an image from the computer or video device onto the big white screen. The images projected by a projector are larger in size as compared to the original images. A projector consists of an optic system, a light source and displays, which contain the original images. The projectors are classified into three categories:

- Ultralight portable projectors
- Conference room projectors
- Fixed installation projectors

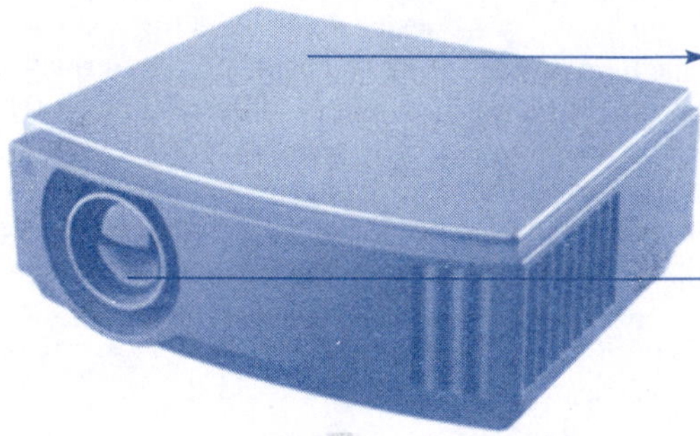

Fig. 5.15 A portable projector

The ultralight projectors are small in size and, are therefore referred as portable projectors. The conference room projectors are the projectors used for projecting the output at large venues such as business meetings and huge gatherings. They are not light weight but have a better projection as compared to the ultralight projectors. The fixed installation projectors are the most expensive projectors. They are fixed permanently at the place of presentation and are capable of projecting images in bright light also.

Projectors were initially used for showing films but now they are used on a large scale for displaying presentations in business organisations and for viewing movies at home. The projectors in home theatres help to project the images of a movie on the white screen at a comparatively large size as compared to the small images displayed on a small television screen. Figure 5.15 shows a portable projector.

5.9 TERMINALS

A terminal is a combination of an input device and an output device that helps a computer in receiving as well as transmitting data. The classification of computer terminals is done on the basis of the data handled by them. A keyboard and a display monitor are respectively the input and the output devices, which are paired together to form a common terminal. The display monitor used in the terminal can be of any of the three types—a CRT, an LCD or a TFT. The terminals are broadly classified into three categories:

- Intelligent terminals
- Smart terminals
- Dumb terminals

An intelligent terminal is a terminal that possesses all the processing power, i.e., the logic required to perform the operations, such as calculations and formatting. It does not require any processor but instead performs all the tasks by itself. A smart terminal is a terminal that contains some logic. It requires the help of a processor to perform complex operations such as performing calculations but is capable of performing simple operations such as making the displayed data appear bold. A dumb terminal is a terminal that does not contain any logic at all. It only displays the data received from the processor. It has the slowest speed as compared to the other two terminals.

Chapter Summary

An output device is the device that is used to pass on the processed data to the end users. The output produced can be in the form of a soft copy or a hard copy. To display a soft copy of the text or graphical output, a display monitor is required. The display monitor is of three types: CRT, LCD and TFT. These monitors differ in their appearance as well as their working. The other commonly used output devices are printers and plotters. Printers are used to produce a hard copy of text and image format output.

On the basis of their mechanism, printers are divided into two types, impact printers and non-impact printers. In impact printers, print head has a mechanical contact between print head and paper, whereas in non-impact printers, there's no mechanical contact between print head and paper. The printers are capable of producing efficient print-outs of text but they cannot produce very clear printouts of images. For image printing, another output device called plotter is used. It is again divided into four categories: drum plotter, flat-bed plotter, ink-jet plotter and electrostatic plotter.

Apart from text format, an output can also have an audio format. The audio format output requires speakers and voice output systems so that it can be communicated to the users. The voice output system includes speech synthesisers, which concatenate small sounds to produce a word of a speech.

Another example of output devices is the projector. Projectors allow the users to view the output on a big screen. Projectors vary on the basis of their sizes such as portable projectors, conference room projectors and fixed installation projectors.

Key Terms to Remember

- **Monitor**: Monitor is the most commonly used output device, which displays the soft copy output of text and graphics to the users.
- **CRT monitors**: CRT monitors use a Cathode Ray Tube (CRT), including an electron beam and a phosphor coated screen for producing an image on the screen.
- **LCD monitors**: LCD monitors use liquid crystals, which are activated by electric field to display the images of high resolution.
- **Printers**: Printers are the output devices that are used to produce a hard copy output of the text or the documents stored in a computer.
- **Impact printers**: Impact printers are the printers in which a mechanical contact exists between print head and paper. The impression of characters is developed on the paper with the help of striking the ink ribbon by the print head.
- **Non-impact printers**: Non-impact printers are the printers in which mechanical contact does not exist between print head and paper and ink is sprayed on the paper with the help of a nozzle to form an impression of the character.
- **Plotters**. Plotters are the output devices attached with computer to plot high quality graphs or images.
- **Drum plotter**: Drum plotter is the plotter that consists of a paper mounted on a drum and pens to plot the graph. Both pens and paper on the drum are moved to produce images.
- **Flat-bed plotter**: Flat-bed plotter consists of a plain surface known as bed on which the paper is fixed and only the pens are moved to produce an image or a graph.
- **Speakers**: Speakers are the output devices used to generate output in an audio format from the computer.
- **Projectors**: Projectors are the output devices that are used to project big picture of the data stored on some storage device such as CD and DVD on a white screen.

- **Terminal**: A terminal is a collection of an input device and an output device that helps a computer in receiving as well as transmitting data.
- **Intelligent terminal**: The terminal, which possesses all processing power, i.e., the logic required to perform operations such as calculations and formatting, is known as intelligent terminal.
- **Smart terminal**: The terminal, which possesses small processing power, is known as smart terminal. It requires the help of a processor to perform certain operations.
- **Dumb terminal**. The terminal, which possesses no processing power, is known as dumb terminal. It does not perform any operation by itself.

Review Questions

Fill in the Blanks

1. ___________ devices are the devices, which help in communicating the processed data to the users.
2. ___________ is one of the most essential and commonly used output devices.
3. ___________, ___________ and ___________ are the three main types of display monitors.
4. The screen in display monitors consists of a number of small dots like structures known as ___________.
5. ___________ printers do not have a mechanical contact between print head and paper.
6. ___________ printers contain an ink ribbon, which is hit by a print head to form an impression of a character on the paper.
7. CRT is an abbreviation for ________ ________ ________.
8. ________ monitor consists of liquid molecules.
9. _________ printers are best suitable for the fields where the content of the printed data is more important than the quality of printing.
10. _________ produce a high quality drawing as compared to printers.
11. _________ are used to generate a sound format output.
12. _________ helps the users to project a big picture of the generated output.
13. _________ terminals contain a built-in logic, which is capable of processing the data.
14. _________ terminals are not capable of processing the output.
15. ________ are the most expensive projectors.
16. The portable projectors are also known as _________ projectors.
17. ________ records the simple messages in human speech form and then combines them to form a single message.
18. In _________ plotters, both pen and paper are moved in opposite directions to plot a graph or an image.
19. ________ printers use a laser beam to produce an image on paper.
20. A daisy wheel printer is the impact printer that produces _________ type printouts.
21. A _______ monitor uses thin film transistor technology to improve the quality of image.
22. The power consumption by an LCD monitor is _________ as compared to a CRT monitor.
23. The quality of image of a _________ monitor is better than the LCD monitor.
24. Special purpose printers are primarily used by _________ .

Multiple Choice Questions

1. Which of the following is not an output device?
   A. Scanner B. Plotter C. Printer D. Speaker
2. Which of the following monitors are commonly used with desktop computers?
   A. CBT monitors B. CRT monitors C. CPT monitors D. None of the above
3. Which of the following are the properties of a printer?
   A. Resolution B. Speed C. Pages per minute D. All of the above
4. Which of the following printers print by spraying ink on the paper?
   A. Daisy wheel printer B. Dot matrix printer C. Drum printer D. Laser printer
5. Which of the following units can be used to measure the speed of a printer?
   A. Characters per inch (cpi) B. Dots per inch (dpi)
   C. Pages per minute (ppm) D. None of the above
6. Which of the following devices are capable of producing large-format drawings like graphs and construction drawings?
   A. Dot matrix printers B. Flat-bed plotters C. Impact printers D. Ink-jet printers
7. Which of the following is a hard copy output device?
   A. Printer B. Speaker C. Display monitor D. Projector
8. Which of the following is an impact printer?
   A. Dot matrix printer B. Ink-jet printer C. Laser printer D. All of the above
9. Which of the following is a non-impact printer?
   A. Daisy wheel printer B. Dot matrix printer C. Laser printer D. All of the above
10. Which of the following is one of the components of a CRT?
    A. Toner B. Liquid crystals C. Electromagnetic coils D. None of the above
11. In which of the following plotters, both pen and papers are moved to produce an image?
    A. Drum plotter B. Electrostatic plotter C. Flat-bed plotter D. Ink-jet plotter
12. In which of the following plotters the graphs are plotted by spraying ink on the paper?
    A. Drum plotter B. Electrostatic plotter C. Flat-bed plotter D. Ink-jet plotter
13. Which of the following are the components of a projector?
    A. Optic system B. Displays C. Electron beam D. Both A and B
14. Which of the following are portable projectors?
    A. Conference room projectors B. Fixed installation projectors
    C. Ultralight projectors D. All of the above
15. Which of the following devices are included in a terminal?
    A. Monitor and printer B. Printer and keyboard C. Keyboard and monitor D. All of the above
16. Which of the following is a type of terminal?
    A. Intelligent terminal B. Dumb terminal C. Both A and B D. All of the above

Discussion Questions

1. What is an output device? Why is it a vital part of computer hardware?
2. Name some of the output devices, which are commonly used with the computer system.
3. Define a display monitor.
4. Name the different types of monitors available in the market.
5. Explain the use of a printer in a computer system.
6. Differentiate between an impact printer and a non-impact printer. Give one example of each.
7. Briefly explain the different types of impact printers.
8. Explain the different types of non-impact printers.
9. What are the advantages and disadvantages of a daisy wheel printer?
10. What are the characteristics of a laser printer?
11. What is the use of plotters?
12. Define a plotter. Explain at least two types of plotters.
13. What are the advantages and disadvantages of a CRT monitor?
14. Which is a better monitor—a CRT or a TFT? State the reasons as well.
15. Explain the term voice response system and list different types used today.
16. What is a projector? Why is it needed?
17. What are the different types of projector?
18. State the characteristics on the basis of which the efficiency of a printer can be measured.
19. Distinguish between a printer and a plotter.
20. Define a terminal.
21. Explain the different types of terminals.
22. What do you mean by speech synthesis?
23. Draw a diagram to show the internal components of a CRT.
24. What are the special purpose printers? What are their applications?
25. State some applications where dumb terminals may be used.

CHAPTER 6

COMPUTER CODES

Chapter Outline

Chapter Objectives

In this chapter, we will learn:

- The concept of positional number system.
- Different types of positional number systems.
- The need of computer codes.
- Different types of 4-bit and 8-bit BCD systems.
- The importance of 16-bit Unicode.
- The conversion of numbers represented in one system into another.

6.1 INTRODUCTION

A computer is a digital system that stores and processes different types of data in the form of 0s and 1s. The different types of data handled by a computer system include numbers, alphabets and some special characters. Therefore, there is a need to change the data entered by the users into a form that the computer system can understand and process. Different types of codes have been developed and used to represent the data entered by the users in the binary format. The binary system represents each type of data in terms of binary digits, 0s and 1s. Since these codes convert the data into the binary form, the computer codes are also referred as *binary codes*.

The decimal system is not the only number system used by computer users. Computer professionals use different number systems according to their requirements to communicate with the computer system. Therefore, before understanding the various computer codes, we need to understand the concept of number systems. All the number systems used by computer professionals to interact with computer systems come under the category of *positional number system*. The positional number system is a number system in which numbers are represented using some symbols called digits and the values of these numbers can be determined by taking the position of digits into consideration. The different number systems, which come under the category of positional number system, are as follows:

- Decimal system
- Binary system
- Hexadecimal system
- Octal system

6.2 DECIMAL SYSTEM

The *decimal system* is the most common number system used by human beings. It is a positional number system that uses 10 as a base to represent different values. Therefore, this number system is also known as *base10 number system*. In this system, 10 symbols are available for representing the values. These symbols include the digits from 0 to 9. The common operations performed in the decimal system are addition (+), subtraction (–), multiplication (×) and division (/).

The decimal system can be used to represent both the integer as well as floating point values. The floating point values are generally represented in this system by using a period called decimal point. The decimal point is used to separate the integer part and the fraction part of the given floating point number. However, there is no need to use a decimal point for representing integer values. The value of any number represented in the decimal system can be determined by first multiplying the weight associated with each digit in the given number with the digit itself and then adding all these values produced as a result of multiplication operation. The weight associated with any digit depends upon the position of the digit itself in the given number. The most common method to determine the weight of any digit in any number system is to raise the base of the number system to a power that initially starts with a 0 and then increases by 1 as we move from right to left in the given number. To understand this concept, let us consider the following floating point number represented in the decimal system:

Decimal point

↓

6 5 4 3 . 1 2 4

In the above example, the value 6543, which comes before the decimal point, is called *integer value* and the value 124, which comes after the decimal point, is called *fraction value*. Table 6.1 lists the weights associated with each digit in the given decimal number.

Table 6.1 Place values in decimal system

Digit	6	5	4	3	.	1	2	4
Weight	10^3	10^2	10^1	10^0		10^{-1}	10^{-2}	10^{-3}

The above table shows that the powers to the base increases by 1 towards the left for the integer part and decreases by 1 towards the right for the fraction part. Using the place values, the floating point number 6543.124 in decimal system can be computed as:

$$6 \times 10^3 + 5 \times 10^2 + 4 \times 10^1 + 3 \times 10^0 + 1 \times 10^{-1} + 2 \times 10^{-2} + 4 \times 10^{-3}$$
$$= 6000 + 500 + 40 + 3 + 0.1 + 0.02 + 0.004$$
$$= 6543.124$$

6.3 BINARY SYSTEM

Among all the positional number systems, the binary system is the most dominant number system that is employed by almost all the modern digital computer systems. The binary system uses base 2 to represent different values. Therefore, the binary system is also known as *base-2 system.* As this system uses base 2, only two symbols are available for representing the different values in this system. These symbols are 0 and 1, which are also known as *bits* in computer terminology. Using binary system, the computer systems can store and process each type of data in terms of 0s and 1s only.

The following are some of the technical terms used in binary system:

- **Bit.** It is the smallest unit of information used in a computer system. It can either have the value 0 or 1. Derived from the words *B*inary dig*IT*.
- **Nibble.** It is a combination of 4 bits.
- **Byte.** It is a combination of 8 bits. Derived from words 'by eight'.
- **Word.** It is a combination of 16 bits.
- **Double word.** It is a combination of 32 bits.
- **Kilobyte (KB).** It is used to represent the 1024 bytes of information.
- **Megabyte (MB).** It is used to represent the 1024 KBs of information.
- **Gigabyte (GB).** It is used to represent the 1024 MBs of information.

We can determine the weight associated with each bit in the given binary number in the similar manner as we did in the decimal system. In the binary system, the weight of any bit can be determined by raising 2 to a power equivalent to the position of bit in the number. To understand this concept, let us consider the following binary number:

Binary point
↓
1 0 1 0 0 1 . 0 1 0 1

In binary system, the point used to separate the integer and the fraction part of a number is known as *binary point.* Table 6.2 lists the weights associated with each bit in the given binary number.

Table 6.2 Place values in binary system

Digit	1	0	1	0	0	1	.	0	1	0	1
Weight	2^5	2^4	2^3	2^2	2^1	2^0		2^{-1}	2^{-2}	2^{-3}	2^{-4}

Like the decimal system, the powers to the base increases by 1 towards the left for the integer part and decreases by 1 towards the right for the fraction part. The value of the given binary number can be determined as the sum of the products of the bits multiplied by the weight of the bit itself. Therefore, the value of the binary number 101001.0101 can be obtained as:

$$1 \times 2^5 + 0 \times 2^4 + 1 \times 2^3 + 0 \times 2^2 + 0 \times 2^1 + 1 \times 2^0 + 0 \times 2^{-1} + 1 \times 2^{-2} + 0 \times 2^{-3} + 1 \times 2^{-4}$$
$$= 32 + 8 + 1 + 0.25 + 0.0625$$
$$= 41.3125$$

The binary number 101001.0101 represents the decimal value 41.3125.

Table 6.3 lists the 4-bit binary representation of decimal numbers 0 through 15.

Table 6.3 Binary representation of first 16 numbers

Decimal number	4-bit binary
0	0000
1	0001
2	0010
3	0011
4	0100
5	0101
6	0110
7	0111
8	1000
9	1001
10	1010
11	1011
12	1100
13	1101
14	1110
15	1111

6.4 HEXADECIMAL SYSTEM

The hexadecimal system is a positional number system that uses base 16 to represent different values. Therefore, this number system is known as *base-16 system*. As this system uses base 16, 16 symbols are available for representing the values in this system. These symbols are the digits 0–9 and the letters A, B, C, D, E and F. The digits 0–9 are used to represent the decimal values 0 through 9 and the letters A, B, C, D, E and F are used to represent the decimal values 10 through 15.

The weight associated with each symbol in the given hexadecimal number can be determined by raising 16 to a power equivalent to the position of the digit in the number. To understand this concept, let us consider the following hexadecimal number:

Hexadecimal point
↓
4A9.2B

In hexadecimal system, the point used to separate the integer and the fraction part of a number is known as *hexadecimal point*. Table 6.4 lists the weights associated with each digit in the given hexadecimal number.

Table 6.4 Place values in hexadecimal system

Digit	4	A	9		2	B
Weight	16^2	16^1	16^0		16^{-1}	16^{-2}

The value of the hexadecimal number can be computed as the sum of the products of the symbol multiplied by the weight of the symbol itself. Therefore, the value of the given hexadecimal number is:

$$4 \times 16^2 + 10 \times 16^1 + 9 \times 16^0 + 2 \times 16^{-1} + 11 \times 16^{-2}$$
$$= 1024 + 160 + 9 + 0.125 + 0.0429$$
$$= 1193 + 0.1679$$
$$= 1193.1679$$

The hexadecimal number 4A9. 2B represents the decimal value 1193.1679.

6.5 OCTAL SYSTEM

The octal system is the positional number system that uses base 8 to represent different values. Therefore, this number system is also known as *base-8 system*. As this system uses base 8, eight symbols are available for representing the values in this system. These symbols are the digits 0 to 7.

The weight associated with each digit in the given octal number can be determined by raising 8 to a power equivalent to the position of digit in the number. To understand this concept, let us consider the following octal number:

Octal point
↓
2 1 5 . 4 3

In octal system, the point used to separate the integer and the fraction part of a number is known as *octal point*. Table 6.5 lists the weights associated with each digit in the given octal number.

Table 6.5 Place values in octal system

Digit	2	1	5		4	3
Weight	8^2	8^1	8^0		8^{-1}	8^{-2}

Using these place values, we can now determine the value of the given octal number as:

$$2 \times 8^2 + 1 \times 8^1 + 5 \times 8^0 + 4 \times 8^{-1} + 3 \times 8^{-2}$$
$$= 128 + 8 + 5 + 0.5 + 0.0469$$
$$= 141 + 0.5469$$
$$= 141.5469$$

The octal number 215.43 represents the decimal value 141.5469.

Table 6.6 lists the octal representation of decimal numbers 0 through 15.

Table 6.6 Octal representation of first 16 numbers

Decimal number	Octal representation
0	0
1	1
2	2
3	3
4	4
5	5
6	6
7	7
8	10
9	11
10	12
11	13
12	14
13	15
14	16
15	17

6.6 4-BIT BINARY CODED DECIMAL (BCD) SYSTEMS

The BCD system is employed by computer systems to encode the decimal number into its equivalent binary number. This is generally accomplished by encoding each digit of the decimal number into its equivalent binary sequence. The main advantage of BCD system is that it is a fast and efficient system to convert the decimal numbers into binary numbers as compared to the pure binary system. However, the implementation of this coding system requires a lot of circuits that makes the design of the computer systems very complicated.

The 4-bit BCD system is usually employed by the computer systems to represent and process numerical data only. In the 4-bit BCD system, each digit of the decimal number is encoded to its corresponding 4-bit binary sequence. The two most popular 4-bit BCD systems are:

- Weighted 4-bit BCD code
- Excess – 3 (XS – 3) BCD code

6.6.1 Weighted 4-Bit BCD Code

The weighted 4-bit BCD code is more commonly known as 8421 weighted code. It is called weighted code because it encodes the decimal system into binary system by using the concept of positional weighting into consideration. In this code, each decimal digit is encoded into its 4-bit binary number in which the bits from left to right have the weights 8, 4, 2, and 1 respectively. Table 6.7 lists the weighted 4-bit BCD code for decimal digits 0 through 9.

Table 6.7 Weighted 4-bit BCD codes

Decimal digits	Weighted 4-bit BCD code
0	0000
1	0001
2	0010
3	0011
4	0100
5	0101
6	0110
7	0111
8	1000
9	1001

Note: *Apart from 8421, some other weighted BCD codes are 4221, 2421 and 5211.*

Example 6.1 *Represent the decimal number 5327 in 8421 BCD code.*

Solution

The given decimal number is 5327.
The corresponding 4-bit 8421 BCD representation of decimal digit 5 is 0101.
The corresponding 4-bit 8421 BCD representation of decimal digit 3 is 0011.
The corresponding 4-bit 8421 BCD representation of decimal digit 2 is 0010.
The corresponding 4-bit 8421 BCD representation of decimal digit 7 is 0111.
Therefore, the 8421 BCD representation of decimal number 5327 is 0101 0011 0010 0111.

Example 6.2 *Convert the decimal number 159 to 8421 BCD code.*

Solution

The given decimal number is 159.
The corresponding 4-bit 8421 BCD representation of decimal digit 1 is 0001.
The corresponding 4-bit 8421 BCD representation of decimal digit 5 is 0101.
The corresponding 4-bit 8421 BCD representation of decimal digit 9 is 1001.
Therefore, the 8421 BCD representation of decimal number 159 is 0001 0101 1001.

Example 6.3 *Convert the decimal number 87. 34 to 8421 BCD code.*

Solution

The given decimal number is 87.34.
The corresponding 4-bit 8421 BCD representation of decimal digit 8 is 1000.
The corresponding 4-bit 8421 BCD representation of decimal digit 7 is 0111.
The corresponding 4-bit 8421 BCD representation of decimal digit 3 is 0011.
The corresponding 4-bit 8421 BCD representation of decimal digit 4 is 0100.
Therefore, the 8421 BCD representation of decimal number 87.34 is 1000 0111. 0011 0100.

We can also transform a number represented in 8421 BCD code into its corresponding decimal representation. To accomplish this, we first need to divide the BCD number into sets of 4-bit binary digits starting from the Least Significant Bit (LSB) and then write the corresponding decimal number for each set. To understand this concept, let us consider the following examples:

Example 6.4 *Determine the decimal number corresponding to the 8421 BCD code 01001001.*

Solution

The given 8421 BCD code is 01001001.

To determine the equivalent decimal number, simply divide the 8421 BCD code into sets of 4-bit binary digits as:

0100 1001

The decimal number corresponding to the binary digits 0100 is 4.

The decimal number corresponding to the binary digits 1001 is 9.

Therefore, the decimal number equivalent to 8421 BCD code 0100 1001 is 49.

Example 6.5 *Determine the decimal number corresponding to the 8421 BCD code 0111010000100110.*

Solution

The given 8421 BCD code is 0111010000100110.

To determine the equivalent decimal number, simply divide the 8421 BCD code into sets of 4-bit binary digits as:

0111 0100 0010 0110

The decimal number corresponding to binary digits 0111 is 7.

The decimal number corresponding to binary digits 0100 is 4.

The decimal number corresponding to binary digits 0010 is 2.

The decimal number corresponding to binary digits 0110 is 6.

Therefore, the decimal number equivalent to 8421 BCD code 0111010000100110 is 7426.

Example 6.6 *Determine the decimal number corresponding to the 8421 BCD representation 010100100001.0110.*

Solution

The given 8421 BCD code is 010100100001.0110.

To determine the equivalent decimal number, simply divide the 8421 BCD code into sets of 4-bit binary digits as:

0101 0010 0001 . 0110

The decimal number corresponding to binary digits 0101 is 5.

The decimal number corresponding to binary digits 0010 is 2.

The decimal number corresponding to binary digits 0001 is 1.

The decimal number corresponding to binary digits 0110 is 6.

Therefore, the decimal number equivalent to 8421 BCD representation 010100100001.0110 is 521.6.

6.6.2 Excess-3 BCD Code

The Excess-3 (XS-3) BCD code does not use the principle of positional weights into consideration while converting the decimal numbers to 4-bit BCD system. Therefore, we can say that this code is a non-weighted BCD code. The function of XS-3 code is to transform the decimal numbers into their corresponding 4-bit BCD code. In this code, the decimal number is transformed to the 4-bit BCD code by first adding 3 to all the digits of the number and then converting the excess digits, so obtained, into their corresponding 8421 BCD code. Therefore, we can say that the XS-3 code is strongly related with 8421 BCD code in its functioning. Table 6.8 lists the XS-3 BCD code for decimal digits 0 through 9.

Table 6.8 Excess-3 BCD codes

Decimal digits	Excess-3 BCD code
0	0011
1	0100
2	0101
3	0110
4	0111
5	1000
6	1001
7	1010
8	1011
9	1100

Note: *Apart from XS-3 code, the other non-weighted BCD code is 4-bit Gray code.*

Example 6.7 *Convert the decimal number 85 to XS-3 BCD code.*

Solution

The given decimal number is 85.
Now, add 3 to each digit of the given decimal number as:
8 + 3 = 11
5 + 3 = 8
The corresponding 4-bit 8421 BCD representation of the decimal digit 11 is 1011.
The corresponding 4-bit 8421 BCD representation of the decimal digit 8 is 1000.
Therefore, the XS-3 BCD representation of the decimal number 85 is 1011 1000.

Example 6.8 *Represent the decimal number 173 in XS-3 BCD code.*

Solution

The given decimal number is 173.
Now, add 3 to each digit of the given decimal number as:
1 + 3 = 4
7 + 3 =10
3 + 3 = 6
The corresponding 4-bit 8421 BCD representation of the decimal digit 4 is 0100.
The corresponding 4-bit 8421 BCD representation of the decimal digit 10 is 1010.
The corresponding 4-bit 8421 BCD representation of the decimal digit 6 is 0110.
Therefore, the XS-3 BCD representation of the decimal number 173 is 0100 1010 0110.

Example 6.9 *Convert the decimal number 3456 into XS-3 BCD code.*

Solution

The given decimal number is 3456.

Now, add 3 to each digit of the given decimal number as:

3 + 3 = 6

4 + 3 = 7

5 + 3 = 8

6 + 3 = 9

The corresponding 4-bit 8421 BCD representation of decimal digit 6 is 0110.

The corresponding 4-bit 8421 BCD representation of decimal digit 7 is 0111.

The corresponding 4-bit 8421 BCD representation of decimal digit 8 is 1000.

The corresponding 4-bit 8421 BCD representation of decimal digit 9 is 1001.

Therefore, the XS – 3 BCD representation of decimal number 3456 is 0110 0111 1000 1001.

Note: *4-bit BCD systems are inadequate for representing and handling non-numeric data. For this purpose, 6-bit BCD and 8-bit BCD systems have been developed.*

6.7 8-BIT BCD SYSTEMS

The 8-bit BCD systems were developed to overcome the limitations of 6-bit BCD systems. The 6-bit BCD systems can handle numeric as well as non-numeric data but with few special characters. The 8-bit BCD systems can handle numeric as well as nonnumeric data with almost all the special characters such as +, - , *, /, @, $, etc. Therefore, the various codes under the category of 8-bit BCD systems are also known as *alphanumeric codes*. The three most popular 8-bit BCD codes are:

- Extended Binary Coded Decimal Interchange Code (EBCDIC)
- American Standard Code for Information Interchange (ASCII)
- Gray code

6.7.1 EBCDIC Code

The EBCDIC code is an 8-bit alphanumeric code that was developed by IBM to represent alphabets, decimal digits and special characters, including control characters. Control characters are the special characters that are used to perform a specific function. For example, the control character FF is used to feed the next page into the printer or eject the current page from the printer. The EBCDIC codes are generally the decimal and the hexadecimal representation of different characters. This code is rarely used by non IBM-compatible computer systems.

Table 6.9 lists some important EBCDIC characters and their corresponding decimal and hexadecimal representation.

Table 6.9 EBCDIC codes

Characters	Decimal representation	Hexadecimal representation
NUL	0	00
SOH	1	01
STX	2	02
ETX	3	03
HT	5	05
DEL	7	07
VT	11	0B
FF	12	0C
CR	13	0D
SO	14	0E
SI	15	0F
DLE	16	10
IUS	31	1F
ESC	39	27
BEL	47	2F
SUB	63	3F
[	74	4A
.	75	4B
<	76	4C
(	77	4D
+	78	4E
&	80	50
$	91	5B
*	92	5C
-	96	60
/	97	61
%	108	6C
?	111	6F
=	126	7E
a – i	129 – 137	81 – 89
j – r	145 – 153	91 – 99
s – z	162 – 169	A2 – A9
A – I	193 – 201	C1 – C9
J – R	209 – 217	D1 – D9
S – Z	226 – 233	E2 – E9
0 – 9	240 – 249	F0 – F9

6.7.2 ASCII Code

The ASCII code is pronounced as ASKEE and is used for the same purpose for which the EBCDIC code is used. However, this code is more popular than EBCDIC code as unlike the EBCDIC code this code can be implemented by most of the non-IBM computer systems. Initially, this code was developed as a 7-bit BCD code to handle 128 characters but later it was modified to an 8-bit code. We can check the value of any ASCII code by just holding down the Alt key and typing the ASCII code. For example, when we hold down the Alt key and type 66 from the keyboard, then the character B appears on the screen. This shows that the ASCII decimal code 66 represents the character B.

Table 6.10 lists some important ASCII codes and their corresponding decimal and hexadecimal representations.

Table 6.10 ASCII codes

Characters	Decimal representation	Hexadecimal representation
NUL	0	0
SOH	1	1
STX	2	2
ETX	3	3
EOT	4	4
ENQ	5	5
ACK	6	6
BEL	7	7
BS	8	8
HT	9	9
CAN	24	18
SUB	26	1A
ESC	27	1B
RS	30	1E
US	31	1F
!	33	21
#	35	23
$	36	24
%	37	25
&	38	26
*	42	2A
+	43	2B
/	47	2F
0 – 9	48 – 57	30 – 39
<	60	3C
=	61	3D

Contd...

Table 6.10 continued

Characters	Decimal representaion	Hexadecimal representation
>	62	3E
?	63	3F
A – I	65 – 73	41 – 49
J – O	74 – 79	4A – 4F
P – Z	80 – 90	50 – 5A
a – i	97 – 105	61 – 69
j – o	106 – 111	6A – 6F
p – z	112 – 122	70 – 7A

6.7.3 Gray Code

Gray code is another important code that is also used to convert the decimal number into 8-bit binary sequence. However, this conversion is carried in a manner that the contiguous digits of the decimal number differ from each other by one bit only. Table 6.11 lists the 8-bit Gray code for decimal numbers 0 through 9.

Table 6.11 8-Bit Gray code

Decimal number	8-Bit Gray code
0	00000000
1	00000001
2	00000011
3	00000010
4	00000110
5	00000111
6	00001111
7	00001011
8	00001001
9	00001101

We can convert the Gray coded number to its binary equivalent by remembering the following two major rules:

- The Most Significant Bit (MSB) of the Gray coded number and the equivalent binary number is always the same.
- The next-to-most significant bit of the binary number can be determined by adding the MSB of the binary number to the next-to-most significant bit of the gray coded number.

Example 6.10 *Convert the Gray coded number 11010011 to its binary equivalent.*

Solution

The given Gray coded number is 11010011.

The following table lists the steps showing the conversion of the Gray coded number into its binary equivalent:

S.No.	Gray coded digit	Binary addition operation	Binary digit
1	1		1
2	1	1 + 1	0
3	0	0 + 0	0
4	1	1 + 0	1
5	0	0 + 1	1
6	0	0 + 1	1
7	1	1 + 1	0
8	1	1 + 0	1

Hence, the binary equivalent of Gray coded number 11010011 is 10011101.

Example 6.11 *Convert the Gray coded number 10101110 to its binary equivalent.*

Solution

The given Gray coded number is 10101110.

The following table lists the steps showing the conversion of the Gray coded number into its binary equivalent:

S.No.	Gray coded digit	Binary addition operation	Binary digit
1	1		1
2	0	0 + 1	1
3	1	1 + 1	0
4	0	0 + 0	0
5	1	1 + 0	1
6	1	1 + 1	0
7	1	1 + 0	1
8	0	0 + 1	1

Hence, the binary equivalent of Gray coded number 10101110 is 11001011.

We can also convert a number represented in the binary form to Gray code representation. For carrying out this conversion, we need to remember the following two rules:

- The Most Significant Digit (MSD) of the binary number and the gray coded number is always the same.
- The next MSD of the gray coded number can be obtained by adding the subsequent pair of bits of the binary number starting form the left.

Note: *We need to ignore the carry, if it is generated while adding the subsequent pairs of bits of the binary number.*

Example 6.12 *Convert the binary number 10100011 to its equivalent Gray coded number.*

Solution

The given binary number is 10100011.

The following table lists the steps showing the conversion of binary number to its equivalent Gray coded number:

S.No.	Binary digit	Binary addition operation	Gray coded digit
1	1		1
2	0	1 + 0	1
3	1	0 + 1	1
4	0	1 + 0	1
5	0	0 + 0	0
6	0	0 + 0	0
7	1	0 + 1	1
8	1	1 + 1	0

Hence, the Gray coded equivalent of the binary number 10100011 is 11110010.

Example 6.13 *Convert the binary number 01010010 to its equivalent Gray coded number.*

Solution

The given binary number is 01010010.

The following table lists the steps showing the conversion of binary number to its equivalent Gray coded number:

S.No.	Binary digit	Binary addition operation	Gray coded digit
1	0		0
2	1	0 + 1	1
3	0	1 + 0	1
4	1	0 + 1	1
5	0	1 + 0	1
6	0	0 + 0	0
7	1	0 + 1	1
8	0	1 + 0	1

Hence, the Gray coded equivalent of the binary number 01010010 is 01111011.

6.8 16-BIT UNICODE

The computer systems can only understand data in the form of numbers. Therefore, each character should be first coded into a specific number before being processed by the computer systems. Many 7-bit and 8-bit character codes are developed to encode only the well-known characters, such as letters a–z in lower as well as upper case, digits 0–9 and some special symbols. These character sets can represent a maximum of 256 different characters only. These 7-bit and 8-bit character codes are confined to represent the characters used by the popular languages around the globe. Therefore, there was always a need of a character code that could contain all the characters used by almost all the languages in the world.

The 16-bit Unicode is an International 16-bit character set that contains a maximum of 2^{16} = 65,536 different characters. These characters are sufficient to represent almost all the technical and special symbols used by the major languages of the world. The 16-bit Unicode, (also called *16-bit universal character set*), encodes the different characters by assigning them a unique value. In computer terminology, this unique value is referred as *code point*. The code assigned to each character of different languages is universal and can be used on any platform without any modification. Therefore, we can say that the 16-bit Unicode allows the computer systems to deal with almost all the characters belonging to different languages used in the world.

The 16-bit Unicode is a character code that is supported by almost all the operating systems such as MS Windows, Linux and Mac OS X. For example, MS Windows operating system allows the use of all the Unicode characters through an accessory called Character Map. Figure 6.1 shows the user interface of the character map.

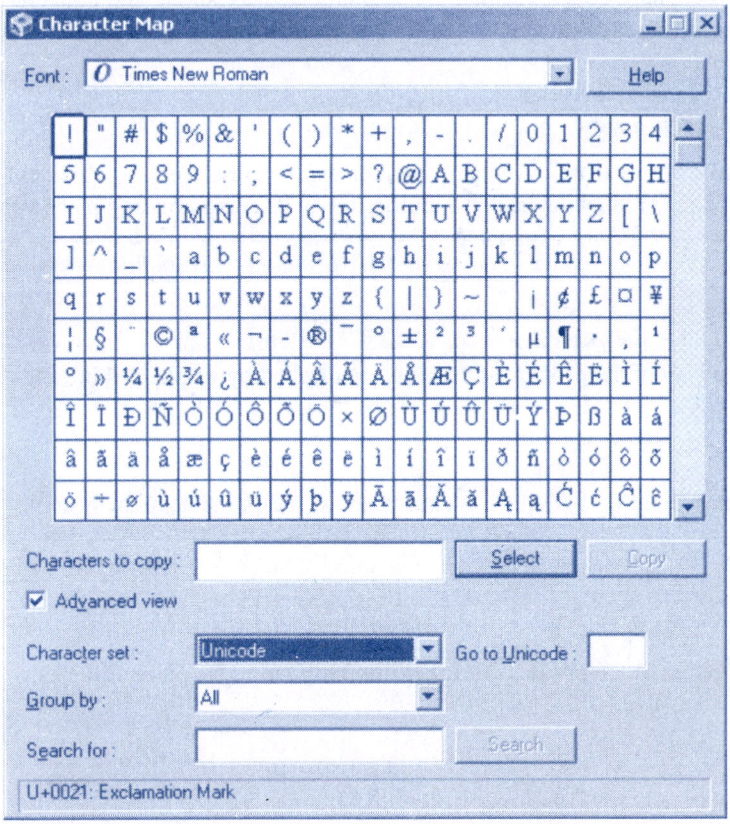

Fig. 6.1 The character map window

Using the Character Map window, we can select any of the Unicode character and copy it to the clipboard. After copying it to the clipboard, we can use the selected Unicode character in any application running under MS Windows operating system.

6.9 CONVERSION OF NUMBERS

The computer systems accept the data in decimal form, whereas they store and process the data in binary form. Therefore, it becomes necessary to convert the numbers represented in one system into the numbers represented in another system. The different types of number system conversions can be divided into the following major categories:

- Non-decimal to decimal
- Decimal to non-decimal
- Octal to hexadecimal

6.9.1 Non-Decimal to Decimal

The non-decimal to decimal conversions can be implemented by taking the concept of place values into consideration. The non-decimal to decimal conversion includes the following number system conversions:

- Binary to decimal conversion
- Hexadecimal to decimal conversion
- Octal to decimal conversion

Binary to decimal conversion A binary number can be converted to equivalent decimal number by calculating the sum of the products of each bit multiplied by its corresponding place value.

Example 6.14 *Convert the binary number 10101101 into its corresponding decimal number.*

Solution

The given binary number is 10101101.

Now, calculate the sum of the products of each bit multiplied by its place value as :

$$(1 \times 2^7) + (0 \times 2^6) + (1 \times 2^5) + (0 \times 2^4) + (1 \times 2^3) + (1 \times 2^2) + (1 \times 2^1) + (1 \times 2^0)$$
$$= 128 + 0 + 32 + 0 + 8 + 4 + 0 + 1$$
$$= 173$$

Therefore, the binary number 10101101 is equivalent to 173 in the decimal system.

Example 6.15 *Convert the binary number 1101 into its equivalent in decimal system.*

Solution

The given binary number is 1101.

Now, calculate the sum of the products of each bit multiplied by its place value as:

$$(1 \times 2^3) + (1 \times 2^2) + (1 \times 2^1) + (1 \times 2^0)$$
$$= 8 + 4 + 1$$
$$= 13$$

Therefore, the binary number 1101 is equivalent to 13 in the decimal system.

Example 6.16 *Convert the binary number 10110001 into its equivalent in decimal system.*

Solution

The given binary number is 10110001.

Now, calculate the sum of the products of each bit multiplied by its place value as:

$$(1 \times 2^7) + (1 \times 2^6) + (1 \times 2^5) + (1 \times 2^4) + (0 \times 2^3) + (0 \times 2^2) + (0 \times 2^1) + (0 \times 2^0)$$

$= 128 + 0 + 32 + 16 + 0 + 0 + 0 + 1$
$= 177$

Therefore, the binary number 10110001 is equivalent to 177 in the decimal system.

Example 6.17 *Convert the binary number 1011.010 into its equivalent in decimal system.*

Solution

The given binary number is 1011.010.

Now, calculate the sum of the products of each bit multiplied by its place value as:

$$(1 \times 2^3) + (0 \times 2^2) + (1 \times 2^1) + (1 \times 2^0) + (0 \times 2^{-1}) + (1 \times 2^{-2}) + (0 \times 2^{-3})$$
$$= 8 + 2 + 1 + \frac{1}{4}$$
$$= 11 + 0.25$$
$$= 11.25$$

Therefore, the binary number 1011.010 is equivalent to 11.25 in the decimal system.

Example 6.18 *Convert the binary number 11011.0110 to its equivalent in decimal system.*

Solution

The given binary number is 11011.0110.

Now, calculate the sum of the products of each bit multiplied by its place value as:

$$(1 \times 2^4) + (1 \times 2^3) + (0 \times 2^2) + (1 \times 2^1) + (1 \times 2^0) + (0 \times 2^{-1}) + (1 \times 2^{-2}) + (1 \times 2^{-3}) + (0 \times 2^{-4})$$
$$= 16 + 8 + 1 + \frac{1}{4} + \frac{1}{8}$$
$$= 27 + 0.25 + 0.125$$
$$= 27.375$$

Therefore, the binary number 11011.0110 is equivalent to 27.375 in the decimal system.

Hexadecimal to decimal conversion A hexadecimal number can be converted into its equivalent number in decimal system by calculating the sum of the products of each symbol multiplied by its corresponding place value.

Example 6.19 *Convert the hexadecimal number A53 into its equivalent in decimal system.*

Solution

The given hexadecimal number is A53.

Now, calculate the sum of the products of each symbol multiplied by its place value as:

$$(10 \times 16^2) + (5 \times 16^1) + (3 \times 16^0)$$
$$= 2560 + 80 + 3$$
$$= 2643$$

Therefore, the hexadecimal number A53 is equivalent to 2643 in the decimal system.

Example 6.20 *Convert the hexadecimal number 6B39 into its equivalent in the decimal system.*

Solution

The given hexadecimal number is 6B39.

Now, calculate the sum of the products of each symbol multiplied by its place value as:

$$(6 \times 16^3) + (11 \times 16^2) + (3 \times 16^1) + (9 \times 16^0)$$

$= 24576 + 2816 + 48 + 9$
$= 27449$

Therefore, the hexadecimal number 6B39 is equivalent to 27449 in the decimal system.

Example 6.21 *Convert the hexadecimal number 5A6D into its equivalent in the decimal system.*

Solution

The given hexadecimal number is 5A6D.

Now, calculate the sum of the products of each symbol multiplied by its place value as:

$(5 \times 16^3) + (10 \times 16^2) + (6 \times 16^1) + (13 \times 16^0)$
$= 20480 + 2560 + 96 + 13$
$= 23149.$

Therefore, the hexadecimal number 5A6D is equivalent to 23149 in the decimal system.

Example 6.22 *Convert the hexadecimal number AB21.34 into its equivalent in the decimal system.*

Solution

The given hexadecimal number is AB21.34.

Now, calculate the sum of the products of each symbol multiplied by its place value as:

$(10 \times 16^3) + (11 \times 16^2) + (2 \times 16^1) + (1 \times 16^0) + (3 \times 16^{-1}) + (4 \times 16^{-2})$

$$= 40960 + 2816 + 32 + 1 + \frac{3}{16} + \frac{4}{256}$$

$= 43809 + 0.1875 + 0.015625$
$= 43809.203$

Therefore, the hexadecimal number AB21.34 is equivalent to 43809.203 in the decimal system.

Example 6.23 *Convert the hexadecimal number 6A11.3B into its equivalent in the decimal system.*

Solution

The given hexadecimal number is 6A11.3B.

Now, calculate the sum of the products of each symbol multiplied by its place value as:

$(6 \times 16^3) + (10 \times 16^2) + (1 \times 16^{-1}) + (1 \times 16^0) + (3 \times 16^{-1}) + (11 \times 16^{-2})$

$$= 24576 + 2560 + 16 + 1 + \frac{3}{16} + \frac{11}{256}$$

$= 27153 + 0.1875 + 0.043$
$= 27153.2305$

Therefore, the hexadecimal number 6A11.3B is equivalent to 27153.2305 in the decimal system.

Octal to decimal conversion An octal number can be converted into its equivalent number in decimal system by calculating the sum of the products of each digit multiplied by its corresponding place value.

Example 6.24 *Convert the octal number 5324 into its equivalent in decimal system.*

Solution

The given octal number is 5324.

Now, calculate the sum of the products of each digit multiplied by its place value as:

$(5 \times 8^3) + (3 \times 8^2) + (2 \times 8^1) + (4 \times 8^0)$

$= 2560 + 192 + 16 + 4$
$= 2772$

Therefore, the octal number 5324 is equivalent to 2772 in the decimal system.

Example 6.25 *Convert the octal number 13256 into its equivalent in decimal system.*

Solution

The given octal number is 13256.

Now, calculate the sum of the products of each digit multiplied by its place value as:

$(1 \times 8^4) + (3 \times 8^3) + (2 \times 8^2) + (5 \times 8^1) + (6 \times 8^0)$
$= 4096 + 1536 + 128 + 40 + 6$
$= 5806$

Therefore, the octal number 13256 is equivalent to 5806 in the decimal system.

Example 6.26 *Convert the octal number 4567 into its equivalent in decimal system.*

Solution

The given octal number is 4567.

Now, calculate the sum of the products of each digit multiplied by its place value as:

$(4 \times 8^3) + (5 \times 8^2) + (6 \times 8^1) + (7 \times 8^0)$
$= 2048 + 320 + 48 + 7$
$= 2423$

Therefore, the octal number 4567 is equivalent to 2423 in the decimal system.

Example 6.27 *Convert the octal number 325.12 into its equivalent in decimal system.*

Solution

The given octal number is 325.12.

Now, calculate the sum of the products of each digit multiplied by its place value as:

$(3 \times 8^2) + (2 \times 8^1) + (5 \times 8^0) + (1 \times 8^{-1}) + (2 \times 8^{-2})$

$$= 192 + 16 + 5 + \frac{1}{8} + \frac{2}{64}$$

$= 213 + 0.125 + 0.03125$
$= 213.15625$

Therefore, the octal number 325.12 is equivalent to 213.15625 in the decimal system.

Example 6.28 *Convert the octal number 7652.01 into its equivalent in decimal system.*

Solution

The given octal number is 7652.01.

Now, calculate the sum of the products of each digit multiplied by its place value as:

$(7 \times 8^3) + (6 \times 8^2) + (5 \times 8^1) + (2 \times 8^0) + (0 \times 8^{-1}) + (1 \times 8^{-2})$

$$= 3584 + 384 + 40 + 2 + \frac{1}{64}$$

$= 4010 + 0.015625$
$= 4010.0156$

Therefore, the octal number 7652.01 is equivalent to 4010.0156 in the decimal system.

6.9.2 Decimal to Non-Decimal

The decimal to non-decimal conversions are carried out by continually dividing the decimal number by the base of the desired number system till the decimal number becomes zero. After the decimal number becomes zero, we may note down the remainders calculated at each successive division from last to first to obtain the decimal number into the desired system. The decimal to non-decimal conversion includes the following number system conversions:

- Decimal to binary conversion
- Decimal to hexadecimal conversion
- Decimal to octal conversion

Decimal to binary conversion The decimal to binary conversion is performed by repeatedly dividing the decimal number by 2 till the decimal number becomes zero and then reading the remainders from last to first to obtain the binary equivalent of the given decimal number. The following examples illustrate the method of converting decimal number to its binary equivalent:

Example 6.29 *Convert the decimal number 30 into its equivalent binary number.*

Solution

The given decimal number is 30.

The following table lists the steps showing the conversion of the given decimal number to its binary equivalent:

Decimal number	Divisor	Quotient	Remainder
30	2	15	0
15	2	7	1
7	2	3	1
3	2	1	1
1	2	0	1

Now, read the remainders calculated in the above table in upward direction to obtain the binary equivalent, which is 11110.

Therefore, the binary equivalent of the decimal number 30 is 11110.

Example 6.30 *Convert the decimal number 111 into its equivalent binary number.*

Solution

The given decimal number is 111.

The following table lists the steps showing the conversion of the given decimal number to its binary equivalent:

Decimal number	Divisor	Quotient	Remainder
111	2	55	1
55	2	27	1
27	2	13	1
13	2	6	1
6	2	3	0
3	2	1	1
1	2	0	1

Now, read the remainders calculated in the above table in upward direction to obtain the binary equivalent, which is 1101111.

Therefore, the binary equivalent of the decimal number 111 is 1101111.

Example 6.31 *Convert the decimal number 215 into its equivalent binary number.*

Solution

The given decimal number is 215.

The following table lists the steps showing the conversion of the given decimal number to its binary equivalent:

Decimal number	Divisor	Quotient	Remainder
215	2	107	1
107	2	53	1
53	2	26	1
26	2	13	0
13	2	6	1
6	2	3	0
3	2	1	1
1	2	0	1

Now, read the remainders calculated in the above table in upward direction to obtain the binary equivalent, which is 11010111.

Therefore, the binary equivalent of the decimal number 215 is 11010111.

The procedure of converting the fractional part of the given decimal number to its binary equivalent is different. In this procedure, we need to continually multiply the fractional part by 2 and then note down the whole number part of the result. The multiplication process will terminate when the fractional part becomes zero or when we have achieved the desired number of bits.

Example 6.32 *Convert the decimal number 45796 to its equivalent octal number.*

Solution

The given decimal number is 45796.

The following table lists the steps showing the conversion of the given decimal number to its octal equivalent:

Decimal number	Divisor	Quotient	Remainder
45796	8	5724	4
5724	8	715	4
715	8	89	3
89	8	11	1
11	8	1	3
1	8	0	1

Now, read the remainders calculated in the above table in upward direction to obtain the octal equivalent, which is 131344.

Therefore, the corresponding octal equivalent of 45796 is 131344.

Example 6.33 *Convert the decimal number 9547 into its equivalent octal number.*

Solution

The given decimal number is 9547.

The following table lists the steps showing the conversion of the given decimal number to its octal equivalent:

Decimal number	Divisor	Quotient	Remainder
9547	8	1193	3
1193	8	149	1
149	8	18	5
18	8	2	2
2	8	0	2

Now, read the remainders calculated in the above table in upward direction to obtain the octal equivalent, which is 22513.

Therefore, the corresponding octal equivalent of 9547 is 22513.

Example 6.34 *Convert the decimal number 1567 into its equivalent hexadecimal number.*

Solution

The given decimal number is 1567.

The following table lists the steps showing the conversion of the given decimal number to its hexadecimal equivalent:

Decimal number	Divisor	Quotient	Remainder
1567	16	97	15
97	16	6	1
6	16	0	6

Now, read the remainders calculated in the above table in upward direction to obtain the hexadecimal equivalent, which is 61F.

Therefore, the hexadecimal equivalent of the given decimal number is 61F.

Example 6.35 *Convert the decimal number 9463 into its equivalent hexadecimal number.*

Solution

The given decimal number is 9463.

The following table lists the steps showing the conversion of the given decimal number to its hexadecimal equivalent:

Decimal number	Divisor	Quotient	Remainder
9463	16	591	7
591	16	36	15
36	16	2	4
2	16	0	2

Now, read the remainders calculated in the above table in upward direction to obtain the hexadecimal equivalent, which is 24F7.

Therefore, the hexadecimal equivalent of the given decimal number is 24F7.

Decimal to octal conversion The decimal to octal conversion is performed by repeatedly dividing the decimal number by 8 till the decimal number becomes zero and reading the remainders from last to first to obtain the octal equivalent of the given decimal number. The following examples illustrate the method of converting decimal number to its octal equivalent:

Example 6.36 *Convert the decimal number 45796 to its equivalent octal number.*

Solution

The given decimal number is 45796.

The following table lists the steps showing the conversion of the given decimal number to its octal equivalent:

Decimal number	Divisor	Quotient	Remainder
45796	8	5724	4
5724	8	715	4
715	8	89	3
89	8	11	1
11	8	1	3
1	8	0	1

Now, read the remainders calculated in the above table in upward direction to obtain the octal equivalent, which is 131344.

Therefore, the corresponding octal equivalent of 45796 is 131344.

Example 6.37 *Convert the decimal number 9547 into its equivalent octal number.*

Solution

The given decimal number is 9547.

The following table lists the steps showing the conversion of the given decimal number to its octal equivalent:

Decimal number	Divisor	Quotient	Remainder
9547	8	1193	3
1193	8	149	1
149	8	18	5
18	8	2	2
2	8	0	2

Now, read the remainders calculated in the above table in upward direction to obtain the octal equivalent, which is 22513.

Therefore, the corresponding octal equivalent of 9547 is 22513.

6.9.3 Octal to Hexadecimal

The given octal number can be converted into its equivalent hexadecimal number in two different steps. Firstly, we need to convert the given octal number into its binary equivalent. After obtaining the binary equivalent, we need to divide the binary number into 4-bit sections starting from the LSB.

The octal to binary conversion is a simple process. In this type of conversion, we need to represent each digit in the octal number to its equivalent 3-bit binary number. Table 6.12 lists the binary representation of all the digits used in an octal system.

Table 6.12 Binary representation of octal symbols

Octal	Binary representation
0	000
1	001
2	010
3	011
4	100
5	101
6	110
7	111

Example 6.38 *Convert the octal number 365 into its equivalent hexadecimal number.*

Solution

Octal number:	3	6	5	
↓	↓	↓	↓	
Binary equivalent:	011	110	101	*Step 1*
↓				
Regrouping into 4-bit sections:	0000	1111	0101	*Step 2*
↓	↓	↓	↓	
Hexadecimal equivalent:	0	F	5	*Step 3*

Hexadecimal number is F5

Example 6.39 *Convert the octal number 6251 into its equivalent hexadecimal number.*

Solution

Octal number:	6	2	5	1	
↓	↓	↓	↓	↓	
Binary equivalent:	110	010	101	001	*Step 1*
↓					
4-bits grouping:	1100	1010	1001		*Step 2*
↓	↓	↓	↓		
Hexadecimal equivalent:	C	A	9		*Step 3*

Hexadecimal number is CA9

Chapter Summary

Computer systems represent and process the data in binary form only. However, they can accept the data in many forms. Therefore, it is very necessary to implement a mechanism in the computer system that can convert the data from the accepted form to the binary form. Computer codes help the computer system to convert the data received in a different number system to the data in the binary form so that it can be stored and processed in an efficient manner. In computer terminology, the number system used to represent data is generally known as positional number system. It is called positional number system because the value of the number represented in this system depends upon the position of the digits in the given number. The positional number system can be of four different types, namely, decimal system, binary system, hexadecimal system and octal system. We can easily convert the number represented in one system to its equivalent in another system. The major number system conversions are non-decimal to decimal, decimal to non-decimal and octal to hexadecimal.

The different computer codes usually come under the category of BCD systems, which are mainly of 4-bit or 8-bit. The 4-bit BCD systems include the weighted 4-bit BCD code and XS-3 BCD code. On the other hand, the 8-bit BCD system includes the EBCDIC code, ASCII code and Gray code.

Key Terms to Remember

- **Computer codes**: The computer codes are the codes that help in converting the data entered by the users into the binary form.
- **Positional number system**: The positional number system is a system in which numbers are represented using certain symbols called digits and the values of these numbers is determined by taking the position of digits into consideration.

- **Decimal system**: The decimal system is a positional number system that uses base 10 to represent different values.
- **Binary system**: The binary system is a positional number system that uses base 2 to represent different values.
- **Bit**: Bit is the smallest unit of information used in a computer system. It can have either have 0 or 1 as its value.
- **Byte**: Byte is the combination of 8 bits.
- **Hexadecimal system**: The hexadecimal system is a positional number system that uses base 16 to represent different values.
- **Octal system**: The octal system is a positional number system that uses base 8 to represent different values.
- **BCD system**: The BCD system is used to encode decimal number into its equivalent binary number.
- **Weighted 4-bit BCD code**: The weighted 4-bit BCD code is used to encode the decimal digits into binary sequence by specifying the weights 8, 4, 2, and 1 respectively to the bits from left to right.
- **Digital codes**: Digital codes allow the computer to handle numeric as well as non-numeric data in an efficient manner.
- **EBCDIC code**: The EBCDIC code is an 8-bit alphanumeric code that was developed by IBM to represent alphabets, decimal digits and special characters including control characters.
- **ASCII code**: The ASCII code is also used to represent alphabets, decimal digits and some special characters. However, this code is usually implemented by the non-IBM computer systems.
- **16-bit Unicode**: The 16-bit Unicode is an International 16-bit character set that can represent a maximum of $2^{16} = 65{,}536$ different characters.

Review Questions

Fill in the Blanks

1. Human beings generally employ the _________ number system to carry out their routine computations.
2. The most common system used by computer systems is _________.
3. The weight of any digit in the number system generally depends upon its _________ in the given number.
4. The binary system represents each type of data in the form of _________ and _________.
5. The digits in binary system are referred as _________.
6. The base of any number system depends upon the number of _________ in the system.
7. Computer designers and professionals generally deal with _________ number system.
8. The octal system is also known as _________ system.
9. The octal number 5624 is equivalent to _________ in decimal system.
10. The binary number 1001010 represents a decimal value of _________.
11. The hexadecimal system consists of _________ symbols.
12. Human beings usually supply data to the computer system in the _________ form.
13. Computer codes help computer systems convert the decimal data into _________ data.
14. BCD stands for _________.
15. _________ and _________ are the two most popular 4-bit BCD codes.
16. The 8421 BCD representation of the decimal number 3569 is _________.
17. The 4-bit BCD systems are suitable for handling _________ data only.
18. The 16-bit _________ is an international standard for representing characters from various languages.
19. The hexadecimal number B45A is equivalent to _________ in decimal system.
20. The hexadecimal representation of the octal number 2564 is _________.

Multiple Choice Questions

1. Computer codes are also more commonly known as:
A. Octal codes B. Digital codes C. Binary codes D. None of the above

2. Which of the following is not a positional number system?
A. Octal system B. Decimal system C. Binary system D. Roman number system

3. Human beings usually employ the following number system for their routine computations:
A. Decimal system B. Octal system C. Binary system D. Hexadecimal system

4. The number system with base 2 is known as:
A. Decimal system B. Binary system C. Octal system D. Hexadecimal system

5. The smallest unit of information in binary system is:
A. Bit B. Byte C. Word D. Kilobyte

6. The combination of 8 bits is known as:
A. Kilobyte B. Bit C. Byte D. Word

7. The 4-bit binary equivalent of the decimal number 6 is:
A. 0111 B. 1000 C. 0010 D. 0110

8. The octal representation of 15 is:
A. 17 B. 16 C. 15 D. 14

9. Which of the following form of data is processed more efficiently by the computer system?
A. Binary data B. Octal data C. Hexadecimal data D. Decimal data

10. The point used to separate the integer part and the fractional part in octal system is referred as:
A. Decimal point B. Binary point C. Hexadecimal point D. None of the above

11. The system implemented by the computer systems to convert the decimal numbers into equivalent binary numbers is known as:
A. BCD system B. Octal system C. Weighted system D. Gray code system

12. Which of the following codes come under the category of 4-bit BCD system?
A. Gray code B. Excess-3 code C. ASCII code D. None of these

13. The weighted 4-bit BCD code is commonly known as:
A. 8421 code B. 4221 code C. 5211 code D. 6211 code

14. The 8-bit BCD codes are better known as:
A. Digital codes B. Alphanumeric codes C. Numeric codes D. None of the above

15. Which of the following code is a type of digital code?
A. ASCII code B. Packed code C. 8421 code D. None of the above

16. EBCDIC code was developed by:
A. Microsoft B. IBM
C. Both by Microsoft and IBM D. None of the above

17. Which of the following keys helps in displaying the value of the ASCII code?
A. Alt key B. Shift key C. Ctrl key D. Tab key

18. Which of the following is not a valid computer number system conversion?
A. Non-decimal to decimal B. Decimal to non-decimal
C. Octal to hexadecimal D. Roman to decimal

19. The hexadecimal equivalent of the octal number 4263 is:
A. 8B3 B. A42 C. 923 D. BA31

Discussion Questions

1. What do you understand by positional number system and why is it called a positional system?
2. What are the different types of positional number systems? Which of the positional systems is mostly used by the computer systems?
3. Explain the different technical terms associated with the binary system.
4. What is the weight of digit 5 in the decimal number 9536?
5. What is the 4-bit binary representation of the decimal number 12?
6. Explain in detail the concept of hexadecimal system.
7. What is BCD system and why is it called BCD?
8. List the two different 4-bit BCD codes.
9. Why is 8421 code called weighted code?
10. How is decimal number converted into its excess-3 representation?
11. What is the difference between 4-bit BCD systems and 8-bit BCD systems?
12. Why are binary codes used by computer systems?
13. What do you understand by digital codes? Explain the two different types of digital codes.
14. Explain in detail the concept of Gray code.
15. Why is the 16-bit Unicode most significant among all the computer codes?
16. Why are the number system conversions implemented in a computer system?
17. Explain in detail the different categories of number system conversions.
18. How is binary number converted into its decimal equivalent?
19. What is the hexadecimal representation of octal number 6235?
20. What is the binary equivalent of 859.238?

CHAPTER 7

COMPUTER ARITHMETIC

Chapter Outline

Chapter Objectives

In this chapter, we will learn:

- The concept of computer arithmetic and different types of arithmetic operations
- The concept of signed and unsigned number representation
- The importance of complement system for the representation of negative integers
- The methods of performing binary subtraction using complements
- The different types of representations for integer and floating-point numbers
- The methods of performing integer as well as floating-point arithmetic.

7.1 INTRODUCTION

A computer system stores and processes billions of instructions in a second that involves a lot of arithmetic computations. The different arithmetic operations in the computer system are performed by the Arithmetic and Logic Unit (ALU), which is an important component of the CPU. Besides performing arithmetic operations, the ALU of the computer system also performs various logical operations.

The computer arithmetic is also referred as *binary arithmetic* because the computer system stores and processes the data in the binary form only. Various binary arithmetic operations can be performed in the same way as the decimal arithmetic operations, but by following a predefined set of rules. Each binary arithmetic operation has an associated set of rules that should be adhered to while carrying out that operation. The binary arithmetic operations are usually simpler to carry out as compared to the decimal operations because one needs to deal with only two digits, 0 and 1, in the binary operations. The different binary arithmetic operations performed in a computer system are:

- Binary addition
- Binary multiplication
- Binary subtraction
- Binary division

7.2 BINARY ADDITION

Binary addition is the simplest arithmetic operation performed in the computer system. Like decimal system, we can start the addition of two binary numbers column-wise from the right most bit and move towards the left most bit of the given numbers. However, we need to follow certain rules while carrying out the binary addition of the given numbers. Table 7.1 lists the rules for binary addition.

Table 7.1 Binary addition rules

A	B	A + B	Carry
0	0	0	0
0	1	1	0
1	0	1	0
1	1	0	1

In the above table, the first three entries do not generate any carry. However, a carry would be generated when both A and B contain the value, 1. The carry, if it is generated, while performing the binary addition in a column would be forwarded to the next most significant column.

Example 7.1 *Perform the binary addition operation on the following binary numbers:*
0 0 1 0
0 1 1 1

Solution

The given binary numbers are 0010 and 0111.

Now, perform the binary addition of the given numbers as:

Binary number	Decimal value
0 0 1 0	2
0 1 1 1	7
1 0 0 1	9

Therefore, the result of the binary addition performed on 0010 and 0111 is 1001.

Note: *In the above example, a carry is generated in the 2nd and the 3rd column only.*

Example 7.2 *Perform the binary addition of the following binary numbers:*

1 0 1 0 1 0
0 1 0 0 1 1

Solution

The given binary numbers are 101010 and 010011.

Now, perform the binary addition of the given numbers as:

Binary number	Decimal value
1 0 1 0 1 0	42
0 1 0 0 1 1	19
1 1 1 1 0 1	61

Therefore, the result of the binary addition performed on 101010 and 010011 is 111101.

Note: *In the above example, a carry is generated in the 2nd column only.*

Example 7.3 *Evaluate the binary sum of the following numbers:*

00011010
10001100

Solution

The given binary numbers are 00011010 and 10001100.

Now, perform the binary addition of the given numbers as:

Binary number	Decimal value
0 0 0 1 1 0 1 0	26
1 0 0 0 1 1 0 0	140
1 0 1 0 0 1 1 0	166

Therefore, the result of the binary addition performed on 00011010 and 10001100 is 10100110.

Note: *In the above example, a carry is generated in the 4th and the 5th column only.*

We can also perform the binary addition on more than two binary numbers. Table 7.2 lists the rules for adding three binary numbers.

Table 7.2 Rules for adding three binary numbers

A	B	C	A + B + C	Carry
0	0	0	0	0
0	0	1	1	0
0	1	0	1	0
0	1	1	0	1
1	0	0	1	0
1	0	1	0	1
1	1	0	0	1
1	1	1	1	1

To understand the concept of triple binary addition, let us consider the following examples:

Example 7.4 *Perform the binary addition operation on the following three numbers:*

0 0 1 0
0 0 0 1
0 1 1 1

Solution

The given binary numbers are 0010, 0001 and 0111.
Now, perform the binary addition of the given numbers as:

Binary number	Decimal value
0 0 1 0	2
0 0 0 1	1
0 1 1 1	7
1 0 1 0	10

Therefore, the result of the binary addition performed on 0010, 0001 and 0111 is 1010.

Note: *In the above example, a carry is generated in the 1st and the 2nd column only.*

Example 7.5 *Evaluate the binary sum of the following numbers:*

0 1 0 1 0
0 0 1 1 0
0 1 1 1 1

Solution

The given binary numbers are 01010, 00110 and 01111.
Now, perform the binary addition of the given numbers as:

Binary number	Decimal value
0 1 0 1 0	10
0 0 1 1 0	6
0 1 1 1 1	15
1 1 1 1 1	31

Therefore, the result of the binary addition performed on 01010, 00110 and 01111 is 11111.

Note: *In the above example, a carry is generated in the 2nd, 3rd and 4th column only.*

7.3 BINARY MULTIPLICATION

The multiplication of two binary numbers can be carried out in the same manner as the decimal multiplication. However, unlike decimal multiplication, only two values are generated as the outcome of multiplying the multiplicand bit by 0 or 1 in the binary multiplication. These values are either 0 or 1. The binary multiplication can also be considered as repeated binary addition. For instance, when we are multiplying 7 with 3, it simply means that we are adding 7 to itself 3 times. Therefore, the binary multiplication is performed in conjunction with the binary addition operation. Table 7.3 lists the rules for binary multiplication.

Table 7.3 Binary multiplication rules

A	B	A×B
0	0	0
0	1	0
1	0	0
1	1	1

The above table clearly shows that binary multiplication does not involve the concept of carry. To understand the concept of binary multiplication, let us consider the following examples:

Example 7.6 *Perform the binary multiplication of the decimal numbers 12 and 10.*

Solution

The equivalent binary representation of the decimal number 12 is 1100.
The equivalent binary representation of the decimal number 10 is 1010.
Now, perform the binary multiplication of the given numbers as:

```
      1 1 0 0      Multiplicand
      1 0 1 0      Multiplier
    ---------
      0 0 0 0      First partial product
    1 1 0 0
  0 0 0 0
1 1 0 0
-------------
1 1 1 1 0 0 0      Final product
-------------
```

Therefore, the result of the binary multiplication performed on the decimal numbers 12 and 10 is 1111000.

Example 7.7 *Evaluate the binary product of the decimal numbers 15 and 14.*

Solution

The equivalent binary representation of the decimal number 15 is 1111.
The equivalent binary representation of the decimal number 14 is 1110.
Now, perform the binary multiplication of the given numbers as:

```
        1 1 1 1      Multiplicand
        1 1 1 0      Multiplier
      ---------
        0 0 0 0      First partial product
      1 1 1 1
    1 1 1 1
  1 1 1 1
---------------
1 1 0 1 0 0 1 0      Final product
---------------
```

Therefore, the result of the binary multiplication performed on the decimal numbers 15 and 14 is 11010010.

Example 7.8 *Perform the binary multiplication of the following numbers:*
1101
111

Solution

The given binary numbers are 1101 and 111.
Now, perform the binary multiplication of the given numbers as:

```
       1 1 0 1      Multiplicand
         1 1 1      Multiplier
      --------
       1 1 0 1      First partial product
     1 1 0 1
   1 1 0 1
 -------------
 1 0 1 1 0 1 1      Final product
 -------------
```

Therefore, the result of the binary multiplication performed on the numbers 1101 and 111 is 1011011.

Example 7.9 *Evaluate the binary product of the following numbers:*
100010
10010

Solution

The given binary numbers are 100010 and 10010.
Now, perform the binary multiplication of the given numbers as:

```
         1 0 0 0 1 0      Multiplicand
           1 0 0 1 0      Multiplier
       --------------
         0 0 0 0 0 0      First partial product
       1 0 0 0 1 0
     0 0 0 0 0 0
   0 0 0 0 0 0
 1 0 0 0 1 0
 -------------------
 1 0 0 1 1 0 0 1 0 0      Final product
 -------------------
```

Therefore, the result of the binary multiplication performed on the numbers 100010 and 10010 is 1001100100.

7.4 BINARY SUBTRACTION

The binary subtraction is performed in the same way as the decimal subtraction. Like binary addition and binary multiplication, binary subtraction is also associated with a set of rules that need to be followed while carrying out the operation. Table 7.4 lists the rules for binary subtraction.

Table 7.4 Binary subtraction rules

A	B	A – B	Borrow
0	0	0	0
0	1	1	1
1	0	1	0
1	1	0	0

The above table shows that the binary subtraction like the decimal subtraction uses the borrow method to subtract one number from another. To understand the concept of binary subtraction, let us consider the following examples:

Example 7.10 *Subtract the following binary numbers:*
0 1 0 1
0 0 1 0

Solution

The given binary numbers are 0101 and 0010.

Now, perform the binary subtraction of the given numbers as:

```
    1        Borrow
0 1 0 1      Minuend
0 0 1 0      Subtrahend
-------
0 0 1 1      Difference
-------
```

Therefore, the result of the binary subtraction performed on the numbers 0101 and 0010 is 0011.

Example 7.11 *Perform the binary subtraction of the following numbers:*
1 0 1 0 1
0 1 1 1 0

Solution

The given binary numbers are 10101 and 01110.

Now, perform the binary subtraction of the given numbers as:

```
  1 1 1        Borrow
1 0 1 0 1      Minuend
0 1 1 1 0      Subtrahend
---------
0 0 1 1 1      Difference
---------
```

Therefore, the result of the binary subtraction performed on the numbers 10101 and 01110 is 00111

Example 7.12 *Perform the binary subtraction of the following numbers:*
10111011
01001001

Solution

The given binary numbers are 10111011 and 01001001.

Now, perform the binary subtraction of the given numbers as:

```
  1                 Borrow
1 0 1 1 1 0 1 1     Minuend
0 1 0 0 1 0 0 1     Subtrahend
---------------
0 1 1 1 0 0 1 0     Difference
---------------
```

Therefore, the result of the binary subtraction performed on the numbers 10111011 and 01001001 is 111001.

Example 7.13 *Perform the binary subtraction of the following numbers:*
101110101010
001111011100

Solution

The given binary numbers are 101110101010 and 001111011100.
Now, perform the binary subtraction of the given numbers as:

```
  1 1 1 1 1   1 1 1         Borrow
1 0 1 1 1 0 1 0 1 0 1 0     Minuend
0 0 1 1 1 1 0 1 1 1 0 0     Subtrahend
-----------------------
0 1 1 1 1 1 0 0 1 1 1 0     Difference
-----------------------
```

Therefore, the result of the binary subtraction performed on the numbers 101110101010 and 001111011100 is 11111001110.

7.5 BINARY DIVISION

Binary division is also performed in the same way as we perform decimal division. Like decimal division, we also need to follow the binary subtraction rules while performing the binary division. The dividend involved in binary division should be greater than the divisor. The following are the two important points, which need to be remembered while performing the binary division:

- If the remainder obtained by the division process is greater than or equal to the divisor, put 1 in the quotient and perform the binary subtraction.
- If the remainder obtained by the division process is less than the divisor, put 0 in the quotient and append the next most significant digit from the dividend to the remainder.

Example 7.14 *Divide 14 by 7 in binary form.*

Solution

The equivalent binary representation of the decimal number 14 is 1110.
The binary representation of 7 is 111.
Now, perform the binary division of the given numbers as:

```
1 1 1 ) 1 1 1 0 (10   (Quotient)
        1 1 1
        -------
        0 0 0 0
        -------
```

Therefore, the result of the binary division performed on the decimal numbers 14 and 7 is 10.

Example 7.15 *Perform the binary division of the decimal numbers 18 and 8.*

Solution

The equivalent binary representation of the decimal number 18 is 10010.
The equivalent binary representation of the decimal number 8 is 1000.
Now, perform the binary division of the given numbers as:

```
1 0 0 0 ) 1 0 0 1 0 ( 1 0     (Quotient)
          1 0 0 0
          ---------
          0 0 0 1 0
          0 0 0 0 0
          ---------
          0 0 0 1 0            (Remainder)
          ---------
```

Therefore, the result of the binary division performed on the decimal numbers 18 and 8 is 10 with a remainder of 10.

Example 7.16 *Perform the binary division of the decimal numbers 11011 and 1001.*

Solution

The given binary numbers are 11011 and 1001.
Now, perform the binary division of the given binary numbers as:

```
1 0 0 1 ) 1 1 0 1 1 ( 1 1     (Quotient)
          1 0 0 1
          -------
            1 0 0 1
            1 0 0 1
            -------
            0 0 0 0
            -------
```

Therefore, the result of the binary division performed on the numbers 11011 and 1001 is 11.

Example 7.17 *Perform the binary division of 217 and 12.*

Solution

The equivalent binary representation of the decimal number 217 is 11011001.
The equivalent binary representation of the decimal number 12 is 1100.
Now, perform the binary division of the given numbers as:

```
1 1 0 0 ) 1 1 0 1 1 0 0 1 ( 1 0 0 1 0     (Quotient)
          1 1 0 0
          -------
          0 0 0 1 1
          0 0 0 0 0
          ---------
              0 1 1 0
              0 0 0 0
              -------
              1 1 0 0
              1 1 0 0
              -------
              0 0 0 1                      (Remainder)
              -------
```

Therefore, the result of the binary division performed on the decimal number 217 and 12 is 10010 with a remainder of 1.

7.6 SIGNED/UNSIGNED NUMBERS

The unsigned binary number is the number with a magnitude of either zero or greater than zero. The unsigned binary numbers are usually represented using the unsigned-magnitude representation. The unsigned-magnitude representation only represents the magnitude of the numbers. This type of representation does not take the sign of the binary numbers into consideration while representing these numbers. Therefore, we can say that the unsigned-magnitude representation is used to represent the positive numbers only.

The signed binary numbers are the numbers that are always associated with a sign. This sign helps in identifying whether the given binary number is a positive quantity or a negative quantity. Signed-magnitude representation is a method used in the computer system for representing the signed binary numbers. In this method, an extra bit called *sign bit* is associated with the magnitude of the given number. This sign bit is used to indicate whether the given binary number is positive or negative. The value of the sign bit is 0 for the positive numbers and 1 for the negative numbers. The signed-magnitude representation method can be used to represent both the positive and the negative numbers. However, the unsigned numbers or the positive numbers in the computer system are usually represented with the help of unsigned-magnitude representation. This is because the numbers represented in the unsigned-magnitude representation can be processed more efficiently and rapidly by the computer system as compared to the signed-magnitude representation.

In the signed-magnitude representation, the number of bits assigned to the signed numbers depends upon the word size of the microprocessor of the computer system. For instance, consider the 8-bit word size computer system of representing integers. The 8-bit word size computer system can represent the numbers between – $(2^8 - 1)$ to $(2^8 - 1)$, i.e., – 255 to 255. Figure 7.1 shows the storage system of an 8-bit word size computer system.

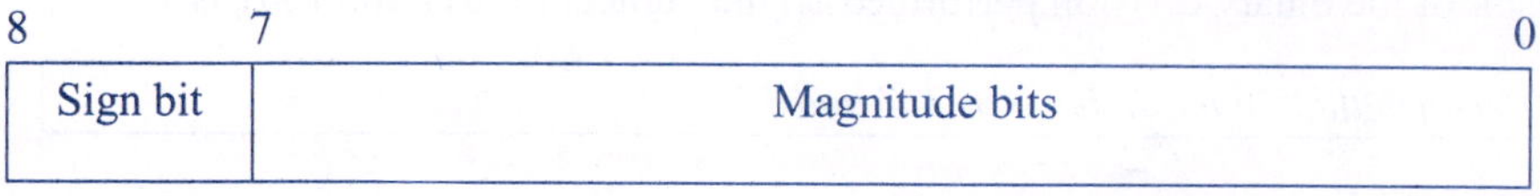

Fig. 7.1 The 8-bit signed-magnitude representation

In Fig. 7.1, the first 7 bits of the 8-bit word size computer system are used to represent the magnitude of the number and the last bit, is used to indicate the sign of the number. This bit is known as the sign bit.

Figure 7.2 shows the signed-magnitude representation of the decimal number 50 in an 8-bit word size computer system. Here, the sign bit contains 0 indicating that the number is positive.

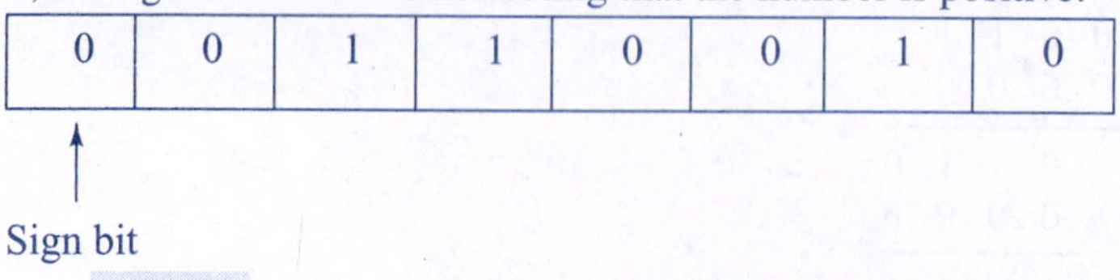

Fig. 7.2 The 8-bit signed-magnitude representation of 50

Figure 7.3 shows the signed-magnitude representation of –50 in an 8-bit word size computer system.

1	0	1	1	0	0	1	0

↑
Sign bit

Fig. 7.3 The 8-bit signed-magnitude representation of –50

Here, the sign bit contains 1 indicating that the number is a negative number.

The following are some of the advantages of the signed-magnitude representation:

- The main advantage of the signed-magnitude representation is its simplicity. It is very easy to represent and understand positive as well as negative numbers using this representation.
- The binary multiplication and the binary division of the signed binary numbers can be easily performed.
- The signed-magnitude representation can represent equal number of positive and negative quantities that makes it a very symmetrical method of representation.

The following are some of the disadvantages of the signed-magnitude representation:

- The implementation of the signed-magnitude representation in the computer system requires the use additional digital circuits that make the internal architecture of the computer system little more complicated.
- It is not an easy task to perform the binary addition and the binary subtraction using this representation.
- It provides two different representations of zero, one for plus zero and another for negative zero but actually they are the same values. This could lead to some confusion while performing various arithmetic operations.

7.7 COMPLEMENTS OF BINARY NUMBERS

The complement system can also be used to represent the signed binary numbers apart from the signed-magnitude representation method. In the complement system, the positive integers are represented in a similar manner as they are represented in the signed-magnitude representation. The following are the two most popular complement methods used in the computer system:

- One's complement
- Two's complement

7.7.1 One's Complement

One's complement method can be used to represent negative binary numbers. A negative number can be represented using one's complement method by first computing the binary equivalent of that number and then changing all the zeros with ones and all the ones with zeros. For example, the binary equivalent of the decimal number 15 is 00001111. Therefore, –15 can be represented using one's complement method as 11110000.

Figure 7.4 shows the one's complement representation of 15 in an 8-bit word size computer system.

1	1	1	1	0	0	0	0

↑
Sign bit

Fig. 7.4 The one's complement representation of –15

The one's complement method also uses the left most bit as the sign bit to indicate the sign of the number. Like the signed magnitude representation, the values, 0 and 1 indicate positive and negative numbers respectively. In the above figure, the value of the sign bit is 1 which shows that the represented number is a negative value.

Table 7.5 lists the one's complement representation of the integers from – 7 to 7.

Table 7.5 One's complement representation

Integers	One's complement representation
–7	1000
–6	1001
–5	1010
–4	1011
–3	1100
–2	1101
–1	1110
–0	1111
+0	0000
+1	0001
+2	0010
+3	0011
+4	0100
+5	0101
+6	0110
+7	0111

Note: *The one's complement method of representing signed numbers also has two different representations for the number, zero.*

Example 7.18 *Represent –25 in the one's complement system in byte size.*

Solution

The given number is –25.

The equivalent binary representation of 25 in byte size is 00011001.

Now, change all the zeros to ones and all the ones to zeros in order to obtain the one's complement representation as:

0 0 0 1 1 0 0 1

↓ ↓ ↓ ↓ ↓ ↓ ↓ ↓

1 1 1 0 0 1 1 0

Therefore, the one's complement representation of –25 is 11100110.

Example 7.19 *Represent –32 in the one's complement system in byte size.*

Solution

The equivalent binary representation of 32 in byte size is 00100000.

Now, change all the zeros to ones and all the ones to zeros in order to obtain the one's complement representation as:

0 0 1 0 0 0 0 0

↓ ↓ ↓ ↓ ↓ ↓ ↓ ↓

1 1 0 1 1 1 1 1

Therefore, the one's complement representation of –32 is 11011111.

Example 7.20 *Represent –32 in the one's complement system in byte size.*

Solution

The given number is –54.

The equivalent binary representation of 54 in byte size is 00110110.

Now, change all zeros to ones and all ones to zeros to obtain the one's complement representation as:

0 0 1 1 0 1 1 0

↓ ↓ ↓ ↓ ↓ ↓ ↓ ↓

1 1 0 0 1 0 0 1

Therefore, the one's complement representation of -54 is 11001001.

7.7.2 Two's Complement

Two's complement is the most widely used method for representing negative numbers in the computer system. The two's complement of the given integer can be obtained by adding 1 to the one's complement of that number. For example, the two's complement representation of –15 can be obtained by adding 1 to 11110000, which is the one's complement representation of –15. Therefore, the two's complement representation of –15 is 11110001.

Figure 7.5 shows the two's complement representation of –15 in an 8-bit word size computer system. Like the one's complement method, the two's complement method also uses the left most bit to represent the sign of the given integer.

1	1	1	1	0	0	0	1

↑

Sign bit

Fig. 7.5 The two's complement representation of –15

Table 7.6 lists the two's complement representation of integers from – 7 to 7.

Table 7.6 Two's complement representation

Integers	Two's complement representation
–7	1001
–6	1010
–5	1011
–4	1100
–3	1101
–2	1110
–1	1111
–0	0000
+0	0000
+1	0001
+2	0010
+3	0011
+4	0100
+5	0101
+6	0110
+7	0111

Example 7.21 *Represent –33 in the 2's complement system in byte size.*

Solution

The given number is –33.

The equivalent binary representation of 33 in a byte is 00100001.

Now, change all the zeros to ones and all the ones to zeros in order to obtain the one's complement representation as:

0 0 1 0 0 0 0 1

↓ ↓ ↓ ↓ ↓ ↓ ↓ ↓

1 1 0 1 1 1 1 0

Therefore, the one's complement representation of –33 is 11011110.

Now, add 1 to the one's complement representation in order to obtain the two's complement representation of the given number as:

```
  1 1 0 1 1 1 1 0
                1
-----------------
  1 1 0 1 1 1 1 1
-----------------
```

Therefore, the two's complement representation of –33 is 11011111.

Example 7.22 *Represent –11 in the 2's complement system.*

Solution

The given number is –11.

The equivalent binary representation of 11 is 00001011.

Now, change all the zeros to ones and all the ones to zeros in order to obtain the one's complement representation as:

```
0 0 0 0 1 0 1 1
↓ ↓ ↓ ↓ ↓ ↓ ↓ ↓
1 1 1 1 0 1 0 0
```

Therefore, the one's complement representation of –11 is 11110100.

Now, add 1 to the one's complement representation in order to obtain the two's complement representation of the given number as:

```
  1 1 1 1 0 1 0 0
                1
  ---------------
  1 1 1 1 0 1 0 1
  ---------------
```

Therefore, the two's complement representation of –11 is 11110101.

Example 7.23 *Represent –59 in the 2's complement system.*

Solution

The given number is –59.

The equivalent binary representation of 59 in byte size is 00111011.

Now, change all the zeros to ones and all the ones to zeros in order to obtain the one's complement representation as:

```
0 0 1 1 1 0 1 1
↓ ↓ ↓ ↓ ↓ ↓ ↓ ↓
1 1 0 0 0 1 0 0
```

Therefore, the one's complement representation of –59 is 11000100.

Now, add 1 to the one's complement representation in order to obtain the two's complement representation of the given number as:

```
  1 1 0 0 0 1 0 0
                1
  ---------------
  1 1 0 0 0 1 0 1
  ---------------
```

Therefore, the two's complement representation of –59 is 11000101.

7.8 BINARY SUBTRACTION USING COMPLEMENTS

The complement methods can be used to perform the binary subtraction of the signed integers. The binary subtraction of the signed integers can be divided into the three following categories:

- Smaller number from larger one
- Larger number from smaller one
- Positive number from negative number

Note: *We can use both the one's complement and two's complement method to perform all the categories of binary subtraction.*

7.8.1 Smaller Number from Larger One

Using one's complement To subtract a smaller number from the larger one using the one's complement method, we need to perform the following steps:

1. Obtain the one's complement of the smaller number.
2. Perform the binary addition on the one's complement and the larger number.
3. If a carry is generated, add it to the calculated result for obtaining the final result.

Consider the following examples for understanding the method of subtracting a smaller number from a larger number using one's complement system:

Example 7.24 *Subtract 3 from 8 using the one's complement method.*

Solution

The equivalent binary representation of the decimal number 8 is 1000.
The equivalent binary representation of the decimal number 3 is 0011.
The one's complement representation of the smaller number 3 is 1100.
Now, perform the binary addition of the one's complement and the larger number as:

```
 1 0 0 0
 1 1 0 0
---------
1 0 1 0 0
---------
```

Add the generated carry to the calculated result as:

```
0 1 0 0
      1
-------
0 1 0 1
-------
```

Therefore, the result of the binary subtraction performed on the given numbers using one's complement method is 0101.

Example 7.25 *Subtract 4 from 7 using the one's complement method.*

Solution

The equivalent binary representation of the decimal number 4 is 0100.
The equivalent binary representation of the decimal number 7 is 0111.
The one's complement representation of the smaller number 4 is 1011.
Now, perform the binary addition of the one's complement and the larger number as:

```
  0 1 1 1
  1 0 1 1
---------
1 0 0 1 0
---------
```

Add the carry to the calculated result as:

```
  0 0 1 0
        1
---------
  0 0 1 1
---------
```

Therefore, the result of the binary subtraction performed on the given numbers using one's complement method is 0011.

Using two's complement To subtract a smaller number from a larger number using the two's complement method, we need to perform the following steps:

1. Obtain the two's complement of the smaller number.
2. Perform the binary addition of the two's complement and the larger number.
3. Discard the carry to obtain the final answer.

Consider the following examples for understanding the method of subtracting a smaller number from a larger number using two's complement system:

Example 7.26 *Subtract 13 from 15 using the two's complement method.*

Solution

The equivalent binary representation of the decimal number 15 is 1111.
The equivalent binary representation of the decimal number 13 is 1101.
The two's complement representation of the smaller number 13 is 0011.
Now, perform the binary addition of the two's complement and the larger number as:

```
    1 1 1 1
    0 0 1 1
-----------
  1 0 0 1 0
-----------
```

Discard the carry to obtain the final answer, which is 0010.

Therefore, the result of the binary subtraction performed on the given numbers using two's complement method is 0010.

Example 7.27 *Subtract 4 from 8 using two's complement method.*

Solution

The equivalent binary representation of the decimal number 4 is 0100.
The equivalent binary representation of the decimal number 8 is 1000.
The two's complement representation of the smaller number 4 is 1100.
Now, perform the binary addition of the two's complement and the larger number as:

```
    1 0 0 0
    1 1 0 0
-----------
  1 0 1 0 0
-----------
```

Discard the carry to obtain the final answer, which is 0100.

Therefore, the result of the binary subtraction performed on the given numbers using two's complement method is 0100.

7.8.2 Larger Number from Smaller One

Using one's complement To subtract a larger number from a smaller number using the one's complement method, we need to perform the following steps:

1. Obtain the one's complement of the larger number.
2. Perform the binary addition on the one's complement and the smaller number to obtain the final answer.

Consider the following examples for understanding the method of subtracting a larger number from a smaller number using one's complement system:

Example 7.28 *Subtract 8 from 3 using the one's complement method.*

Solution

The equivalent binary representation of the decimal number 8 is 1000.
The equivalent binary representation of the decimal number 3 is 0011.
The one's complement representation of the larger number 8 is 0111.
Now, perform the binary addition of the one's complement and the smaller number as:

```
0 1 1 1
0 0 1 1
-------
1 0 1 0
-------
```

Therefore, the result of the binary subtraction performed on the given numbers using one's complement method is 1010.

Example 7.29 *Subtract 11 from 7 using one's complement method.*

Solution

The equivalent binary representation of the decimal number 11 is 1011.
The equivalent binary representation of the decimal number 7 is 0111.
The one's complement representation of the larger number 11 is 0100.
Now, perform the binary addition on the one's complement and the smaller number as:

```
0 1 0 0
0 1 1 1
-------
1 0 1 1
-------
```

Therefore, the result of the binary subtraction performed on the given numbers using one's complement method is 1011.

Using two's complement To subtract a larger number from the smaller one using two's complement method, we need to perform the following steps:

1. Obtain the two's complement of the larger number.
2. Perform the binary addition of the two's complement and the smaller number to obtain the final answer.

Consider the following examples for understanding the method of subtracting a larger number from a smaller number using two's complement system:

Example 7.30 *Subtract 6 from 4 using two's complement method.*

Solution

The equivalent binary representation of the decimal number 6 is 0110.
The equivalent binary representation of the decimal number 4 is 0100.
The two's complement representation of the larger number 6 is 1010.

Now, perform the binary addition on the two's complement and the smaller number as:

```
 1 0 1 0
 0 1 0 0
--------
 1 1 1 0
--------
```

Therefore, the result of the binary subtraction performed on the given numbers using two's complement method is 1110.

Example 7.31 *Subtract 12 from 11 using two's complement method.*

Solution

The equivalent binary representation of the decimal number 12 is 1100.

The equivalent binary representation of the decimal number 11 is 1011.

The two's complement representation of the larger number 12 is 0100.

Now, perform the binary addition on the two's complement and the smaller number as:

```
 0 1 0 0
 1 0 1 1
--------
 1 1 1 1
--------
```

Therefore, the result of the binary subtraction performed on the given numbers using two's complement method is 1111.

7.8.3 Positive Number from Negative Number

Using one's complement The subtraction of a positive number from a negative number always yields a negative integer. To subtract a positive number from a negative number using the one's complement method, we need to perform the following steps:

1. Obtain the one's complement of both the numbers.
2. Perform the binary addition on the one's complement representation of both the given numbers.
3. If a carry is generated, add it to the calculated result to obtain the final result.

Consider the following examples for understanding the method of subtracting a positive number from a negative number using one's complement system:

Example 7.32 *Subtract 7 from –3 using the one's complement method.*

Solution

The one's complement representation of –7 is 1000.

The one's complement representation of –3 is 1100.

Now, perform the binary addition on the one's complement representation of both the given numbers as:

```
   1 0 0 0
   1 1 0 0
----------
 1 0 1 0 0
----------
```

Add the carry to the calculated result as:

```
 0 1 0 0
       1
--------
 0 1 0 1
--------
```

Therefore, the result of the binary subtraction performed on the given numbers using one's complement method is 101.

Example 7.33 *Subtract 9 from –5 using the one's complement method.*

Solution

The one's complement representation of –9 is 0110.

The one's complement representation of –5 is 1010.

Now, perform the binary addition on the one's complement representation of both the given numbers as:

```
  0 1 1 0
  1 0 1 0
---------
1 0 0 0 0
---------
```

Add the carry and add it to the calculated result as:

```
0 0 0 0
      1
-------
0 0 0 1
-------
```

Therefore, the result of the binary subtraction performed on the given numbers using one's complement method is 0001.

Using two's complement To subtract a positive number from a negative number using the two's complement method, we need to perform the following steps:

1. Obtain the two's complement of both the numbers.
2. Perform the binary addition on the two's complement representation of both the given numbers.
3. Discard the carry to obtain the final answer.

Consider the following examples for understanding the method of subtracting a positive number from a negative number using two's complement system:

Example 7.34 *Subtract 9 from –3 using two's complement method.*

Solution

The two's complement representation of –9 is 0111.

The two's complement representation of –3 is 1101.

Now, perform the binary addition on the two's complement representation of both the given numbers as:

```
  0 1 1 1
  1 1 0 1
---------
1 0 1 0 0
---------
```

Discard the carry to obtain the final answer, which is 0100.

Therefore, the result of the binary subtraction performed on the given numbers using two's complement method is 0100.

Example 7.35 *Subtract 3 from –12 using two's complement method.*

Solution

The two's complement representation of –3 is 1101.

The two's complement representation of –12 is 0100.

Now, perform the binary addition on the two's complement representation of both the given numbers as:

```
   1 1 0 1
   0 1 0 0
 ---------
 1 0 0 0 1
 ---------
```

Discard the carry to obtain the final answer, which is 0001.

Therefore, the result of the binary subtraction performed on the given numbers using two's complement method is 0001.

7.9 REPRESENTING NUMBERS

The numbers processed by the computer system are of two types, integer and floating-point. Therefore, the number representations used in the computer system are also of two types. These are known as:

- Integer representation
- Floating-point representation

7.9.1 Integer Representation

Integer numbers are those numbers which do not have fractional parts. Integer numbers include both positive numbers and negative numbers. They can be handled using any of the following representations:

- Unsigned magnitude representation
- Signed magnitude representation
- One's complement representation
- Two's complement representation
- Biased representation

We have already discussed about the unsigned, signed, one's complement and two's complement representation of integers. The unsigned-magnitude representation is used to represent the positive integers only. The signed magnitude representation uses an extra bit called sign bit to represent the sign of the given number. Therefore, this representation can be used by computer system to represent positive as well as negative integers. The one's complement and two's complement representation is mostly suitable for representing negative integers only.

Apart from these integer representations, there is one more integer representation called biased representation, which is not commonly used. The biased representation is basically an unsigned representation but can also be used to represent the negative integers. This can be accomplished by using the concept of a bias, which is actually a positive value added to the given integer to obtain an unsigned value. The value chosen for a bias depends upon the number of bits required to represent the given integer. The bias value for any biased system can be determined by using the formula 2^{n-1}, where n is the number of bits required to represent the integer. For example, for a 4-bit system the bias would be equal to 8. This type of biased system would be called biased-8 representation. In biased system, the number of values that can be represented depends upon the bias value. For instance, we can represent integers from –8 to 7 using biased-8 system.

The biased-8 representation of the integer –8 can be determined by adding the bias value 8 to the given integer; this gives the output as 0. Therefore, the biased-8 representation of the integer –8 is 0000. Similarly, the biased-8 representation of the integer 7 is 1111 which is determined by adding 8 to 7.

7.9.2 Floating-point Representation

Floating-point numbers are the numbers containing two different parts, integer part and fractional part.

The floating-point numbers are also referred as *real numbers*. Some of the examples of the floating-point numbers are 0.5, 3.8 and –102.8. A notation known as *scientific notation* is used to represent the real numbers in the computer system. The scientific notation is usually applied for the real numbers, which are either very small or very large. The scientific notation, also called *exponential notation*, represents the real numbers in the following form:

$m \times b^e$

where,

m is the real value called mantissa

b is the base of the number system

e is the intger value called exponent

Therefore, in the scientific notation, the real numbers are expressed as the product of some real value and the base of the number system, where the base is raised to some integer value. For example, the floating-point representation for the real number 325.123 is 3.25123×10^2. Similarly, the number 0.000000245 can be represented using floating-point representation as 2.45×10^{-7}.

A binary number can be represented in the scientific notation by using base 2. For example, the binary number 1000.0101 can be represented using scientific notation as 1.0000101×2^3.

A given number can be stored in the scientific notation in different forms. For example, the number 4333.123 can be represented in the scientific notation in any one of the following forms:

4.333123×10^3

43.33123×10^2

433.3123×10^1

The modern computer systems usually employ the *normalized scientific notation* to represent real numbers. The following are some of the examples of the real numbers represented in the normalized scientific notation:

0.324521×10^2

0.523×10^{-3}

-0.5469×10^5

The format used to store the binary numbers in the computer system is known as *binary floating-point format*. In this format, the binary numbers are stored in the normalised scientific form. The binary floating-point format stores the binary number by dividing it into the following three parts:

Sign The sign part is always 1-bit long and is used to store the information pertaining to the sign of the number. This part stores either 0 or 1 value for the positive and negative numbers respectively.

Exponent The exponent part is always stored using excess-N notation. The value of N depends upon the number of bits available for storing the exponent. For example, if the exponent is to be stored in 7 bits, excess-64 notation would be used. If the exponent is to be stored in 8 bits, excess-127 notation would be used. Therefore, if 6 is to be stored as the exponent value in a 7-bit word size, it would be stored using excess-64 notation and its value would be 70. Therefore, the exponent value that is actually stored in the computer system is determined by adding the value of N to the actual value of the exponent.

Mantissa The mantissa part of the binary number is always stored in the normalised scientific notation in the computer system.

Figure 7.6 shows the storage layout of the 32-bit binary floating-point number in the computer system.

Sign bit	Exponent bits	Mantissa bits
1 bit	7/8 bits	24/23 bits

Fig. 7.6 Storing binary numbers in the computer system

To understand the storage layout of the binary numbers, let us consider the following binary floating point number:

1000100.1

Before storing the given binary floating-point number in the computer system, we need to normalise its mantissa as:

0.10001001×2^7

Now, the mantissa part of the given number is 0.10001001 and the exponent part of the given number is 7.

Suppose the number of bits available for storing the exponent is 7. In this case, the excess-64 notation would be implemented by the computer system to store the exponent part of the given number.

The excess-64 notation for the decimal number 7 is 71.

The equivalent binary representation of the decimal number 71 is 1000111.

Therefore, the following are the binary values stored in the sign, the exponent and the mantissa parts in the computer system:

- 0 in the sign part
- 1000111 in the exponent part
- .10001001 in the mantissa part

Figure 7.7 shows the storage layout of the binary floating point number 1000100.1 in the computer system.

0	1000111	100010010000000000000000
1 bit	7 bits	24 bits

Fig. 7.7 Storing of the binary number 1000100.1 in the computer system

7.10 INTEGER ARITHMETIC

The integer arithmetic involves a number of arithmetic operations, which are performed on the unsigned and the signed binary numbers. We have already covered the binary addition, binary subtraction, binary multiplication and binary division operations on the unsigned binary numbers. We can perform these arithmetic operations on the signed binary numbers as well. The signed numbers can be represented in the computer system using any one of the following systems:

- Signed-magnitude
- One's complement
- Two's complement

7.10.1 Signed-magnitude System

In the signed-magnitude system, the binary addition can be performed by using the same basic rules that are used with the unsigned binary numbers. However, while performing the binary addition in the signed-magnitude system, we need to take care of two additional rules related to the sign of the binary numbers. These rules are as follows:

- If both the given numbers have the same sign bit, perform the binary addition on the magnitude of the numbers and use the same sign bit in the final result.
- If the sign bits are opposite, instead of binary addition, binary subtraction would be performed on the given numbers.

Consider the following examples for understanding the method of adding binary numbers in the signed-magnitude system:

Example 7.36 *Add 4 and 3 using signed-magnitude system.*

Solution

The signed-magnitude representation of the decimal number 4 is 0 0100.
The signed-magnitude representation of the decimal number 3 is 0 0011.
Now, perform the binary addition as:

```
0   0 1 0 0
0   0 0 1 1
-----------
0   0 1 1 1
-----------
```

Therefore, the result of the binary addition performed on the given numbers in the signed-magnitude system is 0 0111.

Example 7.37 *Add –5 and –4 using signed-magnitude system.*

Solution:

The signed-magnitude representation of the decimal number –5 is 1 0101.
The signed-magnitude representation of the decimal number –4 is 0 0100.
Now, perform the binary addition as:

```
1   0 1 0 1
1   0 1 0 0
-----------
1   1 0 0 1
-----------
```

Therefore, the result of the binary addition performed on the given numbers in the signed-magnitude system is 1 1001.

While performing the binary subtraction in the signed-magnitude system, the following two considerations about the sign bits should be kept in mind:

- If both the given numbers have opposite sign bits, perform the binary addition on the magnitudes of the numbers.
- If the sign bits are the same, compare the magnitudes of the given numbers. The smaller number should always be subtracted from the larger number. If minuend is the smaller number and subtrahend is the larger number, the value of the sign bit would be 1. However, if the minuend is the larger number and subtrahend is the smaller number, the value of the sign bit would be 0.

Consider the following examples for understanding the method of subtracting binary numbers in the signed-magnitude system:

Example 7.38 *Subtract 12 from 5 using signed-magnitude representation.*

Solution

The signed-magnitude representation of 12 is 0 1100.

The signed-magnitude representation of 5 is 0 0101.

As the sign bits are same, larger magnitude would be subtracted from smaller magnitude as:

```
0    1 1 0 0
0    0 1 0 1
------------
1    0 1 1 1
```

As the larger number is to be subtracted from the smaller number, we have kept the value of the sign bit as 1.

Therefore, the result of the binary subtraction performed on the given numbers in the signed-magnitude system is 1 0111.

Example 7.39 *Subtract 5 from 12 using signed-magnitude representation.*

Solution

The signed-magnitude representation of 5 is 0 0101.

The signed-magnitude representation of 12 is 0 1100.

Now, perform the binary subtraction by subtracting the smaller number from the larger number as:

```
0    1 1 0 0
0    0 1 0 1
------------
0    0 1 1 1
```

As the smaller number is to be subtracted from the larger number, we have kept the value of the sign bit as 0.

Therefore, the result of the binary subtraction performed on the given numbers in the signed-magnitude system is 0 0111.

While performing the binary multiplication in the signed-magnitude system, the following two considerations about the sign bits should be kept in mind:

- If the both the numbers have same sign bits, perform the binary multiplication on the magnitudes of the numbers only. The sign bit to represent the positive result would always be zero.
- If both the numbers have opposite sign bits, perform the binary multiplication on the magnitudes of the numbers. The sign bit to represent the negative result would always be one.

Consider the following examples to understand the method of multiplying binary numbers in the signed-magnitude system:

Example 7.40 *Perform the binary multiplication of 5 and 4 using signed-magnitude system.*

Solution

The signed-magnitude representation of 5 is 0 0101.

The signed-magnitude representation of 4 is 0 0100.

Now, perform the binary multiplication only on the magnitudes of the given numbers as:

```
   0 1 0 1     Multiplicand
   0 1 0 0     Multiplier
  --------
   0 0 0 0     First partial product
 0 0 0 0
```

```
  0 1 0 1
0 0 0 0
-------------
0 0 1 0 1 0 0      Final product
-------------
```

As the sign bits of both the given numbers are same, keep the sign bit in the final result as 0.
Therefore, the binary product of the given numbers in signed-magnitude system is 0 10100.

Example 7.41 *Perform the binary multiplication of –6 and 2 using signed-magnitude system.*

Solution

The signed-magnitude representation of –6 is 1 0110.
The signed-magnitude representation of 2 is 0 0010.
Now, perform the binary multiplication only on the magnitudes of the given numbers as:

```
      0 1 1 0      Multiplicand
      0 0 1 0      Multiplier
-------------
      0 0 0 0      First partial product
    0 1 1 0
  0 0 0 0
0 0 0 0
-------------
0 0 0 1 1 0 0      Final product
-------------
```

As, the sign bits of both the given numbers are opposite, keep the sign bit in the final result as 1.
Therefore, the binary product of the given numbers in signed-magnitude system is 1 1100.

While performing the binary division in the signed-magnitude system, the following two considerations about the sign bits should be kept in mind:

- If the both the numbers have same sign bits, perform the binary division on the magnitudes of the numbers only. The sign bit to represent the positive result would always be zero.
- If both the numbers have opposite sign bits, perform the binary multiplication on the magnitudes of the numbers only. The sign bit to represent the negative result would always be one.

Consider the following examples to understand the method of dividing the binary numbers in the signed-magnitude system:

Example 7.42 *Evaluate the binary division of the decimal numbers –18 and –9.*

Solution

The signed-magnitude representation of –18 is 1 10010.
The signed-magnitude representation of –9 is 1 01001.
Now, perform the binary division only on the magnitudes of the given numbers as:

```
1 0 0 1) 1 0 0 1 0(1 0     (Quotient)
         1 0 0 1
         ---------
         0 0 0 0 0         (Remainder)
         ---------
```

As the sign bits of both the numbers are same, keep the sign bit in the final result as 0.
Therefore, the binary division output of the given numbers in the signed-magnitude system is 0 10.

Example 7.43 *Evaluate the binary division of the decimal numbers 6 and –3.*

Solution

The signed-magnitude representation of 6 is 0 0110.
The signed-magnitude representation of –3 is 1 0011.
Now, perform the binary division only on the magnitudes of the given numbers as:

```
0 1 1) 0 1 1 0(1  0     (Quotient)
       0 1 1
       -------
       0 0 0 0          (Remainder)
       -------
```

As the sign bits of both the numbers are opposite, keep the sign bit in the final result as 1.
Therefore, the binary division output of the given numbers in the signed-magnitude system is 1 10.

7.10.2 One's Complement System

The one's complement system can also be used to perform various arithmetic operations. We have already discussed the method of performing binary subtraction using one's complement. Apart from binary subtraction, the other two major arithmetic operations, which we can perform in one's complement system, are binary addition and binary multiplication. The binary addition can be performed in one's complement system by following the same rules as followed in the unsigned binary system. If any carry is generated while performing binary addition, it should be added to the calculated result to obtain the final result.

Consider the following examples for understanding the method of adding the binary numbers in the one's complement system:

Example 7.44 *Perform the binary addition of –2 and –4 using one's complement system.*

Solution

The one's complement representation of –2 is 1101.
The one's complement representation of –4 is 1011.
Now, perform the binary addition of the given numbers as:

```
  1 1 0 1
  1 0 1 1
---------
1 1 0 0 0
---------
```

Discard the carry by adding it to the final result as:

```
1 0 0 0
      1
-------
1 0 0 1
-------
```

Therefore, the result of the binary addition performed on the given numbers in one's complement system is 1001.

Example 7.45 *Perform the binary addition of 3 and –6 using one's complement system.*

Solution

The one's complement representation of 3 is 0011.
The one's complement representation of –6 is 1001.
Now, perform the binary addition of the given numbers as:

```
  0 0 1 1
  1 0 0 1
  -------
  1 1 0 0
  -------
```

Therefore, the result of the binary addition performed on the given numbers in one's complement system is 1100.

The binary multiplication in one's complement system can be performed by using the concept of sign bit extension. According to this concept, when the signed integer is to be represented in the larger bit system, the additional bits on the left side of the number are filled with the sign bit value. We can use this concept in one's complement multiplication by extending the bits in the first partial product. The other binary multiplication rules are the same as used with the unsigned integers.

Consider the following examples to understand the method of multiplying the binary numbers in the one's complement system:

Example 7.46 *Multiply –2 and 2 using one's complement method.*

Solution

The one's complement representation of –2 is 101.

The one's complement representation of 2 is 010.

Now, perform the binary multiplication as:

```
        1 0 1
        0 1 0
    ---------
    1 1 0 0 0
      1 0 1
    0 0 0
  -----------
  1 0 0 0 1 0
  -----------
```

Add the carry to the final product as:

```
  0 0 0 1 0
          1
  ---------
  0 0 0 1 1
  ---------
```

Therefore, the result of the binary multiplication performed on the given numbers in one's complement system is 011.

7.10.3 Two's Complement System

We can also perform the binary addition and the binary multiplication operations in two's complement system. The binary addition can be performed in two's complement system in the same way as it is performed in one's complement system. However, if any carry is generated while performing the binary addition, it should be discarded completely without adding it to the final result.

Consider the following examples to understand the method of adding the binary numbers in the two's complement system:

Example 7.47 *Perform the binary addition of 4 and –5 in two's complement system.*

Solution

The two's complement representation of 4 is 0100.

The two's complement representation of –5 is 1011.

Now, perform the binary addition as:

```
0 1 0 0
1 0 1 1
-------
1 1 1 1
```

Therefore, the result of the binary addition performed on the given numbers in two's complement system is 1111.

Example 7.48 *Perform the binary addition of –8 and –2 in two's complement system.*

Solution

The two's complement representation of –8 is 1000.

The two's complement representation of –2 is 1110.

Now, perform the binary addition as:

```
  1 0 0 0
  1 1 1 0
---------
1 0 1 1 0
```

Discard the carry to obtain the final result, which is 0110.

Therefore, the result of binary addition performed on the given numbers in two's complement system is 0110.

The binary multiplication can also be performed in two's complement system by using the concept of sign bit extension. Consider the following examples for understanding the method of multiplying the binary numbers in the two's complement system:

Example 7.49 *Multiply –14 and 5 using two's complement method.*

Solution

The two's complement representation of –14 is 0010.

The two's complement representation of 5 is 0101.

Now, perform the binary multiplication as:

```
    0 0 1 0     Multiplicand
    0 1 0 1     Multiplier
-----------
1 1 0 0 1 0     First Partial Product

0 0 0 0 0
0 0 1 0
-----------
1 1 1 0 1 0     Final Product
```

Therefore, the result of binary multiplication performed on the given numbers in two's complement system is 111010.

Example 7.50 *Multiply 2 and –4 using two's complement method.*

Solution

The two's complement representation of 2 is 0010.

The two's complement representation of –4 is 1100.

Now, perform the binary multiplication as:

```
        0 0 1 0
        1 1 0 0
  -------------
  1 1 1 0 0 0 0
        0 0 0 0
      0 0 1 0
    0 0 1 0
---------------
1 0 0 0 1 0 0 0
---------------
```

Discard the carry to obtain the final result as 1000.

Therefore, the result of binary multiplication performed on the given numbers in two's complement system is 1000.

7.11 FLOATING-POINT ARITHMETIC

The various floating-point arithmetic operations are performed in the computer system usually on the numbers represented in the normalised floating-point notation. We can perform four basic arithmetic operations: addition, subtraction, multiplication, and division, on the normalised binary floating-point numbers.

7.11.1 Addition

The addition operation is performed on the normalised floating-point numbers by making the exponents of both the numbers equal. This can be accomplished by shifting the mantissa of the smaller number to the right by a number equal to the difference between the exponents of the given numbers.

Consider the following examples for understanding the method of adding binary numbers represented in the normalized binary floating-point format:

Example 7.51 *Perform the addition operation on the following numbers:*
0.001010110E0101000
0.010001001E0100011

Solution

The given binary floating-point numbers are 0.001010110E0101000 and 0.010001001E0100011.

As the difference between the exponents of both the numbers is 5, shift the mantissa of the second number to the right by 5 places.

Now, the second number becomes:

0.000000100E0101000

Now, add the mantissa of both the given numbers as:

0.001010110 + 0.000000100 = 0.001011010

Therefore, the result of the addition operation performed on the given numbers is 0.001011010E0101000

Example 7.52 *Perform the addition operation on the following numbers:*
0.110110100E0100011
0.110001010E0100001

Solution

The given binary floating-point numbers are 0.110110100E0100011 and 0.110001010E0100001.

As the difference between the exponents of both the numbers is 2, shift the mantissa of the second number to the right by 2 places.

Now, the second number becomes:

0.001100010E0100011

Now, add the mantissa of both the given numbers as:

0.110110100 + 0.001100010 = 1.000010110

Therefore, the addition of the given numbers is 1.000010110E0100011

Transform this result into normalised binary floating-point form as:

0.100001011E0100100

Therefore, the result of the addition operation performed on the given numbers is 0.100001011E0100100.

7.11.2 Subtraction

The subtraction operation is also performed on the given numbers after making their exponent parts equal. The subtraction operation is carried out by calculating the two's complement of the subtrahend and adding it to the minuend for obtaining the final result.

Consider the following examples for understanding the method of subtracting binary numbers represented in the normalized binary floating-point format:

Example 7.53 *Perform the binary subtraction of the following numbers:*
0.101100011E0001001
0.011011011E0000110

Solution

The given binary floating-point numbers are 0.101100011E0001001 and 0.011011011E0000110.

As the difference between the exponents of both the numbers is 3, shift the mantissa of the second number to the right by 3 places.

Now, the second number becomes:

0.000011011E0001001

The two's complement of the second number is 0.111100101E0001001

Add the two's complement of the second number to the first number as:

0.111100101E0001001 + 0.101100011E0001001

= 1.101001000E0001001

Discard the overflow bit to obtain the final result as:

0.101001000E0001001

Therefore, the result of the binary subtraction performed on the given numbers is 0.101001000E0001001.

7.11.3 Multiplication

The multiplication operation can be performed on the normalised binary floating-point numbers by multiplying the mantissa and adding the exponent parts. Consider the following example for understanding the method of multiplying binary numbers represented in the normalised binary floating-point format:

Example 7.54 *Perform the multiplication operation on the following numbers:*
0.110011110E0010101
0.110000100E0001001

Solution

The given binary floating-point numbers are 0.110011110E0010101 and 0.110000100E0001001.

Firstly multiply the mantissa of the given numbers and obtain the result in the normalised floating-point form as:

0.110011110 × 0.110000100 = 0.100111000

Now, add the mantissas of both the given numbers as:

0010101 + 0001001 = 0011110

Therefore, the result of the binary multiplication performed on the given numbers is 0.100111000E0011110

7.11.4 Division

The division operation can be performed on the normalised binary floating-point numbers by dividing the mantissa of the first number by the mantissa of the second number and subtracting the exponent of the second number from the exponent of the first number. Consider the following example for understanding the method of dividing binary numbers represented in the normalised binary floating-point format:

Example 7.55 *Evaluate the division of the following numbers:*
0.101110111E0011011
0.001001011E0010001

Solution

The given binary floating-point numbers are 0.101110111E0011011 and 0.001001011E0010001.

First, divide the mantissa of first number by the mantissa of the second number and obtain the result in the normalised floating-point form as:

0.101110111/0.00100101 = 0.000001010

Now, subtract the mantissa of the first number from the mantissa of the second number as:

0011011 – 0010001 = 0001010

Therefore, the result of the binary division performed on the given numbers is 0.000001010E0001010.

7.12 ERRORS IN ARITHMETIC

Computer arithmetic errors can be divided into two categories, integer arithmetic errors and floating-point arithmetic errors. The integer arithmetic errors are the errors generated by the computer system while performing various integer arithmetic operations. On the other hand, the floating-point arithmetic errors may arise in the computer system while performing various floating-point arithmetic operations.

The following are some important types of integer arithmetic errors in the computer system:

- **Overflow** The overflow error may occur when the computer system attempts to use a number in the integer arithmetic that is too large to be handled. This type of error may also be generated as the final result of the integer arithmetic operations. Therefore, the computer users should always use the numbers only within the range that the computer system can handle.

- **Underflow** The underflow error may occur when the computer system attempts to use a number in the integer arithmetic that is too small to be handled. The binary subtraction and the binary division operations may generate this type of error in the computer system.
- **Truncation** The truncation errors may occur in the computer system when the computer system attempts to convert an integer from one data type to another. If the value of the given integer is beyond the range of the desired data type, the given integer would be truncated by preserving the low-order bits only. The binary division operation may generate this kind of error in the computer system.
- **Sign** The sign errors may occur in the computer system when the computer system attempts to represent an unsigned number into signed representation and vice versa.

The floating-point arithmetic errors may also occur in the computer system while carrying out various floating-point arithmetic operations. Overflow and underflow errors also come under the category of floating-point arithmetic errors. Apart from overflow and underflow, the following are some other important reasons that may cause floating-point arithmetic errors:

- The shifting of mantissa to the right for the purpose of representing the real number in the normalised scientific floating-point form may alter the value of the number.
- The conversion of a floating-point decimal number to its equivalent floating-point binary form may generate a binary number containing some repeated sequence of bits in the fraction part. This repeated sequence may sometimes be truncated by the computer system resulting in the wrong output.
- The rounding-off of a very large fraction to the desired number of digits may also generate the floating-point errors.

Example 7.56 *Multiply the numbers 0.200000 E4 and 0.400000 E–2.*

Solution

$$\begin{aligned} f_z &= 0.200000 \times 0.400000 \\ &= 0.080000 \\ E_z &= 4 - 2 = 2 \\ z &= 0.080000 \text{ E2} \\ &= 0.800000 \text{ E1 (normalised)} \\ &= 0.800000 \end{aligned}$$

Example 7.57 *Divide the number 0.8765453 E–5 by 0.200000 E–3.*

Solution

$$\begin{aligned} f_z &= 0.876543 \div 0.200000 \\ &= 4.382715 \\ E_z &= -5 - (-3) = -2 \\ z &= 4.382715 \text{ E–2} \\ &= 0.438271 \text{ E–1 (normalised)} \end{aligned}$$

Note that the mantisa of the result is shortened.

Example 7.58 *Add the numbers 0.500000 E1 and 0.100000 E–7.*

Solution

$$\begin{aligned} \text{Let } x &= 0.500000 \text{ E1 and } y = 0.100000 \text{ E–7} \\ E_z &= 1 \end{aligned}$$

$f_y = 0.000000001$
$f_z = 0.500000001 = 0.500000$
$z = 0.500000 \text{ E1}$

Note that the value of z is the same as that of x.

Example 7.59 *Multiply the number 0.350000 E40 by 0.500000 E70.*

Solution

$E_z = 110$
$f_y = 0.175000$
$z = 0.175000 \text{ E110}$

If the maximum value of exponent is 99, then the result overflows.

Example 7.60 *Divide the number 0.875000 E–18 by 0.200000 E95.*

Solution

$E_z = -18 - 95 = -113$
$f_z = 0.875000 \div 0.200000$
$= 4.375000$
$z = 4.375000 \text{ E}-113$
$= 0.437500 \text{ E}-114$

If the minimum value of exponent is –99, then the result underflows.

Example 7.61 *Subtract 0.499998 from 0.500000.*

Solution

$f_x = 0.500000$
$f_y = 0.499998$
$f_x - f_y = 0.000002$
$E_z = 0$

Thus, $z = 0.000002 \times 10^0$
$= 0.200000 \times 10^{-5}$

Example 7.62 *Associative law for addition.*

Solution

Let $x = 0.456732 \times 10^{-2}$,
$y = 0.243451$,
$z = -0.248000$

$$(x + y) = 0.004567 + 0.243451 = 0.248018$$
$$(x + y) + z = 0.248018 - 0.248000 = 0.000018 = 0.180000 \times 10^{-4}$$
$$(y + z) = 0.243451 - 0.248000 = -0.004549 = -0.4549 \times 10^{-2}$$
$$x + (y + z) = (0.456732 - 0.454900)\, 10^{-2} = 0.183200 \times 10^{-2}$$

Thus,

$$(x + y) + z \neq x + (y + z)$$

7.13 LAWS OF ARITHMETIC

The different arithmetic laws hold true for addition as well multiplication operations. The arithmetic laws can be divided into the following four major categories:

- Identity laws
- Commutative laws
- Associative laws
- Distributive laws

7.13.1 Identity Laws

The two basic identity laws are as follows:

- $a \times 1 = a$
- $a + 0 = a$

The first identity law, $a \times 1 = a$, holds true for the multiplication operation. It states that the multiplication of a number with 1 always yields the same number. For example, 5×1 always yields 5.

The second identity law $a + 0 = a$ holds true for the addition operation. It states that the addition of 0 to a number always yields the same number. For example, $5 + 0$ always yields 5.

7.13.2 Commutative Laws

The two basic commutative laws are as follows:

- $a \times b = b \times a$
- $a + b = b + a$

The first commutative law, $a \times b = b \times a$, holds true for the multiplication operation. It states that multiplying a by b or b by a yields the same result. For example, the multiplication of 3 by 7 and the multiplication of 7 by 3 always yield 21.

The second commutative law $a + b = b + a$ holds true for the addition operation. It states that the addition of the two numbers always yields the same result irrespective of the ordering of the numbers. For example, adding 3 to 5 and adding 5 to 3 always yields 8.

7.13.3 Associative Laws

The two basic associative laws are as follows:

- $a \times (b \times c) = (a \times b) \times c$
- $a + (b + c) = (a + b) + c$

The first associative law holds true for the multiplication operation. It states that the multiplication operation always yields the same result irrespective of the grouping of the numbers. For example, the multiplication operations, $3 \times (5 \times 2)$ and $(3 \times 5) \times 2$ always yield the same result 30.

The second associative law holds true for the addition operation. It states that the addition operation always yields the same result irrespective of the grouping of the numbers. For example, the addition operations, $3 + (5 + 2)$ and $(3 + 5) + 2$ will always yield the same result, i.e., 10.

Example 7.63 *Associative law for multiplication.*

Solution

Let $x = 0.400000 \times 10^{+40}$, $y = 0.500000 \times 10^{+70}$,

$z = 0.300000 \times 10^{-30}$

$(x \times y) \times z = (0.200000 \times 10^{+110})(0.300000 \times 10^{-30})$

Note that $(x \times y)$ causes overflow and so the result will be erroneous.

$$x \times (y \times z) = (0.400000 \times 10^{40}) \times (0.1500000 \times 10^{40})$$
$$= 0.060000 \times 10^{80}$$
$$0.600000 \times 10^{79}$$

This gives the correct result assuming that the exponent can take a value upto +99.

Note that the associative law of arithmetic is *not always* satisfied as illustrated by the Example 7.62.

7.13.4 Distributive Laws

The two basic distributive laws are as follows:

- $a \times (b + c) = a \times b + a \times c$
- $(a + b) \times (c + d) = ac + ad + bc + bd$

The distributive laws hold true for the addition as well as multiplication operations. These laws help solve the complicated multiplication operations involving large numbers by breaking down the numbers into smaller numbers.

For example, the multiplication operation 29×9 can also be performed as:

$= (20 + 9) \times 9$

$= (20 \times 9) + (9 \times 9)$

$= 180 + 81$

$= 261$

Chapter Summary

The main function of the computer system is to process the data. The processing of data by the computer system involves a lot of arithmetic, which is usually of binary type. The basic arithmetic operations performed by the computer system are binary addition, binary multiplication, binary subtraction and binary division.

The basic arithmetic operations can be performed on the integer data as well on floating-point data. The integers in the computer system can be represented by using four different systems: unsigned, signed-magnitude, one's complement and two's complement. The unsigned system is used to represent positive integers only. The other systems can be used to represent positive as well negative integers. The complement system can also be used to perform the binary subtraction in an efficient manner. The floating-point numbers can be represented in the computer system using normalized binary floating-point form. The computer system can generate different types of errors while performing different arithmetic operations. Therefore, a suitable mechanism should be adopted to prevent the occurrence of these errors.

Key Terms to Remember

- **ALU:** ALU is an important component of CPU that is used to perform various arithmetic and logical operations in the computer system.
- **Integer arithmetic:** Integer arithmetic refers to various arithmetic operations involving integer operands only.
- **Floating-point arithmetic:** Floating-point arithmetic refers to various arithmetic operations involving floating-point operands only.
- **Unsigned binary number:** Unsigned binary number is the number with a magnitude of either zero or greater than zero.
- **Signed binary number:** Signed binary number is the number that is always associated with a sign.

- **Sign bit.** Sign bit is an additional bit indicating the sign of the number. It has the value 0 for the positive integers and value 1 for the negative integers.
- **One's complement:** One's complement is a system of representing negative integers. Any negative number can be represented in this system by complementing the bits of its equivalent binary number.
- **Two's complement:** Two's complement is another system of representing negative integers. Any negative integer can be represented in this system by first calculating the one's complement of that number and then adding 1 to it.

Review Questions

Fill in the Blanks

1. The arithmetic operations are usually performed in the computer system by _________ and _________ unit of the CPU.
2. The computer arithmetic is also referred to as the _________ arithmetic.
3. The binary multiplication can be considered as the _________ process of binary _________.
4. Unsigned binary number is a number with a magnitude of either _________ or _________.
5. The unsigned-magnitude representation only represents the _________ of the numbers.
6. The _________ most bit of the given signed number is used to represent the sign of that number.
7. The signed binary numbers always associate a _________ bit with them.
8. The signed-magnitude representation can represent _________ as well as _________ numbers.
9. _________ system can also be used for representing negative integers.
10. The two's complement of any negative number can be obtained by adding _________ to the one's complement of that number.
11. The biased representation of integers uses the concept of a_________.
12. A bias is actually a _________ that is added to the given integer to obtain an unsigned value.
13. The bias value depends upon the number of _________ required to represent the number.
14. The floating-point numbers consist of two major parts, _________ and _________.
15. The floating-point representation is a _________ notation of representing real numbers in the computer system.
16. The scientific notation is usually applied for the real numbers, which are either very _________ or very _______.
17. The different arithmetic laws hold true for _________ as well _________ operations.

Multiple Choice Questions

1. Which of the following unit performs the arithmetic operations in the computer system?
   A. Control unit   B. ALU   C. Shift unit   D. None of the above
2. Which of the following operation is not performed by the ALU of the computer system?
   A. Binary addition   B. AND operation   C. Storing the data   D. Binary division
3. Which of the following is not an appropriate operand for arithmetic operations?
   A. Integers   B. Strings   C. Real   D. None of the above

4. Which of the following is not a valid binary addition rule?
   A. 0 + 0 = 0 B. 1 + 0 = 1 C. 1 + 1 = 0 with a carry 1 D. 1 + 1 = 0 with no carry
5. What is the result of the binary addition performed on the numbers 1001 and 0101?
   A. 0010 B. 1110 C. 1010 D. 1111
6. The binary multiplication can be considered as the repetitive process of:
   A. Binary addition B. Binary subtraction C. Binary division D. Binary multiplication
7. Which of the following is not a valid binary multiplication rule?
   A. 0 × 0 = 1 B. 0 × 1 = 0 C. 1 × 1 = 1 D. 1 × 0 = 0
8. What is the result of the binary multiplication performed on the numbers 12 and 10?
   A. 101011 B. 0111101 C. 1111000 D. 1010000
9. Which of the following is not a valid binary subtraction rule?
   A. 0 – 0 = 0 B. 1 – 0 = 1 with no borrow
   C. 1 – 1 = 0 D. 0 – 1 = 1 with no borrow
10. What is the result of binary subtraction performed on the numbers 1001 and 0101?
    A. 0001 B. 0101 C. 1000 D. 0011
11. Binary division is closely related with the arithmetic operation:
    A. Binary addition B. Binary subtraction C. Binary multiplication D. Binary division
12. Unsigned binary number are the numbers with a magnitude of:
    A. Exactly zero B. Either zero or greater than zero
    C. Less than zero D. None of the above
13. The signed-magnitude representation is used to represent:
    A. Positive numbers only B. Negative numbers only
    C. Numbers with magnitude zero only D. Both the positive and negative numbers
14. The sign bit is used in the signed-magnitude system for representing:
    A. Value of the number B. Whether the number is positive or negative
    C. Whether the number is zero D. None of the above
15. What is the value of sign bit for positive numbers?
    A. 1 B. Not defined C. 0 D. None of the above
16. Which of the following bit is reserved for the sign bit in signed-magnitude representation?
    A. MSB B. LSB
    C. Exactly the middle of the bits D. None of the above
17. Which of the following statement is true for one's complement?
    A. One's complement of a binary number can be obtained by replacing 0 by 1 and 1 by 0.
    B. One's complement is only used to represent negative numbers.
    C. One's complement of a binary number can be obtained by subtracting the number from 9999.
    D. None of the above.
18. Two's complement of a number can be obtained by adding:
    A. 0 to the one's complement of the number
    B. 1 to the one's complement of the number

C. 9 to the signed magnitude representation of the number

D. 1 to the octal representation of the number

19. Which of the following is also known as the scientific notation of representing real numbers?

A. Exponential notation
B. Power notation
C. Zero notation
D. None of the above

20. Which of the following is not an arithmetic law?

A. Identity law
B. Distributive law
C. Commutative law
D. Law of negation

Discussion Questions

1. What do you understand by computer arithmetic? Are the rules for performing computer arithmetic and decimal arithmetic same?
2. What are the different computer arithmetic operations? Explain all of them with their associated set of rules.
3. Perform the binary addition of 1000010, 0111010 and 11110101.
4. Why is binary multiplication considered as the process of repetitive addition?
5. Perform the binary multiplication of 15 and 17.
6. Perform the binary division of 141 and 21.
7. What is the difference between signed and unsigned binary numbers? Is it possible to represent negative numbers with unsigned-magnitude representation?
8. What is the purpose of a sign bit?
9. List the advantages and the disadvantages of signed-magnitude representation.
10. What is a complement system and why is it used in the computer system?
11. What is the difference between one's complement and two's complement system?
12. How the binary subtraction is performed using complements?
13. Perform the binary subtraction of 25 and 15 using two's complement method.
14. What are the different types of integer representations? Explain all of them with examples.
15. What do you understand by floating-point representation? Which notation is best suited for representing real numbers?
16. What are the different rules for performing binary multiplication in signed-magnitude system?
17. Perform the binary multiplication of 12 and 8 using signed-magnitude system.
18. What do you understand by floating-point arithmetic?
19. What do you mean by computer arithmetic errors? What are the different sources of computer arithmetic errors in the computer system
20. What are the different laws of arithmetic?

CHAPTER 8

BOOLEAN ALGEBRA OF SWITCHING CIRCUITS

Chapter Outline

Chapter Objectives

In this chapter, we will learn:

- The concept of Boolean algebra.
- Use of Boolean algebra in designing switching circuits.
- Different elements of Boolean algebra.
- Basic postulates and laws of Boolean algebra.
- Different operations used in Boolean algebra.
- The two different types of Boolean expressions.
- Importance of Venn diagrams.

8.1 INTRODUCTION

We face many situations where there are only two possible decisions 'YES' or 'NO' or two possible outcomes 'TRUE' or 'FALSE'. For instance, consider the following situations:

- A student can get admission in an engineering college *if and only if* he has studied mathematics in school and has secured an average of more than 60% of marks.
- A cheque is valid only if it is signed by the accounts officer and the director.
- The fire alarm in the office will sound if it senses heat or smoke.

Each of these statements contains three parts known as *propositions*. In the first one, the proposition 'student can get admission' connects two propositions—'he has studied mathematics' and 'he has secured more than 60% marks'. We can call the 'admission' proposition as output and the other two as inputs. Here, the output proposition is TRUE if both the input propositions are TRUE. Similarly in the third statement, the output proposition 'alarm will sound' is TRUE if either one of the output propositions is TRUE. This type of logic, called *propositional logic*, was originally observed by the Greek Philosopher **Aristotle**.

In 1854, the English mathematician **George Boole** proposed a symbolic form to the Aristotle's propositional logic, using symbols 1 for TRUE and 0 for FALSE. This system of logic has come to be known as the *Boolean algebra*. This algebra is therefore a form of algebra in which all propositions (values) are reduced to either 1 or 0, known as *Boolean numbers*. A description of all input propositions necessary to get a desired output proposition is known as a *Boolean expression*. The evaluation of a Boolean expression will always result in either 1 or 0.

In 1938, **Claude Shannon** (of MIT, USA) applied Boolean algebra to solve the problems associated with the operations of relay and switching circuits. Switches can exist only in one of the two states, closed or open, as shown in Fig. 8.1. When the switch is closed, the light is 'on' and when the switch is open, the light is 'off'. The on-condition is represented by 1 and the off-condition by 0. Switching circuits and networks used in the computer systems contain a combination of such connected switches. We can therefore apply the concept of binary states 1 and 0 to these switching networks and arrive at a conclusion using the concepts of Boolean algebra. As Boolean algebra is applied to the design of switching circuits, it is also referred to as *switching algebra*.

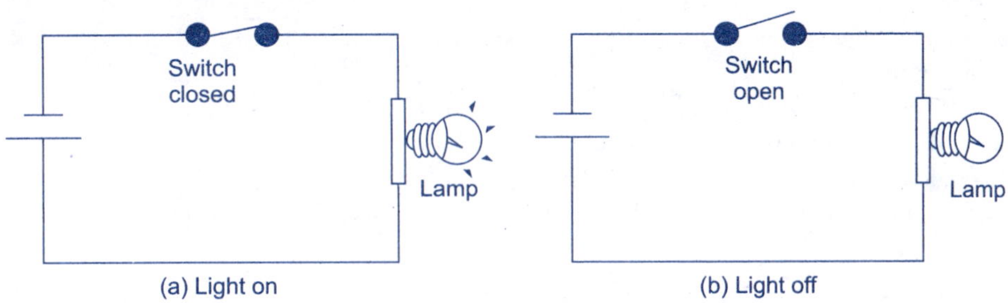

Fig. 8.1 A simple switching circuit

In this chapter, we shall discuss the fundamentals of Boolean algebra such as basic assumptions, Boolean operators, laws governing the Boolean algebra and evaluation of Boolean expressions.

8.2 ELEMENTS OF BOOLEAN ALGEBRA

As stated earlier, Boolean algebra is an algebraic system that is specially evolved for handling the binary number system. As it strictly deals with the binary number system, the variables used in the Boolean expressions can only have two values, 0 and 1. For example, consider the following Boolean expression:

$$P + Q = R$$

In this expression, the variables P, Q and R can take only one of the two values, 0 and 1. The variables used in the Boolean expressions are called Boolean variables. Unlike usual algebraic variables, Boolean variables may only hold either of the two values, 0 or 1. (These values are actually used to represent the state of the signals used by the switching circuits.)

Apart from the Boolean variables, another important element used in the Boolean algebra is Boolean operators. The following are the three important Boolean operators used in Boolean algebra:

- **Logical addition operator** It is denoted by the symbol, '+'. This operator usually operates on two variables to produce a third variable. The logical addition operator is a binary operator as it operates on two variables. The value of the variable produced by this operator strictly depends upon the values of its input variables.
- **Logical multiplication operator** It is denoted by the symbol, '.'. Like the logical addition operator, it is also a binary operator as it operates on two variables. The value of the output variable of the logical multiplication operator also depends upon the values of its input variables.
- **Logical complement operator** Unlike the logical addition and the logical multiplication operators, the logical complement operator operates on a single variable only. Therefore, it is a unary operator and is used to switch the value of the input variable. For example, if the value of its input variable is 1, the logical complement operator switches it to 0 and vice-versa.

Another important concept of the Boolean algebra is the evaluation of the Boolean expressions. Boolean expressions are made of Boolean variables and Boolean operators. There are some primary rules, which should be followed while evaluating the Boolean expressions. These primary rules are as follows:

- The scanning order for the Boolean expressions like the normal algebraic expressions should be from left to right.
- If the Boolean expressions consist of parenthesis, the expressions included in the parenthesis should be evaluated first.
- The logical complement operator should be carried out first.
- The logical multiplication operator should be carried out next.
- The logical addition operator should be carried out at last.

To understand the primary rules for the Boolean expressions, let us consider the following Boolean expression:

$$P + (Q.\overline{R} + S)$$

The above Boolean expression will be evaluated in the following order:

1. As the given Boolean expression contains parenthesis, the expression included in the parenthesis will be evaluated first.
2. The logical complement operator on the variable, R will be performed first inside the parenthesis.
3. The logical multiplication operator will then be performed on the variable, Q as well as on the variable generated by the logical complement operator.
4. The logical addition operator inside the parenthesis will be performed next on the variable, S as well as on the variable generated by the evaluation of expression $Q.\overline{R}$.
5. The logical addition operation will again be performed in the end on the variable, P as well as on the variable generated by the evaluation of expression $(Q.\overline{R} + S)$.

Some basic rules of Boolean algebra are also helpful in evaluating the Boolean expressions. These rules of Boolean algebra are fundamental in nature and used in the simplification or evaluation of complex Boolean expressions. Table 8.1 lists the basic rules of Boolean algebra.

Table 8.1 The basic rules of Boolean algebra

Rule No.	*Rule*
1	$A + 0 = A$
2	$A + 1 = 1$
3	$A.0 = A$
4	$A.1 = A$
5	$A + A = A$
6	$A + \overline{A} = 1$
7	$A.A = A$
8	$A.\overline{A} = 0$
9	$\overline{\overline{A}} = A$
10	$A + AB = A$
11	$A + \overline{A}B = A + B$
12	$(A + B)(A + C) = A + BC$

8.3 BASIC POSTULATES OF BOOLEAN ALGEBRA

Each algebraic system is provided with some postulates, which are also called assumptions. These postulates can be used to determine the additional theorems and properties for the related algebraic system. Like other algebraic systems, the Boolean algebra is also provided with some initial assumptions. These assumptions are generally related to the operators used in the Boolean algebra. The following are some of the basic postulates of the Boolean algebra:

- As the type of inputs accepted by the Boolean operators and the type of output produced by the Boolean operators are same, therefore, the Boolean algebra is closed under the Boolean operators. For example, the logical addition operator '+' accepts only Boolean values and produces a Boolean result. This fact also holds true for the other two Boolean operators.
- The identity element for the logical addition operator is zero. The identity element in any algebra is the element that, when combined with another element, say A, produces A only. For example, the Boolean expression $A + 0$ always produces A, where A is any Boolean variable.
- The identity element for the logical multiplication operator is one. For example, the Boolean expression $A.1$ always produces A, where A is any Boolean variable.
- There exists no identity element for the logical complement operator.

- The logical addition and the logical multiplication operators always produce the same results irrespective of the ordering of the operands. For example, the result produced by the Boolean expression $A + B$ is same as the result produced by the Boolean expression $B + A$. Here, A and B are any Boolean variables.
- The logical addition and the logical multiplication operators always produce the same results, irrespective of the grouping of the operands. For example, all the three Boolean expressions $A.B.C$, $(A.B).C$ and $A.(B.C)$ produce the same result. Here, A, B and C are any Boolean variables.

8.4 BOOLEAN OPERATIONS

The Boolean algebra, like other algebraic systems, consists of some operations that are helpful in simplifying the design of the switching circuits. The following are the three basic operations in Boolean algebra:

- The AND operation
- The OR operation
- The NOT operation

8.4.1 The AND Operation

The AND operation is implemented using the logical multiplication operator and two input variables. Since the logical multiplication operator is used in the AND operation, it is also known as the AND operator. Figure 8.2 shows an electric circuit and the corresponding truth table for the AND operation implemented in the Boolean algebra.

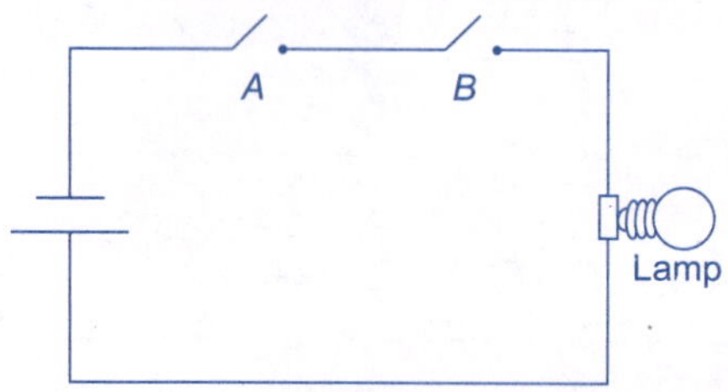

(a) Electric circuit

A	B	A.B
0	0	0
0	1	0
1	0	0
1	1	1

(b) Truth table

Fig. 8.2 Illustration of AND operation

A and B are the Boolean variables. These Boolean variables can only hold one of the two logical values, 0 and 1. The truth table lists the two important facts about the AND operation:

- The AND operation produces 0 as the output if either of its input variables contains the value 0.
- The AND operation produces 1 as the output only if both the input variables contain the value 1.

Note that, in the electric circuit, a closed switch represents 1 while an open switch represents 0.

8.4.2 The OR Operation

The OR operation is implemented using the logical addition operator and two input variables. As the logical addition operator is used in the OR operation, it is also known as the OR operator. Figure 8.3 shows an electric circuit and the corresponding Boolean algebra.

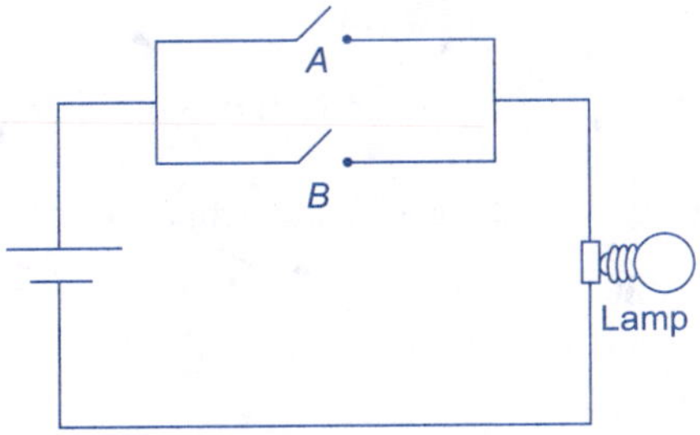

(a) Electric circuit

A	B	A + B
0	0	0
0	1	1
1	0	1
1	1	1

(b) Truth table

Fig. 8.3 Illustration of OR operation

A and *B* are the Boolean variables containing either the value 0 or 1. The truth table lists the two important facts about the OR operation:

- The OR operation produces 1 as the output if either of its input variables contains the value 1.
- The OR operation produces 0 as the output if both the input variables contain the value 0.

8.4.3 The NOT Operation

The NOT operation is implemented using the logical complement operator. Unlike the operations, AND and OR, the NOT operation is applied to a single variable only. As the logical complement operator is used in the NOT operation, it is also known as NOT operator. Table 8.2 lists the truth table for the NOT operation implemented in the Boolean algebra. In Boolean algebra, the NOT operation is denoted by an overscore or bar as shown.

Table 8.2 The NOT operation

A	$\overline{A}$
0	1
1	0

The table clearly depicts the inverting behaviour of the NOT operation. The NOT operation is used to invert the value of its input variable. If the input variable holds a value 1, then the NOT operation changes it to 0 and vice-versa.

8.5 PRINCIPLE OF DUALITY

In the Boolean algebra, the principle of duality helps in deducing new theorems and statements without proving them, if the dual of these theorems and statements has already been proved. According to the principle of duality, the swapping of 0 and 1 and '+' and '.' in any statement of the Boolean algebra does not change the trueness of that statement. Therefore, the principle of duality can be used to deduce the dual of any statement in the Boolean algebra if the statement is known to be true.

For example, consider the following statement in Boolean algebra:

$$(A + 1)\ (A + B.C) = 0$$

The dual of this statement can be determined by just interchanging the elements, 0 and 1 and the operators, '+' and '.'.

Applying the principle of duality, we get the dual of the given statement as:

$$(A.0)\ (A.B + C) = 1$$

Similarly, the dual of the statement $(A + B)\ (A.C) = 1.C + B$ is as follows:

$$(A.B)\ (A + C) = (0 + C).B$$

The operations, AND and OR of Boolean algebra are also dual of each other. Table 8.3 lists the truth table for the AND operation.

Table 8.3 The AND operation

A	B	$A.B$
0	0	0
0	1	0
1	0	0
1	1	1

If we swap the elements, 0 and 1 and the operators, '+' and '.' in the Table 8.3, then the newly obtained table will be the truth table of the OR operation, as shown in Table 8.4.

Table 8.4 The OR operation

A	B	$A + B$
1	1	1
1	0	1
0	1	1
0	0	0

The newly obtained table is clearly the truth table of the OR operation. Similarly, if we start with the truth table of the OR operation and apply the principle of duality on it, we obtain the truth table of the AND operation.

Hence, we can say that the operations, AND and OR in Boolean algebra are dual of each other.

8.6 BASIC LAWS OF BOOLEAN ALGEBRA

Boolean algebra is associated with a set of rules that help in simplifying any type of complicated Boolean expression representing the complex switching circuit. If the Boolean expression of any complex switching circuit can be reduced to a simpler one using the Boolean algebra laws, then a simplified switching circuit with minimum number of logic elements can be obtained. This also results in the reduction of the overall cost of the switching circuit. The following are some important laws of Boolean algebra:

- Laws of multiplication

- Laws of addition
- Commutative laws
- Associative laws
- Distributive laws
- Absorption laws
- Involution laws
- Uniqueness to complement law

8.6.1 Laws of Multiplication

Each law of multiplication states that if a Boolean variable is multiplied with itself any number of times, the result obtained will be the original Boolean variable. The laws of multiplication can be explained using the following expression:

$$A.A = A$$

Figure 8.4 illustrates the laws of multiplication using the electrical circuits.

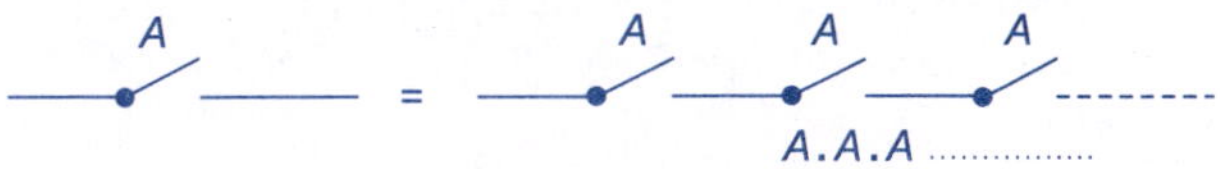

Fig. 8.4 Illustrating the laws of multiplication using electrical circuits

Table 8.5 lists the laws of multiplication for the Boolean algebra.

Table 8.5 Laws of multiplication

A	A	$A.A$
0	0	0
1	1	1

Table 8.5 lists two important laws of multiplication. The first law of multiplication states that the multiplication of 0 with itself any number of times will produce 0 only. The second law of multiplication states that the multiplication of 1 with itself any number of times will produce 1 only.

8.6.2 Laws of Addition

Each law of addition states that if a Boolean variable is added any number of times to itself, the result produced will be the original Boolean variable. The laws of addition can be explained using the following expression:

$$A + A = A$$

Figure 8.5 illustrates the laws of addition using the electrical circuits.

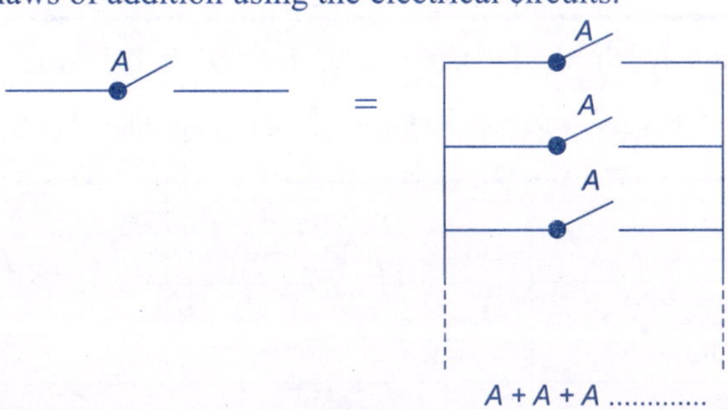

Fig. 8.5 Illustrating the laws of addition using electrical circuits

Table 8.6 lists the laws of addition for the Boolean algebra.

Table 8.6 Laws of addition

A	*A*	*A* + *A*
0	0	0
1	1	1

Table 8.6 lists two important laws of addition. The first law of addition states that the addition of 0 any number of times to itself in the Boolean algebra gives only 0 as the output. The second law of addition states that the addition of 1 to itself any number of times in the Boolean algebra gives the output as 1 only.

8.6.3 Commutative Laws

The commutative laws state that the resultant of the multiplication (AND operation) and the addition (OR operation) performed on two or more Boolean variables will be same irrespective of the order of the variables. The commutative law for multiplication says that:

$$A.B = B.A$$

Figure 8.6 illustrates the commutative law of multiplication using electrical circuits.

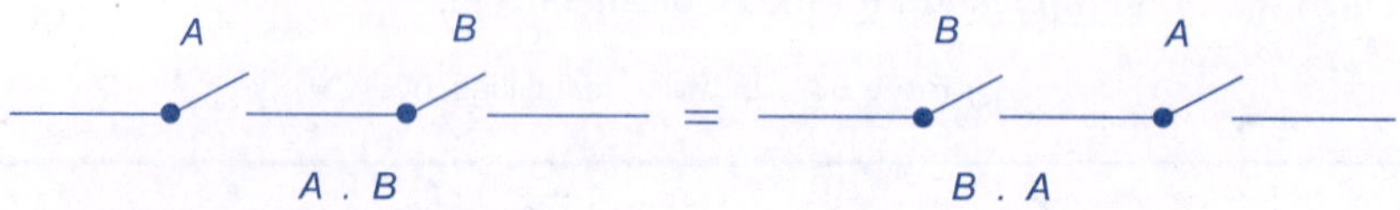

Fig. 8.6 Illustrating the commutative law of multiplication using electrical circuits

We can also verify the commutative law for multiplication using truth tables. Table 8.7 lists the truth table for the AND operation performed on the variables, *A* and *B*.

Table 8.7 AND operation involving the variables, *A* and *B*

A	*B*	*A.B*
0	0	0
0	1	0
1	0	0
1	1	1

Table 8.8 lists the truth table for the AND operation performed on the variables, *B* and *A*.

Table 8.8 AND operation involving the variables *B* and *A*

B	*A*	*B.A*
0	0	0
1	0	0
0	1	0
1	1	1

The truth tables Table 8.7 and Table 8.8 verify the commutative law for multiplication.
The commutative law for addition says that:

$$A + B = B + A$$

Figure 8.7 illustrates the commutative law for addition using electrical circuits.

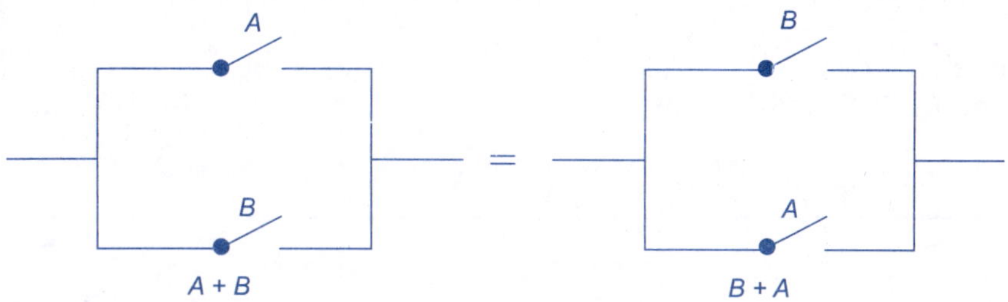

Fig. 8.7 Illustrating the commutative law for addition using electrical circuits

The commutative law for addition can also be verified using the truth tables. Table 8.9 lists the truth table for the OR operation performed on the variables, *A* and *B*.

Table 8.9 OR operation involving the variables, *A* and *B*

A	B	$A+B$
0	0	0
0	1	1
1	0	1
1	1	1

Table 8.10 lists the truth table for the OR operation performed on the variables, *B* and *A*.

Table 8.10 OR operation involving the variables, *B* and *A*

B	A	$B+A$
0	0	0
1	0	1
0	1	1
1	1	1

The truth tables Table 8.9 and Table 8.10 verify the commutative law for addition.

8.6.4 Associative Laws

The associative laws state that the resultant of the multiplication (AND operation) and the addition (OR operation) performed on two or more Boolean variables will be same irrespective of the grouping of the Boolean variables. The associative law for multiplication can be expressed as:

$$A.\ B.\ C = (A.B).C = A.(B.C)$$

Figure 8.8 illustrates the associative law for multiplication using electrical circuits.

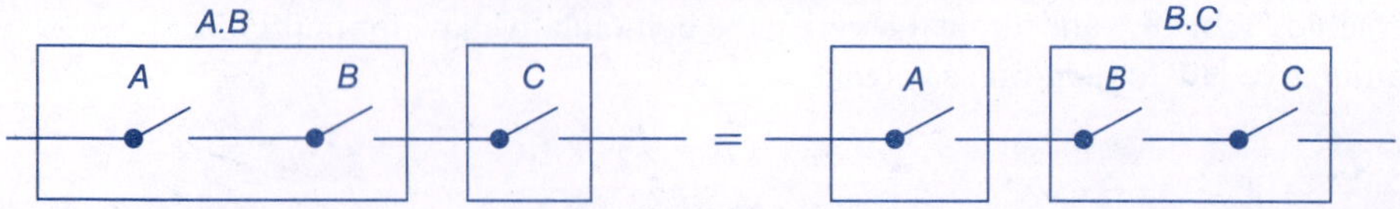

Fig. 8.8 Illustrating the associative law for multiplication using electrical circuits

The associative laws can also be verified using the truth tables. Table 8.11 lists the truth table for the Boolean operation, $(A.B).C$.

Table 8.11 Truth table for the operation, $(A.B).C$ operation

A	B	C	$A.B$	$(A.B).C$
0	0	0	0	0
1	0	0	0	0
0	1	0	0	0
1	1	0	1	0
0	0	1	0	0
1	0	1	0	0
0	1	1	0	0
1	1	1	1	1

Table 8.12 lists the truth table for the Boolean operation, $A.(B.C)$

Table 8.12 Truth table for the operation, $A(B.C)$ operation

A	B	C	$B.C$	$A.(B.C)$
0	0	0	0	0
1	0	0	0	0
0	1	0	0	0
1	1	0	0	0
0	0	1	0	0
1	0	1	0	0
0	1	1	1	0
1	1	1	1	1

The truth tables Table 8.11 and Table 8.12 verify the associative law for multiplication.

The associative law for addition can be expressed as:

$$A + B + C = (A + B) + C = A + (B + C)$$

Figure 8.9 illustrates the associative law for addition using electrical circuits.

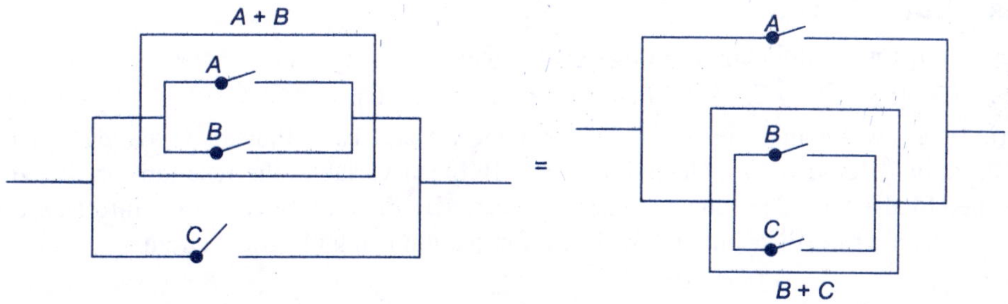

Fig. 8.9 Illustrating the associative law for addition using electrical circuits

Like the associative law for addition, the associative law for multiplication can also be verified using the truth tables.

Table 8.13 lists the truth table for the Boolean operation, $(A + B) + C$.

Table 8.13 Truth table for the operation, $(A + B) + C$

A	B	C	$A + B$	$(A + B) + C$
0	0	0	0	0
1	0	0	1	1
0	1	0	1	1
1	1	0	1	1
0	0	1	0	1
1	0	1	1	1
0	1	1	1	1
1	1	1	1	1

Table 8.14 lists the truth table for the Boolean operation, $A + (B + C)$.

Table 8.14 Truth table for the Boolean operation, $A + (B + C)$

A	B	C	$B + C$	$A + (B + C)$
0	0	0	0	0
1	0	0	0	1
0	1	0	1	1
1	1	0	1	1
0	0	1	1	1
1	0	1	1	1
0	1	1	1	1
1	1	1	1	1

The truth tables shown in Table 8.13 and Table 8.14 verify the associative law for addition.

8.6.5 Distributive Laws

The distributive law for multiplication can be expressed as:

$$A.(B + C) = (A.B) + (A.C)$$

The distributive law for multiplication states that if we add two Boolean variables and multiply the addition of these two Boolean variables with a third Boolean variable, the resultant produced will be the same as obtained by the sum of products of each Boolean variable multiplied by the third Boolean variable.

Figure 8.10 illustrates the distributive law for multiplication using electrical circuits.

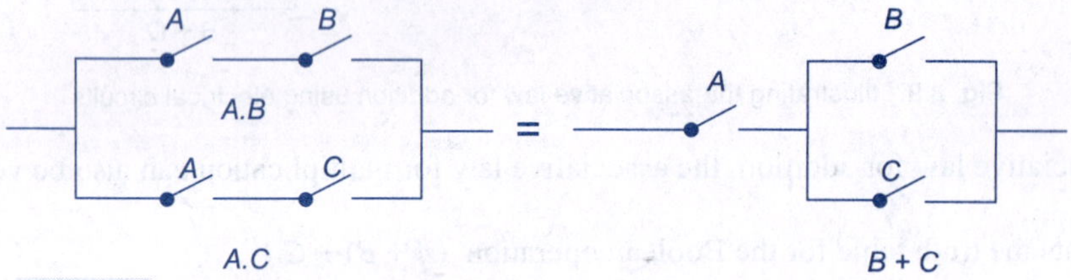

Fig. 8.10 Illustrating the distributive law for multiplication using electrical circuits

The distributive law for multiplication can also be verified using the truth tables. Table 8.15 lists the truth table for the Boolean operation, $(A.B) + (A.C)$.

Table 8.15 Truth table for the operation, (A.B) + (A.C)

A	*B*	*C*	*A.B*	*A.C*	*(A.B) + (A.C)*
0	0	0	0	0	0
1	0	0	0	0	0
0	1	0	0	0	0
1	1	0	1	0	1
0	0	1	0	0	0
1	0	1	0	1	1
0	1	1	0	0	0
1	1	1	1	1	1

Table 8.16 lists the truth table for the Boolean operation, $A.(B + C)$.

Table 8.16 Truth table for the operation, A.(B + C)

A	*B*	*C*	*B + C*	*A.(B + C)*
0	0	0	0	0
1	0	0	0	0
0	1	0	1	0
1	1	0	1	1
0	0	1	1	0
1	0	1	1	1
0	1	1	1	0
1	1	1	1	1

The truth tables shown in the Table 8.15 and Table 8.16 verify the associative law for multiplication. The distributive law for addition can be expressed as:

$$A + (B.C) = (A + B).\ (A + C)$$

Figure 8.11 illustrates the distributive law for addition using electrical circuits.

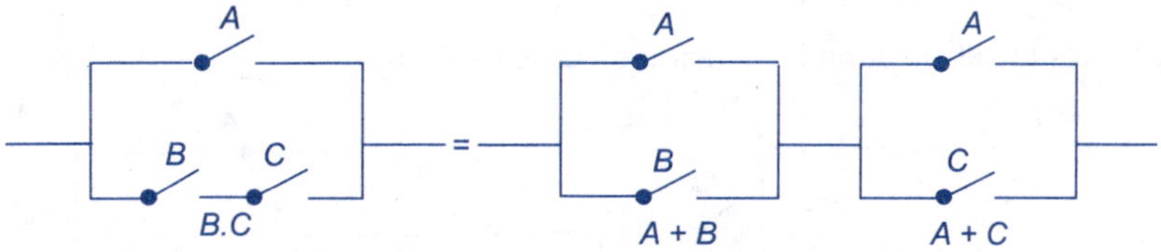

Fig. 8.11 Illustrating the distributive law for addition using electrical circuits

Like the distributive law for multiplication, the distributive law for addition can also be verified using the truth tables. Table 8.17 lists the truth table for the Boolean operation, $(A + B).(A + C)$.

Table 8.17 Truth table for the operation, $(A + B).\ (A + C)$

A	B	C	$A + B$	$A + C$	$(A + B).(A + C)$
0	0	0	0	0	0
1	0	0	1	1	1
0	1	0	1	0	0
1	1	0	1	1	1
0	0	1	0	1	0
1	0	1	1	1	1
0	1	1	1	1	1
1	1	1	1	1	1

Table 8.18 lists the truth table for the Boolean operation, $A + (B.C)$.

Table 8.18 Truth table for the operation, $(A + B).(A + C)$

A	B	C	$B.C$	$A+ (B.C)$
0	0	0	0	0
1	0	0	0	1
0	1	0	0	0
1	1	0	0	1
0	0	1	0	0
1	0	1	0	1
0	1	1	1	1
1	1	1	1	1

The truth tables shown in Table 8.17 and Table 8.18 verify the distributive law for addition.

8.6.6 Absorption Laws

The absorption laws are also known as redundancy laws because they are used to remove the redundant functions in the Boolean expressions. The absorption laws can be expressed as follows:

$$A.(A + B) = A$$
$$A + A.B = A$$

Figure 8.12 illustrates the absorption laws using electrical circuits.

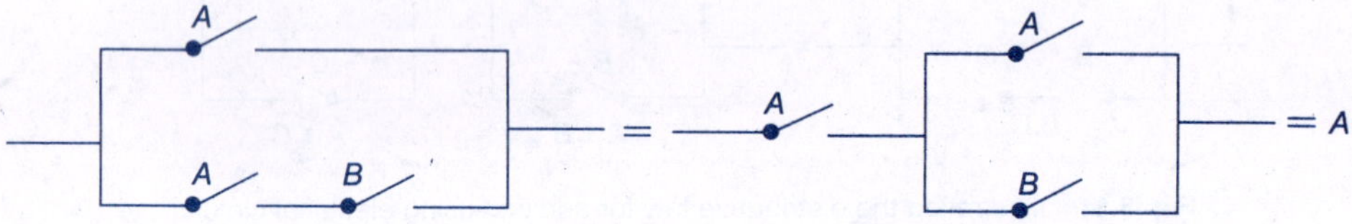

Fig. 8.12 Illustrating the absorption laws using electrical circuits

The absorption laws can also be verified using the truth tables. Table 8.19 lists the truth table for the Boolean operation, $A + (A.B)$.

Table 8.19 Truth table for the operation, $A + (A.B)$

A	B	$A.B$	$A + (A.B)$
0	0	0	0
0	1	0	0
1	0	0	1
1	1	1	1

Table 8.20 lists the truth table for the Boolean operation, $A. (A + B)$.

Table 8.20 Truth table for the operation, $A + (A.B)$

A	B	$A + B$	$A. (A + B)$
0	0	0	0
0	1	1	0
1	0	1	1
1	1	1	1

The truth tables shown in Table 8.19 and Table 8.20 verify the absorption laws of Boolean algebra.

8.6.7 Involution Law

The involution law is also known as the law of double complementation. The involution law states that the double complement of a Boolean variable always gives the Boolean variable itself. The involution law can be expressed as follows:

$$\overline{(\overline{A})} = A$$

Table 8.21 lists the truth table for the verification of the involution law.

Table 8.21 Truth table for involution law

A	$\overline{A}$	$\overline{(\overline{A})}$
0	1	0
1	0	1

8.6.8 Uniqueness to Complement Law

The uniqueness to complement law for addition (OR operation) says that

$$A + \overline{A} = 1$$

The uniqueness to complement law for addition states that the OR operation performed on the Boolean variable and its complement always yields a logical value, 1.

The uniqueness to complement law for multiplication (AND operation) is:

$$A.\overline{A} = 0$$

The uniqueness to complement law for multiplication states that the AND operation performed on the Boolean variable and its complement always yields a logical value, 0.

The uniqueness to complement laws can also be verified using the truth tables. Table 8.22 lists the truth table for the Boolean operation, $A.\overline{A}$.

Table 8.22 Truth table for the operation, $A.\overline{A}$

A	$\overline{A}$	$A.\overline{A}$
0	1	0
1	0	0

Table 8.23 lists the truth table for the Boolean operation, $A + \overline{A}$.

Table 8.23 Truth table for the operation, $A.\overline{A}$

A	$\overline{A}$	$A + \overline{A}$
0	1	1
1	0	1

The truth tables shown in the Table 8.22 and Table 8.23 verify the uniqueness to complement law.

8.7 DEMORGAN'S THEOREM

DeMorgan, a mathematician, provided two important rules for addition (OR operation) and multiplication (AND operation). The DeMorgan's law for addition says that

$$\overline{A+B} = \overline{A}.\overline{B}$$

The first part of the law states that the complement of the sums is equal to the product of the complements of the individual elements. According to the first part of DeMorgan's law, the inverted output of OR operation is equal to the output of the inverted inputs of the AND operation.

Figure 8.13 illustrates the DeMorgan's law for addition using electrical circuits.

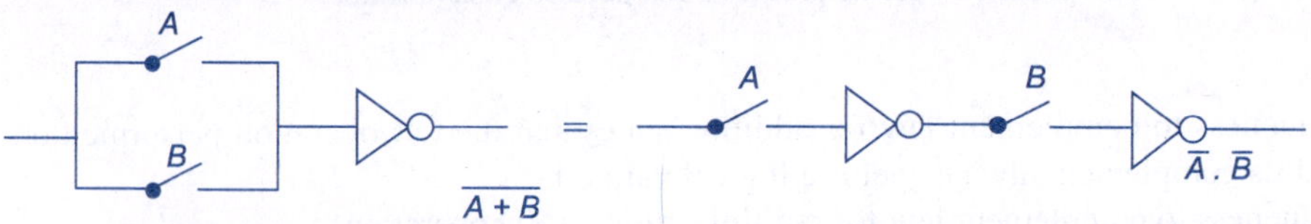

Fig. 8.13 Illustrating the DeMorgan's law for addition using electrical circuits

DeMorgan's law for addition can also be verified using the truth tables. Table 8.24 lists the truth table for the Boolean operation, $\overline{A+B}$.

Table 8.24 Truth table for the operation, $\overline{A+B}$

A	B	$A+B$	$\overline{A+B}$
0	0	0	1
0	1	1	0
1	0	1	0
1	1	1	0

Table 8.25 lists the truth table for the Boolean operation, $\overline{A}.\overline{B}$.

Table 8.25 Truth table for the operation, $\overline{A}.\overline{B}$

A	B	$\overline{A}$	$\overline{B}$	$\overline{A}.\overline{B}$
0	0	1	1	1
0	1	1	0	0
1	0	0	1	0
1	1	0	0	0

The truth tables shown in the Table 8.24 and Table 8.25 verify the DeMorgan's law for addition.

The DeMorgan's law for multiplication says that

$$\overline{A.B} = \overline{A} + \overline{B}$$

The DeMorgan's law for multiplication states that the complement of a product is equal to the sum of the complements of the individual elements. According to this part of the DeMorgan's theorem, the inverted output of AND operation is equal to the output of the inverted inputs of the OR operation.

Figure 8.14 illustrates the DeMorgan's law for multiplication using electrical circuits.

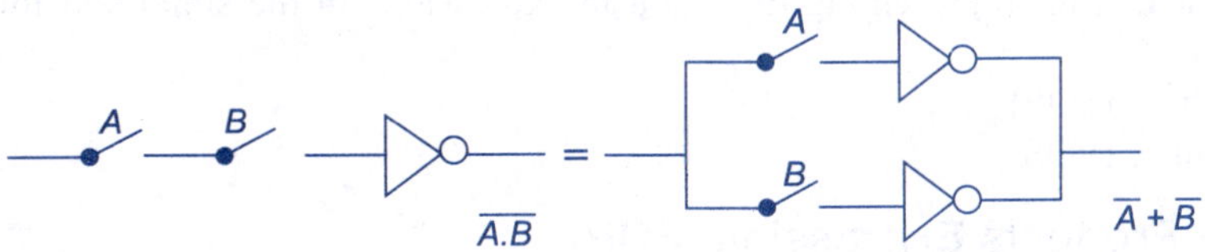

Fig. 8.14 Illustrating the DeMorgan's law for multiplication using electrical circuits

Like DeMorgan's law for addition, DeMorgan's law for multiplication can also be verfied using truth tables. Table 8.26 lists the truth table for the Boolean operation, $\overline{A.B}$.

Table 8.26 Truth table for the operation, $\overline{A.B}$

A	B	$A.B$	$\overline{A.B}$
0	0	0	1
0	1	0	1
1	0	0	1
1	1	1	0

Table 8.27 lists the truth table for the Boolean operation, $\overline{A} + \overline{B}$.

Table 8.27 Truth table for the operation, $\overline{A} + \overline{B}$

A	B	$\overline{A}$	$\overline{B}$	$\overline{A} + \overline{B}$
0	0	1	1	1
0	1	1	0	1
1	0	0	1	1
1	1	0	0	0

The truth tables shown in the Table 8.26 and Table 8.27 verify the DeMorgan's law for multiplication.

8.8 BOOLEAN EXPRESSIONS

Boolean expressions are made up of Boolean variables and Boolean operators. A Boolean expression determines the number of the logic gates required to create an electrical, a digital or a logical circuit. The more the complexity of the Boolean expression, the more is the complexity of the electrical, the digital or the logical circuit. So, in order to create simpler circuits, the Boolean expressions should be simplified. There are two standards for representing the Boolean expressions in the simplified form. These standard forms are as follows:

- Sum-of-Products (SOP)
- Product-of-Sums (POS)

8.8.1 Sum-of-Products Expression (SOP)

The SOP expression is a simplified Boolean expression represented as a combination of the sum of the products of one or more Boolean variables. For example, the following equation represents the SOP form:

$$ABC + B\overline{C} + \overline{A}B$$

The product terms like ABC, $B\overline{C}$ available in the SOP form are called minterms and are represented as m_0, m_1, m_2 and so on. In these minterms, the lowest term, i.e., 0 will be represented in the complemented form and 1 will be represented in the non-complemented form.

A Boolean expression is said to be in canonical SOP form if each product term in the SOP form contains all the Boolean variables. However, these variables may appear in the product terms in any of the two forms, complemented or uncomplemented. For example, if the Boolean function contains three variables, the product terms in the canonical SOP form should contain each of these three variables either in the complemented or the uncomplemented form. Any given SOP expression can be converted into a canonical SOP form. To convert any SOP expression into the canonical SOP form, the following steps should be followed:

1. Analysing the Boolean expression to determine the product terms of the expression.
2. Ensuring that each product term contains all the variables used in the Boolean expression. For example, if the Boolean expression is composed of three variables, namely, A, B and C, then it is checked whether each of the terms contains A, B and C.
3. Multiplying the terms by the sum of the missing variables and their complements, if all the variables are not present in the term.
4. Expanding the Boolean expression and deleting the repeated terms from the expression.

Example 8.1 *Convert* $F(A, B, C) = \overline{A}B + \overline{B}C + \overline{A}C$ *into the canonical SOP form.*

Solution

The given SOP expression is:

$$\overline{A}B + \overline{B}C + \overline{A}C$$

By multiplying each term by the sum of the missing variables and its complement, we obtain:

$$= \overline{A}B\,(C + \overline{C}) + \overline{B}C(A + \overline{A}) + \overline{A}C(B + \overline{B})$$
$$= \overline{A}BC + \overline{A}B\overline{C} + \overline{B}CA + \overline{B}C\overline{A} + \overline{A}CB + \overline{A}C\overline{B}$$

$$= \bar{A}BC + \bar{A}B\bar{C} + A\bar{B}C + \bar{A}\bar{B}C + \bar{A}BC + \bar{A}\bar{B}C$$

$$= \bar{A}BC + \bar{A}B\bar{C} + A\bar{B}C + \bar{A}\bar{B}C, \text{ using the rule } A + A = A$$

$$= 011 + 010 + 101 + 001$$

$$= m_3 + m_2 + m_5 + m_1$$

This is the canonical SOP form of the given Boolean function.
The canonical SOP form of the given Boolean function can also be represented as:

$$F(A, B, C) = \sum(1, 2, 3, 5)$$

Example 8.2 *Convert* $F(A, B, C) = \bar{A}B + A\bar{B} + C$ *to canonical SOP.*

Solution

The given SOP expression is $\bar{A}B + A\bar{B} + C$.
By multiplying each term by the sum of the missing variables and its complement, we obtain:

$$= \bar{A}B(C + \bar{C}) + A\bar{B}(C + \bar{C}) + C(A + \bar{A})(B + \bar{B})$$

$$= \bar{A}BC + \bar{A}B\bar{C} + A\bar{B}C + A\bar{B}\bar{C} + ABC + \bar{A}BC + A\bar{B}C + \bar{A}\bar{B}C$$

$$= \bar{A}BC + \bar{A}B\bar{C} + \bar{A}\bar{B}C + A\bar{B}C + ABC + A\bar{B}\bar{C}$$

$$= 011 + 010 + 001 + 101 + 111 + 100$$

$$= m_3 + m_2 + m_1 + m_5 + m_7 + m_4$$

This is the canonical SOP form of the given Boolean function.
The canonical SOP form of the given Boolean function can also be represented as:

$$F(A, B, C) = \sum(1, 2, 3, 4, 5, 7)$$

8.8.2 Product-of-Sums Expression (POS)

The POS expression is a simplified Boolean expression represented as a combination of the products of the sums of one or more Boolean variables. For example, the following equation represents the POS form:

$$(A + B)\ (A + \bar{B} + C)\ (A + B + \bar{C})$$

The sum terms like $(A + B)$, $(A + \bar{B} + C)$ present in the POS form are called maxterms and are represented as M_0, M_2, M_3 and so on. In these maxterms, the lowest term, i.e., 0 will be represented in the non-complemented form and 1 will be represented in the complemented form.

A Boolean expression is said to be in the canonical POS form if each sum term in the POS form contains all the Boolean variables. To convert any POS expression into a canonical POS form, the following steps should be followed:

1. Analysing the Boolean expression to determine the sum terms in the expression.
2. Ensuring that each sum term contains all the variables used in the Boolean expression. For example, if the Boolean expression is composed of three variables, namely, A, B and C, then checking that each of the terms contains A, B and C.

3. Adding the term by the product of the missing variable and its complement, if all the variables are not present in the term.
4. Expanding the Boolean expression and deleting the repeated terms from the expression.

Example 8.3 *Convert* $F(A,B,C) = (\overline{A} + \overline{B})(\overline{B} + C)$ *to the canonical POS.*

Solution

The given POS expression is:

$$(\overline{A}+\overline{B})\ (\overline{B}+C)$$

By adding the product of the missing variable and its complement to the given expression, we obtain:

$$[(\overline{A}+\overline{B})+C\overline{C}][(\overline{B}+C)+A\overline{A}]$$
$$=(\overline{A}+\overline{B}+C\overline{C})\ (\overline{B}+C+A\overline{A})$$
$$=(\overline{A}+\overline{B}+C)\ (\overline{A}+\overline{B}+\overline{C})\ (\overline{B}+C+A)\ (\overline{B}+C+\overline{A}) \text{ Applying distributive law}$$
$$=(\overline{A}+\overline{B}+C)\ (\overline{A}+\overline{B}+\overline{C})\ (A+\overline{B}+C)\ (\overline{A}+\overline{B}+C)$$
$$=\ (\overline{A}+\overline{B}+C)\ (\overline{A}+\overline{B}+\overline{C})\ (A+\overline{B}+C)$$
$$=\ (110)\ (111)\ (010)$$
$$=(M_6)\ (M_7)\ (M_2)$$

The canonical POS form of the given Boolean function can also be represented as:

$$F(A,B,C) = \prod(2,6,7)$$

8.9 VENN DIAGRAM

Venn diagram is an important graphics model used to explain the various laws and theorems of Boolean algebra. The Venn diagrams are used to illustrate the different Boolean operations using a rectangle consisting of a number of circles inside it, where each circle represents a Boolean variable. The internal and the external areas of the circle in the rectangle represent the Boolean variable and its complement respectively.

Figure 8.15 shows the Venn diagram for two Boolean variables, *A* and *B*. Various regions are marked as ①, ②, ③, ④ that represent the following Boolean operations:

Region ① $= A.\overline{B}$

Region ② $= A.B$

Region ③ $= \overline{A}.B$

Region ④ $= \overline{A}.\overline{B}$

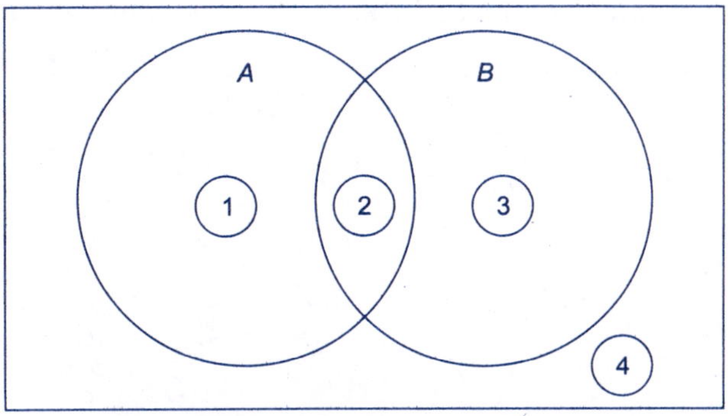

Fig. 8.15 Venn diagram for two variables

Note that (1) + (2) = $A.\overline{B} + A.B = A\,(B + \overline{B}) = A$

The various operations of Boolean algebra can also be illustrated using the Venn diagrams. Figure 8.16 shows the Venn diagram for the Boolean AND operation.

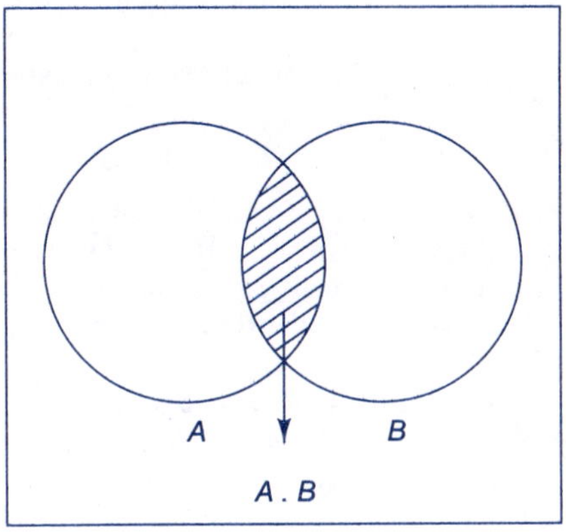

Fig. 8.16 The Venn diagram illustrating the AND operation

The Boolean AND operation is represented by the overlapped area of the circles. The overlapped area of the circles will contain 1 as the value if both the Boolean variables hold the value 1. The other area in the Venn diagram will contain 0 as the value if one of the Boolean variables holds the value 0.

Figure 8.17 shows the Venn diagram for the Boolean OR operation.

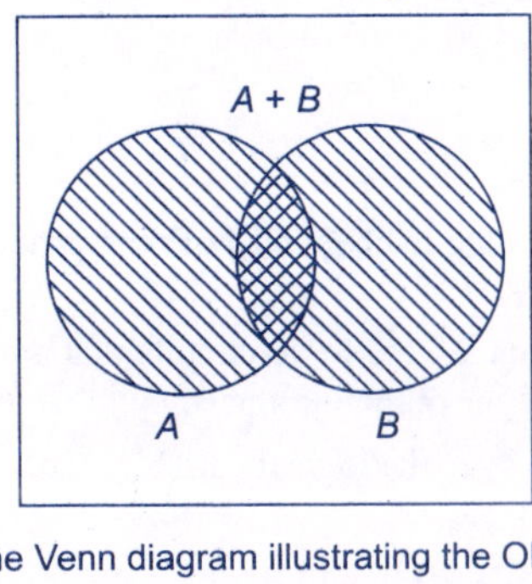

Fig. 8.17 The Venn diagram illustrating the OR operation

The Boolean OR operation is represented by the internal areas of both the circles as well as by the overlapped area of the circles.

Figure 8.18 shows the Venn diagram for the Boolean NOT operation.

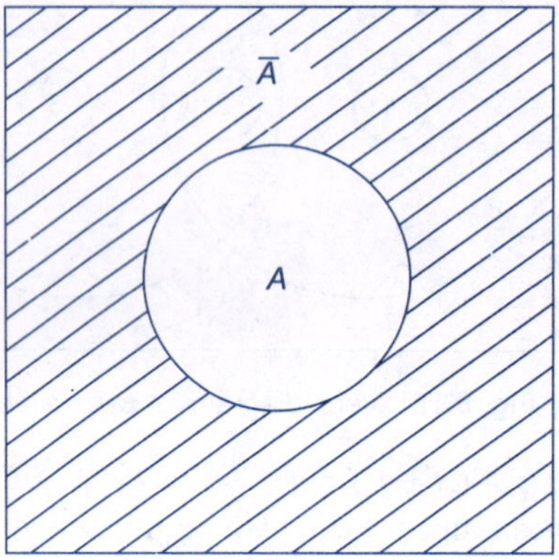

Fig. 8.18 The Venn diagram illustrating the NOT operation

The Boolean NOT operation is represented by the whole of the external area of the circle.

Chapter Summary

George Boole developed a system of logic known as Boolean algebra in 1854. Claude Shannon applied this logic to simplify the designing of the switching circuits, which are also called logic circuits, in the digital system. The logic circuits can be designed by first deriving the Boolean expressions and then simplifying them by using different laws and postulates of Boolean algebra. The Boolean expressions are made up of Boolean variables and Boolean operators. The Boolean variables unlike the numeric variables can hold only two values, 0 and 1. The different Boolean operators in Boolean algebra are logical addition operator, logical multiplication operator and logical complement operator. These operators are used to perform three basic Boolean operations: AND operation, OR operation and NOT operation. The Boolean expressions can be simplified using the various laws of Boolean algebra such as laws of multiplication, laws of addition, commutative laws, associative laws, distributive laws and DeMorgan's laws.

The two standard forms of Boolean expressions are SOP and POS. In SOP, the Boolean expression is represented as the sum of the products of one or more Boolean variables. In POS, the Boolean expression is represented as the product of the sums of one or more Boolean variables. In the Boolean algebra, the Venn diagrams can also be used to illustrate the various Boolean operations graphically.

Key Terms to Remember

- **Boolean algebra**: Boolean algebra is the mathematics of representing the operations performed on the switching circuits in the form of expressions.
- **Switching circuits**: Switching circuits are the logic circuits that are built from various logic gates such as AND, OR, and NOT and are used to change the output produced by the logic gates from one state to another.
- **Boolean variables**: Boolean variables are the logical variables that can take only one of the two numerical values, 0 and 1.

- **Logical addition operator**: Logical addition operator is denoted by the symbol, '+' and is used to produce the value 1 if either of the Boolean variables holds a value 1.
- **Logical multiplication operator**: Logical multiplication is a Boolean operator denoted by the symbol, '.' and is used to produce the value 1 only if both the Boolean variables hold the value 1.
- **Logical complement operator**: Logical complement operator is a Boolean operator denoted by the symbol, '—' and is used to complement the value of its input Boolean variable.
- **Boolean expressions**: Boolean expressions are the logical expressions made up of Boolean variables and Boolean operators.
- **Boolean algebra postulates**: Boolean algebra postulates are the assumptions used to determine the additional theorems and properties for the Boolean algebra.
- **Principle of duality**: Principle of duality states that the swapping of 0 and 1 and '+' and '.' in any statement of the Boolean algebra does not change the trueness of that statement.
- **SOP expression**: It is a simplified Boolean expression form in which a Boolean expression is represented as a combination of the sum of the products of one or more Boolean variables.
- **POS expression**: It is a simplified Boolean expression form in which a Boolean expression is represented as a combination of the products of the sums of one or more Boolean variables.
- **Venn diagrams**: Venn diagrams are the graphical models used to explain the various laws and theorems of Boolean algebra.

Review Questions

Fill in the Blanks

1. Boolean algebra is an _______ system used for designing logic circuits.
2. The Boolean algebra is also known as _______.
3. The concept of Boolean algebra was developed by _______.
4. Boolean variables can hold only _______ values.
5. The logical addition operator is denoted by the symbol _______.
6. The logical multiplication operator is denoted by the symbol _______.
7. The logical complement operator is also known as _______ operator.
8. The identity element for the logical multiplication operator is _______.
9. The rules of Boolean algebra help in _______ the complicated Boolean expressions.
10. The law of multiplication states that if a Boolean variable is multiplied with itself any number of times, then the result will be the _______ Boolean variable.
11. Commutative law states that the resultant of the operations, AND and OR performed on two or more Boolean variables will be the same, irrespective of the _______ of the variables.
12. Associative law states that the resultant of the operations AND and OR performed on two or more Boolean variables will be the same irrespective of the _______ of the Boolean variables.
13. Absorption laws are also known as _______ laws.
14. The involution law is also known as the law of _______.
15. According to the DeMorgan's law, the complement of the sums is equal to the _______ of the _______ of the individual elements.

16. _______ and _______ are the two standards for representing the Boolean expressions in the simplified form.
17. Venn diagram is an important _______model that can be used to explain the various laws and theorems of Boolean algebra.

Multiple Choice Questions

1. What is the purpose of Boolean algebra?
   A. To perform mathematical calculations
   B. To simplify any algebraic expressions
   C. To minimise number of switches in designing logic circuits
   D. None of the above
2. Who was the inventor of Boolean algebra?
   A. George Boole B. Claude Shannon C. Aristotle D. Von Neumann
3. The variables in Boolean algebra can hold:
   A. Any decimal value B. Either 0 or 1 C. Any octal value D. Any numeric value
4. Which of the following symbols is used to denote the logical addition operator in Boolean algebra?
   A. '.' B. '&' C. '+' D. '++'
5. Which of the following symbols is used to denote the logical multiplication operator in Boolean algebra?
   A. '.' B. '&' C. '+' D. '*'
6. How many variables can the logical complement operator have?
   A. Exactly one B. Exactly two C. Either one or two D. None of the above
7. What is the purpose of using Boolean operations in Boolean algebra?
   A. Simplifying the design of switching circuits B. Changing the values of Boolean variables
   C. Constructing the switching circuits D. None of the above
8. In the circuit given below, which of the following conditions will cause the flow of current from X to Y?

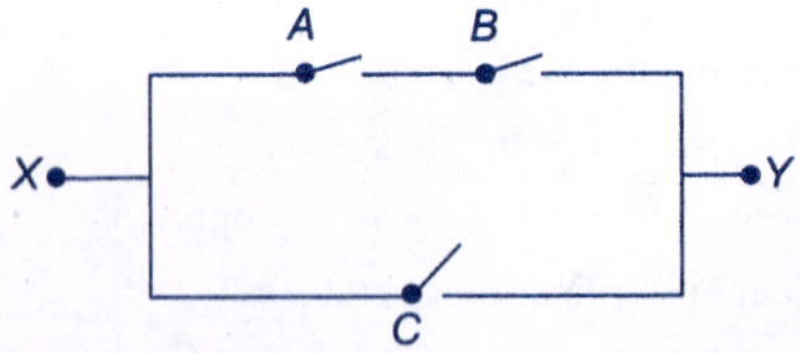

   A. $A = 1, B = 0, C = 0$ B. $A = 0, B = 0, C = 1$ C. $A = 0, B = 1, C = 0$ D. $A = 0, B = 0, C = 0$
9. What is the output of the Boolean operation 1 + 1?
   A. 0 B. 2 C. 1 D. None of the above
10. What is the purpose of the NOT operation in Boolean algebra?
    A. To increment the value of its input variable by 1
    B. To keep the value of its input variable same
    C. To decrement the value of its input variable by 1
    D. To switch the value of its input variable
11. Which of the following statements about the principle of duality is true?

A. It is used to simplify the Boolean expressions.

B. It is used to change the logical addition operator with logical complement operator.

C. It is used to derive the new theorems and statements without actually proving them.

D. None of the above

12. Which of the following expressions represents the law of multiplication?

A. $A + A = A$ B. $A.A = A$ C. $A.B = B.A$ D. $A + B = B + A$

13. What is the purpose of absorption laws?

A. To switch the values of all the Boolean variables in the Boolean expressions

B. To remove the redundant functions in the Boolean expressions

C. To verify the trueness of the Boolean expressions

D. None of the above

14. The involution law is also known as:

A. Law of double complementation B. Law of single complementation

C. Law of one's complement D. Law of two's complement

15. Which of the following expressions represents the uniqueness to complement law for addition operation?

A. $A + \overline{A} = 1$ B. $A.\overline{A} = 0$ C. $A + B = 1$ D. None of the above

16. Which of the following is not a valid SOP expression?

A. $ABC + B\overline{C} + \overline{A}BC$ B. $(A + B)(B + C) + B\overline{C} + \overline{A}BC$

C. $AB + \overline{A}B\overline{C} + \overline{A}BC$ D. None of the above

17. What is the purpose of Venn diagrams in Boolean algebra?

A. The Venn diagrams are used to explain the various laws and theorems of Boolean algebra.

B. The Venn diagrams are used to prove the laws of Boolean algebra.

C. The Venn diagrams are used to derive new theorems and laws in Boolean algebra.

D. All of the above

Discussion Questions

1. What is the importance of Boolean algebra in the designing of switching circuits?
2. What are the different elements of Boolean algebra? Explain all of them in detail.
3. What is the purpose of logical complement operator? Can the logical complement operator be used on two Boolean variables at the same time?
4. What are the different primary rules for evaluating Boolean expressions?
5. What is the use of the postulates of Boolean algebra in designing switching circuits?
6. Explain all the operations of Boolean algebra in detail.
7. Explain the usefulness of the principle of duality in Boolean algebra.
8. What is the dual of the Boolean expression, $A + \overline{A}B + A\overline{B}$?
9. What do you understand by the laws of Boolean algebra?
10. What is the difference between the laws of multiplication and the laws of addition?
11. Why are the absorption laws also called redundancy laws?

12. What do you understand by involution law? Why is it called the law of double complementation?
13. What is the importance of DeMorgan's theorem in Boolean algebra?
14. Which are the two different standards available for representing the Boolean expressions?
15. What is the canonical SOP form? What are the different steps required for converting the SOP expression into the canonical SOP form?
16. What is the canonical POS form? What are the different steps required for converting the POS expression into the canonical POS form?
17. What is the canonical SOP form of the Boolean function, $\overline{A}BC + \overline{A}C + \overline{A}B$?
18. What is the canonical POS form of the Boolean function, $A.B + \overline{A}C$?
19. Explain the importance of Venn diagrams in Boolean algebra.
20. Explain the associative law of Boolean algebra using a Venn diagram.
21. Prove that $(A + B).(A + C)$ is equivalent to $A + (B.C)$, using the method of simplification, without using truth tables or electric circuits.
22. Obtain a Boolean expression for the switching circuit shown below:

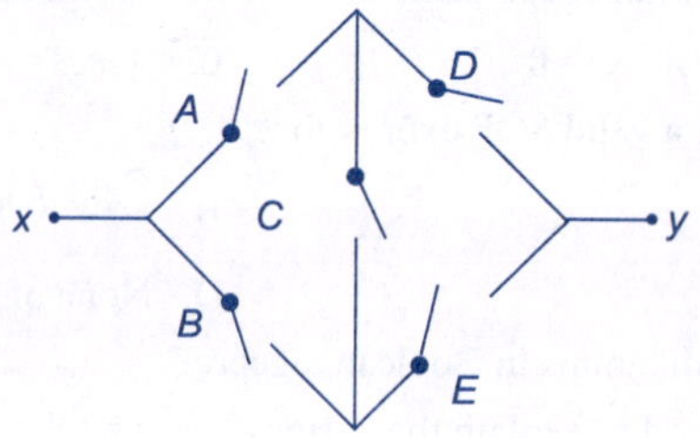

23. Draw the switching circuit and prepare the truth table for each of the following Boolean expressions:
    (a) $A. (B + C)$
    (b) $A + \overline{A}.B$
24. Simplify the following expressions.
    (a) $ABC + A\overline{B}C + \overline{A}\overline{B}C$
    (b) $A (B + C) + A + AB$
25. Given below is a Venn diagram for three variables *A*, *B*, and *C*. Indicate the regions depicted by the following expressions.

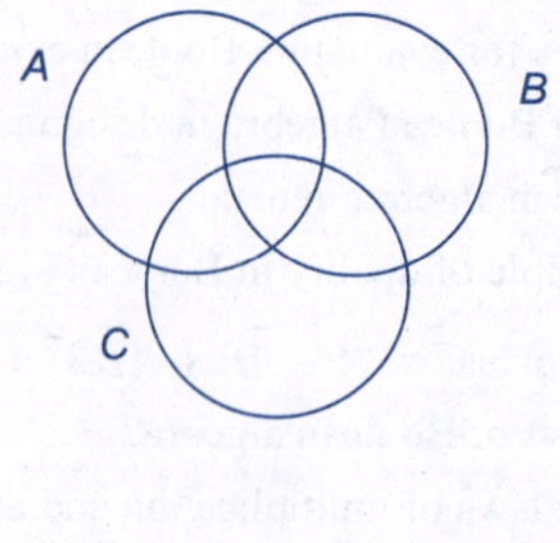

    (a) $A + BC$
    (b) $(A + B) (A + C)$

CHAPTER 9

LOGIC GATES AND DIGITAL CIRCUITS

Chapter Outline

Chapter Objectives

In this chapter, we will learn:

- Basic concepts related to logic gates.
- Steps required to convert the Boolean functions into logic diagrams and vice versa.
- Fundamentals of adder and flip-flop circuits.
- Different application areas of the flip-flops.

9.1 INTRODUCTION

Logic gates and digital circuits play a very important role in the working of a computer system. A computer system basically comprises of two types of components—software and hardware. The software components refer to the programs that act as an interface between the end user and the hardware components. The hardware components refer to the electronic circuitry, which is actually responsible for executing an instruction. The electronic circuitry comprises of various digital components such as basic logic gates, derived logic gates and flip-flops that accept binary input and produce binary output. These components are used in designing the execution unit of a computer system that performs arithmetic and logical operations.

A logic gate is an electronic switch which produces an electrical output signal (representing 0 or 1) based on one or more input signals (representing 0 or 1) using the principle of Boolean logic, such as AND, OR, or NOT.

The logic gates are used to design various combinational circuits, such as half adders and full adders. These circuits produce output on the basis of the input provided to the digital circuit. Another type of circuits, known as sequential circuits can also be designed using logic gates. The output generated by these circuits depends on the present input value as well as on the previous output of the circuit. Sequential circuits are used in designing registers and counters, which perform special tasks such as storing the data and counting the clock cycles.

9.2 BASIC LOGIC GATES

Basic logic gates are building blocks of digital circuits that perform various logical operations such as AND, OR and NOT on binary input. The value of the inputs as well as the output is either 0 or 1. The value 0 represents low signal while the value 1 represents high signal. Low signal indicates that no power is being supplied to the circuit while high signal indicates that a power supply of +5 volts is being supplied to the circuit. The values of inputs and the corresponding output of the logic gates can be represented using a table called truth table. The following are the basic logic gates:

- AND
- OR
- NOT

9.2.1 AND Gate

The AND gate contains two input lines, *A* and *B* and one output line, *Y*. The output of AND gate is true if and only if both the inputs are true. Figure 9.1 shows the circuit symbol of the AND gate.

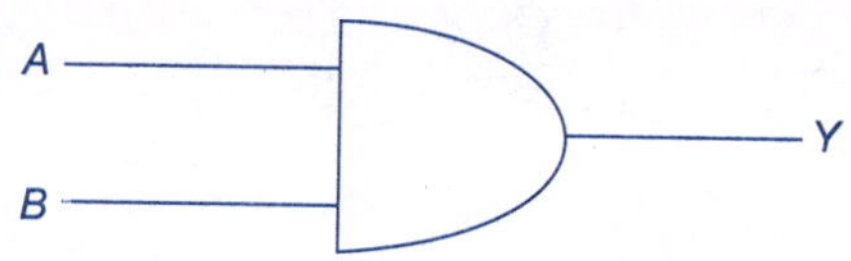

Fig. 9.1 The circuit symbol of AND gate

Note: *An AND gate can have more than two inputs.*

AND gate can be logically expressed as:

$$Y = A.B$$

Table 9.1 shows the truth table of AND gate.

Table 9.1 The truth table of AND gate.

Input *A*	Input *B*	Output *Y* (*A.B*)
0	0	0
0	1	0
1	0	0
1	1	1

An AND gate can be considered as a *coincidence detector* for the HIGH condition. The HIGH output is produced only when all the inputs coincide at the HIGH level.

9.2.2 OR Gate

The OR gate contains two input lines, *A* and *B* and one output line, *Y*. The output of OR gate is true if any one of the inputs is true. However, if both the inputs are false then the output is also false. Figure 9.2 shows the circuit symbol of OR gate.

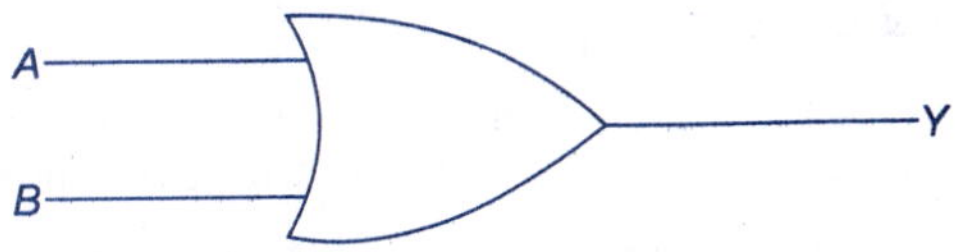

Fig. 9.2 The circuit symbol of OR gate

Note: *An OR gate can have more than two inputs.*

OR gate can be logically expressed as:

$$Y = A + B$$

Table 9.2 shows the truth table of OR gate.

Table 9.2 The truth table of OR gate

Input A	Input B	Output Y $(A + B)$
0	0	0
0	1	1
1	0	1
1	1	1

An OR gate can be thought of as a coincidence detector for the LOW condition. A LOW output results only when all the inputs available coincide at the LOW level.

9.2.3 NOT Gate

The NOT gate, contains only one input line, i.e., *A* and one output line, i.e., *Y*. The NOT gate inverts the value of the input for producing the output. For example, if 1 is provided as an input to the NOT gate then the output will be 0 and vice-versa. The NOT gate is therefore popularly known as an *inverter*. Figure 9.3 shows the circuit symbol of NOT gate.

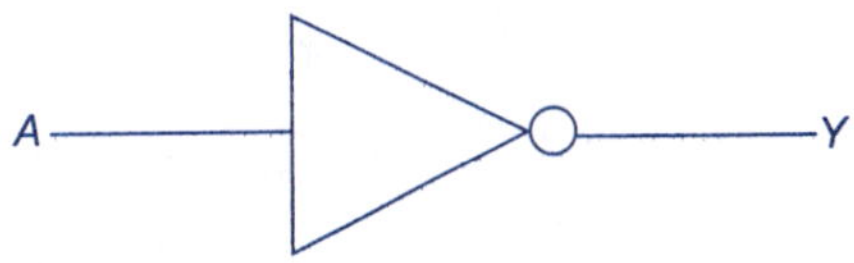

Fig. 9.3 The circuit symbol of NOT gate

The NOT gate can be logically expressed as:

$$Y = \overline{A}$$

Table 9.3 shows the truth table of NOT gate.

Table 9.3 The truth table of NOT gate

Input A	Output Y $(\overline{A})$
0	1
1	0

9.2.4 Practical Logic Circuits

The basic logic gates are implemented with the help of circuits belonging to different logic families. These circuits are constructed using different combinations of electronic components such as diode, resistor and transistor. Diode is a semiconductor device that allows the current to pass through it in only one direction. Resistor is an electrical device that controls the flow of current in an electronic circuit. Transistor is a semiconductor device that acts as a switch for controlling the flow of electricity in an electronic circuit.

The working of a logic gate depends on the logic family that is used to design the logic gate. On the basis of the various combinations of diode, resistor and transistor, the logic families are categorised into the following types:

- Diode Logic (DL)
- Diode-Transistor Logic (DTL)
- Transistor-Transistor Logic (TTL)

Diode Logic In a DL logic gate, the diode acts as a logical switch that allows the current to pass in only one direction. DL family can be used to implement AND and OR logic gates. In a DL logic gate, each input line is connected with a diode. In the AND gate implementation, both the diodes are connected in the reverse directions. While in the OR gate implementation, both the diodes are connected in the forward direction. A register is also connected in the circuit to set the output at logic 1 state.

Figure 9.4 shows the AND and OR gate implementation in the DL logic family.

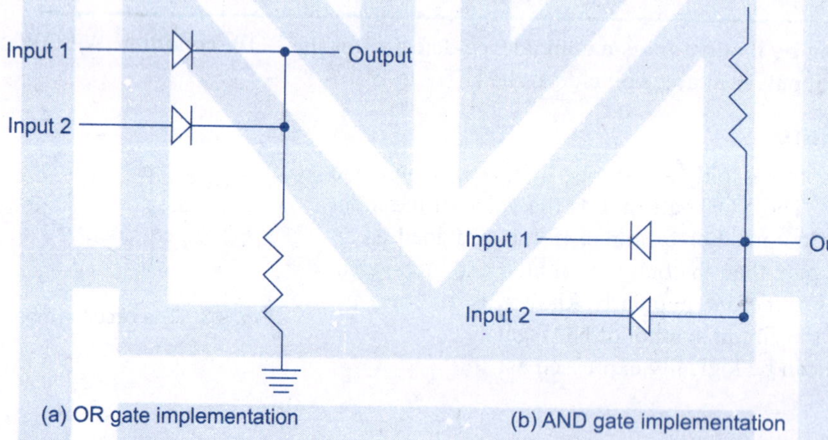

Fig. 9.4 AND and OR gate implementation in the DL logic family

The disadvantages associated with DL family are:

- The output signal is degraded.
- It cannot be used for the implementation of NOT gate.

Diode-transistor Logic The DTL family uses a transistor to amplify and preserve the output signal of a circuit. It also supports the inversion of a signal, which helps to implement NOT gate. Thus, DTL family eliminates both the disadvantages associated with the DL family. The only difference between the DL and the DTL family is the use of an extra transistor for maintaining the stability of the output signal. Except for the additional transistor, the logic circuit for the AND and OR gate implementation remains same in DTL.

The disadvantage associated with the DTL logic family is that the diode construction occupies more space on the Integrated Chip (IC).

Transistor-transistor Logic In the TTL family, all the diodes connected with the input lines are replaced with a transistor. The smaller size of the transistor eliminates the disadvantage of diode occupying more space in the ICs. The TTL family is used as a standard for the manufacturing if ICs.

9.3 DERIVED LOGIC GATES

The derived logic gates are those logic gates that perform logical operations on binary inputs with the help of combination of two or more basic logic gates. The various derived logic gates are:

- NAND
- NOR
- XOR
- XNOR

9.3.1 NAND Gate

NAND gate is a series combination of AND and NOT gates. The output of NAND gate is true if any one of the inputs or both the inputs are false. On the other hand, the output is false if both the inputs are true. Figure 9.5 shows the circuit symbol of NAND gate. The circle at the output denotes the logical inversion.

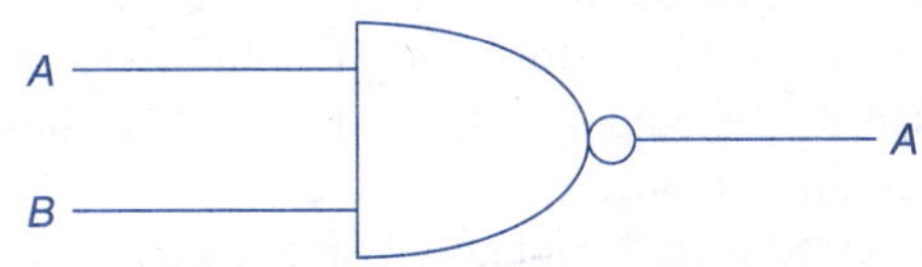

Fig. 9.5 The circuit symbol of NAND gate

The NAND gate can be logically expressed as:

$$Y = \overline{A.B}$$

Table 9.4 shows the truth table of NAND gate.

Table 9.4 The truth table of NAND gate

Input A	Input B	Output Y
0	0	1
0	1	1
1	0	1
1	1	0

As with AND, a NAND gate can have more inputs.

9.3.2 NOR Gate

The NOR gate is a series combination of OR and NOT gates. The output of NOR gate is true if and only if both the inputs are false. Figure 9.6 shows the circuit symbol of NOR gate. The circle at the output denotes the logical inversion.

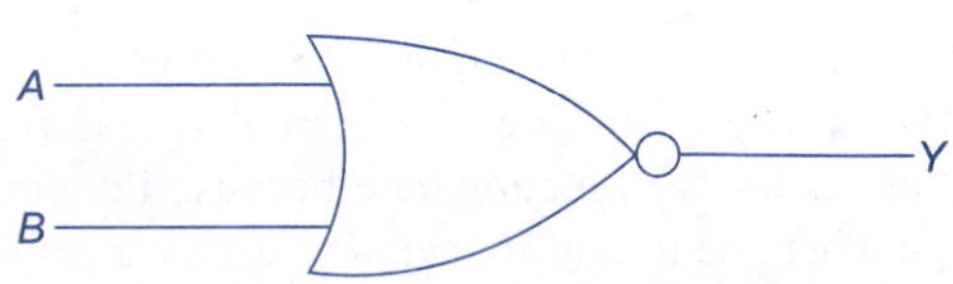

Fig. 9.6 The circuit symbol of NOR gate

The NOR gate can be logically expressed as:

$$Y = \overline{A + B}$$

Table 9.5 shows the truth table of NOR gate.

Table 9.5 The truth table of NOR gate

Input A	Input B	Output Y
0	0	1
0	1	0
1	0	0
1	1	0

A NOR gate can also have more than two inputs.

9.3.3 XOR Gate

The XOR gate is also called Exclusive-OR gate. The output of XOR gate is true if any one of the inputs is true. However, if both the inputs are same, the output is false. Figure 9.7 shows the circuit symbol of XOR gate. The XOR is also referred to as "inequality" function gate because the output is true when the inputs are *not equal*.

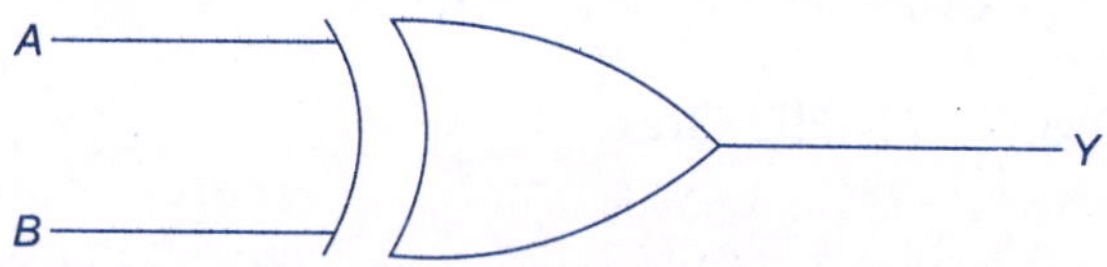

Fig. 9.7 The circuit symbol of XOR gate

The XOR gate can be logically expressed as:

$$Y = A \oplus B$$

Table 9.6 shows the truth table of XOR gate.

Table 9.6 The truth table of XOR gate

Input A	Input B	Output Y
0	0	0
0	1	1
1	0	1
1	1	0

9.3.4 XNOR Gate

The XNOR gate is a combination of XOR and NOT gates. The output of XNOR gate is true if both the inputs are same. Figure 9.8 shows the circuit symbol of XNOR gate. The XNOR is also referred to as "equality" function gate because the output is true when the inputs are *equal* to each other.

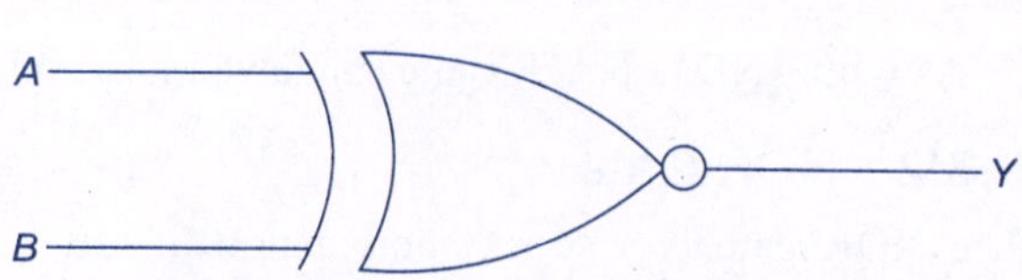

Fig. 9.8 The circuit symbol of XNOR gate

The XNOR gate can be logically expressed as:

$$\overline{A \oplus B}$$

Table 9.7 shows the truth table of XNOR gate.

Table 9.7 The truth table of XNOR gate

Input A	Input B	Output Y
0	0	1
0	1	0
1	0	0
1	1	1

9.4 CONVERSION OF BOOLEAN FUNCTIONS

All logical operations—such as AND and OR—can be expressed in the form of Boolean expressions. Boolean expressions enable a designer to express the complete logic of a digital circuit. Boolean expressions can be simplified or reduced in order to reduce the size and complexity of a digital circuit. Boolean expressions can be converted into an equivalent logic diagram and vice versa.

9.4.1 Boolean Expression to Logic Diagram

Before learning the process of creating an equivalent logic diagram of a Boolean expression, we must understand the types of Boolean expressions. A Boolean expression can be of two types, Sum Of Product (SOP) and Product Of Sum (POS). In the SOP Boolean expression, different product terms are combined with the addition operators, while in the POS Boolean expression, different sum terms are combined with the product operator. The product terms in SOP Boolean expression are called minterms, while the sum terms in POS Boolean expression are called maxterms.

To draw a logic circuit diagram from a Boolean expression, we need to perform the following steps:

1. Simplify the given Boolean expression using Karnaugh map (k-map).
2. Identify the variables present in the simplified Boolean expression.
3. Draw an input line corresponding to each of the input variables.
4. Draw the corresponding logic gates for the terms contained in the Boolean expression.

Table 9.8 lists the terms and symbols related to the logic gates.

Table 9.8 The terms and symbols related to logic gates

Terms	Logic gate	Symbol
Product term	AND gate	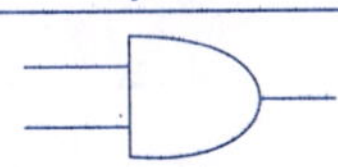
Sum term	OR gate	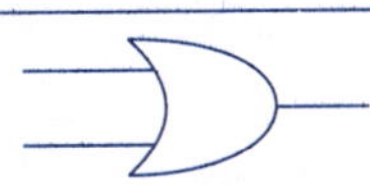
Inversion	NOT gate	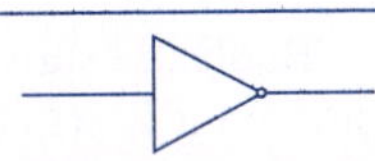

Simplification of Boolean Expression using the k-map K-map is a technique of simplifying the Boolean expressions using graphical representation method. It simplifies the expressions by combining the similar expressions and deleting the repeated variables. K-map expresses all the input and the output values given in the truth table in the form of a graphical representation. Figure 9.9 shows a truth table and its corresponding k-map.

Input *A*	Input *B*	Output *Y*
0	0	0
0	1	1
1	0	0
1	1	1

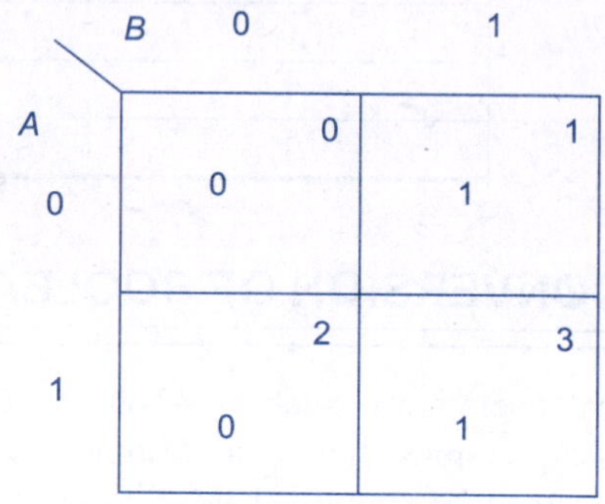

Fig. 9.9 The truth table and its k-map

In Fig. 9.9, the 0's and 1's written at the top of the k-map represent the values of the input variables, *A* and *B*. The values written inside the boxes of the k-map represent the values of the output *Y*. For example, the lower left corner contains the output corresponding to the inputs $A = 1$, $B = 0$. Moreover, the decimal value corresponding to each block is also written inside the block.

The k-map shown in Fig. 9.9 can also be termed as a two-variable k-map. Depending on the number of variables used in a Boolean expression, a k-map can have three or four variables, as shown in Fig. 9.10.

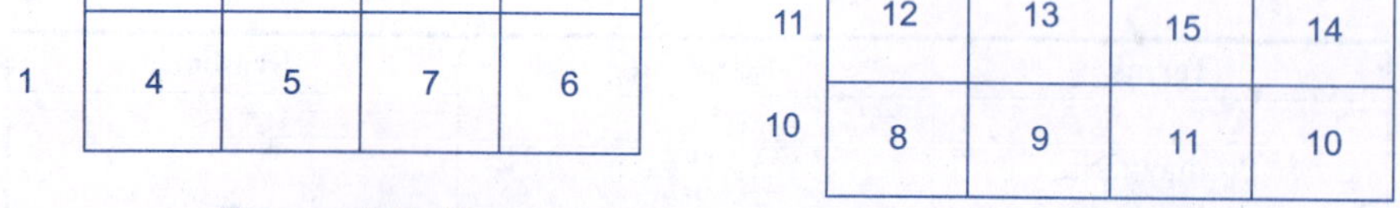

Three-variable K-map

Four-variable K-map

Fig. 9.10 Three and four variable k-maps

The plotting of a Boolean expression on the k-map is the first step in simplifying the expression. To plot a Boolean expression on a k-map, we first need to draw the k-map depending upon the number of input variables present in the expression. Then, we need to fill the k-map with 1's at all those places for which a product or sum term is present in the expression.

The next step in simplifying the Boolean expression is to group the 0's and 1's present in the k-map. When adjacent 1's are grouped, SOP form of Boolean expression is obtained and when adjacent 0's are grouped, POS form of Boolean expression is obtained. Don't care conditions can also be grouped with 1's or 0's. Don't care conditions refer to those outputs, whose values cannot be determined from the given inputs. The simplification of Boolean expression involves grouping of two, four and eight adjacent 1's and 0's.

After the groups of 1's and 0's are marked in a k-map, the groups are analysed for change of state of input variables. If a variable changes its state from 1 to 0 or vice versa then this variable is eliminated from the term of the simplified Boolean expression.

Group of two adjacent 1's In a k-map, two adjacent 1's can be grouped in different ways. Figures 9.11(a), (b), (c) and (d) represent the various ways of grouping two adjacent 1's.

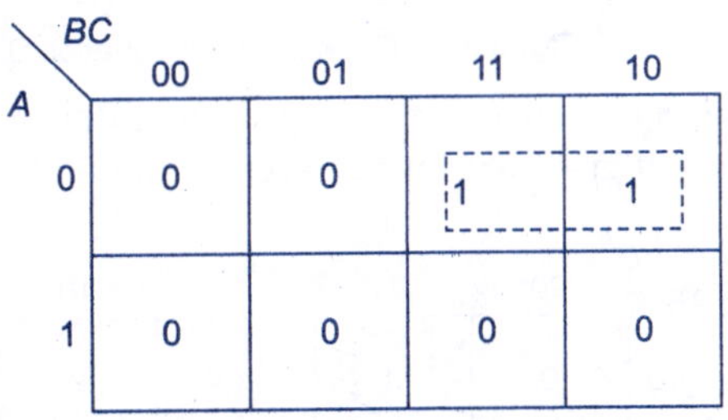

Fig. 9.11(a) The grouping of two horizontal 1's

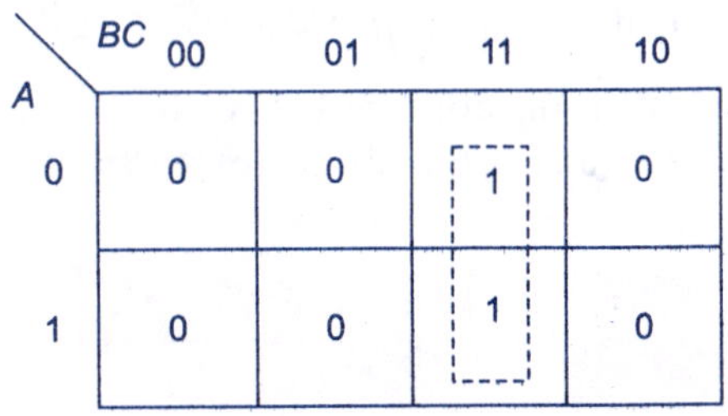

Fig. 9.11(b) The grouping of two vertical 1's

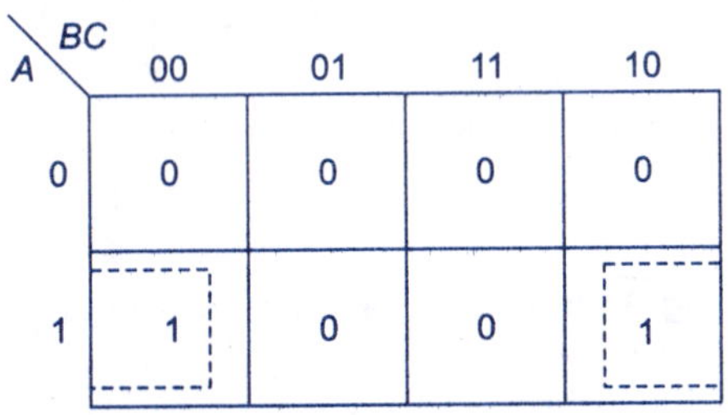

Fig. 9.11(c) The grouping of 1's at corners

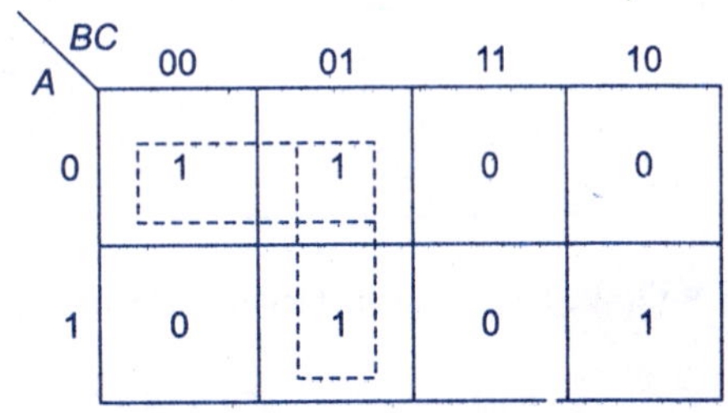

Fig. 9.11(d) The grouping of two overlapped 1's

Example 9.1 *Simplify the following Boolean expression using the k-map.*

$$\bar{A}\bar{B}CD + \bar{A}BCD + AB\bar{C}\bar{D} + A\bar{B}\bar{C}\bar{D}$$

Solution The given expression is:

$$\bar{A}\bar{B}CD + \bar{A}BCD + AB\bar{C}\bar{D} + A\bar{B}\bar{C}\bar{D} \qquad \ldots(9.1)$$

Figure 9.12 shows the k-map for the given expression.

In Fig. 9.12, there are two pairs of 1's that correspond to the following two equations:

$$\bar{A}B\bar{C}D + \bar{A}BCD \quad \text{...(9.2)}$$

$$AB\bar{C}\bar{D} + A\bar{B}\bar{C}\bar{D} \quad \text{...(9.3)}$$

In Eq. 9.2, only the variable C is changing its state; hence it is eliminated to obtain the simplified term $\bar{A}BD$.

In Eq. 9.3, only the variable B is changing its state; hence it is eliminated to obtain the simplified term $A\bar{C}\bar{D}$.

So, the equation $\bar{A}B\bar{C}D + \bar{A}BCD + AB\bar{C}\bar{D} + A\bar{B}\bar{C}\bar{D}$ is reduced to the equation $\bar{A}BD + A\bar{C}\bar{D}$.

AB \ CD	00	01	11	10
00	0	0	0	0
01	0	1	1	0
11	1	0	0	0
10	1	0	0	0

Fig. 9.12 The k-map for Equation 9.1

Group of four adjacent 1's In a k-map, four adjacent 1's can be grouped in different ways. Figures 9.13(a), (b), (c), (d) and (e) represent the various ways of grouping four adjacent 1's.

A \ BC	00	01	11	10
0	1	1	1	1
1	0	0	0	0

Fig. 9.13(a) The grouping of four horizontal 1's

AB \ CD	00	01	11	10
00	0	1	0	0
01	0	1	0	0
11	0	1	0	0
10	0	1	0	0

Fig. 9.13(b) The grouping of four vertical 1's

A \ BC	00	01	11	10
0	1	1	0	0
1	1	1	0	0

Fig. 9.13(c) The grouping of four 1's in the form of a block

A \ BC	00	01	11	10
0	1	0	0	1
1	1	0	0	1

Fig. 9.13(d) The grouping of four random 1's at corners

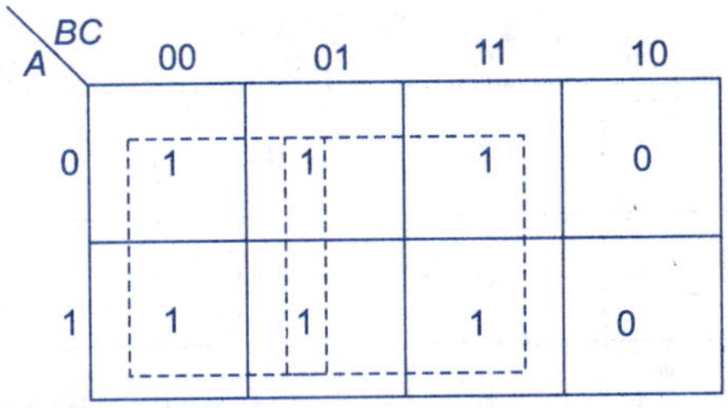

Fig. 9.13(e) The grouping of overlapped 1's

Example 9.2 *Reduce the expression* $\sum m(0, 2, 3, 4, 5, 6)$ *using k-map.*

Solution The given expression is:

$$\sum m(0,\ 2,\ 3,\ 4,\ 5,\ 6)$$

The given SOP expression contains 6 values and therefore, the k-map will be drawn for 3 variables. The k-map will contain 8 cells as shown in Fig. 9.14. As the k-map is drawn for SOP expression, the grouping of adjacent 1's is done.

The given Boolean expression is:

$$\overline{A}\,\overline{B}\,\overline{C} + \overline{A}BC + \overline{A}B\overline{C} + A\overline{B}\,\overline{C} + A\overline{B}C + AB\overline{C}$$

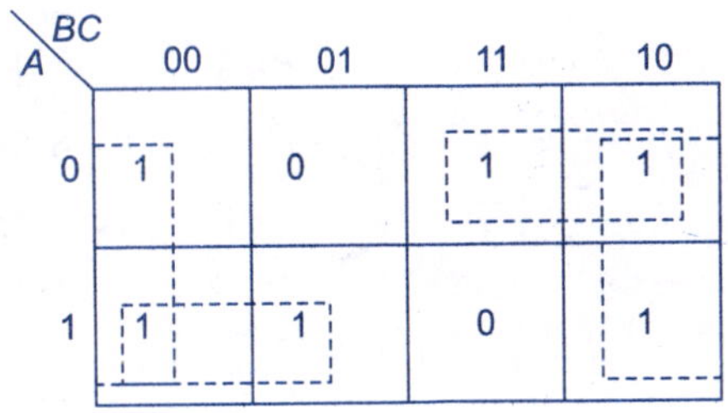

Fig. 9.14 The k-map for Example 9.2

Now, grouping the various minterms as per the groups of 1's in the k-map, we obtain:

$$\overline{A}BC + \overline{A}B\overline{C} \qquad \text{...(9.4)}$$

$$A\overline{B}\,\overline{C} + A\overline{B}C \qquad \text{...(9.5)}$$

$$\overline{A}\,\overline{B}\,\overline{C} + A\overline{B}\,\overline{C} + \overline{A}B\overline{C} + AB\overline{C} \qquad \text{...(9.6)}$$

In Eq. 9.4, only the variable C is changing its state; hence it is eliminated to obtain the simplified term $\overline{A}B$.

In Eq. 9.5, only the variable C is changing its state; hence it is eliminated to obtain the simplified term $A\overline{B}$.

In Eq. 9.6, both the variables A and B are changing their states; hence they are eliminated to obtain the simplified term $\overline{C}$.

So, the equation $\overline{A}\,\overline{B}\,\overline{C} + \overline{A}BC + \overline{A}B\overline{C} + A\overline{B}\,\overline{C} + A\overline{B}C + AB\overline{C}$ is reduced to the equation $\overline{A}B + A\overline{B} + \overline{C}$.

Group of Eight Adjacent 1's In a k-map, eight adjacent 1's can be grouped in different ways. Figures 9.15(a), (b) and (c) represent the various ways of grouping eight adjacent 1's.

AB \ CD	00	01	11	10
00	0	1	1	0
01	0	1	1	0
11	0	1	1	0
10	0	1	1	0

Fig. 9.15(a) The grouping of eight vertical 1's

AB \ CD	00	01	11	10
00	1	1	1	1
01	1	1	1	1
11	0	0	0	0
10	0	0	0	0

Fig. 9.15(b) The grouping of eight horizontal 1's

AB \ CD	00	01	11	10
00	1	0	0	1
01	1	0	0	1
11	1	0	0	1
10	1	0	0	1

Fig. 9.15(c) The grouping of eight 1's at corners

Example 9.3 *Simplify a four-variable Boolean expression using k-map, whose truth table is shown in Fig. 9.16.*

A	B	C	D	Y
0	0	0	0	0
0	0	0	1	1
0	0	1	0	0
0	0	1	1	0
0	1	0	0	1
0	1	0	1	1
0	1	1	0	1
0	1	1	1	1
1	0	0	0	0
1	0	0	1	1
1	0	1	0	0
1	0	1	1	0
1	1	0	0	1
1	1	0	1	1
1	1	1	0	1
1	1	1	1	1

Fig. 9.16 The truth table of Example 9.3

Solution Figure 9.17 shows the k-map of the given truth table.

Now, grouping the various minterms as per the groups of 1's in the k-map, we obtain:

AB \ CD	00	01	11	10
00	0	1	0	0
01	1	1	1	1
11	1	1	1	1
10	0	1	0	0

Fig. 9.17 The k-map of Example 9.3

$$\overline{A}\,\overline{B}\,\overline{C}D+\overline{A}B\overline{C}D+AB\overline{C}D+A\overline{B}\,\overline{C}D \quad ...(9.7)$$

$$\overline{A}B\overline{C}\,\overline{D}+\overline{A}B\overline{C}D+\overline{A}BCD+\overline{A}BC\overline{D}+AB\overline{C}\,\overline{D}+AB\overline{C}D+ABCD+ABC\overline{D} \quad ...(9.8)$$

In Eq. 9.7, both the variables A and B are changing their states; hence they are eliminated to obtain the simplified term $\overline{C}D$.

In Eq. 9.8, the variables A, C and D are changing their states; hence they are eliminated to obtain the simplified term B.

Hence, the simplified equation for given truth table is $\overline{C}D + B$.

Example 9.4 *Draw a logic diagram for the following Boolean expression:*

$$ABC\overline{D}+A\overline{B}CD+\overline{A}\,\overline{B}\,\overline{C}\,\overline{D}+A\overline{B}C\overline{D}+\overline{A}B\overline{C}D+A\overline{B}\,\overline{C}D+\overline{A}\,\overline{B}CD+AB\overline{C}D+A\overline{B}\,\overline{C}\,\overline{D}$$

Solution Before drawing the logic diagram for the given equation, we need to first simplify the given expression using the k-map. Figure 9.18 shows the k-map for the given Boolean expression.

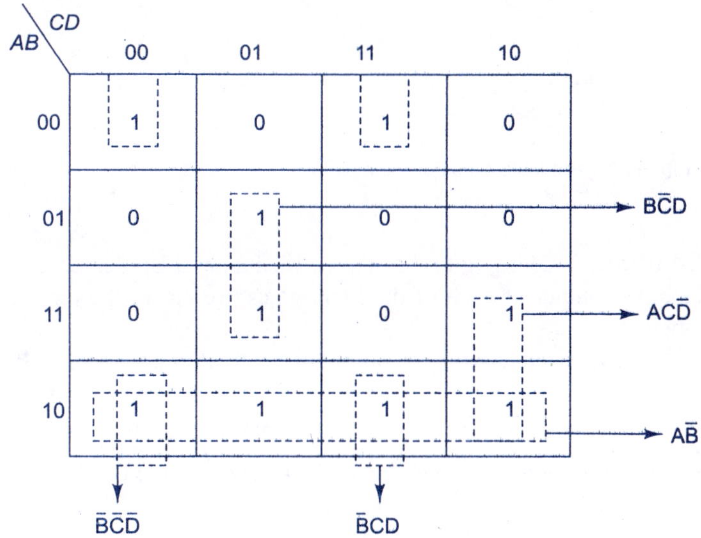

Fig. 9.18 The k-map for Example 9.4

The following simplified equation is deduced from the above k-map:

$$\overline{B}\,\overline{C}\,\overline{D}+\overline{B}CD+A\overline{B}+AC\overline{D}+B\overline{C}D$$

To draw the logic diagram for the above equation, we need to use four input lines and an inverter for complementing the input variable. Since, the equation is in SOP form, each minterm is realised using AND gates and the output of the AND gates is fed into an OR gate for implementing the logic.

Figure 9.19 shows the logic diagram for the simplified Boolean expression.

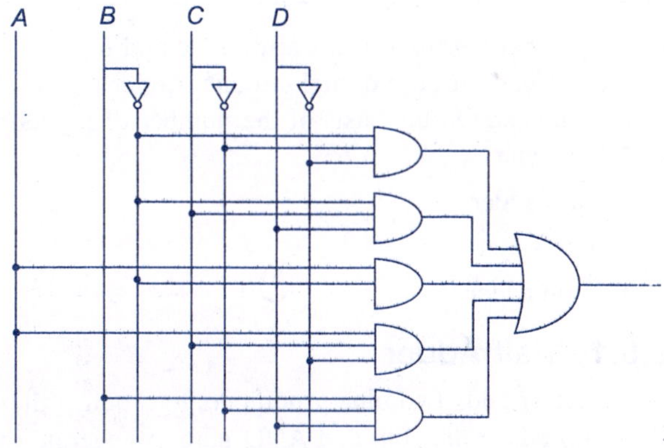

Fig. 9.19 The logic diagram for the simplified Boolean expression

9.4.2 Logic Diagram to Boolean Expression

Each logic diagram is a logic implementation of a Boolean expression. A logic diagram can be analysed to obtain the Boolean expression that is being realised by the logic diagram.

To obtain the Boolean expression from a logic diagram, we need to perform the following steps:

1. Analyse the circuit and label the output of each of the gates present in the logic circuit.

2. Write the output of the last gate of the circuit to obtain the Boolean expression.

Example 9.5 *Determine the Boolean expression for the logic circuit shown in Fig. 9.20.*

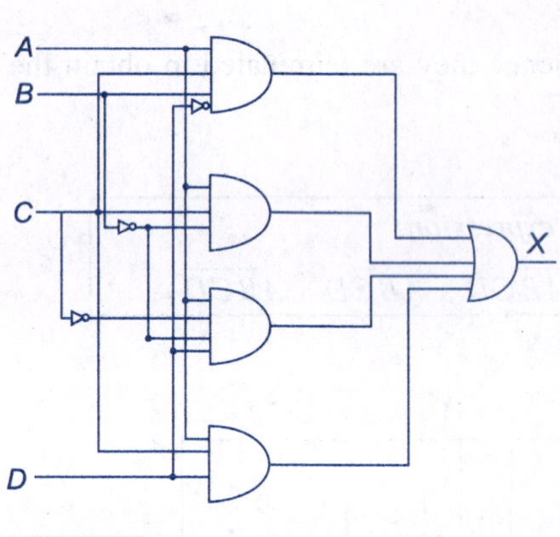

Fig. 9.20 The logic circuit of Example 9.5

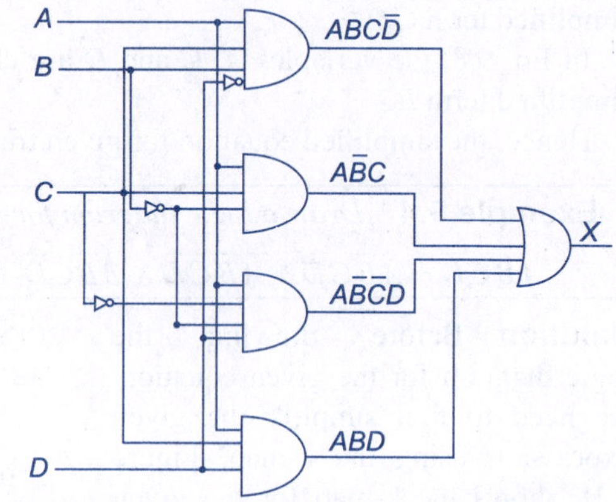

Fig. 9.21 The logic circuit with labelled outputs

Solution According to the steps of deducing a Boolean expression from a logic circuit, we first need to label the output of each of the logic gates present in the circuit. Figure 9.21 shows the logic circuit with labelled outputs.

Now, we need to write the output of the final logic gate that produces the final output X, as shown under:

$$X = ABC\overline{D} + A\overline{B}C + \overline{A}\overline{B}\overline{C}D + ABD$$

Therefore, $ABC\overline{D} + A\overline{B}C + \overline{A}\overline{B}\overline{C}D + ABD$ is the Boolean expression for the given logic circuit.

9.5 ADDER CIRCUITS

A computer performs various arithmetic and logical operations, such as addition and comparison with the help of special-purpose digital circuits. Adder is one of these digital circuits that can be used to add two or more numbers. On the basis of the number of inputs provided to a digital circuit, the adder is categorised into three types:

- Half adder
- Full adder
- 4-bit adder

9.5.1 Half Adder

A half adder adds two binary numbers to produce the sum and carry. The half adder circuit uses the XOR gate to produce the sum and AND gate to generate the carry. Figure 9.22 shows the circuit diagram of a half adder.

Input 1 and Input 2 are the two inputs that are provided to both the logic gates, XOR and AND. The XOR gate produces the sum of the two numbers and the AND gate generates the carry for the addition operation. Table 9.9 shows the truth table of a half adder circuit.

Table 9.9 The truth table of a half adder circuit

Input		Output	
A	*B*	Sum	Carry
0	0	0	0
0	1	1	0
1	0	1	0
1	1	0	1

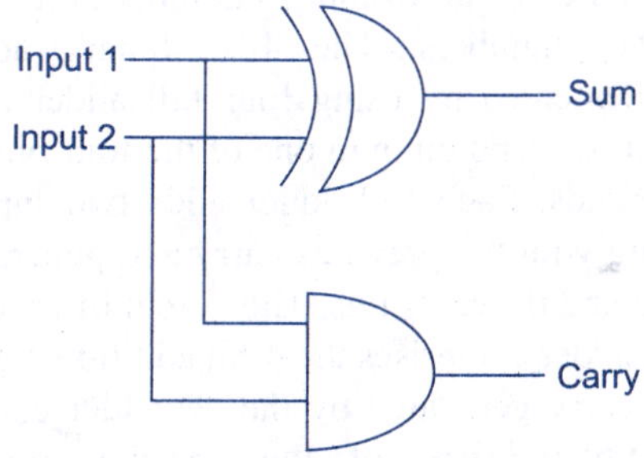

Fig. 9.22 The circuit diagram of a half adder

9.5.2 Full Adder

A full adder is a digital circuit that adds three binary numbers and produces the sum and carry. The circuitry of full adder comprises of two XOR gates to produce the sum of the input values and an AND gate to produce the carry. In other words, in a full adder circuit, two half adder circuits are combined to generate the result of addition of three binary numbers. Figure 9.23 shows the circuit diagram of a full adder.

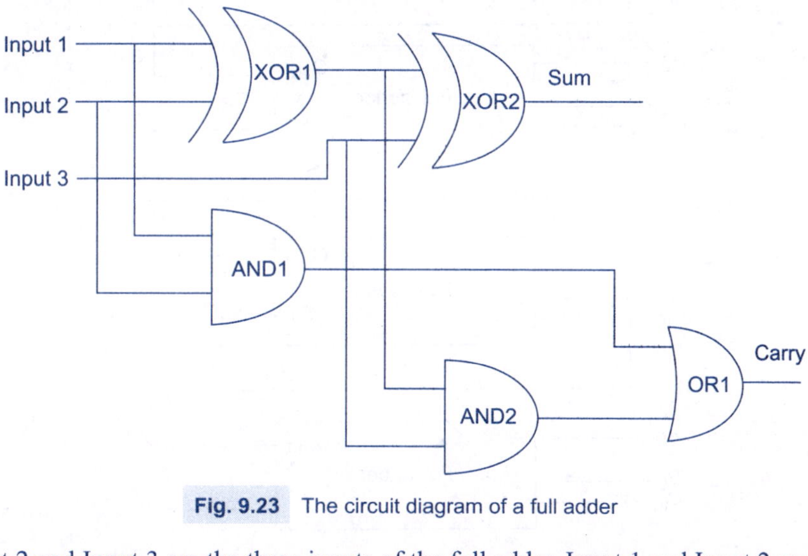

Fig. 9.23 The circuit diagram of a full adder

Input 1, Input 2 and Input 3 are the three inputs of the full adder. Input 1 and Input 2 are provided to the first XOR gate, XOR1, which produces the sum of the first two numbers. The output of the XOR1 gate is applied to another XOR gate, XOR2 along with the third input, Input 3. The XOR2 gate produces the final sum of three inputs.

Similarly, Input 1 and Input 2 are provided to the first AND gate, AND1, which produces the carry for the addition of the first two numbers. The output of the AND1 gate is applied to another AND gate, AND2 along with the third input, Input 3. The AND2 gate produces the final carry for the addition of three inputs. Table 9.10 shows the truth table of a full adder circuit.

9.5.3 4-bit Adder

A 4-bit adder is a digital circuit that helps the CPU in performing addition of two 4 bit binary numbers. The 4-bit binary adder is implemented by using four full adder circuits, each corresponding to one of the four bits of the operands. Each full adder adds two input bits along with the previous carry and generates the sum and the carry bits. The output of each of the full adder comprises the 4-bit addition result and the carry generated by the 4th adder comprises the final carry of the addition operation. Figure 9.24 shows the logic circuit of the 4-bit binary adder.

Table 9.10 The truth table of full adder

Input			Output	
A	*B*	*C*	Sum	Carry
0	0	0	0	0
0	0	1	1	0
0	1	0	1	0
0	1	1	0	1
1	0	0	1	0
1	0	1	0	1
1	1	0	0	1
1	1	1	1	1

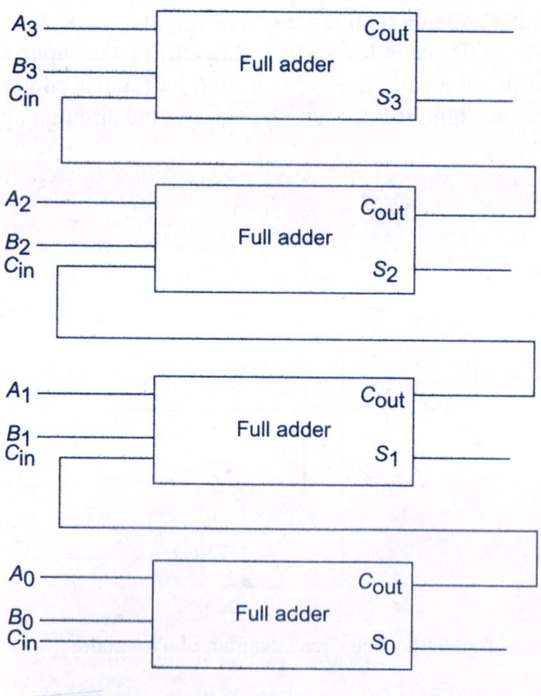

Fig. 9.24 The logic circuit of 4-bit binary adder

9.6 FLIP-FLOP CIRCUITS

Flip-flop is a sequential electronic circuit that is used to store 1-bit information, i.e., either 0 or 1. A sequential electronic circuit produces the output on the basis of the present input as well as the previous output of the circuit.

To store information in a flip-flop, two stable states, set or reset are used along with a clock signal. The set state represents the value 1 and the reset state represents the value 0. All flip-flops generate two outputs, one is the present output of the circuit and the other is the complemented value of the present output.

The various types of flip-flop are:

- SR
- JK
- D type
- T type

9.6.1 SR Flip-flop

SR flip-flop consists of two NAND gates, which accept two inputs. One input is externally provided to each of the NAND gates while the other input is provided by connecting the previous outputs of the NAND gates. Figure 9.25 shows the basic circuit of SR flip-flop.

Table 9.11 shows the truth table of SR flip-flop. In the truth table, Q_n and $\overline{Q_n}$ represent the outputs at the *n*th clock pulse.

Table 9.11 The truth table of SR flip-flop

Inputs		**Output**	
Set	***Reset***	Q_n	$\overline{Q_n}$
0	0	Q_{n-1}	$\overline{Q_{n-1}}$
0	1	0	1
1	0	1	0
1	1	Not used	

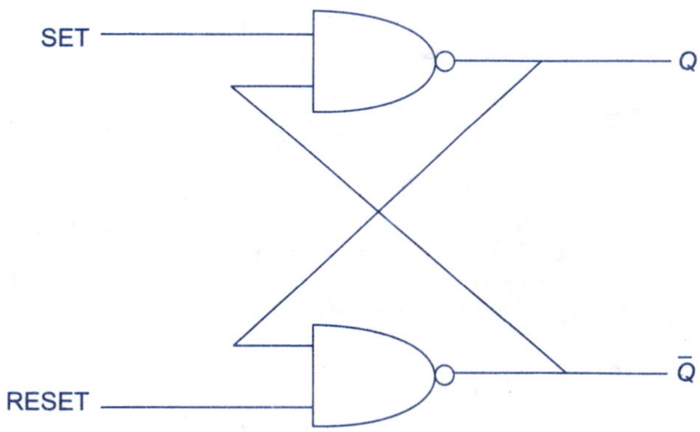

Fig. 9.25 The basic circuit of SR flip-flop

9.6.2 D Type Flip-flop

D type flip-flop is an enhanced version of the clocked SR flip-flop. In the clocked SR flip-flop, the two inputs *S* and *R* are connected to an AND gate along with a clock input. The output of each of the AND gate is then applied as an input to the NAND gates. The inclusion of clock signal ensures that the flip-flop can be set or reset only when a clock pulse is also provided to the circuit. The circuit will work only when both the AND gates receive a positive clock pulse. Figure 9.26 shows the circuit of clocked SR flip-flop.

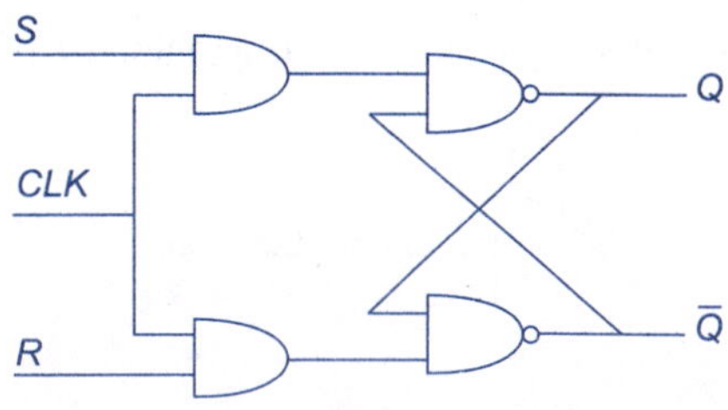

Fig. 9.26 The circuit of the clocked SR flip-flop

In the D type flip-flop, the input *S* is directly applied to the first AND gate and a complement of *S* is applied to the second AND gate. Figure 9.27 shows the circuit diagram of D type flip-flop.

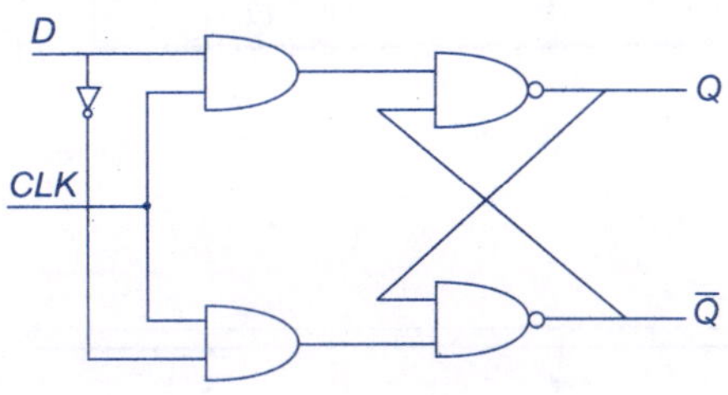

Fig. 9.27 The circuit of D type flip-flop

Table 9.12 shows the truth table of the D type flip-flop.

Table 9.12 The truth table of the D type flip-flop

Input	Output
0	0
1	1

9.6.3 JK Flip-flop

The disadvantage of SR flip-flop is that its output is undefined when both the inputs are 1. This situation is called race condition. JK flip-flop is an advancement over the SR flip-flop. It eliminates the race condition that is encountered in SR flip-flops.

Figure 9.28 shows the circuit of JK flip-flop.

Table 9.13 shows the truth table of JK flip-flop.

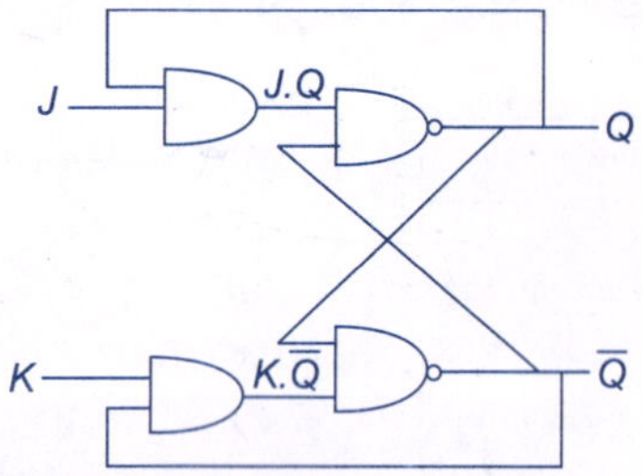

Fig. 9.28 The basic circuit of the JK flip-flop

Table 9.13 The truth table of JK flip-flop

Inputs		Output	
J	K	Q_n	$\overline{Q_n}$
0	0	Q_{n-1}	$\overline{Q_{n-1}}$
0	1	0	1
1	0	1	0
1	1	$\overline{Q_{n-1}}$	Q_{n-1}

9.6.4 T Type Flip-flop

T type flip-flop is an enhanced version of the JK flip-flop that accepts only one input. In T type flip-flop, same input is applied to both the AND gates of the JK flip flop. Figure 9.29 shows the circuit diagram of the T type flip-flop.

Table 9.14 shows the truth table of T type flip-flop.

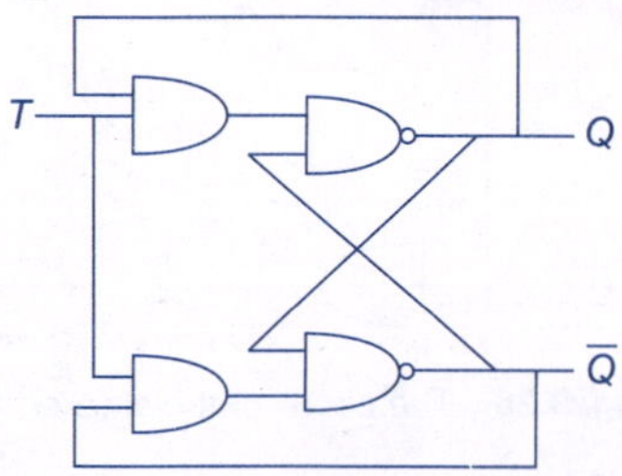

Fig. 9.29 The circuit diagram of T type flip-flop

Table 9.14 The truth table of T type flip-flop

Input T	Output Q_n
0	Q_n
1	$\overline{Q_n}$

9.7 APPLICATION OF FLIP-FLOPS

Flip-flop is one of the most important components of electronic circuits. One or more flip-flops are combined together for constructing digital circuits like counters and registers.

9.7.1 Counter

Counters are used as timers in digital circuits that help to count the clock pulses. The counter circuit consists of flip-flops and basic gates logically arranged for counting the clock pulses. The counters can be categorised on the following basis:

- On the basis of the counting order, i.e., ascending or descending. The counter that counts in ascending order is called up counter while the counter that counts in descending order is called down counter. Both up and down counters can be realised in a single circuit called up-down counter.
- On the basis of the type of clock used, i.e., synchronous or asynchronous. The counter that uses synchronous clock is called synchronous counter while the counter that uses asynchronous clock is called asynchronous counter. In a synchronous counter, each flip-flop receives the clock pulse simultaneously from an external clock device. In an asynchronous counter, each flip-flop receives the clock pulse from the previous flip-flop, with the first flip-flop receiving its clock pulse from an external source.

Up-down Counter The up-down counter counts the values in both ascending as well as descending order. It provides a selector line for choosing the mode of the counter, i.e., up or down. Figure 9.30 shows the circuit diagram of the up-down counter.

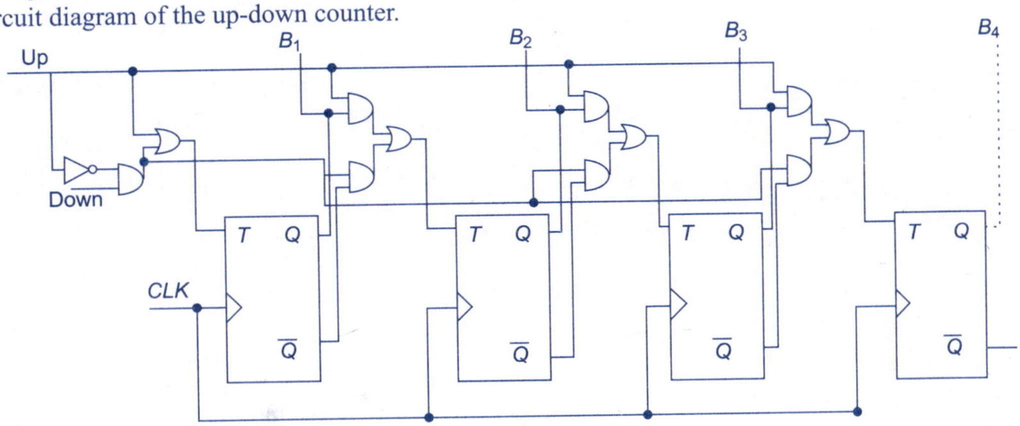

Fig. 9.30 The circuit diagram of the up-down counter

Asynchronous Counter An asynchronous counter can either be constructed using T type or JK flip-flop. If the counter consists of T type flip-flops, then value 1 is applied to all the inputs of the flip-flops. If the counter consists of JK flip-flops, then value 1 is applied to both J and K inputs of all the flip-flops. The output of the first flip-flop is used as the clock signal for the second flip-flop, the output of second flip-flop is used as the clock signal for the third flip-flop and so on. Therefore, in asynchronous counter each flip-flop receives the clock signal at different times. An asynchronous counter is also known as ripple counter.

Figure 9.31 shows the circuit diagram of asynchronous counter.

Synchronous Counter In synchronous counter, each flip-flop receives the clock input at the same time. Hence, all flip-flops in the synchronous counter change their states at the same time. A synchronous counter logically arranges the flip-flops and AND gates for implementing the counting functionality. Figure 9.32 shows the circuit diagram of synchronous counter.

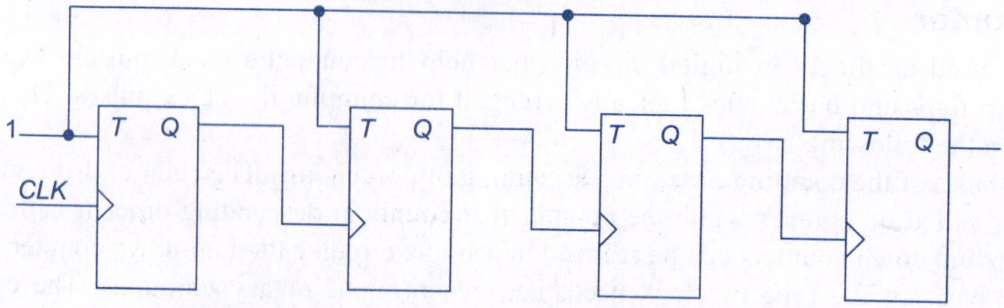

Fig. 9.31 The circuit diagram of asynchronous counter

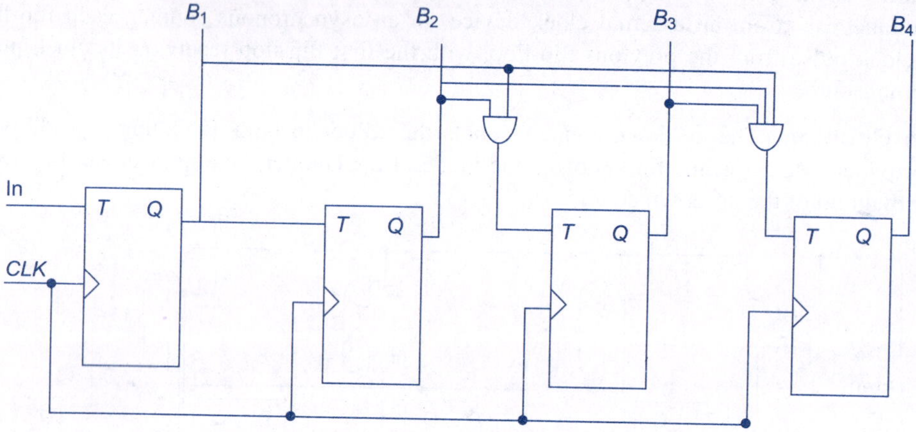

Fig. 9.32 The circuit diagram of synchronous counter

9.7.2 Register

Register is a group of flip-flops used for storing multiple bits of binary information. The most common application area of a register is inside the CPU where the CPU uses several registers for temporary storage of data. Each flip-flop used in a register is used to store one bit of a binary digit. Therefore, the number of flip flops used in a register signifies the number of bits of data that the register can store. Registers use D type flip-flop because the output value of the D type flip flop is same as the input value. Figure 9.33 shows the block diagram of a four bit register containing four D type flip-flops.

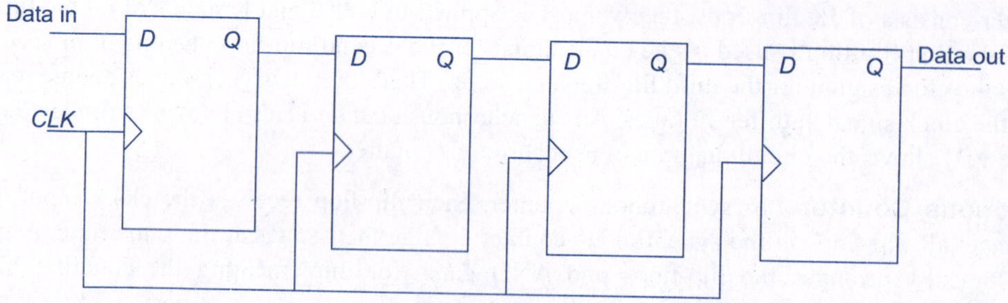

Fig. 9.33 The block diagram of a four bit register

Chapter Summary

Whenever an end-user gives a command to the computer system, it performs various operations with the help of the hardware components of the computer system. The basic unit of the hardware components of a computer system is the logic gate, which is of two types—basic logic gate and derived logic gate. Logic gates are used in designing combinational as well as sequential circuits. In combinational circuits, the output does not depend on the previous state of the circuit, whereas in case of sequential circuits the output depends on the present input as well as the previous state of the circuit. Examples of combinational circuits are adder circuits which add two or more numbers. Examples of the sequential circuits include flip-flops, which are the basic components of counters and registers. The flip-flops are used to store one bit of binary information. The counters are used to count the clock pulses of an electronic circuit. Therefore, the counter is used as a timer in an electronic circuit. The registers are used to store information produced during the execution of instructions.

Key Terms to Remember

- **Basic logic gates:** Basic logic gates are the building blocks of digital circuits that perform logical operations such as AND, OR and NOT, on the binary inputs.
- **Derived logic gates:** Derived logic gates are those logic gates that perform logical operations on the binary inputs with the help of two or more basic logic gates.
- **K-map:** K-map is a technique of simplifying the Boolean expressions using graphical representation method.
- **Adder:** Adder is a digital circuit that adds two or more binary numbers.
- **Half adder:** Half adder adds two binary numbers to produce the sum and carry.
- **Full adder:** Full adder is a digital circuit that adds three binary numbers and produces the sum and carry.
- **Flip-flop:** Flip-flop is a sequential electronic circuit that is used to store 1-bit information, i.e., either 0 or 1.
- **Sequential electro*nic circuit:** Sequential electronic circuit produces the output on the basis of the present input as well as the previous output of the circuit.
- **Counters:** Counters are used as timers in digital circuits that help to count the clock pulses.
- **Register:** Register is a set of two or more flip-flops that stores binary numbers.

Review Questions

Fill in the Blanks

1. Logic gates are the building blocks of digital circuits that perform various ______________ on the binary input.
2. The values of the input and the corresponding output of the logic gates can be represented using a table called ______________.
3. The output of the ______________ gate is true if any one of the inputs is true.
4. The ______________ inverts the value of the input for producing the ouput.
5. Derived logic gates are those logic gates that perform logical operations on the binary inputs with the help of two or more ______________.
6. The output of ______________ gate is true if both the inputs are same.

7. In the SOP Boolean expression, different product terms are combined with the _____________ operator.
8. K-map is a technique of simplifying the _____________ using graphical representation method.
9. The product terms in SOP Boolean expression are called _____________ while the sum terms in POS Boolean expression are called _____________ .
10. Each _____________ is a logic implementation of a Boolean expression.
11. _____________ is one of the digital circuits that can be used to add two or more numbers.
12. Half adder adds _____________ binary numbers to produce the sum and carry.
13. In a full adder circuit, two _____________ circuits are combined to generate the result of addition of three binary numbers.
14. A 4-bit adder is a digital circuit that helps the CPU in performing the addition of two _____________ binary numbers.
15. A sequential electronic circuit produces the output on the basis of the present input as well as the _____________ of the circuit.
16. D type flip-flop is an enhanced version of _____________ flip-flop.
17. In T type flip-flop, same input is applied to both the inputs of the _____________ flip-flop.
18. Counters are used as _____________ in digital circuits that help to count the clock pulses.
19. A _____________ counter is also known as ripple counter.
20. _____________ is a group of flip-flops used for storing multiple bits of binary information.

Multiple Choice Questions

1. Which of the following components is actually responsible for executing an instruction?
   A Software B. Hardware C. Flip-flops D. Counter
2. Which of the following are the building blocks of digital circuit?
   A. Flip-flops B. Logic gates C. Register D. None of the above
3. Which of the following types of operations can be performed by logic gates?
   A. Assignment operation B. Arithmetical operation
   C. Logical operation D. Shift operation
4. Which of the following digital circuits is used to add binary numbers?
   A. Register B. Logic gates C. Adder D. All of the above
5. Which of the following techniques enables a user to simplify the Boolean expression?
   A. Logic diagram B. Flip-flop C. Truth table D. Karnaugh-map
6. Which of the following digital circuits is used as the basic component for storing data?
   A. Flip-flop B. Registers C. Counters D. Derived logic gates
7. Which of the following logic gate is also known as inverter?
   A. AND B. OR C. NAND D. NOT
8. Which of the following components is used to perform the logical operation in the derived logic gates?
   A. Flip-flop B. Basic logic gate C. Register D. All of the above
9. Which of the following logic gates generates false output only when both of the inputs have the same value?
   A. NAND B. XNOR C. XOR D. AND

10. Which of the following combinations of logic gates is included in the NAND gate?
   A. NOT and OR B. AND and OR C. NOT and AND D. NOT and XOR
11. Which of the following circuits is used to add two bits?
   A. Adder B. Half adder C. Full adder D. 4-bit adder
12. Which of the following statements is not true for a full adder?
   A. It is a digital circuit.
   B. It adds three binary numbers and generates a sum as well as a carry.
   C. It uses half adder circuits to implement is functionality.
   D. It is used to store information.
13. Which of the following options can be used to express all logical operations?
   A. K-map B. Truth table C. Boolean expression D. All of the above
14. Which of the following logic gates produces true output while receiving false value for both its inputs?
   A. XNOR B. NAND C. NOR D. All of the above
15. Which of the following digital circuits is used to add two binary numbers having more than one bit?
   A. Full Adder B. Register C. 4-bit adder D. None of the above
16. In which of the following digital circuits, the output of the circuit depends on the present input as well as the previous output of the circuit?
   A. Electronic circuit B. Combinational circuit C. Sequential circuit D. Flip-flop circuit
17. In which of the following flip-flops, both input signals of the JK flip flop are connected with the same input variable?
   A. SR flip-flop B. D type flip-flop C. T type flip-flop D. None of the above
18. Which of the following components is used for temporary storage of data?
   A. Counter B. Flip-flop C. Register D. Logic gates
19. In which of the following counter, all the flip-flop are clocked at different time?
   A. Asynchronous counter B. Synchronous counter
   C. Up-down counter D. None of the above
20. Which of the following counters enables us to perform both increment and decrement count using a single circuit?
   A. Ripple counter B. Up counter C. Synchronous counter D. Up-down counter

Discussion Questions

1. What are logic gates? Why are they important?
2. Explain the different types of basic logic gates.
3. What do you understand by derived logic gates? Explain the different types of derived logic gates.
4. Explain the basic concept of truth table and also describe the truth tables of all the basic logic gates.
5. Differentiate between logic gates and derived gates.
6. Explain the basic steps required to convert a Boolean expression into logic gates.

7. Simplify the following Boolean expression and also draw its logic diagram:

$$\overline{A}BC\overline{D}+AB\overline{C}+\overline{B}CD+A\overline{B}C\overline{D}+\overline{A}CD+A\overline{B}\overline{C}D+A\overline{B}D$$

8. Explain the working of a half-adder circuit with the help of a neatly labelled diagram.
9. How can two half adder circuits be combined to design a full adder circuit?
10. Explain the working of a 4-bit adder circuit.
11. Explain the basic working of a flip-flop circuit.
12. Explain the various types of flip-flops with the help of a neatly labelled diagram.
13. What do you know about clocked SR flip-flop?
14. What is the disadvantage of SR flip-flop?
15. What is a register? How do registers play an important role in the computer system?
16. How does a register store a value during the execution of an operation?
17. Explain the purpose of a counter circuit used in the digital circuit.
18. What do you understand by the up-down counter?
19. Explain the working of the synchronous counter with the help of a neatly labelled diagram.
20. Explain the working of the ripple counter with the help of a neatly labelled diagram.
21. Give Boolean expressions and truth tables for the following logic circuits:

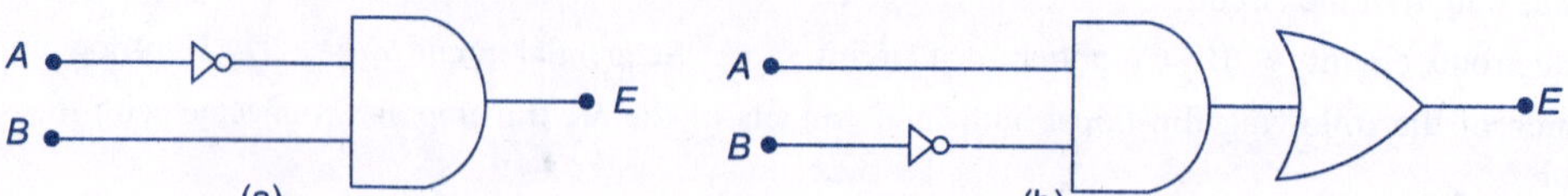

(a) (b)

22. Draw logic circuits for the following expressions:
    (a) $X1 = AB\overline{C} + A\overline{B}$
    (b) $X2 = \overline{A + BC} + C$
23. Show that the circuit diagram given behaves like a NOR circuit.

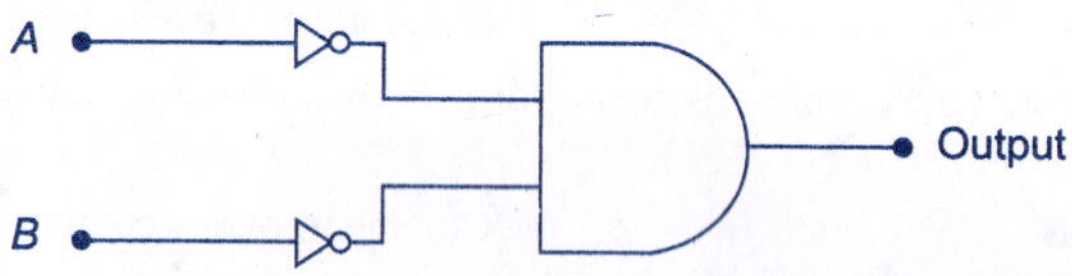

24. In the circuit shown, show that the output is 1 when two inputs 'disagree' and 0 when they 'agree'.

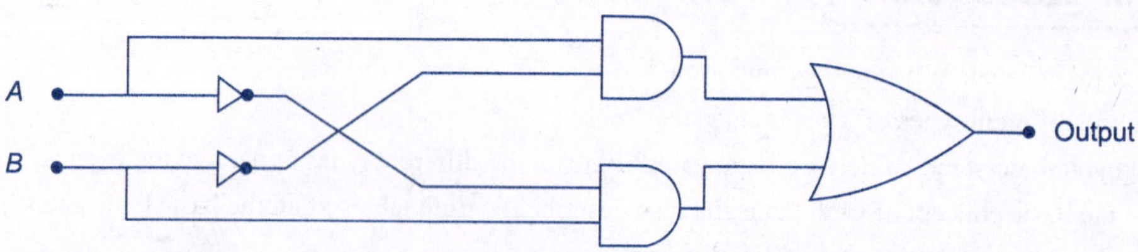

25. Examine what happens when AND is changed to OR and OR is changed to AND in Question 24.

CHAPTER 10

COMPUTER SOFTWARE

Chapter Outline

Chapter Objectives

In this chapter, we will learn:

- Fundamentals of computer software
- Types of software
- Role of system software
- Types of system software and their functions
- Functions of operating system
- Different types of application software
- Basic steps in solving a problem
- Basic steps in developing a program

10.1 INTRODUCTION

All computer systems consist of two major components, namely, hardware and software. The hardware refers to the physical equipments that are necessary for performing various operations, such as reading and processing data, storing results and providing output to the users in a desired form. The software refers to a set of computer programs that are required to enable the hardware to work and perform these operations effectively.

A computer program is basically a set of logical instructions, written in a computer programming language that tells the computer how to accomplish a task. The software is therefore an essential interface between the hardware and the user as shown in Fig. 10.1.

We can say that software gives life to the hardware and therefore, the software is popularly referred to as the "soul" of the computer system while the hardware as the "heart". There is an array of computer programs available for operating and controlling the computer. It is the judicious combination of these programs that gives the computer its power and versatility, and the users their satisfaction.

In this chapter, we shall discuss the various types of computer software and their functions and utility.

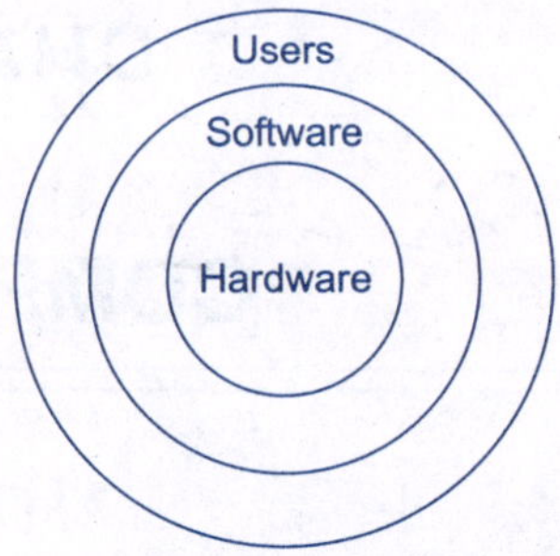

Fig. 10.1 Software interface between hardware and software

10.2 TYPES OF COMPUTER SOFTWARE

As stated earlier, a computer software performs two distinctive tasks. The first task is to control and coordinate the hardware components and manage their performances and the second one is to enable the users to accomplish their required tasks. The software that is used to achieve the first task is known as the *system software* and the software that is used to achieve the second task is known as the *application software*. While the system software is essential for a computer to work, the application software is the additional software required for the user to perform a specific job. The system software not only controls the hardware functions but also enables the hardware to interact with the application software as well as the users as illustrated in Fig. 10.2.

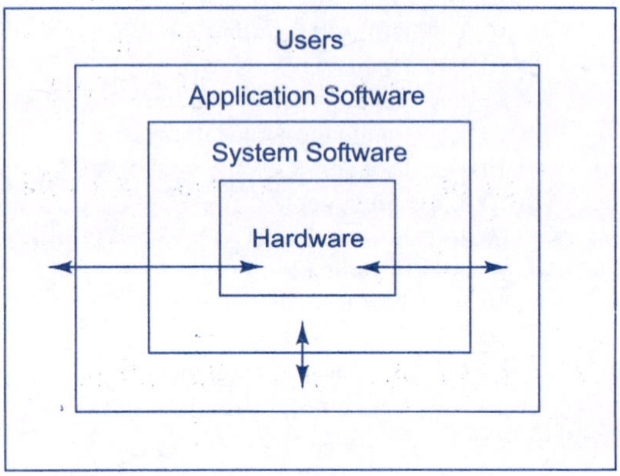

Fig. 10.2 Layers of software and their interactions

10.2.1 System Software

System software consists of many different programs that manage and support different tasks. Depending upon the task performed, the system software can be classified into two major groups:

- *System management programs* used for managing both the hardware and software systems.
- *System development programs* used for developing and executing application software.

10.2.2 Application Software

Application software includes a variety of programs that are designed to meet the information processing needs of end users. They can be broadly classified into two groups:

- *Standard application programs* that are designed for performing common application jobs.
- *Unique application programs* that are developed by the users themselves to support their specific needs.

Figure 10.3 illustrates the major categories of computer software.

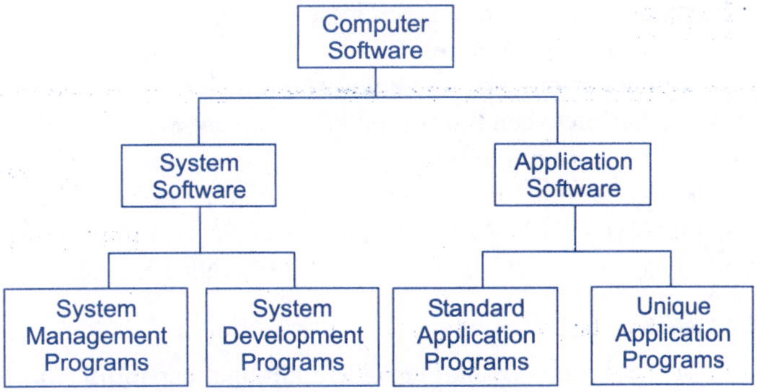

Fig. 10.3 Major categories of computer software

10.3 SYSTEM MANAGEMENT PROGRAMS

System management programs are those programs that are meant for operating the hardware system and managing their resources effectively. They also enable the users to perform certain utility functions, such as creating backup files, recovering damaged files and merging files. They minimise the human intervention during processing and aid in maximising the productivity of a computer system. System management programs include:

- Operating system
- Utility programs
- Device drivers

These programs work in close interaction with each other as shown in Fig. 10.4.

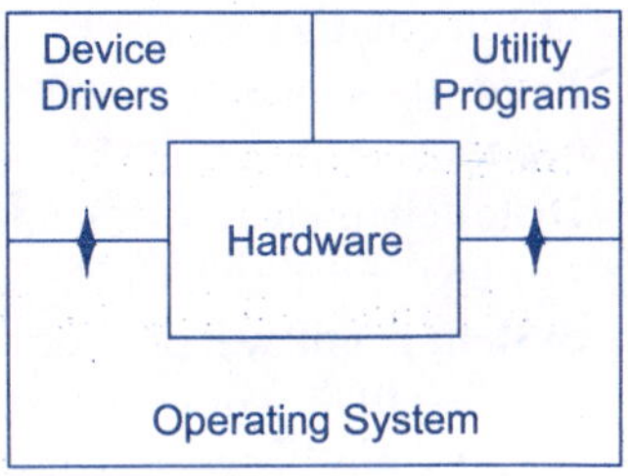

Fig. 10.4 System Management Programs

10.3.1 Operating System

Operating System (OS) is the principal component of system software and is responsible for overall management of computer resources. It also provides an interface between the computer and the user and helps in implementing the application programs as illustrated in Fig. 10.5.

Major functions of an operating system are:

- Scheduling and execution of all processes.
- Allocation and management of main memory and other storage areas to the programs.
- Coordination and assignment of different hardware devices to the programs.
- Creation, storage and manipulation of files required by the various processes.

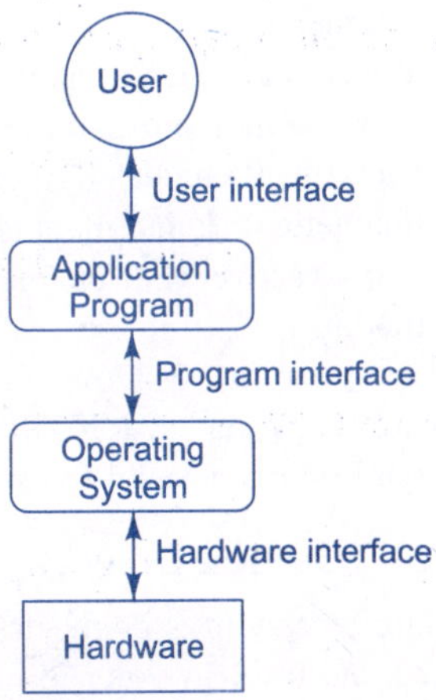

Fig. 10.5 Hardware-OS-User interface

- Determining and maintaining the order of execution of programs.
- Interpretation of commands and instructions.
- Coordination and assignment of other development and utility programs.
- Providing a friendly interface between the computer and the user.
- Ensuring security of access to computer resources.

Operating systems are usually supplied by the hardware manufacturers and are rarely developed by the users due to its technical complexity. The operating system is discussed in more detail in the next chapter. The most popular operating system, MS-DOS, is discussed in Chapter 12.

10.3.2 Utility Programs

Utility programs refer to small programs, which provide additional capabilities to the computer system in addition to the ones provided by the operating system. They enable an operating system to perform some additional tasks, such as searching and printing the files and scanning the viruses, etc. A utility program is not an essential part of an operating system, because it does not help the operating system in the execution of a command or a program. A utility program only provides the additional features to the computer system. In other words, an operating system can execute most of the programs without having the utility programs. Utility programs are added to an operating system to perform many different tasks, that include:

- **Search and replace.** It enables the operating system to search a file on the basis of the specified search criteria.
- **Print.** It enables an operating system to initiate the print operation of the printer connected with the computer system.
- **Disk defragmenter.** It helps in defragmenting the memory space. Defragmentation is the process of storing the data at a single place in the memory instead of disjointed memory locations.
- **System profiler.** It provides the information related to the various hardware and software components installed in the computer system. In other words, it provides a list of the hardware components, which are presently connected with the computer system, and the software components, which are currently installed in the computer system.
- **Encryption.** It enables the operating system to generate the encrypted format of the messages or the files, which have to be transmitted from one system to another system over the network or the Internet.
- **Virus scanner.** It enables the operating system to detect viruses and bugs, which may affect the correct functioning of the computer system.
- **Backup.** It enables the creation of a copy of various files and folders on a secondary medium such as magnetic disk and magnetic tape, in order to keep the original data safe.
- **Data recovery.** It enables the retrieval of lost data from a corrupted or damaged primary storage medium.

Like operating systems, utility programs are prewritten by manufacturers and supplied with the hardware. They may also be obtained from standard software vendors. A good range of utility programs can make the life much easier for the user.

10.3.3 Device Drivers

A computer system is connected with multiple input and output (I/O) devices, so that it can communicate with the end user. In order to interact with the I/O devices, the computer system requires special software called device driver. The device driver acts as a translator between the I/O devices and the computer. A device driver of the input device interprets the input provided by the user into the computer understandable form and directs it to the operating system. Similarly, the device drivers of the output devices translate the output generated by the computer into the user understandable format and display it on the screen. In other words, a device driver is special software that enables a hardware device, such as keyboard, monitor and printer to perform an operation according to the command given by the end user.

Whenever a program needs to use a connected hardware device, it issues a command to the operating system. The operating system calls the respective routine or process of the device driver, which instructs the device to perform the task. For providing instruction to the devices, the device driver sends various control and data signals through buses and cables to the device. In order to acknowledge the device driver's signal, the device sends the acknowledgment signals to the device driver. After performing the task, the device sends a message to the device driver, which returns the value to the calling program of the operating system. In other words, a device driver instructs a hardware device the way it should accept the input from the operating system and the way in which it should communicate with the other units of the computer system. Figure 10.6 illustrates the working of the device driver.

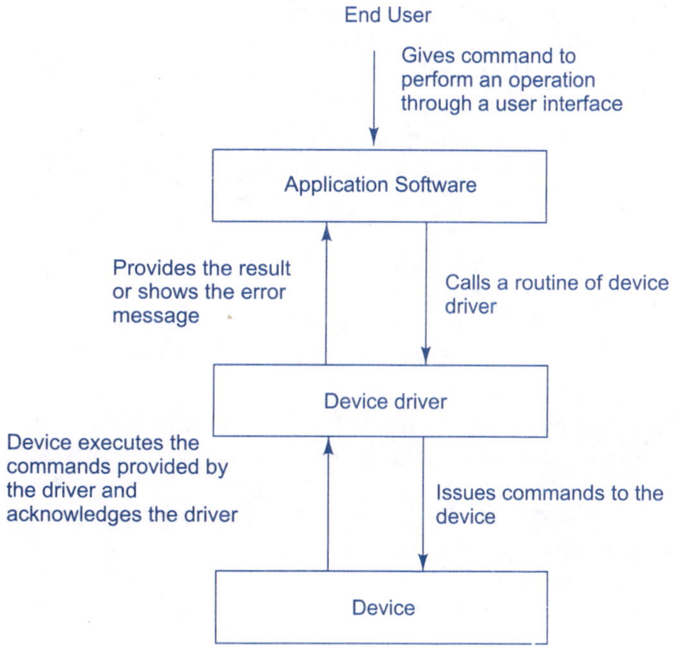

Fig. 10.6 Working of a device driver

10.4 SYSTEM DEVELOPMENT PROGRAMS

System development programs known as *programming software* allow the users to develop programs in different programming languages. The process of developing and executing a program involves the following tasks:

- Debugging the program
- Linking the various variables and objects with the libraries files
- Translating the code from one language to another
- Running the machine code to perform the desired task

In order to carry out these tasks, we need the following system development tools:

- Language translators
- Linkers
- Debuggers
- Editors

10.4.1 Language Translators

Language translator is used to convert the program code written in one language to another language. The program code provided as an input to the language translator is known as *source code*. The source code is a high-level or an assembly language program. The language translator converts the high-level language program into the low-level language program called *object code*. Compiler, interpreter and assembler are the most common examples of language translator. A compiler translates a high-level program into a low-level program and an assembler translates an assembly language program into a low-level program. An interpreter also produces a low-level program from a high-level program, but the working of the interpreter is not similar to that of the compiler. An interpreter processes the high-level program line-by-line and simultaneously, produces the low-level program. On the other hand, a compiler compiles the high-level program in one go. Figure 10.7 shows the input and the output of the various language translators.

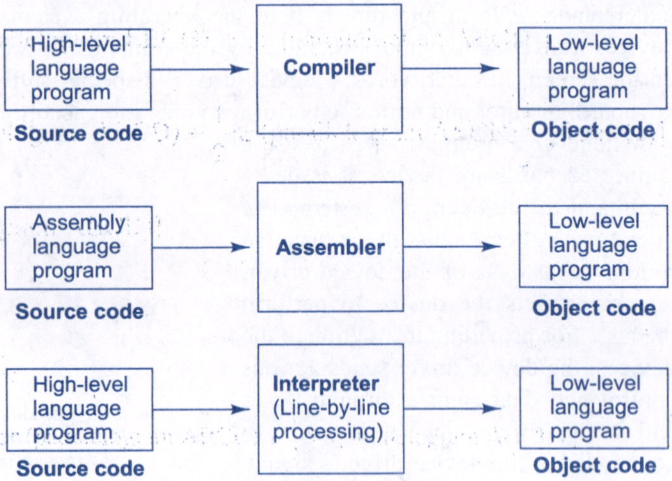

Fig. 10.7 Language translators

10.4.2 Linkers

Most of the high-level languages allow the developer to develop a large program containing multiple modules. Linker arranges the object code of all the modules that have been generated by the language translator into a single program. The execution unit of the computer system is incapable of linking all the modules at the execution time and therefore, linker is regarded as one of the important software because of its ability to combine all the modules into a single program. Linker assembles the various objects generated by the compiler in such a manner that all the objects are accepted as a single program during execution. Linker also includes the links of various objects, which are defined in the runtime libraries. In many cases, linker inserts the symbolic address of the objects in place of their real address. Figure 10.8 illustrates the working of a linker.

10.4.3 Debuggers

Debugger is the software that is used to detect the errors and bugs present in the programs. The debugger locates the position of the errors in the program code with the help of what is known as the *Instruction Set Simulator (ISS)* technique. ISS is capable of stopping the execution of a program at the point where an erroneous statement is encountered.

Debugger is divided into two types, namely, *machine-level debugger* and *symbolic debugger*. The machine-level debugger debugs the object code of the program and shows all the lines where bugs are detected. On the other hand, the symbolic debugger debugs the original code, i.e., the high-level language code of the program. It shows the position of the bug in the original code of the program developed by the programmer.

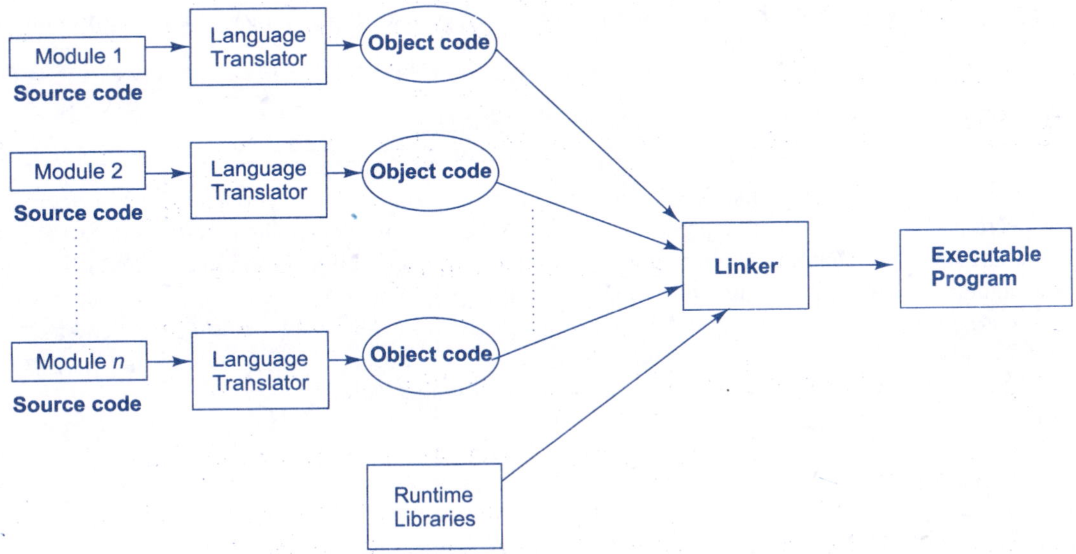

Fig. 10.8 Working of linker

While debugging a program, the debugger performs a number of functions other than debugging, such as inserting breakpoints in the original code, tracking the value of specific variables, etc. In order to debug the program, a debugger helps us to perform the following tasks:

- Step-by-step execution of a program
- Back tracking for checking the previous steps
- Stopping the execution of the program until the errors are corrected

10.4.4 Editors

Editor is a special program that allows the user to work with text in the computer system. It is used for the documentation purposes and enables us to edit the information present in an existing document or a file. The editor enables us to perform the various editing operations such as copy, cut and paste while editing the text. On the basis of the content edited by the editors, they are divided into the following categories:

- **Text editor** It is used to edit plain text. An operating system always includes a text editor for updating the configuration files.
- **Digital audio editor** It is used to edit the information related to the audio components of a multimedia application. These editors are used in audio applications where editing the music and the sound signals is necessary.
- **Graphics editor** It is used to edit the information related to the graphical object. These editors are generally used in the multimedia applications where the user is working with multiple animation objects.
- **Binary file editor** It is used to edit the digital data or the binary data, i.e., data having strings of 0s and 1s.
- **HTML editor** It is used to edit the information included in the web pages.

- **Source code editor** It is used to edit the source code of a program written in a programming language such as C, C++ and Java.

10.5 STANDARD APPLICATION PROGRAMS

Standard application programs, also known as *general-purpose application programs*, are programs that perform certain common information processing tasks for the users. For example, preparing documents such as letters and notes are common among almost all organisations as well as individuals. Similarly, creating and managing databases of products and employees are very common activities in large organisations. Ready-to-use programs for such applications are available from hardware or software vendors. These programs would not only increase significantly the productivity of users but also decrease the investment in terms of time and cost. Examples of standard application programs include:

- Word processor
- Spreadsheet
- Database Manager
- Desktop Publisher
- Web Browser

We shall briefly discuss some of these programs in this section.

10.5.1 Word Processor

Word processor is an application software that is generally used to create documents such as letters, reports, etc. It is one of the most commonly used computer applications. Word processor enables us to enter text in a document in a particular format. It also allows us to modify the existing text and apply the formatting features, such as boldface and italic, change the colour of the text, change the writing style of the text, etc. The word processor application software also allows us to perform different operations, such as cut-paste for moving the text within the document, copy-paste for copying the text within a document or from one document to another document, etc. MS Word is the most common example of a word processor. Figure 10.9 shows the default window of MS Word.

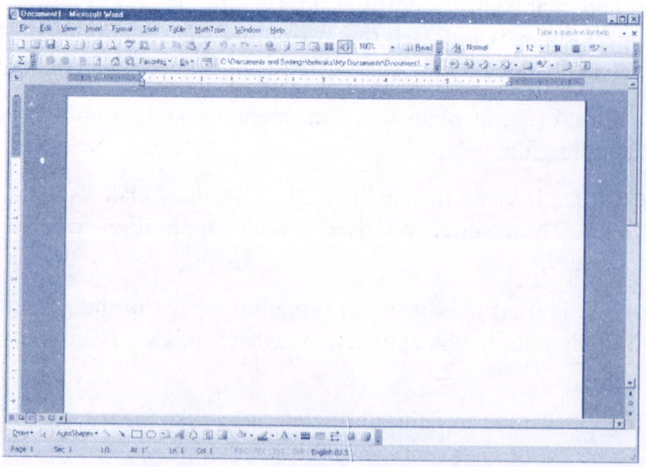

Fig. 10.9 The default window of MS Word

10.5.2 Spreadsheet

Spreadsheet is an application software that enables the user to maintain a worksheet in which information is stored in different cells. Each cell in the spreadsheet can contain numeric and alphanumeric data. Spreadsheet is also used as a computational tool by applying formulas on the values of cells. If we change the value of a cell in a spreadsheet, then all the values, which are dependent on that value, get automatically updated according to the new value. As a result, the users, who need to store and maintain financial information, always prefer a spreadsheet for storing the information.

MS Excel is the most common example of the spreadsheet software. Figure 10.10 shows the default window of MS Excel.

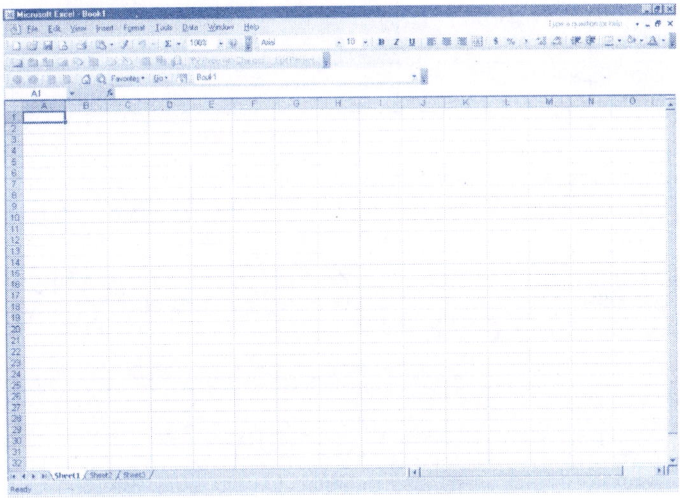

Fig. 10.10 The default window of MS Excel

10.5.3 Database Management System

Database Management System (DBMS) is a computer software that helps us to store and maintain records in a database. Database refers to a set of records, which are stored in a structured manner in the computer system. Record refers to a set of similar or dissimilar values related to an entity such as student and employee. DBMS allows a user to perform various operations such as search, update and delete on the data stored in the database. With the help of DBMS an end user can store, retrieve, and modify the data in an easy manner. The advantages of DBMS are as follows:

- It enables the user to organise all the information in a strategic manner.
- It helps the users in maintaining consistency in the information stored in the database.
- It helps the user in maintaining data integrity while performing the various operations on the database values.
- It allows the user to maintain the security of the confidential information by password-protecting the database.
- It helps in accessing information from any system connected in a networked system environment.

The DBMS used for maintaining a database always uses specific data model such as relational, hierarchical and network that describes the physical and the logical arrangement of data in the database. In the relational data model, different records are arranged in the form of tables containing rows and columns. In the hierarchical model, records are arranged in the form of a tree where each record is attached with one parent node and one or more child nodes. In the network model, data is arranged in the form of a network where each node is connected with one or more parent nodes as well as child nodes. Figure 10.11 shows the arrangement of records in different data models of the DBMS.

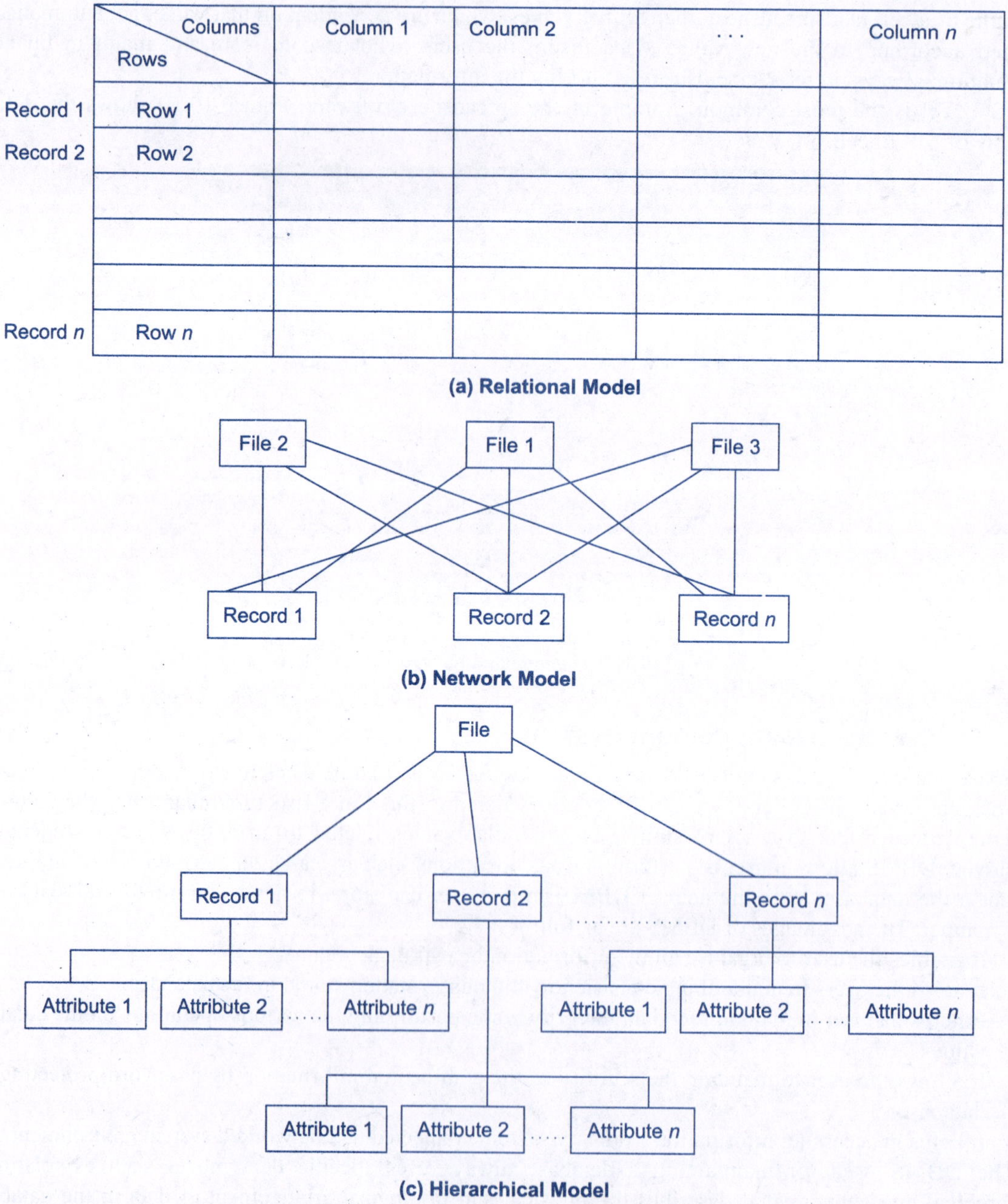

Fig. 10.11 Different data models used to design DBMS

DBMS comprises of different components, which are responsible for performing a specific task in the database system. Some of the components of DBMS are as follows:

- **Data structure** Data structure refers to a storage mechanism that is used to store multiple values as a single entity. In DBMS, different types of data structures are used to store the information related to an entity. These data structures include:
  - ***File*** It refers to a collection of multiple records.
  - ***Record*** It refers to a collection of multiple values of different data types related to one entity.
  - ***Field*** It refers to a set of different values having similar data type.
- **Transaction mechanism** DBMS always includes a transaction mechanism, which ensures that the basic properties of the database system are not affected by the processing of the transactions. A transaction mechanism included in a database system consists of the following properties:
  - ***Atomicity*** The transaction mechanism should complete either all tasks included in a transaction processing or none of them.
  - ***Consistency*** The transaction mechanism should be capable of maintaining consistency in the information stored in the multiple files of DBMS after the processing of a transaction.
  - ***Isolation*** The transaction mechanism should not allow any sub process of the transaction to use the intermediate data of another transaction.
  - ***Durability*** The transaction mechanism should be capable of providing information related to the transactions, which have been processed to change the information stored in the database.
- **Database query language** DBMS includes a query language system, which enables a user to perform various operations such as searching and updating the information stored in the database.

10.5.4 Desktop Publishing System

Desktop publishing system enables the user to perform various activities required for publishing of a page or set of pages. These activities include organising the content layout by setting margins and justification properties of the page. In the desktop publishing system, a page layout software is installed on a computer system that enables the end users to view the changes done at the time of designing the document. The page layout software uses the 'What You See Is What You Get (WYSIWYG)' technique for displaying the preview of the page being designed. Desktop publishing system is also referred as DTP.

Desktop publishing system is generally used in the publishing industry, where there is a need to publish information either through print media or display media. It helps the users to design the desired page layout containing different components such as text, graphics and images. Some of the commonly used DTP application software include: Quark XPress, InDesign, Microsoft Publisher, Apple Pages.

10.6 UNIQUE APPLICATION PROGRAMS

There are situations where organisations need to develop their own programs to accomplish certain tasks that are unique to their areas of operations. Similarly, individuals like scientists, engineers, accountants, teachers and other professionals write their own programs to solve their problems. Such programs are known as *unique application programs* or application-specific programs. These programs are also referred to as end-user application programs. Examples of unique applications include:

- Managing the inventory of a store
- Preparing pay-bills of employees in an organisation
- Processing examination results of students
- Reserving seats in trains or airlines
- Analysing mathematical models
- Computing personal income tax
- And many more

These programs are usually developed in one of the high-level languages, such as C, C++ or Java and therefore, developing such programs in-house would require skilled programmers with deep knowledge not only in programming languages but also in programming environment.

We will discuss below in this section two applications which are usually developed in-house to suit the user's unique requirements.

10.6.1 Inventory Management System

Inventory management system helps in keeping a record of the huge amount of items stored in warehouse and storerooms. In order to keep a record of inventory or items, application software called inventory management system, which makes use of DBMS, is used. DBMS is responsible for storing the information related to the items in the form of various files and tables. It also helps in storing the information related to the location, where a particular item is placed. Inventory management system enables a user to get a report on the items stored in the warehouse or storeroom on the basis of the different conditions, such as availability of items, shipping date of item, etc.

The database of the inventory management system identifies each item by a unique identification number. The identification number is used as the primary key of an item in the database. Primary key refers to an attribute, which must contain a unique value for each item of the database. The identification number can be dependent on the various properties, such as type, model and manufacturing date of the items, etc. Nowadays, the identification number of an item is specified on the barcodes printed on each item. Barcode is a group of small and black vertical lines of varying widths. The barcodes are not understandable by a human being and is always read by an input device called barcode reader. A barcode reader is similar to the handheld scanner that scans the barcode of the item in order to enter the barcode in the database. Figure 10.12 shows the sample barcode of an item.

Fig. 10.12 Barcode of an item

The use of barcode technology with inventory management system saves a lot of time as the user is not required to manually enter the item details. These details are automatically read by the barcode scanner and stored in the database of the inventory management system. An inventory management system finds its application in those organisations where a constant maintenance and updation of inventory information is required.

10.6.2 Pay-roll System

Pay-roll system is the application software that enables us to perform the various activities related to pay-roll accounting and pay-roll administration process. It is used by the HR department of an organisation for the purpose of computation of salary of employees. A typical pay-roll processing system provides an interface to the user through which the user can enter salary related details, such as attendance, tax deduction, etc. A pay-roll system is an effective and efficient way of computing the salary of employees as it eliminates the manual task of performing computations and automates most of the tasks related to pay-roll processing.

A pay-roll system can be custom built or it can be an off-the-shelf application software. Several ERP products include a dedicated module on pay-roll processing which is particularly used in enterprise-wise implementation of pay-roll processing. A pay-roll system can also be used to print or e-mail the salary slips of employees.

10.7 PROBLEM SOLVING

Problems that can be solved through a computer may range in size and complexity. Since computers do not possess any common sense and cannot make any unplanned decisions, the problem, whether it is simple or complex, has to be broken into a well-defined set of solution steps for the computer to implement.

Problem solving is the process of solving a problem in a computer system by following a sequence of steps. The major steps that we need to follow for solving a problem are:

1. **Preparing hierarchy chart** A hierarchy chart shows the top-down solution of a problem. In case of large problems, we can break them into parts representing small tasks, prepare several algorithms and later combine them into one large algorithm.
2. **Developing algorithm** An algorithm is a sequence of steps written in the form of English phrases that specify the tasks that are performed while solving a problem. It involves identifying the variable names and types that would be used for solving the problem.
3. **Drawing flowchart** A flowchart is the graphical representation of the flow of control and logic in the solution of a problem. The flowchart is a pictorial representation of an algorithm.
4. **Writing Pseudocode** Pseudocode is pretty much similar to algorithms. It uses generic syntax for describing the steps that are to be performed for solving a problem. Along with the statements written using generic syntax, pseudocode can also use English phrases for describing an action.

10.7.1 Hierarchy Chart

Hierarchy chart is a solution approach that suggests a top-down solution of a problem. We very often come across large problems to be solved using computers. It may be very difficult to comprehend the solution steps of such large problems at one go. In such situations, we can decompose the problem into several parts, each representing a small task which is easily comprehensible and solvable. We can then prepare solution steps for each task independently and later combine them into one large solution algorithm. Figure 10.13 illustrates a hierarchy chart for computing

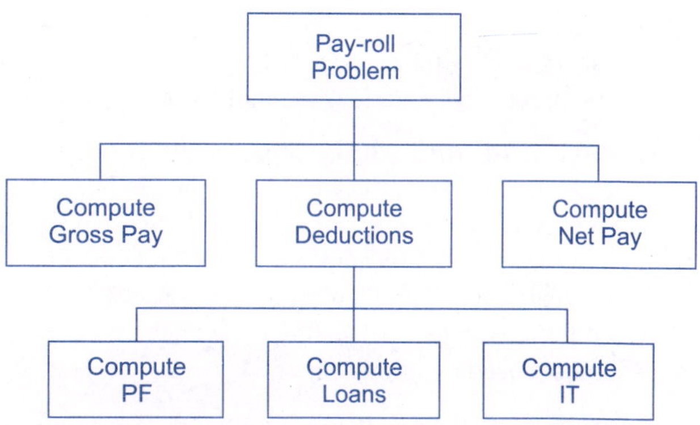

Fig. 10.13 Hierarchy chart for pay-roll problem

pay of an employee in an organisation. Since the chart graphically illustrates the structure of a program, it is also known as a *structure chart*.

While developing a computer program, we may treat each subtask as a module and prepare computer code for testing independently. This approach is popularly known as *modular programming*. Note that the hierarchy chart does not provide any detail about program logic. We have to use the tools discussed below to prepare logic for each task.

10.7.2 Algorithms

Algorithms help a programmer in breaking down the solution of a problem into a number of sequential steps. Corresponding to each step a statement is written in a programming language; all these statements are collectively termed as a program. The following is an example of an algorithm to add two integers and display the result:

```
Algorithm to add two integers and display the result
Step 1 - Accept the first integer as input from the user.
         (integer1)
Step 2 - Accept the second integer as input from the user.
         (integer2)
Step 3 - Calculate the sum of the two integers.
         (integer3 = integer1 + integer2)
Step 4 - Display integer3 as the result.
```

There is a time and space complexity associated with each algorithm. Time complexity specifies the amount of time required by an algorithm for performing the desired task. Space complexity specifies the amount of memory space required by an algorithm for performing the desired task. When solving a complex problem, it is possible to have more than one algorithm to provide the required solution. The algorithm that takes less time and requires less memory space is the best one.

10.7.3 Flowcharts

A flowchart can be defined as the pictorial representation of a process, which describes the sequence and flow of the control and information in a process. The flow of information is represented in a flowchart in a step-by-step form. This technique is mainly used for developing business workflows and solving problems using computers.

Flowchart uses different symbols for depicting different activities, which are performed at different stages of a process. The various symbols used in a flowchart are as follows:

- **Start and end** It is represented by an oval or a rounded rectangle in a flowchart. It is used to represent the starting and the ending of a process. Every process starts and ends at some point so a flowchart always contains one start as well as one end point. Figure 10.14 shows the start and the end symbols used in a flowchart.

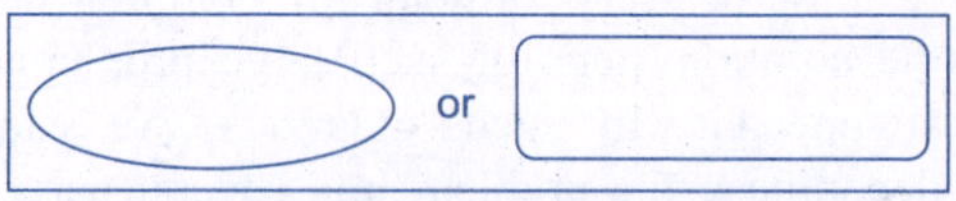

Fig. 10.14 Start and end symbol

- **Input or output** It is represented by a parallelogram in a flowchart. It is used to represent the inputs given by the user to the process and the outputs given by the process to the user. Figure 10.15 shows the input or output symbol.

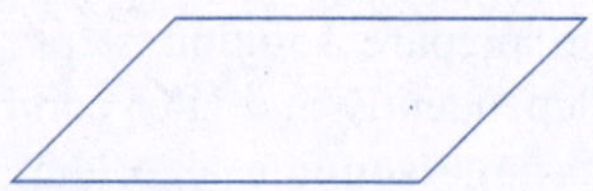

Fig. 10.15 Input or output symbol

- **Action or process** It is represented by a rectangle. It represents the actions, logics and calculations taking place in a process. Figure 10.16 shows the action or process symbol.

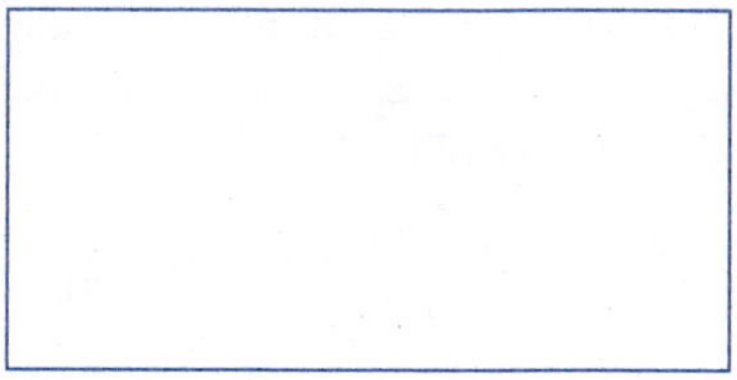

Fig. 10.16 Action or process symbol

- **Decision or condition** It is represented by a rhombus or a diamond shape in a flowchart. It represents the condition or the decision-making step in the flowchart. The result of the decision is a Boolean value, which is either true or false. Each of these values takes the flow of the program to a certain point, which is shown with the help of arrows. Figure 10.17 shows the decision or condition symbol.

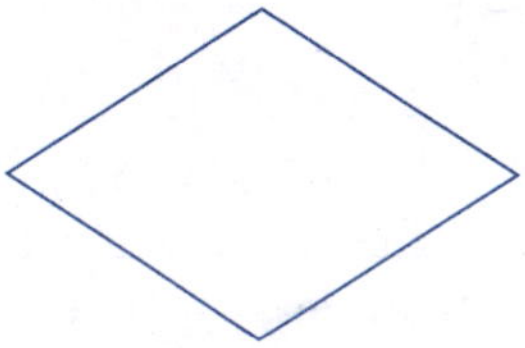

Fig. 10.17 Decision or condition symbol

- **Arrow** It is represented by a directed line in a flowchart. It represents the flow of process and the sequence of steps in the flowchart. It guides the process about the direction and the sequence, which is to be followed while performing the various steps in the process. Figure 10.18 shows the arrow symbol.
- **Connector** It is represented by a circle in a flowchart. It represents the continuation of the flow of steps when a flowchart continues to the next page. A character, such as an alphabet (a to z) or a symbol (α, β or χ), etc. can be placed in the circle at the position where the flow is broken and the same character is also placed in the circle at the position from where the flowchart continues. Figure 10.19 shows the connector symbol.

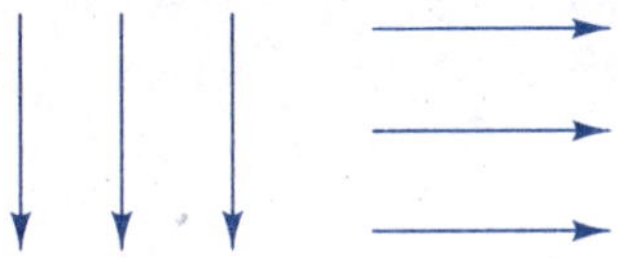

Fig. 10.18 Arrow symbol

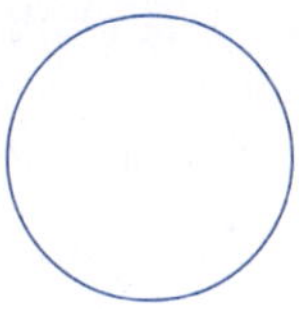

Fig. 10.19 Connector symbol

In order to understand how a flowchart represents flow of information, consider an example of flowchart in which addition of two numbers is represented. Figure 10.20 shows the flowchart for addition of two numbers.

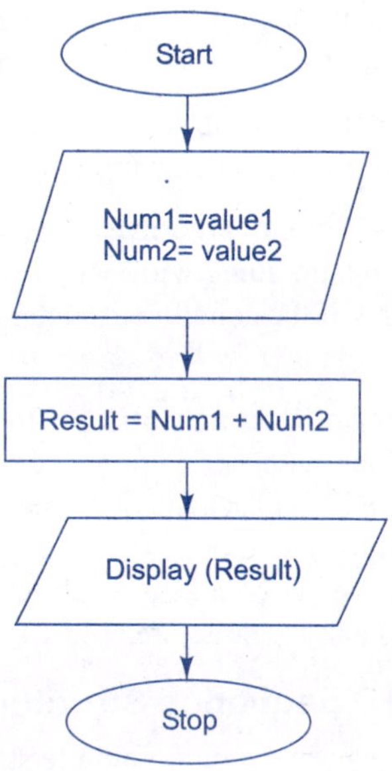

Fig. 10.20 Flowchart of addition of two numbers

10.7.4 Pseudocodes

Analysing a detailed algorithm before developing a program is very time consuming. Hence, there arises a need of a specification that only focuses on the logic of the program. Pseudocodes serve this purpose by specifying only the logic, which is used by the programmer for developing a computer program.

Pseudocode is not written using specific syntax of a programming language rather it is written with a combination of generic syntax and normal English language.

It helps the programmer understand the basic logic of the program after which it is the programmer's choice to write the final code in any programming language.

The example of a pseudocode to add two numbers and display the result is shown below:

```
A pseudocode to add two numbers and display the result
Define: Integer num1, num2, result.
Input: Integer num1.
Input: Integer num2.
Sum: result = num1 + num2
Output: Display(result).
```

After the pseudocode for a computer program has been written, it is used to develop the source code for the computer program. The source code is developed using a programming language, which can be an assembly language or a high level programming language. After the source code has been written, the programmer detects and eliminates any errors in the program so that the program generates the desired output after its execution.

10.8 STRUCTURING THE LOGIC

While writing the pseudocode for a problem, it is necessary to define all the logics used in the pseudocode for developing the program. Pseudocode of a problem should be able to describe the sequence of execution of statements and procedures specified in the program. The sequence of the execution of instructions determines the basic structure of a program or the logic used to solve a problem.

The basic structure of a program comprises of different sets of the statements, whose execution is dependent on some conditions and decisions. These conditions and decision-making statements are specified in a control structure. Depending upon the sequence of the execution of the statements, the control structures are categorised into the following types:

- **Sequence structure** The execution of the statements in a sequence structure is done sequentially, i.e., all the statements are executed in the same order as they are written in the program.
- **Selection structure** In the selection structure, two sets of statement blocks are written in a program along with one or more conditions. The execution of a particular block's statements occurs only if the conditional statement specified at the beginning of the block is true. A selection structure is also known as *branching structure*.
- **Repetition structure** In the repetition structure, a block of two or more instructions is specified along with a conditional statement. The execution of these instructions is repeated many times if the conditional statement is true. This structure is also known as *looping structure*.

We must incorporate these program constructs into the program design, whether as a flowchart or as a pseudocode. We can also combine the constructs, if necessary. For example, a selection structure can be a part of a looping structure.

10.8.1 Sequence Structure

In a sequence structure, multiple statements are written in a simple sequence in the program. The execution of these statements is not affected by any condition. Generally, sequence structure is used for performing simple computations, which do not require any decision-making. Figure 10.21 shows the representation of statements in the sequence structure.

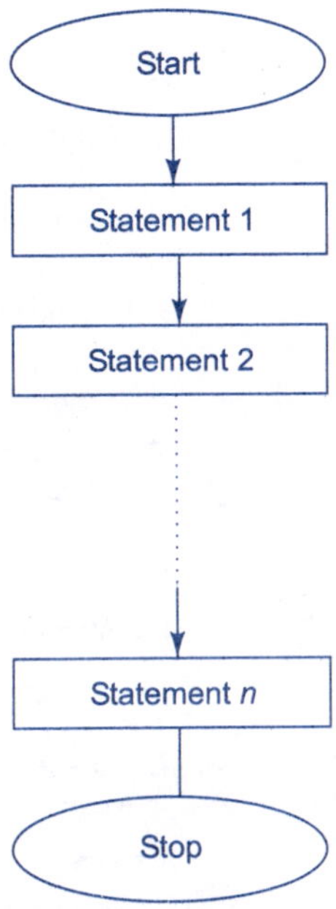

1. Begin
2. Statement 1
3. Statement 2
⋮
n–1. Statement *n*
n. End

Flowchart **Pseudocode**

Fig. 10.21 Representation of statements in the sequential structure

10.8.2 Selection Structure

In the selection structure, the execution of a set of statements is done according to a pre-specified condition. The selection structure is also known as decision-making structure because the decision to execute a particular set of statements is made on the basis of the conditional statement. The selection structure is categorised into the following types:

- **If-Then** In this selection structure, If and Then clauses are used to represent a condition as well as set of statements. In the If clause, the conditional statement is written, while in the Then clause the set of statements to be executed are specified. The execution of the statements specified in the Then clause occurs only if the condition is true.
- **If-Then-Else** This selection structure is very much similar to the If-Then selection structure. The only difference between the two is that in If-Then-Else selection structure two sets of statements are specified. One set of statements is represented in the Then clause and another is represented in the Else clause. If the condition given in the If clause is true, then all the statements specified in the Then clause are executed; otherwise statements given in the Else clause are executed.
- **Case Type** In this selection structure, multiple sets of statements are specified. Each block of statements is associated with a value. The selection of a particular set of statements is made on the basis of the value of the variable given at the beginning of the selection structure.

Figure 10.22 shows the representation of statements in the If-Then-Else selection structure.

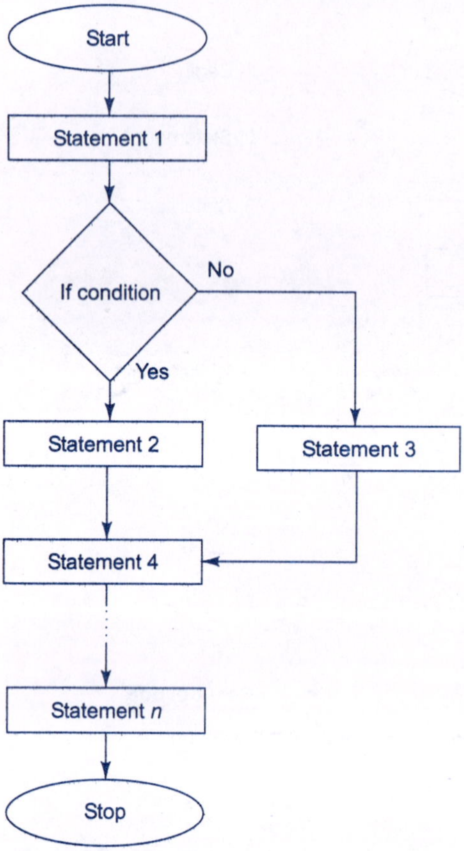

Flowchart

```
1. Begin
2. Statement 1
3. If (Condition1)
      Then
         Statement 2
      Else
         Statement 3
4. Statement 4
   ⋮
n–1. Statement n
n. End
```

Pseudocode

Fig. 10.22 Representation of statements in the If-Then-Else selection structure

10.8.3 Repetition Structure

In the repetition structure, only one set of multiple statements is specified. The same set of statements is executed several times on the basis of the condition specified along with the structure. The various types of repetition structure are as follows:

- **Do-while** In the Do-while structure, a set of statements is given in the Do block and a condition is given in the While block. The statements given in the Do block are executed till the given condition is true. At each instance of execution of block statements, the condition is checked. If the condition is true, then only the block statements are executed; otherwise the repetition structure is terminated.
- **Repeat-until** The Repeat-until structure is opposite to the Do-while repetition structure. In this structure, the repetitive execution of statements given in the Repeat clause occurs only when the condition given in the Until clause is false.

Figure 10.23 shows the representation of statements in the Do-while repetition structure.

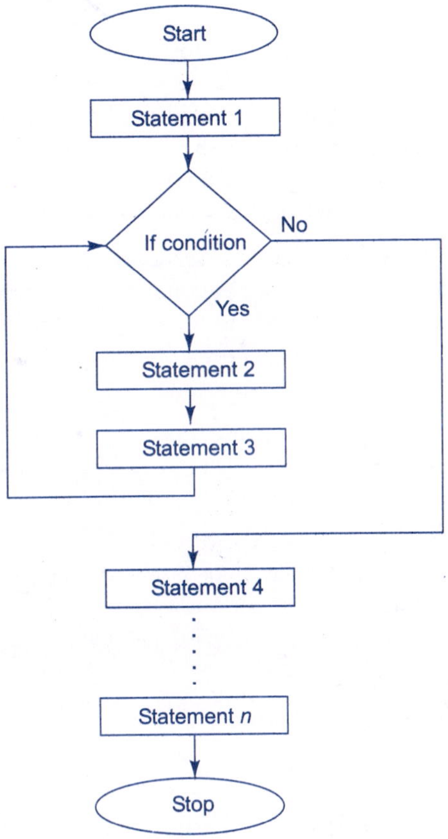

Flowchart

```
1. Begin
2. Statement 1
3. Do while condition
        is true
        Statement 2
        Statement 3
        End do
4. Statement 4
   .
   .
   .
n–1. Statement n
n End
```

Pseudocode

Fig. 10.23 Representation of the statements in the Do-while repetition structure

10.9 USING THE COMPUTER

Whenever a user wants to use a computer for solving a problem, he/she has to perform various interrelated tasks in a systematic manner. A user can not get the solution of a problem by simply providing input to the computer without preparing the base for solving the problem. The working process of a computer is similar to the human mind, which first analyses the complete situation of a problem, its causes and its parameters, and then decides the way to solve the problem on the basis of available parameters. All the activities, which have to be performed by a user in order to solve a problem using computer, are grouped into three phases:

- Understanding the problem
- Developing a program
- Executing the program

1. **Understanding the problem** It is the first stage of problem solving using a computer. In this stage, two basic activities are performed by the user. These activities are as follows:
   - ***Identifying parameters and constraints*** A user has to identify the role of different parameters in solving the problem, i.e., the user must have the knowledge about the relation between the various parameters and the problem itself. After identifying the problem and its parameters, the user has to identify the associated constraints that need to be considered in order to generate an accurate solution of the problem. The identification of parameters and constraints help in choosing the most appropriate method to solve the problem.
   - ***Collecting information*** After analysing the problem and choosing the solution method, a user has to collect the information related to the identified parameters of the problem. In order to collect the information, a user can use the documents and reports pertaining to the previous versions of the problem. The collected information helps in designing the layout of the output or solution of the problem.
2. **Developing a program** After analysing the problem, a user has to plan for developing the program, which will provide the solution of the program after execution. A program includes multiple instructions having a specific syntax. For developing a program, a user has to perform the following activities:
   - ***Identifying the logical structure*** It is the most important activity in which a user prepares the logical structure of the program by analysing the various tasks that need to be performed for solving the problem. In order to prepare the logical structure of a program, a user performs the following task:
     (i) Writing algorithm to list the various steps.
     (ii) Drawing flowchart to represent the flow of information.
     (iii) Writing pseudocode to specify the programming specifications.
   - ***Writing the computer program*** After preparing the logic, a user has to write the program code in a particular programming language. The program code should be syntactically and semantically correct in order to generate the desired result.
   - ***Debugging the program*** After writing the complete program, a user has to apply the debugging techniques for removing any possible errors in the program. Several programming environments provide debugging tools that aid the users in effectively and efficiently remove the errors in a program.
3. **Executing the program** After developing an error free program, it needs to be executed in order to view the solution of the original problem.

Chapter Summary

Computer software is one of the most important components of a computer system. The other component of a computer system is computer hardware. Computer software helps the computer hardware in carrying out their functions in an effective manner. Computer software can be either system software or application software.

System software is responsible for managing and controlling the hardware resources of a computer system. System software can be further divided into two major categories, which are system management programs and system development programs. Operating system, utility programs and device drivers are some of the examples of system management programs. Typical examples of system development programs include linkers, debuggers, and editors.

Application software is specially designed to cater the information processing needs of end users. Like system software, application software can be further divided into two major categories, which are standard application programs and unique application programs. Word processor, spreadsheet, database manager, desktop publisher and web browser are some of the standard application programs. The unique application programs are specially developed by the users to meet their specific requirements. For examples, inventory management system and pay-roll system comes under the category of unique application programs.

Computer based problem solving requires a series of steps such as preparing hierarchy charts, developing algorithms, drawing flowcharts, writing pseudocodes, and developing and executing programs.

Key Terms to Remember

- **Hardware:** Hardware refers to various electronic and mechanical devices, which are responsible for performing various operations, such as storing data into the storage devices, transferring data through buses and cables, etc.
- **Software:** Software is a set of programs and procedures containing a number of instructions for processing the data.
- **System software:** System software is the program that directly controls the working of hardware components of the computer system, and enables implementation of application software.
- **Application software:** Application software is the software that enables the end user to perform various tasks, such as creating documents, preparing presentations, creating databases, developing graphics and images, etc.
- **Operating system:** Operating system is a set of various small system software, which control the execution of various sub processes in a computer system.
- **Utility program:** Utility program refers to a small program that helps perform utility tasks in a computer system.
- **Device driver:** Device driver is a special software that enables a hardware device such as keyboard, monitor and printer to perform an operation according to the command given by the end user.
- **Editor:** Editor is a program that allows the user to write and edit text in the computer system.
- **Spreadsheet:** Spreadsheet is a computer program that enables the user to maintain a worksheet in which information is stored in different cells.
- **Hierarchy chart:** Hierarchy chart is a design tool that shows the top-down design of a problem solution.
- **Pseudocode:** Psuedocode is a set of instructions that describe the logic of a solution.
- **Algorithm:** Algorithm is a sequential structure of steps, which are performed to solve a particular problem.
- **Flowchart:** Flowchart is a pictorial representation of a process, which describes the sequence and flow of the control and information in a process.
- **Language translator:** It is a program that converts a high-level language program into a low-level language program. Compilers, assemblers and interpreters are examples of language translator.
- **Compiler:** It is a program that translates a high-level program into a machine language program.
- **Assembler:** It is a program that translates a program written in the assembly language into a machine language program.
- **Interpreter:** It is a program that translates a high-level program into machine code statement-by-statement. That is, a translated statement is executed before the next statement is translated.
- **Linker:** A program that combines several object code files into a single executable program.
- **Debugger:** It is a program used to detect errors and bugs in a program.

Review Questions

Fill in the Blanks

1. A computer system consists of two types of components, ______________ components and ______________ components.
2. Computer software is classified into two categories, namely, ______________ and ______________.
3. System software consists of two groups of programs: ______________ and ______________.
4. ______________ is responsible for managing the allocation of devices and resources to the various processes.
5. Device driver acts as a translator between the ______________ and the ______________.
6. A computer system requires special software called ______________ in order to interact with the I/O devices.
7. Language translator converts the high-level language program into the low-level program called ______________.
8. Application software includes two types programs: ______________ and ______________.
9. ______________ enables you to enter text in the document in a particular format.
10. Spreadsheet is generally used to calculate the values stored in a cell by applying ______________ on the values of other cells.
11. Database refers to a set of records, which are stored in a ______________ in the computer system.
12. In the hierarchical model, records are arranged in form of a ______________ in which each record is attached with one parent node and one or more children node.
13. Desktop publishing system is also known as ______________.
14. Pseudocode is not written using any specific ______________ of a programming language.
15. ______________ is a pictorial representation of a process, which describes the sequence and flow of the control and information in a process
16. In the ______________ structure, multiple statements are written in a simple sequence in the program.

Multiple Choice Questions

1. Which of the following is a hardware device?
   A. Device driver B. Barcode reader C. Interpreter D. Linker
2. A device driver acts as an interface between:
   A. End-user and I/O device B. Application software and I/O device
   C. Application software and operating system D. Operating system and I/O device
3. Which of the following software components enables a user to store data in the form of tables?
   A. Spreadsheet B. Editor C. DBMS D. Word processor
4. Which of the following is not a system software?
   A. Linkers B. Device drivers C. Operating system D. Word processor
5. Which of the following software helps the users to detect the errors while executing a program?
   A. Language Translator B. Debugger C. Loader D. Linker
6. Which of the following software runs at the basic level of computer system?
   A. Application software B. System software C. User software D. All of the above

7. A program in which multiple instructions of high-level language or assembly language instructions are written is generally known as:
   A. Psuedocode B. Source code C. Object code D. Machine code
8. A small program, which provides additional capabilities to the operating system, is known as:
   A. Application program B. System development program
   C. Utility program D. Translator program
9. A software, which links different elements of an object code with the library files, is known as:
   A. Editor B. Linker C. Loader D. Debugger
10. Which of the following options is not a utility system?
    A. Virus scanner B. System profiler C. Disk defragmenter D. Debugger
11. Which of the following is not a data structure?
    A. Record B. Table C. File D. Field
12. Which of the following data models enables us to arrange data files in the tree structure?
    A. Network model B. Relational model C. Hierarchical model D. None of the above
13. The software, which enables an end user to edit text and other components of a publishing document, is known as:
    A. Word processor B. Editor
    C. Desktop publishing system D. Debugger
14. A control structure in which only a single set of instructions executes several times is known as:
    A. Repetition structure B. Sequence structure C. Selection structure D. None of the above
15. Which of the following structure executes the set of instruction only when the given condition is false?
    A. If-Then B. Do-While C. If-Then-Else D. Repeat-Untill

Discussion Questions

1. What do you know about the components of a computer system?
2. Explain the different types of computer software.
3. What do you understand by the term system software?
4. Explain the major functions of an operating system.
5. What is the purpose of translator programs?
6. List a few popular standard application programs.
7. Explain the application of system development programs.
8. What does utility program mean?
9. What are the basic functions of DBMS?
10. What do you know about inventory management system?
11. What is meant by unique application program?
12. What is a language translator?
13. Differentiate between a compiler, an assembler and an interpreter.
14. What is a debugger?

15. Explain the basic features of a word processor application.

16. Explain the basic features of spreadsheet software.

17. Write down an algorithm to add a series of integer.

18. What do you understand by pseudocode?

19. List the various types of control structures.

20. List the different symbols used in a flowchart.

21. Write a short note on the following:

A. Graphic editor B. Disk defragmenter C. HTML editor D. System profiler E. Data model

22. Describe an algorithm for calculating the average of n numbers.

23. Develop a flowchart for finding the greatest among the given three numbers.

24. Write a psuedocode for solving the quadratic equation for x where $x = \dfrac{-b \pm \sqrt{b^2 - 4ac}}{2a}$

If ($b^2 - 4ac$) is negative, do not calculate the roots but instead print 'NEGATIVE'.

25. Draw a flowchart for solving the quadratic equation discussed above.

CHAPTER 11

OPERATING SYSTEMS

Chapter Objectives

In this chapter, we will learn:

- The concept of operating systems.
- Various functions of operating systems.
- Different types of operating systems.
- How user interfaces are provided in an operating system.
- Highlights of some important operating systems.

Chapter Outline

11.1 INTRODUCTION

An operating system (OS) is a software that makes the computer hardware to work. While the hardware provides 'raw computer power', the OS is responsible for making the computer power useful for the users. As discussed in the previous chapter, the OS is the main component of system software and therefore must be loaded and activated before we can accomplish any other task.

The operating system provides an interface for users to communicate with the computer. It also manages the use of hardware resources and enables proper implementation of application programs. In short, the operating system is the master control program of a computer. Figure 11.1 shows the different roles performed by an operating system. The main functions include:

- Operates CPU of the computer.
- Controls input/output devices that provide the interface between the user and the computer.
- Handles the working of application programs with the hardware and other software systems.
- Manages the storage and retrieval of information using storage devices such as disks.

Every computer, irrespective of its size and application, needs an operating system to make it functional and useful. Operating systems are usually prewritten by the manufacturers and supplied with the hardware and are rarely developed in-house owing to its technical complexity. There are many operating systems developed during the last few decades but the popular among them are MS-DOS, Windows 2000, Windows XP, Windows Server 2003, UNIX and Linux.

In this chapter we shall discuss in detail the various functions of operating systems, different types of operating systems and their services, and the types of user interfaces available.

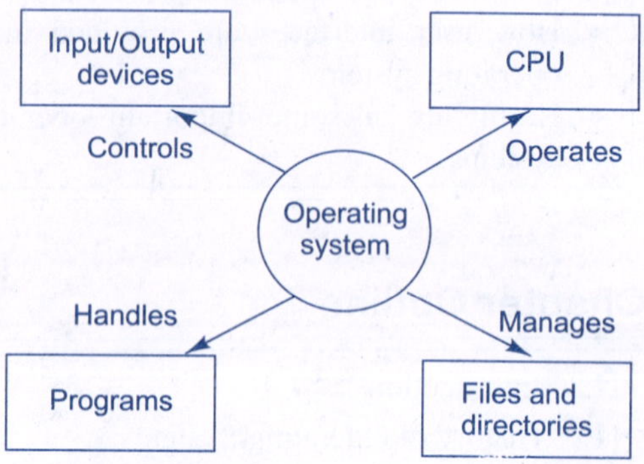

Fig. 11.1 The roles of an operating system

11.2 HISTORY OF OPERATING SYSTEMS

A series of developments in the computer architecture led to the evolution of the operating system during the later half of the 20th century. During the 1940's, there was no operating system and assembly language was used to develop programs that could directly interact with the hardware. The computer systems during this period were mainly used by the researchers, who were both the programmers as well as the end users of the computer system.

During the 1950s, more number of people started using the computer systems. This led to a repetition of tasks as everyone started developing their own programs and device drivers. Different people created device drivers for the same input and output devices. To avoid this repetition of tasks, various batch processing operating systems such as BKY, CAL and Chios were developed during this period. FORTRAN Monitor System, General Motors Operating System and Input Output System are the other operating systems developed in the 1950s. The operating systems developed during this period were capable of performing only a single task at a time.

During the 1960s, multi-tasking operating systems were developed. These operating systems ensured better utilisation of resources by allowing the multiple tasks to be performed simultaneously. They also allowed multiple programs to remain in memory at the same time. Central Processing Unit (CPU) executed multiple processes at a single time and also handled the hardware devices attached to the computer system. These operating systems used the concepts of spooling and time-sharing model for achieving the multi-tasking functionality. The various operating systems developed during the 1960s include Admiral, Basic Executive System, Input Output Control System and SABRE (Semi-Automatic Business Related Environment).

During the 1970s, a major breakthrough was achieved in the development of operating system with the introduction of UNIX by AT&T Bell Labs. UNIX supported a multi-user environment where multiple users could work on a computer system. The core functionality of UNIX resided in a kernel that was responsible for performing file, memory and process management. UNIX also came bundled with utility programs for performing specific tasks. The other operating systems that were introduced in the 1970s include DOS/VS, OS/VS1and OpenVMS.

During the 1980s, some key operating systems were developed including MS-DOS, HP-UX and Macintosh. MS-DOS was developed by Microsoft and could be installed on desktop Personal Computers (PCs), such as Intel 80x86 PCs. HP-UX was similar to UNIX and was developed by Hewlett Packard. This operating system could be installed on the HP PA RISC computer systems. Macintosh was developed by Apple computers and could be installed on the desktop PCs such as Motorola 680x0. MS DOS and Macintosh became quite popular in the 1980's and are still in use.

A number of operating systems were developed during the 1990s including Windows 95, Windows 98, Windows NT, FreeBSD and OS/2. Windows 95, Windows 98 and Windows NT were GUI based operating systems developed by Microsoft. FreeBSD was similar to UNIX and was available free of cost. OS/2 was introduced by IBM and could be installed on Intel/AMD Pentium and Intel 80x86 based computer systems. The decade of 1990 revolutionised the way of computing through robust GUI-based operating systems and fast processing devices.

The first decade of 21st century has seen the development of operating systems such as MAC OS X, Windows 2000, Windows Server 2003, Windows ME and Windows XP. With the advent of Internet, security has been the prime focus of the operating systems of this era.

11.3 FUNCTIONS OF OPERATING SYSTEMS

The main function of an operating system is to manage the resources such as memory and files of a computer system. The operating system also resolves the conflicts that arise when two users or programs request the same resource at the same time. Therefore, the operating system is also called the resource manager of a computer system. The currently used operating systems such as Windows 2000, Windows Server 2003 and Linux also support networking that allows the sharing of files and resources such as printer and scanner. The following are some of the important functions of an operating system:

- **Process management** It manages the processes running in a computer system. A process is basically a program that is being currently run by a user on a computer system. For example, a word processor application program such as Microsoft Word runs as a process in a computer system.
- **Memory management** It manages the memory resources of a computer system. There are various memory resources of a computer system including primary memory or Random Access Memory (RAM) and secondary memory like hard disk and Compact Disk (CD). All the programs

are loaded in the main memory before their execution. It is the function of the operating system to determine how much memory should be provided to each process.

- **File management** It manages the files and directories of a computer system. A file can be defined as a collection of information or data that is stored in the memory of a computer system. Every file has a unique name associated with it. The organisation of files and directories in a computer system is referred as file system. An operating system allows us to create, modify, save, or delete files in a computer system.
- **Device management** This function of operating system deals with the management of peripheral devices, such as printer, mouse and keyboard attached to a computer system. An operating system interacts with the hardware devices through specific device drivers. The primary task of an operating system is to manage the input/output operations performed by the end users.
- **Security management** It ensures security for a computer system from various threats such as virus attacks and unauthorised access. An operating system uses various techniques, such as authentication, authorisation, cryptography, etc for ensuring security of a computer system.

Figure 11.2 depicts the various functions of an operating system.

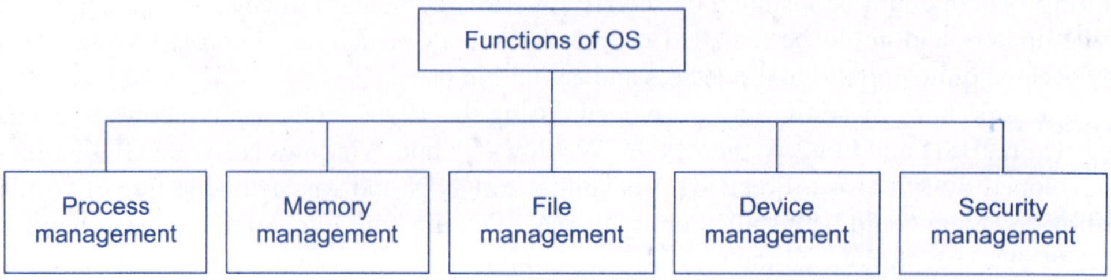

Fig. 11.2 The functions of an operating system

11.4 PROCESS MANAGEMENT

Process management involves the execution of various tasks such as creation of processes, scheduling of processes, management of deadlocks and termination of processes. When a process runs in a computer system, a number of resources such as memory and CPU of the computer system are utilised. It is the responsibility of an operating system to manage the running processes by performing tasks such as resource allocation and process scheduling. The operating system also has to synchronise the different processes effectively in order to ensure consistency of shared data.

Generally, only a single process is allowed to access the CPU for its execution at a particular instant of time. When one process is being processed by the CPU, the other processes have to wait until the execution of that particular process is complete. After the CPU completes the execution of a process, the resources being utilised by that process are made free and the execution of the next process is initiated. All the processes that are waiting to be executed are said to be in a queue. In some cases, a computer system supports parallel processing allowing a number of processes to be executed simultaneously.

A process consists of a set of instructions to be executed called *process code*. A process is also associated with some data that is to be processed. The resources that a process requires for its execution are called *process components*. There is also a state associated with a process at a particular instant of time called *process state*. Similar to these concepts, there are a number of concepts associated with the process management function of an operating system. Some of these key concepts are:

- Process state
- Process Control Block (PCB)
- Process operations
- Process scheduling
- Process synchronisation
- Interprocess communication
- Deadlock

11.4.1 Process State

A process state can be defined as the condition of a process at a particular instant of time. There are basically seven states of a process:

- **New** It specifies the time when a process is created.
- **Ready** It specifies the time when a process is loaded into the memory and is ready for execution.
- **Waiting** It specifies the time when a process waits for the allocation of CPU time and other resources for its execution.
- **Executing** It is the time when a process is being executed by the CPU.
- **Blocked** It specifies the time when a process is waiting for an event like I/O operation to complete.
- **Suspended** It specifies the time when a process is ready for execution but has not been placed in the ready queue by the operating system.
- **Terminated** It specifies the time when a process is terminated and the resources being utilised by the process are made free.

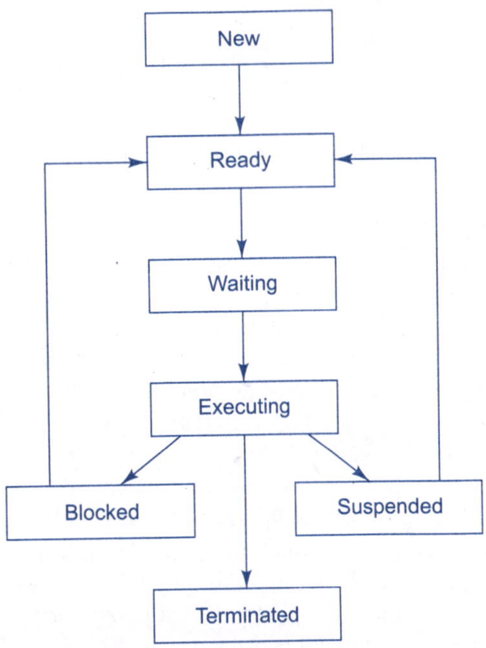

Fig. 11.3 The different states of a process

Figure 11.3 illustrates the various process states.

The Fig. 11.3 shows that a process is initially in the new state when it is created. After the process has been created, the state of the process changes from new to ready state where the process is loaded into the memory. The state of the process changes from ready to the waiting state when the process is loaded into the memory. The process state changes from waiting to the executing state after the CPU time and other resources are allocated to it and the process starts running. After the process has executed successfully, it is terminated and its state changes to terminated.

11.4.2 Process Control Block (PCB)

PCB is a data structure associated with a process that provides complete information about the process. PCB is important in a multiprogramming environment as it captures information pertaining to a number of processes running simultaneously. PCB comprises of the following:

- **Process id** It is an identification number that uniquely identifies a process.
- **Process state** It refers to the state of a process such as ready and executing.
- **Program counter** It points to the address of the next instruction to be executed in a process.
- **Register information** It comprises of the various registers, such as index and stack that are associated with a process.
- **Scheduling information** It specifies the priority information pertaining to a process that is required for process scheduling.
- **Memory related information** This section of the PCB comprises of page and segment tables. It also stores the data contained in base and limit registers.
- **Accounting information** This section of the PCB stores the details relate to CPU utilisation and execution time of a process.
- **Status information related to I/O** This section of the PCB stores the details pertaining to resource utilisation and the files opened during process execution.

The operating system maintains a table called *process table*, which stores the PCBs related to all the processes. Figure 11.4 shows the structure of PCB.

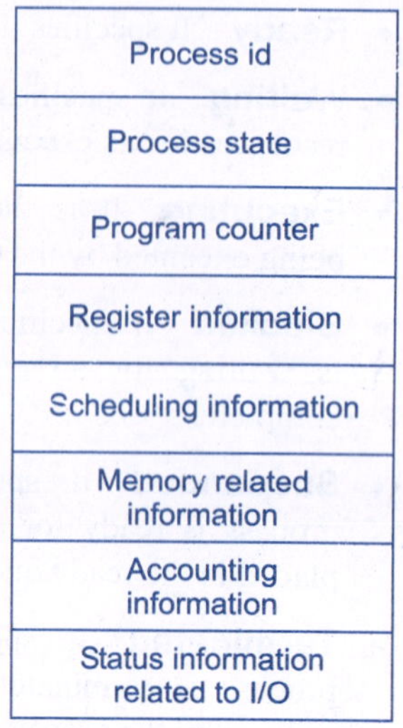

Fig. 11.4 The structure of a PCB

11.4.3 Process Operations

The process operations carried out by an operating system are primarily of two types, *process creation* and *process termination*. Process creation is the task of creating a new process. There are different situations in which a new process is created. A new process can be created during the time of initialisation of operating system or when system calls such as create-process and fork( ) are initiated by other processes. The process, which creates a new process using system calls, is called *parent process* while the new process that is created is called *child process*. The child processes can further create new processes using system calls. A new process can also be created by an operating system based on the request received from the user. Figure 11.5 shows the hierarchical structure of multiple processes running in a computer system.

The process creation operation is very common in a running computer system because corresponding to every task that is performed there is a process associated with it. For instance, a new process is created every time a user logs on to a computer system, an application program such as MS Word is initiated, or when a document is printed.

Process termination is an operation in which a process is terminated after it has executed its last instruction. When a process is terminated, the resources that were being utilised by the process are released by the operating system. When a child process terminates, it sends the status information back to the parent process before terminating. The child process can also be terminated by the parent process if the task performed by the child process is no longer needed. In addition, when a parent process terminates, it has to terminate the child process as well because a child process cannot run when its parent process has been terminated.

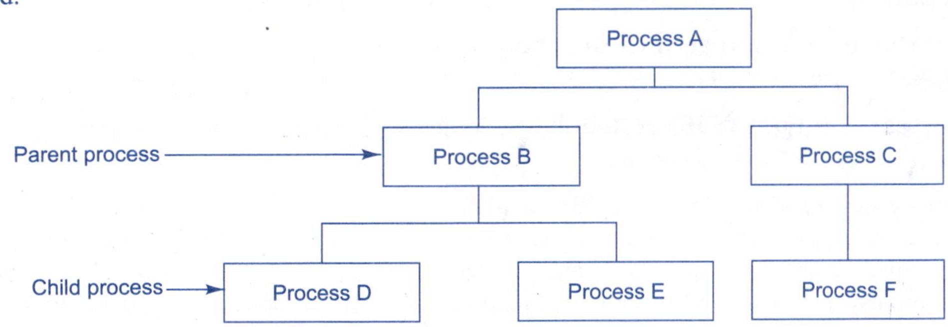

Fig. 11.5 The hierarchical structure of processes

The termination of a process when all its instructions have been executed successfully is called *normal termination*. However, there are instances when a process terminates due to some error. This is called *abnormal termination* of a process.

11.4.4 Process Scheduling

Process scheduling is the task performed by an operating system for deciding the priority in which the processes, which are in ready and waiting states, are allocated the CPU time for their execution. Process scheduling is very important in multiprogramming and multitasking operating systems where multiple processes are executed simultaneously. Process scheduling ensures maximum utilisation of CPU because a process is always running at a specific instant of time. At first, the processes that are to be executed are placed in a queue called *job queue*. The processes, which are present in the main memory and are ready for CPU allocation, are placed in a queue called *ready queue*. If a process is waiting for an I/O device then that process is placed in a queue called *device queue*.

An operating system uses a program called *scheduler* for deciding the priority in which a process is allocated the CPU time. Scheduler is of three types:

- **Long term scheduler** It selects the processes that are to be placed in the ready queue. The long term scheduler basically decides the priority in which processes must be placed in the main memory.
- **Mid term scheduler** It places the blocked or suspended processes in the secondary memory of a computer system. The task of moving a process from the main memory to the secondary memory is referred as swapping out. The task of moving back a swapped-out process from the secondary memory to the main memory is referred as swapping in. The swapping of processes is performed to ensure the best utilisation of main memory.
- **Short term scheduler** It decides the priority in which processes in the ready queue are allocated the CPU time for their execution. The short term scheduler is also referred as CPU scheduler.

An operating system uses two types of scheduling policies for process execution, preemptive and non preemptive. In the preemptive scheduling policy, a low priority process has to suspend its execution if a high priority process is waiting in the queue for its execution. However in the non preemptive scheduling policy, processes are executed in first come first serve basis, which means the next process is executed only when currently running process finishes its execution. The selection of the next process, however, may be done considering the associated priorities. Operating systems perform the task of assigning priorities to processes based on certain scheduling algorithms. Some of the key scheduling algorithms are:

- **First Come First Served (FCFS) scheduling** In this scheduling algorithm, the first process in a queue is processed first.
- **Shortest Job First (SJF) scheduling** In this scheduling algorithm, the process that requires shortest CPU time is executed first.
- **Priority scheduling** In this scheduling algorithm, a priority is assigned to all the processes and the process with highest priority is executed first. Priority assignment of processes is done on the basis of internal factors such as CPU and memory requirements or external factors such as user's choice. The priority scheduling algorithm can support either preemptive or non-preemptive scheduling policy.
- **Round Robin (RR) scheduling** In this scheduling algorithm, a process is allocated the CPU for a specific time period called time slice or time quantum, which is normally of 10 to 100 milliseconds. If a process completes its execution within this time slice then it is removed from the queue otherwise it has to wait until the next time slice.

11.4.5 Process Synchronisation

Process synchronisation is the task of synchronising the execution of processes in such a manner that no two processes have access to the same shared data or resource. When multiple processes are concurrently running then they may attempt to gain access to the same shared data or resource. This can lead to inconsistency in the shared data as the changes made by one process in the shared data may not be reflected when another process accesses the same shared data. In order to avoid such inconsistency of data, it is important that the processes are synchronised with each other.

One of the important concepts related to process synchronisation is that of critical section problem. Each process contains a set of code called critical section through which a specific task, such as changing the value of a global variable and writing certain data to a file, is performed. To ensure that only a single process enters its critical section at a specific instant of time, the processes need to coordinate with other by sending requests for entering the critical section. When a process is in its critical section no other process is allowed to enter the critical section.

Peterson's solution is one of the solutions to critical section problem involving two processes. Peterson's solution states that when one process is executing its critical section then the other process executes the rest of the code and vice versa. This ensures that only one process is in the critical section at a particular instant of time.

Locking is another solution to critical section problem in which a process acquires a lock before entering its critical section. When the process finishes executing its critical section, it releases the lock. The lock is then available for any other process that wants to enter the critical section. The locking mechanism also ensures that only one process is in the critical section at a particular period of time.

Another solution to the critical section problem is that of *Semaphore*. It is basically a synchronisation tool in which the value of an integer variable called semaphore is retrieved and set using wait and signal operations. Based on the value of the Semaphore variable, a process is allowed to enter its critical section.

11.4.6 Interprocess Communication

Interprocess communication is the method of communication between processes through which processes interact with each other for gaining access to shared data and resources. There are two methods of interprocess communication, *shared memory* and *message passing*.

In the shared memory method, a part of memory is shared between the processes. A process can write the data that it wants to share with other processes in to the memory. Similarly, another process can read the data that has been written by another process. Figure 11.6 shows the shared memory method of interprocess communication.

In Fig. 11.6, P1 and P2 represent the two processes. P1 writes the data that it needs to share with P2 in the shared memory. P2 then reads the data written by P1 from the shared memory.

In the message passing method, a process sends a message to another process for communication. This method allows the sharing of data between processes in the form of messages. Figure 11.7 shows the message passing method of interprocess communication.

In Fig. 11.7, P1 sends the shared data in the form of a message to the kernel and then the kernel sends the message sent by P1 to P2.

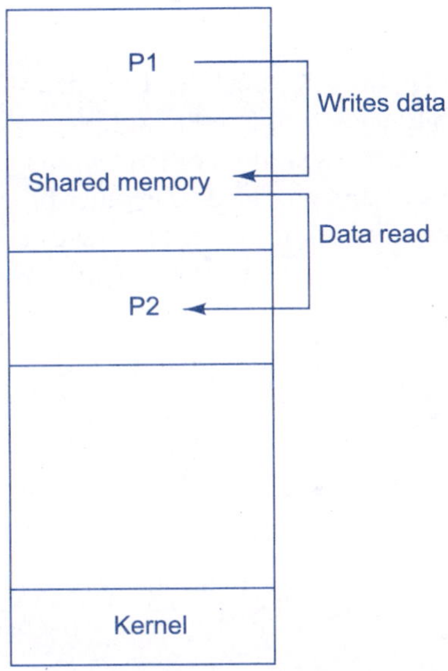

Fig. 11. 6 The shared memory method of interprocess communication

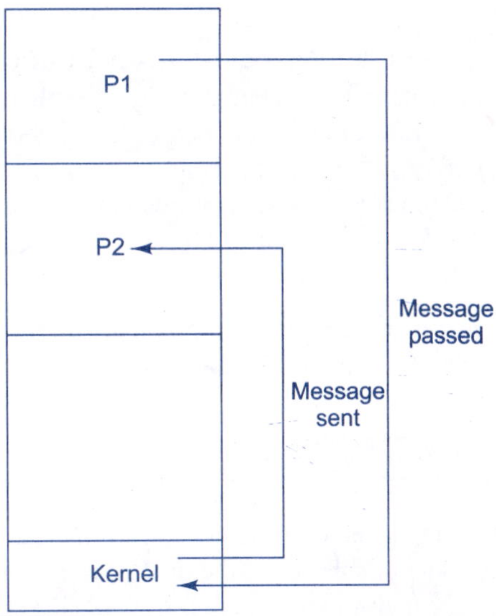

Fig. 11.7 The message passing method for the interprocess communication

11.4.7 Deadlock

Deadlock is a condition that occurs when multiple processes wait for each other to free up resources and as a result all the processes remain halted. Let us understand the concept of deadlock with the help of an example. Suppose there are two processes P1 and P2 running in a computer system. P1 requests for a resource, such as printer that is being utilised by the P2 process. As a result, the P1 process has to wait till the time P2 completes its processing and frees the resource. At the same time, the P2 process requests for a resource, such as shared data that has been locked by the process P1. Thus, both the processes end up waiting for each other to free up the required resources. This situation is called a deadlock.

The following are some of the reasons due to which a deadlock situation may arise.

- **Mutual exclusion** In mutual exclusion, processes are not allowed to share resources with each other. This means that if one process has control over a resource, then that resource cannot be used by another process until the first process releases the resource.
- **Hold and wait** In this condition, a process takes control of a resource and waits for some other resource or activity to complete.
- **No preemption** In this condition, a process is not allowed to force some other process to release a resource.

There are a number of methods through which the deadlock condition can be avoided. Some of these methods are:

- **Ignore deadlock** In this method, it is assumed that a deadlock would never occur. There is a good chance that a deadlock may not occur in a computer system for a long period of time. As a result, the ignore deadlock method can be useful in some cases.
- **Detect and recover from deadlock** In this method, the deadlock is first detected using allocation/request graph. This graph represents the allocation of resources to different processes. After a deadlock has been detected, a number of methods can be used to recover from the deadlock. One way is preemption in which a resource held by one process is provided to another process. The second way is rollback in which the operating system keeps a record of the process states and makes a process roll back to its previous state; thus eliminating the deadlock situation. The third way is to kill one or more processes to overcome the deadlock situation.
- **Avoid deadlock** In this method, a process requesting a resource is allocated the resource only if there is no possibility of deadlock occurrence.

11.5 MEMORY MANAGEMENT

Memory management function of an operating system helps in allocating the main memory space to the processes and their data at the time of their execution. Along with the allocation of memory space, memory management also perform the following activities:

- Upgrading the performance of the computer system
- Enabling the execution of multiple processes at the same time
- Sharing the same memory space among different processes

Memory management is one of the most important functions of operating system because it directly affects the execution time of a process. The execution time of a process depends on the availability of data in the main memory. Therefore, an operating system must perform the memory management in such a manner that the essential data is always present in the main memory. An effective memory management system ensures accuracy, availability and consistency of the data imported from the secondary memory to the main memory.

An effective memory management system must ensure the following:

- **Correct relocation of data** The data should be relocated to and from the main memory in such a manner that the currently running processes are not affected. For example, if two processes are sharing a piece of data then the memory management system must relocate this data only after ensuring that the two processes are no longer referencing the data.
- **Protection of data from illegal change** The data present in the main memory should be protected against unauthorised access or modifications. The memory management system should ensure that a process is able to access only that data for which it has the requisite access and it should be prohibited from accessing data of other processes.
- **Provision to share the information** An ideal memory management system must facilitate sharing of data among multiple processes.
- **Utilisation of small free spaces** A memory management system should be able to apply appropriate defragmentation techniques in order to utilise small chunks of scattered vacant spaces in the main memory.

Segmentation, paging and swapping are the three key memory management techniques used by an operating system.

11.5.1 Segmentation

Segmentation refers to the technique of dividing the physical memory space into multiple blocks. Each block has a specific length and is known as a segment. Each segment has a starting address called the base address. The length of a segment determines the available memory spaces in the segment. Figure 11.8 shows the organisation of segments in a memory unit.

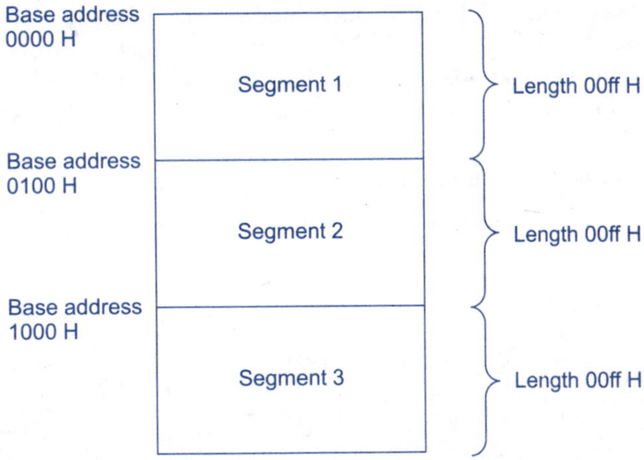

Fig. 11.8 Memory unit having segments

The location of data values stored in a segment can be determined by the distance of the actual position of data value from the base address of the segment. The distance between the actual position of data and the base address of segment is known as displacement or offset value. In other words, whenever it is required to obtain data from the segmented memory then the actual address of the data is calculated by adding the base address of the segment and with offset value. The base address of the segment and the offset value is specified in a program instruction itself. Figure 11.9 shows how the actual position of an operand in a segment is obtained by adding the base address and the offset value.

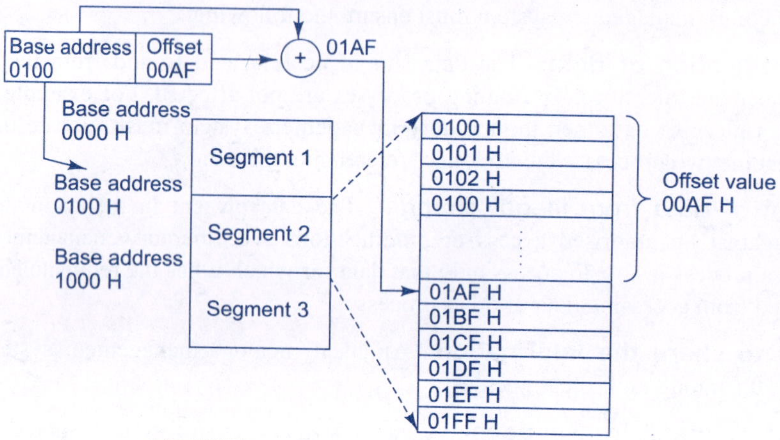

Fig. 11.9 Obtaining the actual address of data

11.5.2 Paging

Paging is a technique in which the main memory of the computer system is organised in the form of equal sized blocks called pages. In this technique, the addresses of the occupied pages of the physical memory are stored in a table, which is known as page table.

Paging enables the operating system to obtain data from the physical memory location without specifying its lengthy memory address in the instruction. In this technique, a virtual address is used to map the physical address of the data. The length of the virtual address is specified in the instruction and is smaller than the physical address of the data. It consists of two different numbers, first number is the address of a page called virtual page in the page table and second number is the offset value of the actual data in the page. Figure 11.10 shows how the virtual address is used to obtain the physical address of an occupied page of physical memory using a page table.

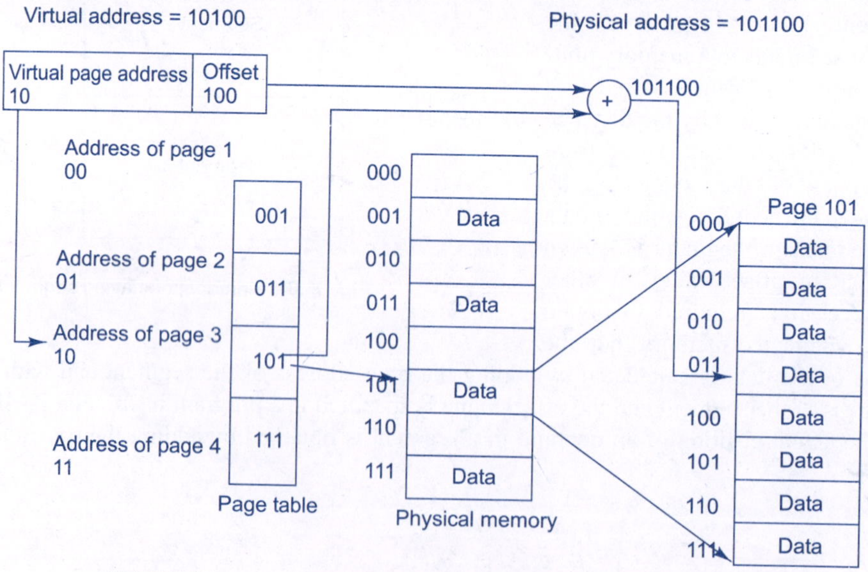

Fig. 11.10 Obtaining data from a page using the paging technique

11.5.3 Swapping

Swapping is a technique used by an operating system for efficient management of memory space of a computer system. Swapping involves performing two tasks called swapping in and swapping out. The task of placing the pages or blocks of data from hard disk to the main memory is called swapping in. On the other hand, the task of removing pages or blocks of data from main memory to hard disk is called swapping out. The swapping technique is useful when a large program has to be executed or some operations have to be performed on a large file.

The main memory in a computer system is limited. Therefore, to run a large program or to perform some operation on a large file, the operating system swaps in certain pages or blocks of data from the hard disk. To make space for these pages or blocks of data in the main memory, the operating system swaps out the pages or blocks of data that are no longer required in the main memory. The operating system places the swapped out pages or blocks of data in a swap file. A swap file is the space in the hard disk that is used as an extension to the main memory by the operating system. Figure 11.11 shows the technique of swapping used by the operating system for memory management.

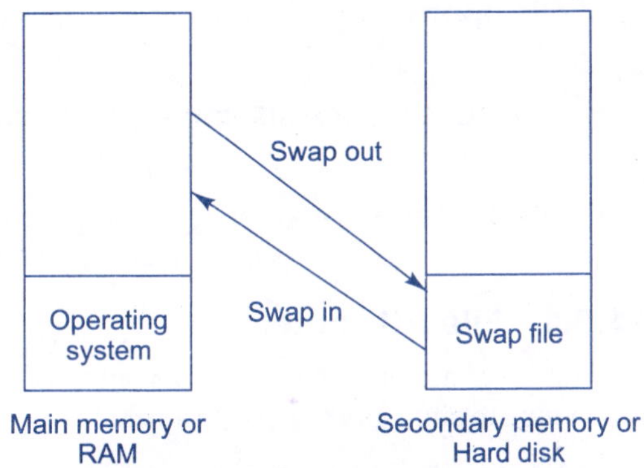

Fig. 11.11 Swapping of pages

11.6 FILE MANAGEMENT

File management is defined as the process of manipulating files in a computer system. A file is a collection of specific information stored in the memory of the computer system. File management includes the process of creating, modifying and deleting the files. The following are some of the tasks performed by the file management function of operating system:

- It helps in creating new files and placing them at a specific location.
- It helps in easily and quickly locating the files in the computer system.
- It makes the process of sharing the files among different users easy.
- It helps store the files in separate folders known as directories that ensure better organisation of data.
- It helps modify the content as well as the name of the file as per the user's requirement.

Figure 11.12 shows the general hierarchy of file storage in an operating system.

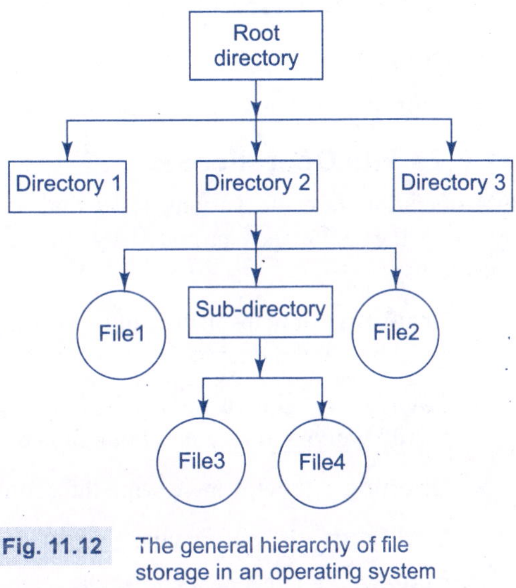

Fig. 11.12 The general hierarchy of file storage in an operating system

In Fig. 11.12, the root directory is present at the highest level in the hierarchical structure. It includes all the subdirectories in which the files are stored. Subdirectory is a directory present inside another directory in the file storage system. The directory based storage system ensures better organisation of files in the memory of the computer system.

The file management function of OS is based on the following concepts:

- **File attributes** It specifies the characteristics, such as type and location that completely describe a file.
- **File operations** It specifies the tasks that can be performed on a file such as opening and closing a file.
- **File access permissions** It specifies the access permissions related to a file such as read and write.
- **File systems** It specifies the logical method of file storage in a computer system. Some of the commonly used file systems include FAT and NTFS.

11.6.1 File Attributes

File attributes are the properties associated with a file that specify different information related to a file. The following are some of the key file attributes:

- **Name** It specifies the name of a file given by the user at the time of saving it.
- **File type** It specifies the type of a file such as a Word document or an Excel worksheet.
- **Location** It specifies the location of a file where it is stored in the memory.
- **Size** It specifies the size of the file in bytes.
- **Date and time** It specifies the date and time when the file was created, last modified and last accessed.
- **Read-only** It specifies that the file can be opened only for reading purpose.
- **Hidden** If this attribute of a file is selected, then the file is hidden from the user.
- **Archive** If this attribute of a file is selected, then the back up of a file is created.

11.6.2 File Operations

File operations are the various tasks that are performed on files. A user can perform these operations by using the commands provided by the operating system. The following are some of the typical file operations:

- **Creating** It helps in creating a new file at the specified location in a computer system. The new file could be a Word document, an image file or an Excel worksheet.
- **Saving** It helps in saving the content written in a file at some specified location. The file can be saved by giving it a name of our choice.
- **Opening** It helps in viewing the contents of an existing file.
- **Modifying** It helps in changing the existing content or adding new to an existing file.
- **Closing** It helps in closing an already open file.

- **Renaming** It helps in changing the name of an existing file.
- **Deleting** It helps in removing a file from the memory of the computer system.

11.6.3 File Access Permissions

File access permissions help specify the manner in which a user can access a file. These are the access rights that allow us to read, write or execute a file. The following are some of the typical file access permissions:

- **Read** It allows a user to only read the content of an existing file.
- **Write** It allows a user to only modify the content of an existing file.
- **Execute** It allows a user to run an existing file stored in the computer system.

11.6.4 File Systems

File systems are used by an operating system to store and organise the various files and their information on a hard disk. The following are the two different file systems that are used to organise files in a computer system:

- **File Allocation Table (FAT)** It is a method used for organising the files and folders in the form of a table, which is known as FAT. This type of system is used for disks that are smaller in size and contain simple folders. The different types of FAT systems are FAT12, FAT16 and FAT32.
- **New Technology File System (NTFS)** This file system is specifically designed for large hard disks for performing basic file operations, such as reading, writing, modifying, saving, etc., quickly and efficiently. NTFS overcomes the drawbacks of the FAT system.

11.7 DEVICE MANAGEMENT

Device management is another important function of the operating system. Device management is responsible for managing all the hardware devices of the computer system. It may include the management of the storages devices as well as the management of all the input/output devices of the computer system. It is the responsibility of the operating system to keep a track of the status of all the devices in the computer system. The status of any computer device, internal or external, may be either free or busy. If a device requested by a process is free at a specific instant of time, the operating system allocates it to the process.

An operating system manages the devices in a computer system with the help of device controllers and device drivers. Each device in the computer system is equipped with a corresponding device controller. For example, the various device controllers in a computer system may be disk controller, printer controller, tape-drive controller and memory controller. All these device controllers are connected with each other through a system bus. The device controllers are actually the hardware components that contain some buffer registers to store the data temporarily. The transfer of data between a running process and the various devices of the computer system is accomplished only through these device controllers.

Apart from device controllers, device drivers also help the operating system to manage and allocate the devices to different processes in an efficient manner. Device drivers are the software programs that are used by the operating system to control the functioning of various devices in a uniform manner. An operating system communicates with the device controllers with the help of device drivers while allocating the devices to the various processes running on the computer system. The device drivers may also be regarded as the software programs acting as an intermediary between the processes and the device controllers.

Figure 11.13 shows the mechanism of allocating a device to a process by the operating system.

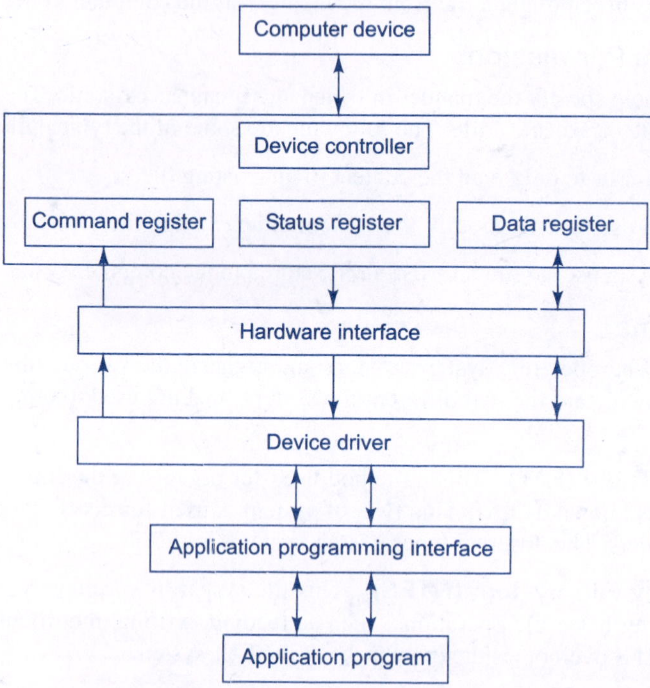

Fig. 11.13 Device management

Figure 11.3 shows how a device or resource can be allocated to an application program by the operating system. If an application program or process, during its execution, requires a device to perform a specific task, it generates a request. This request is handled by the operating system through the corresponding device driver and device controller.

The device controller used in the device management operation usually includes three different registers: command, status and data. The command register is used to contain the information regarding the request issued by an application program. It is the only register of device controller that specifies the type of service requested by the application program. The status register is used to keep track of the status of the device. It contains information about whether or not the device is free to service the request of an application program. The data register holds the necessary data required to be transferred between the application program and the corresponding device.

Apart from handling the commands issued by the application program, the other major responsibility of the device management function is to implement the Application Programming Interface (API). API is the only interface through which the application programs running on the computer system can communicate with the kernel of the operating system to issue the various device-related requests. It can also be regarded as the set of functions or routines that can be called by the application programs to access various services required for their proper execution. This API provides a uniform interface for accessing all the device controllers in the computer system.

11.8 SECURITY MANAGEMENT

The security management function of an operating system helps in implementing mechanisms that secure and protect the computer system internally as well as externally. Therefore, an operating system is responsible for securing the system at two different levels, which are internal security and external security.

Internal security refers to the protection of activities of one process from the activities of another process. The term internal security may also be regarded as system protection. The internal security of the computer system also ensures the reliability of the computer system. There may be a number of processes running in the computer system concurrently. It is the responsibility of the operating system to make sure that only one process at a time has access to a particular resource of the computer system. Most of the operating systems use the concept of least privilege to implement internal security. In this concept, each process or program running in the computer system is assigned enough privileges to access the various resources of the computer system. If two processes running on the computer system send a request to the operating system for the allocation of same device or resource, the kernel of the operating system checks the privileges of both the processes. The process with more privileges will be serviced by the operating system. The process with fewer privileges will be blocked by the operating system from gaining access to the particular computer device.

External security refers to the implementation of mechanisms for securing the data and programs stored in the computer system as well as the various resources of the computer system against unauthorised access. The term external security may also be regarded as system security. External security is particularly required when a computer system is either on a network or connected to the Internet. The system security can be desecrated either intentionally or accidentally. It is easier for the operating system to implement the security mechanisms for accidental security breaches. Most of the external security mechanisms implemented by the operating system are only to prevent the computer system against accidental misuse. The various external threats, accidental or intentional, to the computer system may include reading, writing or deletion of computer data by an unauthorised user and accessing of computer resources or devices by an unauthorised user. It is not possible to prevent the computer system from external threats only at the operating system level. Apart from the operating system, the three other major levels at which external security should be implemented are physical, human and network. The most common external security mechanism employed by most operating systems is a software firewall. The software firewall is software included in the operating system that is specially designed to prevent the computer system against unauthorised users or programs from gaining access to the data and programs stored in the computer system.

11.9 TYPES OF OPERATING SYSTEMS

Many different types of operating systems have evolved till date. As the computers have improved in terms of speed, reliability, and cost so have the operating systems in terms of their capabilities. The operating systems supported by first generation computers were not very powerful. They were only designed and developed to cater the needs of a single user at a time. Also, the users of these operating systems were capable of performing only one task at a time. However, there has been a tremendous amount of improvement in operating systems in the recent years. The modern-day operating systems allow multiple users to carry out multiple tasks simultaneously. Based on their capabilities and the types of applications supported, the operating systems can be divided into the following six major categories:

- Batch processing operating systems

- Multi-user operating systems
- Multitasking operating systems
- Real-time operating systems
- Multiprocessor operating systems
- Embedded operating systems

11.9.1 Batch Processing Operating Systems

The batch processing operating systems are capable of executing only one job at a time. The jobs or the programs submitted by different users are grouped into batches and one batch of jobs is provided as input to the computer system at a time. The jobs in the batch are processed on the first-come-first-serve basis. After getting an appropriate command from the operator, the batch processing operating system starts executing the jobs one-by-one. The execution of a particular job generally involves three major activities, which are reading the job from the input device, executing the job by the system and printing the calculated result on to the output device. After the execution of one job is complete, the operating system automatically fetches the next job from the batch without any human intervention.

The following are some of the advantages of batch processing operating systems:

- The computer systems employing the batch processing operating systems were very efficient computer systems of their times because the idle time for these systems was very small.
- These operating systems facilitated the execution of jobs in an organised manner.

The following are some of the disadvantages of batch processing operating systems:

- The jobs are processed only in the order in which they are placed in a batch and not as per their priority.
- The debugging of a program at execution time is not possible in these operating systems.
- The executing jobs may enter an infinite loop, as each job is not associated with a proper timer.

11.9.2 Multi-user Operating Systems

The multi-user operating systems enable multiple users to use the resources of a computer system at the same time. In other words, a multi-user operating system allows a number of users to work simultaneously on the same computer system. These types of operating systems are specially designed for the multi-user systems. A multi-user system is usually implemented by following the multi-terminal configuration. In this type of configuration, a single powerful computer system is connected to multiple terminals though serial ports. This computer system is responsible for processing the different requests generated by the various terminals at the same time. The devices connected with the various terminals are keyboard, mouse, and monitor. The central computer system is equipped with a fast processor and a memory of large capacity for catering to the multiple requests of the end users. Examples of multi-user operating system include Unix, Linux, Windows 2000 and VM-386

The following are some of the advantages of the multi-user operating systems:

- It allows the resources of the computer system to be utilised in an efficient manner.
- It enhances the overall productivity of the various users by providing simultaneous access to the various computer resources.

The following are the disadvantages of the multi-user operating systems:

- The configuration of the computer system employing multi-user operating system is complex and hence, is difficult to handle and maintain.
- This type of system may result in an inconsistent data if the activities of one user are not protected from another user.
- This type of operating system is required to have robust security mechanisms.

11.9.3 Multitasking Operating Systems

The multitasking operating systems allow a user to carry out multiple tasks at the same time on a single computer system. The multitasking operating systems are also known as by several other names, such as multiprocessing, multiprogramming, concurrent or process scheduling operating systems. The first multitasking operating systems evolved during 1960s. The number of tasks or processes that can be processed simultaneously in this type of operating system depends upon various factors, such as the speed of the CPU, the capacity of the memory, and the size of the programs.

In this type of operating system, the different processes are executed simultaneously by implementing the concept of time slicing. According to this concept, a regular slice of CPU time is provided to each of the processes running in the computer system. Multitasking operating systems can be of two different types, which are preemptive multitasking operating systems and cooperative multitasking operating systems. In preemptive multitasking operating system, slices of CPU time are allocated to the various processes on some priority basis. These priorities are assigned to the various processes in such a manner that the overall efficiency of the system is maintained. In cooperative multitasking operating system, it strongly depends upon the processes whether or not to relinquish CPU control for other running processes. Examples of multitasking operating system include Unix, Linux, Windows 2000, and Windows XP.

The following are some of advantages of multitasking operating systems:

- It helps in increasing the overall performance of the computer system.
- It helps in increasing the overall productivity of the user by performing a number of tasks at the same time.

The following are some of the disadvantages of multitasking operating systems:

- A large amount of memory is required to execute several programs at the same time.
- Some mechanism needs to be implemented to ensure that the activities of one process do not interfere with the activities of another process.

11.9.4 Real-time Operating Systems

The real-time operating systems are similar to multitasking operating systems in their functioning. However, these operating systems are specially designed and developed for handling real-time applications or embedded applications. The real time applications are those critical applications that are required to be executed within a specific period of time. Therefore, time is the major constraint for these applications. The different examples of real-time applications are industrial robots, spacecrafts, industrial control applications and scientific research equipments.

The real-time operating systems can be of two different types, hard real-time operating system, and soft real-time operating system. In the hard real-time operating system, it is necessary to perform a task in the specified amount of time, i.e. within the given deadline. On the other hand, in the soft real-time operating system, a task can be performed even after its allocated time has elapsed.

The following are some of the examples of real-time operating system:

- MTOS
- Lynx
- RTX

The following are some of the advantages of the real-time operating systems:

- It is easy to design and develop and execute real-time applications under real-time operating system as compared to other types of operating systems.
- The real-time operating systems are usually more compact as compared to other operating systems. Thus, these systems require less memory space.

The following are some of the disadvantages of real-time operating systems:

- It is primarily focused on optimising the execution time of an application and thus, it sometimes overlooks some of the other critical factors related to the overall efficiency of the computer system.
- It is only used for providing some dedicated functionality, and thus, cannot be used as a general-purpose operating system.

11.9.5 Multiprocessor Operating Systems

The multiprocessor operating system allows the use of multiple CPUs in a computer system for executing multiple processes at the same time. By using more than one CPU, the processes are executed in a faster manner as compared to the computer systems performing multiprocessing with a single CPU.

The following are some of the examples of the multiprocessor operating system:

- Linux
- Unix
- Windows 2000

The following are some of advantages of multiprocessor operating systems:

- It helps in improving the overall performance and throughput of the computer system.
- It helps in increasing the reliability of the computer system. If one CPU of the computer system fails, the other CPU takes control and executes the currently running process.

The following are some of disadvantages of the multiprocessor operating systems:

- The cost of the computer systems employing multiprocessor operating systems is very high.
- A large amount of memory is required for running and executing several user programs.

11.9.6 Embedded Operating Systems

The embedded operating systems are somewhat similar to real-time operating systems. The embedded operating system is installed on an embedded computer system, which is primarily used for performing computational tasks in electronic devices. These operating systems provide limited functionality that is required for the corresponding embedded computer system. The other common functions that a usual operating system supports are not found in these operating systems.

The following are some of the examples of embedded operating systems:

- Palm OS
- Windows CE

The following are some of the advantages of embedded operating systems:

- These operating systems allow the implementation of embedded systems in an efficient manner.
- The computer system with embedded operating system is easy to use and maintain.

The following are some of the disadvantages of embedded operating systems:

- It is only possible to perform some specific operations with these operating systems.
- These operating systems cannot be used in frequently changing environments.

11.10 PROVIDING USER INTERFACE

User Interface (UI) facilitates communication between an application and its users by acting as an intermediary between them. Each application including the operating system is provided with a specific UI for effective communication. The two basic functions of the UI of any application are to take the inputs from the user and to provide the outputs to the user. However, the types of inputs taken by the UI and the types of outputs provided by the UI may vary from one application to another.

The UI of any operating system can be classified into one of the following types:

- Graphical User Interface (GUI)
- Command Line Interface (CLI)

11.10.1 Graphical User Interface

GUI is a type of UI that enables the users to interact with the operating system by means of point-and-click operations. GUI contains several icons representing pictorial representation of the various objects such as file, directory and device. The graphical icons provided in the UI can be manipulated to perform different types of tasks. These UI graphical icons are usually manipulated by the users using a suitable pointing device, such as mouse, trackball, touch screen and light pen. The other input devices like keyboard can also be used to manipulate these graphical icons. GUIs are considered to be very user-friendly interfaces because each object is represented with a corresponding icon. Unlike the other UIs, the users need not provide text commands for executing tasks.

Figure 11.14 shows the GUI of Windows XP operating system.

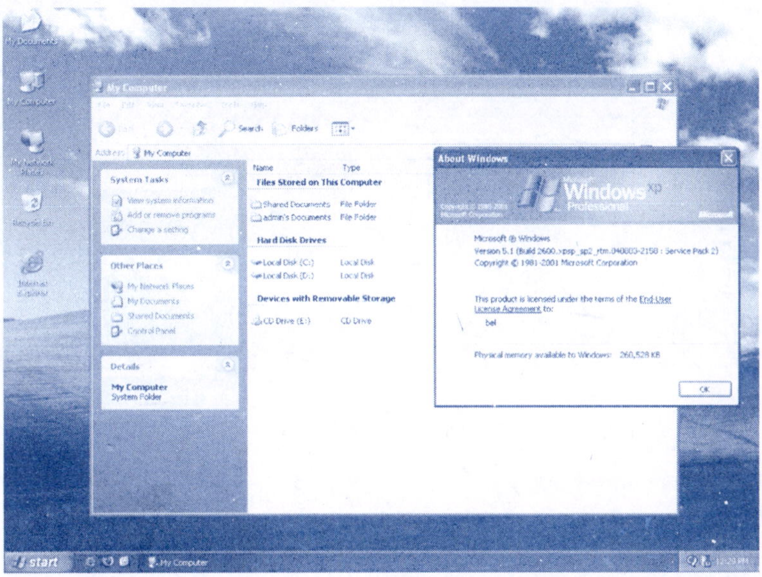

Fig. 11.14 The user interface of Windows XP operating system

The following are some of the advantages of GUI-based operating systems:

- The GUI interface is easy to understand and even the new users can operate on them on their own.
- The GUI interface visually acknowledges and confirms each type of action performed by the users. For example, when the user deletes a file in the Windows operating system, then the operating system asks for the confirmation before deleting it.
- The GUI interface enables the users to perform a number of tasks at the same time. This feature of operating system is also known as multitasking.

11.10.2 Command Line Interface

CLI is a type of UI that enables the users to interact with the operating system by issuing some specific commands. In order to perform a task in this interface, the user needs to type a command at the command line. As soon as the user presses the Enter key, the command is received by the command line interpreter. The command line interpreter is a software program that is responsible for receiving and processing the commands issued by the user. After processing the command, the command line interpreter displays the command prompt again along with the output of the previous command issued by the user. The disadvantage of the CLI is that the user needs to remember a lot of commands to interact with the operating system. Therefore, these types of interfaces are not considered very friendly from the user's perspective.

Fig. 11.15 The command line interface of MS-DOS

Figure 11.15 shows the command line user interface of MS-DOS. In order to perform a task, we need to type a command at the command prompt denoted by C:\>. For example, to copy a text file, say, a1.txt, from the C drive of our computer system. to the D drive, we need to type the copy command at the command prompt, as shown in Fig. 11.16.

Figure 11.16 shows that a text file from the C drive of the computer system has been copied to the D drive of the computer system. However, before typing the copy command at the command prompt, we need to make sure that the file, a1.txt, exists in the C drive of the computer system.

11.11 POPULAR OPERATING SYSTEMS

To date, many operating systems have been developed that suit different requirements of the users. Some of these operating systems became quite popular while others did not do well. The following are some of the popular operating systems:

- MS-DOS

- UNIX
- Windows

Fig. 11.16 Copying a file in MS-DOS

11.11.1 MS-DOS

MS-DOS was developed and introduced by Microsoft in 1981. It is a single-user and single-tasking operating system developed for personal computers. MS-DOS was specifically designed for the family of Intel 8086 microprocessors. This operating system provides a command line user interface, which means that a user needs to type a command at the command line for performing a specific task. The CLI of MS-DOS is more commonly known as DOS prompt. The user interface of MS-DOS is very simple to use but not very user-friendly because of its non-graphical nature. The user has to issue a command to carry out even a simple task.

The command prompt of MS-DOS only allows the execution of the files with the extensions: .COM (Command files), .BAT (Batch files) and .EXE (Executable file). The structure of MS-DOS comprises the following programs:

- **IO.SYS** It is an important hidden and read only system file of MS-DOS that is used to start the computer system. It is also responsible for the efficient management and allocation of the hardware resources through the use of appropriate device drivers.
- **MSDOS.SYS** It is another hidden and read only system file that is executed immediately after the execution of IO.SYS file is finished. MSDOS.SYS acts as the kernel of MS-DOS. It is responsible for managing the memory, processors and the input/output devices of the computer system.
- **CONFIG.SYS** It is a system file that is used to configure various hardware components of the computer system so that they can be used by the various applications.

- **COMMAND.COM** It is the command interpreter that is used to read and interpret the various commands issued by the users.
- **AUTOEXEC.BAT** It is a batch file consisting of a list of commands that is executed automatically as the computer system starts up.

The use of various features of MS-DOS is discussed in Chapter 12.

11.11.2 UNIX

UNIX is an operating system that allows several users to perform a number of tasks simultaneously. The first version of UNIX was introduced during the 1970s. However, since then, it is in constant development phase for further improving its functionality. UNIX operating system provides a GUI that enables its users to work in a more convenient environment. UNIX is most suitable for the computers that are connected to a Local Area Network (LAN) for performing scientific and business related operations. It can also be implemented on personal computers. The following are the core components of the UNIX operating system:

- **Kernel** It is the central part of the UNIX operating system that manages and controls the communication between the various hardware and software components of the computer system. The other major functions performed by the kernel are process management, memory management and device management.
- **Shell** It is the user interface of the UNIX operating system that acts as an intermediary between the user and the kernel of the operating system. Shell is the only program in UNIX operating system that takes the commands issued by the users and interprets them in an efficient manner to produce the desired result.
- **Files and processes** The UNIX operating system arranges everything in terms of files and processes. The directory in this operating system is also considered as a file that is used to house other files within it. The process is usually a program executed under the UNIX operating system. Several processes can be executed simultaneously in this operating system and are identified by a unique Process Identifier (PID) assigned to them.

Figure 11.17 shows the directory structure of UNIX operating system.

The UNIX operating system supports hierarchical directory structure in the form of a tree for arranging different files in the computer system. The root of the tree is always denoted by slash (/). The current working directory of the user is denoted by home. There can be several home directories corresponding to the different users of the UNIX operating system. All the files and directories under the home directory belong to a particular user. The path of any file or directory in UNIX operating system always starts with the root (/). For example, the full path of the file word.doc can be represented as /home/its/ag2/mmdata/word.doc.

The following are some of the significant features of UNIX operating system:

- It allows multiple users to work simultaneously.
- It allows the execution of several programs and processes at the same time to ensure efficient utilisation of the processor.

It implements the concept of virtual memory in an efficient manner. This feature enables the UNIX operating system to execute a program whose size is larger than the main memory of the computer system.

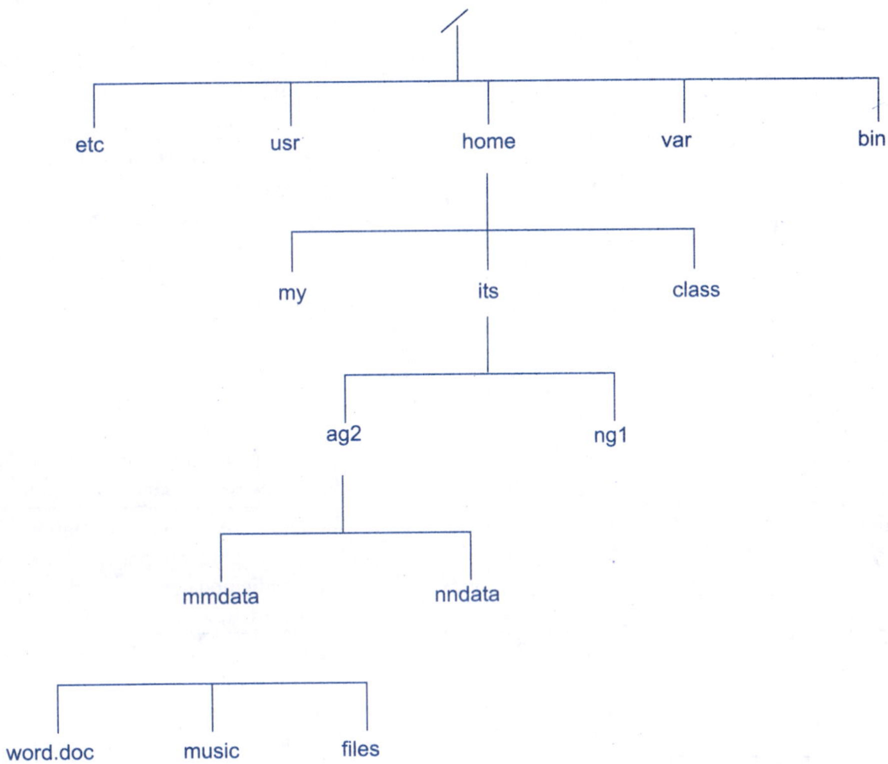

Fig. 11.17 UNIX directory structure

11.11.3 Windows

Microsoft has provided many operating systems to cater the needs of different users. Microsoft is a well known name in the development of operating system as well as various software applications. Initially, Microsoft introduced Windows 1.x, Windows 2.x and Windows 386 operating systems. However, these operating systems lacked certain desirable features, such as networking and interactive user interface. Microsoft continued to work towards developing an operating system that met the desirable features of users and came up with a new operating system in the year 1993, which was known as Windows NT 3.1. This operating system was specially designed for the advanced users performing various business and scientific operations. After the release of Windows NT 3.1, several other operating systems were introduced by Microsoft in the successive years with their own unique features. Table 11.1 lists some of other important Windows operating system introduced by Microsoft with their release dates and significant features.

Table 11.1 Microsoft Windows operating system

Name of operating system	Date of release	Significant features
Windows 95	August, 1995	• 32-bit file system • Multitasking • Object Linking and Embedding (OLE) • Plug and play • Optimised memory management
Windows 98	June, 1998	• 32-bit Data Link Control (DLC) protocol • Improved GUI • Improved online communication through various tools, such as outlook express, personal web server and web publishing wizard • Multiple display support • Windows update
Windows 2000	February, 2000	• More reliable against application failures • Improved Windows explorer • Secure file system using encryption • Microsoft Management Console (MMC) • Improved maintenance operations
Windows ME	September, 2000	• System restoration against failure • Universal plug and play • Automatic updates • Image preview
Windows XP	October, 2001	• Attractive desktop and user interface • System restore • Windows firewall • Files and settings transfer wizard
Windows Server 2003	April, 2003	• Enhanced Internet Information Services (IIS) • Enhanced Microsoft Message Queuing (MSMQ) • Enhanced active directory support • Watchdog timer
Windows Vista	November, 2006	• Multilingual user interface • Enhanced search engine • Enhanced Internet explorer • Enhanced Windows media player • Enhanced Windows update • Windows system assessment tool

Chapter Summary

Operating system is a system software installed on a computer system that performs several key tasks, such as process management, memory management, device management, file management, etc. An operating system also secures the computer system from various threats such as virus and unauthorised access. There are different types of operating system available such as multi-user, batch processing and embedded. The multi-user operating system allows multiple users to use the computer system simultaneously. The batch processing operating system processes the jobs in groups called batches. The embedded operating system is installed on an embedded computer system, which is primarily used for performing computational tasks in electronic devices.

An end user interacts with an operating system through a user interface, which is of two types, GUI or CLI. A GUI interface allows the end users to issue commands through point-and-click operations while a CLI interface allows the end users to issue commands only by typing them at the command prompt. Windows, UNIX and MS-DOS are some of the most popular operating systems. Windows is a GUI based operating system, while MS-DOS is a CLI based operating system.

Key Terms to Remember

- **Operating system:** It is a system software that manages the hardware and other resources of a computer system and enables effective user interaction.
- **Process management:** Process management involves the execution of various tasks, such as creation of processes, scheduling of processes, management of deadlocks and termination of the processes.
- **Process state:** Process state is the condition of a process at a particular instant of time.
- **Process Control Block:** PCB is a data structure associated with a process that provides complete information about the process.
- **Process scheduling:** Process scheduling is a task performed by an operating system for deciding the priority in which the processes are allocated the CPU time for their execution.
- **Process synchronisation:** Process synchronisation is the task of synchronising the execution of processes in such a manner that no two processes have access to the same shared data or resource.
- **Interprocess communication:** Interprocess communication is the method of communication between processes through which processes interact with each other for gaining access to shared data and resources.
- **Deadlock:** It is a condition that occurs when multiple processes wait for each other to free up resources and as a result all the processes remain halted.
- **Memory management:** Memory management function of an operating system helps in allocating the main memory space to the processes and their data at the time of their execution.
- **File management:** File management is defined as the process of manipulating files in a computer system.
- **Security management:** Security management function of an operating system helps in implementing mechanisms that secure and protect the computer system internally as well as externally.
- **Batch processing operating system:** This operating system processes the jobs by organising them in groups called batches. It processes only one job at a time.
- **Multi-user operating system:** It allows multiple users to work simultaneously on the same computer system.
- **Multitasking operating system:** It allows a user to carry out multiple tasks at the same time on a single computer system.
- **Real-time operating system:** It is used for processing critical applications that are required to be executed within a specific period of time.
- **Multiprocessor operating system:** It allows the use of multiple CPUs in a computer system for executing multiple processes at the same time.
- **Embedded operating system:** It is installed on an embedded computer system, which is primarily used for performing computational tasks in electronic devices.
- **User Interface (UI):** UI facilitates communication between an application and its users by acting as an intermediary between them.

- **Graphical User Interface:** GUI is a type of UI that enables the users to interact with the operating system by means of point-and-click operations.
- **Command Line Interface:** CLI is a type of UI that enables the users to interact with the operating system by issuing some specific commands.
- **Kernel:** Kernel is the central part of the UNIX operating system that manages and controls the communication between the various hardware and software components.
- **Shell:** Shell is the user interface of the UNIX operating system that acts as an intermediary between the user and the kernel of the operating system.

Review Questions

Fill in the Blanks

1. ____________ is a system software that allows the users to interact with the hardware and other resources of a computer system.
2. In ____________ interface, users type the commands pertaining to the tasks that they want to perform.
3. In ____________ interface, commands are given by means of point-and-click operations performed using a pointing device, such as mouse.
4. The process of managing the files and directories contained in a computer system is known as ____________.
5. The ____________ state specifies the time when a process is ready for execution but has not been placed in the ready queue by the operating system.
6. ____________ is a data structure associated with a process that provides complete information about the process.
7. The operating system maintains a table called ____________, which stores the PCBs related to all the processes.
8. The process, which creates a new process using the system call, is called ____________.
9. ____________ is the task performed by an operating system for deciding the priority in which the processes, which are in ready and waiting states, are allocated the CPU time for their execution.
10. An operating system uses a program called ________ for deciding the priority in which a process is allocated the CPU time.
11. In ____________ scheduling algorithm, a process is allocated the CPU for a specific time period called time slice or time quantum.
12. ____________ is the task of synchronising the execution of processes in such a manner that no two processes have access to the same shared data or resource.
13. ____________ is a condition that occurs when multiple processes wait for each other to free up resources and as a result all the processes remain halted.
14. The ____________ function of an operating system helps in allocating the main memory space to the processes and their data at the time of their execution.
15. Paging is a technique in which the main memory of the computer system is organized in the form of equal sized blocks called ______.
16. ________ management is responsible for managing all the hardware devices of the computer system.
17. The ______________ function of an operating system helps in implementing mechanisms that secure and protect the computer system internally as well as externally.
18. In __________ operating system, jobs are grouped into groups called batches and assigned to the computer system with the help of a card reader.

19. In ____________ operating system, multiple users can make use of computer system's resources simultaneously.
20. UI facilitates communication between a _________ and its ______ by acting as an intermediary between them.
21. ___________ is the central part of the UNIX operating system that manages and controls the communication between the various hardware and software components.

Multiple Choice Questions

1. Which of the following program is essential for the functioning of a computer system?
   A. MS Word B. Operating system C. MS Excel D. System software
2. Which of the following operating systems makes use of CLI?
   A. MS-DOS B. Windows 2000 C. Windows Server 2003 D None of the above
3. Which of the following operating systems makes use of GUI?
   A. Windows 2000 B. Windows Server 2003 C. Windows Vista D. All of the above
4. Which of the following operating systems makes use of both command line interface and GUI?
   A. Windows 2000 B. Linux C. Windows Vista D. None of the above
5. Which of the following functions is provided by an operating system?
   A. Process management B. Security management
   C. File management D. All of the above
6. Which of the following provides complete information related to a process?
   A. Process state B. Process scheduling C. Process communication D. PCB
7. Which of the following is an operation related to a process?
   A. Process creation B. Process execution C. Process completion D. None of the above
8. Which of the following is responsible for ascertaining the order in which processes are executed?
   A. Scheduler B. Process schedule manager
   C. Operating system scheduler D. Process Scheduler
9. Which one of the following scheduling algorithm is the simplest algorithm for the scheduling of processes?
   A. FCFS scheduling algorithm B. RR scheduling algorithm
   C. Priority scheduling algorithm D. SJF scheduling algorithm
10. Which of the following methods is used for interprocess communication?
    A. Shared cache memory B. Shared region
    C. Message passing D. Cache memory
11. Which one of the following methods is used for handling of deadlocks?
    A. Detect and recover deadlock B. Mutual exclusion
    C. No preemption D. All of the above
12. Which one of the following is a file operation?
    A. Opening a file B. Manipulating a file C. Resising a file D. All of the above
13. Which one of the following software components is used by an operating system for device management function?
    A. Driver B. Device driver C. Program driver D. Application driver

14. Which one of the following types of the operating systems allows multiple users to work simultaneously?

A. Multitasking operating system
B. Multi-user operating system
C. Multiprocessor operating system
D. None of the above

15. Which of the following type of UI allows a user to enter commands at command line?

A. GUI
B. CLI
C. Both GUI and CLI
D. Neither GUI nor CLI

16. Which of the following is a part of MS-DOS?

A. DOS.SYS
B. CONFIGURATION.SYS
C. EXEC.BAT
D. COMMAND.COM

17. Which of the following is the core component of UNIX?

A. Command shell
B. Kernel
C. Directories and programs
D. None of the above

Discussion Questions

1. What is an operating system? Explain briefly with the help of examples.
2. Briefly state the history of operating system.
3. Briefly explain the various functions of an operating system.
4. What is a process state? Explain the various states of a process with the help of a figure.
5. What is a PCB and what information is contained in it?
6. Explain the process creation and process termination operations related to a process.
7. Briefly explain the term process scheduling.
8. Explain the three types of schedulers that help in process scheduling.
9. Which scheduling algorithms are used in process scheduling? Explain each one of them briefly.
10. Briefly explain the task of process synchronisation performed by an operating system.
11. What is interprocess communication? Explain the two methods used for interprocess communication.
12. What is a deadlock? Explain briefly the methods that can be used to handle this condition.
13. What is memory management? Explain briefly.
14. Briefly explain the function of file management performed by an operating system.
15. Briefly explain the device management function of an operating system. Also, describe the role of device drivers in device management.
16. Briefly explain any three types of operating system.
17. What is a UI? Explain the two types of UI.
18. State the programs that are a part of the MS-DOS structure.
19. Explain the core components of UNIX operating system.
20. Briefly explain why Windows operating system is one of the most popular operating systems.

CHAPTER 12

MICROSOFT SOFTWARE

Chapter Outline

Chapter Objectives

In this chapter, we will learn:

- The various internal and external commands of MS-DOS.
- How to create, save, edit, format and print a document in the MS Word system.
- How to create, save, modify, rename, delete and move a worksheet in the MS Excel system.
- How to create, save, add, navigate and print a presentation in the MS PowerPoint system.
- How to create a database, table, query and relationship in the MS Access system.
- How to use MS Publisher to produce documents, such as news letters and brochures.

12.1 INTRODUCTION

Personal computers are becoming increasingly powerful, versatile and popular among organisations and individuals alike not because of reduction in their cost and increase in memory size but primarily due to the tremendous power and variety of software available. In fact, it is the software that makes a computer useful as well as user-friendly. Although there are a number of software vendors in the market, the main driving force behind the software revolution is the Microsoft Corporation.

The first major software project of Microsoft Corporation was the development of an operating system known as Disk Operating Systems (DOS) for the original IBM personal computer in the year 1980. This software, popularly referred to as Microsoft Disk Operating System (MS-DOS), became instantly popular among IBM and the IBM clone computer users and put the Microsoft on its meteoric rise not only in revenues but also in popularity. This encouraged Microsoft eventually to develop a series of sophisticated operating systems, each one with enhanced features as discussed in chapter 11.

Although originally seen as a supplier of operating systems, Microsoft went on to develop a variety of successful application packages, thus becoming a leading software company in the world. Microsoft today has a suite of software packages that would meet many of the standard applications requirements of most organisations. This software suite, popularly known as Microsoft Office, includes the following application packages:

- **Microsoft Word** Developed in 1983, it provides powerful tools for creating and manipulating word processing documents.
- **Microsoft Excel** Developed in 1985, it enables to create detailed spreadsheets for viewing and collaboration.
- **Microsoft PowerPoint** Developed in 1988, it provides a complete set of tools for creating presentations.
- **Microsoft Publisher** Developed in 1991, it helps in publishing materials, such as news letters, brochures and catalogs.
- **Microsoft Access** Developed in 1992, it gives powerful tools for creating and managing databases.

In this chapter, we shall discuss briefly how to use the various features of these packages.

12.2 MS-DOS

MS-DOS is an operating system that uses Command Line Interface (CLI) for interacting with the end users. It was developed in 1980 by Microsoft (MS) Corporation for IBM Personal Computers (PCs). It is a single-user and single-tasking operating system that helps in handling the files of a computer system. The commands of MS-DOS are not case sensitive that means we can write commands either in capital letters or small letters. A command is defined as an instruction provided by a user to perform some specific tasks on the computer system.

MS-DOS consists of three layers, which manage the services provided by the computer system. The lowest layer includes the Basic Input/Output System (BIOS), which is stored in Read-Only Memory (ROM) and provides the basic low-level services, such as managing the I/O devices and disk drives of the computer system. The second layer provides high-level services with the help of low-level services of BIOS. These high-level services include referring to files by names instead of referring to some particular sector or track of the disk drive. The third layer includes the command interpreter or shell, which is used to display the Command Prompt on the computer's screen. A shell is a program that provides a text-only user interface for typing commands. Its function is to read the commands typed by the user on the Command Prompt and execute them.

12.2.1 Accessing MS-DOS

For working with MS-DOS, we need to install MS-DOS in our computer system. After installing, start MS-DOS using any of the following two ways:

- Start menu
- Run command

Using Start menu We can start MS-DOS by performing the following steps using the Start menu:

1. Select Start → Programs → Accessories → Command Prompt, as shown in Fig. 12.1.

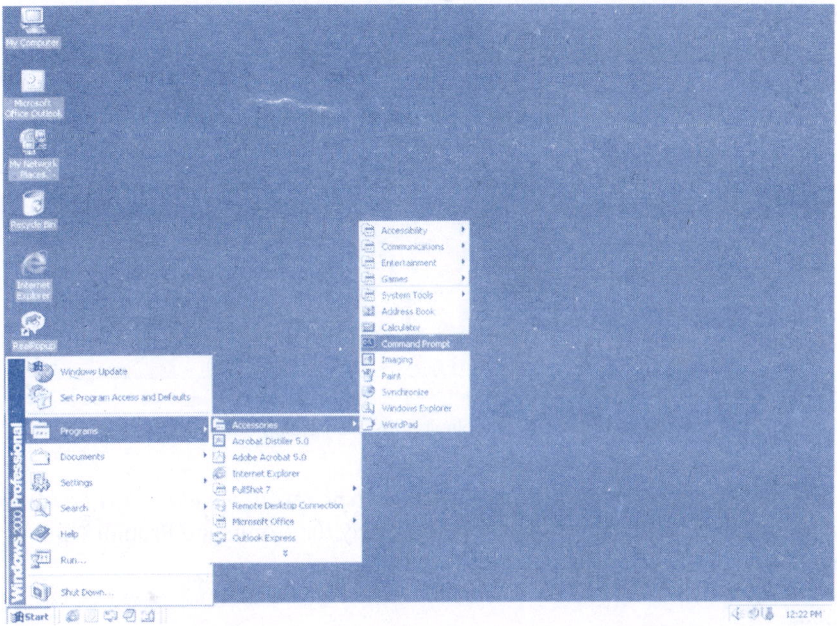

Fig. 12.1 Starting MS-DOS using the Start menu

2. Click the Command Prompt option to display the Command Prompt window of MS-DOS, as shown on Fig. 12.2.

Fig. 12.2 Displaying the Command Prompt window of MS-DOS

Using Run command We can also start MS-DOS by performing the following steps using the Run command:

1. Select Start → Run to display the Run dialog box, as shown in Fig. 12.3.

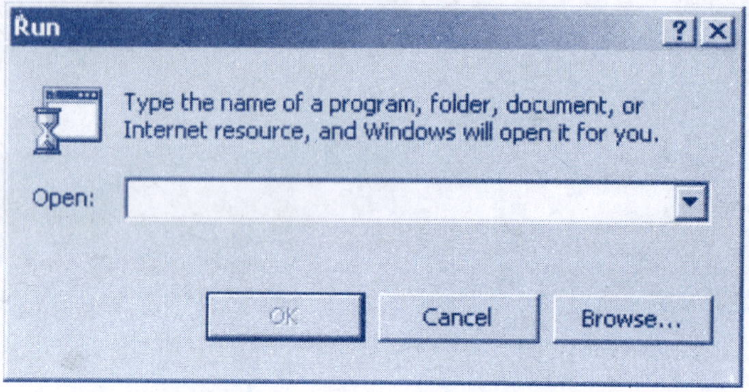

Fig. 12.3 Displaying the Run dialog box

Note: *By default, the Ok button is disabled, but when we type text in the Open text box it gets enabled.*

2. Type cmd in the Open text box and click OK to display the Command Prompt window of MS-DOS.

The various commands of MS-DOS can be categorised as:

- Internal commands
- External commands
- Batch commands

12.2.2 Internal Commands

Internal commands are those commands that are stored in the command interpreter of MS-DOS. These commands get automatically loaded into the memory when a computer system is started. Some of the key internal commands of MS-DOS are as follows:

- DIR
- COPY
- TYPE
- MD
- CD
- RD
- DEL
- DATE
- TIME
- CLS

DIR The DIR command is used to display the names of files and subdirectories present in a directory along with their size in bytes and the date and time of last modification performed. To run the DIR command, we need to type the following command at the Command Prompt and then press enter:

C:\ >DIR

The execution of the above command will display a list of all the files and subdirectories stored in the main or root directory. The list can also be displayed in the form of pages on the screen. To display the list of files and subdirectories in the form of pages, type the following command and then press Enter:

C:\ >DIR /P

The execution of the above command will display a list containing the files and subdirectories, in the page format. The list can also be displayed in the wide format on the screen. To display the list of files and subdirectories in the wide format, type the following command and then press Enter:

C:\ >DIR /W

The execution of the above command will display the available files and subdirectories in the current directory, in the wide format. We can also display only a set of files having same extension with the help of wildcard characters, such as asterisk represented by * and question mark represented by ? The wildcard character * is used for substituting one or more characters including zero, and the wildcard character ? is used for substituting a single character. To display all the files in the current directory using a wildcard character, type the following command and then press Enter:

C:\ >DIR *.*

The execution of the above command will display all the available files and subdirectories in the current working directory.

COPY The COPY command is used to copy a file from one location to another on the computer system. To copy a file from one directory to another, type the following command and press Enter:

C:\ >COPY abc D:

The execution of the above command will copy the file abc available in the C drive to the D drive. We can also copy a file in the current directory with the same content but with a different name. To copy a file with a new name in the current directory, type the following command and press Enter:

C:\ >COPY abc def

The execution of the above command will copy the file abc with a new name def at the same location, i.e. C drive. The COPY command can also be used for copying and concatenating two files in to a new third file. To copy and combine two files in to a new file at the same location, type the following command and press Enter:

C:\ >COPY abc+def C:xyz

The execution of the above command will copy and concatenate the abc and def files in the C drive with a new name xyz.

TYPE The TYPE command is used to view the contents of an existing file. To view the contents of an existing file, type the following command and press Enter:

C:\ >TYPE abc

The execution of the above command will display the contents of the file abc present in the C drive. The

TYPE command can also be used to view the contents of a file present at a location other than the current working directory. To view the contents of a file present at a different location, type the following command and press Enter:

C:\ >TYPE d:abc

The execution of the above command will display the contents of the file abc present in the D drive.

MD The MD command is used to create a new directory at the specified location in the computer system. MD stands for make directory and it is also known as the MKDIR command. To create a new directory, type the following command and press Enter:

C:\ >MD dir1

The execution of the above command will create a new directory with name dir1 in the current directory, i.e. C:\. To create a new directory at a location other than the current directory, type the following command and press Enter:

C:\ >MD D:\dir1

The execution of the above command will create a new directory with name dir1 at the specified location, i.e. D drive.

CD The CD command is used to move from one directory to another specified directory on the computer system. CD stands for change directory and it is also known as CHDIR command. To change directory, type the following command and press Enter:

C:\ >CD dir1

The execution of the above command will make dir1 as the current working directory. This will change the Command Prompt in the Command Prompt window as shown below:

C:\ dir1>

The CD command can also be used to move from the current working directory to the root directory of the computer system. To change the current working directory to the root directory, type the following command and press Enter:

C:\ dir1>CD\

The execution of the above command will change from the current working directory dir1 to the root directory, i.e. C.

RD The RD command is used to remove an empty directory from the computer system. RD stands for remove directory and it is also known as RMDIR command. To remove an empty directory, type the following command and press Enter:

C:\ >RD dir1

The execution of the above command will remove the empty directory dir1 from the specified location, i.e. C drive. However, in the later versions of Windows operating system, i.e. Windows 2000 and Windows XP, a directory containing files and subdirectories can also be removed by using the following command:

C:\ >RD dir1/S

The execution of the above command will remove the directory dir1 along with its files and subdirectories.

DEL The DEL command is used to delete one or more files from the computer system. DEL stands for delete and it is similar to ERASE command. To delete a file from a specified directory, type the following command and press Enter:

C:\ >DEL abc

The execution of the above command will delete the abc file from the C drive. To delete a file from a location other than the current working directory, type the following command and press Enter:

C:\ >DEL D:\def

The execution of the above command will delete the def file from the specified location, i.e. D drive.

DATE The DATE command is used to display the current date stored in the computer system. To check the current date, type the following command and press Enter:

C:\ >DATE

The execution of the above command will display the current date of the computer system. It also enables us to enter new date, if we want to change the current date of the computer system.

TIME The TIME command is used to display the current time. To check the current time, type the following command and press Enter:

C:\ >DATE

The execution of the above command will display the current time. It also enables us to enter new time, if we want to change the current time of the computer system.

CLS The CLS command is used to clear the screen of the command prompt window. To clear the screen, type the following command and press Enter:

C:\ >CLS

The execution of the above command will clear the screen and place the cursor at the top-left side of the command prompt window.

12.2.3 External Commands

External commands are those commands, which are stored on a disk and are not in the command interpreter. These commands have an extension of .COM, .EXE or .BAT and are less frequently used as compared to the internal commands. Some of the important external commands of MS-DOS are as follows:

- ATTRIB
- CACLS
- EDIT
- TREE
- DELTREE
- CHKDSK
- COMP

- FIND
- HELP

ATTRIB ATTRIB is used to display the attributes of a file and change those attributes, if required. A file can have any of the four attributes, i.e. read-only, system, archive or hidden. To display the attributes of a file present in the current directory, type the following command and press Enter:

C:\ >ATTRIB

The execution of the above command will display the attributes of all the files present in the current directory. If we want to add or remove any attribute to or from a particular file, then we have to use + and – symbol respectively with this command. To add an attribute to a file present in the current directory, type the following command and then press enter:

C:\ >ATTRIB +R abc

The execution of the above command will add a read-only attribute to the abc file present in the current directory. This means that the abc file cannot be modified further by any user. However, we can modify the contents of abc file by removing this attribute from the file. To remove the read only attribute from the abc file present in the current directory, type the following command and then press enter:

C:\ >ATTRIB –R abc

The execution of the above command will remove the read-only attribute from the abc file. As a result, its contents can be modified by a user.

CACLS The CACLS command is used to display the Access Control Lists (ACLs) of the specified file. An ACL is a list that provides information to a computer system about the user access rights pertaining to a file. To display the ACLs of a file, type the following command and then press enter:

C:\ >CACLS abc

The execution of the above command will display the ACLs of the abc file present in the C-drive.

EDIT The EDIT command is used to create, open or edit a particular file. It helps in creating a new file in the specified directory and also enables us to open and edit the contents of an existing file. To edit a particular file, type the following command and press Enter:

C:\ >EDIT abc

The execution of this command will open the MS-DOS editor displaying the contents of the abc file, if this file is present in the C drive. However, if the file abc does not already exist, then the execution of this command will create a new file with the name abc and open the MS-DOS editor for adding contents to this file.

TREE The TREE command is used to view the files and subdirectories of the current directory in the form of a tree. It helps view the structure of the current directory in an easier way. To view the files and subdirectories of the current directory, type the following command and press Enter:

C:\ >TREE

The execution of the above command will display the structure of C drive, i.e., it will display all the available files and subdirectories in the C drive, in tree format. To view the files and subdirectories of a particular directory, type the following command and press Enter:

C:\ >TREE dr

The execution of the above command will display the tree structure of the dr directory present in the C drive.

DELTREE The DELTREE command is used to delete a directory and all the files present in that directory permanently from the computer system. It removes a directory from the computer system along with its files and subdirectories. To delete all the available files and subdirectories from a directory, type the following command and press Enter:

C:\ >DELTREE dir

The execution of this command will delete all the files and subdirectories present in the directory dir.

CHKDSK The CHKDSK command is used to check the status of hard disk drives on the computer system for errors. If there are any errors on the disk then it helps in correcting those errors. We should run this command frequently in order to detect any errors on the disk. To check the status of the current disk, type the following command and press Enter:

C:\ >CHKDSK

The execution of the above command will display the status of the current disk.

COMP The COMP command is used to compare two existing files. To display the comparison between two files, type the following command and press Enter:

C:\ >COMP abc def

The execution of the above command will compare only the size of the two files, i.e. abc and def. This command can be used with various options such as /L, /N and /D for comparing the contents and other attributes of the two files.

FIND The FIND command is used to search and display a string of characters in the specified file. The string to be searched is placed inside double quotes. To search a string, type the following command and press Enter:

C:\ >FIND “hello” abc

The execution of the above command will search the string hello in file abc and display the results. There are various options such as /V, /I and /N that can be used with this command. The /V option is used to display the lines that do not contain the specified string. The /I option is used to search the specified string without considering the case of the characters in the string. The /N option is used to display the line number that contains the specified string in the file.

HELP The HELP command is used to display information related to various commands in MS-DOS. To display information about all the commands available in MS-DOS, type the following command and press Enter:

C:\ >HELP

The execution of the above command will display the commands and their description on the command prompt. We can also find information related to a single command by using the HELP command. To get information about the TREE command, type the following command and press Enter:

C:\ >HELP TREE

The execution of the above command will display information related to the TREE command.

12.2.4 Batch Commands

Batch commands are used to execute a sequence of commands in MS-DOS. The sequence of commands, which could be internal or external are stored in a file called batch file. A batch file is stored with .BAT extension. Some of the important batch commands of MS-DOS are as follows:

- @
- %DIGIT
- CALL
- ECHO

@

The @ command is used to hide the display of a batch command on the screen and display only the output produced by the batch command. The syntax of using the @ command is as follows:

```
@[command]
```

Here, command specifies the batch command, which will not be displayed but its output will be displayed on the Command Prompt. For example, suppose batchfile.bat is a batch file with which we want to use the @ command. To create the batchfile.bat batch file, type the following command and press Enter:

C:\ >EDIT batchfile.bat

The execution of the command will open the MS-DOS editor and create a batch file with name batchfile.bat. In this batch file, we can write different commands in a specific sequence. To hide the display of the batch command at the Command Prompt, type the following command inside the batchfile.bat file and then close this file after saving:

@ DIR

To display the output of the above command, type the following command at the Command Prompt and press Enter:

C:\ >batchfile.bat

The execution of the above command will display the output of DIR command at the Command Prompt but will not display the DIR command.

%DIGIT The %DIGIT command is used to specify the batch parameters, which can be instantiated by the user at the time of execution of the batch command. These parameters are in the form of digits ranging from 0 to 9 where %0 represents the batch command itself. The syntax of %DIGIT command is as follows:

[Command] % DIGIT

Here, Command specifies the command with which we want to define the batch parameters and %DIGIT specify the batch parameters. To specify the batch parameters, type the following command in the batchfile. bat file and then close it after saving:

MD %1 %2

To display the output of the above command, type the following command at the Command Prompt and then press enter:

C:\ >batchfile.bat dir1 dir2

The execution of the above command will display the following command at the Command Prompt:

C:\ >MD dir1 dir2

The execution of the above command will create two directories with names dir1 and dir2 in the D drive. Here, %1 is replaced by dir1 and %2 is replaced by dir2.

CALL The CALL command is used to call a batch program at the Command Prompt. It is also used to call or execute one batch program from another in such a manner that the first batch program is not interrupted. The syntax of the CALL command is as follows:

CALL[drive:] [path] filename [batch parameters]

Here, [drive:][path] specifies the location of the batch program and filename specifies the name of the batch file. The batch parameters specify the command-line information required by the batch program. For example, to call the batchfile.bat file, type the following command at the Command Prompt and press Enter:

C:\ >CALL batchfile.bat

The execution of the above command will call the batchfile.bat file and execute the commands contained in it. To call a batch file from inside the batchfile.bat file, type the following command in the batchfile.bat and then close it after saving:

CALL a.bat

Here, a.bat is another batch file. Now, when the batchfile.bat file is executed, it will automatically execute the a.bat file and the commands present in it.

ECHO The ECHO command is used to display or print a message on the command prompt. It is also used to turn on or off the display of the batch file commands on the command prompt. The syntax of the ECHO command to display a message on the command prompt is as follows:

C:\ >ECHO Welcome to MS-DOS

The execution of the above command will display the message 'Welcome to MS-DOS' on the command prompt.

12.3 MS WORD SYSTEM

MS Word is an application software that can be used to create, edit, save and print personal as well as professional documents in a very simple and efficient manner. MS Word is an important tool of the MS office suite that is mainly designed for word processing. Therefore, it is also referred as the word processing program.

MS Word is not the only word processing program available in the market. There are many other word processing applications available, such as Open Office Writer and Google Docs. However, MS Word is the most popular word processing program among all.

12.3.1 Accessing MS Word

For working in MS Word, we need to install MS Office in a computer system. After installing MS Office, we can start MS Word using any of the following two ways:

- Start menu
- Run command

Using Start menu We can start MS Word by performing the following steps using the Start menu:

1. Select Start → Programs → Microsoft Office, as shown in Fig. 12.4.

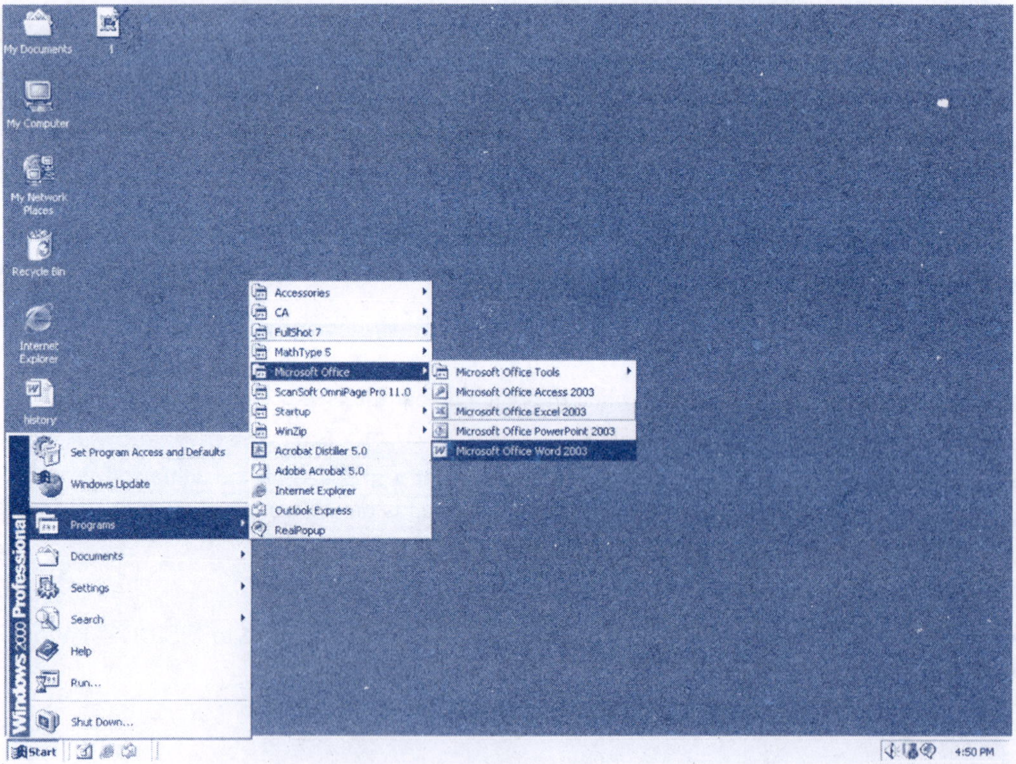

Fig. 12.4 Starting MS Word using the Start menu

2. Select the Microsoft Office Word 2003 option to display the Graphical User Interface (GUI) of MS Word, as shown in Fig. 12.5.

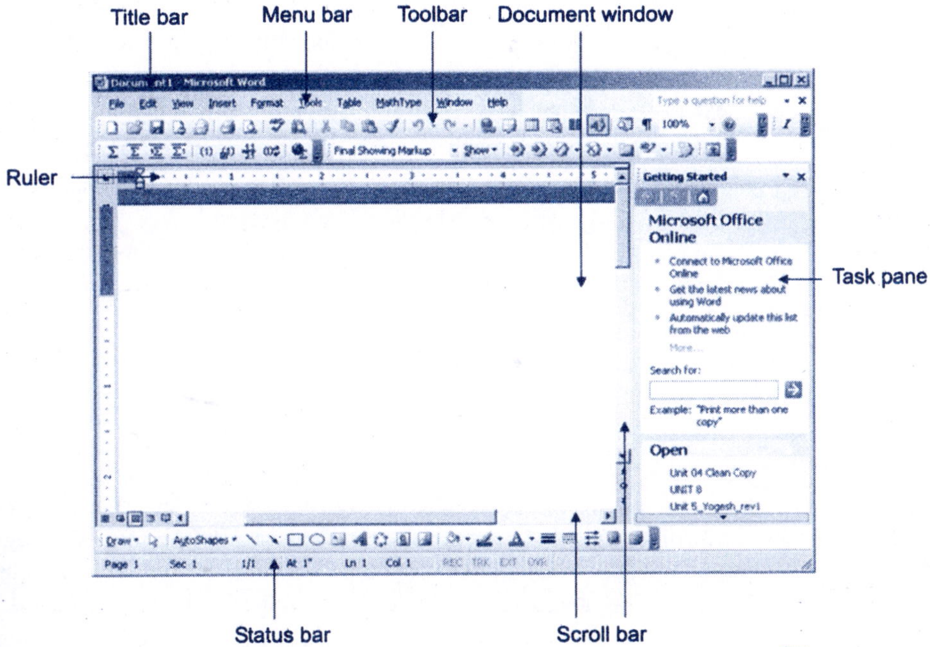

Fig. 12.5 The Document1 – Microsoft Word window

Using Run command We can also start MS Word by performing the following steps using the Run command:

1. Select Start → Run to display the Run dialog box.
2. Type winword in the Open text box and click OK to display the Document1 – Microsoft Word window.

Figure 12.5 shows the GUI of MS Word with the following major components:

- ***Title bar*** It is a horizontal bar at the top of the window that displays the name of the currently opened MS Word document. By default, MS Word assigns names to new documents as Document1, Document2, Document3 and so on. However, we can also save our document with some other name of our choice.
- ***Menu bar*** It is located right below the title bar. The Menu bar is used to house a set of commands that can be used to perform various operations such as opening a file, closing a file and creating a table. The Menu bar of MS Word contains the following menus:
  - *File menu* It contains a set of commands that can be used to perform various file handling operations. The file handling operations in MS Word are usually known as document handling operations. The various operations that can be performed using the options available in the File

menu are opening a new document, opening an existing document, saving the current document, printing the current document, etc.

- *Edit menu* It contains a set of commands that can be used to perform various operations related to content editing and manipulation. The various operations that we can perform using the options available in the Edit menu are copying the currently selected text to clipboard, moving the currently selected text to some other location in the currently opened document, pasting the text from clipboard to the currently opened document, deleting the selected text, etc.
- *View menu* It contains a set of commands that can be used to display the document in different views. The different views available in MS Word are Normal, Web Layout, Print Layout, Document Map, Full Screen and Zoom. Apart from changing the view of a document, we can also perform various other tasks using the View menu like displaying or hiding the toolbar, setting the header and footer for a document and displaying or hiding the rulers.
- *Insert menu* It contains a set of commands that can be used to insert various objects such as clip art, auto shapes, organisation chart, word art and text box in a document to make it more attractive. Apart from these objects, we can also insert date and time, page numbers, symbols, page break and column break in the document.
- *Format menu* It contains a set of commands that can be used to alter the look and layout of the content present in the document. The various tasks that can be performed using the options available in the Format menu are changing the font type, font colour, font size and font style of the selected text, indenting a paragraph, inserting bullets and numbering in the document, etc.
- *Tools menu* It contains a set of commands that can be used to perform advanced operations in the MS Word document. The various tasks that can be performed using the options available in the Tools menu are checking and correcting spelling and grammatical mistakes, counting the number of words and characters, protecting a document and using mail merge, etc.
- *Table menu* It contains a set of commands that can be used to perform various operations related to the creation, modification and deletion of tables in a document.
- *Window menu* It contains a set of commands that can be used to perform various tasks related to the active window in which we are working. Using this menu, we can open a new window containing the same content as the active window, split the active window into different panes and arrange all the opened documents into separate windows in such a manner that all the windows can be viewed at the same time by the user.
- *Help menu* It assists the user by providing information related to MS Word from various sources such as Office Assistant tool and Microsoft Office Web site etc. In addition, it can also be used to detect and repair the errors contained in MS Word files.

- ***Toolbar*** It is located right below the menu bar. A number of toolbars are provided in MS Word for a quick and easy access to the various commands housed in the Menu bar. The three most commonly used toolbars in MS Word are as follows:
  - *Standard toolbar* It provides quick access to the various operations related to the file handling and content editing and manipulation. However, this is not the only purpose of this toolbar. There are certain icons present on this toolbar with the help of which we can perform many other tasks

such as spelling and grammar check, applying the formatting of certain section to some other section in the currently opened document and creating and editing tables.

Note: *If the Standard toolbar is not visible in the MS Word window, then we need to select View → Toolbars → Standard to make it visible.*

- *Formatting toolbar* As its name implies, it is used to perform various operations related to the look and the layout of the document content. Using the icons available on this toolbar, we can change the font size, style and colour of the selected text, align the selected text to left, center or right of the screen, create numbered and bulleted list, etc.

Note: *If the Formatting toolbar is not visible in the MS Word window, then we need to select View → Toolbars → Formatting to make it visible.*

- *Drawing toolbar* It is located at the bottom of the screen just above the status bar. Using the different icons available on the drawing toolbar, we can draw and manipulate different types of graphics in a document. The various shapes that we can draw using the drawing toolbar are line, rectangle, oval, etc. We can also insert clip art, wordart and pictures in a document using this toolbar.

Note: *If the Drawing toolbar is not visible in the MS Word window, then we need to select View → Toolbars → Drawing to make it visible.*

- ***Document window*** It is the actual area in the MS Word window where we can enter text and draw graphics. The document window of MS Word can also be considered as a text editor because yo.. can edit and apply different types of formatting to the text in this window. The document window is also called the text area of the MS Word window.
- ***Status bar*** It is located at the bottom of the MS Word window. The status bar provides some helpful information related to the document that we are currently working with. The information provided by the status bar includes:
  - Total number of pages in the document.
  - Page number of the active page.
  - Line number of the line of text where the cursor is currently positioned.
  - Column number of the character in the line of text where the cursor is currently positioned.
  - Status of various modes such as track mode, extend selection mode and overtype mode.
- ***Scroll bar*** The term scroll bar usually refers to the horizontal and the vertical bars placed at the right and the bottom of the MS Word window. These bars allow the user to view those portions of the document that cannot fit on the screen at one time.
- ***Ruler*** It is located below the toolbars. The ruler bar in MS Word is used to set the alignment for the content in the document.

Note: *If the ruler bar is not displayed in the MS Word window, then we can make it visible by selecting View → Ruler.*

- ***Task pane*** It is a rectangular pane placed at the right side of the MS Word window. The Getting Started task pane appears by default. We can consider the task pane as an open menu that can be used to open a new as well as an existing document. Using the Getting Started task pane, we can open recent documents, create a new document and search for some information using the Microsoft Office Online tool. Apart from the Getting Started task pane, the other task panes that we can view are Assistance, Search Results, Clip Art, Clipboard, etc.

Note: *If the Task Pane is not visible, then we can open it by selecting View → Task Pane or by pressing the Ctrl and F1 keys simultaneously.*

12.3.2 Basic Operations Performed in MS Word

The following are the key operations that we can perform in MS Word:

- Creating a document
- Saving a document
- Editing a document
- Formatting a document
- Printing a document

Creating a document We can create a document by performing the following steps:

1. Open the Document1 — Microsoft Word window.
2. Type some text; say, "This is my word document", in the document window, as shown in Fig. 12.6.

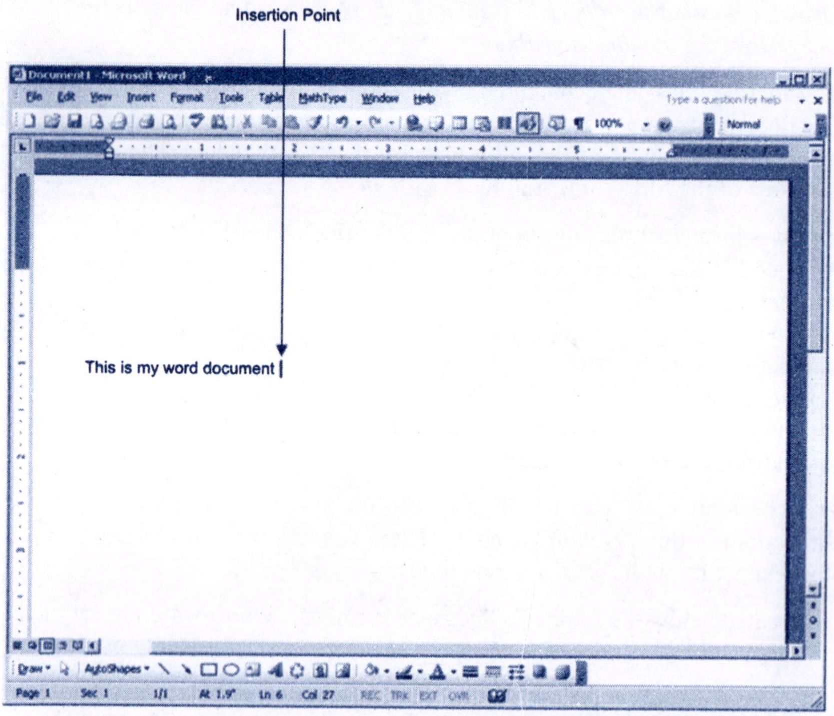

Fig. 12.6 The Document1 – Microsoft Word window with the entered text

Figure 12.6 shows the insertion point, which is actually a vertical blinking bar. In MS Word, the insertion point is more commonly known as a cursor. The insertion point usually defines the place in the document window from where we start typing the text.

Saving the document After we have finished creating a document, we need to save it at some appropriate location in the computer system for future reference.

To save a document, we need to perform the following steps:

1. Select File → Save to display the Save As dialog box, as shown in Fig. 12.7.

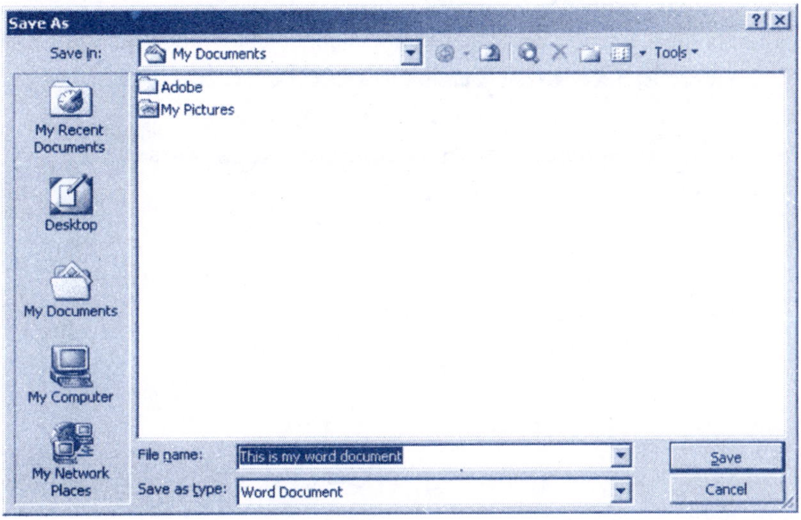

Fig. 12.7 The Save As dialog box

Figure 12.7 shows the Save As dialog box in which you can specify the document name and location where you want to save the document.

2. Select a location from the Save in list for saving the document.

Note: *By default, the My Documents location appears in the Save in list.*

3. Type a name, say mydoc, in the File name text box and click the Save button to save the document. The specified name, mydoc appears in the title bar, as shown in Fig. 12.8.

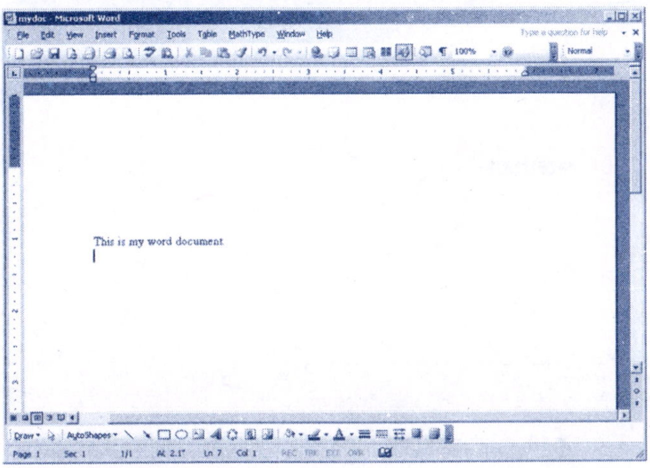

Fig. 12.8 The mydoc—Microsoft Word document

Editing the document Editing a document generally involves the operations, such as selecting the text, moving and copying the text and deleting either the selected text or the entire text in the document window. For selecting the text, say "This is my word", in the mydoc document, we need to perform the following steps:

1. Open the mydoc — Microsoft Word window.
2. Set the insertion point before the word "This" in the document window, as shown in Fig. 12.9.

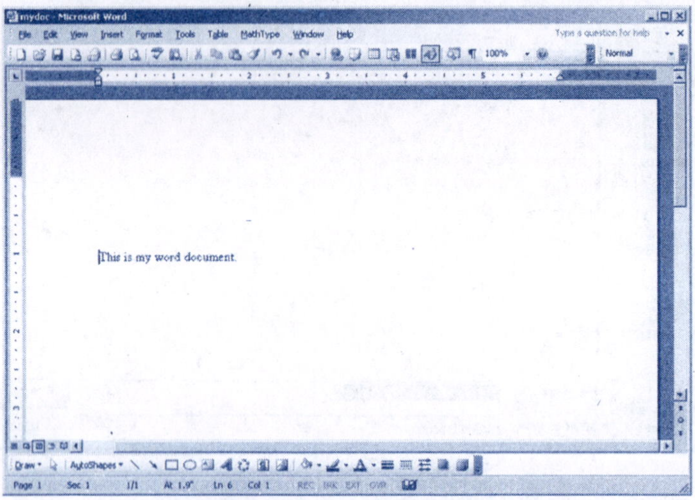

Fig. 12.9 Placing the insertion point

3. Press the left mouse button and drag the mouse pointer up to the desired level of the selection.
4. Release the left mouse button to complete the selection, as shown in Fig. 12.10.

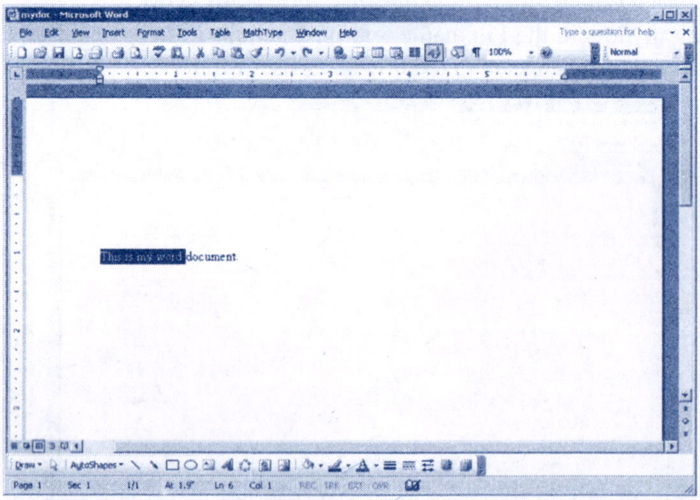

Fig. 12.10 Selecting the desired text in the document window

Note: *We can select the entire content of the document by either selecting Edit → Select All option or by pressing the Ctrl and A keys simultaneously.*

After selecting, we can copy the selected text, by performing the following steps:

1. Right-click the selected text to display a shortcut menu.
2. Select the Copy option to copy the selected text to the clipboard.

Note: *We can also copy the selected text to the clipboard by either selecting Edit → Copy or by pressing the Ctrl and C keys simultaneously.*

After copying, we can paste the selected text either in the same document window or in another document window, by performing the following steps:

1. Set the insertion point where the selected text needs to be pasted, as shown in Fig. 12.11.

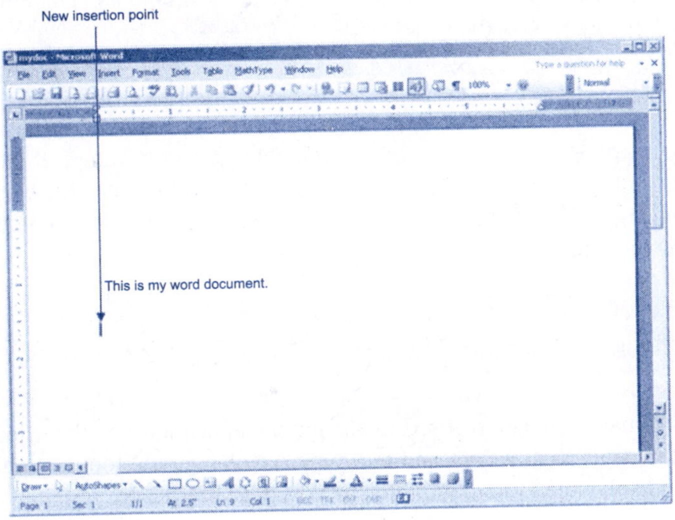

Fig. 12.11 Placing the insertion point for pasting the copied text

2. Right-click to display a shortcut menu and select the Paste option to paste the selected text at the new position in the document window, as shown in Fig. 12.12.

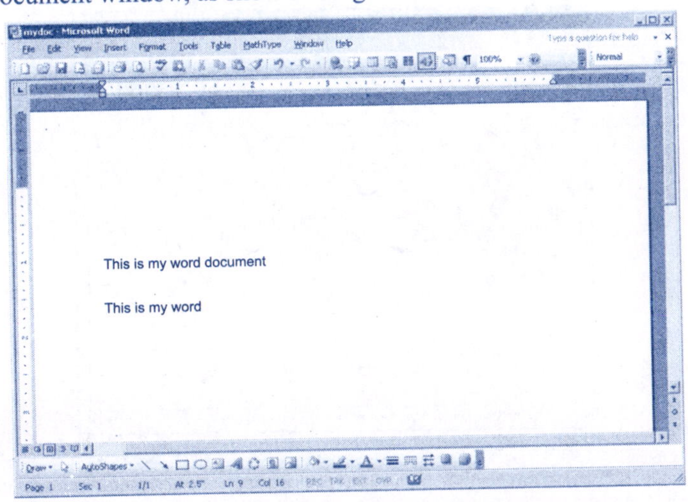

Fig. 12.12 The mydoc—Microsoft Word containing the text pasted at new position

Note: *We can also paste the selected text by either selecting Edit → Paste or by pressing the Ctrl and V keys simultaneously.*

Moving the text around the document window generally refers to the process of cutting the selected text from its original location and pasting it at some new place in the document window. To cut the selected text, select the Cut option from the shortcut menu that appears when we right-click on the selected text. Alternatively, we can also cut the selected text by selecting Edit → Cut option or by pressing the Ctrl and X keys simultaneously.

We can also delete either the selected text or the entire text of the document window. To perform the delete operation in the document window, select Edit → Clear → Contents. The content in the document window can also be deleted by pressing the Delete key.

Note: *We can get back the most recently deleted text by selecting Edit → Undo Clear or by pressing the Ctrl and Z keys simultaneously.*

Formatting the document The formatting of a document generally refers to the method of changing the layout and the design of the text according to the requirements. We can use the various options available in the Format menu to change the look and layout of the text in the document. Some of the options that can be used to format a document are as follows:

- Font
- Paragraph
- Bullets and Numbering

Font

The Font option in the Format menu can be used to change the appearance of the selected text by assigning it a different font size, font style, font colour and font type. To change the font settings of the selected text, select Format → Font to display the Font dialog box, as shown in Fig. 12.13.

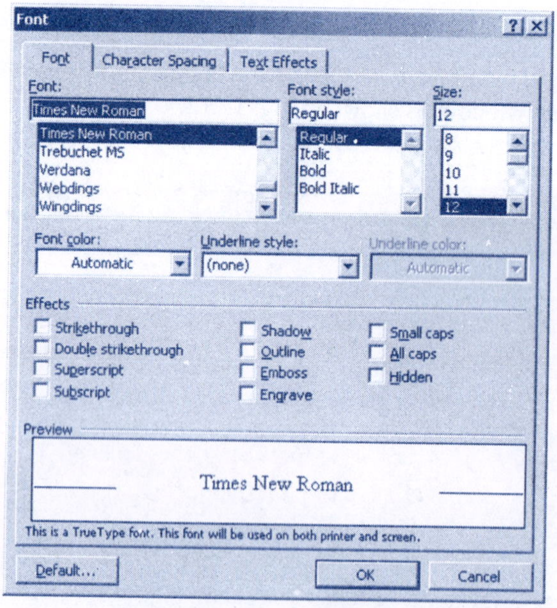

Fig. 12.13 The Font dialog box

Figure 12.13 shows the Font dialog box in which we can select various options for applying different formatting styles to the text in a document.

Paragraph
The Paragraph option in the Format menu can be used to apply different types of formatting to the paragraphs in the document window. In order to apply paragraph formatting, select Format → Paragraph to display the Paragraph dialog box, as shown in Fig. 12.14.

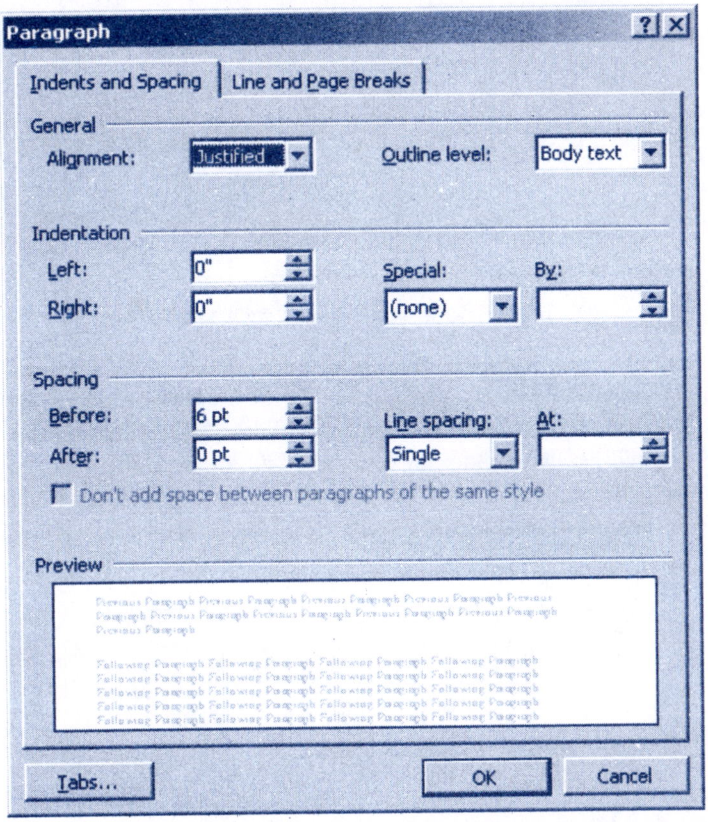

Fig. 12.14 The Paragraph dialog box

Figure 12.14 shows the Paragraph dialog box in which we can select various formatting styles either for the whole paragraph or for the selected text in a paragraph. We can change the alignment of the text in a paragraph by clicking Alignment drop down list and selecting an appropriate alignment for the selected text.

The different types of alignment styles available in the Paragraph dialog box are Left, Centered, Right and Justified. We can also indent a paragraph either in the left or right direction by selecting the indentation value in the Left and Right lists under the Indentation section.

Bullets and Numbering
The Bullets and Numbering option in the Format menu can be used to create the bulleted and numbered list in a document. To create these lists, select Format → Bullets and Numbering to display the Bullets and Numbering dialog box, as shown in Fig. 12.15.

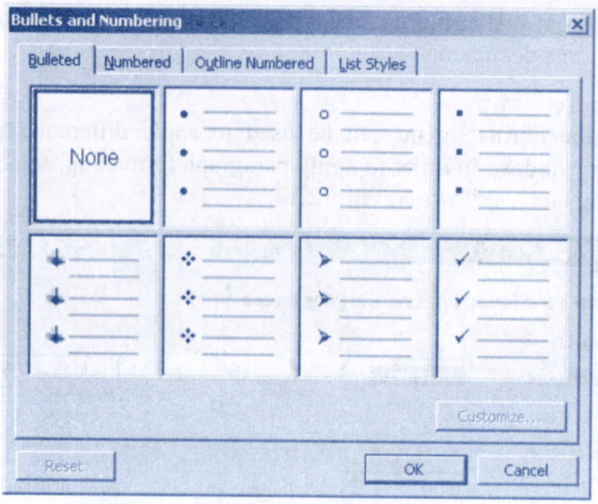

Fig. 12.15 The Bullets and Numbering dialog box

Note: *We can also create the bulleted list by clicking the Bullets icon on the Formatting toolbar.*

By default, the bulleted tabbed page appears in the Bullets and Numbering dialog box. As per our requirement, we can select the bullet style from the various bullet styles available in the bulleted tabbed page.

You can create a numbered list by clicking the Numbered tab in the Bullets and Numbering dialog box. The Numbered tabbed page allows us to select a numbering style, as shown in Fig. 12.16.

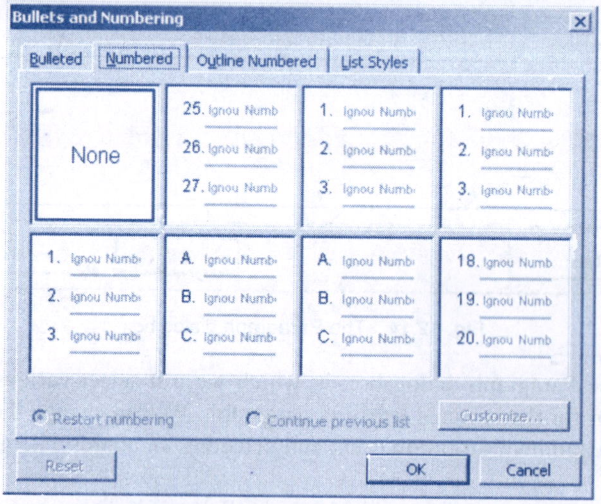

Fig. 12.16 The Numbered tabbed page

Note: *We can also create the Numbered list by clicking the Numbering icon on the Formatting toolbar.*

We can also create a numbered list with multiple levels, which is known as outline numbered list.

To create an outline numbered list, click the Outline Numbered tab to display the Outline Numbered tabbed page, as shown in Fig. 12.17.

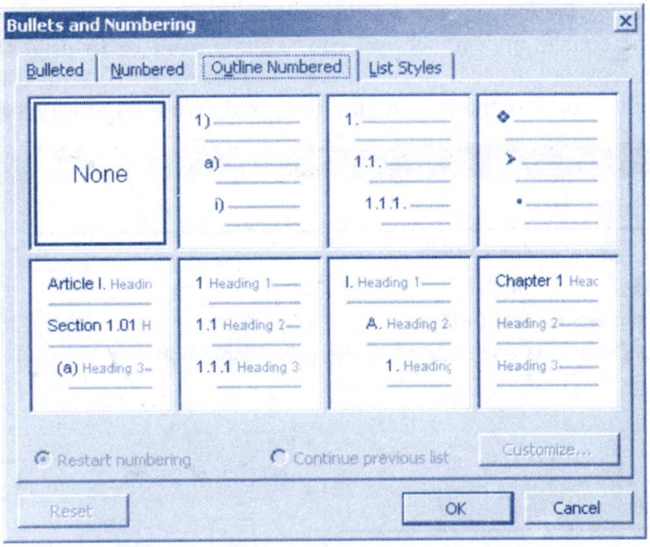

Fig. 12.17 The Outline Numbered tabbed page

After this, select the outline numbered style from the various styles available in the Outline Numbered tabbed page.

Printing the document After creating, editing, formatting and saving a document, we can print a copy of the document. However, before printing a document, we need to ensure that the printer is properly connected to the computer system and the appropriate print drivers have been installed. MS Word also provides a feature called Print Preview, which enables the user to get an idea of exactly how the document will appear after printing. This feature also provides the user a chance to make the last-minute changes before actually printing the document.

You can preview the content appearance, by selecting File → Print Preview option to display the preview window, as shown in Fig. 12.18.

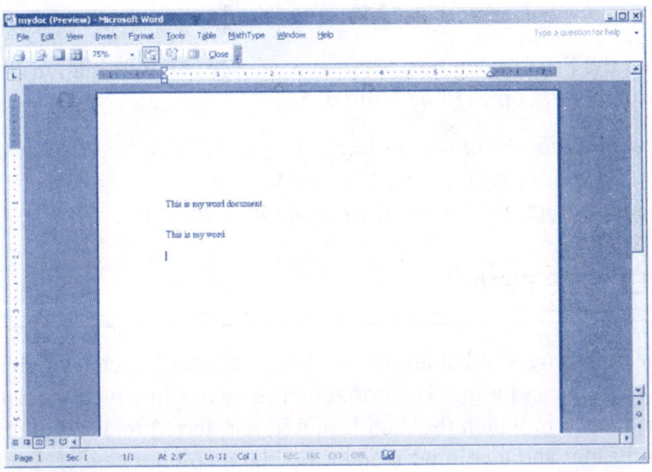

Fig. 12.18 The mydoc (Preview)—Microsoft Word window

Note: *We can also display the Preview window by clicking the Print Preview icon on the Standard toolbar.*

After previewing the content appearance, we can actually print it. To print the document, we need to perform the following steps:

1. Select File → Print to display the Print dialog box, as shown in Figure 12.19.

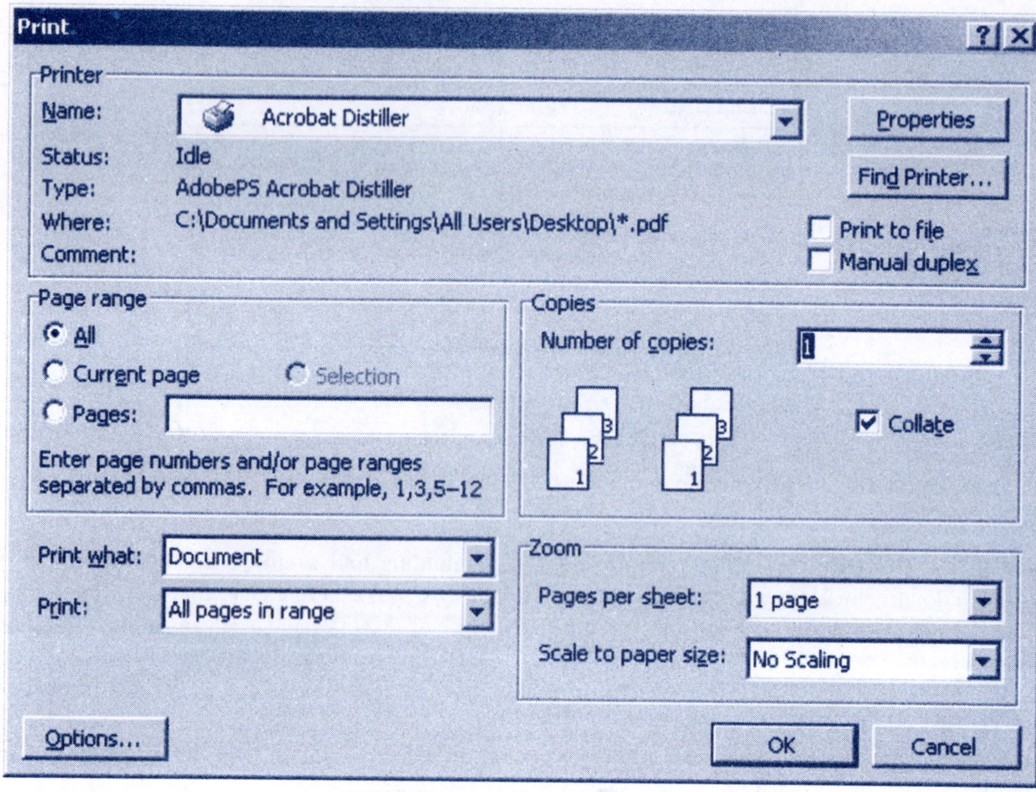

Fig. 12.19 The Print dialog box

Figure 12.19 shows the Print dialog box where we can specify information like printer name, number of pages to be printed, number of copies to be printed, etc.

Note: *We can also display the Print dialog box either by pressing the Ctrl and P keys simultaneously or by clicking the Print icon on the Standard toolbar.*

2. Accept the default settings and click OK to print the document.

12.4 MS EXCEL SYSTEM

MS Excel is an application program that allows us to create spreadsheets, which are represented in the form of a table containing rows and columns. The horizontal sequence in which the data is stored is referred to as a row. The vertical sequence in which the data is stored is referred to as a column. In a spreadsheet, a row is identified by a row header and a column is identified by a column header. Each value in a spreadsheet is stored in a cell, which is the intersection of rows and columns. A cell can contain either numeric value or a character string. We can also specify the contents of a cell using formulas. In a spreadsheet, we can perform various mathematical operations using formulas, such as addition, subtraction, multiplication, division, average, percentage, etc.

MS Excel also allows us to represent the complex data pictorially in the form of graphs. These are generally used to represent the information with the help of images, colours etc so that their presentation is simple and more meaningful. Some of the graphs available in spreadsheet are bar graphs, line graphs, 3-D graphs, area graphs, etc.

12.4.1 Accessing MS Excel

For working with MS Excel, we first need to install MS Office in our computer system. After installing MS Office, we can start MS Excel using any of the following two ways:

- Start menu
- Run command

Using Start menu We can start MS Excel by performing the following steps using the Start menu:

1. Select Start → Programs → Microsoft Office, as shown in Fig. 12.20.

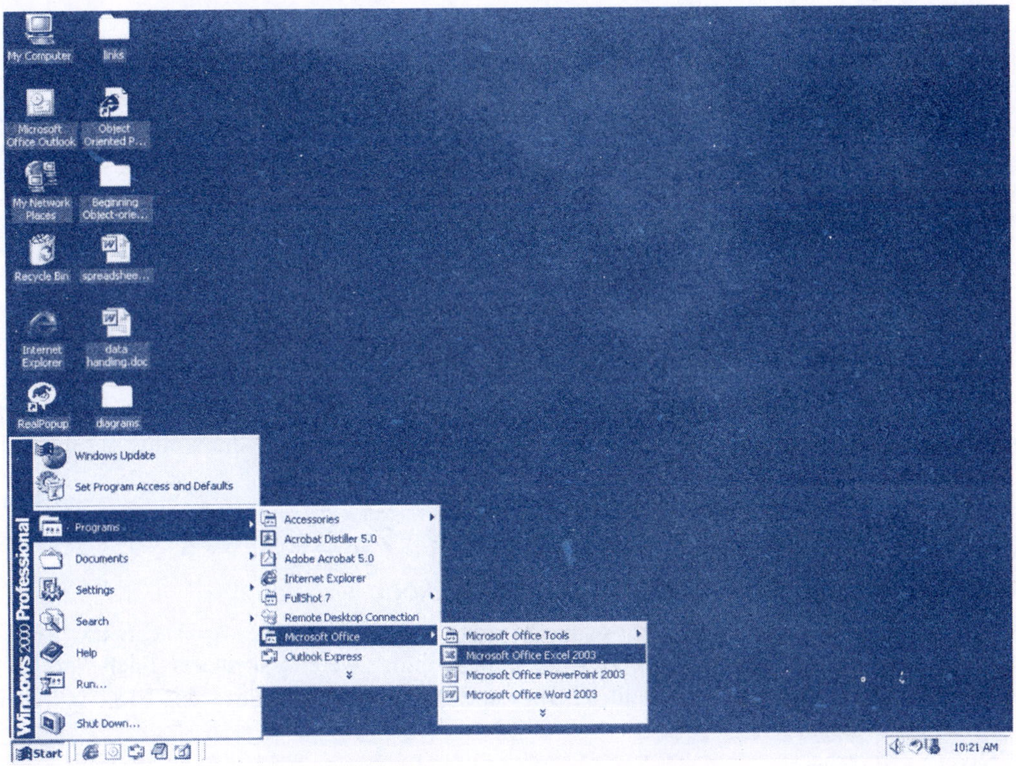

Fig. 12.20 Starting MS Excel using the Start menu

2. Select the Microsoft Office Excel 2003 option to display the GUI of MS Excel, as shown in Fig. 12.21.

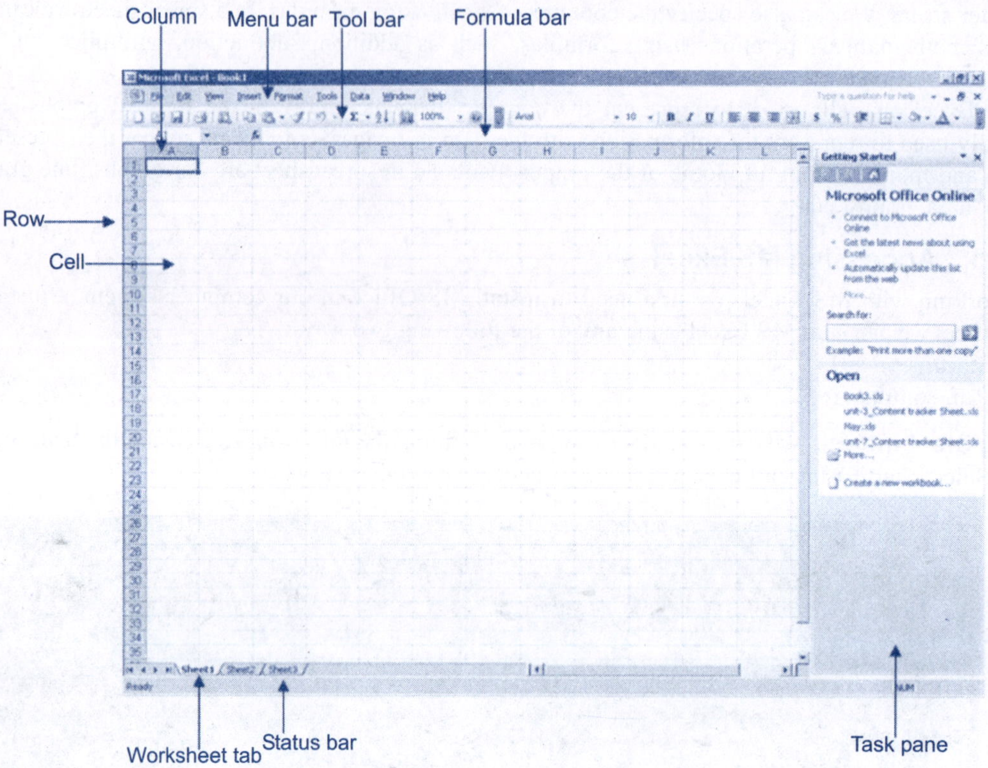

Fig. 12.21 The Microsoft Excel—Book1 window

Figure 12.21 shows the initial workbook of MS Excel, which in turn contains worksheets. Each worksheet contains rows and columns where we can enter data.

Using Run command We can also start MS Excel by performing the following steps using the Run command:

1. Select Start → Run to display the Run dialog box.
2. Type excel in the Open text box and click OK to display the Microsoft Excel – Book1 window.

12.4.2 Basic Operations Performed in MS Excel

Worksheet is the actual working area consisting of rows and columns. The worksheets are also known as the spreadsheets. A workbook in MS Excel is a combination of several worksheets. Each workbook of MS Excel contains three worksheets by default. The key operations that are performed in MS Excel include:

- Creating a worksheet
- Saving a worksheet
- Modifying a worksheet
- Renaming a worksheet
- Deleting a worksheet
- Moving a worksheet
- Editing a worksheet

Creating the worksheet We can create a worksheet in MS Excel by simply inserting the data in the cells of the worksheet. To create a worksheet, perform the following steps:

1. Open the Microsoft Excel - Book1 window.
2. Insert the data into the cells according to the requirement, as shown in Fig. 12.22.

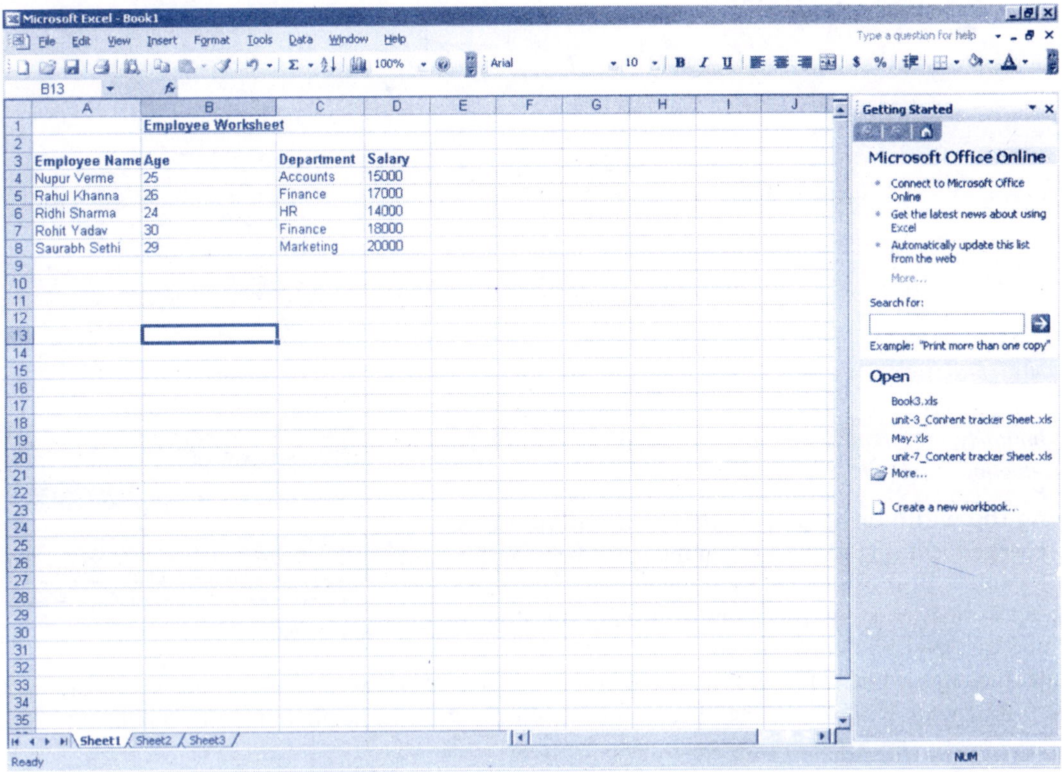

Fig. 12.22 Entering data in the Microsoft Excel—Book1 window

Saving the worksheet After entering the data in the worksheet, we need to save the worksheet at the desired location in the computer system. To save a worksheet, perform the following steps:

1. Select File → Save As to display the Save As dialog box.
2. Select a location from the Save in list where the worksheet is to be saved.
3. Enter the name of the file in the File name text box.
4. Click the Save button to save the file.

Modifying the worksheet A worksheet in MS Excel can be modified in the following two ways:

- By inserting rows and columns in the existing worksheet.
- By changing the width or height of rows and columns.

Inserting rows and columns In order to insert a row in the worksheet, select Insert → Rows, as shown in Fig. 12.23.

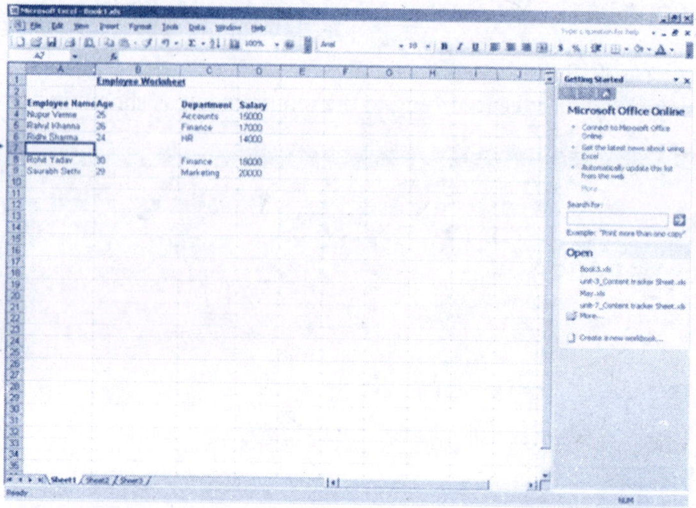

Fig. 12.23 Inserting a row in Microsoft Excel—Book1

Note: *Similarly, we can insert a column in the worksheet by selecting Insert → Columns.*

Changing the width or height of the rows and columns In order to change the height of the rows in the worksheet, perform the following steps:

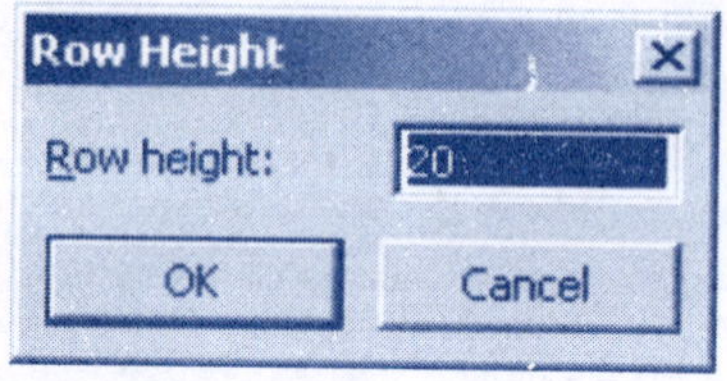

Fig. 12.24 The Row Height dialog box

1. Select Format → Row → Height to display the Row Height dialog box, as shown in Fig. 12.24.
2. Enter the required height in the Row Height text box and click OK to apply height specifications to the rows. Figure 12.25 shows the Microsoft Excel-Book1 with the height of the row modified to 20.

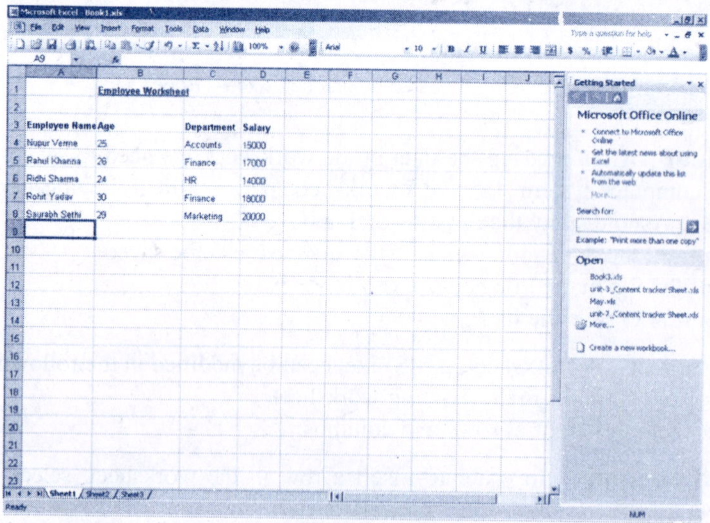

Fig. 12.25 Formatting rows in the Microsoft Excel—Book1 window

Renaming the worksheet Usually the default names of the worksheet in MS Excel are Sheet1, Sheet2, Sheet3 etc. In order to rename the worksheet, we need to perform the following steps:

1. Open the Microsoft Excel - Book1 window.
2. Right-click the Sheet1 tab to display a shortcut menu.
3. Select the Rename option and change the name of worksheet.

Figure 12.26 shows the Microsoft Excel – Book1 window in which Sheet1 has been renamed to Employee Worksheet.

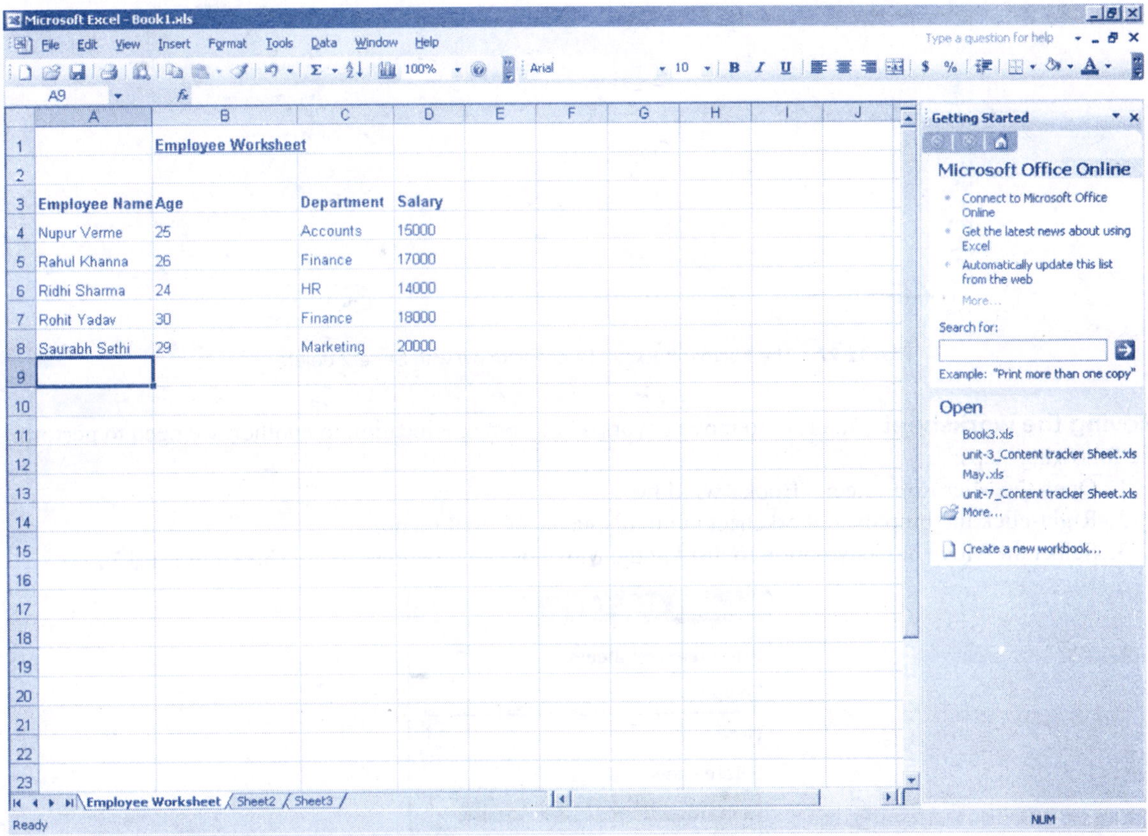

Fig. 12.26 Renaming the Microsoft Excel – Book1

Deleting the worksheet In order to delete a worksheet from the workbook, we need to perform the following steps:

1. Open the Microsoft Excel - Book1 window.
2. Right-click the Sheet2 tab to display the shortcut menu.
3. Select the Delete option to delete the Sheet2 worksheet.

Figure12.27 shows the Microsoft Excel - Book1 window with Sheet2 deleted.

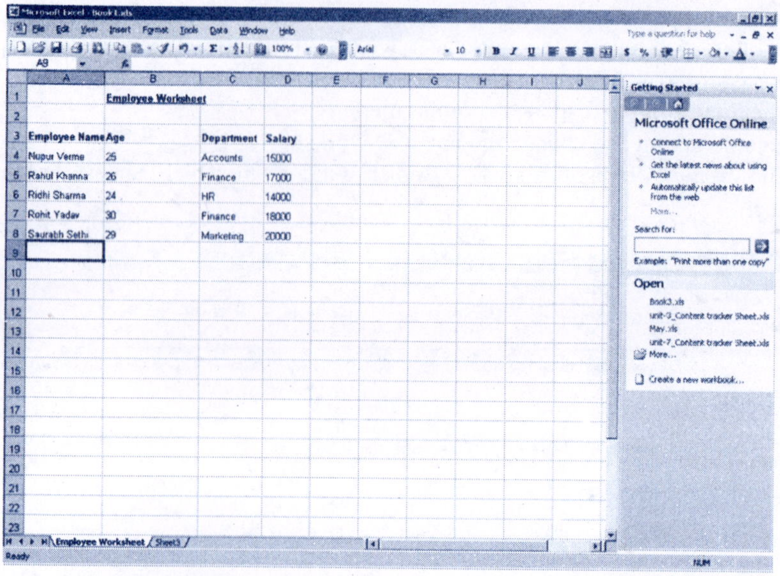

Fig. 12.27 The Microsoft Excel–Book1 window with Sheet2 deleted

Moving the worksheet In order to move a worksheet from one location to another, we need to perform the following steps:

1. Open the Microsoft Excel – Book1 window.
2. Right-click the Employee Worksheet tab to display a shortcut menu.
3. Select the Move or Copy option to display the Move or Copy dialog box, as shown in Fig.12.28.

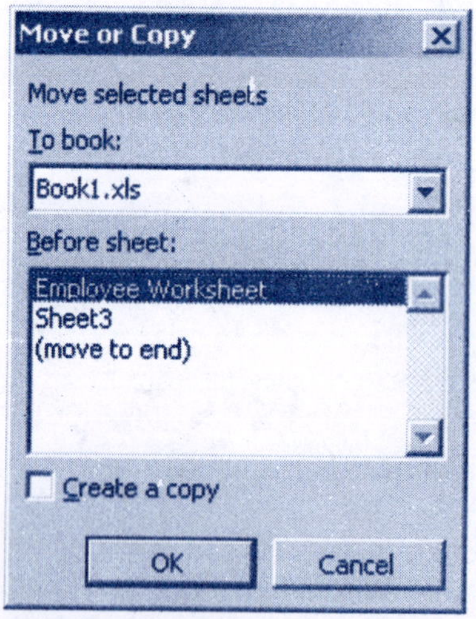

Fig. 12.28 The Move or Copy dialog box

4. Select the location, say (move to end), from the Before sheet list, to move the current sheet before the selected one and press OK.

Figure 12.29 shows that the Employee Worksheet moved to the end.

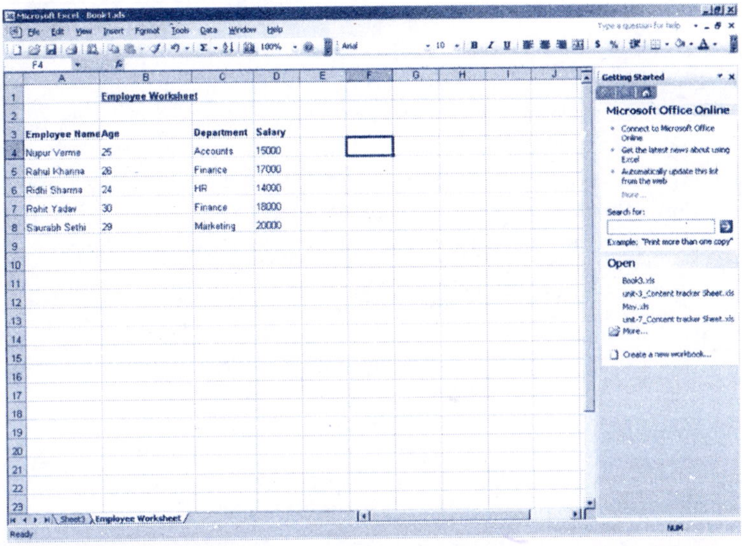

Fig. 12.29 Displaying the changed position of the Employee Worksheet

Editing the worksheet In order to edit a worksheet in the workbook, we need to perform the following steps:

1. Open the Microsoft Excel – Book1 window.
2. Double-click the cell in which we want to make the changes.
3. Enter the new data in the cell.

Figure 12.30 shows the Microsoft Excel – Book1 with modified data.

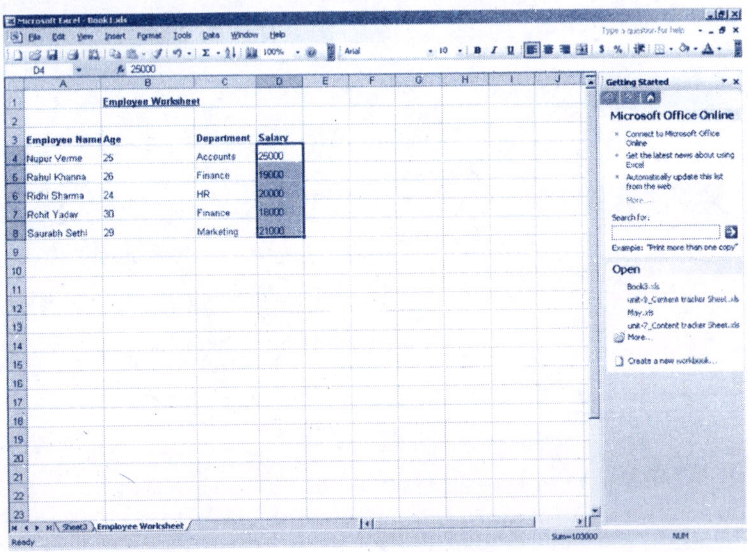

Fig. 12.30 Editing the Microsoft Excel—Book1

12.5 MS POWERPOINT SYSTEM

MS PowerPoint is a software application included in the MS Office package that allows us to create presentations. PowerPoint provides a GUI with the help of which we can create attractive presentations quickly and easily. The presentation may include slides, handouts, notes, outlines, graphics and animations. A slide in PowerPoint is a combination of images, text, graphics, charts, etc that is used to convey some meaning information. The presentations in MS PowerPoint are usually saved with the extension .ppt. The interface of MS PowerPoint is similar to the other interfaces of MS Office applications. PowerPoint presentations are commonly used in business, schools, colleges, training programmes, etc.

12.5.1 Accessing MS PowerPoint

For working in MS PowerPoint, we need to first install the MS Office package in our computer system. After installing MS Office, we can start MS PowerPoint using any of the following two ways:

- Start menu
- Run command

Using Start menu We can start MS PowerPoint by performing the following steps using the Start menu:

1. Select Start → Programs → Microsoft Office, as shown in Fig. 12.31.

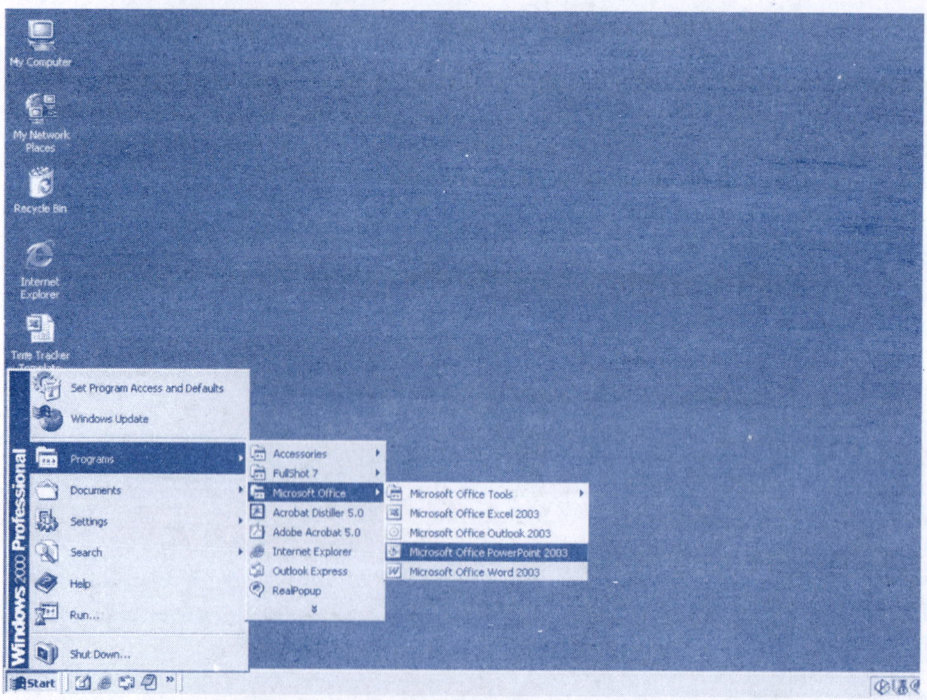

Fig. 12.31 Starting MS PowerPoint using the Start menu

2. Select the Microsoft Office PowerPoint 2003 option to display the GUI of MS PowerPoint, as shown in Fig. 12.32.

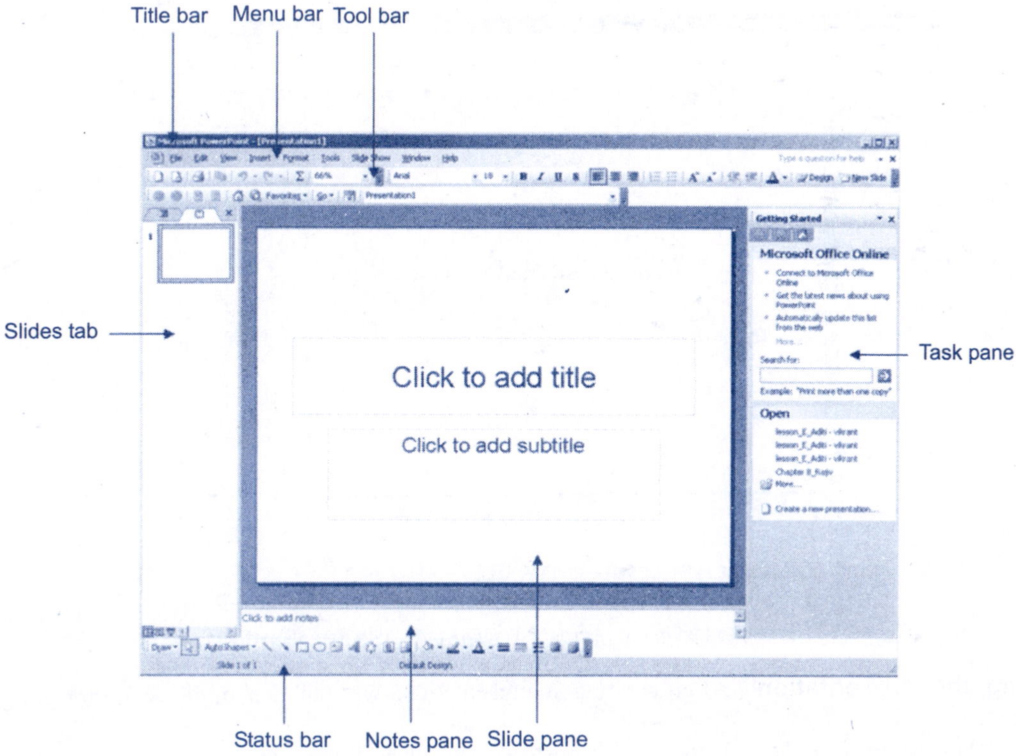

Fig. 12.32 The Microsoft PowerPoint—[Presentation1] Window

Using Run command We can also start MS PowerPoint by performing the following steps using the Run command:

1. Select Start → Run to display the Run dialog box.
2. Type powerpnt in the Open text box and click OK to display the Microsoft PowerPoint – [Presentation1] window.

12.5.2 Basic Operations Performed on a Presentation

The following are the key operations that can be performed in MS PowerPoint:

- Creating a new presentation
- Designing the presentation
- Saving a new presentation
- Adding slides to the presentation
- Printing the presentation

Creating a new presentation We can create a new presentation in MS PowerPoint by performing the following steps:

1. Open the Microsoft PowerPoint – [Presentation1] window.
2. Enter some text in the slide, as shown in Fig. 12.33.

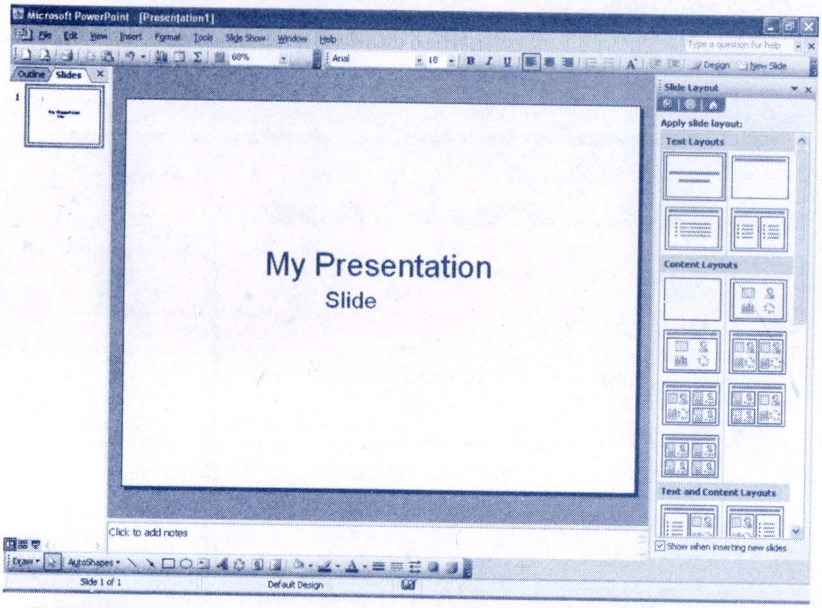

Fig. 12.33 Entering text in the Microsoft PowerPoint—[Presentation1] window

Designing the presentation After creating a presentation, we can design it by performing the following steps:

1. Select Format → Slide Design to display the Slide Design task pane at the right-hand side of the Microsoft PowerPoint – [Presentation1] window, as shown in Fig. 12.34.

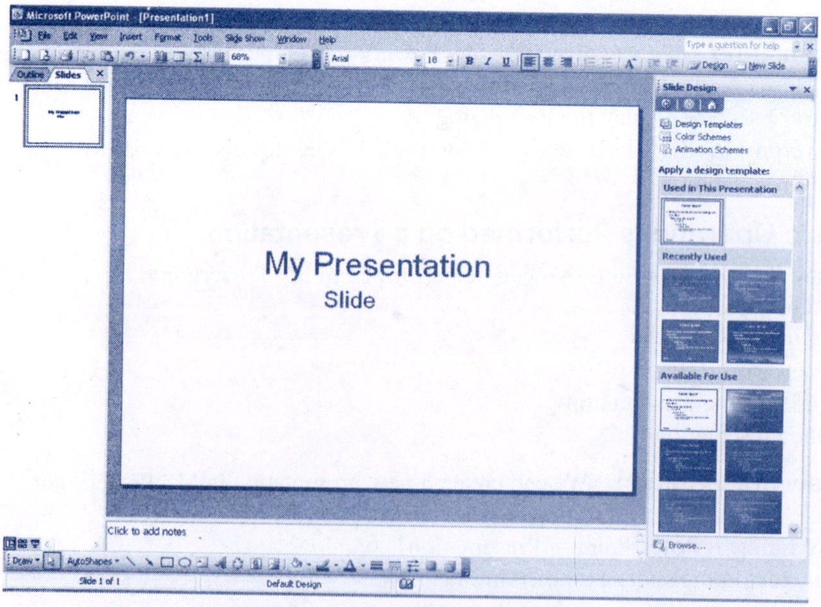

Fig. 12.34 The Slide Design task pane

2. Select a slide design, say Maple, from the Apply a design template section, as shown in Fig. 12.35.

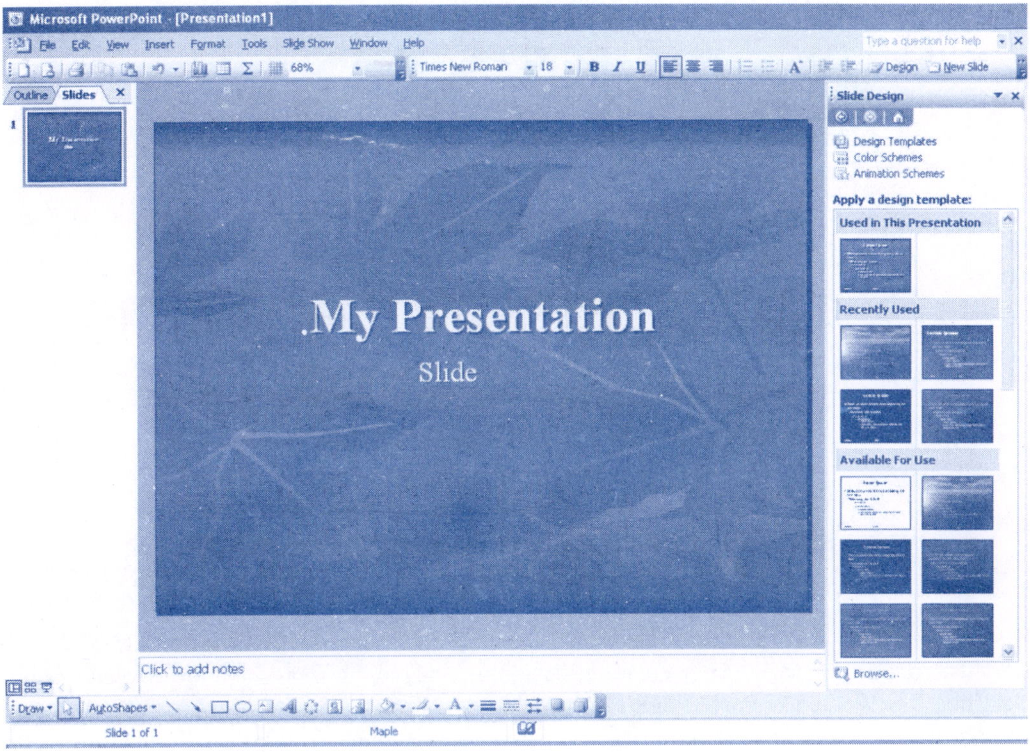

Fig. 12.35 Designing the presentation

Saving the presentation After we have finished creating and designing a presentation, we need to save it at some appropriate location in the computer system for future reference. To save the presentation, we need to perform the following steps:

1. Select File → Save to display the Save As dialog box in which the File name text box contains the default name suggested by MS PowerPoint. However, we can change the name as per our requirement.
2. Select a location from the Save in list for saving the presentation.
3. Type a name, say My Presentation1, in the File name text box and click the Save button to save the presentation.

Adding slides to the presentation You can add a new slide to the presentation by performing the following steps:

1. Open the Microsoft PowerPoint – [My Presentation1] window.
2. Select Insert → New Slide option to add a new slide, as shown in Fig. 12.36.

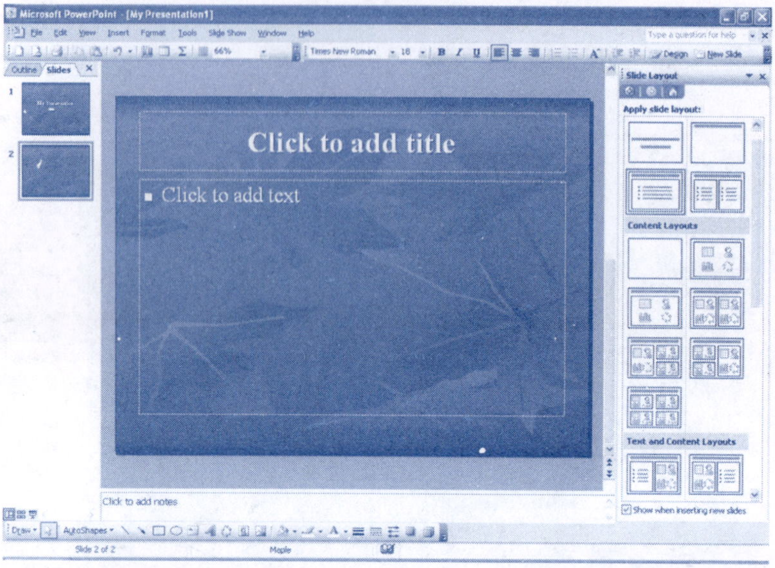

Fig. 12.36 The Microsoft PowerPoint—[My Presentation1] window with a new slide

Note: *You can also insert a new slide by right-clicking the slide thumbnail and then selecting the New Slide option.*

Printing the presentation After creating, designing and saving a presentation, we can print a copy of it. Just like MS Word, MS PowerPoint also provides the feature of print preview. We can preview the content appearance before issuing the print command by selecting File → Print Preview to display the preview window, as shown in Fig. 12.37.

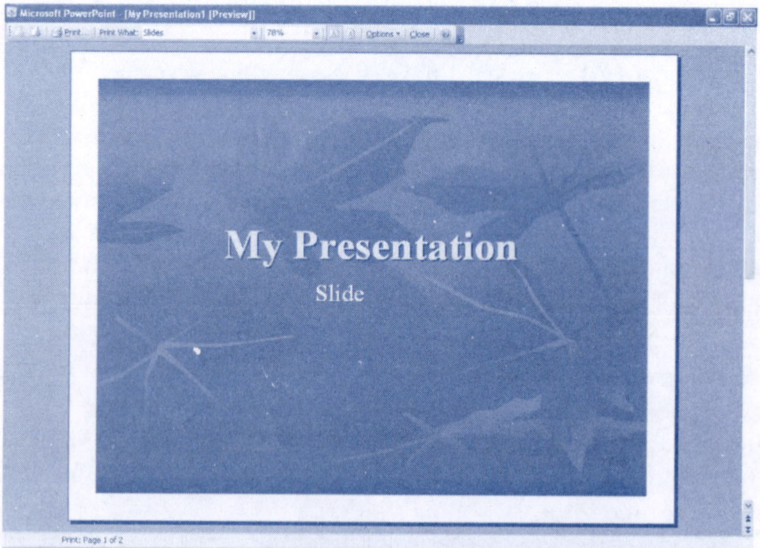

Fig. 12.37 The Microsoft PowerPoint—[My Presentation1 [Preview]] window

After previewing, we need to perform the following steps to print the MS PowerPoint presentation:

1. Select File → Print to display the Print dialog box.
2. Specify the number of pages and numbers of copies of each page to be printed and click OK to print the presentation.

12.6 MS ACCESS SYSTEM

Microsoft Access (MS Access) is a Relational Database Management System (RDBMS) that allows the users to create a database and store the data in the form of rows and columns i.e. in the form of tables. MS Access comprises of a database engine known as Microsoft Jet Database Engine and a GUI. It also supports various tools that help the users in creating and managing databases. MS Access is used by business organisations and programmers for creating an organised database system.

12.6.1 Accessing MS Access

For working in MS Access, we need to install first install MS Office in our computer system. After installing MS Office, we can start MS Access using any of the following two ways:

- Start menu
- Run command

Using Start Menu We can start MS Access by performing the following steps using the Start menu:

1. Select Start → Programs → Microsoft Office, as shown in Fig. 12.38.

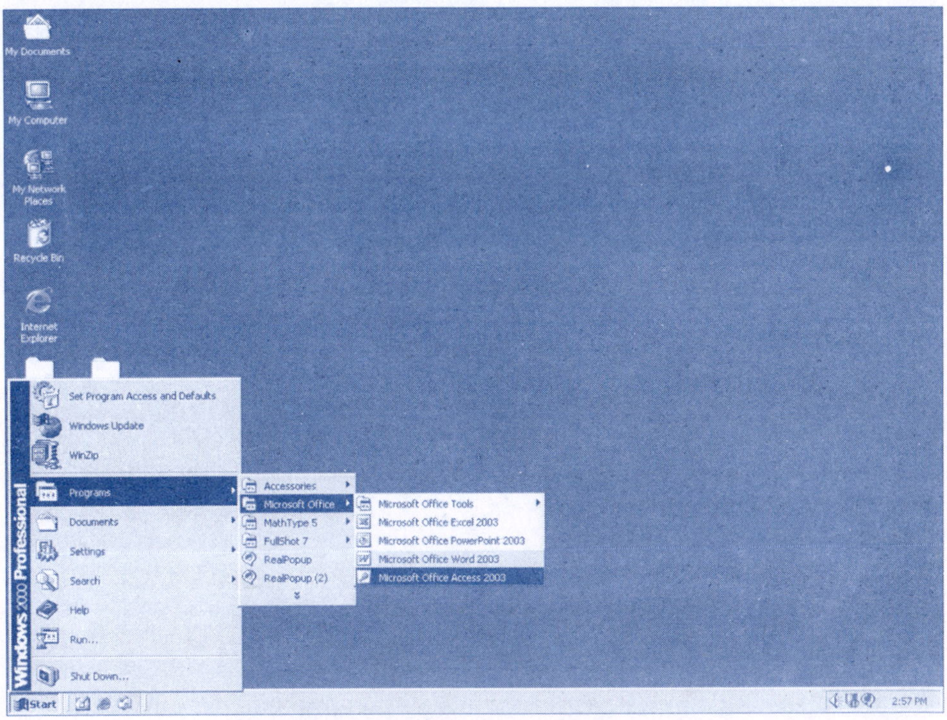

Fig. 12.38 Starting MS Access using the Start menu

2. Select the Microsoft Office Access 2003 option to display the GUI of MS Access, as shown in Fig. 12.39.

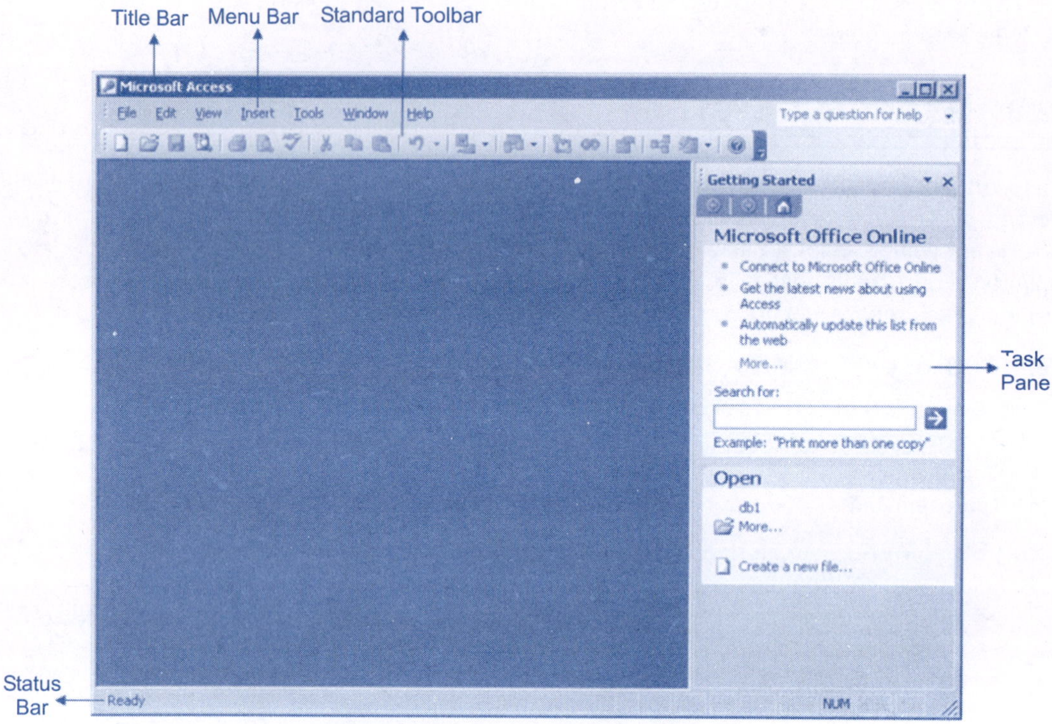

Fig. 12.39 The Microsoft Access window

Using Run command We can also start MS Access by performing the following steps using the Run command:

1. Select Start → Run to display the Run dialog box.
2. Type msaccess in the Open text box and click OK to display the Microsoft Access window.

Note: *The basic functions of the GUI components of MS Access are same as that of MS Word.*

12.6.2 Basic Operations Performed in MS Access

MS Access is a database management system that can be used for creating databases. We can perform various operations in MS Access for storing the data in an efficient manner. The following are some of the key operations that can be performed in MS Access:

- Creating a database
- Creating a database table
- Defining relationships
- Creating a database query

Creating a database We can create a database in MS Access by performing the following steps:

1. Open the Microsoft Access window.

2. Select File → New to display the New File task pane on the right side of the Microsoft Access window, as shown in Fig. 12.40.

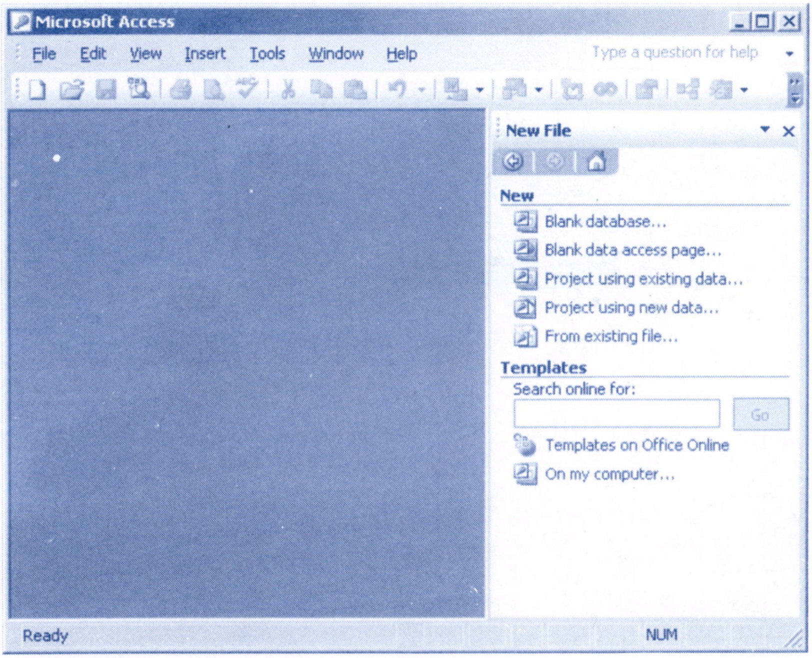

Fig. 12.40 The Microsoft Access window containing the New File task pane

3. Click the Blank database icon under the New section to display File New Database dialog box, as shown in Fig. 12.41.

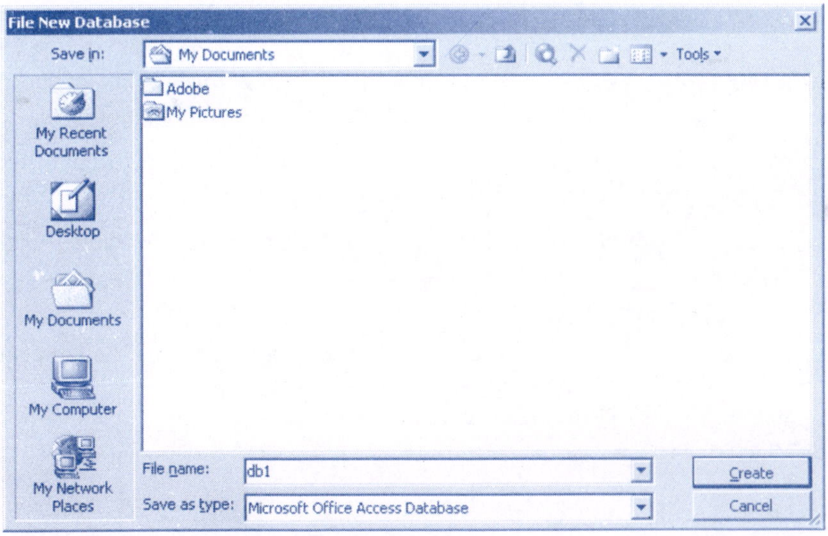

Fig. 12.41 The File New Database dialog box

4. Select the location from the Save in list for saving the database.
5. Enter the name of the database such as Student Database in the File name text box and click the Create button to create the Student Database. Figure 12.42 shows the Student Database: Database (Access 2000 file format) window.

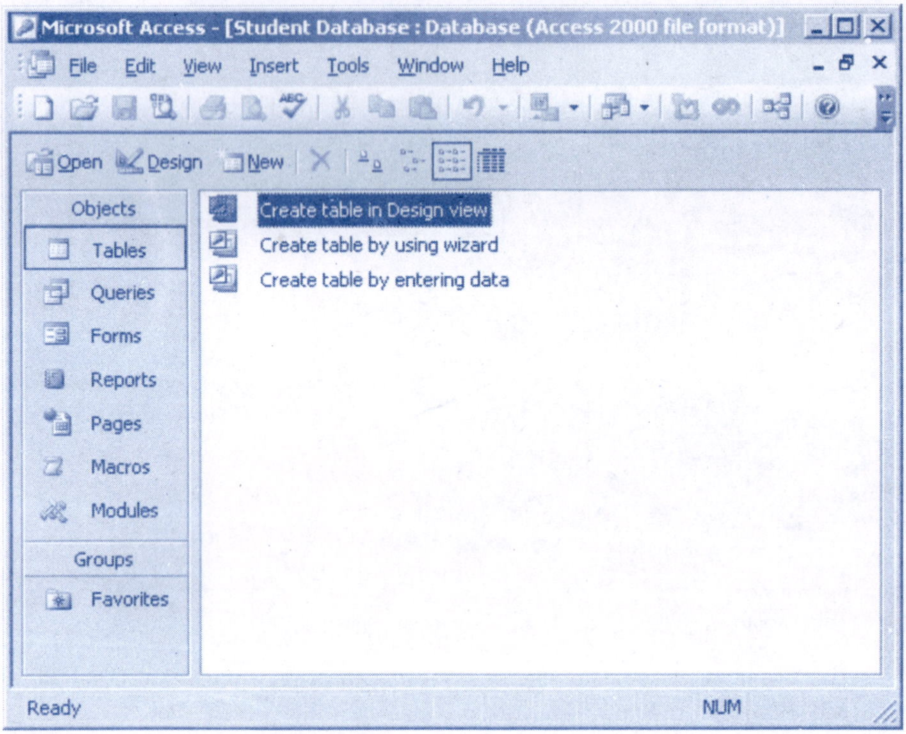

Fig. 12.42 The Student Database window

Creating a database table We can create a table in MS Access using any of the following three options available in the Student Database: Database (Access 2000 file format) window:

- ***Create table in Design view*** This option allows us to first create the design of the table, i.e., the fields of the table along with its data type and then enter data into it.
- ***Create table by using wizard*** This option provides some sample tables to the user. These sample tables are divided into two categories, business and personal. After selecting a sample table and its fields, the users can enter data in to the newly created table.
- ***Create table by entering data*** This option allows the user to design the table and enter data in the table simultaneously. There is no need to specify the data type for the fields.

The most commonly used method for creating a table in MS Access is the Create table in Design view option. For creating a table in MS Access using the Create table in Design view option, we need to perform the following the steps:

1. Double-click the Create table in Design view option in Student Database: Database (Access 2000 file format) window to display the Table1: Table page, as shown in Fig. 12.43.

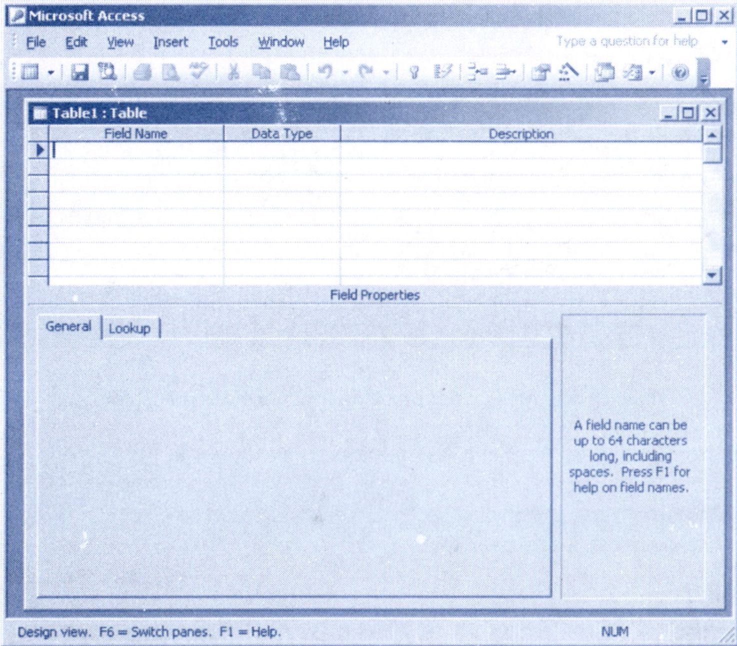

Fig. 12.43 The design view of Table1—Table page in the Microsoft Access window

2. Enter the name of the fields in the Field Name column and the data types in the Data Type column, as shown in Fig. 12.44.

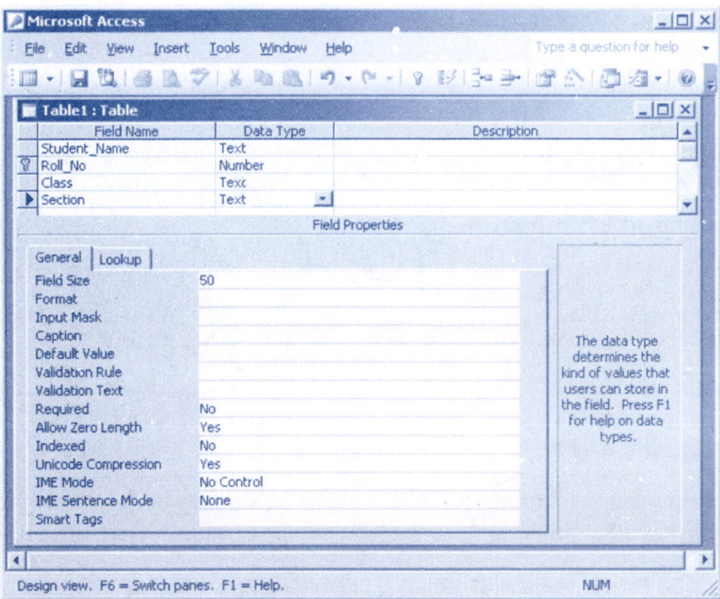

Fig. 12.44 The Table1—Table page with field names and their data types

3. Close the Table1 : Table page. Before closing the Table1 : Table page, a message prompt appears, as shown in Fig. 12.45.

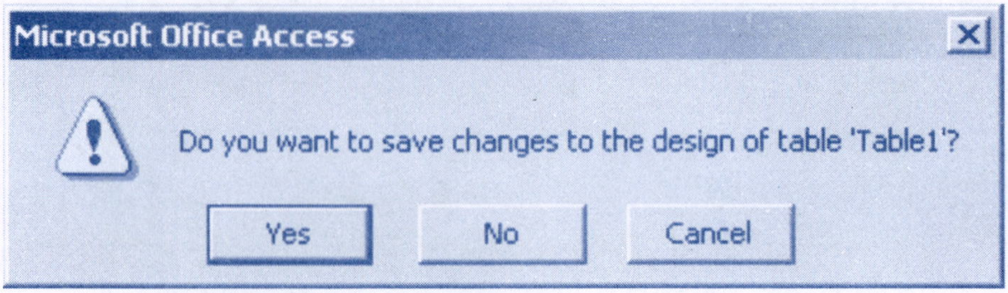

Fig. 12.45 Message Prompt for saving the design of table

4. Click the Yes button to display the Save As dialog box, as shown in Fig. 12.46.

Fig. 12.46 Saving the design of the table

5. Enter the name of the table, say Student_Details, in the Table Name text box and click OK. A message prompt again appears, as shown in Fig. 12.47.

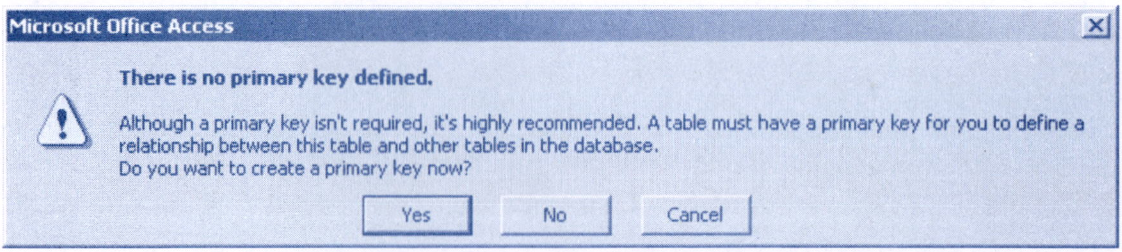

Fig. 12.47 Prompting whether to define a primary key or not

In Fig. 12.47, we can either select the Yes or No option depending upon our requirement of defining a primary key. A primary key is a single field or a combination of multiple fields that are used to uniquely identify a record in the database table.

6. Click the NO button to display the Microsoft Access – [Student Database: Database (Access 2000 file format)] window, as shown in Fig. 12.48.

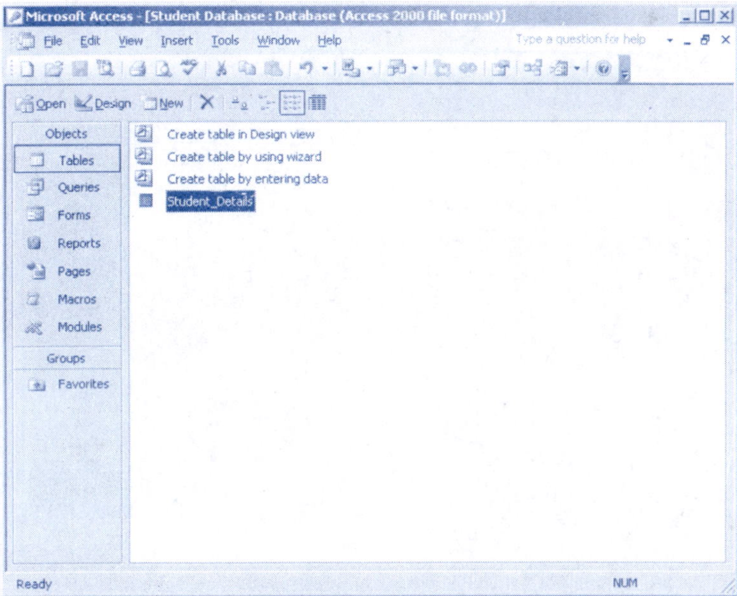

Fig. 12.48 The Microsoft Access—[Student Database: Database (Access 2000 file format)] with the Student_Details table

Entering data in a table In order to enter data in the Student_Details table, we need to perform the following steps:

1. Double-click the Student_Details icon to display the Microsoft Access – [Student_Details:Table] window, as shown in Fig. 12.49.

Fig. 12.49 The Microsoft Access—[Student_Details:Table] window

2. Enter data in the table, as shown in Fig. 12.50.

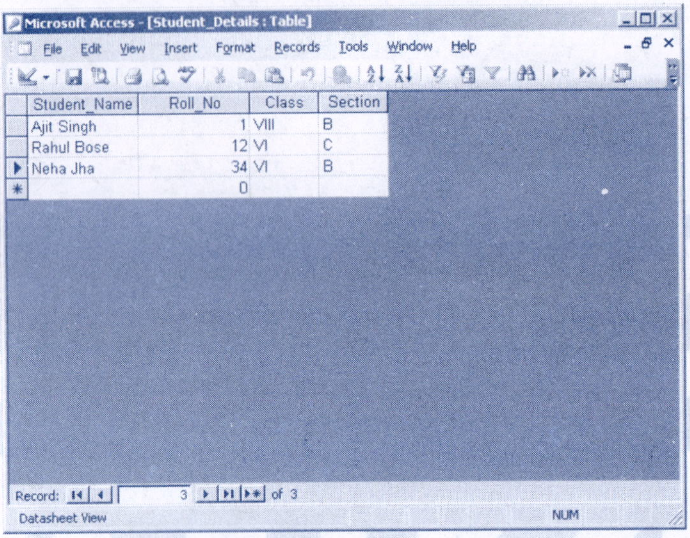

Fig. 12.50 The Microsoft Access—[Student_Details:Table] window with the entered data

3. Close the Microsoft Access – [Student_Details:Table] window to display the Microsoft Access – [Student Database: Database (Access 2000 file format)] window.

Manipulating a table Manipulating a table involves the addition of new rows and columns to the table. A row represents a record in the table whereas a column represents a field. For adding a record, we need to perform the following steps:

1. Open the Student_Details table to add new records.
2. Enter the data in the empty record marked with an asterisk (*), as shown in Fig. 12.51.

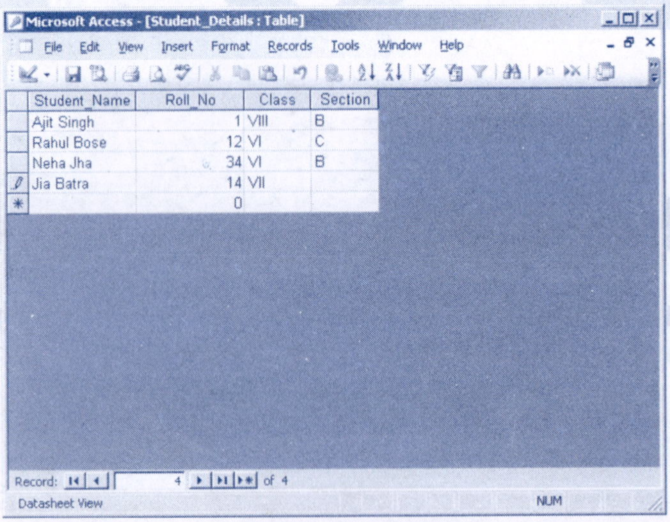

Fig. 12.51 The Microsoft Access—[Student_Details:Table] window a New Record Added

Note: *The asterisk (*) shifts to the next record as soon as data is entered in the new record.*

3. Close the Microsoft Access–[Student_Details:Table] window to display the Microsoft Access [Student Database: Database (Access 2000 file format)] window.

For adding a new column, we need to perform the following steps:

1. Open the Student_Details table.
2. Select a field, say Class, before which the new field is to be added.
3. Select Insert → Column to insert a new blank field before the Class field, as shown in Fig. 12.52.

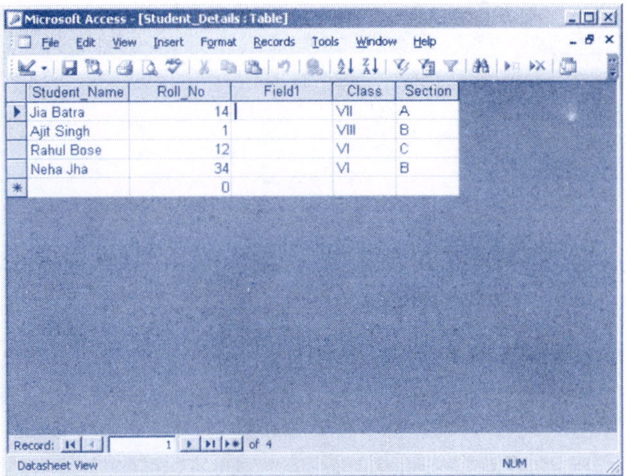

Fig. 12.52 A new blank field inserted before the Class field

4. Enter D_o_Admission as the name of the field by double-clicking Field1 column header.
5. Enter data in the D_o_Admission field, as shown in Fig. 12.53.

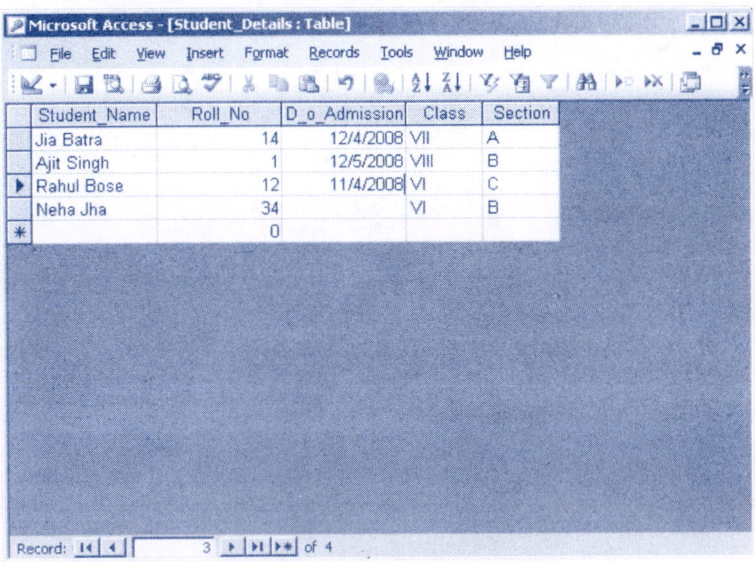

Fig. 12.53 The newly inserted field

6. Close the Microsoft Access – [Student_Details:Table] window to display the Microsoft Access – [Student Database: Database (Access 2000 file format)] window.

Editing a table Editing a table involves changing the existing data in the table. For editing a table, we need to perform the following steps:

1. Open the Student_Details table for editing the records.
2. Select the cell for which the value has to be changed, for example we can change the Roll_No of Ajit Singh from 1 to 39, as shown in Fig. 12.54.

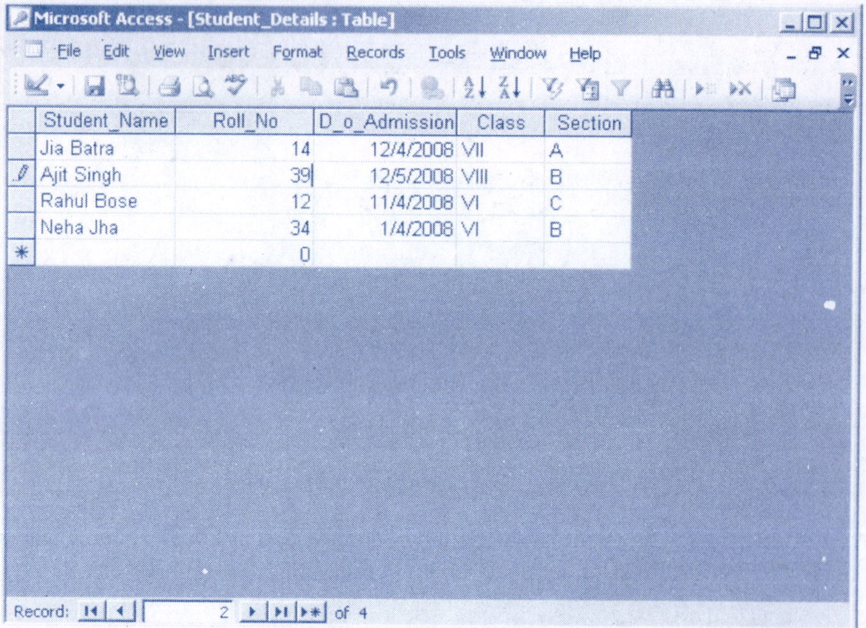

Fig. 12.54 The Microsoft Access—[Student_Details:Table] window with the changed value

3. Close the Microsoft Access – [Student_Details:Table] window to display the Microsoft Access – [Student Database: Database (Access 2000 file format)] window.

Deleting a record In order to delete a record, we need to perform the following steps:

1. Select the record that is to be deleted.
2. Select Edit → Delete Record to display a message prompt confirming the deletion of record, as shown in Fig. 12.55.

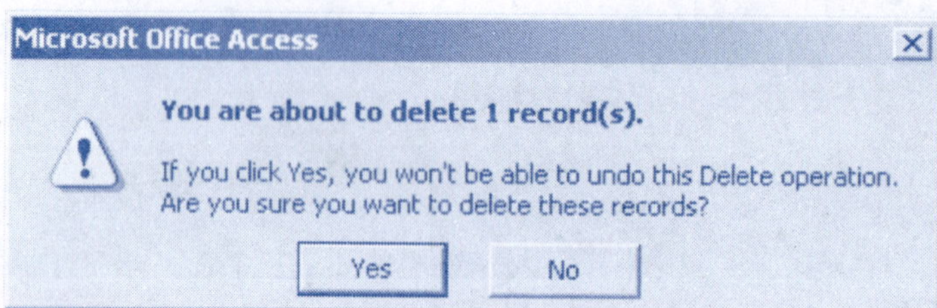

Fig. 12.55 Message prompt confirming the deletion of record

3. Click the Yes button to permanently delete the record. Figure 12.56 shows the Microsoft Access – [Student_Details:Table] window after the deletion of the third record.

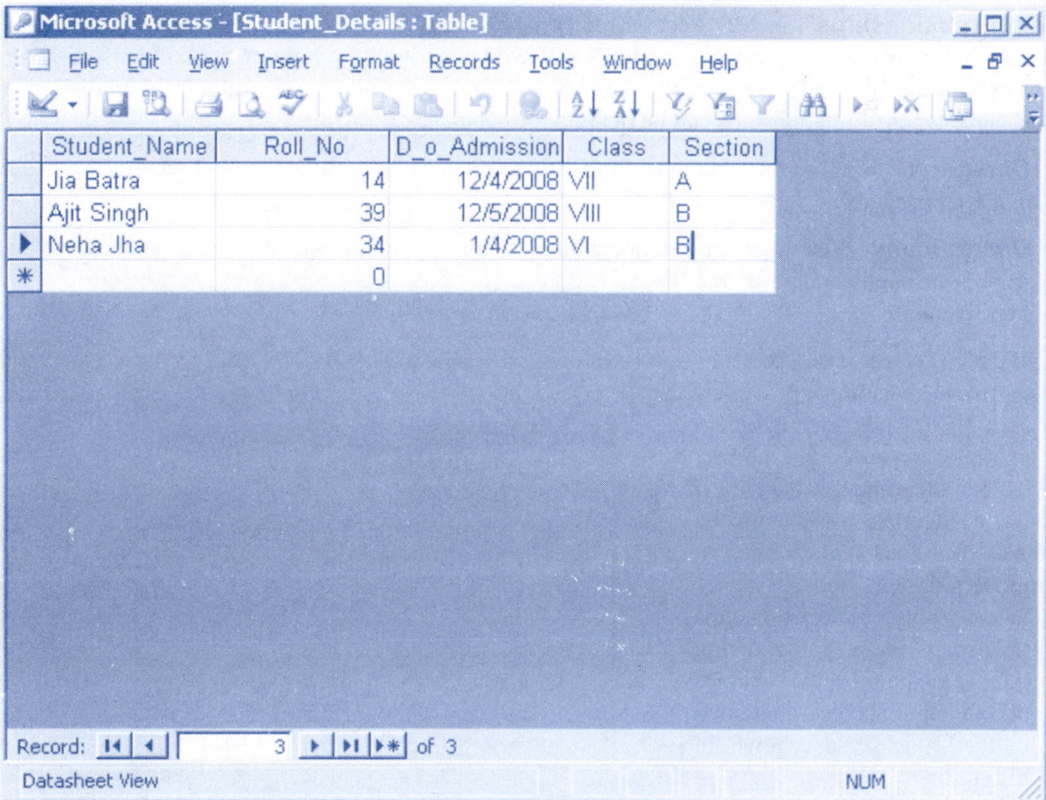

Fig. 12.56 The Microsoft Access—[Student_Details:Table] window after the deletion of a record

4. Close the Microsoft Access – [Student_Details:Table] window to display the Microsoft Access – [Student Database: Database (Access 2000 file format)] window.

Deleting a table In order to delete a table from the database, we need to perform the following steps:

1. Open the Students database.
2. Right-click on the table that is to be deleted to display a shortcut menu.
3. Select the Delete option to delete the Student_Details table. A message prompt appears confirming the deletion of table, as shown in Fig. 12.57.

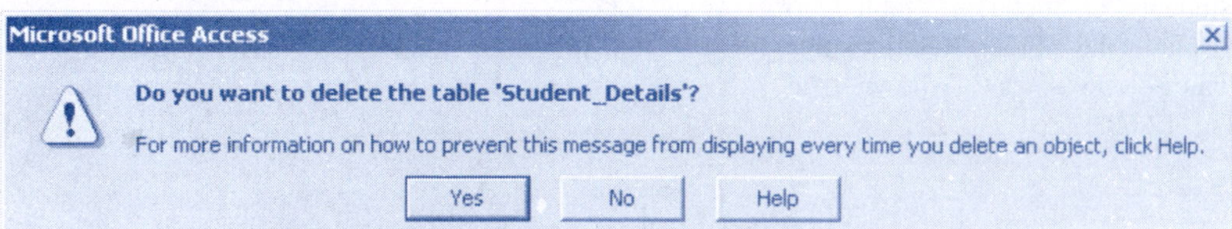

Fig. 12.57 Message prompt confirming the deletion of table

4. Click the Yes button to delete the table permanently. The Microsoft Access – [Student Database: Database (Access 2000 file format)] window appears.

Defining relationships In MS Access, relationships between two or more tables of a database help to create a link between the two tables. It links the two tables with the help of the columns of same types present in both the tables. The linking of same columns helps in reducing the duplicacy and inconsistency of data. Three types of relationships can be defined for databases:

- ***One-to-one*** One-to-one relationship maps one record of a table to a single record of another table in the same database.
- ***One-to-many*** One-to-many relationship maps one record of a table in a database to multiple records of another table in the same database.
- ***Many-to-many*** Many-to-many relationship maps multiple records of a table to multiple records of another table in the same database.

To create a relationship between two tables of a database, we need to perform the following steps:

1. Select Tools → Relationships to display Show Table dialog box containing the names of all the tables contained in the database, as shown in Fig. 12.58.
2. Select a table name and click the Add button to add a relationship to it.
3. Click the Close button to close the Show Table dialog box and display the Relationships window, as shown in Fig. 12.59.
4. Drag the Roll_No field, which is present in the Student_Details table to the Roll_No field in the Student_PersonelData table to display the Edit Relationships dialog box, as shown in Fig. 12.60.

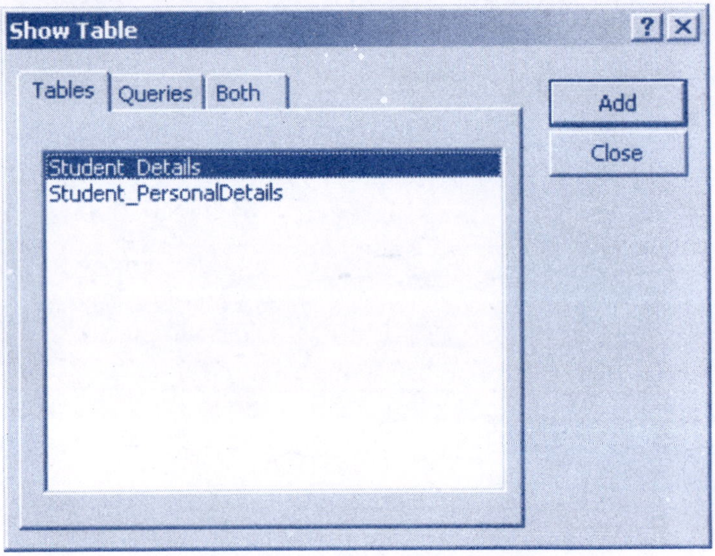

Fig. 12.58 The Show Table dialog box

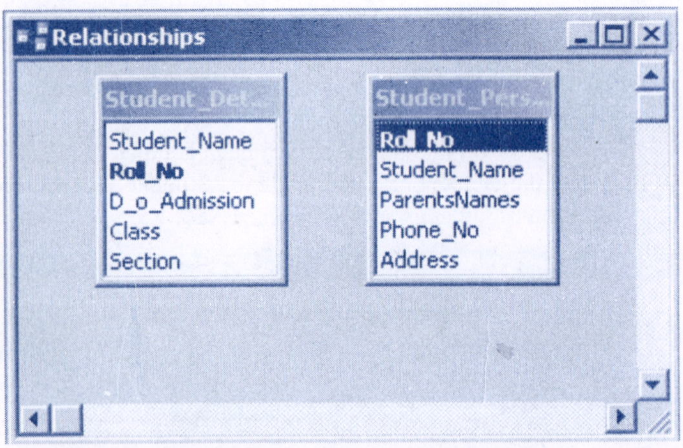

Fig. 12.59 The Relationships window

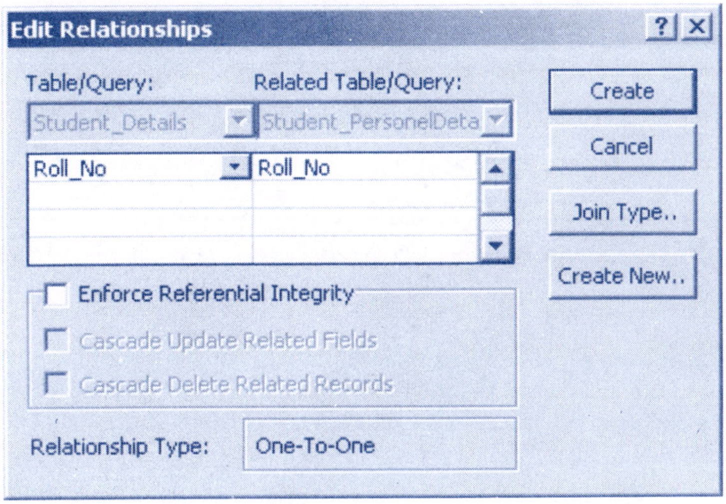

Fig. 12.60 The Edit Relationships dialog box

Note: *The Enforce Referential Integrity option present in the Edit Relationships dialog box ensures that the relationships are valid and prevents the accidental deletion of data from the database.*

5. Click the Create button to establish a relationship between the two tables. Figure 12.61 shows the Relationships window displaying a relation created between the two tables.

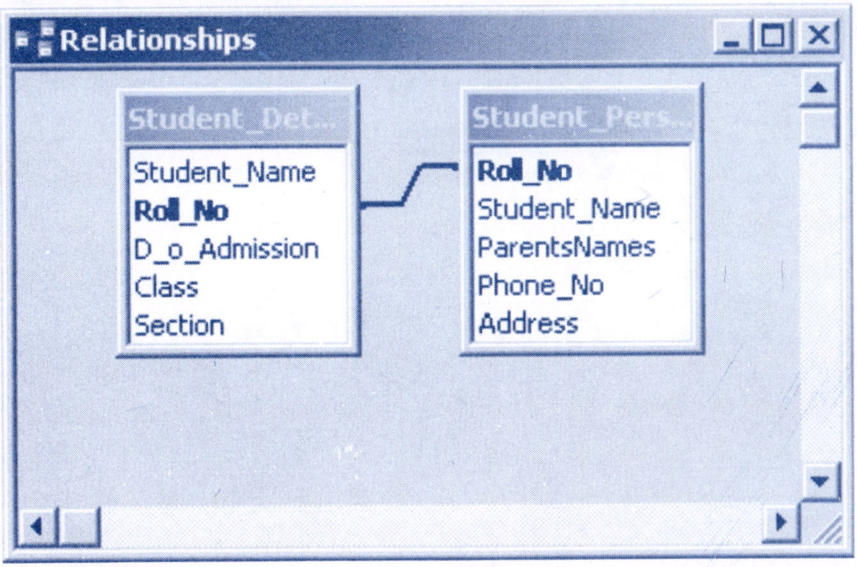

Fig. 12.61 The Relationships window showing a one-to-one relationship

6. Close the Relationships window. A message prompt appears asking whether to save the changes or not, as shown in Fig. 12.62.

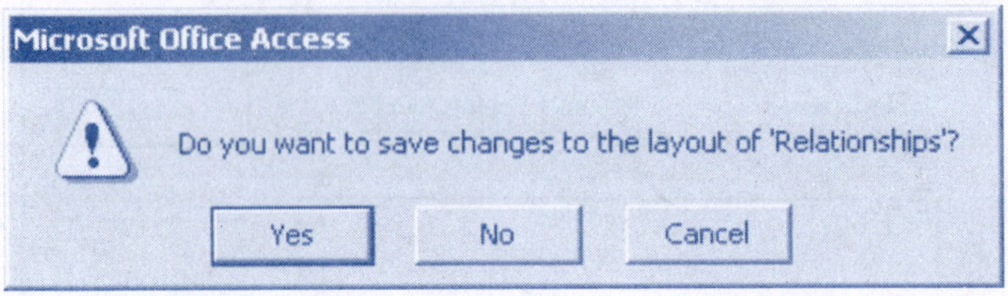

Fig. 12.62 Message prompt asking whether to save the changes or not

7. Click the Yes button to save the relationship.

Creating a database query Query is a request through which a record or a set of records can be accessed conditionally from a database. On the basis of the query, only the records fulfilling the specified condition are displayed in the result. There exists two ways of creating a query, which are as follows:

- Create a query in Design view
- Create a query using wizard

The most commonly used method for creating a query in MS Access is by using the Create query in Design view option. For creating a query in MS Access using the Create query in Design view option, we need to perform the following the steps:

1. Click the Queries button in left pane of the Microsoft Access - [Student Database: Database (Access 2000 file format)] window to display the various query options, as shown in Fig. 12.63.

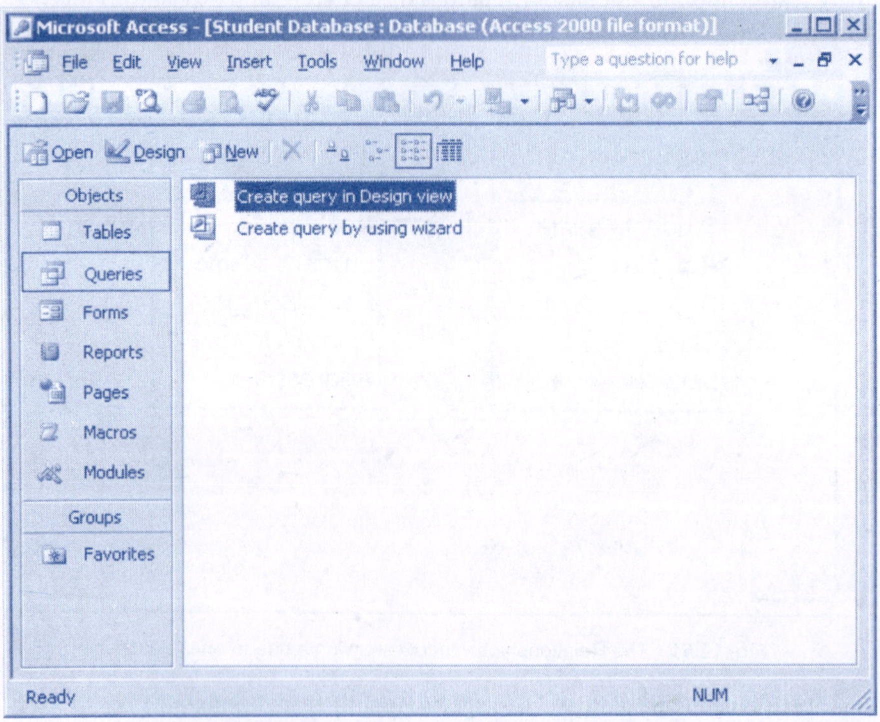

Fig. 12.63 Displaying the available query options

2. Double-click the Create query in Design view option to display the Show Table window.
3. Click the Add button to add the tables from which data is to be extracted.
4. Click the Close button to close the Show Table window. The Microsoft Access - [Query1: Select Query] window appears, as shown in Fig. 12.64.

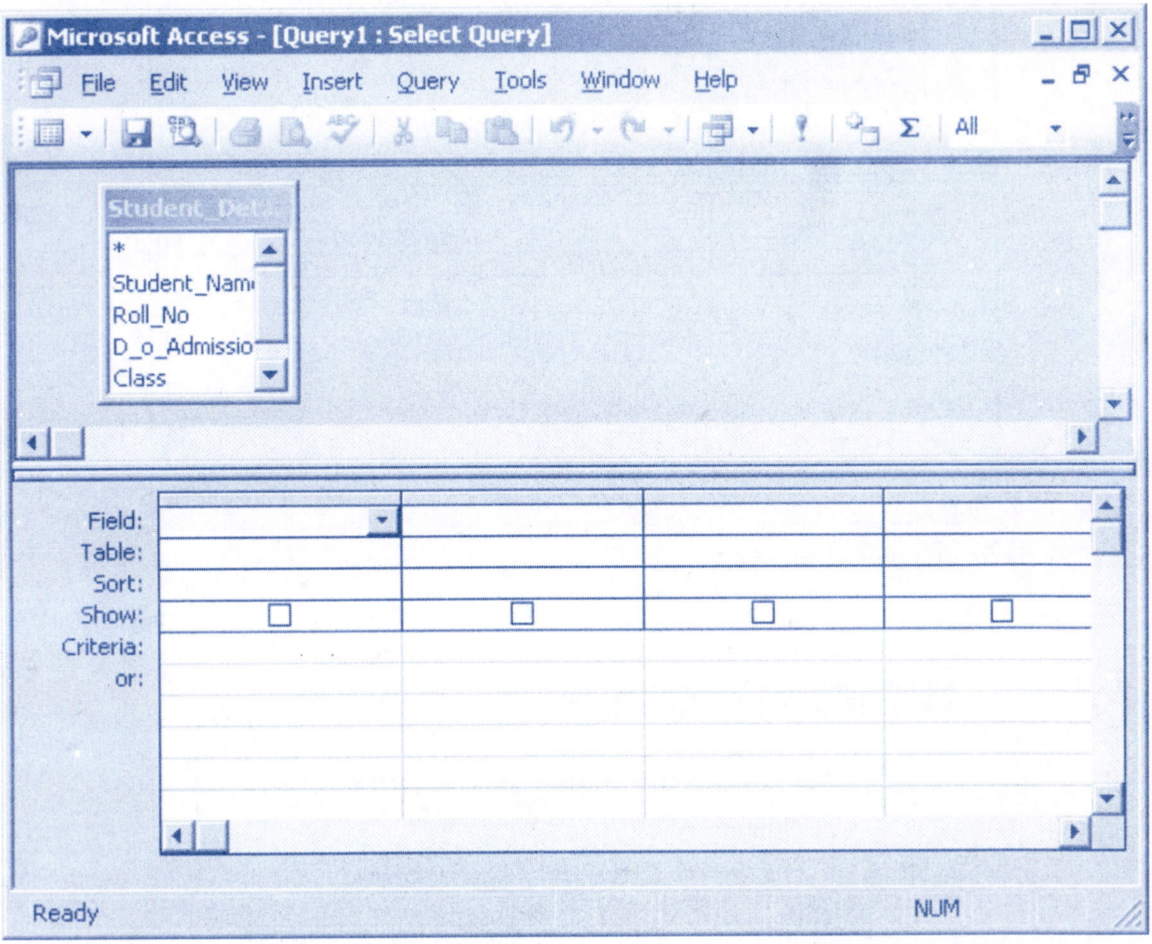

Fig. 12.64 The Microsoft Access—[Query1: Select Query] window

5. Select the field name to be displayed from the Field list and the table name from the Table list.
6. Specify the condition on the basis of which data is to be extracted in the Criteria field, as shown in Fig. 12.65.

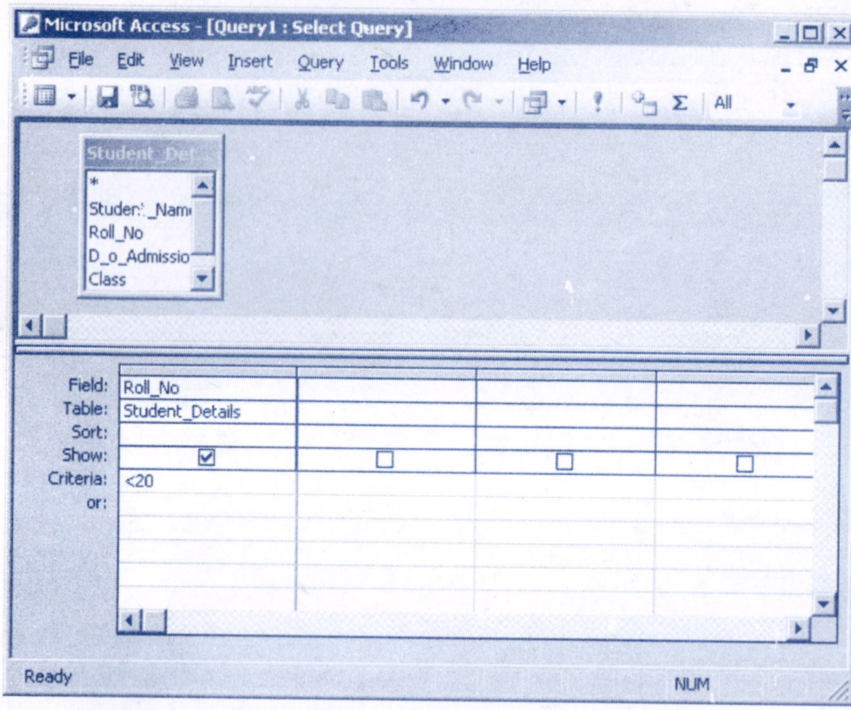

Fig. 12.65 The Microsoft Access—[Query1:Select Query] window with field names and specified criteria

7. Close the Microsoft Access - [Query1: Select Query] window. A message prompt appears asking whether to save the changes pertaining to the query or not, as shown in Fig. 12.66.

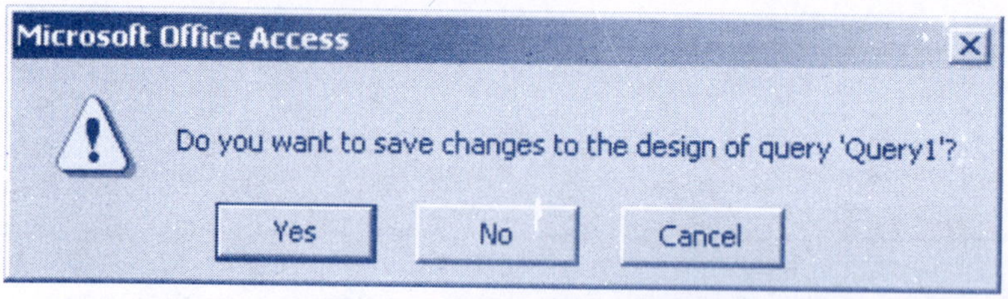

Fig. 12.66 Prompting whether to save changes pertaining to the query

8. Click the Yes button to save the query. Figure 12.67 shows the Save As dialog box.

Fig. 12.67 Saving the query name

9. Enter the name of the query, say Query_Roll in the Query Name text box.
10. Click OK to save the query. The Microsoft Access-[Student Database: Database (Access 2000 file format)] window appears containing the name of the query.

To view the result of the query, perform the following steps:

1. Double-click the query name, Query_Roll in the Microsoft Access-[Student Database: Database (Access 2000 file format)] window to display the results of the query, as shown in Fig. 12.68.

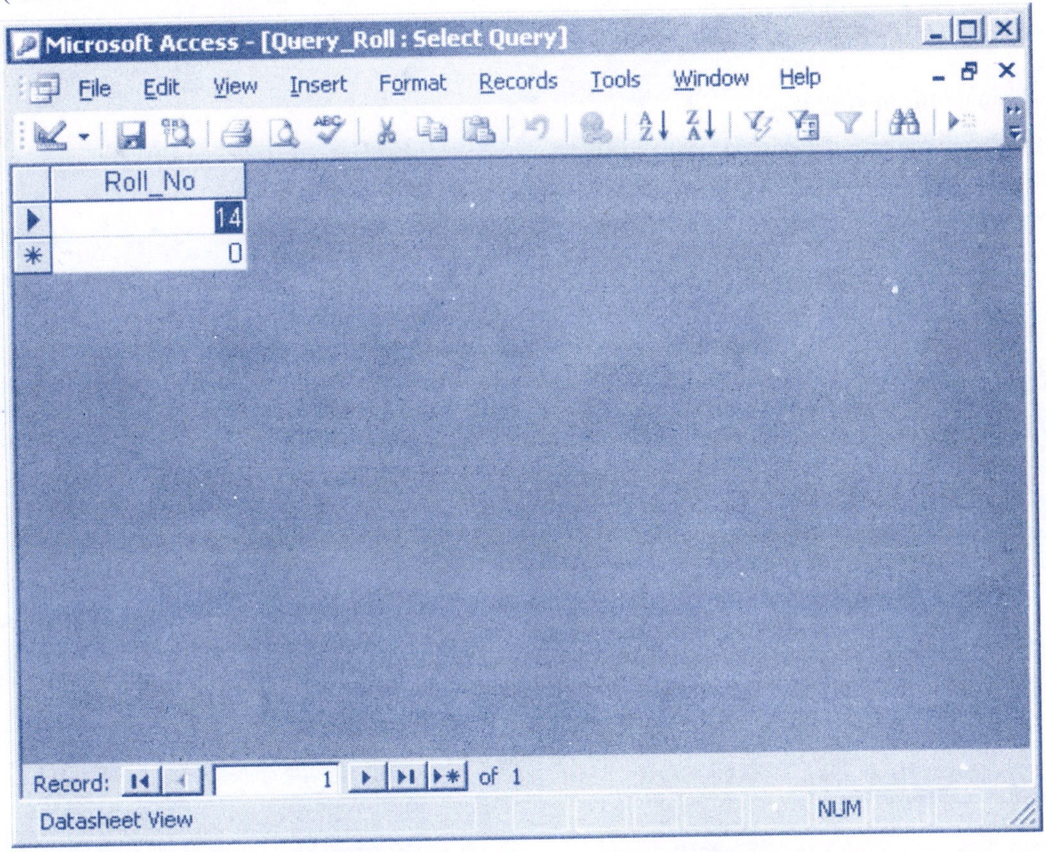

Fig. 12.68 The results of the Query_Roll query

12.7 MS PUBLISHER

MS Publisher is a desktop publishing software package that helps in creating as well as publishing different types of materials, such as newsletters, brochures, catalogs, postcards and calendars. The publications created in MS Publisher can be published through a variety of modes, such as a desktop printer, commercial printer or a printing press. We can also publish the created publications over the Internet. In MS Publisher, a publication can be created either from the scratch by using a blank publication, or by selecting an appropriate pre-defined template depending upon the requirements.

In this section, we shall discuss the following four major concepts related to MS Publisher:

- Starting MS Publisher
- Creating a publication
- Creating a table
- Printing a publication

12.7.1 Starting MS Publisher

MS Publisher is a part of the MS Office suite. After installing MS Office, we can start MS Publisher using one of the following two ways:

- Using Start menu
- Using Run command

Using Start menu To start MS Publisher using start menu, we need to select Start → Programs → Microsoft Office → Microsoft Office Publisher 2003 as shown in Fig. 12.69.

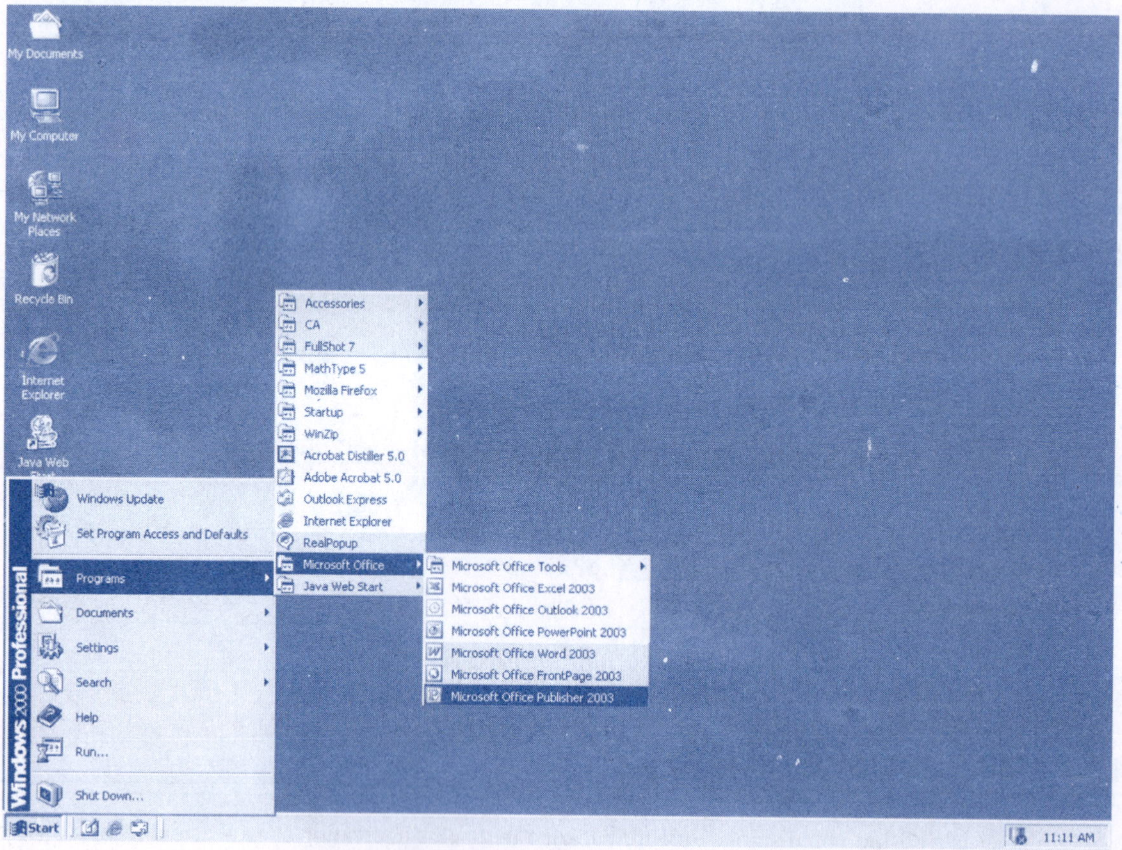

Fig. 12.69 Starting MS Publisher

Using Run command To start MS Publisher using Run command, we need to perform the following steps:

1. Select Start → Run to display the Run dialog box, as shown in Fig. 12.70.

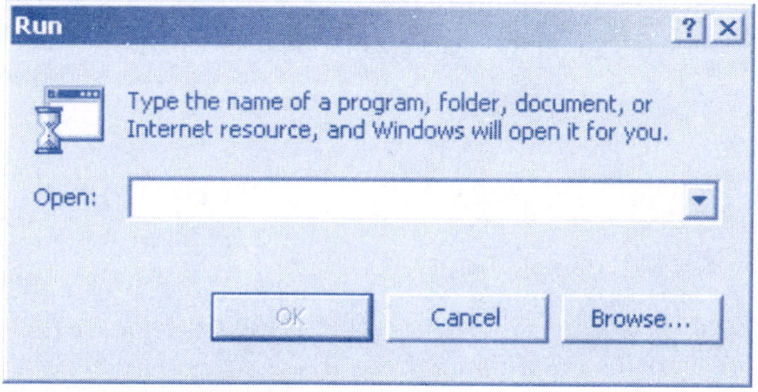

Fig. 12.70 The Run Dialog Box

2. Type mspub in the Open textbox and click OK to display the Microsoft Publisher window, as shown in Fig. 12.71.

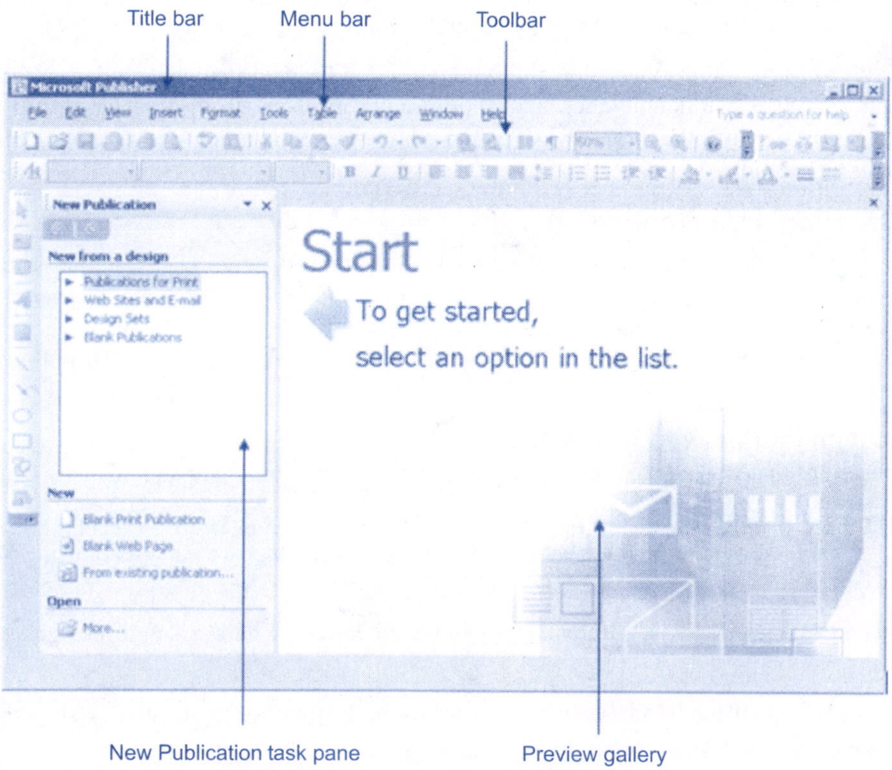

Fig. 12.71 The Microsoft Publisher Window

Figure 12.71 shows the GUI of MS Publisher with the following five major components:

- ***Title bar*** It is used to display the name of the publication.

- ***Menu bar*** It provides access to various functions related to the designing and publishing of publications. The various items of the menu bar of MS Publisher are:
  - File
  - Edit
  - View
  - Insert
  - Format
  - Tools
  - Table
  - Arrange
  - Window
  - Help
- ***Toolbar*** It provides quick access to the most frequently used commands. The various toolbars in MS Publisher include Standard toolbar, Formatting toolbar, Drawing toolbar and Picture toolbar.
- ***New Publication task pane*** It helps in creating a new publication. Using New Publication task pane, we can design and publish a variety of publications.
- ***Preview gallery*** It displays the different types of designs available under different types of publications. When we double-click any option under the New from a design section in the New Publication task pane, the preview gallery displays the number of designs available under that particular publication.

12.7.2 Creating a Publication

To create a new publication, we need to use the New Publication task pane. The New Publication task pane is visible by default; if it is not, then we can display it by selecting File → New. Alternatively, the New Publication task pane can also be displayed by pressing Ctrl and N keys simultaneously.

Using New Publication task pane, we can basically create four important types of publications. These include:

- **Publication for Print** It allows us to create a publication that we want to print. The different types of publications that we can create using this option are banner, brochure and business card.
- **Web sites and E-mail** It allows us to create a Web site or a publication that we want to send through e-mail. Newsletter is the best example of publication that we can create using Web sites and e-mail option.
- **Design sets** It allows us to create different publications where a single design is consistently followed.
- **Blank publications** It allows us to create a publication from scratch. Using this option, a publication can be designed by adding our own text, images or any other objects.

To create a publication from scratch, we need to perform the following steps:

1. Select the Blank Publications option under the New from a design section in the New Publication task pane to display the preview gallery as shown in Fig. 12.72.

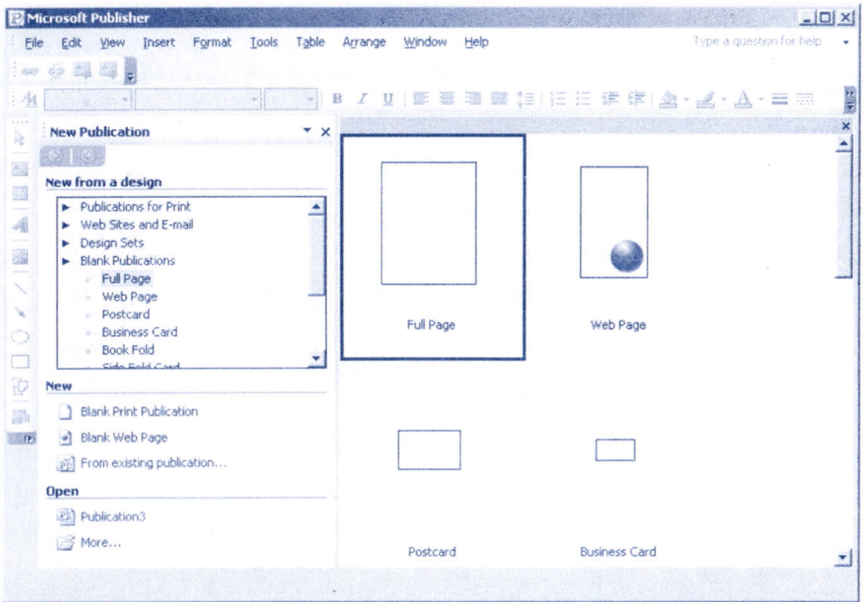

Fig. 12.72 The Microsoft Publisher Window with the New Publication Task Pan

2. Select the Full Page publication from the preview gallery to display the Publication1 – Microsoft Publisher – Print Publication window, as shown in Fig. 12.73.

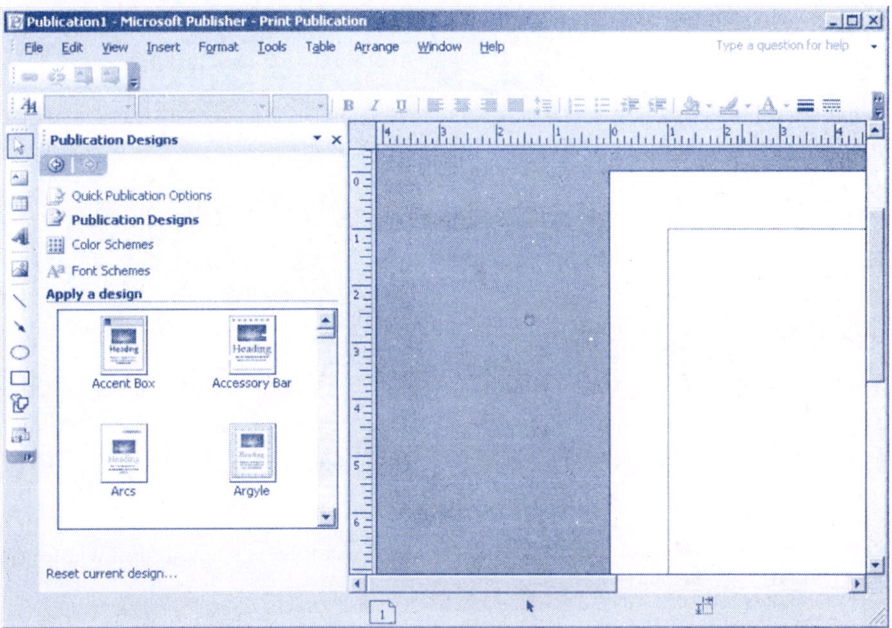

Fig. 12.73 The Publication1—Microsoft Publisher—Print Publication Window

3. Add some objects in the publication according to your requirements, as shown in Fig. 12.74.

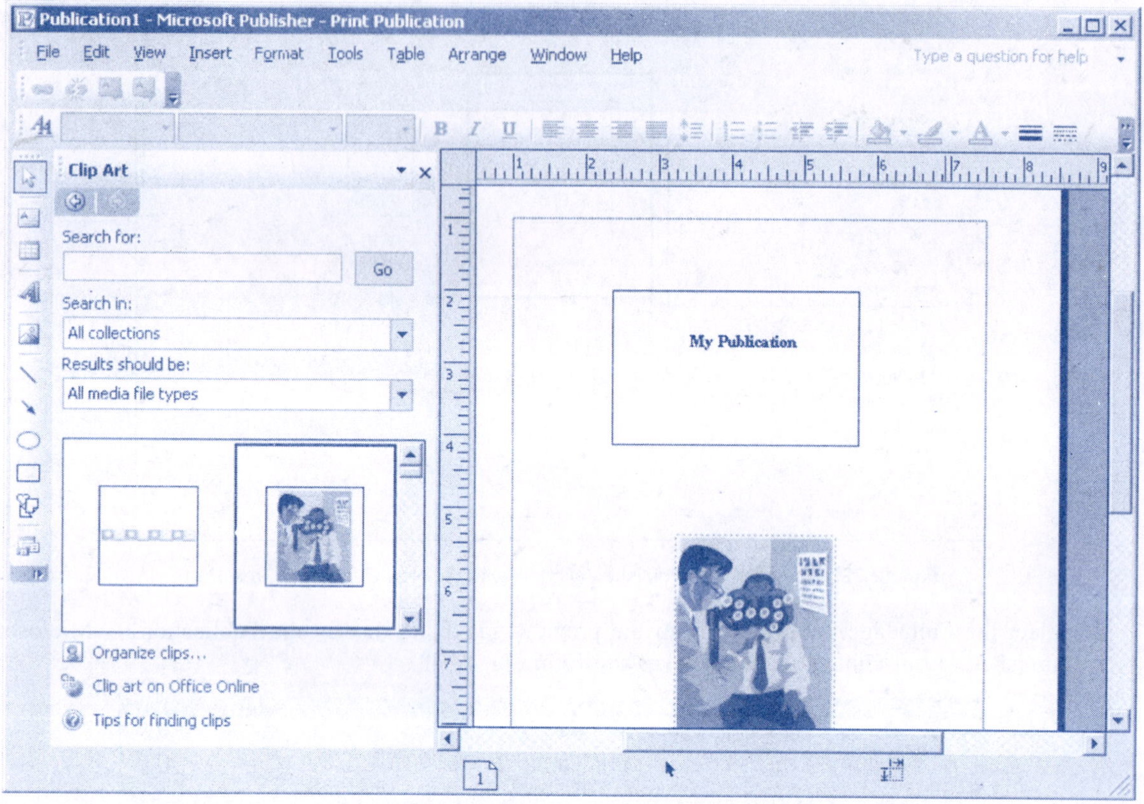

Fig. 12.74 Adding objects to the publication

4. Save the publication using the Save As dialog box.

Note: *Make sure that the Save as type list in the Save As dialog box contains the Publisher Files option.*

We can also create a publication by using a pre-defined template. We can either download a template from the MS Office online Web site or save an existing publication as a template. MS Publisher requires the templates to be saved at the default template location of MS Word. In case, the default template location in MS Word is not set, the location where we save the template becomes the default location for templates.

After we have downloaded or created a template publication, we need to restart MS Publisher to display the templates in the New Publication task pane. We can organise these templates into different categories by changing the Category property of the template files. To change the property of a template file, we need to perform the following steps:

1. Select the Templates → My Templates to display all the templates in the preview gallery, as shown in Fig. 12.75.

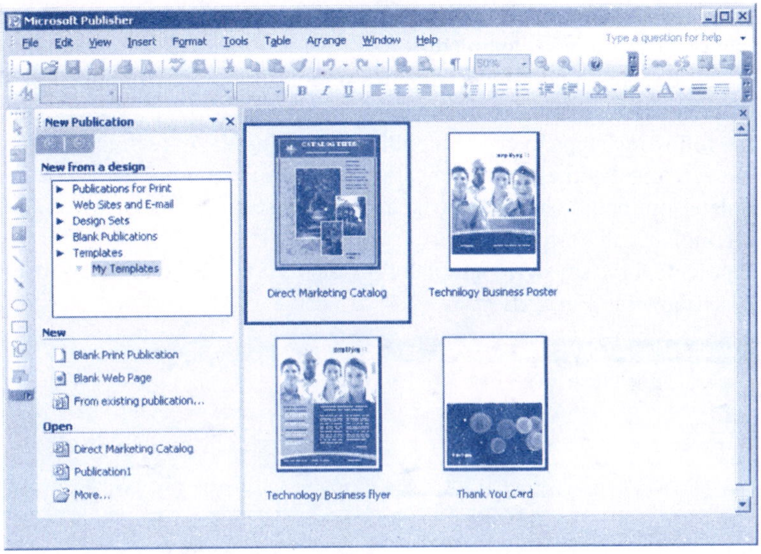

Fig. 12.75 Templates displayed in the preview gallery

2. Select the template to be categorised, say Direct Marketing Catalog. The template opens in the form of a publication document.
3. Select File → Properties to display the Properties dialog box for the publication document, as shown in Fig. 12.76.

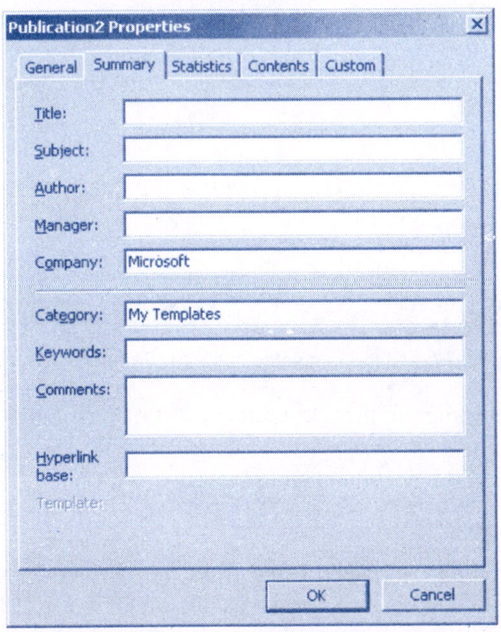

Fig. 12.76 The Properties dialog box

4. Enter the category, say Catalog, under which the template should be categorised and click OK.
5. Save the Publication2 document a., template.

The new category will be listed under the Templates option in the New publication task pane when we restart MS Publisher.

We can perform the following steps to create a publication using the predefined template:

1. Select File → New to display the New Publication task pane.
2. Select the Templates option under the New from a design section in the New Publication task pane to view the list of template categories.
3. Select a template category, say My Templates to display all the templates in this category in the preview gallery as shown in Fig. 12.77.

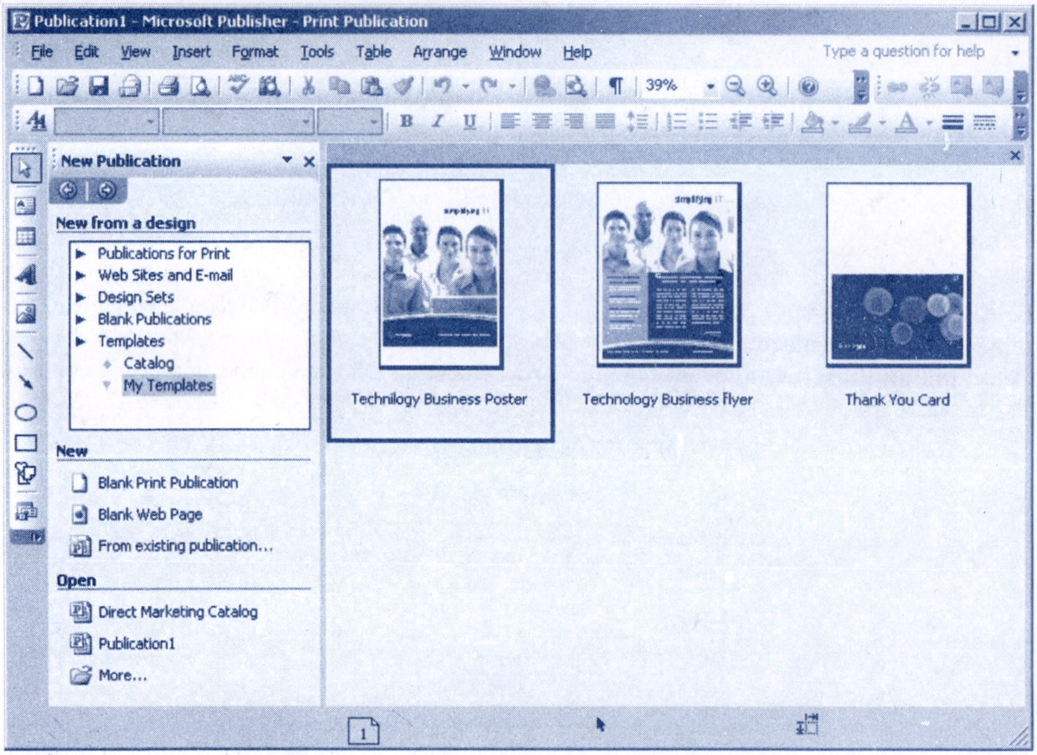

Fig. 12.77 All the templates in the My Templates category

4. Select the template according to the requirements to open the template as a new publication document.
5. Add the required content to the document and save it.

12.7.3 Creating a Table

To create a table, we need to click on **Insert Table** from the **Objects** toolbar, and then click inside our publication. The **Create Table** dialog box will appear as illustrated in Fig. 12.78.

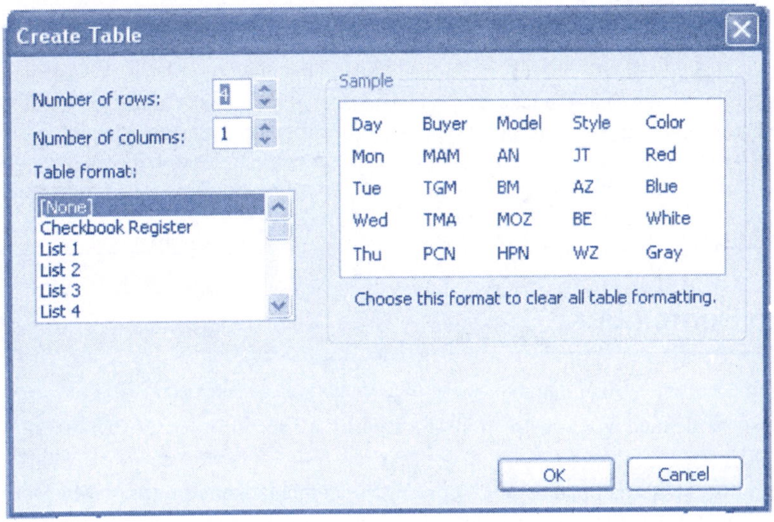

Fig. 12.78 Create Table dialog box

From the **Table Format**, we can choose the various formats as per our requirements. After doing so, we click on **OK** and start typing the text.

To resize the table, we place the mouse pointer over a selection handle until the **Resizer** icon can be seen. We can resize the table by dragging the pointer.

12.7.4 Printing a Publication

The publication that we have designed can be printed on the desktop printer in the same manner as other Office documents are printed. We can also publish the publication document in a PDF file. For this, we need to select the Acrobat Distiller in the Name list box under the Printer section instead of the name of the printer. This will save the publication document in a PDF file.

Chapter Summary

In the past two decades, Microsoft has developed robust, efficient, and user-friendly operating systems and application software. MS-DOS is the first operating system launched by Microsoft. It supports a CLI interface for user interaction. MS-DOS supports various internal, external and batch commands for performing specific tasks. Internal commands are stored in the command interpreter while external commands are stored on a disk. The batch commands of MS-DOS are used with a batch file for the execution of multiple commands simultaneously.

Some of the commonly used Microsoft-based application softwares for performing utility tasks include MS Word, MS Excel, MS PowerPoint and MS Access. MS Word is generally used for creating professional as well as personal documents in an efficient manner. The basic operations performed in MS Word include saving, editing, formatting and printing a document. MS Excel is a spreadsheet application program that allows us to create spreadsheets. A spreadsheet comprises of rows and columns with the data stored in the intersection of rows and columns, i.e., cells. MS PowerPoint is an application software that enables us to create presentations. A PowerPoint presentation comprises of slides that contain text, images, charts, tree-diagrams etc. for presenting the information in an attractive and concise manner. The basic operations that can be performed in MS PowerPoint include creating a presentation, saving a presentation, adding slides to a presentation, printing a presentation etc.

In addition to Word, Excel, and PowerPoint, MS Office Suite also comes bundled with a very handy database management system, MS Access. It is a relational database management system that allows us to create databases and also define relationships between the various tables of the databases. In order to access records from a database, queries are created. A query retrieves the data from the database on the basis of some pre-defined criteria.

The need of creating and publishing different types of publications, such as newsletters, postcards, brochures and catalogs is fulfilled by the software package MS Publisher. It is a popular desktop publishing software that facilitates creation of the publications through a variety of modes such as a desktop printer, commercial printer and a printing press. It also supports publishing over the Internet.

Key Terms to Remember

- **MS-DOS**: It is an operating system that makes use of Command Line Interface (CLI) for interacting with the users.
- **Command**: It can be defined as an instruction provided by a user in order to perform some specific task on the computer system.
- **Internal commands**: These commands are stored in the command interpreter of MS-DOS and loaded into the computer system's memory automatically.
- **External commands**: These commands are stored on a disk and are not stored in the command interpreter.
- **Batch commands**: These commands are used with a batch file in MS-DOS for executing multiple commands simultaneously.
- **Batch file**: It is a text file containing internal and external commands.
- **MS Word**: It is an application software bundled in MS Office package that allows us to create edit, save and print personal as well as professional documents in a very simple and efficient manner.
- **MS Excel**: MS Excel is a spreadsheet application program that enables the users to create the spreadsheets.
- **Row**: It is a horizontal sequence of data stored in a spreadsheet.
- **Column**: It is a vertical sequence of data stored in a spreadsheet.
- **Worksheet**: Worksheet is the actual working area of a spreadsheet program that comprises of rows and columns.
- **Workbook**: Workbook is a combination of multiple worksheets in MS Excel.
- **Graphs**: Graphs are the pictorial representation of complex data.
- **MS Access**: MS Access is a database management system that allows the users to create databases.
- **Database**: Database is a collection of data that is organised in the form of tables.
- **Table**: Table is a collection of rows and columns where data is actually stored.
- **MS PowerPoint**: MS PowerPoint is an application software included in the MS Office package that allows us to create presentations.
- **Slide**: A slide is the fundamental unit of a PowerPoint presentation containing a combination of images, text, graphics, charts, etc.
- **MS Publisher**: It is a desktop publishing software package that helps in creating as well as publishing different types of materials, such as newsletters, brochures, catalogs, postcards and calendars.

Review Questions

Fill in the Blanks

1. MS-DOS is an operating system that makes use of ___________ interface.
2. _________ commands are stored in the command interpreter of MS-DOS.
3. RD, TYPE and DEL are _________ commands.
4. _________ commands are stored on a disk instead of command interpreter.
5. _________ and _________ are external commands.
6. The commands used with a batch file in MS-DOS are known as _________ commands.
7. _____________ is an application software included in MS Office for working with documents.
8. MS Word can be accessed either using ___________ or _____________.
9. MS Word uses a ___________ interface to interact with the users.
10. The horizontal bar at the top of the MS Word window is called ___________.
11. The blinking bar in MS Word that indicates the position of the next key stroke or the character to be inserted is called ___________.
12. The feature in the MS Word that helps the user to view the appearance of the document before printing is called ____________.
13. _________________ is a spreadsheet application program that is widely used in business applications.
14. The horizontal sequence of data stored in a spreadsheet is known as ______________.
15. The vertical sequence of data stored in a spreadsheet is known as ______________.
16. Complex data in MS-Excel is stored pictorially in the form of ______________.
17. _____________ is an application software included in MS Office package for creating presentations.
18. The presentations in the MS PowerPoint are usually saved with the ___________ extension.
19. __________________ is the Microsoft-based database management system that allows the users to create databases.
20. ____________ is a desktop publishing software package that helps in creating as well as publishing different types of publication materials, such as newsletters, brochures, catalogs, postcards and calendars.

Multiple Choice Questions

1. Which of the following is a feature of MS-DOS operating system?
   A. 16-bit B. Single-user C. Single tasking D. All of the above
2. Which of the following commands are used in MS-DOS operating system?
   A. Internal commands B. External commands C. Batch commands D. All of the above
3. Which of the following commands is used for viewing the contents of a file in MS-DOS operating system?
   A. DIR B. TYPE C. MD D. CD
4. Which of the following commands is used print a message on the command prompt?
   A. %DIGIT B. %VARIABLE% C. ECHO D. REM

5. Which of the following makes use of CLI?
   A. MS Excel B. MS PowerPoint C. MS-DOS D. MS Access
6. Which one of the following is typed in the Run dialog box to access MS Word?
   A. winword B. word C. msword D. wordprogram
7. Which of the following is a word processing program?
   A. MS Excel B. MS-DOS C. MS Word D. MS PowerPoint
8. Which of the following is a spreadsheet application program?
   A. MS Access B. MS Word C. MS Excel D. MS-DOS
9. Which of the following is the extension used for MS PowerPoint files?
   A. doc B. ppt C. cpp D. pwpt
10. Which of the following is a database management system used for creating tables?
    A. MS Access B. MS-Excel C. MS-Dos D. All of the above
11. Which of the following is a desktop publishing software package that is used for creating as well as publishing different types of publication materials such as newsletters, calendars and postcards?
    A. MS-DOS B. MS Excel C. MS Publisher D. None of the above
12. What is the run command for opening MS Publisher window?
    A. mspublish B. mspublisher C. winpub D. mspub
13. MS Word is basically used for _______.
    A. Analysing the data B. Preparing the various documents
    C. Preparing the slides D. None of the above
14. What text should be typed in the Run dialog box for accessing MS Excel?
    A. msexcel B. excel C. xcel D. msspreadsheet
15. What text should be typed in the Run dialog box for accessing MS PowerPoint?
    A. powerpoint B. powerpnt C. mspowerpnt D. ppt
16. What is the name of the task pane used for designing slides in MS PowerPoint?
    A. Slide Design B. Slide Layout C. Design Slide D. None of the above
17. Which publication type of MS Publisher is used for creating different publications where a single design is consistently followed?
    A. Publication for Print B. Web sites and E-mail C. Design Sets D. Blank Publications
18. What is the intersection of row and column called in MS Excel?
    A. Cell B. Worksheet C. Workbook D. None of the above
19. What is correct expansion of MS DOS?
    A. Microsoft Data Operating system B. Microsoft Disk Operating system
    C. Microsoft Digital Operating system D. None of the above
20. What is the combination of worksheets in MS Excel called?
    A. Workbook B. Spread sheet C. Excel sheet D. None of the above

Discussion Questions

1. Explain the features of MS-DOS operating system.
2. Differentiate between internal and external commands of MS-DOS.
3. What do you mean by command interpreter?
4. Write a short note on the following commands:
   A. DIR B. COPY C. MD
   D. TREE E. COMP
5. What are batch commands? Explain with the help of an example.
6. What is the basic use of MS Word? Explain with the help of an example.
7. What are the different methods of accessing MS Word?
8. What are the basic operations performed on a word document? Explain all of them in detail.
9. What do you mean by MS-Excel? Explain the different ways of starting MS-Excel from our computer system?
10. What are the different operations possible on a worksheet in MS-Excel?
11. What are the different methods of accessing MS PowerPoint?
12. What is the difference between creating and designing a new presentation in MS PowerPoint?
13. How can a new slide be added to a presentation in MS PowerPoint
14. What is MS Access? How can we create database in MS Access?
15. Explain the method of creating tables in MS Access with design view.
16. What do you mean by queries? How can we create queries in MS Access?
17. What is the function of Slide Design option in MS PowerPoint?
18. Explain the basic operations performed on a presentation.
19. Define the following terms pertaining to MS-PowerPoint:
    A. Slide pane B. Task pane C. Notes pane D. Status bar
20. Explain the two ways of launching MS Publisher.
21. Briefly explain the various types of publications available in the New Publication task pane of MS Publisher window.

CHAPTER 13

PROGRAMMING LANGUAGES

Chapter Outline

Chapter Objectives

In this chapter, we will learn:

- The concept of programming languages.
- The evolution of programming languages.
- The different generatins of programming languages.
- The concept of high-level languages and their types.
- Some of the popular high-level languages.
- The process of developing and running a program.

13.1 INTRODUCTION

Computers can perform a variety of tasks. However, they cannot perform any of them on their own. As we know, computers have no commonsense and they cannot think. They need clear-cut instructions to tell them *what to do, how to do and when to do.* A set of instructions to carry out these functions is called a *computer program*.

The communication between two parties, whether they are machines or human beings, always needs a common language or terminology. The language used in the communication of instructions to a computer is known as *computer language* or *programming language.* There are many different types of languages available today. A computer program can be written using any of the programming languages depending upon the task to be performed and the knowledge of the person developing the program. The process of writing instructions using a computer language is known as *programming or coding.* The person who writes such instructions is referred as a *programmer.*

We know that natural languages such as English, Hindi or Tamil have a set of characters and use some rules known as *grammar* in framing sentences and statements. Similarly, set of characters and rules known as *syntax* that must be adhered to by the programmers while developing computer programs.

Although, during the intial years of computer programming. All the instructions were written in the machine language, a large number of different type of programming languages have been developed during the last six decades. Each one of them has its own unique features and specific applications. In this chapter, we shall discuss briefly the various types of programming languages, their evolution and characteristics and how they are used to solve a problem using a computer.

13.2 HISTORY OF PROGRAMMING LANGUAGES

The history of programming languages is interlinked with the evolution of computer systems. As the computer systems became smaller, faster and cheaper with time, the programming languages also became more and more user friendly. Ada Augusta Lovelace, a companion of Charles Babbage, was considered as the *first computer programmer* in the history of programming languages. In the year 1843, Ada Augusta Lovelace wrote a set of instructions to program the *analytical engine* designed by Charles Babbage. This computer program was used to transform the data entered by the users into binary form before being processed by the computer system. This program increased the efficiency and the productivity of the analytical engine by automating various mathematical tasks. Later, in the year 1946, Konrad Zuse, a German engineer, developed a programming language known as **Plankalkul**. It was developed to target the various scientific, business and engineering needs of the users. It was considered as the first complete programming language that supported various programming constructs and the concept of data structures as well. The various programming constructs were implemented in this programming language with the help of Boolean algebra.

During the 1940s, *machine languages* were developed to program the computer system. The machine languages which used binary codes 0s and 1s to represent instructions were regarded as *low-level programming languages.* The instructions written in the machine language could be executed directly by the CPU of the computer system. These languages were hardware dependent languages. Therefore, it was not possible to run a program developed for one computer system in another computer system. This is because of the fact that the internal architecture of one computer system may be different from that of another. The development of programs in machine languages was not an easy task for the programmers. One was required to have thorough knowledge of the internal architecture of the computer system before developing a program in machine language.

During the 1950s, *assembly language*, which is another low-level programming language, was developed to program the computer systems. The assembly language used the concept of mnemonics to write the instructions of a computer program. Mnemonics refer to the symbolic names that are used to replace the machine language code. The programmers enjoyed working with this programming language because it was easy to develop a program in the assembly language as compared to the machine language. However, unlike machine language programs, assembly language programs could not be directly executed by the CPU of the computer system and required some a software program to convert these programs into machine understandable form.

During the period between 1950 and 1960, many high-level programming languages were developed to cater to the needs of the users of various disciplines, such as business, science and engineering. In 1951, Grace Hopper, an American computer scientist, started working towards designing a compiler called **A-0**, and in the year 1957, developed a high-level programming language known as **MATH-MATIC**. In 1952, another programming system known as **AUTOCODE** was developed by Alick E. Glennie. Grace Hopper was considered as the first person who had put some serious efforts towards the development of a high-level programming language.

In the year 1957, another popular high-level programming language known as **FORTRAN** (FORmula TRANslation) was developed. During its era, it was the only high-level programming language that became hugely popular among its users. FORTRAN was developed by John Backus and his team at International Business Machines (IBM). FORTAN was best suited for solving problems related to scientific and numerical analysis field. Another high-level programming language known as **ALGOL** (Algorithm Language) was developed in the year 1958. Some other high-level languages that evolved during this era were LISt Processing (LISP) in 1958, Common Business Oriented Language (COBOL) in 1959 and ALGOL 60 in 1960.

In the next decade, from 1960 to 1970, more high-level programming languages evolved. In the year 1964, the Beginners All-Purpose Symbolic Instruction Code (BASIC) was designed by John G. Kemeny and Thomos E. Kurtz at Dartmouth college. It was a general-purpose programming language that was very simple to use. In the same year, another powerful high-level programming language, **PL/1** with many rich programming features such as complex data type and methods, was designed for developing engineering and business applications. PL/I was considered to have the best features of its ancestor programming languages: COBOL, FORTRAN, and ALGOL 60. The other programming languages that evolved during this era were **Simula I, Simula 67, Algol 68 and APL**.

The period between 1970 and 1980 was actually the golden era for the development high-level programming languages. This period saw the birth of many general-purpose and powerful high-level programming languages. In the early 1970s, a procedural programming language, **Pascal** was developed by Niklaus Wirth. This programming language was provided with strong data structures and pointers, which helped in utilizing the memory of the computer system in an efficient manner. In the year 1972, Dennis Ritchie developed a powerful procedural and block structured programming language known as **C**. C is still very popular among the users for developing system as well as application software. In 1974, IBM developed Structured Query Language (SQL) that was used for performing various operations on the databases, such as creating, retrieving, deleting and updating. Apart from these programming languages, some other high-level programming languages that evolved during this era were **Forth**, **Smalltalk**, and **Prolog**.

During the next decade, from 1980 to 1990, the focus of development of high-level programming languages shifted towards enhancing the performance and design methodology. The languages of this period used modular approach for designing large-scale applications. The modular approach of program design can be regarded as a design methodology, which divides the whole system into smaller parts that could be developed independently. This approach of designing software applications is still employed by modern programming languages. Some of the high-level programming languages that evolved during this era include **Ada, C++, Perl** and **Eiffel**.

The high-level programming languages developed and designed in the 1990s are considered as the fifth generation programming languages. During this period, Internet technology evolved tremendously. Therefore, the basic purpose of the programming languages of this period was to develop web-based applications. However, these languages could also be used for the development of desktop applications. The important high-level programming languages of this era are **Java, VB** and **C#**. Most of the programming languages of this era employed object-oriented programming paradigm for designing and developing robust and reliable software applications.

Table 13.1 summarises the history of development of programming languages:

Table 13.1 The evolution of programming languages

Period of employment	Programming language	Characteristics
1940s	Machine language	• Machine dependent • Faster execution • Difficult to use and understand • More prone to errors
1950s	Assembly language	• Machine dependent • Faster execution • More prone to errors • Relatively simple to use
1950–1970	FORTRAN, LISP, COBOL, ALGOL 60, BASIC, APL	• High-level languages • Easy to develop and understand programs • Less prone to errors
1970–1990	C, C++, Forth, Prolog, Smalltalk, Ada, Perl, SQL	• Very high-level languages • Easier to learn • Highly portable
1990s	Java, HTML, VB, PHP, XML, C #	• Internet-based languages • Object-oriented languages • More efficient • Reliable and robust

13.3 GENERATIONS OF PROGRAMMING LANGUAGES

Programming languages have been developed over the years in a phased manner. Each phase of development has made the programming languages more user-friendly, easier to use and more powerful. Each phase of improvement made in the development of the programming languages can be referred as a *generation*. The programming languages, in terms of their performance, reliability and robustness can be grouped into five different generations.

- First generation languages (1GL)
- Second generation languages (2GL)
- Third generation languages (3GL)
- Fourth generation languages (4GL)
- Fifth generation languages (5GL)

13.3.1 First Generation: Machine Languages

The first generation programming languages are also called *low-level programming language* because they were used to program the computer systems at a very low level of abstraction, i.e., at the machine-level. The machine language, also referred as the native language of the computer system, is the first generation programming language. In the machine language, a programmer can issue the instructions to the computer system in the binary form only. Therefore, machine language programming only deals with two numbers, 0 and 1. The machine language programs are entered into the computer system by setting the appropriate switches available in the front panel system. These switches are actually the devices used to alter the course of the flow of electric current. The enable state of the switch represents the binary value, 1 and the disable state of the switch represents the binary value, 0. The programs written in the machine language are directly executed by the CPU of the computer system and therefore, unlike the modern programming languages, there is no need of using a translator in a machine language. Figure 13.1 shows the typical instruction format of the machine language instruction.

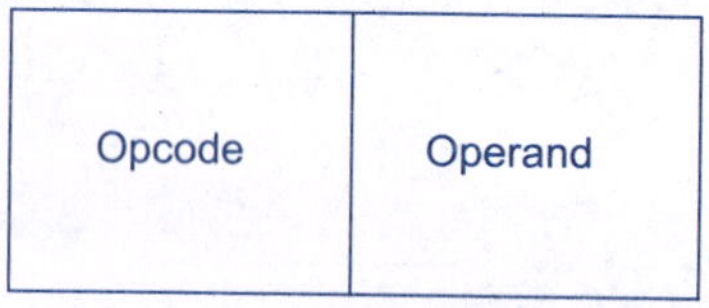

Fig. 13.1 Machine instruction format

As seen in the figure, the instruction in the machine language is made up of two parts only, opcode and operand. The opcode part of the machine language instruction specifies the operation to be performed by the computer system and the operand part of the machine language instruction specifies the data on which the operation is to be performed. However, the instruction format of any instruction in the machine language strongly depends upon the CPU architecture.

The advantages of the first generation programming languages are:

- They are translation free and can be directly executed by the computers.
- The programs written in these languages are executed very speedily and efficiently by the CPU of the computer system.
- The programs written in these languages utilise the memory in an efficient manner because it is possible to keep track of each bit of data.

There are many disadvantages of using the first generation programming languages. They include:

- It is very difficult to develop a program in the machine language.
- The programs developed in these languages cannot be understood very easily by a person, who has not actually developed these programs.
- The programs written in these languages are so prone to frequent errors that they are very difficult to maintain.
- The errors in the programs developed in these languages cannot be detected and corrected easily.
- A programmer has to write a large number of instructions for executing even a simple task in these languages. Therefore, we can say that these languages result in poor productivity while developing programs.
- The programs developed in these languages are hardware dependent and thus they are non-portable.

Due to these limitations, machine languages are very rarely used for developing application programs.

13.3.2 Second Generation: Assembly Languages

Like the first generation programming languages, the second generation programming languages also belong to the category of *low-level programming languages*. The second generation programming languages comprise of assembly languages that use the concept of mnemonics for writing programs. Similar to the machine language, the programmer of assembly language needs to have internal knowledge of the CPU registers and the instructions set before developing a program. In the assembly language, symbolic names are used to represent the opcode and the operand part of the instruction. For example, to move the contents of the CPU register, **a1** to another CPU register, **b1** the following assembly language instruction can be used:

```
mov b1, a1
```

The above code shows the use of symbolic name, **mov** in an assembly language instruction. The symbolic name, **mov** instructs the processor to transfer the data from one register to another. Using this symbolic name, a value can also be moved to a particular CPU register.

The use of symbolic names made these languages little bit user-friendly as compared to the first generation programming languages. However, the second generation languages were still machine-dependent. Therefore, one was required to have adequate knowledge of the internal architecture of the computer system while developing programs in these languages.

Unlike the machine language programs, the programs written in the assembly language cannot be directly executed by the CPU of the computer system because they are not written in the binary form. As a result, some mechanism is needed to convert the assembly language programs into the machine understandable form. A software program called *assembler* is used to accomplish this purpose. An assembler is a *translator program* that converts the assembly language program into the machine language instructions. Figure 13.2 shows the role of an assembler in executing an assembly language program.

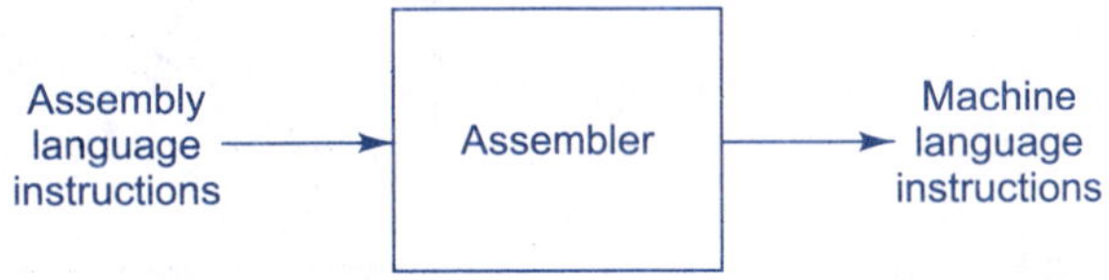

Fig. 13.2 Functioning of an assembler

An assembler acts as an intermediary between the assembly language program and the machine language program. It takes a program written in the assembly language as input and generates the corresponding machine language instructions as output.

The following are some of the advantages of second generation programming languages:

- It is easy to develop, understand and modify the programs developed in these languages as compared to those developed in the first generation programming languages.
- The programs written in these languages are less prone to errors, and therefore can be maintained with great ease.
- The detection and correction of errors is relatively easy in these languages in comparison to the first generation programming languages.

The following are some of the disadvantages of the second generation programming languages:

- The programs developed in these languages are not executed as quickly as the programs developed in the machine language. This is because of the fact that the computer system needs to convert these programs into machine language before executing them.

- The programs developed in these languages are not portable as these languages are machine dependent.
- The programmer of these languages needs to have thorough knowledge of the internal architecture of the CPU for developing a program.
- The assembly language programs, like the machine language programs, still result in poor productivity.

13.3.3 Third Generation: High-level Languages

The third generation programming languages were designed to overcome the various limitations of the first and second generation programming languages. The languages of the third and later generations are considered as *high-level programming languages* because they enable the programmer to concentrate only on the logic of the program without concerning about the internal architecture of the computer system. In other words, we can also say that these languages are machine independent languages.

The third generation programming languages are also quite user-friendly because they relieve the programmer from the burden of remembering operation codes and instruction sets while writing a program. The instructions used in the third and later generations of languages can be specified in English-like sentences, which are easy to comprehend for a programmer. The programming paradigm employed by most of the third generation programming languages was *procedural programming*, which is also known as *imperative programming*. In the procedural programming paradigm, a program is divided into a large number of procedures, also known as *subroutines*. Each procedure contains a set of instructions for performing a specific task. A procedure can be called by the other procedures while a program is being executed by the computer system.

The third generation programming languages were considered as domain-specific programming languages because they were designed to develop software applications for a specific field. For example, the third generation programming language, COBOL, was designed to solve a large number of problems related to the business field only.

Unlike the assembly language, the programs developed in the third and the later generation of programming languages were not directly executed by the CPU of the computer system. These programs require *translator programs* for converting them into machine language. There are two types of translator programs, namely, *compiler* and *interpreter*. Figure 13.3 shows the translation of a program developed in the high-level programming language into the machine language program.

Fig. 13.3 Functioning of a compiler and an interpreter

A program written in any high-level language can be converted by the compiler or the interpreter into the machine-level instructions. Both the translator programs, compiler and interpreter, are used for the same purpose except for one point of difference. The compiler translates the whole program into the machine language program before executing any of the instructions. If there are any errors, the compiler generates error messages which are displayed on the screen. All errors must be rectified before compiling again. On the other hand, the interpreter executes each statement immediately after translating it into the machine language instruction. Therefore, the interpreter performs the translation as well as the execution of the instructions simultaneously. If any error is encountered, the execution is halted after displaying the error message.

The following are some of the popular third generation programming languages:

- FORTRAN
- ALGOL
- BASIC
- COBOL
- C/C++

The following are some of the advantages of the third generation programming languages:

- It is easy to develop, learn and understand the programs.
- The programs developed in these languages are highly portable as compared to the programs developed in the first and second generation programming languages. Hence, we can also say that the third generation programming languages are machine independent programming languages.
- The programs written in these languages can be developed in very less time as compared to the first and second generation programming languages. This is because of the fact that the third generation programming languages are quite user-friendly and provide necessary inbuilt tools required for developing an application.
- As the programs written in these languages are less prone to errors, they are easy to maintain.
- The third generation programming languages provide more enhanced documentation and debugging techniques as compared to the first and the second generation programming languages.

The following are some of the disadvantages of the third generation programming languages:

- As compared to the assembly and the machine language programs, the programs written in the third generation programming languages are executed slowly by the computer system.
- The memory requirement of the programs written in these programming languages is more as compared to the programs developed using the assembly and machine languages.

13.3.4 Fourth Generation: Very High-level Languages

The languages of this generation were considered as very high-level programming languages. The process of developing software using the third generation programming languages required a lot of time and effort that affected the productivity of a programmer. Moreover, most of the third generation programming languages were domain-specific. The fourth generation programming languages were designed and developed to reduce the time, cost and effort needed to develop different types of software applications. Most of the fourth generation programming languages were general-purpose programming languages. This means that most of the fourth generation programming languages could be used to develop software applications related to any domain. During this generation, the concept of Database Management System (DBMS) also evolved tremendously. Therefore, most of the fourth generation programming languages had database related features for working with databases. These languages have simple, English-like syntax rules. Since 4GLs are non-procedural languages, they are easier to use and therefore more user-friendly. We need to specify WHAT is required rather than specifying How to do it.

The following are some of the fourth generation programming languages:

- PowerBuilder
- SQL
- XBase++
- CSS
- ColdFusion

Apart from being machine independent, the following are some of the other important advantages of the fourth generation programming languages:

- The fourth generation programming languages are easier to learn and use as compared to the third generation programming languages.
- These programming languages require less time, cost and effort to develop different types of software applications.
- These programming languages allow the efficient use of data by implementing various database concepts.
- As compared to the third generation programming languages, these languages required less number of instructions for performing a specific task.
- The programs developed in these languages are highly portable as compared to the programs developed in the languages of other generations.

The following are some of the disadvantages of the fourth generation programming languages:

- As compared to the programs developed in the programming languages of previous generations, the programs developed in the 4GLs are executed at a slower speed by the CPU.
- As compared to the third generation programming languages, the programs developed in these programming languages require more space in the memory of the computer system.

13.3.5 Fifth Generation: Artificial Intelligence Languages

The programming languages of this generation mainly focus on constraint programming. The constraint programming, which is somewhat similar to declarative programming, is a programming paradigm in which the programmer only needs to specify the solution to be found within the constraints rather than specifying the method or algorithm of finding the desired solution. The major fields in which the fifth generation programming languages are employed are Artificial Intelligence (AI) and Artificial Neural Network (ANN). AI is the branch of computer science in which the computer system is programmed to have human intelligence characteristics. It helps make computer system so intelligent that it can take decisions on its own while solving various complicated problems. On the other hand, ANN refers to a network that is used to imitate the working of a human brain. ANN is widely used in voice recognition systems, image recognition systems and industrial robotics.

The following are some of the fifth generation programming languages:

- Mercury
- Prolog
- OPS5

The following are two important advantages of fifth generation programming languages:

- The fifth generation languages allow the users to communicate with the computer system in a simple and an easy manner. Programmers can use normal English words while interacting with the computer system.
- These languages can be used to query the databases in a fast and efficient manner.

13.4 CHARACTERISTICS OF A GOOD PROGRAMMING LANGUAGE

The popularity of any programming language depends upon the useful features that it provides to its users. A large number of programming languages are in existence around the world but not all of them are popular. The following are some of the important characteristics of a good programming language:

- The language must allow the programmer to write simple, clear and concise programs.
- The language must be simple to use so that a programmer can learn it without any explicit training.

- The glossary used in the language should be very close to the one used in human languages.
- The function library used in the language should be well documented so that the necessary information about a function can be easily obtained while developing an application.
- The various programming constructs supported by the language must match well with the application area it is being designed for.
- The language must allow the programmer to focus only on the design and the implementation of the different programming concepts without requiring the programmer to be well acquainted with the background details of the concepts being used.
- The programs developed in the language must make efficient use of memory as well as other computer resources.
- The language must provide necessary tools for development, testing, debugging and maintenance of a program. All these tools must be incorporated into a single environment known as Integrated Development Environment (IDE), which enables the programmer to use them easily.
- The language must be platform independent, i.e., the programs developed using the programming language can run on any computer system.
- The Graphical User Interface (GUI) of the language must be attractive, user-friendly and self explanatory.
- The language must be object-oriented in nature so as to provide various features such as inheritance, information hiding, and dynamic binding to its programmers.
- The language must be consistent in terms of both syntax and semantics.

13.5 CATEGORISATION OF HIGH-LEVEL LANGUAGES

The high-level languages can be categorised into different types on the basis of the application areas in which they are employed, as well as the different design paradigms supported by them. Figure 13.4 shows the different types of high-level languages categorised on the basis of application areas and design paradigms.

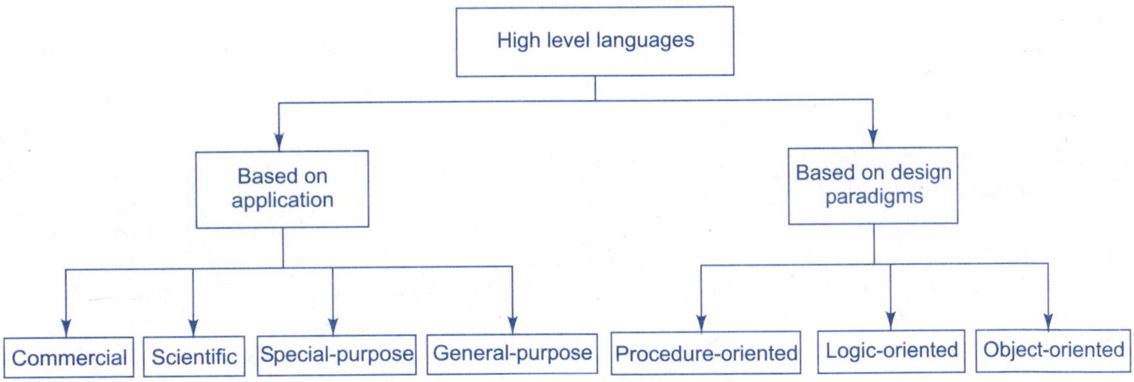

Fig. 13.4 Types of high-level languages

The figure clearly shows that the high-level programming languages are designed for use in a number of areas. Each high-level language is designed by keeping its target application area in mind. Some of the high-level languages are best suited for business domain, while others are apt in scientific domain only.

The high-level programming languages can also be categorised on the basis of the various programming paradigms supported by them. The programming paradigm refers to the approach employed by the programming languages for solving the different types of problems.

13.5.1 Categorisation Based on Application

On the basis of application area, the high-level programming languages can be divided into the following types:

- **Commercial languages.** These programming languages are dedicated to the commercial domain and are specially designed for solving business-related problems. These languages can be used in organisations for processing and handling the data related to payroll, accounts payable and tax handling applications. COBOL is the best example of the commercial-based high-level programming language employed in the business domain. This language was developed with strong file handling capabilities and support for business arithmetic operations. Another example of business-oriented programming language is Programming Language for Business (PL/B), which was developed by Datapoint during the 1970s.
- **Scientific languages.** These programming languages are dedicated to the scientific domain and are specially designed for solving different scientific and mathematical problems. These languages can be used to develop programs for performing complex calculations during scientific research. FORTRAN is the best example of the scientific-based high-level programming language. This language is capable of performing various numerical and scientific calculations.
- **Special-purpose languages.** These programming languages are specially designed for performing some dedicated functions. For example, SQL is a high-level language specially designed to interact with the database programs only. Therefore, we can say that the special-purpose high-level programming languages are designed to support a particular domain area only.
- **General-purpose languages.** These programming languages are used for developing different types of software applications regardless of their application area. The various examples of general-purpose high-level programming languages are BASIC, C, C++ and Java.

13.5.2 Categorisation Based on Design Paradigm

On the basis of design paradigm, the high-level programming languages can be categorised into the following types:

- **Procedure-oriented languages.** These programming languages are also called *imperative programming languages*. In these languages, a program is written as a sequence of procedures. Each procedure contains a series of instructions for performing a specific task. Each procedure can be called by the other procedures during the program execution. In this type of programming paradigm, a code once written in the form of a procedure can be used any number of times in the program by only specifying the corresponding procedure name. This approach also makes the program structure relatively very simple to follow as compared to the other programming paradigms. We can also say that the major emphasis of these languages is on the procedures and not on the data. Therefore, the procedure-oriented languages allow the data to move freely around the system. The various examples of procedure-oriented languages are FORTRAN, ALGOL, C, BASIC and Ada.
- **Logic-oriented languages.** These languages use *logic programming paradigm* as the design approach for solving various computational problems. In this programming paradigm, predicate logic is used to describe the nature of a problem by defining relationships between rules and facts. Prolog is the best example of the logic-oriented programming language.

- **Object-oriented languages.** These languages use *object-oriented programming paradigm* as the design approach for solving a given problem. In this programming paradigm, a problem is divided into a number of objects, which can interact by passing messages to each other. The other features included in the object-oriented languages are encapsulation, polymorphism, inheritance and modularity. C++, JAVA and C# are the examples of object-oriented programming language.

13.6 POPULAR HIGH-LEVEL LANGUAGES

Today, a large number of high-level programming languages are available for developing different types of software applications. However, only few of these programming languages are popular among programmers. The following are some of the popular high-level programming languages used around the world:

- FORTRAN
- LISP
- COBOL
- BASIC
- PASCAL
- C
- C++
- Java
- Python
- C#

13.6.1 FORTRAN

FORTRAN is the most dominant high-level programming language employed in the science and engineering domain. As mentioned earlier, FORTRAN was initially developed by a team led by John Backus at IBM in the 1950s. Since then several new versions of FORTRAN have evolved. They include FORTRAN II, FORTRAN IV, FORTRAN 77 and FORTRAN 90. FORTRAN 90, which is approved by the International Organisation for Standardisation, is more portable, reliable and efficient as compared to its earlier versions. The following are some of the important applications areas where FORTRAN can be employed:

- Finding solutions to partial differential equations
- Predicting weather
- Solving problems related to fluid mechanics
- Solving problems related to physics and chemistry

Some of the most significant characteristics of FORTRAN are enumerated as under:

- It is easier to learn as compared to the other scientific high-level languages.
- It has a powerful built-in library containing some useful functions, which are helpful in performing complex mathematical computations.
- It enables the programmers to create well-structured and well-documented programs.
- The internal computations in this language are performed rapidly and efficiently.
- The programs written in this language can be easily understood by other programmers, who have not actually developed the programs.

13.6.2 LISP

LISP (List Processing) was developed by John McCarthy in the year 1958 as a functional programming language for handling data structures known as *lists*. LISP is now extensively used for research in the field of artificial intelligence (AI). Some of the versions of LISP are Standared LISP, MACLISP, Inter LISP, Zeta LISP and Common LISP.

Some good features of LISP are:

- Easy to write and use.
- Recursion, that is a programming calling itself, is possible.
- Supports grabage collection.
- Supports interactive computing.
- Most suitable for AI applications.

Some negative aspects of LISP are:

- Poor reliability.
- Poor readability of programs.
- Not a general-purpose language.

13.6.3 COBOL

COBOL is a high-level programming language developed in the year 1959 by COnference on DAta SYstems Languages (CODASYL) committee. This language was specially designed and developed for the business domain. Apart from the business domain, COBOL can also be used to develop the programs for the various other applications. However, this language cannot be employed for developing various system software such as operating systems, device drivers etc. COBOL has gone through a number of improvement phases since its inception and, as a result, several new versions of COBOL have evolved. The most significant versions of COBOL, which are standardised by American National Standards Institute (ANSI), are COBOL-68, COBOL-74 and COBOL-85.

Some of the most significant characteristics of COBOL are enumerated as follows:

- The applications developed in this language are simple, portable and easily maintainable.
- It has several built-in functions to automate the various tasks in business domain.
- It can handle and process a large amount of data at a time and in a very efficient manner.
- As compared to the other business-oriented high-level programming languages, the applications can be developed rapidly.
- It does not implement the concept of pointers, user-defined data types, and user-defined functions and hence is simple to use.

13.6.4 BASIC

BASIC (Beginner's All-purpose Symbolic Instruction Code) was developed by John Kemeny and Thomas Kurty at Dartmaith Collge, USA in the year 1964. The language was extensively used for microcomputers and home computers during 1970s and 1980s. BASIC was standardized by ANSI in 1978 and became popular among business and scientific users alike. BASIC continues to be widely used because it can be learned quickly.

During the last four decades, different versions of BASIC have appeared. These include Altair BASIC, MBASIC, GWBASIC, Quick BASIC, Turbo BASIC and Visual BASIC. Microsoft's Visual BASIC adds object-oriented features and a graphical user interface to the standard BASIC.

Main features of BASIC are:

- It is the first interpreted language.

- It is a general-purpose language.
- It is easy to learn as it uses common English words.

13.6.5 PASCAL

PASCAL is one of the oldest high-level programming languages developed by Niklaus Wirth in the year 1970. It was the most efficient and productive language of its time. The programming paradigm employed by PASCAL is procedural programming. A number of different versions of PASCAL have evolved since 1970 that help in developing the programs for various applications such as research projects, computer games and embedded systems. Some of the versions of PASCAL include USCD PASCAL, Turbo PASCAL, Vector PASCAL and Morfik PASCAL. This programming language was also used for the development of various operating systems such as Apple Lisa and Mac.

Some of the most significant characteristics of PASCAL are enumerated as under:

- It is simple and easy to learn as compared to the other high-level programming languages of its time.
- It enables the programmers to develop well-structured and modular programs that are easy to maintain and modify.
- The data in this language is stored and processed efficiently with the help of strong data structures.
- It enables the programmer to create the data types according to their requirements that are also referred as user-defined data types.
- The PASCAL compiler has strong type checking capability that prevents the occurrence of data type mismatch errors in a program.

13.6.6 C

C is a general-purpose high-level programming language developed by Dennis Ritchie and Brain Kernighan at Bell Telephone Laboratories, the USA in the year 1972. C is a well-known high-level programming language that is used for developing the application as well as system programs. It is also block-structured and procedural, which means that the code developed in C can be easily understood and maintained. C is the most favourite language of system programmers because of its several key characterises, that are hardly found in other high-level programming languages. The first major system program developed in C was the UNIX operating system. C is also regarded as a middle-level language because it contains the low-level as well as the high-level language features.

Some of the most significant characteristics of C are:

- C is machine and operating system independent language. Therefore, the programs developed in C are highly portable as compared to the programs developed in the other high-level programming languages.
- It is a highly efficient programming language because the programs developed in this language are executed very rapidly by the CPU of the computer system. Also, the memory requirement for the storage and the processing of C programs is comparatively less. Therefore, C is considered to be equivalent to assembly language in terms of efficiency.
- It can be used to develop a variety of applications; hence, it is considered to be quite flexible.
- It allows the programmer to define and use their own data types.
- C allows the use of pointers that allows the programmers to work with the memory of the computer system in an efficient manner.

13.6.7 C++

C++ is a general-purpose, object-oriented programming language developed by Bjarne Stroustrup at Bell Labs in the year 1979. Initially, Bjarne Stroustrup named his new language as C with classes because this new language was the extended version of the existing programming language, C. Later, this new language was renamed as C++. It is also regarded as the superset of the C language because it retains many of its salient features. In addition to having the significant features of C, C++ was also expanded to include several object-oriented programming features, such as classes, virtual functions, operator overloading, inheritance and templates.

Some of the most significant characteristics of C++ are as follows:

- It uses the concept of objects and classes for developing programs.
- The code developed in this language can be reused in a very efficient and productive manner.
- Like C, C++ is also a machine and operating system independent language. Therefore, the programs developed in this language are highly portable.
- It is a highly efficient language in terms of the CPU cycles and memory required for executing different programs.
- The number of instructions required to accomplish a particular task in C++ is relatively lesser as compared to some of the other high-level programming languages.
- It follows the modular approach of developing the programs for the different types of applications. Therefore, the programs developed in C++ can be understood and maintained easily.
- C++ is highly compatible with its ancestor language, i.e., C because a program developed in C can be executed under the C++ compiler with almost no change in the code.

13.6.8 JAVA

JAVA is an object-oriented programming language introduced by Sun Microsystems in the year 1995. It was originally developed in the year 1991 by James Gosling and his team. The syntax and the semantics of JAVA are somewhat similar to C++. However, it is regarded as more powerful than C++ and the other high-level programming languages. In the current scenario, JAVA is the most dominant object-oriented programming language for developing web-based applications. Apart from the web-based applications, JAVA can also be employed to develop other types of applications, such as desktop applications and embedded systems applications.

JAVA is a highly platform independent language because it uses the concept of *just-in-time* compilation. In this type of compilation, the JAVA programs are not directly compiled into the native machine code. Instead, an intermediate machine code called *bytecode* is generated by the JAVA compiler that can be interpreted on any platform with the help of a program known as *JAVA interpreter*.

Some of the most significant characteristics of JAVA are enumerated as under:

- It is a highly object-oriented and platform independent language.
- The programs written in this language are compiled and interpreted in two different phases.
- The programs written in this language are more robust and reliable.
- It is more secure as compared to the other high-level programming languages because it does not allow the programmer to access the memory directly.
- It assists the programmers in managing the memory automatically with a feature called garbage collection.
- It also implements the concept of dynamic binding and threading in a better and efficient manner as compared to other object-oriented languages.

13.6.9 Python

Python is a high-level and object-oriented programming language developed by Guido Van Rossum in the year 1991. It is a general-purpose programming language that can be used to develop software for a variety of applications. Python is also regarded as the successor language of ABC programming language. ABC was a general-purpose programming language developed by a team of three scientists, leo Geurts, Lambert Meertens, and Steven Pemberton. Several versions of Python have been evolved since 1991. Some of the versions of Python are Python 0.9, Python 1.0, Python 1.2, Python 1.4, Python 1.6 and Python 2.0.

Python has a strong built-in library for performing various types of computations. This built-in library also makes Python simple and easy to learn. Python is an interpreted language and its interpreter as well as other standard libraries are freely available on the Internet. The programs developed in this language can be run on different platforms and under different operating systems. Hence, Python is regarded as platform independent language.

Some of the salient features of Python are:

- It is an interpreted and object-oriented programming language.
- It implements the concept of exception handling and dynamic binding better than the other languages of its time.
- The syntax and the semantics of this language are quite clear and concise.
- It is a platform independent language.

13.6.10 C#

C#, pronounced as "C-sharp" is a new object-oriented programming language developed by Microsoft late in the 1990s. It combines the power of C++ with the programming ease of Visual BASIC. C# is directly descended from C++ and contains features similar to those of JAVA.

C# was specially designed to work with Microsoft's **.NET** platform launched in 2000. This platform offers a new software-development model that allows applications developed in different languages to communicate with each other. C# includes several modern programming features that include:

- concise, lean and modern language
- object-oriented visual programming
- component-oriented language
- multimedia (audio, animation and video) support
- very good exception handling
- suitable for Web-based applications
- language interoperability
- more type safe than C++.

As C# has been built upon widely used languages such as C and C++, it is easy to learn. Using the Integrated Development Environment (IDE), it is very easy and much faster to develop and test C# programs.

13.7 FACTORS AFFECTING THE CHOICE OF A LANGUAGE

A large number of programming languages are available for developing programs for different types of applications. To develop software for a specific application, one needs to carefully choose a programming language so as to ensure that the programs can be developed easily and efficiently in a specific period of time. There are certain factors that must be considered by a programmer while choosing a programming language for software development. These factors are described as follows:

- **Purpose** It specifies the objective for which a program is being developed. If a commercial application is to be developed, some business-oriented programming language such as COBOL is preferred. Similarly, if some scientific application is to be developed, then it is best to use some scientific-oriented language such as FORTRAN. The programs related to the AI field can be developed efficiently in the LISP or Prolog programming languages. Some object-oriented language should be preferred for developing web-based applications. A middle-level language such as C should be chosen for developing system programs.
- **Programmer's experience** If more than one programming language is available for developing the same application, then a programmer should choose a language as per his comfort level. Generally, the programmer should go for the language in which he has more experience. For this, the programmer can also compromise with the power of the programming language.
- **Ease of development and maintenance** The programmer should always prefer the language in which programs can be easily developed and maintained. Generally, the object-oriented languages are preferred over the procedural-oriented programming languages because the code developed in these languages can be reused and maintained with great ease.
- **Performance and efficiency** These are the two important factors, which need to be considered while selecting a programming language for software development. The language in which programs can be developed and executed rapidly should always be preferred. In addition, the languages, which require less amount of memory for the storage of programs, should be chosen.
- **Availability of IDE** The language with an IDE (Integrated Development Environment) of well-supported development, debugging and compilation tools should be preferred. A powerful IDE helps in increasing the productivity of a programmer.
- **Error checking and diagnosis** These two factors involve finding the errors and their causes in a program. A programmer must choose a programming language, which contains efficient error handling features. For example, JAVA provides an efficient error handling mechanism of try/catch block. The try/catch block in JAVA programs can be used to handle the unexpected errors that may occur during the execution of a program. Error checking and diagnosis is very important for developing quality and error free programs. A programming language with efficient and robust error detection and correction mechanism eases the task of code development and testing.

13.8 DEVELOPING A PROGRAM

Developing a program in any programming language refers to the process of writing the source code for the required application by following the syntax and the semantics of that language. The syntax and the semantics refer to a set of rules that a programmer needs to adhere while developing a program.

Before actually developing a program, the aim and the logic of the program should be very clear to the programmer. Therefore, the first stage in the development of a program is the detailed study of the objectives of the program. The objectives make the programmer aware of the purpose of the program for which it is being developed. After determining the objectives of the program, the programmer prepares a detailed theoretical structure of the steps to be followed for the development of the program. This detailed structure is known as *algorithm*.

The programmer may also use a graphical model known as *flowchart* to represent the steps needed to perform a specific task. It can also be regarded as the pictorial representation of the steps defined in the algorithm of the program.

After the logic of the program has been developed either by an algorithm or a flowchart, the next step is to choose a programming language for the actual development of the program. The factors, which we have discussed in the previous section, should be taken into consideration while selecting the programming language.

Each programming language is provided with an IDE, which contains the necessary tools for developing, editing, running and debugging a computer program. The tool to develop and edit a computer program in the IDE is usually known as *source code editor*. The source code editor is a text editor containing various features such as search and replace, cut, copy and paste, undo, redo, etc. For example, C is provided with a strong and powerful IDE to develop, compile, debug and run the programs. Figure 13.5 shows the IDE of C language.

Most of the programming languages uncover the syntactical errors in the program during its compilation. However, some programming languages also provide a feature known as *background compilation*, in which we can check the errors related to the syntax of the programming language while developing a program in the source code editor.

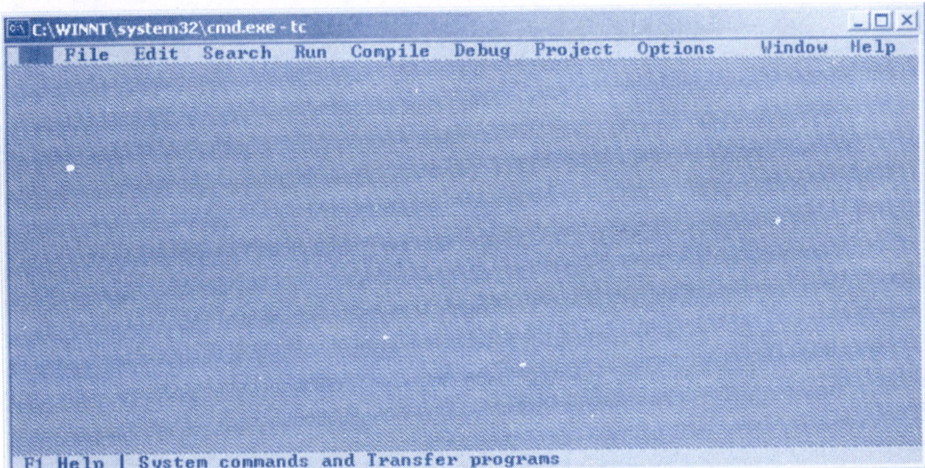

Fig. 13.5 The IDE of C Language

Suppose we need to develop a program for calculating the percentage of marks of two subjects of a student and display the output. The first step in the development of a program for this problem is the preparation of an algorithm. The following code shows the algorithm for calculating the percentage of marks in two different subjects:

```
//Algorithm for calculating the percentage and displaying the result
Step 1 - Input the marks for first subject. (mark1)
Step 2 - Input the marks for second subject. (mark2)
Step 3 - Calculate the percentage.
         percentage = (mark1 + mark2)/2
Step 4 - If percentage > 40,
         Display Pass
Step 5 - Else,
         Display Fail
```

Figure 13.6 shows the flowchart for the algorithm.

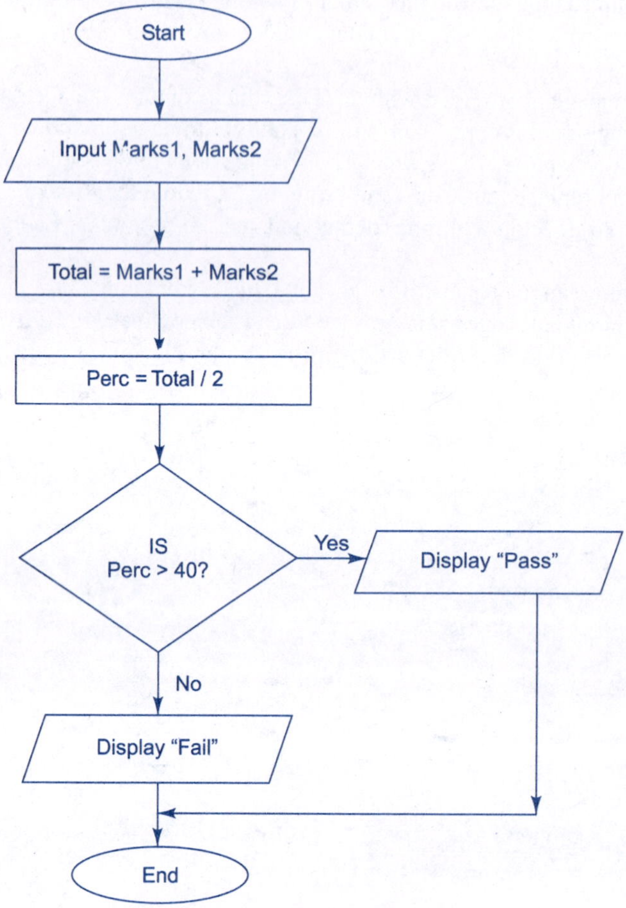

Fig. 13.6 Flowchart for calculating the percentage of marks and displaying the result

After developing the algorithm and flowchart, the actual development of the program can be started in the source code editor of C language. The following code shows the C language program for calculating the percentage of marks in two different subjects of a student.

```
#include<stdio.h>
#include<conio.h>
void main()
{
      float mark1,mark2;
      float percentage;
      clrscr();
```

```
    printf("\n Enter marks of first subject:");
    scanf("\n %f", &mark1);
    printf("\n Enter marks of second subject:");
    scanf("\n %f", &mark2);
    percentage =(mark1+mark2)/2;
    if(percentage>40)
          printf("\n The student is passed");
      else
          printf("\n The student is failed");
      getch();
}
```

Figure 13.7 shows the actual development of the program in the source code editor of C language.

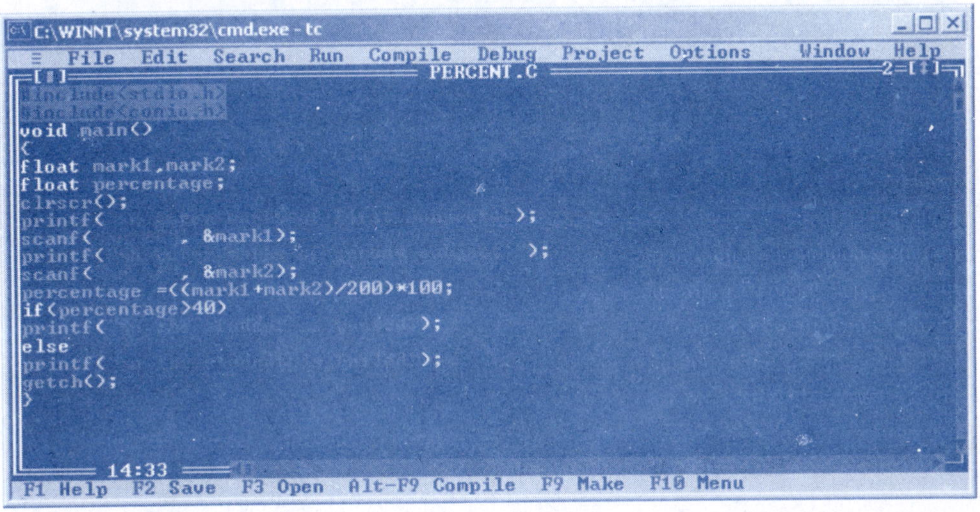

Fig. 13.7 Developing a program in the source code editor of C language

13.9 RUNNING A PROGRAM

After developing a program, the next step to be carried out in the program development process is to compile the program. The program is compiled in order to find the syntactical errors in the program code. If there are no syntax errors in the source code, then the compiler generates the object code. It is the machine language code that the processor of the computer system can understand and execute.

Once the corresponding object code or the executable file is built by the compiler of the language, the program should be run in order to check the logical correctness of our program and generate the output. The logical errors also called semantic errors might cause the program to generate undesired outputs. The programming languages provide various mechanisms such as exception handling for handling these logical errors. If the output generated by the program corresponding to the given inputs matches with the desired result, then the purpose of developing the program is solved. Otherwise, the logic of the program should be checked again to obtain the correct solution for the given problem

Figure 13.8 shows the output of the program developed in the Fig. 13.7.

Fig. 13.8 Running a program

Chapter Summary

Programming languages help perform a specific task by providing a set of instructions to the computer system. Programming languages have evolved a lot over the years. The evolution of the programming languages is divided in five different generations. The first generation programming languages comprise of machine language, which is a fast and efficient programming language but not very easy to use. The second generation programming languages comprise of assembly language. The first and second generation languages are also known as low level languages. The third, fourth and fifth generation of languages comprise of various high-level languages. The high-level languages are machine independent languages in which a program can be developed with great ease. Some popular high-level languages are FORTRAN, BASIC, PASCAL, C, C++, and Java.

There are various high-level languages in existence that can be used for developing programs. Therefore, a proper high-level language should be chosen by considering certain factors such as the purpose of the program to be developed, the experience of the programmer, performance and efficiency of the language, and the IDE of the programming language. After selecting the right programming language, a program can be developed and run in the IDE of the selected programming language to obtain the desired result.

Key Terms to Remember

- **Programming languages**: The programming languages are used to write computer programs in order to instruct the computer system for performing a specific task.
- **Low-level programming languages**: These languages are the machine dependent languages and were used in the early stages of the development of programming languages. The low-level programming languages include machine language and assembly language.

- **High-level programming languages**: These languages are the machine independent languages that use English-like words for developing software applications.
- **Machine language**: It is a low level programming language in which the instructions are specified in terms of 0s and 1s only. The programs developed in this language are directly executed by the computer system.
- **Assembly language**: It is also a low level programming language that uses the concept of mnemonics for writing instructions of a program.
- **Assembler**: It is a software program that converts the assembly language program into machine language instructions.
- **Interpreter**: It is a translator program that converts a high-level program into machine language program. It executes each statement immediately after its translation before proceeding to the next statement.
- **Compiler**: It is a translator program that converts the entire high-level language program into machine language program before executing any to the statements.
- **Opcode**: It refers to that part of the machine instruction, which specifies the operation to be performed by the computer system.
- **Operand**: It refers to that part of the machine instruction, which specifies the data on which the operation is to be performed.
- **Program development**: It refers to the process of writing the source code of a program by following the syntax and semantics of the programming language.

Review Questions

Fill in the Blanks

1. Programming languages are used to provide _______ to the computer system.
2. The person who uses the programming languages to communicate with the computer system is referred as _______.
3. _______ was considered as the first computer programmer in the history of programming.
4. The _______ of the front panel of the ancient computer systems were used to enter the machine language programs into the computer system.
5. The two important parts of the machine instruction are _______ and _______.
6. The opcode part of the machine instruction specifies the _______ to be performed by the computer system.
7. The operand part of the machine instruction specifies the _______ on which the operation is to be performed by the computer system.
8. The second generation programming languages used the concept of _______ for writing computer programs.
9. An assembler is a software program that converts the assembly language program into _______ language instructions.
10. The programming paradigm employed by most of the third generation programming languages was _______.
11. _______ and _______ are the software programs that can be used to convert the high-level programs into machine language programs.
12. _______ is a good example of scientific-oriented high-level programming language.
13. _______ is a high-level language specially designed to interact with database programs.
14. C language was developed by _______ in the year _______.

15. C++ uses the _______ programming paradigm for developing programs for various applications.
16. Java is best suited for developing _______ applications.
17. A program is developed by following the _______ and _______ of the programming language.
18. A program is compiled for finding the _______ errors in the program.
19. The object code is the _______ code that a processor of the computer system understands and executes.
20. The running of a program may reveal the _______ errors in the source code.

Multiple Choice Questions

1. What is a programming language?
   A. It is the language that instructs the computer system to perform a certain action.
   B. It is used to change the configuration of the computer system.
   C. It is the language for managing computer hardware.
   D. None of the above.
2. The person who uses the programming languages to develop programs is usually known as:
   A. Hardware engineer B. Programmer C. Analyst D. All of the above
3. Who was considered as the first computer programmer in the history of programming languages?
   A. Charles Babbage B. Ada Augusta Lovelace C. Konrad Zuse D. John Backus
4. Which of the following is a low-level programming language?
   A. FORTRAN B. Ada C. C D. Machine language
5. Machine language programs are very efficient because
   A. They are directly executed by the CPU B. The are very easy to develop
   C. Their object code is very small in size D. None of the above
6. What is a machine language?
   A. It is an object-oriented language. B. It is a language of 0s and 1s.
   C. It is a high-level language. D. All of the above
7. Which of the following domain is best suited for FORTRAN?
   A. Engineering B. Medical C. Education D. Business
8. Who developed the SQL language?
   A. Microsoft B. Dell C. Google D. IBM
9. Who was the inventor of C programming language?
   A. Lary Wall B. Roussel C. Dennis Ritchie D. Bjarne Stroustrup
10. Which of the following is a part of the machine instruction?
    A. Data B. Mnemonics C. Opcode D. Address
11. Which of the following languages is considered as the second generation language?
    A. Machine language B. Assembly language C. Ada D. BASIC
12. Which of the following programs is used to convert the assembly programs into machine instructions?
    A. Compiler B. Interpreter C. Assembler D. SQL
13. In which generation were database languages developed?
    A. 2GL B. 3GL C. 4GL D. 5GL

14. What is the full form of FORTRAN?
    A. Form transaction B. Formulation transcription C. Formula transition D. Formula translation
15. Which one of the following is not a programming paradigm?
    A. Procedure-oriented B. Logic-oriented C. Data-oriented D. Object-oriented
16. Who was the developer of PASCAL?
    A. Dannis Ritchie B. Niklaus Wirth C. John Backus D. James Gosling
17. Which of the following operating systems was written in C?
    A. UNIX B. Windows C. Macintosh D. None of the above
18. Which of the following paradigm is employed by C++?
    A. Procedural B. Object-oriented C. Logic-oriented D. None of the above
19. Which of the following errors are detected by the compiler?
    A. Syntax errors B. Logical errors C. Semantics errors D. Data errors

Discussion Questions

1. What do you understand by programming languages?
2. What is the difference between low-level and high-level programming languages? Which one of these is considered more user-friendly and why?
3. Why are the programs developed in low-level programming languages considered as efficient programs? Is it not possible to develop efficient programs in high-level programming languages?
4. Explain in detail the evolution of the programming languages.
5. What do you understand by generations of programming languages?
6. Why the second generation programming languages are considered as more user-friendly than the first generation programming languages?
7. Explain in detail the machine instruction format.
8. What is the function of an assembler in assembly language? Does it affect the efficiency of the programs developed in the assembly language?
9. What is the difference between a compiler and an interpreter?
10. What are the different advantages and disadvantages of third generation programming languages?
11. What do you understand by constraint programming? List out some of the applications in which constraint programming is employed.
12. What are the different characteristics of a good programming language?
13. Explain the difference between different programming paradigms used in programming languages.
14. List out some popular high-level languages and explain in detail any three of them.
15. Why is C++ considered as a superset of C?
16. Do the programming languages, C and C++, use the same programming paradigm?
17. What are the different factors that affect the choice of a language for software development?
18. What are the different points that should be remembered before developing a program?
19. What is the difference between compiling and running of a program? Do these two processes generate the same output?
20. Explain the terms—source code, syntax, semantics and IDE.

CHAPTER 14

DATA COMMUNICATIONS AND NETWORKS

Chapter Outline

Chapter Objectives

In this chapter, we will learn:

- The process of data transmission from the source to the destination.
- The interconnectivity of computers in different types of networks, such as LAN, WAN, Internet etc.
- The use of network protocols and software by computers for communicating with each other.
- How to use network for accessing various resources.

14.1 INTRODUCTION

Computers were originally developed as stand-alone, single-user systems. Stand-alone computers can receive user's data, manipulate them and provide useful information for making decisions. Here, the user uses his own data for his own decision making purposes. When the use of computers spread across government offices and business organisations, a number of issues were raised.

- What if a user wants to share his computer generated information with other colleagues?
- What if a user wants to explore the possibility of using certain information stored elsewhere?

These issues were addressed by the subsequent developments in software, hardware and communication technologies which have enabled the computers to communicate between each other and exchange information quickly and accurately and at any time.

The process of electronic transfer of information between two locations is known as data communication. The five basic elements of data communication are:

- **Message** It is the information to be communicated. It may be in the form of text, pictures, audio, video, or any combination of these.
- **Sender** It is the device that creates and transmits the information.
- **Receiver** It is the device that receives the information.
- **Medium** It is the communication channel through which the information travels from sender to receiver. It could be a physical wire or radio waves.
- **Protocol** It represents a set of rules that governs the communication process between the sender and the receiver.

Figure 14.1 illustrates these five elements of data communication.

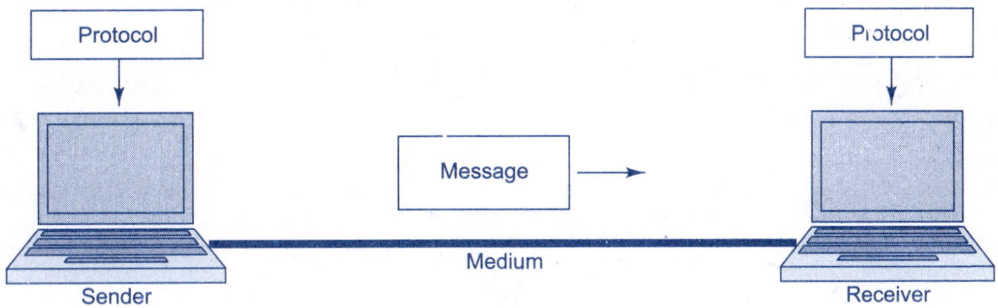

Fig. 14.1 Basic elements of data communication

Data communication may occur in a simple point-to-point mode as shown in Fig. 14.1 or in a multipoint mode where more than two computers are connected together in the form of a *network*. A network is a system of interconnected computers that can communicate with one another to share applications and data.

We shall discuss in this chapter the various forms of networks, their topologies, protocols used and network applications.

14.2 DATA COMMUNICATION USING MODEM

In data communication, data from one computer is transferred to another computer using various channels such as analog transmission channel and satellites. One of the analog transmission channels, which is most commonly used in data communication is the telephone lines. A computer that sends data to another computer is called the *source terminal* and the computer which receives the data from a sender computer is called the *destination terminal*.

The sender computer provides the data for transmission in the form of digital signals. These digital signals have to be first converted into analog signals for transmission through an analog transmission channel such as telephone lines. The process of converting digital signals into analog signals is called *modulation*. The analog signals have to be again converted into digital signals when they reach the destination so that the receiver computer can understand the signals. The process of converting the analog signals again into digital signals is called *demodulation*. The modulation and demodulation processes are performed by a device called *modem* during data transfer between computers. A modem is basically an electronic device that converts the digital signals into analog signals. It also helps to convert analog signals into digital signals.

A modem must be present both at the source and destination for data transmission. This means a sender computer as well as a receiver computer must have a modem for data transmission. If a sender computer does not have a modem then it will not be able to send data to the receiver computer through an analog transmission channel. Similarly, if a receiver computer does not have a modem then it will not be able to receive the data sent by a sender computer through analog transmission channel. Figure 14.2 shows the use of modem in data communication.

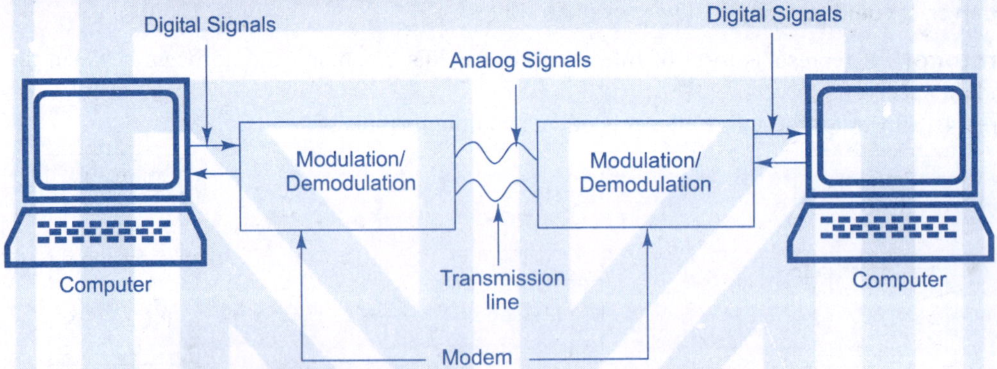

Fig. 14.2 Data Communication through Modem

Figure 14.2 shows that data in the form of digital signals are passed from the sender computer to the modem. Modem then converts the digital signals into analog signals. The converted analog signals are transferred from source to destination using analog transmission channel such as telephone lines. At the destination, a modem again converts the analog signal to digital signals. The converted digital signals are then passed to the receiver computer.

When using a modem in data communication, there are two factors that are of importance, modem speed and modem type. *Modem speed* refers to the time period that a modem takes to convert digital signals into analog signals or analog signals into digital signals. The speed of the modem is very important for data transmission between the sender computer and receiver computer. If a modem is able to convert digital signals into analog signals or analogs signals into digital signals at a high speed then data will also be transmitted at high speed. A modem's speed is measured in bits per second (bps). *Modem type* refers to the type of a modem. There are basically two types of modems: internal modem and external modem. *Internal modem* is the modem that is present on the expansion board, which is contained in a computer. An *external modem* on the other hand is a modem that is connected externally to the COM port of the computer through a cable. Normally internal modems are considered better than external modems because these types of modems are present inside a computer and save desktop space.

Windows operating system provides built-in mechanism for setting up a connection using modem. We can either set up a direct connection or a dial-up connection using a modem. In Windows operating system, a new connection through a modem is established using the New Connection Wizard. Figure 14.3 shows the welcome screen of the New Connection Wizard.

Fig. 14.3 The New Connection Wizard

The New Connection Wizard provides explicit information in each of its screen to guide the end user on setting up the desired connection using modem.

14.3 COMPUTER NETWORK

Computer network is a system of interconnected computers that enable the computers to communicate with each other and share their resources, data and applications. The physical location of each computer is tailored to personal and organisational needs. A network may include only personal computers or a mix of PCs, minis and mainframes spanning a particular geographical area. Computer networks that are commonly used today may be classified as follows:

- Based on geographical area:
    - o Local Area Networks (LANs)
    - o Wide Area Networks (WANs)

- Metropolitan Area Networks (MANs)
- International Network (Internet)
- Intranet

- Based on how computer nodes are used:
  - Client Server Networks (CSNs)
  - Peer-to-peer Networks (PPNs)
  - Value-added Networks (VANs)

14.3.1 Local Area Network (LAN)

LAN is a group of computers, as shown in Fig. 14.4, that are connected in a small area such as building, home, etc. Through this type of network, users can easily communicate with each other by sending and receiving messages. LAN is generally used for connecting two or more personal computers through some medium such as twisted pair, coaxial cable etc. Though the number of computers connected in a LAN is limited, the data is transferred at an extremely faster rate.

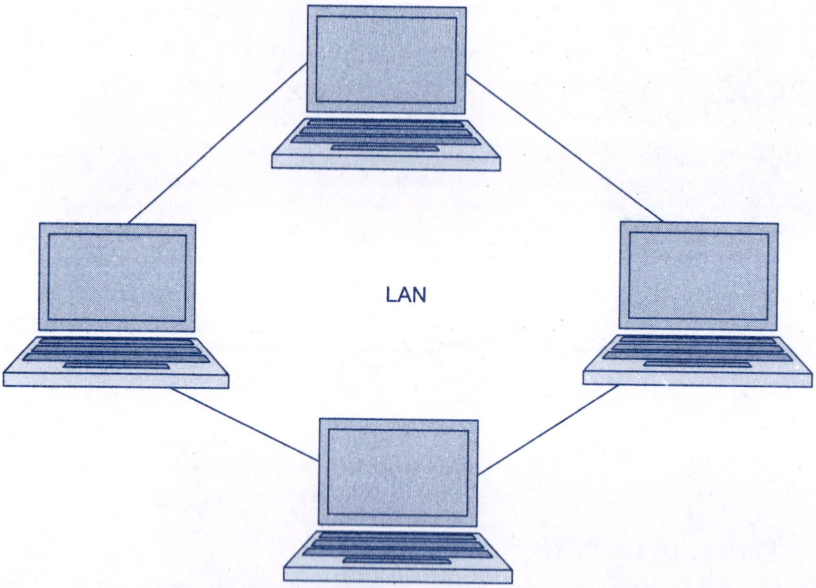

Fig. 14.4 A LAN

14.3.2 Wide Area Network (WAN)

WAN is a group of computers that are connected in a large area such as continent, country, etc. WAN is generally used for connecting two or more LANs through some medium such as leased telephone lines, microwaves, etc. In WAN, data is transferred at slow rate. A typical WAN network is shown in Fig. 14.5.

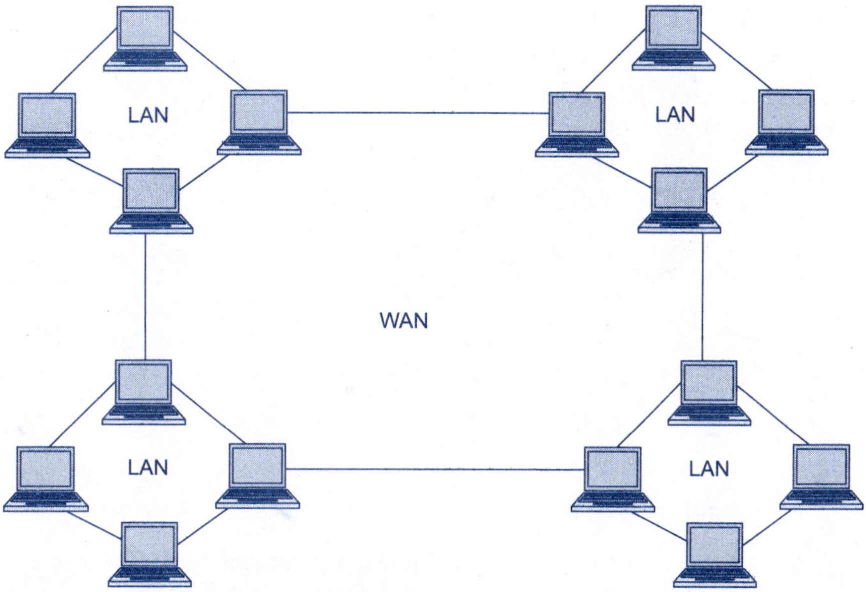

Fig. 14.5 A WAN system

14.3.3 Metropolitan Area Network (MAN)

MAN is a network of computers that covers a large area like a city. The size of the MAN generally lies between that of LAN and WAN, typically covering a distance of 5 Km to 50 Km. The geographical area covered by MAN is comparatively larger than LAN but smaller than WAN. MAN is generally owned by private organisations. MAN is generally connected with the help of optical fibres, copper wires etc. One of the most common example of MAN is cable television network within a city as shown in Fig. 14.6. A network device known as *router* is used to connect the LANs together. The router directs the information packets to the desired destination.

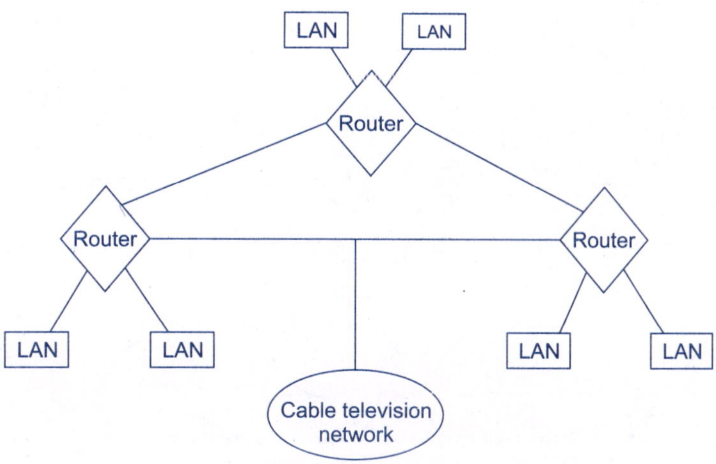

Fig. 14.6 A typical MAN system

14.3.4 The Internet

The Internet is a global area network that allows computers connected over the network to share resources and information using different protocols. It is basically a network of networks across the globe. Users at different locations can very easily communicate with each other via the Internet. They can access data and information from other computers if they are permitted to do so. The Internet basically uses a set of protocols such as Transmission Control Protocol/ Internet Protocol (TCP/IP) for transferring the data over the network. The following are the different types of services provided by the Internet to the users:

- **E-mail** E-mail is the widely used service of the Internet through which users can send and receive messages in an efficient way. It allows an individual to send the message even if the other individual is offline. The e-mail messages are sent to and from a unique e-mail address. The series of the characters usually in the form username@hostname for sending the messages to a person is known as the e-mail address.
- **Online chat** The online chat generally allows one-to-one communication between the individuals over the Internet. Users can communicate directly by sending and receiving messages to there fellow friends easily. Online chat is possible only when the sender and receiver both are online.
- **Online shopping** The Internet has become popular by providing shopping of different products online. Now, it is very easy and simple to buy the products from the other parts of the country or from anywhere across the world. A user can purchase an item with the use of personal computer, Internet and special softwares such as shopping cart and e-cash. The shopping cart is used for selecting the items online whereas e-cash is used for making the online payment of the items purchased.
- **Usenet** Usenet is the Internet based newsgroup that allows individuals to share their views regarding a specific topic or subject over the network. People accessing the usenet can receive these views through private or public e-mail.

There are various advantages of using the Internet:

- **Information** The Internet allows users to access large amount of information efficiently. The information could be related to any topic, such as law, marketing, finance, science, technology etc.
- **Availabilty** The Internet is available continuously to the users all the time without any delay. Users can access the information from the Internet at any time.
- **Cost** The Internet provides different facilities to the users at a low cost. Users can access any website over the Internet absolutely free. The cost of sending messages through e-mail is also cheaper as compared to postal messages.

The following are some of the disadvantages of using the Internet:

- **Hacking** The process of illegally accessing the personal information stored over the Internet is called *hacking*. The person who is involved in this activity is called a *hacker*.
- **Virus** The software program that itself gets activated in our computer system and destroys the stored information is called *virus*. Virus usually corrupts the resourses that are connected over the Internet.
- **Bulk e-mail** It is the most common problem of the Internet where the unwanted bulk messages such as subscription mails, advertisement mails, job alert mails etc. are received on the users account. These messages are sometimes frustrating and irritating for the users because the user simply does not require these mails.

14.3.5 The Intranet

Intranet is a private network, which is confined to a single organisation only. This type of computer network allows only the internal users of the organisation to share the resources. However, the users outside the organisation can also access the Intranet but they can do so only if they are authorised. The concept of Intranet was used for sharing the company's information amongst the employees. Certain protocols such as TCP/IP, HTTP, etc. are used by Intranet for enabling the communication between the computer systems. Organisations that use Intranet for transferring the messages generally make use of tunneling, which is a technique used for sending private messages. The website of the Intranet is provided with the firewall, which is a layer that helps in ensuring the security of the information and resources. The only disadvantage of Intranet is that it is relatively insecure as compared to the other networks. The various advantages of using Intranet are as follows:

- It allows the employees of an organisation to access the organisation's information easily and quickly.
- Intranet users can easily communicate with each other within the organisation.
- It is relatively easier to maintain and implement Intranet than the Internet.

14.3.6 Client Server Network (CSN)

CSN basically consists of two computers, client computer and server computer. The client computers are dummy computers, which simply send requests to the server computer, whereas the server computers receive and execute the requests sent by the client computer. CSN is also known as the client server architecture. This architecture is a two-tier architecture, which is divided into two layers. The first layer comprises of the user interface that is located on the client's desktop. On the other hand, the second layer is the database management layer, which is located on the server machine so as to provide services to the clients.

In CSN, a client computer sends a request related to processing of data to the server. The server receives the request from the client computer and processes the data. It then sends the output obtained after the processing of data to the client computer as a response to its request. The following are the advantages of the CSN:

- There is a proper distribution of computing tasks. The task of the client computer is to send request to the server for processing of data. The server receives the request of the client computer, processes the data and sends the result back to the client computer.
- All the important data is stored on the server and only authorised persons are allowed to access the data from the server. As a result, there is greater security of data in a CSN.
- It is easy to manage the data updates as data is stored in a centralised manner on a server.
- Multiple client computers having varying hardware configuration are able to interact with a server.

The following are the disadvantages of the CSN:

- If the server crashes, the complete network breaks down.
- The load on the server increases in a CSN because there are multiple clients sending some request to a server. As a result, the network traffic increases and network congestion occurs.

Figure 14.7 shows a typical CSN.

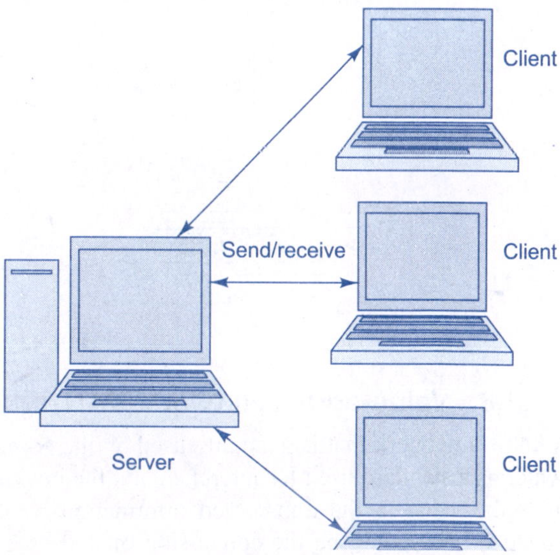

Fig. 14.7 A CSN

14.3.7 Peer-to-peer Network (PPN)

In PPN, there is no separate division as clients and servers. Every computer in the PPN is treated equally and can send as well as receive the messages directly. PPN architecture cannot work under heavy load. This type of architecture is commonly used for file sharing and chatting in real time. Computers connected in this network can easily share their resources with the other computers. PPN is used in a variety of fields such as business, education, telecommunications, military etc. The advantages of PPN are as follows:

- PPN is relatively cheaper than the CSN, as the centralised server is not required.
- PPN is simpler than the CSN because computers connected in the network can communicate efficiently with each other.

The following are the disadvantages of the PPN:

- PPN is less secure because message flows freely between the computers.
- PPN is decentralised as there is no specific space for the storage of files.
- PPN is less expandable as performance and speed of network degrades when more computers are added.

Figure 14.8 shows the PPN.

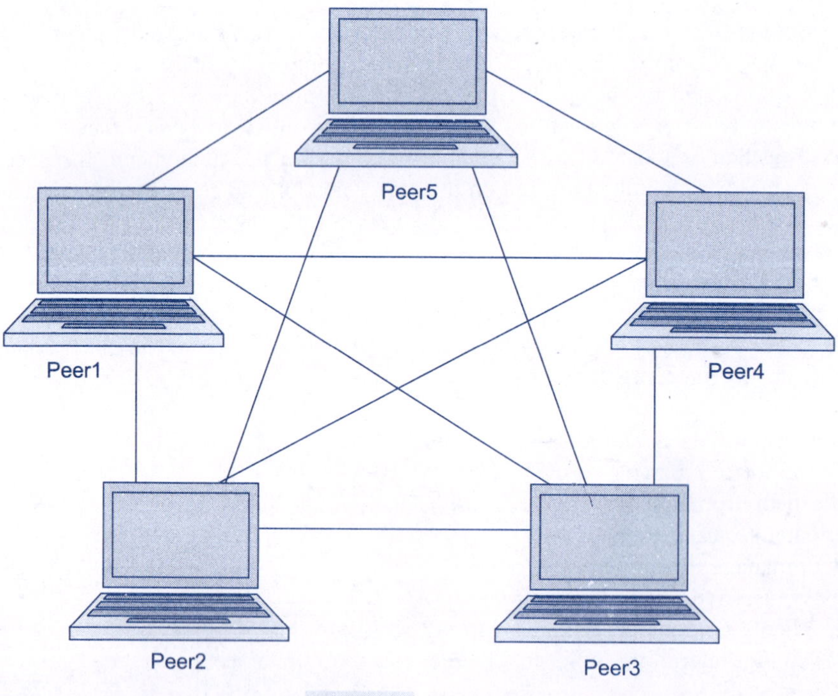

Fig. 14.8 The PPN

14.3.8 Value-added Network (VAN)

VAN is a network that is generally used by the companies privately for Electronic Data Interchange (EDI), which is a standard used for interchanging the business data. In other words, VAN is a network that usually adds the value to the transmitted information by providing value-added services. An example of value added service could be the conversion of data in eXtensible Markup Language (XML) to EDI provided through VAN to specific companies.

Apart from providing value-added services, VAN also provides the auto error detection and correction and protocol conversion services for data modification. Error detection and correction is a technique used for detecting the errors in the transmitted data and then rectifying it. On the other hand, protocol conversion is basically used for converting a message, which has been transferred using a specific protocol to another protocol with the help of protocol converter.

14.4 NETWORK TOPOLOGIES

Network topology refers to the arrangement of computers connected in a network through some physical medium such as cable, optical fibre etc. Topology generally determines the shape of the network and the communication path between the various computers (nodes) of the network. The various types of network topologies are as follows:

- Hierarchical topology
- Bus topology
- Star topology
- Ring topology
- Mesh topology
- Hybrid topology

14.4.1 Hierarchical Topology

The hierarchical topology is also known as tree topology, which is divided into different levels connected with the help of twisted pair, coaxial cable or fibre optics. This type of topology is arranged in the form of a tree structure in which top level contains parent node (root node), which is connected with the child nodes in the second level of hierarchy with the point-to-point link. The second level nodes are connected to the third level nodes, which in turn are connected to the fourth level nodes and so on. Except the top-level node, each level node has a parent node.

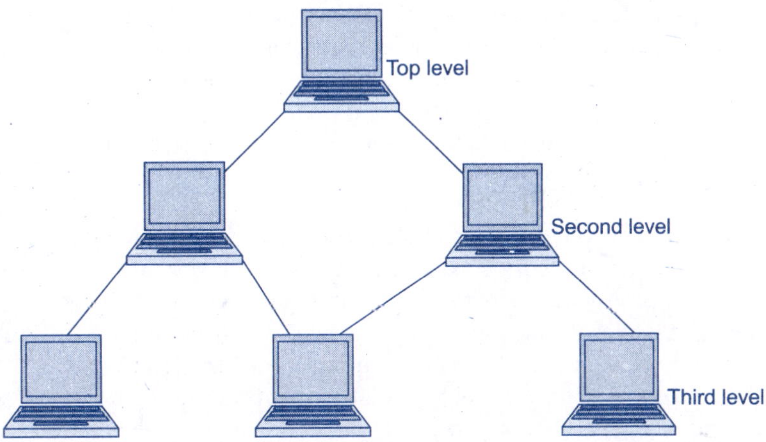

Fig. 14.9 The hierarchical topology

The number of point-to-point links in the hierarchical type of topology is generally one less than the total number of nodes in the structure. The hierarchical topology is symmetrical, having a fixed branching factor, f, associated with each node. The branching factor is the number of point-to-point links between the levels of hierarchy. Figure.14.9 shows the arrangement of computers in hierarchical topology.

Advantages of hierarchical topology are:

- The hierarchical topology is generally supported by most hardware and software.

- In the hierarchical topology, data is received by all the nodes efficiently because of point-to-point link.

The following are the disadvantages of hierarchical topology:

- In the hierarchical topology, when the root node fails, the whole network crashes.
- The hierarchical topology is difficult to configure.

14.4.2 Linear Bus Topology

In the linear bus topology, all the nodes are connected to the single backbone or bus with some medium such as twisted pair, coaxial cable etc. When a node wants to communicate with the other nodes in the network, it simply sends a message to the common bus. All the nodes in the network then receive the message but the node for which it was actually sent only processes it. The other nodes discard the message. Figure 14.10 shows the arrangement of computers in the linear bus topology.

Advantages of linear bus topology are:

- The linear bus topology usually requires less cabling.
- The linear bus topology is relatively simple to configure and install.
- In the linear bus topology, the failure of one computer does not affect the other computers in the network.

The following are the disadvantages of linear bus topology:

- In the linear bus topology, the failure of the backbone cable results in the breakdown of entire network.
- Addition of computers in the linear bus topology results in the performance degradation of the network.
- The bus topology is difficult to reconstruct in case of faults.

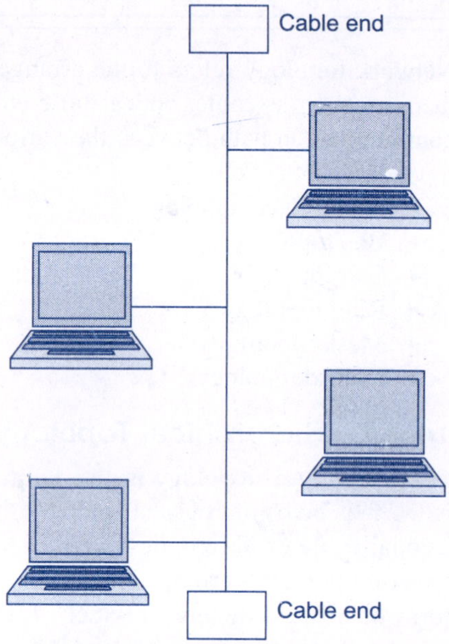

Fig. 14.10 A linear bus topology

14.4.3 Star Topology

In the star topology, all the nodes are connected to a common device known as hub. Nodes are connected with the help of twisted pair, coaxial cable or optical fibre. When a node wants to send a message to the other nodes, it first sends the message to the hub, which in turn forwards the message to the intended node. Each node in the network is connected with a point-to-point link to the centralised hub. The task of hub is to detect the faulty node present in the network. On the other hand, it also manages the overall data transmission in the network. Figure 14.11 shows the arrangement of computers in star topology.

Advantages of star topology are:

- This topology allows easy error detection and correction.
- In the star topology, the failure of one computer does not affect the other computers in the network.
- Star topology is easy to install.

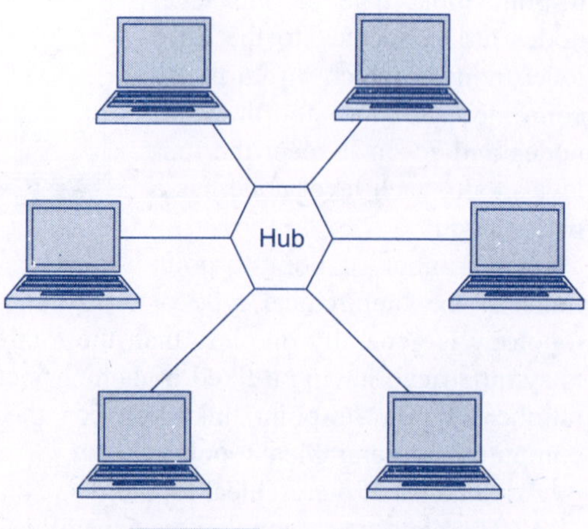

Fig. 14.11 A star topology

The following are the disadvantages of star topology:

- In the star topology, the hub failure leads to the overall network crash.
- The star topology requires more amount of cable for connecting the nodes.
- It is expensive due to the cast of hub.

14.4.4 Ring Topology

In the ring topology, the nodes are connected in the form of a ring with the help of twisted pair. Each node is connected directly to the other two nodes in the network. The node, which wants to send a message, first passes the message to its consecutive node in the network. Data is transmitted in the clockwise direction from one node to another. Figure 14.12 shows the arrangement of computers in the ring topology. Each node incorporates a repeater, which passes the message to next node when the message is intended for another node.

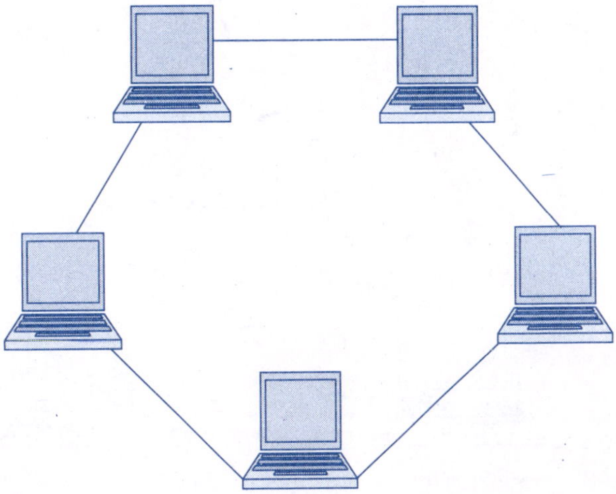

Fig. 14.12 A ring topology

Advantages of ring topology are:

- Each node has an equal access to other nodes in the network.
- Addition of new nodes does not degrade the performance of the network.
- Ring topology is easy to configure and install.

The following are the disadvantages of ring topology:

- It is relatively expensive to construct the ring topology.
- The failure of one node in the ring topology affects the other nodes in the ring.

14.4.5 Mesh Topology

In mesh topology, each computer is connected to every other computer in point-to-point mode as shown in Fig. 14.13. For example, if we have four computers, we must have six links. If we have n computers, we must have $n(n-1)/2$ links. A message can take several possible paths to reach a destination.

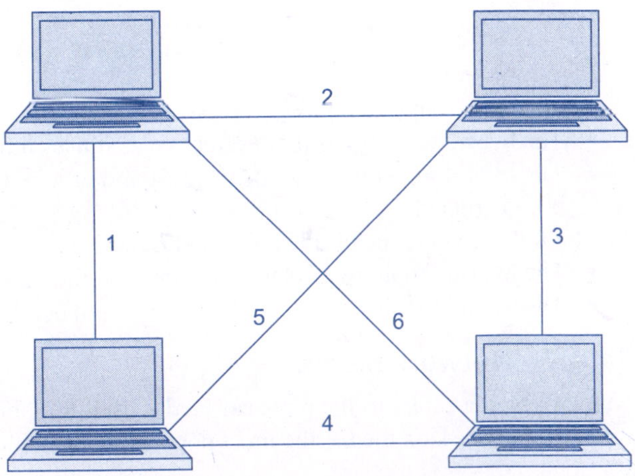

Fig. 14.13 Mesh topology

Advantages of mesh topology are:

- Message delivery is more reliable.
- Network congestion is minimum due to large number of links.

The following are the disadvantages:

- It is very expensive to implement.
- It is very difficult to configure and install.

14.4.6 Hybrid Topology

The hybrid topology is the combination of multiple topologies, used for constructing a single large topology. The hybrid topology is created when two different network topologies are interconnected. If two ring topologies are connected then the resultant topology is not the hybrid topology. On the other hand, if the ring topology is connected to the bus topology then the resulting topology is called the hybrid topology. This topology generally combines the features of the two topologies and is therefore more effective and efficient than the individual topologies. Figure 14.14 shows a typical arrangement of computers in hybrid topology.

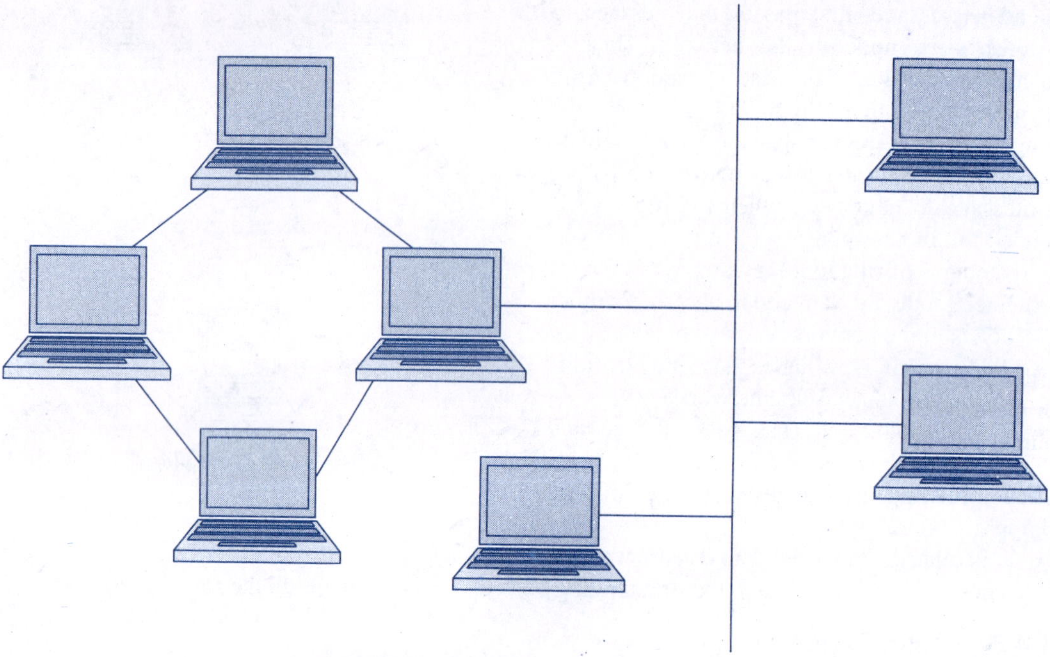

Fig. 14.14 A hybrid topology

Advantages of hybrid topology are:

- The hybrid topology is more effective as it uses multiple topologies.
- The hybrid topology contains the best and efficient features of the combined topologies from which it is constructed.

The following are the disadvantages of hybrid topology:

- The hybrid topology is relatively more complex than the other topologies.
- The hybrid topology is difficult to install and configure.

14.4.7 Network Media

Network media refers to the physical media used to connect the computer nodes together. There are many types of transmission media, the most popular being cables, optical fibre, microwave and satellite.

- **Cables** Cable is one of the easiest methods of transferring messages from one place to another. Some of the commonly used cables are telephone lines, twisted-pair cables and coaxial cables.

Twisted-pair cables are insulated and twisted around each other in order to reduce noise (unwanted signal). They are generally used to connect hubs to nodes in star topology. Coaxial cables have single copper conductor with a shield around it. They are very robust and used for crossing large distances such as the ocean.

- **Optical fibre** An optical fibre is a thin strand of glass that transmits pulsating beams of light rather than electric current. These light pulses carry information. Fibre-optic cables can thus carry information in digital form. They can carry enormous amount of messages at extremely fast speed. These are used for long distance communications. It is a highly secured transmission medium.
- **Microwave** Communication through microwave can be used when the transmitting and receiving ends are located at a large distance from one another. Microwaves are used to transmit analog signals. WANs often use microwave links to connect LANs together. This mode of transmission is greatly affected by the weather conditions.
- **Satellite** Satellites are used for receiving and transmitting analog signals globally. We can send data from one country to another with the help of satellites. WANs that cover long distances often use satellites for linking LANs.

14.5 NETWORK PROTOCOLS AND SOFTWARE

In order to share data between computers, it is essential to have appropriate network protocols and software. With the help of network protocol, computers can easily communicate with each other and can share data, resources etc.

14.5.1 Network Protocol

Network protocols are the set of rules and regulations that are generally used for communication between two networks. Any two networks communicate with each other by sending and receiving messages in the form of packets. The technique that is used separating a message into packets is called packet switching. Each packet contains the address of the computer from which the message was sent and also of the computer, which will receive the message. In order to send the packet, routers and switches are connected over the network path that forwards the packet to the intended receiver. Using network protocol, the following tasks can be performed:

- Identification of the type of the physical connection used
- Error detection and correction of the improper message
- Initiation and termination of the communication session
- Message formatting

Some of the commonly used network protocols are Hyper Text Transfer protocol (HTTP), Simple Mail Transfer Protocol (SMTP), File Transfer Protocol (FTP), Transmission Control Protocol/ Internet Protocol (TCP/IP), Telecommunications Network (Telnet), Domain Name System (DNS) etc.

14.5.2 Network Software

Network software refers to the set of instructions that are given to the computers connected in a network to perform different tasks. These instructions are given in the form of a program, which is usually written in some programming language such as C++, Java, C etc. The network software generally provides support to the computers connected in a network so that they can communicate with each other by exchanging information. Network operating system software is the type of network software that basically controls the network traffic, access to the network resources such as printers, files, etc. This type of software generally provides multiuser, multitasking facilities so as to ensure effective communication between the computers over the network. It also establishes the communication between multiple computers that are performing a single task.

14.6 APPLICATIONS OF NETWORK

Network is the system of computers generally linked together to enable the flow of data between the interconnected computers. With the help of network, we can access the data remotely. Some of the applications of a network are:

- **Data sharing** It is the capability of sharing data with multiple users over the network. In order to share the data among multiple users, it is generally stored on the servers. Different applications can therefore access the data from these servers easily. A special software locking mechanism is maintained over the network, so as to prevent multiple users from modifying the data. The sharing of data among the multiple users in an interactive way is known as data conferencing.
- **Remote data access** Remote data access is the process of accessing the data from remote location in an efficient way. Different software programs are used to provide an interface to the end users for accessing the data remotely.
- **Resource sharing** Resource sharing is the process of sharing the resources such as storage devices, input/output devices, etc. over the network. For example, printer can be shared among the computers connected in a network by attaching it to the server computer. When the users want their documents to be printed they can simply give the print command from there computers and get their document printed. The sharing of a printer on a network is relatively cheaper than attaching separate printers to the individual computers connected in the network.
- **Personal communication** The far-reaching applications of networks are electronic mail and teleconferencing. These applications allow individuals as well as organisations to use networks for exchanging messages (written, voice and video) extensively. Electronic mail enables a person to send and receive instant messages over a computer network with the help of Internet. On the other hand, teleconferencing enables real-time communication over a distance by allowing people at different locations to communicate with each other by seeing the video picture of people at other sites. This is also referred to as virtual meeting.

Chapter Summary

Data communication is the process of sending data to the destination via some communication medium such as cables, satellites, fibre optics, etc. Modem is a device that works as a modulator as well as a demodulator. It receives the outgoing signal in the digital form and converts them into the analog form for transmission. This process is called modulation. The analog signal is then converted back into the digital signal at the receiving end. This process is known as demodulation.

A cluster of computers connected together in order to share resources is termed as a computer network. Computer network comes in a variety of shapes and sizes such as LAN, WAN, MAN, Internet, Intranet, CSN, PPN and value added network. Computers in these networks are connected with each other in some pattern such as star, ring and bus, which is referred as network topology. There are various types of network topologies such as hierarchical topology, bus topology, star topology, ring topology, mesh topology and hybrid topology. The computers connected in a network generally communicate with the help of network protocols. For the computers connected in a network, a proper network software has to be installed so that they can communicate with each other.

Key Terms to Remember

- **Data communication**: It is the process of transmission of data from the source computer to the destination computer.
- **Modem**: It is a device that converts outgoing digital signal into analog signal for onward transmission and converts incoming analog signal into digital signal suitable for the computer.
- **LAN**: It is a group of interconnected computers covering a small area such as a building.
- **WAN**: It usually connects the computers in a large area such as country, continents etc.
- **MAN**: It is the regional area network that typically connects the computers within a city, campus etc.
- **Internet**: It is the global network, which comprises of various networks spread over globally.
- **Intranet**: It is the private network of computers, usually contained within an organisation.
- **CSN**: CSN consists of two computers, client computer and server computer, where the server computer simply receives the request from the client computer and processes these requests.
- **PPN**: In PPN, every computer communicates directly with other computers by sending and receiving the requests.
- **Network topology**: The network topology is the physical arrangement of the computers connected with each other in a network such as ring, star, bus, hierarchical and hybrid.
- **Network protocol**: The network protocol is the standard according to which different computers over the network communicate with each other.
- **Network media**: It is the physical media used to connect the computer nodes together.
- **Network software**: It is a computer program that aids the computers to communicate with each other effectively.

Review Questions

Fill in the Blanks

1. Data communication is the process of sending the data from the ________ to the __________.
2. ______________ is a medium for transmitting the data in digital form from the source to the destination.
3. The process of converting the digital signal into analog signal is termed as __________.
4. ___________ is the method of transforming analog signals into digital signal.
5. ___________ is used for converting digital signal into analog signals and vice versa.
6. When computers are connected together in order to share resources, they are said to be in a __________.
7. ____________ is used for connecting the computers within a few kilometers of area.
8. ____________ is used for connecting the computers in a large geographical area.
9. The size of the MAN generally lies between that of LAN and WAN, typically covering a distance of ____________ to _______________.

10. ______________ is the global area network consisting of many networks world over.
11. ______________ is the Internet based newsgroup that allows individuals to share their views regarding a specific topic or subject over the network.
12. The software program that itself gets activated in our computer system and destroys the stored information is called ______________.
13. The network that is restricted within an organisation is termed as ____________.
14. In the CSN architecture, ___________ sends the request to the ___________.
15. The ______________ architecture does not consist of client computer and the server computer.
16. ______________ is the network used for exchanging the data related to business.
17. Hierarchical topology is also known as ______________.
18. ____________ is the common point where all the nodes of the network are connected in the bus topology.
19. ____________ is used for connecting the nodes in the star topology.
20. The combination of multiple topologies connected in a network is known as ______________.
21. ______________ is the set of rules and regulations based on which computers in a network communicate.
22. ____________ is one of the tasks that can be performed using network protocol.
23. ____________ is used for transferring files from one computer to another over the network.
24. The set of instructions that are given to the computer for performing various tasks is known as ______________

Multiple Choice Questions

1. Which one of the following uses light pulses for carrying information?
   A. Satellite B. Microwave C. Optical fibre D. Coaxial cable
2. The process of converting digital signal into the analog signal is known as ______________.
   A. Demodulation B. Modulation C. Data compression D. None of the above
3. Which one of the following is the factor that must be considered when using modem for data communication?
   A. Modem Speed B. Computer Port C. Modem size D. None of the above
4. Which of the following network is used for connecting the computers in a small geographical area?
   A. MAN B. WAN C. LAN D. Internet
5. What is the full form of TCP?
   A. Transfer Control Protocol B. Transmission Control Protocol
   C. Transmit Control Protocol D. Transfer Communication Protocol
6. Which one of the following Internet services provides one to one communication?
   A. Online chat B. Online messaging C. E-mail D. Usenet
7. A network that is restricted to use by a single organisation is referred to as:
   A. LAN B. WAN C. Internet D. Intranet
8. In which network architecture there are no client computers and server computers?
   A. CSN architecture B. Value added network architecture
   C. PPN architecture D. All of the above
9. In which type of network can network congestion occur?
   A. CSN B. PPN C. Value added network D. LAN

10. Which type network cannot work under heavy load?
    A. MAN B. LAN C. PPN D. VAN
11. Which topology is arranged in the form of a tree structure?
    A. Hybrid topology B. Bus topology C. Star topology D. Hierarchical topology
12. Which of the one of the following topologies is not easy to reconstruct when a fault occurs?
    A. Star topology B. Bus topology C. Ring topology D. Hybrid topology
13. Which of one of the following topologies allow easy error detection and correction?
    A. Linear bus topology B. Hybrid topology C. Ring topology D. Star topology
14. Which device is used for connecting the computers in a star topology?
    A. Router B. Bridge C. Hub D. Repeater
15. Which topology is the combination of multiple topologies?
    A. Star topology B. Bus topology C. Hybrid topology D. Mesh topology
16. In which topology data is transferred in a circular pattern?
    A. Star topology B. Ring topology C. Bus topology D. Hybrid topology
17. Which of the following topologies is the most complex but efficient?
    A. Star topology B. Bus topology C. Ring topology D. Hybrid topology
18. What is the technique used for routing the packets to the destination according to their addresses?
    A. Circuit switching B. Packet switching C. Routing D. None of the above
19. Which one of the following is not a network protocol?
    A. FTP B. HTTP C. SMTP D. NMP
20. A set of rules that are used for communication between two networks is referred to as:
    A. Network software B. Network media
    C. Network protocol D. Network operating system

Discussion Questions

1. Explain the process of data communication with the help of a diagram.
2. What are the different components used in the data communication? Explain each component briefly.
3. How are modems used for the purpose of data communication?
4. What is a computer network?
5. Describe different types of computer networks with the help of illustrations.
6. What is the difference between LAN and WAN?
7. Explain CSN architecture.
8. What is PPN architecture?
9. What is metropolitan area network?
10. What is network topology?
11. What are the different types of network topologies? Explain any two network topologies through suitable illustrations.
12. Explain hybrid topology in detail.
13. How network protocols helps in the communication of messages over the network?
14. What is the difference between ring topology and bus topology?

15. What is network software?
16. What are the advantages and disadvantages of using Internet?
17. What is the importance of value added network in the business?
18. What is the difference between Internet and Intranet?
19. Explain the popular network media used for data transmission.
20. Differentiate among ring, star, bus and hybrid topology with the help of diagrams.

CHAPTER 15

THE INTERNET AND WORLD WIDE WEB

Chapter Outline

Chapter Objectives

In this chapter, we will learn:

- The difference between the Internet and World Wide Web.
- How the Internet has grown from a small network to a large network over the years.
- The use of the Internet in various fields, such as business, education, entertainment and communication.
- How web browser and World Wide Web are used for accessing websites and gathering information.
- The benefit of using search engines for finding information over the Internet.
- How the email service provided by the Internet allows the users to send and receive email messages over the Internet.
- The various protocols used for the Internet and their functions at different levels.

15.1 INTRODUCTION

Internet is a popular buzzword among many people today. Almost everyone working in government offices and business organisations is using the Internet for exchange of information in one form or the other.

World Wide Web is another popular phrase among the computer users. It is commonly referred to as *the Web*. Most people consider the

Internet and the World Wide Web to be synonymous, but they are not. Although these two terms are used interchangeably, they actually describe two different but related things.

The Internet is a massive network of networks that links together thousands of independent networks thus bringing millions of computers on a single network to provide a global communication system. It acts as a facilitator for exchange of information between computers that are connected to the Internet. It is like a network of roads in a country that facilitates the movement of vehicles around the country.

We can create special documents known as *hypertext documents* containing text, graphics, sounds and video on a computer. The storage location of these documents is known as *website*. The World Wide Web is the network of all such websites all around the world. It is popularly known as WWW or Web. The websites are spread across the Internet and therefore, the information contained in the websites can be transmitted through the Internet. It is like transporting the goods stored in the warehouses using the road network. So the Web is just a portion on the Internet and not same as the Internet.

In this chapter, we shall discuss the evolution of the Internet, the basics of World Wide Web, use of Web browsers and search engines and the various Internet applications. We shall also discuss briefly various protocols that are necessary for using the Web and the Internet.

15.2 HISTORY OF INTERNET

The Internet was not a worldwide network initially. It was a small network called ARPAnet, which was developed at the Advanced Research Projects Agency (ARPA) of United States in 1969. ARPAnet was developed to help the researchers at one university to communicate with the researchers at other universities. The computers, which were connected through the ARPAnet, were the computers present at the University of California, Stanford Research Institute (California) and the University of Utah (Nevada).

To transfer data between these computers, the ARPAnet used the concept of packet switching in which the data was divided into small modules known as packets before transmitting. These packets were transmitted individually over the network and were reassembled at the receiver's end. During the process of transmission of packets on the network, some rules and methods known as protocols were followed. The ARPAnet initially used Network Control Protocol (NCP), which allowed the transmission of files, directories and messages between two computers on the network. The use of NCP provided end-to-end networking as the user could only trust the ends, i.e., the sender and the receiver but could not trust the means of transmission, i.e., the network. In 1972, the access to ARPANET was extended and made available to common people and business organisations.

In the year 1974, the scientists developed a new host-to-host protocol, which not only allowed the sharing of files, directories and messages but also helped the users to share software and applications on the network. This protocol was known as Transmission Control Protocol/Internet Protocol (TCP/IP). It was a combination of two protocols, TCP and IP, which worked collectively. The IP was the protocol that guided the packets on the different routes on the network. The IP routed each packet on a different route and the selection of a route for a packet was made in such a manner that the packets should take minimum time to reach their destination. The selection of different routes for different packets also facilitated the transmission of packets even when one of the parts of the network was not working properly. The TCP was the network protocol that was responsible for the reassembling of the packets at the destination.

The congestion on ARPAnet was increasing continuously because of its extensive use by the military. In 1975, the Defence Communications Agency (DCA) took control of the ARPAnet and changed its name to Defence Advanced Research Projects Agency (DARPA). DARPA allowed all the defence related organisations to connect to it but at the same time it denied the connection to all the non-government organisations. This led to the development of other commercial networks such as Telnet.

In 1976, the telephone companies from all over the world broadcasted a new protocol called X.25 with the support of Consultative Committee for International Telegraphy and Telephony (CCITT). The X.25 protocol was similar to the packet switching technique but its implementation was different. The X.25 protocol reduced the packet size and provided a more reliable means of transmission of packets. It used the concept of hop-to-hop networking in which the receiving of packet was acknowledged by the hop at every step. In the X.25 protocol, the information of the path was contained only in the first packet, which helped create a virtual path. The rest of the packets just followed the virtual path created by the first packet. Though this protocol was used for a very short period of time but was crucial for the development of enterprise networks.

In 1979, a research computer network known as Usenet was developed by a group of computer scientists from all over the world. This network allowed computers to connect through a dial-up connection. In the Usenet network, the UNIX-to-UNIX copy protocol was used to transfer data. Usenet provided two main services, Usenet News and mail servers. The Usenet News still continues to be used as NetNews but the mail servers did not prove to be a success. The failure of mail servers was due to the fact that to send a mail through mail servers a user was required to provide the complete path to the destination computer with the help of the UUCP bang addressing format. The UUCP bang addressing format was the format in which the names of different machines were separated using a bang, i.e., an exclamation mark.

In 1982, a new network known as Eunet was developed in Europe to connect the networks of European countries such as UK, Scandinavia and Netherlands. By the year 1983, a number of networks were added to ARPAnet to connect around 300 computers. In the same year, TCP/IP was made the standard protocol for ARPAnet. The TCP/IP protocol allowed communication between computers of different networks and the ARPAnet became capable of internetworking. This was the time when ARPAnet was renamed as the Internet. In 1983, the military part of ARPAnet was split and named as MILNET.

The number of computers connected to ARPAnet increased day-by-day because of which a new problem arose. The mapping of host names to the IP addresses became difficult. The IP addresses were the addresses provided to each host computer on the network. Earlier, the Network Information Center (NIC) maintained a record of the IP addresses and the corresponding host names in a file and every computer downloaded this file whenever required. But with the increase in the number of computers connected to the ARPAnet, it became difficult for the NIC to do so.

In 1984, Domain Name Server (DNS) was developed that helped in the mapping of host names to the IP addresses. The domain names such as .edu for educational, .com for commercial, .gov for governmental and .org for international organisational hosts, were introduced along with a specific code for each country. The DNS converted these domain names into the corresponding IP addresses. The domain names also made it easier for the users to remember the addresses.

In 1987, the National Science Foundation established a network known as NSFNET that linked the computers through a high speed of 56Kbps. NSFNET allowed many organisations to connect to the Internet without following the ARPAnet's policies. By 1990 almost all the organisations, which were connected to ARPAnet shifted to NFSNET and ARPAnet came to an end. The use of the Internet was limited to email, Telnet and FTP till 1990. In 1990, the McGill University introduced an FTP search tool known as Archie, which helped the users search for the information on the Internet. In the next year, i.e., 1991, another application known as Gopher was developed at the University of Minnesota. This service helped the users arrange the documents on the Internet; and to locate these documents a Gopher search tool known as Veronica was used.

In 1992, Tim Berners-Lee, a physicist from Geneva, introduced the World Wide Web, which was a network of websites that could be accessed with the help of a protocol known as HyperText Transfer Protocol (HTTP). HTTP searched the required address from where the web pages had to be accessed and retrieved the web pages for the user. The web page on the WWW had links in the form of text known as hypertext. These links were helpful in accessing other web pages when a user clicked the hypertext with the help of a mouse. In 1995, the commercial Internet providers started controlling the Internet by providing connections to different people for accessing the Internet. Today the Internet is used in almost every field, such as education, entertainment, business, defence and medicine. In all these fields, the Internet is used to share data, gather information and communicate with the other users. According to the Internet world usage statistics, more than 1.4 billion people use the Internet today.

15.3 INTERNET APPLICATIONS

Nowadays the Internet is used in almost all the fields for different purposes. Each and every field uses one or the other services provided by the Internet. The Internet is extensively used in the following fields:

- Business
- Education
- Communication
- Entertainment
- Government

15.3.1 The Internet in Business

In business, the Internet can be used for many purposes. An organisation can provide details about its products on the Internet that can be either used by the other organisations interested in developing business links with it or by the prospective customers. Business transactions such as sale and purchase of products and online payment can also be performed using the Internet. This service of the Internet is called e-business, which can be further classified into the following categories:

- **Business-to-business (B2B)** B2B e-business refers to the business transactions that take place between two business organisations. In B2B, a large website acts as a market place and helps the buyers and suppliers interact at the organisational level. The website acting as a market place helps the buyers to find new suppliers and the suppliers to search for new buyers. It also saves the time and cost of interaction between the organisations. For example, a supplier business organisation can provide certain raw materials to a manufacturing business organisation through its website.

- **Business-to-consumer (B2C)** B2C e-business refers to the business transactions that take place between an organisation and a consumer directly. In B2C, a consumer can shop online for the products offered by a business organisation. It provides all the information regarding the available products through a website and allows the consumers to order and pay for the products online, thus facilitating fast and convenient shopping. For example, the Asian Sky Shop sells the various products offered by different business organisations online and any user who wants to purchase a product can buy it online.

- **Consumer-to-consumer (C2C)** C2C refers to the business transactions that take place between two consumers but with the help of a third party. In C2C, a consumer provides information about a product, which is to be sold, on the website of the third party. Another consumer can buy the same item through bidding on the website of the third party. The consumer, who provides an item for sale on the website, is known as seller; whereas the consumer, who bids for the item, is known as buyer. For example, e-bay is a website on which a consumer can provide information about the products, which s/he needs to sell. The best bidder gets to buy the listed product.

- **Consumer-to-business (C2B)** C2B is a business model that allows individual consumers to offer their products and services to companies in return of which they get payment from the companies. One of the popular examples of C2B model is the online advertising site Google Adsense. It allows individuals to display advertising content or promotional materials on their personal websites. The administration and payment of these ads are done by Google itself. Also, platforms like Google Video and Fotolia are good examples of C2B, where individuals can sell digital content including images, animations, videos, etc. to companies.

15.3.2 The Internet in Education

In the field of education, the Internet is widely used for learning and teaching. The Internet not only helps the students search information on various topics of their interest but also proves useful for the students pursuing distance education. The distance education institutes provide notes, lectures and syllabus to students through their respective websites. The students just have to access the website of the institute to get all the required information from it. If the website of an educational institution supports e-learning, then the students can participate in online lectures through simulations, Web Based Training (WBT), etc.

The Internet also provides the Usenet service, which contains a large number of Newsgroups through which a user can submit as well as obtain the articles on different topics. The members of a newsgroup connect to each other and have discussions through the Usenet network. Usenet contains a number of message boards on which the articles are placed and the software known as newsreader is used to read the articles published on message board. Most of the newsgroups allow the users to submit their articles on the selected topics such as scientific research, social issues, religion and politics. Moreover, some newsgroups also allow the users to submit their articles on a topic of their own choice. Newsgroup not only helps the users in gaining knowledge but also allows them to make online friends.

The Internet also provides an application similar to Newsgroups known as Discussion forum. The discussion forum also allows a large number of people to hold discussions or place their articles on a particular topic similar to Newsgroups. But the only difference between the Discussion forums and Newsgroups is that the Discussion forums display articles according to the time or the thread of receiving the article. The thread refers to the grouping together of all the messages received on a particular topic. Some discussion forums allow the users to place their articles even without having a membership of the Discussion forum, while the other Discussion forums require the users to have membership along with valid username and password. The members of such Discussion forums have special facilities such as to make alterations in their previous articles, to initiate a new topic and to delete the previous articles submitted by them.

Both Newsgroup and Discussion forums are used by students and other users of the Internet to share their knowledge with each other by participating in a discussion on a specific topic. The extensive use of the Internet in education has led to the creation of what are known as Virtual Universities in many countries.

15.3.3 The Internet in Communication

The Internet is mostly used by the people as a fast and cheap means of communication. Many services provided by the Internet such as e-mail and instant messaging help the users to communicate quickly and cheaply over long distances. E-mail is an application of Internet that allows a user to send and receive text messages electronically. To use the email services, a user requires an account on a mail server. The account is created by the user by providing a username; a password and other personal information such as address and contact number. Each time the user wants to access the email service, she/he has to log on to the server using the username and the password provided during account creation. If the username or the password provided by a user is invalid, then that user is considered as an unauthorised user and is prohibited from using the service.

The Internet also provides another easy way of communication, i.e., communication through instant messaging. Instant messaging is a service of the Internet through which it is possible for a user to perform real-time communication with one or more users on the Internet. The real-time communication refers to the communication in which there is an immediate response to a message. In case of instant messaging, the communication between two users takes place by instant sending and receiving of message. To use this service, the users have to log on to the instant messaging server. After a user has successfully logged on to the server, a chat room with a list of online users is made available to the user. An online user is a user who is available for chatting at a specific period of time. The user can then select an online user from the list and then send a message to that online user. If a response is received from the online user to whom a message was sent, then instant sending and receiving of message takes place. Chat rooms not only provide the sharing of text messages but also allow the users to share images and graphics online.

Apart from e-mail and instant messaging, Internet telephony and web conferencing are the other application areas of the Internet that facilitate, quick, cheap and efficient communication over long distances. Through these mediums, the users can talk to the other uses in real-time through an audio-visual interface.

15.3.4 The Internet in Entertainment

The Internet over the period of time has evolved as a great source of entertainment. It provides many entertainment resources to the users such as games, music and movies. The most popular entertainment resources on the Internet are the games, which are either free of cost or can be bought through the payment of a small price. Multi User Dungeon (MUD) is a virtual environment in which fantasy characters such as warriors, priests and thieves are adopted by end users for playing games. Each user represents a specific character and interacts with other characters with the help of text messages. The information regarding the game and the virtual environment is also provided to the users through commands displayed on the screen. MUD is also available with graphics that enhance the background of the game by providing it a 3-dimensional look. This feature is known as virtual reality because the background and the characters in the game resemble the real world entities.

Apart from games, the Internet also provides many other entertainment resources. Several websites provide easy access to any type of music and videos, which can be freely downloaded on the computers. The Internet also enables the users to share videos and photos with other users. Many websites on the Internet also provide information regarding the sports events taking place at specific period of time. These websites allow the users to access continuous score updates.

15.3.5 The Internet in Government

These days, the Internet is playing a crucial role in the functioning of the government organisations. Almost all the government organisations have set up their websites that provide information related to the organisation as well as help them in performing their operations. For example, nowadays people can submit the passport application form and file the income tax returns through the use of Internet. Moreover, Internet also enables the government agencies to share the data with each other.

The vast use of IT and Internet has paved the way for e-governance. More and more government agencies are adopting the concept of e-governance to improve their service delivery capabilities.

15.4 UNDERSTANDING THE WORLD WIDE WEB

World Wide Web is a collection of web servers, which contain several web pages pertaining to different websites. The web pages contain hypertext, simple text, images, videos and graphics. The web pages are designed with the help of HyperText Markup Language (HTML). To view the web pages provided by a web server, the software known as web browser is required. To display the web pages, a web browser runs the HTML code segment written for a particular web page. Each web page on the Internet is provided its own address known as Uniform Resource Identifier (URI) or URL. This URL helps the web browser in locating a web page on the Internet. A URL string begins with the name of a protocol such as http or ftp that represents the protocol through which a web page is accessed. The rest of the URL string contains the domain server name of the web page being accessed and the location of the web page on the local web server.

15.5 WEB BROWSERS

Web browser is the software, which is used to access the Internet and the WWW. It is basically used to access and view the web pages of the various websites available on the Internet. A web browser provides many advanced features that help achieve easy access to the Internet and WWW. When we open a web browser, the first page, which appears in the web browser window, is the home page set for that particular web browser.

The web browsers are categorised into two categories, text based and Graphical User Interface (GUI) based. The text based browsers are the browsers that display unformatted text contained in the HTML files. These types of browsers do not display images, which are inline with the text contained in the HTML files. However, the text based browsers have the ability of displaying the images that are not inline with the text contained in the HTML files. The text based browsers are simple to use and do not require computers with expensive hardware. They allow the downloading of graphic and sound files but only if the computer contains the software and the hardware required for such files. The GUI based browsers, on the other hand, display formatted text along with images, sounds and videos, which are contained in the HTML files. The user has to just click the mouse button to view or download image, sound and video files. The most commonly used web browsers are Internet Explorer (IE), Netscape Navigator and Mozilla Firefox.

The IE is the most widely used web browser that was developed in 1995 by Microsoft. The first version of IE, i.e., IE 2.0 could be installed and run on the computers with Macintosh and the 32-bit Windows operating systems. IE 2.0 was specially designed to access secure websites, and hence had the capabilities of tracing any kind of errors. To trace the errors and provide secure access to websites, IE 2.0 included a new protocol known as Secure Socket Layer (SSL) protocol. In 1996, the next version, i.e., IE 3.0 was developed, which had many advanced features, such as Internet Mail, Windows Address Book and Window Media Player. This version was basically developed for Windows 95 operating system. In 1997, the next version, IE 4.0 was developed that included Microsoft Outlook Express 4.0, which is e-mail software used for sending and receiving e-mail messages. Microsoft Outlook Express was included with IE 4.0 to provide enhanced Internet mail and news features. The latest version of IE is IE 8.0. It is the most secure web browser as it contains many privacy and safety features as compared to any of the previous versions of IE. The IE 8.0 version supports the latest Windows operating system, i.e., Windows Vista.

To access Internet Explorer on a computer, we need to select Start→Programs→Internet Explorer. The Microsoft Internet Explorer window appears with the home page as shown in Fig. 15.1.

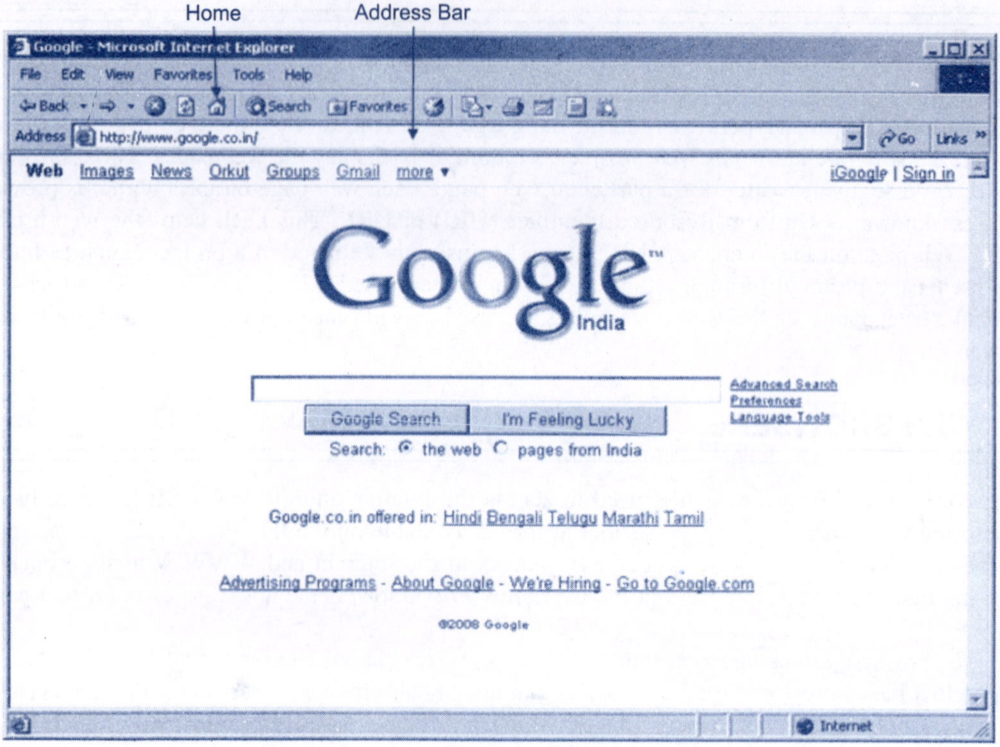

Fig. 15.1 Microsoft Internet Explorer window

Figure 15.1 shows that the home page for the Internet Explorer has been set to the google.com website, which is a search engine that helps in searching information on the Internet. A user can change the home page according to the requirements using the Internet Options option of the Tools menu.

Another commonly used web browser is Netscape Navigator, which was also known as Mozilla during its development phase. This web browser was widely in use in the 1990's. The only advantage of Netscape Navigator over IE is that when a web page is being downloaded, unlike IE in which a blank screen appears some of the text and graphics contained in the web page appears in the case of Netscape Navigator. This prevents the wastage of time as the user can start reading the page even before it is completely downloaded. Initially, Netscape Navigator became very popular because of its advanced features and free availability to all the users. However, its usage declined later in 1995 when it was declared that the web browser was freely available only to the non-profit and educational organisations. Another reason for the decline in the usage of Netscape Navigator is that it was not capable of fixing the errors automatically. On the other hand, IE 4.0 had the feature of automatically fixing errors. As a result, many people suddenly stopped using Netscape Navigator. In order to increase the usage of Netscape Navigator many new features such as mail and news reader were added to its older version. However, these new features affected the speed of the Web browser and increased its size. As a result, Netscape Navigato is rarely being used nowadays.

To access Netscape Navigator, we need to select Start→ Programs→Netscape Communicator Professional Edition→Netscape Navigator. The Netscape window appears with the home page as shown in Fig. 15.2.

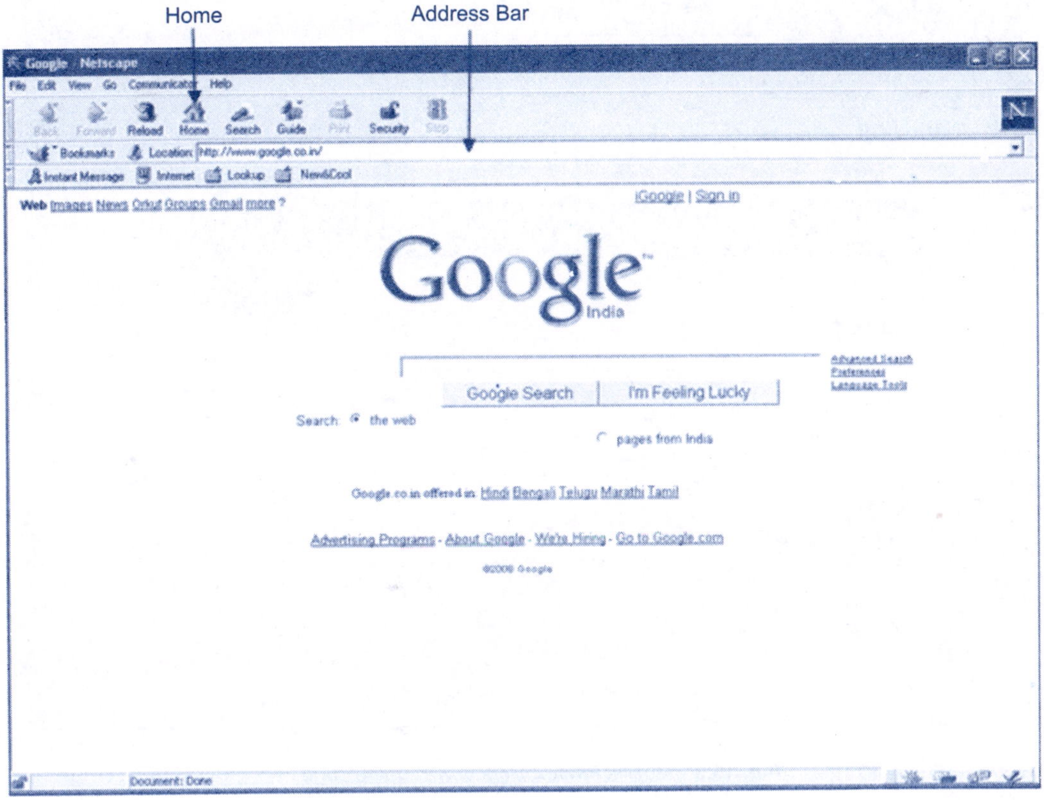

Fig. 15.2 The Netscape window with home page

The third most commonly used web browser is the Mozilla Firefox, which was developed by Dave Hyatt and Blake Ross. Many versions of Mozilla Firefox web browser were developed before it was officially released in November 2004. The latest version of Mozilla Firefox that is currently being used is 2.0.0.14. This version includes many new features such as mail, news and HTML editing. The Firefox web browser uses XML User Interface (XUL), which supports features such as Cascade Spread Sheets (CSS) and JavaScript. XUL provides extensions and themes, which enable a user to increase the capabilities of the Mozilla Firefox web browser. Initially, the Firefox was named as m/b (Mozilla/ Browser) but later its name was changed to Phoenix. The name Phoenix already existed for some BIOS software so the web browser was renamed as Firebird but again the same problem persisted. This was already a name of a popular database server. So, in February 2004 another name, i.e., Mozilla Firefox was given to the web browser that persists till today. To access Mozilla Firefox, we need to select Start → Programs→Mozilla Firefox→Mozilla Firefox. The Mozilla Firefox window appears with the home page as shown in Fig. 15.3.

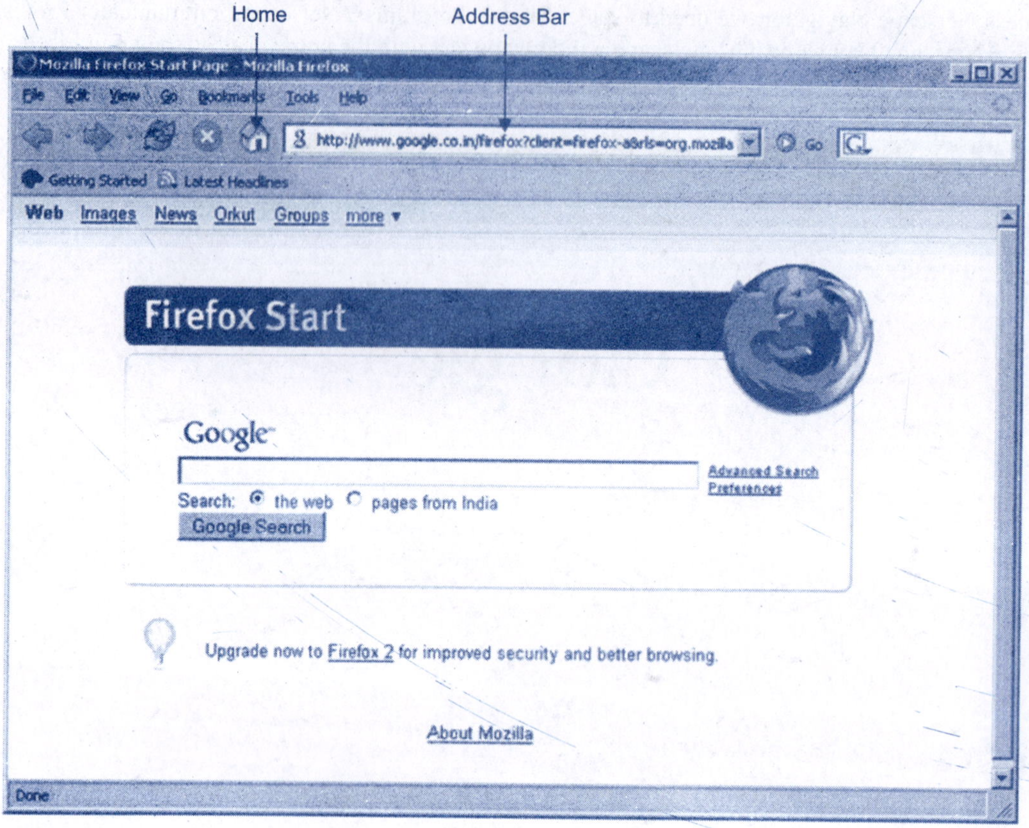

Fig. 15.3 Mozilla Firefox window with home page

15.6 BROWSING THE INTERNET

Browsing the Internet is the process of accessing different websites available on the Internet using a web browser. To browse the Internet, we need to first connect our computer to the Internet through a connection provided by an ISP. To connect to the Internet, a modem is also required. Modem is a device that converts analog signals into digital signals and vice versa. In addition, a telephone line is required for connecting the computer to the server of the ISP. After connecting to the Internet, we can perform the following steps to browse the Internet using IE web browser:

1. Select Start → Programs → Internet Explorer to display the Microsoft Internet Explorer window.
2. Type the URL of the website, which you want to access such as java.sun.com in the address bar that appears at the top in the Microsoft Internet Explorer window.
3. Press the Enter key to display the home page of the java.sun.com website as shown in Fig. 15.4.

Fig. 15.4 Accessing an Internet website

When browsing the Internet, we can use one of the important features, favourites, of the IE web browser. This feature allows us to easily and quickly access the frequently visited websites. In other words, the favourites features allows the users who are browsing the Internet to keep a record of all the websites that are their favourites and are required to be accessed on a frequent basis. This feature also proves to be handy when a user wants to avoid the tedious task of remembering the URL of the websites, which are frequently accessed by that user. Users can simply add the websites, which are frequently accessed by them in the list of favourites so that they can be easily accessed in the future without remembering their URLs. To access a website, which has been added to the favourites, we can use the Favourites menu or the Favourites button, which appears in the Standard toolbar. When we click the Favourites button in the toolbar, the Favourites pane appears as shown in Fig. 15.5.

The Favourites pane contains a list of names of the websites, which have been added to favourites. We can now click a specific name in the Favourites pane to access the corresponding website quickly.

Fig. 15.5 The Favourites pane

We can also use another important feature, i.e., 'search' available in IE web browser when browsing the Internet. The search feature allows us to search for information on a specific topic. If a user is not aware of any website, which contains the desired information, then the user can use the search feature of the IE web browser. When a user searches for information through the search feature of IE, then a list of websites containing the related information is displayed. To search for information using the search feature of IE, we can click the Search button, which appears in the Standard toolbar. The Search pane appears as shown in Fig. 15.6.

In the Search pane, you can type a word in the Find a Web page containing text box related to the topic on which you want to search the information. After typing the word, click the Search button to search the information related to the topic.

Note: *Apart from Favourites and Search features, the Standard toolbar of the IE web browser contains other options like Home, Next, Previous etc, which are used for performing different functions.*

Fig. 15.6 The Search pane

15.7 USING A SEARCH ENGINE

Search engines are the websites that provide the users the facility of searching for information related to some topic. The search engines maintain an index of websites available on the Internet along with a summary of the content contained in these websites. The summary of the content is displayed when a user searches for information on some topic. We can use a number of techniques to make the process of searching the information using search engines efficient and useful. These techniques are as follows:

- **Use of double quotes (" ")** Double quotes are used to search for a phrase collectively. Generally, a search engine provides a list of websites that contains any of the words contained in the text specified for searching of information. However, if a user wants the search engine to consider the entire text specified for searching as a single phrase, then that user should provide the text in double quotes. For example, suppose a user wants to search the information related to the topic, types of computers. In this case, if the user specifies the text, types of computers, without double quotes for searching the information, then the search engine will display all websites, which either contain the word, types or the word, computers. However, if a user wants that a search engine should regard the text, history of the Internet as a single phrase, then the user must provide the text in double quotes as "types of computers". This will make the search more efficient.
- **Use of Boolean operators** Boolean operators such as AND, OR and NOT can also be used in the text specified for searching information in order to make the search process more efficient. The Boolean AND operators can be used to search for websites, which contain the information related to two words such as computer and hard disk. The Boolean OR can be used to search for websites, which contain either of the two words. The Boolean NOT can be used to search for the websites, which contain the information other than the information related to the word specified after the NOT operator. For example, if a user is searching for some information regarding track ball present in the mouse, then the user can specify the text "track ball OR touch ball" for searching the information as

both of the words mean the same. So, now the search engine will search and display all the websites containing either of the words.

- **Use of plus (+) and minus (-) sign** Plus (+) sign is used to search the websites in which all the words included in the text specified for searching are present. Minus (–) sign is used to search all the websites in which the words included in the text specified for searching are not present. For example, suppose a user wants to search the features of a mouse, then the user has to specify the text "features + mouse" for searching the information related to the features of the mouse. The Internet search engine will list all the web pages containing the words, features and mouse.

Some of the search engines that are commonly used by the users are www.google.com, www.altavista.com, www.askjeeves.com, www.search.yahoo.com and www.ask.com. Among these search engines, www.google.com is the most popular search engine, which is used worldwide. To use the google.com search engine for searching information, the user has to perform certain steps, which are as follows:

1. Open IE web browser. The Microsoft Internet Explorer window appears.
2. Type the URL, google.com in the address bar, which appears at the top in the Microsoft Internet Explorer window.
3. Press Enter to open the home page of the google.com search engine as shown in Fig. 15.7.

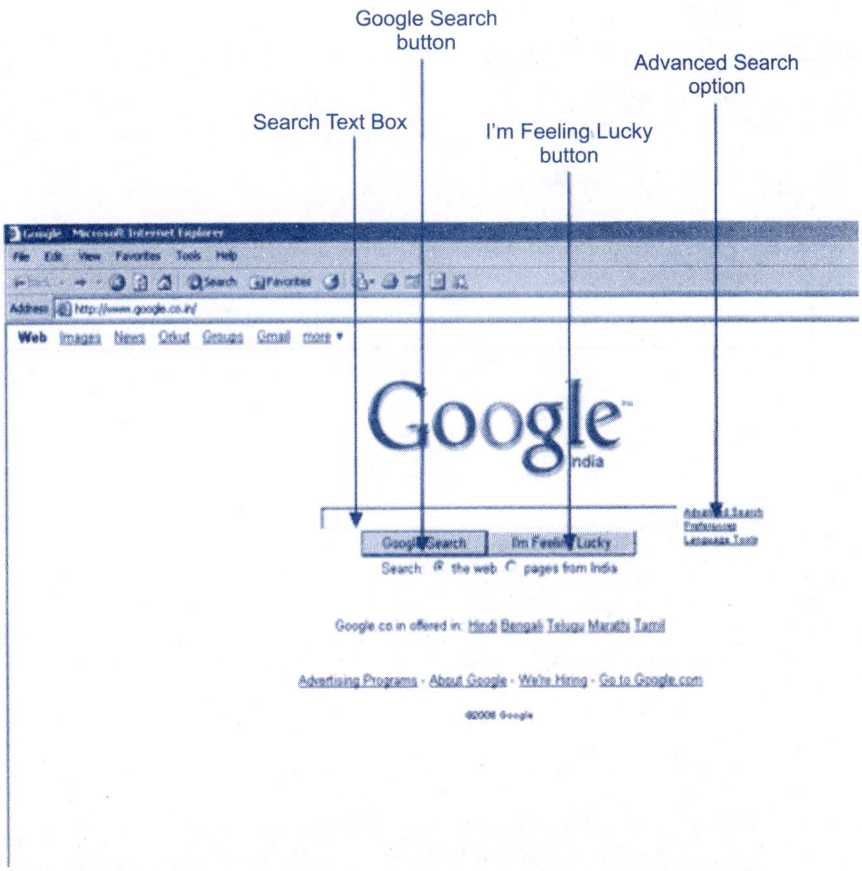

Fig. 15.7 The home page of google.com search engine

Figure 15.7 shows that the home page of the google.com search engine contains a text box in which we can specify the text for searching information. It also contains two buttons, Google Search and I'm feeling Lucky. The Google Search button is used to initiate the searching process using the google.com search engine. I'm Feeling Lucky button is used to display the first website returned as a search result corresponding to the specified text. The home page of the Google.com search engine also contains the following options:

- **The web** This option allows us to search the WWW for getting the information on a specific topic.
- **Pages from India** This option allows us to search the pages submitted from India for information on specific topic.
- **Advanced search** This option allows us to specify certain advanced settings for making the search more specific and efficient.

1. Type some text such as mouse + computers in the search text box to specify the text on the basis of which information will be searched.
2. Click the Google Search button or press the Enter key to initiate the process of searching the information related to mouse. A list of websites containing information related to the specified text such as mouse gets displayed as shown in Fig. 15.8.

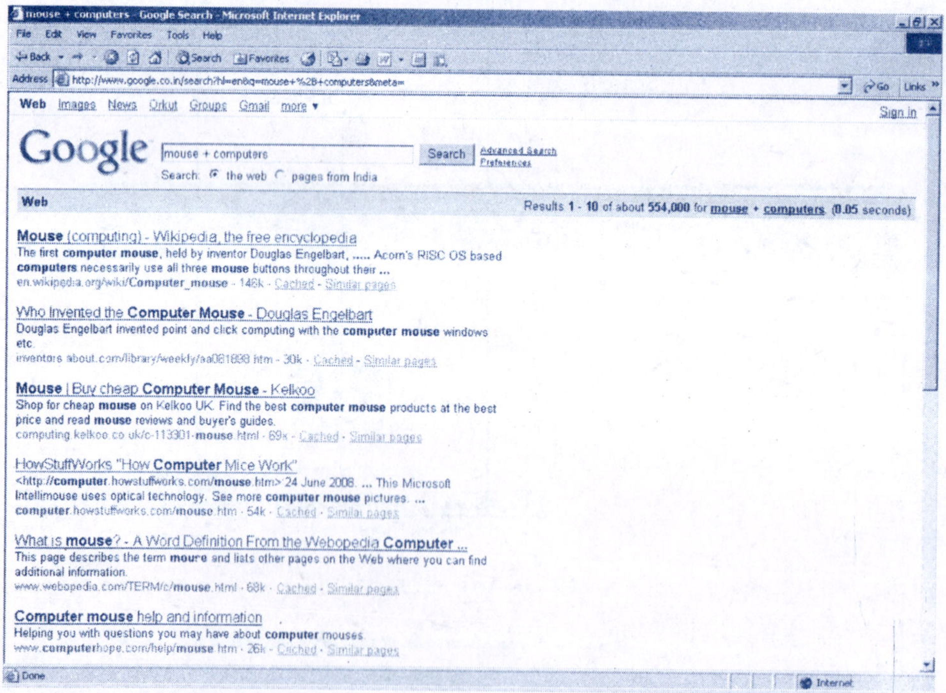

Fig. 15.8 The search results from google.com search engine

In Fig. 15.8, the blue text in the search result is the hypertext through which the web page containing the required information can be accessed and the green text represents the URL of the website to which the web page belongs. The user has to click the hypertext to view the web page containing the required information.

15.8 EMAIL SERVICE

Email service provided by the Internet is a very effective means of communication as it allows two persons in remote places to communicate with each other. To use the e-mail service, a user must have a valid email account. There are two ways in which a user can obtain an email account. The first way is to obtain an email account from an ISP. A user can obtain an email account from an ISP when that user registers with the ISP. To register, a user has to firstly purchase an Internet connection package offered by an ISP.

After purchasing the Internet connection package, the user registers with the ISP by providing information such as name, address, username and password in the registration form available on the website of the ISP. The user is then provided an email account and an email address by the ISP. The email address consists of two parts separated by @ sign such as shruti_garg@yahoo.com. The first part written before @ symbol in the email address is the unique identity of the user who uses the email service on the Internet. The other part written after @ symbol is the name of the website, which provides the email service. In case a user is using the email account of an ISP, the part after the @ sign will consist of the name of the website owned by the ISP. No two users can have the same email addresses.

The second way to obtain an email account is to get registered on one of the websites such as hotmail.com and yahoo.com, which provide free e-mail facility to their users. To register, a user must first access one of these websites using a web browser. After accessing the website, the user must provide information such as username, password, name and address in the registration form and finally the user must submit the form to register on to the website. When the user has successfully registered, an email account is opened for the user and an e-mail address is also provided. The user can now access the email account by providing a valid username and password in the home page of the website such as hotmail.com and yahoo.com for using the email service of the Internet.

The email service can be used by a user to send and receive email messages. An email message has two sections, a header section and a body section. The header section contains the information about the sender, the receiver and the subject of the email message. It consists of the fields such as to, cc and subject. The to field contains the email address of the person to whom the e-mail message is to be sent. The cc field or the carbon copy field contains the email addresses of other persons to whom a copy of the e-mail message has to be sent. The body section contains the actual text message, which has to be sent. This section also contains a signature block at the end where the sender places his/her signature.

15.9 PROTOCOLS USED FOR THE INTERNET

The Internet is a collection of computers, which are connected to each other for the purpose of sharing of information. To share information, data has to be transferred from one computer to another. When data is transferred between computers, certain rules called protocols have to be followed. The protocols perform different tasks, which are arranged in a vertical stack and each task is performed at a different layer. The computer, which sends the data to another computer, is called source computer. On the other hand, the computer, which receives the data from another computer, is called destination computer. At the time of transferring of data from the source to the destination computer, a protocol is responsible for determining the network to which the destination computer belongs. It is also responsible for defining the procedure, which must be followed for dividing the data into packets. The protocols are also responsible for detection of errors in the data packets and the correction of these errors or loss of data packets. In addition, it is the responsibility of the protocols to identify loss of connection between the computers in a network and help the users to establish the connection again.

Each computer on a network has a unique address, which is known as the Internet Protocol (IP) address. An IP address is a group of four numbers and the numbers are separated from each other by a dot. When any data is sent from one computer to another computer over the network, it is divided into small modules known as packets or datagrams. These packets are transmitted on the network by the Internet Protocol. Each packet transmitted on the network contains the addresses of both source and destination computer. A gateway present on the network reads the address of the destination computer and sends the data to the specified address. Gateway is a computer, which contains the software required for the transmission of data over different networks. Each packet on the network is an independent entity, so they are transferred through different routes to reach the destination computer. The packets received at the destination are not in the same sequence in which they were transmitted. As a result, these packets are arranged in a right sequence by a protocol known as Transmission Control Protocol (TCP) and then are merged at the destination to form the complete data. TCP and IP work in coordination with other protocols such as Telnet and User Datagram Protocol (UDP) but are considered as the most fundamental of all protocols. All these protocols are collectively known as TCP/IP suite. A model known as TCP/IP model determines how the protocols of the TCP/IP suite will work together for the transfer of data between computers in a network

15.9.1 TCP/IP Model

The TCP/IP model was initially developed by US Defence Advanced Research Projects Agency (DARPA). This model is also known as the Internet Reference model or DoD model. It consists of four layers, namely, application layer, transport layer, network layer, and physical layer. Figure 15.9 shows the four layers of TCP/IP model.

The physical layer in the TCP/IP model is responsible for interacting with the medium of transmission of data, whereas the application layer helps in interacting with the users. The four layers of TCP/IP and the functions performed by these layers are as follows:

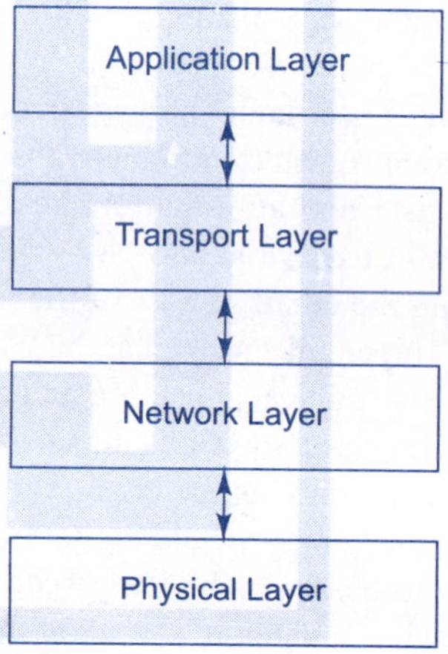

Fig. 15.9 Layers of TCP/IP model

- **Application layer** The application layer is responsible for managing all the user interface requirements. Many of the protocols, such as telnet, FTP, SMTP, DNS, NFS, LPD, SNMP and DHCP work on this layers.
- **Transport layer** The transport layer is responsible for the delivery of packets or datagrams. It also hides the packet routing details from the upper layer, i.e., the application layer. In addition, the transport layer allows detection and correction of errors and helps to achieve end-to-end communication between devices. The transport layer connects the application layer to the network layer through two protocols, namely, TCP and UDP.
- **Network layer** The network layer is also known as Internetworking layer or IP layer. It contains three protocols that perform different functions. The three protocols of Network layer are as follows:
  - **a.** ***Internet Protocol (IP)*** IP is a connectionless protocol that is responsible for the delivery of packets. The IP protocol contains all the address and control information for each transmitted packet.
  - **b.** ***Internet Control Message Protocol (ICMP)*** The ICMP protocol is responsible for reporting errors, sending error messages and controlling the flow of packets. It is more reliable than the IP as it is capable of determining errors during data transmission.

c. ***Address Resolution Protocol (ARP)*** It is responsible for determining the Media Access Control (MAC) address corresponding to an IP address. It sends an ARP request on the network for a particular IP address and the device, which identifies the IP address as its own, returns an ARP reply along with its MAC address.

- **Physical layer** The physical layer is responsible for collecting packets so that the frames, which are transmitted on the network, can be formed. It performs all the functions required to transmit the data on the network and determines the ways for accessing the medium through which data will be transmitted. This layer does not contain any protocols but instead of protocols, it contains some standards such as RS-232C, V.35 and IEEE 802.3.

15.9.2 OSI Model

Open System Interconnection (OSI) is a layered design that defines the functions of the protocols used in a computer network. It consists of seven layers where each layer provides some services to the next layer. Figure 15.10 shows the seven layers of OSI model.

The seven layers of the OSI model and the functions performed by them are as follows:

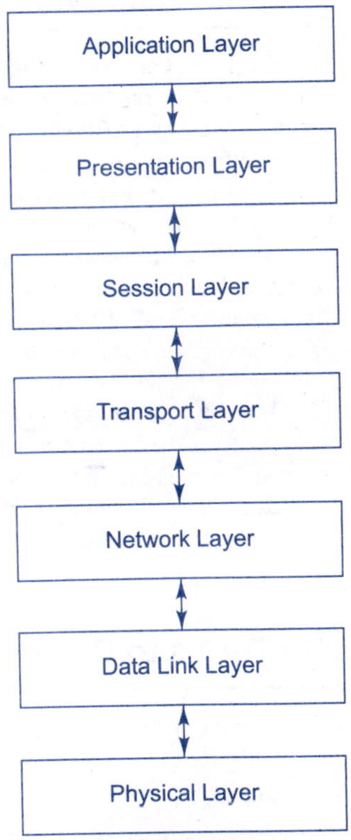

Fig. 15.10 OSI model

- **Application layer** The application layer provides an interface through which users can communicate and transfer data on the network.
- **Presentation layer** The presentation layer determines the way in which the data is presented to different computers. It converts the data into a particular format, which is supported by a specific computer. It is also responsible for encrypting, decrypting, compressing and decompressing of data.
- **Session layer** The session layer manages the communication between the computers on the network. This layer is responsible for notifying the errors, which may have occurred in the layers above it. It is also responsible for setting up and breaking the connection between the computers or devices.
- **Transport layer** The transport layer is responsible for the delivery of packets in a proper sequence. It also provides proper rectification of errors and manages the flow of packets over the network. This layer ensures that data is properly delivered at the destination. It also keeps track of all the packets, which fail to reach the destination, and transmits them again.
- **Network layer** The network layer is responsible for identifying the ways in which the data is transmitted over the network from one device to another. It prevents the overloading of packets on the network and maintains the proper flow so that all the resources on the network can be used efficiently by all. The network layer directs the packets to the destination device on the basis of the IP address of the device. It detects the errors, which occur during the transmission of packets. This layer is also responsible for breaking the large size packets into smaller packets when the device is unable to accept the packets due to their large size.

- **Data link layer** The data link layer specifies the actions, which must be performed to maintain the network communication. It collects the packets to form frames, which are then transmitted over the network. It also finds out and then corrects the errors, which occur during the transmission of packets.
- **Physical layer** The physical layer describes all the physical requirements for the transmission of data between devices on a network. For example, the physical layer can specify the layout of pins, hubs and cables. This layer defines the relation between a single device and the transmission medium. It specifies the way in which a device must transmit data and also the way in which another device must receive data. This layer is responsible for the setting up and ending up of a network connection.

Chapter Summary

A collection of networks in which a large number of computers are connected to each other is known as the Internet. The Internet marked its beginning with a network known as ARPAnet which was developed at Advanced Research Projects Agency (ARPA) of the U S in 1969. The first protocol used on the ARPAnet was TCP/IP. From 1975 to 1982, different scientists developed many new networks, such as Telnet, Usenet and Eunet. All these continuous developments led to the eventual development of the Internet.

The Internet can be used to gather information on a wide variety of topics. Today the Internet is used in many fields such as business, education and entertainment. In business, the most popular use of the Internet is e-business through which an organisation and a consumer can communicate with each other and perform business transactions. In education field, the students use discussion forums and newsgroups on the Internet to gain specific information. The internet also extends its application in communication field by providing services such as e-mail and instant messaging through which a person at one location can communicate to another person located at a remote place. The Internet also provides entertainment through games, music and movies.

To access the Internet and the WWW, the user requires a software known as web browser. Some commonly used web browsers are IE, Netscape Navigator and Mozilla Firefox. To gather information from the Internet, a user has to search for the information on the Internet. This is done with the help of search engines provided on the Internet. The most commonly used search engines are www.google.com, www.altavista.com and www.askjeeves.com.

Key Terms to Remember

- **Internet**: The Internet is a large network of computers placed at different locations around the world that are connected to each other through telephone lines and satellites.
- **WWW**: The WWW is a collection of interlinked hypertext documents stored on computers all around the world.
- **Web page**: Web page is a formatted document stored on a web server that can be accessed to gather information.
- **Web server**: Web server is a computer that contains the web pages corresponding to the websites available on the Internet.
- **Web browser**: Web browser is a software, which is used to access the Internet and the WWW.
- **Search engines**: Search engines are websites, which provide the users the facility of searching for information related to some topic.
- **Email**: Email is a service provided by the Internet that allows two persons in remote places to communicate with each other.
- **ISP**: An ISP is an organisation that provides the Internet connection services to people who want to use Internet.
- **Hypertext**: Hypertext is that text on a web page which when clicked provides an access to the other web pages.

- **Gateway**: Gateway is a computer, which contains all the software required for the transmission of data over different networks.
- **Protocol**: Protocol is the set of rules and methods that are to be followed to transfer data from one computer to another on a network.
- **IP (Internet Protocol)**: IP is a protocol that is responsible for the routing of data on the network.

Review Questions

Fill in the Blanks

1. _________ provides the facility of information sharing and communication between users.
2. WWW refers to _________ __________ __________.
3. Each web page is accessed on a network using __________.
4. _________ was the network founded at the Advanced Research Projects Agency (ARPA) of United States in 1969.
5. ARPAnet used the concept of ____________ to transfer the data from one computer to another.
6. The methods and the rules followed to transfer data on a network are known as _________.
7. _________ is the unique address of a computer on the network.
8. _________ is a network, which provides mail and news services to the users.
9. _________ converts domain names to corresponding IP addresses.
10. _________ refers to the business transactions conducted on the Internet.
11. _________ service of the Internet is used to perform real-time communication on the Internet.
12. _________ allows the users to search for some information on the Internet.
13. An email message consists of two sections _________ and __________.
14. The web pages are designed with the help of ______________.
15. XML User Interface (XUL) supports features such as _________ and __________.
16. The TCP/IP model contains four layers, which are ________, ________, ________ and ________.
17. The two types of web browsers are _______ and ________.
18. An OSI model is also referred as _____________.

Multiple Choice Questions

1. Which of the services of Internet allows the users to gather information from the Internet?
   A. Email B. Discussion forums C. WWW D. Instant messaging
2. What is the address of a computer on a network known as?
   A. URL B. IP address C. Host D. Domain name
3. When was the ARPAnet developed?
   A. 1945 B. 1967 C. 1969 D. 1959
4. Which type of e-business transactions take place on the e-bay website?
   A. B2B B. B2C C. C2C D. C2B

5. Which of the following allows the users to share articles on the Internet?
   A. Newsgroups B. Email C. Instant messaging D. None of the above
6. What is the name of the procedure followed before allowing a user to use email services?
   A. Check in B. Login C. Set in D. None of the above
7. Which service of the Internet provides real-time communication?
   A. Email B. Newsgroup C. Instant messaging D. MUD
8. Which of the following tasks can be performed using the Internet?
   A. Book air tickets B. Shop for clothing
   C. Check the bank statement D. All of the above
9. Which of the following are mentioned in a URL?
   A. Domain name B. IP address C. Hypertext D. None of the above
10. Which of the following are the most commonly used search engines?
    A. www.google.search.com B. www.yahoo.com
    C. www.search.yahoo.com D. www.search. google.com
11. Which of the following are the sections of an email message?
    A. Address B. Message C. Header D. Footer
12. At which layer of the TCP/IP model IP, ICMP and ARP protocols function?
    A. Physical layer B. Application layer C. Network layer D. Transport layer
13. How many layers are there in a TCP/IP model?
    A. 2 layers B. 5 layers C. 7 layers D. 4 layers
14. Which of the following are the protocols that work at the application layer of the TCP/IP model?
    A. FTP B. SMTP C. IP D. ARP
15. How many layers does an OSI model contain?
    A. 2 layers B. 5 layers C. 7 layers D. 4 layers
16. Which layer in the OSI model prevents the overloading of packets on the network?
    A. Data link layer B. Application layer C. Network layer D. Session layer
17. Which of the following are the examples of a web browser?
    A. Net navigator B. Mozilla foxfire
    C. IE D. Netscape communicator
18. What is the function of a DNS?
    A. To convert domain names into IP addresses B. To convert IP addresses into domain names
    C. Both A and B D. None of the above
19. Which layer in a TCP/IP model does not contain any protocols?
    A. Transport layer B. Application layer C. Network layer D. Physical layer
20. The term ISP stands for?
    A. Information System Protocol B. Internet System Protocol
    C. Internet Service Provider D. Information Service Provider

Discussion Questions

1. Define Internet.
2. What do you mean by WWW?
3. Write a short note on the history of the Internet.
4. Explain the layers of TCP/IP model using a diagram.
5. Explain briefly the layers of the OSI model.
6. What are the various applications of the Internet?
7. Explain the various classifications of e-business.
8. Define search engine. Explain the techniques used while searching for information through a search engine.
9. What is a web browser? Write a short note on any one of the most commonly used web browsers.
10. Explain the email service provided by the Internet.
11. What is the difference between discussion forums and newsgroups?
12. What is the use of the Internet in education field?
13. What are the two types of web browsers? Explain.
14. Explain the use of Instant messaging service provided by the Internet.
15. Name some of the most commonly used search engines.
16. What do you mean by URL?
17. Explain the term DNS. Why is it used?
18. Explain the protocols, which work at the transport layer of TCP/IP model.
19. What is the difference between email and instant messaging services of the Internet?
20. Differentiate between the Internet and the WWW.

CHAPTER 16

INTRODUCTION TO C PROGRAMMING

Chapter Outline

Chapter Objectives

In this chapter, we will learn:

- The evolution of C programming language.
- The character set, keywords and data types used in C.
- The use of preprocessor directives in C programs.
- The use of various types of constants and variables in C.
- The different operators and statements used in C.
- The control statements used in C programs.
- The use of arrays and strings in C.
- The concept of functions in C.
- The use of structures and pointers in C programs.
- File handling in C.

16.1 INTRODUCTION

C is a powerful, portable and elegantly structured programming language. It combines the features of a high-level language with the elements of an assembler and therefore, it is suitable for writing both system software and application packages. It is the most widely used general-purpose language today. In fact, C has been used for implementing systems such as operating systems, compilers, linkers, word processors and utility packages.

16.1.1 History of C

C was evolved from the earlier languages such as ALGOL, BCPL and B by **Dennis Ritchie** at the Bell Laboratories in USA in 1972. ALGOL, developed in early 1960s, gave the concept of structured programming to the computer science community. BCPL (Basic Combined Programming Language) was developed by Martin Richards in 1967 primarily for writing system software. In 1970, **Ken Thomson** created a language using many features of BCPL and called it simply B. The earlier versions of UNIX operating system were implemented using B. Both BCPL and B were 'type-less' languages as they did not define and use any data types. C developed in 1972 borrowed many ideas from these languages and added the concept of data types and other powerful features. During 1970s, C has evolved into a powerful language for development of operating systems and compilers. It became popular among the programming community when **Brian Kerningham** and **Dennis Ritchie** published their book 'The C Programming Language' in 1978. In 1983, American National Standards Institute (ANSI) adopted C language to bring in some standards to the language and a version known as *ANSI C* was approved in 1989. This remains as a standard even today. This version of C is also referred to as C89.

During 1990s, some of the features of later languages like C++ and Java were added to C and in 1999, the Standardisation Committee of C announced a new version of C known as *C99*.

16.1.2 Characteristics of C

The increasing popularity of C is probably due to its many desirable qualities. Some of the important characteristics are:

- It is a highly structured language.
- It uses features of high-level languages.
- It can handle bit-level operations.
- C is a machine independent language and therefore highly portable.
- It supports a variety of data types and a powerful set of operators.
- It supports dynamic memory management by using the concept of pointers.
- It enables the implementation of hierarchical and modular programming with the help of functions.
- C can extend itself by addition of functions to its library continuously.

16.1.3 A Simple C Program

A very simple C program is given below:

```
#include<stdio.h>
  void main()
  {
printf("This is a sample C program\n");
  }
```

This program, although a very simple one, illustrates a few important points to note:

- Every C program contains a function called main. This is the starting point of the program.
- **#include <stdio.h>** is a preprocessor directive, which enables the program to interact with the I/O units. We will find this at the beginning of almost every C program.
- **main()** declares the start of the program, while the curly brackets specify the beginning and end of the main function. (In C, curly brackets are used to group statements together.)
- The only executable statement in the program
  printf("This is a sample C program\n");

will print the text enclosed in double quotes on the screen. The **\n** at the end of the text tells the computer to take the cursor to the next line after printing the text.

- Every executable statement in C will end with a semicolon.

In this chapter, we shall discuss briefly the various components and features of C language that are essential to develop useful C programs.

16.2 CHARACER SET, KEYWORDS AND DATA TYPES

Character set, keywords and data types are considered the basic building blocks of C programs. In order to construct a C program, programmers generally make use of character set, keywords and data types. With the help of these building blocks, the intended meaning of the program can be clearly reflected to the user.

16.2.1 Character Set

The character set of C defines the characters, which can be used by the programmers during programming. Figure 16.1 shows the character set used in C.

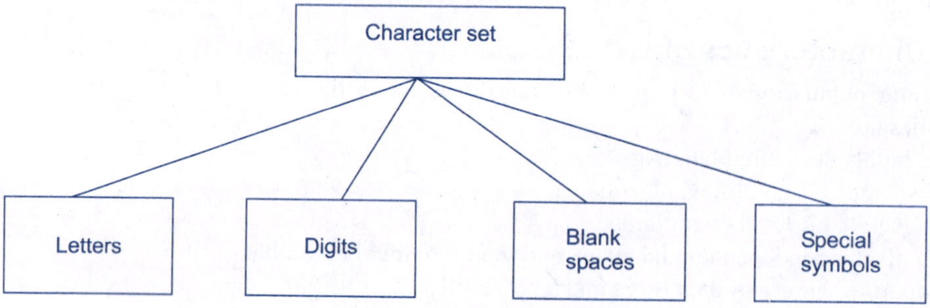

Fig. 16.1 Character set of C

- **Letters and digits** Letters and digits are essential characters required for developing a program. Table 16.1 lists the letters and digits, which can be used in C.

Table 16.1 Letters and digits of a character set

Characters	Format
Letters	A to Z a to z
Digits	0 to 9

- **Blank spaces** Blank spaces hold no relevance in C program, as they are not considered by the compiler during the compilation of a program. It is not allowed to insert blank spaces between keywords and identifiers. The keywords are the special words used in C, and the identifiers are used for naming variables, constants and functions. Blank spaces are used while writing the strings in the program. The following are the different types of blank spaces, which are allowed in C programs:
  - ***Single space*** It creates a gap of single character between two strings.
  - ***Tab*** It creates a gap of 1 inch or 2 inch between the strings depending on the settings of the tab on the ruler.

- o ***Form feed*** It works with printer and causes the printer to skip the current page and move to the starting of the next page.
- o ***Carriage return*** It causes the cursor to move from the current location to the starting of the line.
- o ***New line*** It causes the cursor to move from the current line to the next line.

- **Special symbols** Some special symbols can also be used in C. Table 16.2 lists the special symbols used in C.

Table 16.2 Special symbols

Special symbol	Name	Special symbol	Name
!	Exclamation sign	{	Left braces
#	Pound sign	}	Right braces
$	Dollar sign	[	Left bracket
%	Percentage sign	]	Right bracket
^	Caret	\	Backward slash
&	Ampersand	/	Forward slash
*	Asterisk	,	Comma sign
(	Left parenthesis	.	Period
)	Right parenthesis	;	Semicolon
_	Underscore	:	Colon
-	Minus sign	‘	Apostrophe
+	Plus sign	“	Quotation marks
?	Question mark	~	Tilde

16.2.2 Keywords

Keywords, also known as reserved words, are the special words reserved by C. The meaning of each keyword is pre-defined to the compiler and cannot be changed. Keywords are case sensitive and are written in lower case. The number of keywords supported by C varies depending on the version of C in use but generally 32 keywords are supported by C. Table 16.3 lists the keywords used in C.

Table 16.3 Keywords used in C

auto	else	long	switch
break	else if	register	then
char	extern	Return	typedef
const	float	Short	union
continue	For	signed	unsigned
default	goto	sizeof	void
do	if	static	volatile
double	int	struct	while

16.2.3 Data Types

Data type refers to the structural format of the data used in the program. Data type provides the users with the flexibility of using any type of data while programming. C supports a large number of data types. Figure 16.2 shows the different data types supported by C.

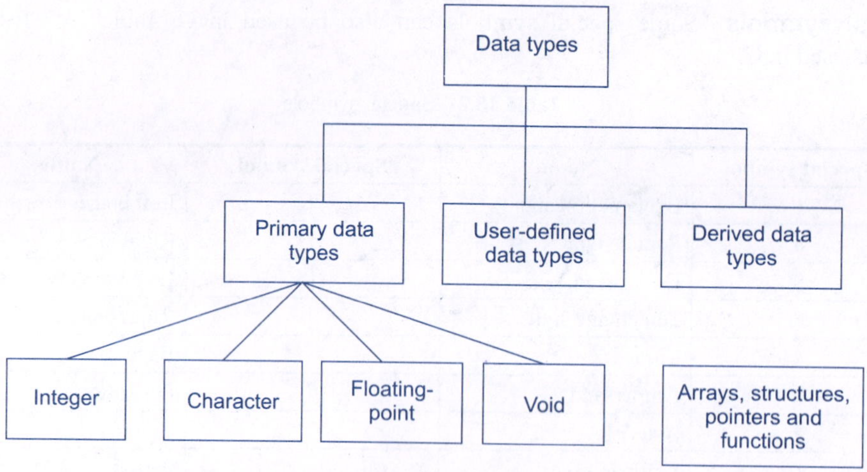

Fig. 16.2 Data types

The main data types supported by C are:

- Primary data types
- Derived data types
- User-defined data types

Primary data types Primary data types are the data types that are supported by all the compilers of C. Primary data types include integer, character, float, double and void that are represented in the programs as **int**, **char**, **float**, **double** and **void** respectively. Each of these data types occupies different amount of space in memory and can store different values of data depending on the range of the particular data type. Table 16.4 lists primary data types, their size and range.

Table 16.4 Size and range of primary data types

Data type	Size (in bytes)	Range of values
int	2	– 32768 to 32767
char	1	– 128 to 127
float	4	3.4e – 38 to 3.4e+e38

Integer data type Integer data type supports integer values within a specific range as defined by the compiler. In C, there are two forms of integers, **signed** and **unsigned**. In the signed form, the integers are represented with a + or – minus sign, and in the unsigned form, no sign is used. If no sign is used with the integer, then by default the integer is considered positive. Integers are stored in the memory using three storage classes, namely, **int**, **short int** and **long int**. Generally, **int** data type is used to store the integer values, **short int** is used to store integers that have small value and **long int** is used to store integers that have large value. All these three classes can hold integers in different ranges. Table 16.5 lists the range of different classes of integer data type.

Table 16.5 Size and range of integer data type

Data type	Size (in bytes)	Range of values
Unsigned integer		
int	2	0 to 65535
short int	1	0 to 255
long int	4	0 to 4, 294, 967, 295
Signed integers		
int	2	– 32768 to 32767
short int	1	– 128 to 127
long int	4	– 2,147,483,648 to 2,147,483,647

The signed and the unsigned integers are represented in the program using the **signed** or the **unsigned** keyword followed by **int**, **short int** or **long int**.

Character data type Character data type is used to store the alphanumeric data, such as letters, digits and symbols. This data type is also available in two forms, signed and unsigned. Both the forms can store the data in different ranges. **Signed char** data type can hold the values in the range of 0 to 255 and the **unsigned char** can hold the values in the range of –128 to 127.

Float data type This data type is used to store the real numbers with 6 digits precision. This data type is further divided into two more data types, **double** and **long double**. If the representation of the number written in float data type is not accurate, then double data type is used. **Double data type** represents the numbers with more accuracy as it uses a 14 digit precision. **Long double data type** is used for the representation of the larger numbers with better accuracy and larger precision. Table 16.6 lists the size and the range of values of float data types.

Table 16.6 Size and range of float data types

Data type	Size (in bytes)	Range of values
float	4	3.4E – 38 to 3.4E+38
double	8	1.7E – 308 to 1.7E+308
long double	10	3.4E – 4932 to 1.1E+4932

Void data type This data type is also known as empty data type as it does not contain any value. **Void** data is generally used for the declaration of the functions, which do not return any value. Variables can also be declared void but they are of no use in the program as they cannot be assigned any value and cannot be casted to any other data type.

16.3 PREPROCESSOR DIRECTIVES

Preprocessor directives are used to specify special instructions in a program which are processed before the actual program is executed. Preprocessor directives are recognised by the hash sign, #, placed before them. Semicolon is not placed at the end of these statements as is done in the case of other statements in C. These statements usually get completed in a single line and are not continued to the next line. The common preprocessor directives are given below:

- **#define** This directive is used to define constants or macros using the following syntax:

```
#define <identifier> <replacement name>
```

The execution of this directive will replace the identifier coming anywhere in the code with the replacement name. For example, suppose max_marks is the identifier, which is to be replaced by 100 everywhere in the program. It can be implemented as follows using the #define directive:

```
#define max_marks 100
int marks1[max_marks];
int marks2[max_marks];
```

The code will now become equivalent to the following statements:

```
int marks1[100];
int marks2[100];
```

- **#undef** This directive is used to undefine a macro, which has been defined before so that it can be defined for a different value. To undefine a defined macro, the following syntax is used:

```
#undef Name
```

For example, the identifier max_marks is undefined as follows:

```
#undef max_marks
```

- **#include** This directive is used to include another file in the program. It can include file using the following two ways:

```
#include <filename>
#include "filename"
```

If the name of the file to be included is specified within <> symbol, then the compiler will search the file in the directory specified as the include directory. So, the standard header files are generally specified within angular quotes. If the name of the file to be included is specified within " " symbol, then the compiler searches the file in all the directories in the current drive.

Some directives are used to compile a part of the program based on certain conditions. It means that if a specific condition is fulfilled, then the program will be executed otherwise not. These conditional directives are # if, # ifdef, # ifndef, # elif, # else and # endif.

- **#ifdef** This directive is used to compile a part of the program only if the macro is defined as a parameter in the program irrespective of its value. The use of #ifdef can be explained with the help of the following example:

```
#ifdef max_marks
int marks[max_marks];
#endif
```

In this example, the second statement will be executed only if the macro max_marks has been defined before in the program. If it has not been defined previously, then the int statement will not be included in the program execution.

- **#ifndef** This directive is the opposite of #ifdef directive. It means that the statements written between #ifndef and #endif will be executed only if the identifier has not been defined previously. The use of #ifnfdef can be explained with the help the following example:

```
#ifndef max_marks
#define max_marks 100
#endif
```

According to this directive, the second statement will be executed only if the macro max_marks has not been defined earlier.

- **#if, #else, #elif** These directives are used in between a program to allow or prevent the further execution of the program. #if is used to check whether the result of a given expression is zero or not. If the result is not zero, then the statements after #if are compiled else not. The use of #if, #else and #elif can be explained with the help of the following example:

```
main()
{
#if AGE<=18
statement 1;
    statement 2;
#elif AGE>=40
    Statement 3;
#else
    statement 4;
    statement 5;
#endif
}
```

- **#line** This directive allows both the file name and the line number at which the error occurred during the compilation of the program to be displayed by the compiler. The syntax of this directive is given below:

```
#line number "filename"
```

- **#error** This directive stops the compilation of the program when the compiler encounters an error, which can be specified as a parameter.

16.4 CONSTANTS AND VARIABLE TYPES

Constants and variables are used in C for holding the data values in a program. Constants hold values, which cannot be changed throughout the program; whereas variables hold values, which can be changed anywhere in the program.

16.4.1 Constants

Constants are the fixed value in a C program that cannot be changed during the execution of the program. The constants in C are divided into four major categories—integer constant, floating point constant, character constant and string constant. Figure 16.3 shows the classification of constants.

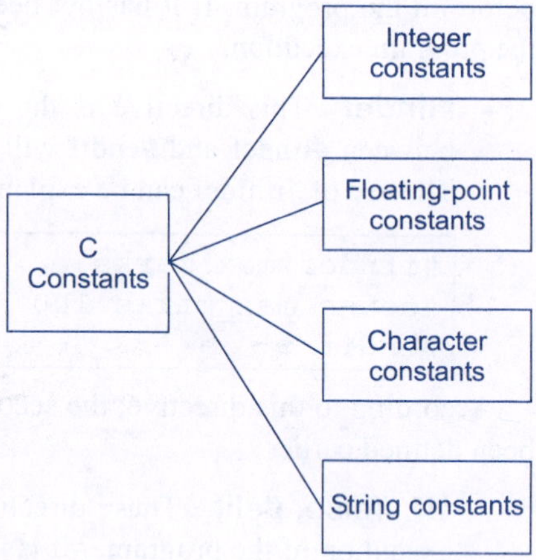

Fig. 16.3 Classification of constants in C

- **Integer constants** Integer constants are the constants that consist of integeral values only. Integer constants can be positive or negative. Negative constants are preceded by a minus sign and a constant without any sign is considered as a positive constant. Integer constants do not contain any special symbol but only digits. The following are the various types of integer constants:
    - o ***Decimal integer constants*** Decimal integer constants contain only digits and the sign symbol. For example, 120, –235, etc.
    - o ***Octal integer constants*** These constants begin with a zero and can contain digits in the range 0–7 only. For example, 032, 05732, etc.
    - o ***Hexadecimal integer constants*** These constants begin with a 0, which is followed by a character ×, and can contain digits in the range 0 to 9 followed by A, B, C, D, E or F. For example, 0×2348, 0×978, etc. are hexadecimal numbers. The alphabets A, B, C, etc. represent the numbers following 9, i.e., 10, 11 and so on till 15.
- **Floating point constants** Floating point constants are the constants that have a decimal point or an exponent part e followed by decimal point. A floating point constant is preceded by a + or – sign and if no sign is mentioned, then it is considered as positive. The exponent part of the floating point constant cannot contain more than three digits lying in the range 0 to 9. Floating point constants are of the following types:
    - o ***Decimal floating point constants*** These constants are just like integer constants having decimal points. For example, –6.45 and 2.32 are decimal floating point constants.
    - o ***Exponential floating point constants*** These constants are composed of two parts, integer part and exponent part. The exponent part represents the power of 10 that should be multiplied with the integer part. For example, 1.3e3 represents an exponential floating point constant that is equivalent to 1.3×10^3.
- **Character constants** Character constants are the constants in which single characters are enclosed within quotes. For example, 'a', '$', '1', etc. represent character constants. Back slash, also called escape sequence, is also used to represent some of the alphabets for serving special purposes. Table 16.7 lists some of the special escape sequences.

Table 16.7 Representing escape sequences

Escape sequence	Function
'\''	Represents the ' character
'\\'	Represents the \ character
'\0'	Represents a null character
'\f'	Represents form feed character
'\b'	Represents backspace character
'\t'	Represents tab character
'\r'	Represents return character
'\n'	Represents new line character

- **String constants** String constants are the constants that contain text strings, which are enclosed within double quotes. For example, "Computer" represents a string constant. String constants also make use of back slash character to break up a line of text strings. For example, if a user wants to type a long line, then it can be broken up into different parts using the back slash character. String constants are stored in the memory in the form of arrays. While storing the string constants, one extra null character is always attached to the end of the string constant. Therefore, if a 5 character string constant is stored in the memory, then 6 spaces will be occupied.

16.4.2 Variables

Variables are the names assigned to different memory locations for storing data. Variables are volatile in nature; so the values stored in them can change. For example, consider a variable x, which can hold value 5 at some point in the program and this value can be changed to 3 at some other point of time in the program. The following rules must be followed while naming a variable:

- A variable name should be composed of a letter, a digit or an underscore and should not contain special characters.
- The name of a variable must start with an alphabet.
- No spaces should be given in the variable name.
- The name of the variable should not be the same as that of a keyword.
- Uppercase and lowercase are significant.

Table 16.8 lists some examples of valid and invalid variables.

Table 16.8 Valid and invalid variables

Valid variables	Invalid variables
Name	$US
_student1	total marks
new3point	25ab
marks_total	struct

In Table 16.8, variable *$US* is invalid because a variable name cannot contain a special symbol. The variable name, total marks is invalid because no space is allowed in the variable name. The variable name, *25ab* is invalid as a variable name cannot start with a digit, whereas the variable name, struct is invalid because struct is a keyword, which is reserved for the use by the compiler and cannot be considered as a variable name.

The different types of variables supported by a language can be determined on the basis of the types of constants supported by the language. Figure 16.4 shows the classification of variables in C.

- **Integer variables** These are the variables, which can hold only integer numbers.
- **Character variables** These are the variables, which can hold only characters such as letters and digits.
- **Float variables** These are the variables, which can hold only decimal point numbers.
- **Double variables** These are the variables, which can hold decimal point numbers and can store larger values than float variables.

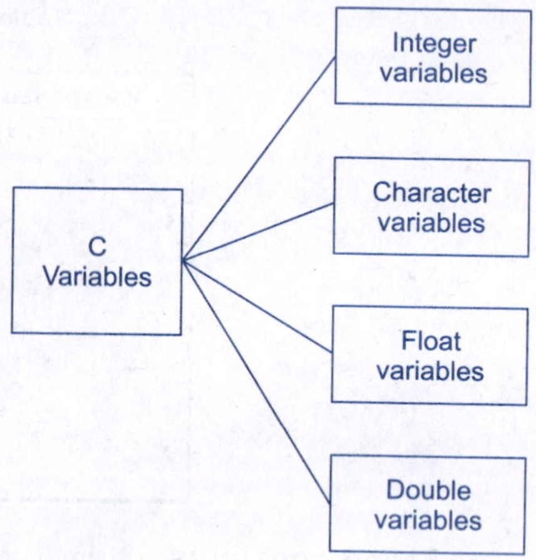

Fig. 16.4 Classification of C variables

In C, a variable is named by using an identifier. An identifier is the combination of letters, digits and underscore that begins with a character. Identifiers are used to name functions, variables, constants and user-defined data types. Identifiers are case sensitive which means that the change in the case of the identifier changes the meaning of the identifier. For example, *mean_1* and *MEAN_1* are treated as separate identifiers and have separate meanings depending on their usage in the program.

16.4.3 Declaration of Variables

All the variables that are used in a program must be declared for their types before they are actually encountered in the program. The syntax of declaring a variable is as follows:

```
type var_name;
```

The *type* represents the data type that can be stored in the variable and *var_name* represents the identifier used to name the variable. We can also declare more than one variable using the same data type. For example, valid declarations are:

```
int count;
int number, total;
double average;
```

Note: *The multiple variables are separated by commas and a declaration statement must end with a semicolon.*

16.5 OPERATORS AND STATEMENTS

The programs written in C make use of different types of operators and statements for processing the data. The operators such as arithmetic and relational are used to operate on data and variables, whereas the statements are used to write instructions in a program.

16.5.1 Operators

Operators are the symbols, which perform certain operations on one or more values. In C, the operators perform mathematical or logical operations on data and variables. The following are the operators, which are used in C:

- **Arithmetic operators** These operators are used to perform arithmetic operations on data and variables. Arithmetic operators are of two types, unary and binary. Unary operators are the operators, which operate on single operand, and binary operators are the operators, which operate on two operands. Table 16.9 lists the arithmetic operators used in C.

Table 16.9 Arithmetic operators

Arithmetic operators	Function
Unary operators	
++	Increments a given number
- -	Decrements a given number
sizeof	Determines the size of a variable in bytes
(type)	Converts the data type of a variable
Binary operators	
+	Performs addition operation
-	Performs subtraction operation
*	Performs multiplication operation
/	Performs division operation
%	Calculates the remainder after division

The arithmetic operators can operate on integers, real numbers and a combination of integer and real numbers. For example, if $a = 1$ and $b = 4$, then the arithmetic operator + will result in the expression, $a + b = 5$. If $a = 2.5$ and $b = 3.6$, then the arithmetic operator + will result in the expression, $a + b = 6.1$. If $a = 4$ and $b = 1.5$, then the arithmetic operator + will result in the expression, $a + b = 5.5$.

- **Relational operators** These operators are used to carry out the comparison between different operands. Relational operators help in decision making process in C. Table 16.10 lists the relational operators supported by C.

Table 16.10 Relational operators

Relational operators	Description
<	Less than
>	Greater than
<=	Less than equal to
>=	Greater than equal to
= =	Is equal to
!=	Not equal to

Relational operators can be used to perform comparison operations between constants, variables and a combination of both constants and variables. For example, the relational operator, > can be used to compare constants as 5 > 3. It can be used to compare variables as $a > b$ and a combination of constants and variable as $a > 8$.

- **Logical operators** These operators are used to perform logical AND, OR and NOT operations on data. Logical operators are generally used to compare Boolean expressions. Table 16.11 lists the logical operators used by C.

Table 16.11 Logical operators

Logical operators	Description
&&	Performs logical AND operation
||	Performs logical OR operation
!	Performs logical NOT operation

The logical operators work with relational operators and operate on the expressions, which are connected using relational operators. For example, consider the expression $a > b$ && $c > d$, this expression will hold true only if both the conditions hold true. The logical NOT operation is performed on a single expression and the expression is considered true if the given condition does not satisfy. For example, consider the expression! ($a > b$), this expression holds true if a is not greater than b.

- **Assignment operators** These operators are used to evaluate an expression and assign the value present at the right hand side of the expression to the left hand side of the expression. The left hand side of the operator must be a variable, whereas the right hand side could be a variable or constant. Table 16.12 lists the main assignment operators used in C.

Table 16.12 Assignment operators

Assignment operators	Description
=	Assigns the right hand side value of the expression to the left hand side value of the expression.
+=	Adds the variables present on either side of the expression.
-=	Subtracts the variables present on either side of the expression.
*=	Multiplies the variables present on either side of the expression.
/=	Divides the variables present on either side of the expression.
%=	Performs the modulus operation on the variables present on either side of the expression.

Table 16.13 lists the expanded form of assignment operators that will help in better understanding.

Table 16.13 Expanded form of the assignment operators

Assignment operators	Expanded form
a += b	$a = a + b$
A –= b	$a = a - b$
a *= b	$a = a * b$
a /= b	$a = a / b$
a %= b	$a = a$ % b

- **Conditional operators** These operators are used to perform certain conditional tests on the expressions. These operators operate on three expressions and contain two symbols ? and :. The syntax of conditional operators is as follows:

```
expression1 ? expression2: expression3
```

- This syntax of conditional operator means that if expression1 is true, then execute expression2 otherwise execute expression3. For example, suppose $a = 1$ and $b = 2$ and the expression implementing the conditional operator is:

  $x = (a > b)\ ?\ a : b.$

  In the above expression, a is less than b, therefore, x will be assigned the value of b, i.e., 2.

- **Bit-manipulation operators** These operators are also known as bitwise operators and operate on each bit of data. These operators are used for testing, shifting and complementing data bits. Table 16.14 lists the bit-manipulation operators.

Table 16.14 Bit-manipulation operators

Bit-manipulation operators	Description
&	Performs AND operation on the bits of the operands.
||	Performs OR operation on the bits of the operands.
~	Performs NOT operation on the bits of the operands.
^	Performs XOR operation on the bits of the operands.
>>	Shifts data bits to the right
<<	Shifts data bits to the left

Precedence of operators Precedence of operators refers to order in which they are operated in a program. Table 16.15 lists the precedence of operators.

Table 16.15 Precedence of operators

Type of operator	Operators	Associativity
Unary operators	+, –, !, ~, ++, —, type, size of	Right to left
Arithmetic operators	*, /, %, +, -	Left to right
Bit-manipulation operators	<<, >>	Left to right
Relational operators	>, <, >=, <=, = =, !=	Left to right
Logical operators	&&, ||	Left to right
Conditional operators	?, :	Left to right
Assignment operators	=, +=, -=, *=, /=, %=	Right to left

16.5.2 Statements

In C, statements are used to perform different functions in a program, such as processing, the input, modifying the value of variable and producing the output. In other words, statements form the basis of a C program and represent a complete instruction. A program contains a series of statements in which punctuation is also used. An expression represents a statement with a semi-colon at the end. An expression is a combination of an operator and an operand, where operator operates on an operand. For example, an expression can be written as:

$a = 5$

In the above expression, variable a is assigned value of 5. This expression can be written in the form of a statement as:

$a = 5;$

The above statement is known as an expression statement. Therefore, any expression in C is considered as a statement if semi-colon is used at the end of that expression. The general form of expression statement can be written as:

```
exp;
```

Here, exp represents the expression to be written in the form of a statement. The expression statement is also used for making a function call and for creating assignment statements. In case of making a function call, expression statement uses expression as a function call. In case of assignment statement, expression statement uses expression as an assignment expression. The general form of an assignment statement can be written as:

```
var = exp;
```

Here, var represents the variable and exp represents the expression. In the above assignment statement, the variable present on the left-hand side of the statement will be assigned the value of the expression present on the right-hand side.

16.5.3 Statements

Arithmetic expressions without parentheses will be evaluated from *left to right* using the rules of precedence of operators. There are two distinct levels of arithmetic operators in C:

High priority : */%
Low priority : + –

The basic evaluation procedure includes 'two' left-to-right passes through the expressions. During the first pass, the high priority operators are applied as they are encountered. During second pass, the low priority operators are applied as they are encountered. Consider the following evaluation statement:

$$x = a-b/3+c*2-1$$

When a=9, b=12, and c=3, the statement becomes

$$x = 9-12/3+3*2-1$$

and is evaluated as follows:

First Pass

Step 1: $x = 9-4+3*2-1$ (Division is applied)

Step 2: $x = 9-4+6-1$ (Multiplication is applied)

Second Pass

Step 3: $x = 5+6-1$ (Minus is applied)

Step 4: $x = 11-1$ (Plus is applied)

Step 5: $x = 10$ (Second minus is applied)

However, the order of evaluation can be changed by introducing parentheses into the expression. Consider the same expression with parentheses as shown below:

$$x = 9-12/(3+3)*(2-1)$$

Whenever parentheses are used, the expressions within parentheses assume highest priority. If two or more sets of parentheses appear as shown above, the expression contained in the left-most set is evaluated first and the right-most in the last. Given below are the new steps.

First Pass

Step 1: 9–12/6*(2–1)

Step 2: 9–12/6*1

Second Pass

Step 3: $x = 9-2*1$

Step 4: $x = 9-2$

Third Pass

Step 5: 7

This time, the procedure consists of three left-to-right passes. However, the number of evaluation steps remain the same as 5. When parentheses are nested, the innermost is evaluated first.

16.6 CONTROL STATEMENTS

Control statements are defined as the statements that are responsible for controlling the execution of various instructions included in a program. A C program is executed on the basis of the sequence in which the instructions are present in the program. In some situations, a particular set of statements needs to be repeated or executed in some specific order. In such situations, the flow of the program needs to be decided using the decision making instructions, which decide the order in which the statements are to be executed or computations are to be performed. Control statements are categorised in three different categories. Figure 16.5 shows the classification of control statements.

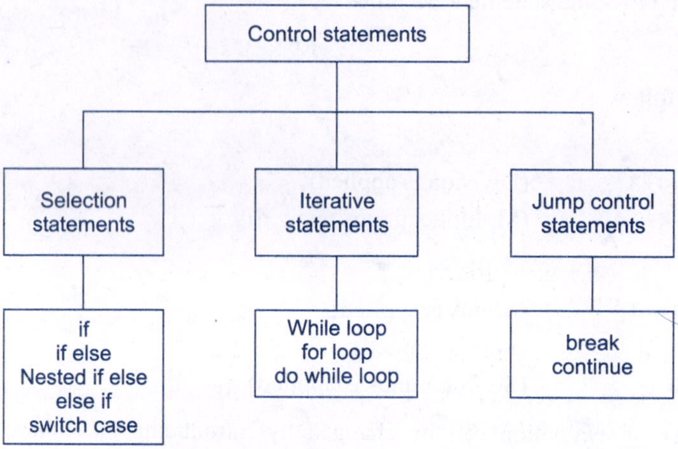

Fig. 16.5 Classification of control statements

16.6.1 Selection Statements

Selection statements are the statements that test a particular condition in a program and cause a change in the flow of the program if the particular condition is met. The following are the various selection statements supported by C:

- **If** statement
- **If else** statement
- Nested **if else** statements
- **Else if** statement
- **Switch case** statements

If statement **If** instruction is used in C programs for the purpose of decision making. This instruction is used to test a particular condition in a program. If the condition is satisfied, then the statements or the code following the **if** statement is executed; otherwise the program skips the **if** statement part of the program. The general structure of **if** statement can be represented as:

```
if (a given condition is true)
{
   Execute these statements;
}
```

As soon as the **if** statement is encountered in the program, the condition written in the pair of parenthesis is checked. The condition in the **if** statement is written using relational operators. Consider the following C program to understand the functioning of the **if** statement:

```
#include<stdio.h>
#include<conio.h>
void main ( )
{
    float percentage;
     clrscr();
     printf("Enter your percentage");
     scanf("%f",&percentage);
     if(percentage<40)
     {
         printf("You are fail");
     }
getch();
}
```

In the above code, *percentage* variable is taken as a **float** type inside the main function. The **printf** statement is used to display the statement written inside its parenthesis and the **scanf** statement is used to accept the input from the user. Here, if the condition given inside the parenthesis of the **if** statement is satisfied, then the statement written inside the parenthesis of **printf** statement will be displayed on the computer's screen. But, if any number greater than 40 is entered as an input in the above program, then no result will be displayed on the computer's screen.

Figure 16.6 shows the output of the above program.

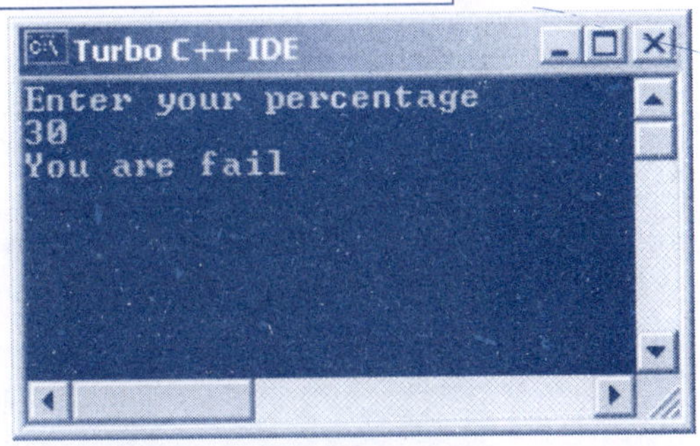

Fig. 16.6 Explaining the usage of if statement

Example 16.1 *Write a program to determine whether a seller has made profit or incurred loss and also the amount of profit or loss, if the cost price and the selling price of an article are entered by the user.*

Solution The following program determines whether a seller has earned profit or incurred loss:

```
#include<stdio.h>
#include<conio.h>
void main ()
{
    float cp, sp, p, l;
    clrscr();
    printf("Enter the cost price and selling price of the article");
    scanf("%f %f",&cp,&sp);
    p=sp-cp;  /*Profit=selling price-cost price*/
    l=cp-sp;  /*loss= cost price- selling price*/
    if(p>0)
```

```
    {
        printf("The seller has made profit of %f Rs.",p);
    }
    if(l>0)
    {
        printf("The seller has made loss of %f Rs.",l);
    }
    if(p==0)
    {
        printf("The seller has made no loss and no profit");
        }
    getch();
}
```

In the above code, *cp* represents the cost price, *sp* represents the selling price, *p* represents the profit and l represents the loss. These variables are taken as **float** data type. In this program, three **if** statements are used for determining the profit earned or loss incurred.

Figure 16.7 shows the output of the above program.

Fig. 16.7 Displaying the profit earned by the seller

The main drawback of using the **if** statement is that if the condition given in the **if** statement is satisfied, then only the given set of instructions or statements is executed. But, if the condition is not satisfied, then no operation is performed.

If else statement **If else** statement is an improvement over **if** statement. In this statement, if the condition given in the **if** statement is satisfied, then the statements given in the **if** block are executed. On the other hand, if the condition is not satisfied, then the instructions given in the **else** block are executed. The general structure of the **if else** statement is:

```
if ( the given condition is true)
{
    Execute these statements;
}
```

```
else
{
    Execute these statements;
}
```

The following program illustrates the functioning of the **if else** statement:

```
#include<stdio.h>
#include<conio.h>
void main ( )
{
    int x,y;
    clrscr();
    printf("Enter any two numbers x and y");
    scanf("%d %d",&x,&y);
    if (x==y)
    {
        printf("Both the numbers are equal");
    }
    if (x>y)
    {
        printf("%d is greater than %d",x,y);
    }
    else
    {
        printf("%d is smaller than %d",x,y);
    }
    getch();
}
```

In the above code, the larger of the two numbers entered by the user is determined. Here, the two variables, *x* and *y* are taken as integer data type and for storing the values entered by the user. The **if else** statement determines the greater value out of the two values and displays it on the screen using the **printf** statement.

Figure 16.8 shows the output of the above program.

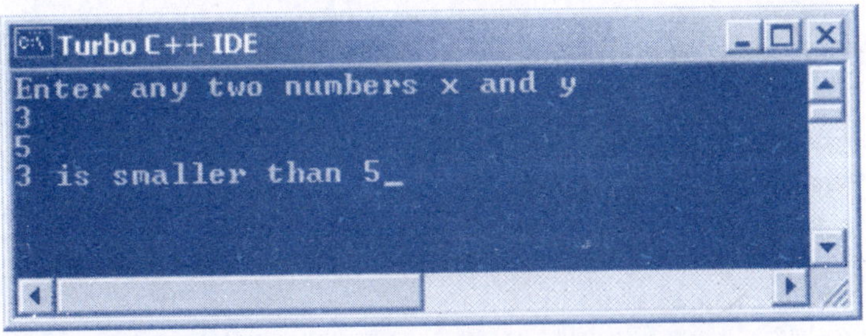

Fig. 16.8 Explaining the usage of **if else** statement

Example 16.2 *Write a program to check whether a given number is odd or even.*

Solution The following program determines whether a number is odd or even:

```
#include<stdio.h>
#include<conio.h>
void main( )
{
     int num;
     clrscr();
     printf("Enter the number");
     scanf("%d",&num);
     if (num%2==0)        /* remainder after division by 2*/
          printf("\nThe number is even");
     else
          printf("\nThe number is odd");
     getch();
}
```

In the above code, variable *num*, which is taken as integer data type is used to store the value of the number entered by the user. The **if else** statement determines whether the number entered by the user is even or odd.

Figure 16.9 shows the output of the above program.

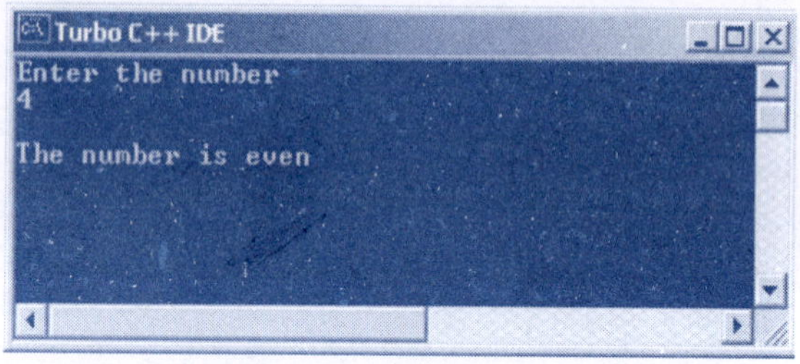

Fig. 16.9 Displaying the even number

Nested if else Statements A large number of **if else** statements are required in complex programs, where they are nested inside each other. The following code shows the general structure of nested **if else** statements:

```
if(a given condition is true)
{
if(a given condition is true)
    Execute this statement;
else
{
    Execute this statements;
}
}
else
    Execute this statement;
```

The basic functioning of the nested **if else** statements can be understood with the help of the following program, which calculates the smallest number among three numbers:

```
#include<stdio.h>
#include<conio.h>
void main()
{
int x,y,z,smaller;
clrscr();
printf("Enter the three numbers");
scanf("%d %d %d",&x,&y,&z);
if(x<z)
{
      if(x<y)
            smaller = x;
      else
            smaller = y;
}
else
{
      if(z<y)
            smaller = z;
      else
            smaller = y;
}
printf("The smallest number is:%d",smaller);
getch();
}
```

In the above code, the smallest number out of the three numbers entered by the user is determined. Here, four variables taken as an integer data type are *x*, *y*, *z* and *smaller*. The nested **if else** statements are used for determining the smallest numbers out of the three numbers entered by the user.

Figure 16.10 shows the output of the above program.

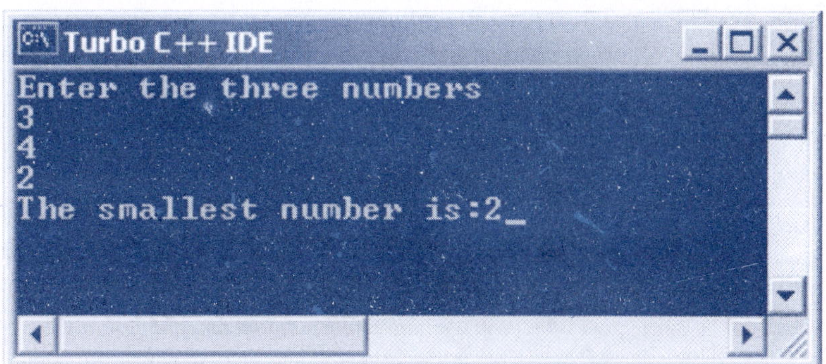

Fig. 16.10 Explaining the usage of nested **if else** statement

Example 16.3 *Write a program to determine whether the year entered by the user is a leap year or not.*

Solution The following program determines whether the year is a leap year or not:

```
#include<stdio.h>
#include<conio.h>
void main()
{
int yr;
clrscr();
printf("Enter the year");
scanf("%d",&yr);
if(yr%100==0)
{
      if(yr%400==0)
            printf("\n Year is leap year");
      else
            printf("\n Year is not leap year");
}
else
{
      if(yr%4==0)
            printf("\n Leap year");
      else
            printf("\n Not a leap year");
}
getch();
}
```

In the above code, variable *yr* is taken as an integer data type that stores the value of the year entered by the user. The nested **if else** statements are used to determine whether the year entered by the user is a leap year or not and the result is displayed on the screen by using the **printf** statement.

Figure 16.11 shows the output of the above program.

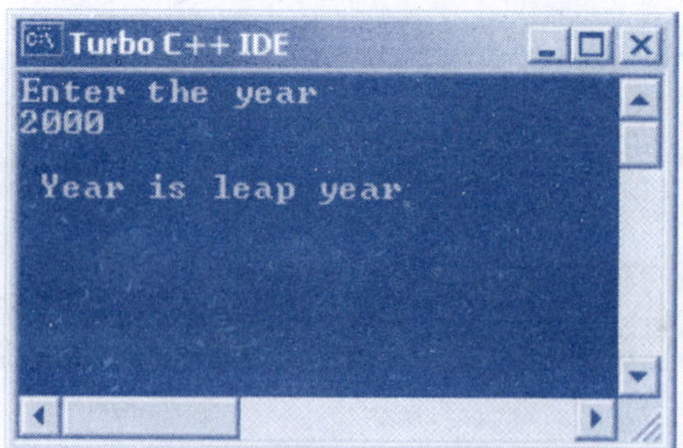

Fig. 16.11 Displaying the leap year

Else if statement It is another selective statement that helps in the decision making process in a simpler way by allowing multiple **else if** statements in the program. The following program illustrates the functioning of **else if** statement:

```
#include<stdio.h>
#include<conio.h>
void main( )
{
long int salary=0;
clrscr();
printf("Enter the salary of the employee:");
scanf("%ld",&salary);
if(salary<=5000)
     printf("The grade of the employee is C");
     else if(salary<40000)
          printf("The grade of the employee is B");
          else if(salary>=40000)
               printf("The grade of the employee is A");
getch();
}
```

In the above code, the grade of an employee is determined by taking salary as an input from the user. The variable, *salary* is taken as an integer data type that is used to store the amount of salary entered by the user. The **else if** statement determines the grade of the employee according to the salary entered by the user.

Figure 16.12 shows the output of the above program.

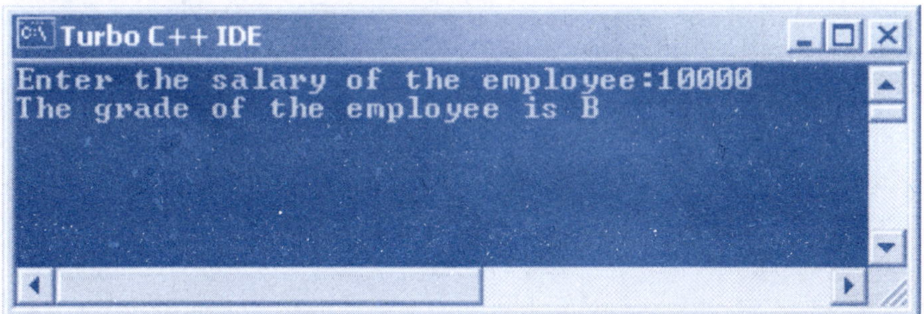

Fig. 16.12 Explaining the usage of the else if statement

Switch case statements **Switch case** statement is a better form of the nested if else statements. The **switch case** statement is used in situations where a selection is to be made from more than two choices. The **switch** statement works by testing a desired case among all the given cases. As soon as the given **case** is found, the block of statements associated with that **case** is executed. The following code shows the general structure of the switch case statement:

```
switch(variable)
{
case const_expr:
      block of statements;
      break;
case const_expr:
      block of statements;
      break;
default:
      block of statements;
}
```

In the above code, const_expr represents the constant expressions. The cases corresponding to the *switch* variable are tested and if none of the case is satisfied, then the case labelled default is executed. The **break** statement is used to cause immediate exit from the **switch** statement as soon as the code under one case is executed.

The following program shows the functioning of the **switch case** statement without the use of **break**:

```
#include<stdio.h>
#include<conio.h>
void main()
{
char ch;
clrscr();
printf("Enter any character:");
scanf("%c",&ch);
switch(ch)
{
      case 'b':
            printf("\nb is in the program");
      case 'c':
            printf("\nc is in the program");
      case 'a':
            printf("\na is in the program");
      default:
            printf("\nnothing is in the program");
}
getch();
}
```

In the above code, variable *ch* is taken as character data type that stores the character entered by the user. The **switch case** statement is used to match the character entered by the user with the cases given inside the switch statement. After matching the character with a particular case, its statements are executed.

Figure 16.13 shows the output of the above program.

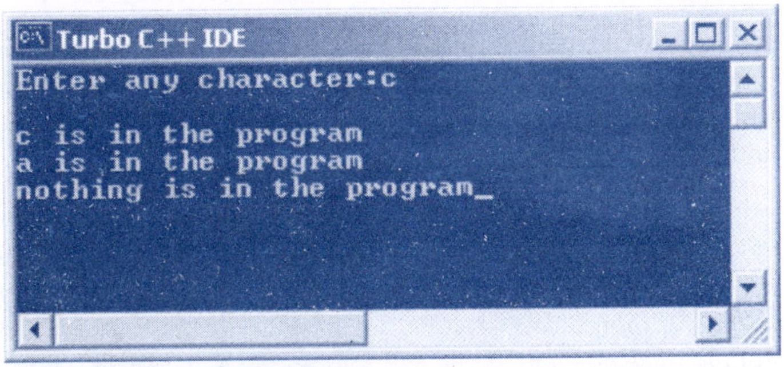

Fig. 16.13 Explaining the usage of switch case statement without break

The actual output of the above program should have been “c is in the program” only. But the above program is executing all the statements following the case a. This is the reason why the **break** statement should be used in the **switch case** statements so that as soon as the matching case is found, the block of the statements is executed and the control of the program is taken out of the **switch case**.

The following program explains the use of the **switch case** statement along with the **break** statements:

```
#include<stdio.h>
#include<conio.h>
void main()
{
char ch;
clrscr();
printf("Enter any character:");
scanf("%c",&ch);
switch(ch)
{
case ‘b’:
     printf("b is in the program");
     break;
case ‘c’:
     printf("c is in the program");
     break;
case ‘a’:
     printf("a is in the program");
     break;
default:
     printf("nothing is in the program");
}
```

```
getch();
}
```

In the above code, the **break** statement is used in the **switch case** statement for returning the control of the program out of the **switch case** statement immediately after executing the statements of the matching case.

Figure 16.14 shows the output of the above program.

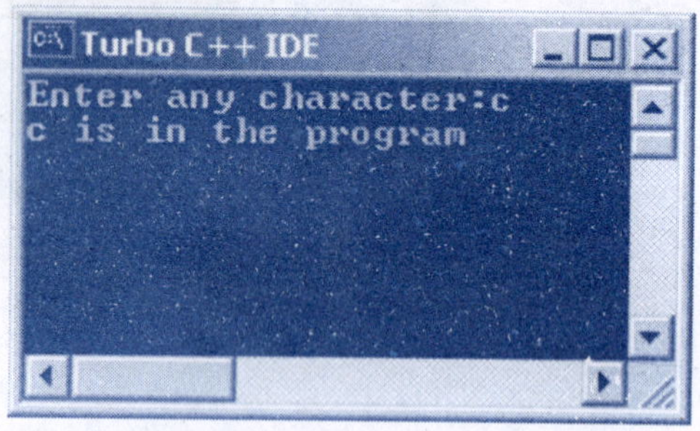

Fig. 16.14 Explaining the usage of switch case statement with break

Example 16.4 *Write a program asking the user to enter the number of a week day and then display the corresponding name of the week day on the computer screen.*

Solution The following program determines the day of the week after taking the number of a week day as an input from the user:

```
#include<stdio.h>
#include<conio.h>
void main()
{
int num;
clrscr();
printf("Enter the number of weekday you want to see:");
scanf("%d",&num);
switch (num)
{
      case 1:
            printf("Monday");
            break;
      case 2:
            printf("Tuesday");
            break;
      case 3:
            printf("Wednesday");
            break;
      case 4:
            printf("Thursday");
            break;
      case 5:
            printf("Friday");
            break;
default:
            printf("It is the weekend or no day");
}
getch();
}
```

In the above code, variable *num* is taken as an integer data type that stores the number entered by the user. The different cases are written in the **switch case** statement and the number entered by the user is matched with these cases. The statements of the matched case are executed and the result is displayed on the screen.

Figure 16.15 shows the output of the above program.

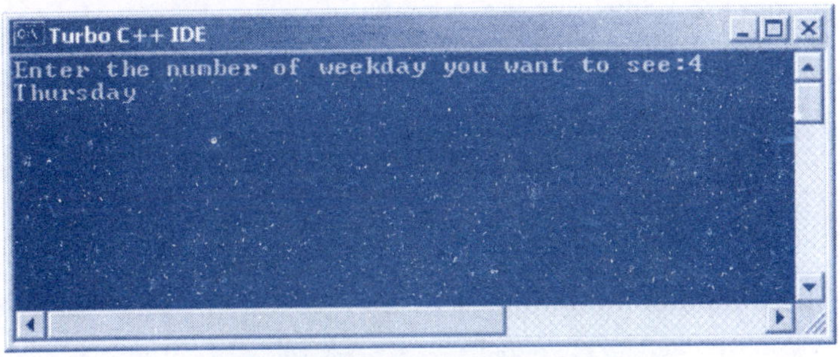

Fig. 16.15 Displaying the day of week

16.6.2 Iterative Statements

Iterative statements are the statements that are used for running a particular set of code for any number of times. Iterative statements consist of two parts, head and body. The head of the statement decides the number of times for which the instructions present in the body of the statement are to be executed. The following iterative statements are supported by C:

- **While** statement
- **For** statement
- **Do while** statement

While statement **While** statement is the simplest of all iterative statements. The main function of the **while** statement is to repeat a particular set of statements for a fixed number of times. The following code shows the general structure of the while statement:

```
Initialize the loop variable
while(test condition)
{
    Execute these statements;
    Increment the loop variable
}
```

In the above code, *loop* variable refers to the variable that is used to run the loop for a particular number of times. The following program to print the numbers from 1 to 10 illustrates the functioning of the **while** statement:

```
#include<stdio.h>
#include<conio.h>
void main ( )
{
int i = 1;
clrscr();
printf(" the ten numbers are:");
while (i<=10)
{
     printf("\n%d\n",i);
     i= i+1;
}
getch();
}
```

In the above code, loop variable *i* is taken as an integer data type and is initialised with value 1. The **while** loop prints the numbers from 1 to 10 by using the loop variable *i*.

Figure 16.16 shows the output of the above program.

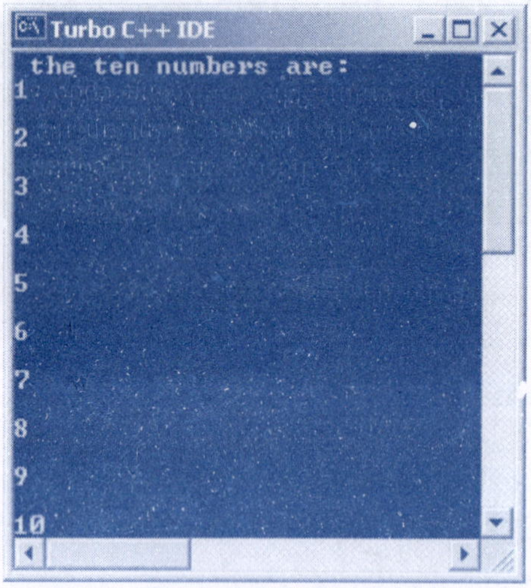

Fig. 16.16 Explaining the usage of while statement

Example 16.5 *Write a program to calculate the value of one number raised to the power of another number when both numbers are entered by the user.*

Solution The following program shows how the value of one number raised to the power of another number is calculated:

```
#include<stdio.h>
#include<conio.h>
void main ( )
{
int x,y,i=1;              /* two numbers*/
int power=1;
clrscr();
printf("Enter two numbers:");
scanf("%d%d",&x,&y);
while(i<=y)
{
     power = power * x;
     i++;
}
printf("\n%d to the power %d is %d",x,y,power);
getch();
}
```

In the above code, variables *x*, *y*, *i* and power are taken as an integer type, where *i* is the loop variable.

The variables, *x* and *y* store the two numbers entered by the user. The **while** loop is used to calculate the value of one number raised to the power of another number when both the numbers are entered by the user.

Figure 16.17 shows the output of the above program.

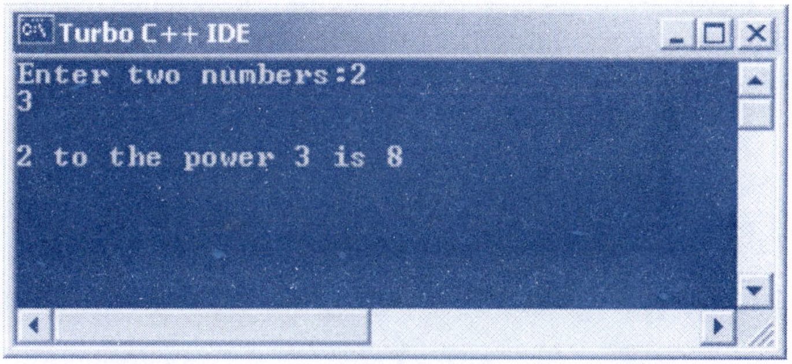

Fig. 16.17 Displaying the result of the number raised to other number

For statement **For** statement can be treated as a compact form of **while** statement. In the **while** statement, the initialisation of looping variable, the testing of a condition and the incrementation of the looping variable occur at different places in the program. But, in the **for** statement, all the three tasks are specified at the same place in the program. The following code shows the general structure of the **for** statement:

```
for( initialization; testing; incrementation)
{
    Execute these statements;
}
```

The following program illustrates the functioning of the **for** statement:

```
#include<stdio.h>
#include<conio.h>
void main ( )
{
int i;
clrscr();
printf("\nTen numbers are:");
for(i=1;i<=10;i++)
{
     printf("\n%d\n",i);
}
getch();
}
```

In the above code, loop variable *i* is taken as an integer data type. The **for** statement comprises of the initialisation of the loop variable, the test condition and the incrementation of the loop variable. This program prints the numbers from 1 to 10 using the for statement. When the **for** statement is executed for the first time, the value of *i* is set to 1. After performing this operation, the condition $i <= 10$ is tested.

As $i = 1$, the condition is satisfied and the control of the program is transferred to the body of the **for** statement. The body of the **for** statement is executed and the **printf** statement is executed to print the number 1. After this, the control of the program is transferred back to the **for** statement, where the value of i is incremented by 1. This whole process is repeated until the test condition remains true. Then, the control of the program is transferred to the set of instructions that immediately follow the for statement.

Figure 16.18 shows the output of the above program.

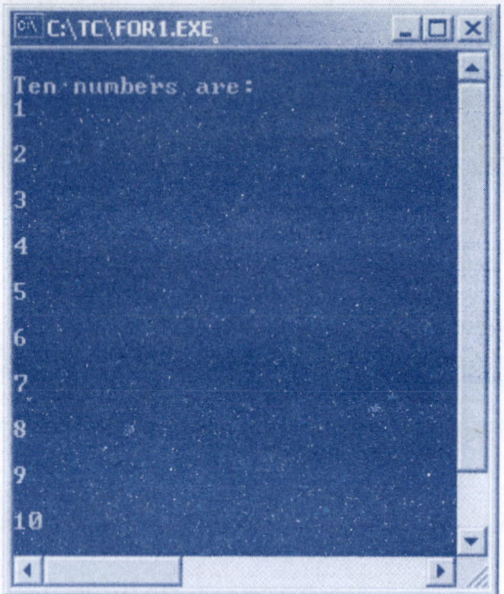

Fig. 16.18 Explaining the usage of for statement

Example 16.6 *Write a program to print the multiplication table of a number entered by the user.*

Solution The following program shows how the multiplication table of a number is calculated:

```
#include<stdio.h>
#include<conio.h>
void main ( )
{
int num,i;
clrscr();
printf("Enter the number");
scanf("%d",&num);
for (i=1;i<=10;i++)
{
      printf("\n%d*%d = %d",num,i,num*i);
}
getch();
}
```

In the above code, variables *num* and *i* are taken as an integer data type. The number entered by the user is stored in the *num* variable and *i* is the loop variable. The **for** statement prints the multiplication table of the number entered by the user and displays the result using the **printf** statement on the screen.

Figure 16.19 shows the output of the above program.

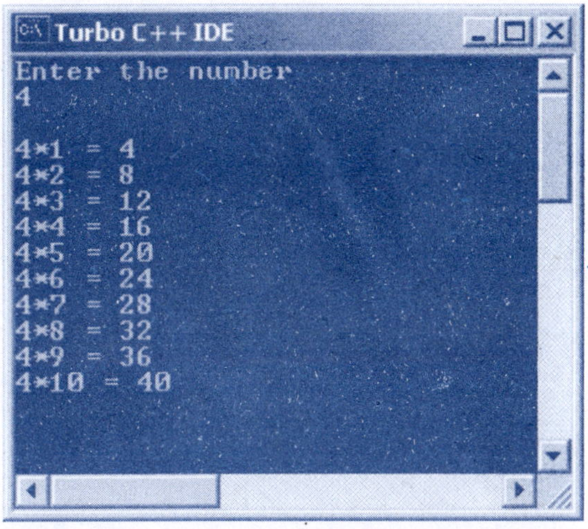

Fig. 16.19 Displaying the multiplication table of a number

Do while statement **Do while** statement is similar to the **while** statement in functioning but the only difference between the two is that the testing condition is present at the end of the **do while** statement body unlike the **while** statement in which it is present in the beginning. The **do while** statement executes at least once even if the condition to be tested is not satisfied. The **do while** statements are used in the situations where some data is to be read. The following code shows the general structure of the **do while** statement:

```
do
{
Execute these statements;
} while (a given condition is true)
```

The following program illustrates the functioning of the **do while** statement:

```
#include <stdio.h>
#include <conio.h>
void main()
{
int num,x,y,sum=0,i=0;
clrscr();
printf("Enter an integer number:");
scanf("%d",&num);
x=num;
```

```
do
{
      y=num%10;
      sum=sum+y;
      i=i*10+y;
      num=num/10;
}
while(num!=0);
printf("The sum of digits of the number
                  is:=%d\n",sum);
printf("The reverse of the number is:=%d\n",i);
if (x==i)
      printf("The number is palindrome\n");
else
      printf("The number is not a palindrome\n");
getch();
}
```

In the above code, variable *num* is taken as an integer data type that stores an integer number entered by the user. The value of *num* variable is also stored in the variable *x* to preserve it for future comparison. Here, the **do while** loop is used for determining the sum and the reverse of the number entered by the user. The program code decides whether the given number is palindrome or not on the basis of the comparison of the computed reverse number and the value stored in the variable *x*. The program code finally displays the appropriate message based on this comparison as an output.

Figure 16.20 shows the output of the above program.

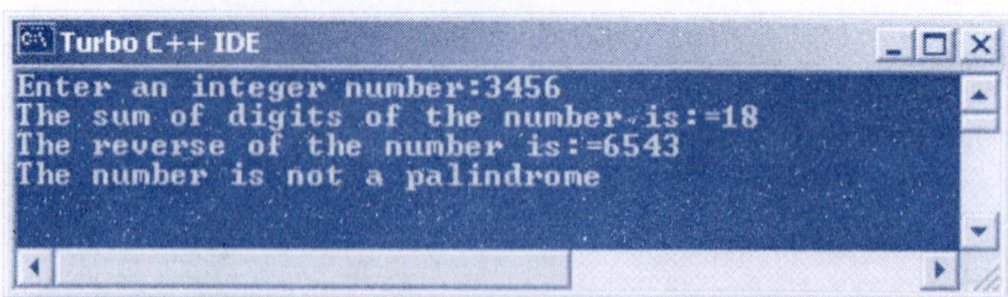

Fig. 16.20 Explaining the usage of do while statement

16.6.3 Jump Control Statements

Jump control statements are the statements that cause the program to jump from a particular location in the program to another specified or unspecified location in the program. The following jump control statements are supported by C:

- **Break**
- **Continue**
- **Goto**

Break statement

Break statement allows the users to terminate an iterative statement. The **break** statement is also used to exit the control from the **switch case** control structure. Whenever the user wants to terminate an iterative statement, the **break** keyword is inserted in the iterative statement. The following program explains the functioning of the **break** statement:

```
#include<stdio.h>
#include<conio.h>
void main()
{
int i,j;
clrscr();
for(i=1;i<=2;i++)
{
     for(j=1;j<=5;j++)
     {
          if(j==4)
             break;/*Jump out of the loop*/
          else
             printf("%d%d\n",i,j);
     }
}
getch();
}
```

In the above code, two variables, *i* and *j* are taken as an integer data type.

Figure 16.21 shows the output of the above program.

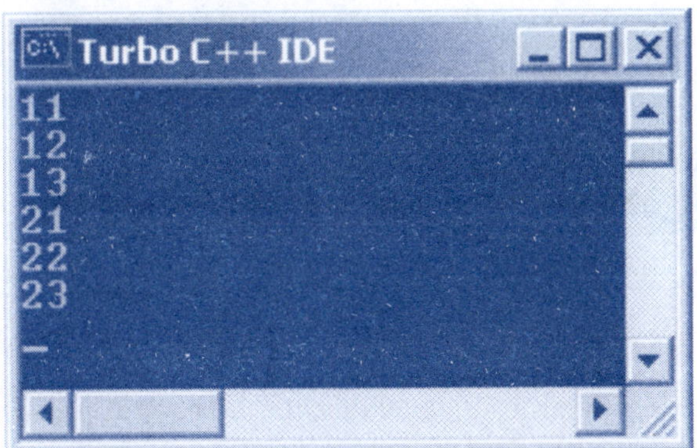

Fig. 16.21 Explaining the usage of break statement

Continue statement This statement is used to take the control of the program to the beginning of the loop and execute the statements, which immediately follow the beginning of the loop. The following program explains the functioning of the **continue** statement:

```
#include<stdio.h>
#include<conio.h>
void main()
{
int x,y;
clrscr();
for(x=1;x<=3;x++)
{
        for(y=1;y<=3;y++)
        {
            if(x==y)
                continue;
            printf(«\n%d\t%d\t»,x,y);
        }
}
getch();
}
```

In the above code, two variables, *x* and *y* are taken as an integer data type. Here, when the value of *x* is equal to *y*, the control of the program is transferred to the inner **for** loop using the **continue** statement.

Figure 16.22 shows the output of the above program.

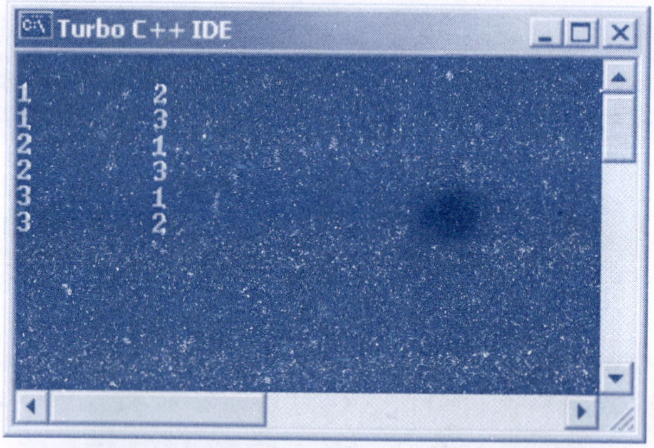

Fig. 16.22 Explaining the use of continue statement

Goto This statement is used to transfer the control of a program to a particular statement during the program execution. The **goto** statement requires a label or a tag, which is followed by a colon (:) in order to locate the particular statement where the control is to be transferred. The label is inserted prior to this particular statement. The syntax of using the **goto** statement in a C program is as follows:

```
goto label-name;
```

If the **goto** statement transfers the control in the upward direction, then a loop will be formed, i.e., some specific statements will be executed again and again. The following program illustrates the functioning of the **goto** statement:

```
#include<stdio.h>
#include <conio.h>
void main()
{
        int x,y;
        char ch;
        clrscr();
        number:
        printf("\nEnter the number:");
        scanf("%d",&x);
        if(x<0)
        {
                printf("\n%d is a negative number, please enter a
                    positive number\n",x);
                goto choice;
        }
        else
        {
                y=x*x;
                printf("\nSquare of %d is: %d\n", x, y);
        }
        choice:
        printf("\nDo you want to get square of more numbers?");
        fflush(stdin);
        scanf("%c", &ch);
        if(ch=='y')
                goto number;
        else
                exit(0);
        getch();
}
```

In the above code, two integer type variables *x* and *y* and a character type variable *ch* have been used. The number whose square is to be determined is entered by the user and stored in the variable *x*. First of all, the value of the variable *x* is checked; if the value is less than 0 then the program displays a message and transfers the control to the choice label. However, if the user enters a positive number, then its square is calculated and the result is displayed on the screen.

Figure 16.23 shows the output of the above program.

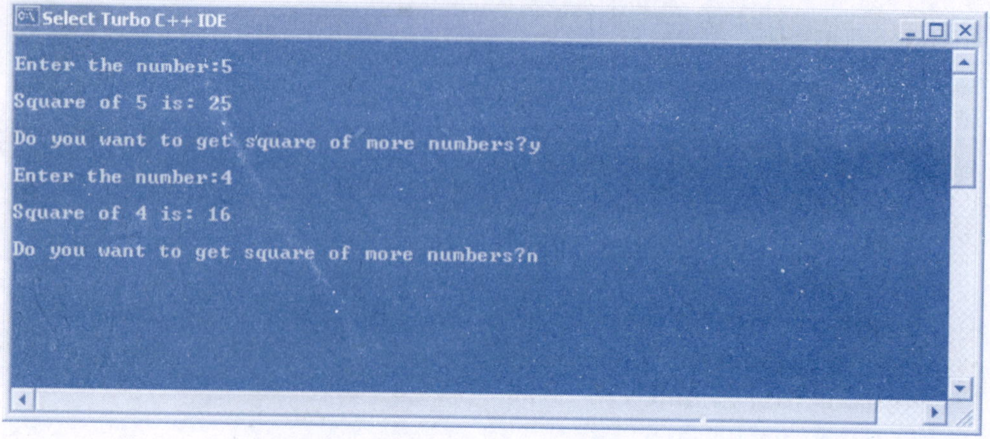

Fig. 16.23 Illustrating the use of **goto** statement

16.7 ARRAYS AND STRINGS

C allows a user to store the elements of same data type in the continuous memory locations using arrays. The arrays of characters that are used to store characters are known as strings.

16.7.1 Arrays

An array is defined as a collection of data elements of same type. It can store values in the form of characters, integers and floats at contiguous memory locations in the memory. The elements in an array can be accessed by using an array index where the first index value always starts from zero. An array of size n can store n values in it with the first value stored at 0 index and the last value stored at $n - 1$. Moreover, the elements present in an array share the same name but a different index number.

The data type and the dimension of an array must be declared before using it in a C program. The general form of array declaration is as follows:

```
data-type arr-name[dimension];
```

Here, data-type represents the data type of the elements to be stored in the array, arr-name represents the name of the array and dimension represents the size of the array. The size of an array specifies the number of elements that can be stored in an array. The square brackets [] are used for delimiting the array size. Example:

```
int students[20];
```

In the above example, **int** represents the integer data type of the elements of the array and *students* represent the name of the array. Here, the size of the array is 20, i.e., 20 elements can be stored in the students array.

The following program illustrates the declaration and the use of an array:

```
#include<stdio.h>
#include<conio.h>
void main()
{
int array[10]; /*Declaration of an array*/
int i;
clrscr();
printf("Enter the elements of an array:\n");
for(i=0;i<10;i++)
{
      scanf("%d",&array[i]);
}
printf("The array elements are:\n");
for(i=0;i<10;i++)
      printf("array[%d]=%d\n",i,array[i]);
getch();
}
```

In the above code, an array, which can hold 10 elements, is declared with the name *array*. The 10 elements are entered by the user and are stored at the contiguous memory locations in the memory. The **printf** statement is used to display the input elements of the array on the screen.

Figure 16.24 shows the output of the above program.

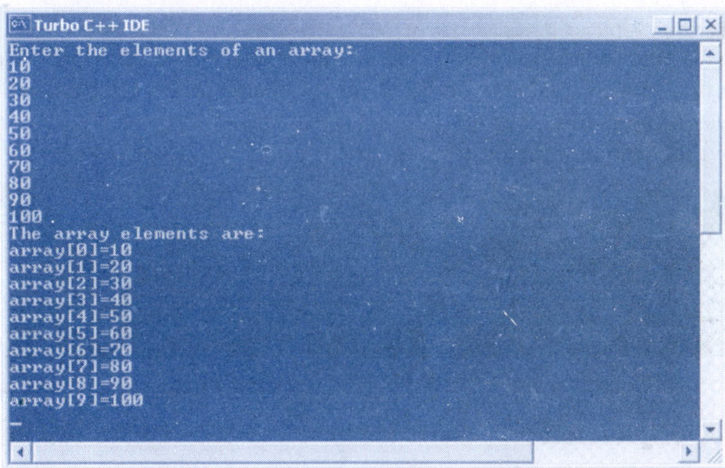

Fig. 16.24 Explaining the usage of arrays

16.7.2 Strings

Strings are defined as the character arrays in which each character is stored using one byte in the memory. In C, the end of the string is denoted by the null character, i.e., \0. The general syntax of declaring a string is as follows:

```
char arr-name[dimension];
```

Here, **char** represents the character data type of array, *arr-name* represents the name of the array and dimension represents the size of the array. Example:

char students_name[5];

In the above example, *students_name* represents the name of the array or string and 5 represents the size of the array. Here, the size is 5, therefore, 5 characters can be stored in *students_name* array.

The following program illustrates the declaration and the use of strings:

```
#include<stdio.h>
#include<conio.h>
void main()
{
char array[11];
int i;
clrscr();
printf("Enter the elements of a character array:\n");
for(i=0;i<11;i++)
{
     scanf("%c",&array[i]);
}
printf("\nThe character array elements are:\n");
for(i=0;i<11;i++)
     printf("%c",array[i]);
getch();
}
```

In the above code, a character array of size 11, i.e., an array, which can store 11 characters including null character '/0' in the memory, is taken. The elements of character array are entered by the user and are displayed on the screen using **printf** statement.

Figure 16.25 shows the output of the above program.

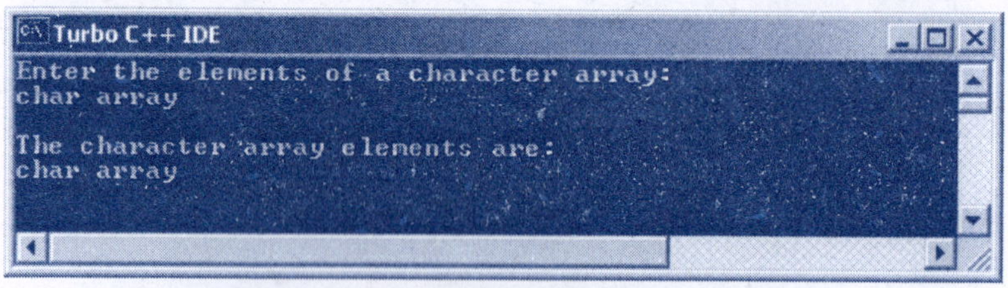

Fig. 16.25 Explaining the usage of character array

16.8 FUNCTIONS

A function refers to a set of statements, which are designed to perform some specific task. The programs written in C are usually composed of more than one function. main is the one of the important functions that is used in every C program. When a C program is executed, the instructions are carried out inside the main function. Functions enable us to break a program into smaller parts, which are executed as separate functions. This technique is known as *modularisation*.

16.8.1 Use of Functions

Functions increase the reusability of code as we can use the same function multiple number of times within a program. We can invoke a function using the function name. When a function is invoked, the compiler transfers the program control to the first statement present in the function. The main advantages of using functions are:

- Functions encapsulate a particular set of instructions and help to avoid the rewriting of a particular set of the instructions again and again.
- Functions break large and complex programs into simpler and smaller programs.
- Functions allow the users to easily modify complex and large programs by introducing the concept of modularisation.

The following program illustrates the creation and the use of functions:

```
#include<stdio.h>
#include<conio.h>
void main()/* Main function */
{
clrscr();
printf("This is the main function");
functA();/* Function call */
functB();/* Function call */
getch();
}
int functA()/* Function definition */
{
printf("\n\nThis is the function A");
return (0); /* Returns to the main */
}
int functB()/* Function definition */
{
printf("\n\nThis is the function B");
return (0); /* Returns to the main */
}
```

In the above code, two functions, **functA** and **functB** are used in the main function. These functions are defined outside the main function.

Figure 16.26 shows the output of the above program.

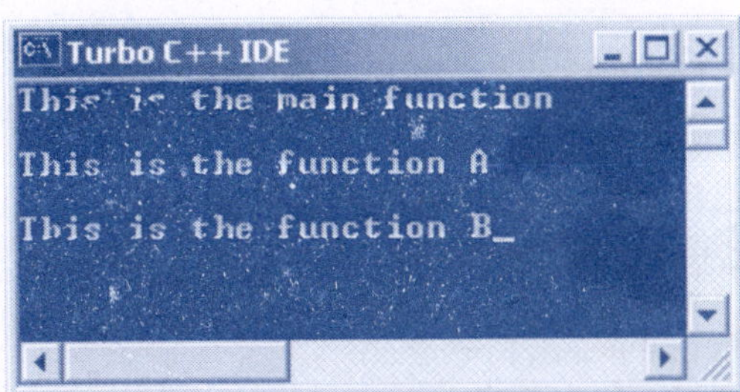

Fig. 16.26 Explaining the usage of functions

When a function is called, it is end with a semicolon and its definition is not followed by semicolon but by the set of statements. A C program can contain any number of functions. The functions are executed in the same sequence in which they are called in the program. Once a function is executed, the control of the program returns to the main function, which after executing all given functions and instructions ends the program.

Functions can also be nested and used within other functions. The following program illustrates the use of nested functions:

```
#include<stdio.h>
#include<conio.h>
void main()
{
clrscr();
printf("This is the main function");
functA();/* Function call */
printf("\n\nBack in main function");
getch();
}
functA()
{
printf("\n\nThis is the function A");
functB();/* Function A calls B */
printf("\n\nBack to function A");
}
functB()
{
printf("\n\nThis is the function B");
functC();/* Function B calls C */
printf("\n\nBack in function B");
}
functC()
{
printf("\n\nThis is the function C");
}
```

In the above code, the nested functions as well as the transfer of control between different functions are shown. The main function calls one of the functions, which in turn call some other functions.

Figure 16.27 shows the output of the above program.

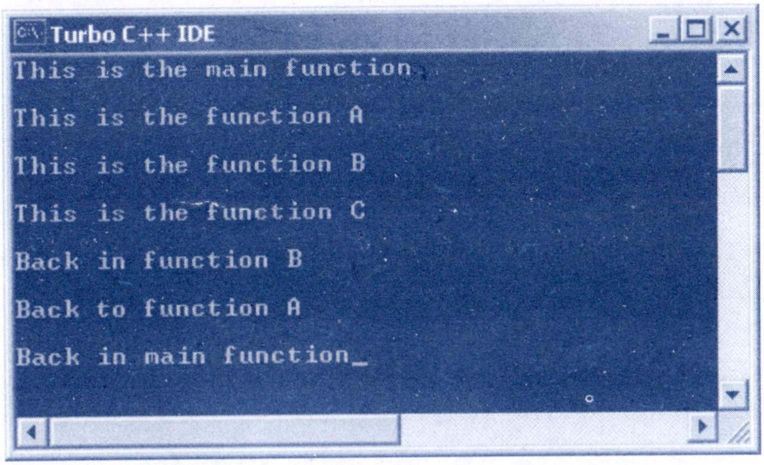

Fig. 16.27 Explaining the usage of nested functions

16.8.2 Function Definition

Functions are of two forms, functions with arguments and functions without arguments. The programs, which we have discussed above, use functions without any arguments. The general structure of the functions with arguments is as follows:

```
Function_type function name(arguments)
Data type of arguments;
{
Block of statements;
Return statement;
}
```

Function type represents the return type of the function that could be **void**, **int**, **char**, **float**, etc. The name of the function could be any variable name but should not be any keyword. A C function can contain any number of arguments. The arguments, which are also known as formal parameters, act as the input data for the functions to carry out a specific task. The data type of the arguments can be specified within the argument list or outside the argument list as shown in the above code. After specifying the arguments, the statements contained in the body of the function are defined. After the execution of the body of the function, the value evaluated by the function is returned to the main program using the return statement. The following program illustrates the creation and the use of functions with arguments:

```
#include<stdio.h>
#include<conio.h>
void main()
{
int a,b,result;
clrscr();
```

```
printf("Enter the two numbers to be added:");
scanf("%d %d",&a,&b);
result=sum(a,b);/* Function call */
printf("\nThe addition of two numbers is:%d",result);
getch();
}
int sum(int x,int y)/* Function definition */
{
int z;/* Local variable*/
z=x+y;
return(z);
}
```

The function **sum( )** which computes the sum of two integer values is defined with two formal parameters **x** and **y**. The function call

```
result = sum(a, b);
```

transfers the control to function **sum( )** which assigns the values of actual parameters **a** and **b** to the formal parameters **x** and **y** respectively. The value of **z**, which is the sum of **x** and **y** is returned back to the main function and assigned to the variable *result*.

Since the value to be returned by the function **sum( )** is of type **int**, the return-type of the function is specified as **int**.

Figure 16.28 shows the output of the program.

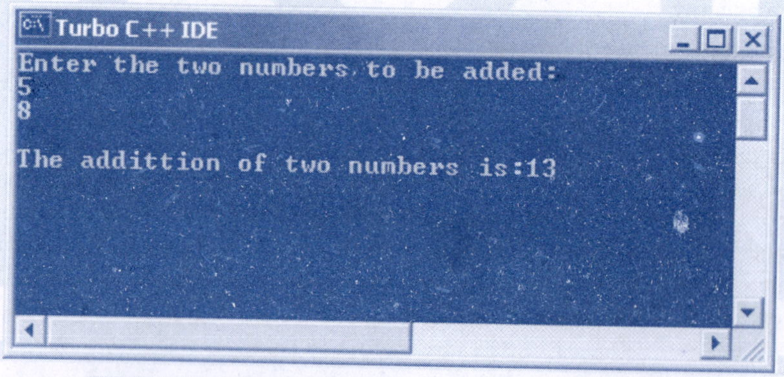

Fig. 16.28 Explaining the usage of functions with arguments

Example 16.7 *Write a program to receive a **float** and an **int** number from **main( )** function. Find the product of these two numbers and return the product, which is printed through the **main( )** function.*

Solution The following program shows how the product is calculated and the product is returned to the **main( )** function:

```
#include<stdio.h>
#include<conio.h>
float product(int,float);/* Function declaration */
void main()
{
int x;
float y,prod;
clrscr();
printf(“Enter the integeral and real numbers:”);
scanf(“%d %f”,&x,&y);
prod=product(x,y);/* Function call */
printf(“Product of %d and %f is = %f”,x,y,prod);
getch();
}
float product(int a, float b)/* Function definition */
{
float p;
p=a*b;
return(p);
}
```

Figure 16.29 shows the output of the above program.

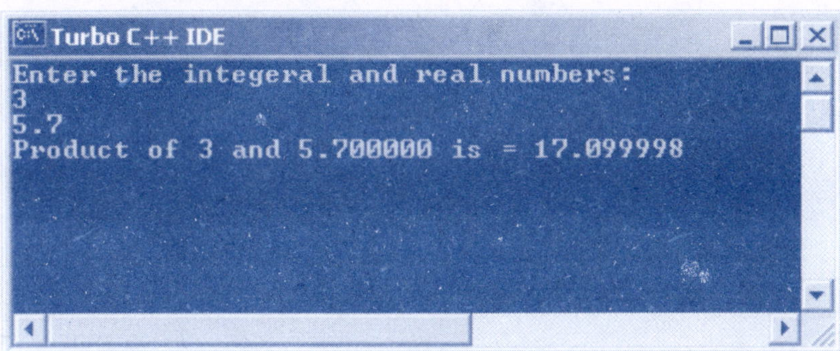

Fig. 16.29 Displaying the two numbers returned to main function

Note: *When the actual parameters are of mixed types, the types must match the types of formal parameters in the function definition, in number and order. In this program, x is of type **int** and y and prod are of type **float**. If the parameters do not match in type and number, the compiler will produce an error message.*

16.9 STRUCTURES

Structure is a user-defined data type that is used to represent a group of data items of different types under a single name. The different types of data items could be characters, integers, strings, etc. For example, a structure can be created to represent employees' personal details like their name, address, salary, etc.

16.9.1 Defining a Structure

A structure consists of different data types grouped together in a single entity. The structures can be defined by using the **struct** keyword as follows:

```
struct employee {
            char name [50];
            char deptt [120];
            int age;
            int salary;
};
```

Here, a new data type employee is defined. The elements, *name*, *deptt*, *age* and *salary* are called structure elements in which *name* and *deptt* belong to **char** data type, while *age* and *salary* belong to **int** data type. Structure definition always ends with a semicolon.

16.9.2 Declaring Structure Variables

After the format of a structured data type has been defined, its variables can be declared. For example, the variables of structure data type, **employee** will be declared as follows:

```
employee emp1, emp2, emp3;
```

Here, *emp1*, *emp2* and *emp3* are the three variables that are declared to be of **employee** data type. The complete declaration of employee structure is as follows:

```
struct employee {
            char name [50];
            char deptt [120];
            int age;
            int salary;
};
employee emp1, emp2, emp3;
```

Each of the employee variables declared above will have all the four elements—*name*, *deptt*, *age* and *salary*.

Example 16.8 *Define a structure, student, which contains elements like student's name, class, rollno, marks1, marks2, marks3, etc. Write a program using structure to read these values, calculate the total marks, the marks percentage and display the complete information on the screen.*

Solution The following program shows how the total marks and the marks percentage of the student is calculated using the structure student:

```
struct student
{
char name[20];
```

```
int std;
int rollno;
float m1, m2, m3;
float total;
float percentage;
};
void main()
{
struct student st;
clrscr();
printf("Enter name: ");
scanf("%s", st.name);
printf("Enter std: ");
scanf("%d", &st.std);
printf("Enter rollno: ");
scanf("%d", &st.rollno);
printf("Enter marks: ");
scanf ("%f %f %f",&st.m1,&st.m2,&st.m3);
st.total=st.m1+st.m2+st.m3;
st.percentage = st.total/3;
printf("Student's name is %s\n", st.name);
printf("%s studies in %d\n", st.name, st.std);
printf("Roll no of %s is %d\n", st.name, st.rollno);
printf("The total marks of %s are %f\n", st.name,
        st.total);
printf("The percentage of %s is %f\n", st.name,
        st.percentage);
getch();
}
```

In the above code, *name*, *std*, *rollno*, *m1*, *m2*, *m3*, *total* and *percentage* represent the elements of the structure **student**. The structure is instantiated inside the **main** function and the information is displayed using **printf** statement. Note that the structure elements are accessed using dot (.) operator with the structure variable name, like *st.name*.

Figure 16.30 shows the output of the above program.

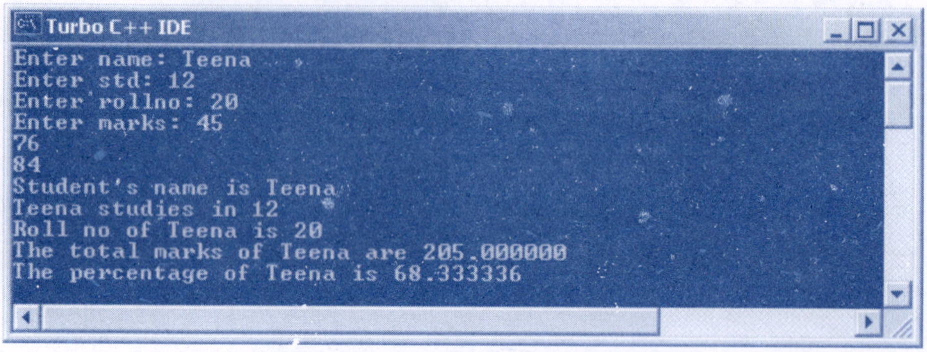

Fig. 16.30 Explaining the usage of structures

16.10 POINTERS

A pointer is defined as a variable that stores the address of another variable. A pointer variable is represented by using asterisk sign, * followed by the pointer variable name. The general syntax of pointer declaration is as follows:

```
data-type *pointer-name;
```

Here, data-type represents the data type of the pointer variable and pointer-name represents the name of the pointer. Example:

```
int *p;
```

Here, **int** represents the integer data type of the pointer variable, **p** represents the name of the pointer and * specifies that the variable declared is a pointer. In C, **p** specifies the address of another variable while ***p** represents the value stored at the address pointed to by **p**.

To assign the address of a variable to a pointer, an address operator, **&** is used before the variable name. The following are the characteristics of pointers:

- Pointers are used to hold only the memory addresses of variables but not their values.
- Pointers are also used to access the elements of an array.
- Pointers are used to allocate the memory dynamically to the elements.

The following program illustrates the use of pointers:

```
#include<stdio.h>
#include<conio.h>
void main()
{
```

```
int i;
int *j;
clrscr();
j=&i;
*j=5;
printf(“Address of i:%u\n”, &i);
printf(“Address pointed to by j:%u\n”, j);
printf(“Value of i:%d\n”, i);
printf(“Value contained in address pointed to by j:%d\n”,*j);
getch();
}
```

In the above code, the variable, *i* is declared as an integer data type and variable *j* is declared as a pointer of integer data type. The memory address of variable, *i* is assigned to the pointer variable, *j* by using the address operator. The location pointed to by the pointer variable *j* is set to 5, which means that *i* also takes the value 5. The **printf** statements are used to display the addresses and values of *i* and *j* variables on the screen.

Figure 16.31 shows the output of the above program.

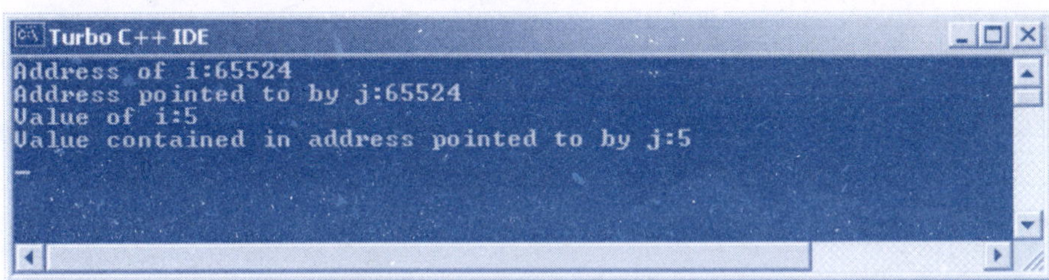

Fig. 16.31 Explaining the usage of pointers

16.11 FILES IN C

A file is defined as a collection of different types of data such as text, symbols and numbers that are stored on a disk. C programs can also make use of files to store and retrieve data. For doing this, C supports the mechanism of file handling. The different functions related to file handling in C are as follows:

- **Opening a file** A file can be opened by using the function fopen. Before opening a file, we must specify the name of the file and the opening mode of the file. The function, fopen takes two arguments, the file name and the opening mode of the file. The different opening modes of a file are as follows:
  - **r.** It opens a file for reading purpose only.
  - **w.** It opens a file for writing purpose only.
  - **a.** It opens a file for appending purpose only.
  - **r+.** It opens a file for both reading and writing. In this mode, read or write operation is performed in the file from the beginning.

- o **w+.** It opens a file for both reading and writing. In this mode, if an existing file is opened, then the data already present in the file is deleted; otherwise a new file is created with the specified name.
- o **a+.** It opens a file for both reading and writing. In this mode, if an existing file is opened, then only new data can be entered in the file and the previous content can not be modified. If the file does not exist then a new file is created with the specified name.

The general syntax for opening a file is as follows:

```
FILE *fptr;
fptr=fopen("file-name", "opening-mode");
```

Here, **FILE** represents the data type and **fptr** represents a file pointer of **FILE** data type. The file pointer, **fptr** points to the file, which is to be opened; and fopen represents the function used for opening a file. The argument file-name represents the name of file, which is to be opened and the opening-mode represents any one of the different modes for opening a file such as r, w or a.

- **Reading a file** A file can be read by using functions such as **fscanf**, **fgets** and **fgetc**. The function **fscanf** reads one or more than one character from the file but cannot read the space characters present in the file. The function **fgets** only reads the data from a file, which has the length up to 1 KB whereas the function fgetc reads only one character at a time from a file.

- **Writing to a file** A file can be written using the function, **fprintf**, which is similar to printf function.

- **Closing a file** A file can be closed by using the function, **fclose**. The function **fclose** is used to close any file that is already open.

The general syntax for closing a file is as follows:

```
fclose(fptr);
```

Here, **fclose** represents the function used for closing any opened file in C and **fptr** represents the file pointer related to the file.

The following program illustrates the **open**, **read** and **close** file operations in C:

```
#include<stdio.h>
#include<conio.h>
void main()
{
    FILE *fptr;
    char arr[50];
    clrscr();
    fptr = fopen("example.txt","r");
    fgets(arr,sizeof(arr),fptr);
    fclose(fptr);
    printf("%s\n", arr);
    getch();
}
```

In the above code, **fptr** is a file pointer, which points to the file that is to be opened and **arr** is a character array declared as a buffer for storing the string read from the file. The file, **example.txt** is opened using the **fopen** function. The contents of the file are read using the **fgets** function. This function takes three parameters, buffer variable, size of the buffer and the file pointer. In the end, the **fclose** function is used for closing the file.

Note: *For successfully running the above program, a file named example.txt containing some sample text needs to be created.*

Figure 16.32 shows the output of the above program.

Fig. 16.32 Illustrating the use of different file functions

Chapter Summary

C is the most popularly used procedure-oriented programming language. To write programs in C, we need to understand the various terms, such as characters, identifiers, keywords, constants, variables and data types. Characters include alphabets, numbers and some special characters such as @, % and &. The combination of the characters forms identifiers. Variables are the elements whose values can be changed during the execution of a program. On the other hand, constants are the values that remain unchanged during the execution of a program. The keywords are the reserved words that cannot be used as a variable name or as a function name. The data types specify the type of a data entity, such as integer, float and character. To perform specific operations in C, we can use different operators such as arithmetic, relational, logical, assignment and conditional.

In C, the control statements are used to transfer the control from one part of a program to another depending on a specific condition. C provides various conditional statements such as **if else**, **switch**, and **break** that help in transferring the control from one part of a program to another. Depending on the conditions given, we can repeat a block of statements by using the **do-while** and **for** statements. Sometimes, in complex programs, the repetition of a particular block of statements increases the size of the program. In order to avoid this situation, functions are used in C programs. Functions are the blocks of code defined to perform a specific task. In a C program, one or more functions can be used. Functions are called in the **main( )** function and are defined outside the main function. We can call a function using the function name with the required number of arguments in the parenthesis. Arguments are specified in the functions to pass the values between the main program and the function.

A variable pointing to another variable is known as pointer. Pointers are used in C to preserve memory space as they help in dynamic memory allocation. Dynamic memory allocation refers to the allocation of memory at run time. C also supports file handling through which different operations on a file can be performed such as opening a file, reading from or writing to a file and closing a file.

SAMPLE PROGRAMS

Sample 16.1 *Write a program to multiply the two numbers taken as input from the user.*

Solution The following program shows how two numbers entered by a user are multiplied:

```
#include<stdio.h>
#include<conio.h>
void main ()
{
int number1, number2;      /* Numbers to be multiplied*/
int result;      /* Result stores the result of multiplication*/
clrscr();
printf ("Enter two numbers");
scanf("%d%d", &number1,&number2);
result=(number1*number2);
printf("The result is:%d", result);
getch();
}
```

Figure 16.33 shows the output of the above program.

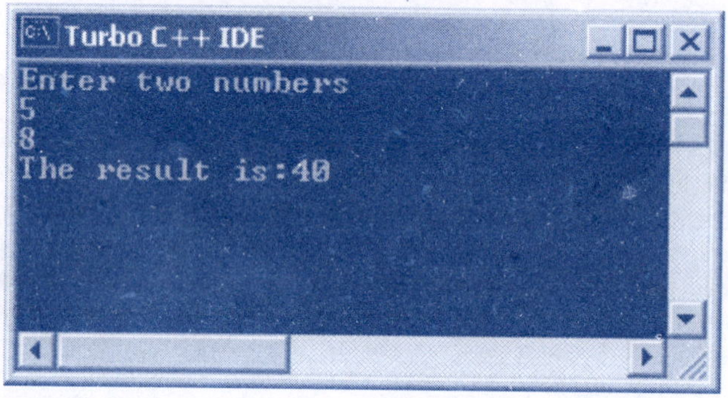

Fig. 16.33 Displaying the result of the multiplication of two numbers

Sample 16.2 *Write a program to enter the marks of five different subjects of a student and display their total and percentage.*

Solution The following program shows how the marks of five different subjects are entered and their total and percentage is calculated:

```
#include<stdio.h>
#include<conio.h>
void main()
{
float m1,m2,m3,m4,m5; /* Marks of the five subjects*/
float total,percentage;   /*Total and percentage of five subjects*/

clrscr();
printf("Enter the marks of five subjects:");
```

```
scanf("%f%f%f%f%f",&m1,&m2,&m3,&m4,&m5);
total=(m1+m2+m3+m4+m5);
percentage=total/5;
printf("\nTotal marks obtained by a student is:%f",total);
printf("\n\nPercentage marks of the student
   is:%f",percentage);
getch();
}
```

Figure 16.34 shows the output of the above program.

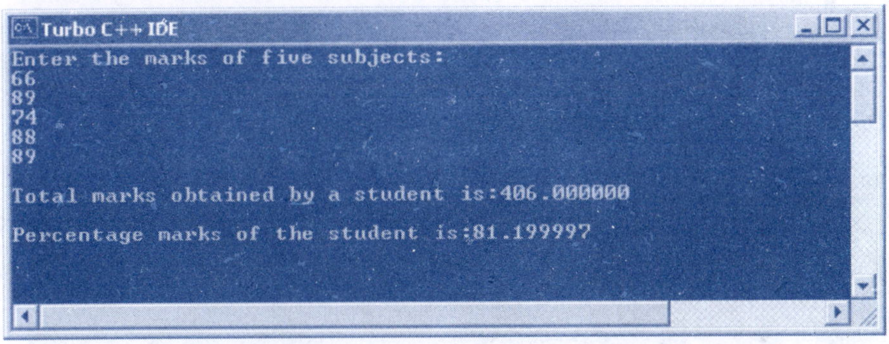

Fig. 16.34 Displaying total marks and percentage

Sample 16.3 *Write a program to generate a pyramid of numbers.*

Solution The following program shows the code to generate a pyramid of numbers:

```
#include<stdio.h>
#include<conio.h>
void main()
{
int n,i,y,x=25;
clrscr();
printf("\nEnter the number:\n");
scanf("%d",&n);

for(y=0;y<=n;y++)
{
        gotoxy(x,y+1);    /*(x-coordinate, y-coordinate)*/
```

```
        for(i=0-y;i<=y;i++)
                printf("%3d",abs(i));
        x=x-3;
}
getch();
}
```

In the above code, four variables, i.e. *n*, *i*, *y* and *x* are taken as integer type inside the **main** function. The value of variable *x* is initialised as 25 and value of variable *n* is entered by the user that specifies the number upto which the pyramid will be displayed. The **for** loop used that contains a **gotoxy** function, an inner for loop and **abs** function. **gotoxy** is a function that is used to move the cursor at a specific (*x*, *y*) location on the screen, where *x* specifies the *x*-coordinate in horizontal direction and *y* specifies the *y*-coordinate in vertical direction. In the above program, `gotoxy(x, y + 1)` means that cursor first go to the position *x* and *y* and then increment *y*-coordinate by 1. The **abs** function is used here to display the absolute value of *i* on the screen.

Figure 16.35 shows the output of the above program.

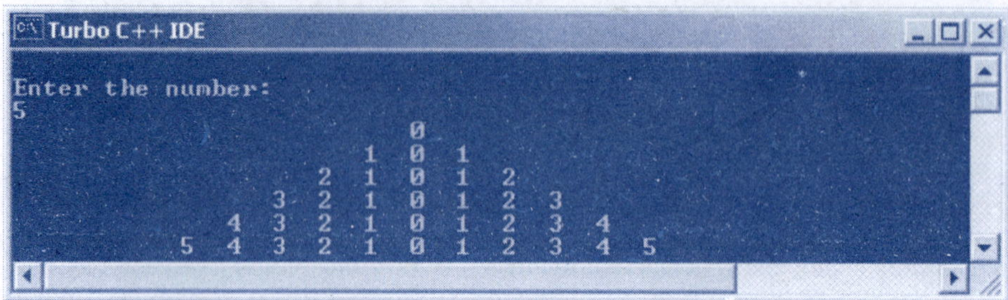

Fig. 16.35 Explaining the usage of data types

Sample 16.4 *Write a program to print prime numbers between 1 to 100.*

Solution The following program shows how prime numbers between 1 to 100 are calculated:

```
#include<stdio.h>
#include<conio.h>
void main()
{
int i,n=1;
clrscr();
printf("Prime numbers between 1 to 100 are:\n");
while(n<=100)
{
        i=2;
        while(i<n)
```

```
        {
                if(n%i==0)
                        break;
                else
                        i++;
        }
        if(i==n)
                printf("%d\t",n);
        n++;
}
getch();
}
```

The above program will display the prime numbers existing between 1 to 100. A prime number is an integer greater than 1 that is divisible only by 1 and itself. Figure 16.36 shows the output of the above program.

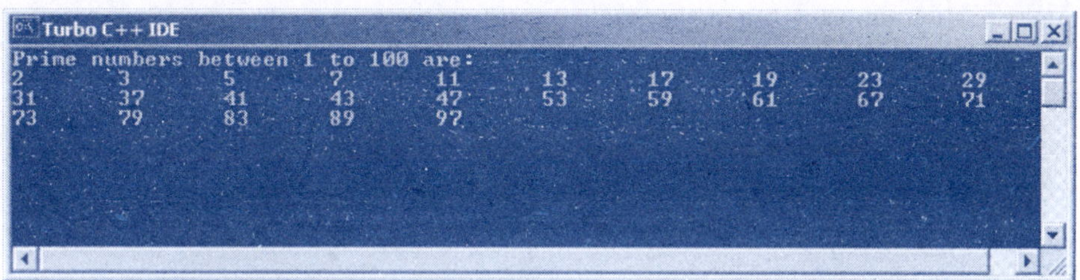

Fig. 16.36 Displaying the prime numbers between 1 to 100

Key Terms to Remember

- **Keywords:** Keywords, also known as reserved words, are the special words reserved by C.
- **Data type:** Data type refers to the structural format of the data used in the program.
- **Primary data types:** Primary data types are the data types, which are supported by all the compilers of C.
- **Constant:** Constant refers to the fixed value, which cannot be changed during the execution of a program.
- **Variables:** Variables are the names, which are assigned to different memory locations for storing the data.
- **Operators:** Operators are the symbols, which perform certain operations on one or more values.
- **Control statements:** Control statements are responsible for controlling the flow of execution of instructions in a program.
- **Selection statements:** Selection statements are the statements, which test for a particular condition in a program and cause a change in the flow of the program if the particular condition is met.
- **Iterative statements:** Iterative statements are the statements, which are used for repeating the execution of a particular set of statements for a specific number of times.

- **Jump control statements:** Jump control statements are the statements, which cause the program to jump from a particular location in the program to another specified location.
- **Array:** Array is defined as a collection of different elements having similar data type.
- **Strings:** Strings are defined as the character arrays in which each character is stored using one byte in the memory.
- **Function:** Function is a set of statements, which are used to perform some specific task.
- **Structure:** Structure is a user-defined data type, which is used to represent a group of data items having different types under a single name.
- **Pointer:** Pointer is defined as a variable that stores the address of another variable.
- **File:** A file is a collection of related data items stored on a disk.

Review Questions

Fill in the Blanks

1. C is a _______ language.
2. C was developed in _______ by _________.
3. ________, ________ and ________ are the basic building blocks of C.
4. Keywords are also known as ________ words.
5. The total number of keywords available in C is ________.
6. Constants are divided in ______ major categories.
7. A variable declared as long int occupies ___________bytes of memory.
8. A variable in C can be declared as float if it is within the range of ________ to __________.
9. ________ assignment operator assigns the right hand side value of the expression to the left hand of the expression.
10. The logical NOT operation is performed by _______ operator.
11. Bit-manipulation operators are also known as __________.
12. The data bits are shifted to the right using _______ operator.
13. ________ operators have highest priority.
14. ________ operators have lowest priority.
15. The long double data type holds ________ bytes in the memory.
16. Iterative statements include _______, ________ and ________ statements.
17. Jump control statements include _______ and ________ statements.
18. An ________ is a collection of different elements having similar data type.
19. An array of character is known as _______.
20. __________ is a user-defined data type, which is used to represent a group of data items of different types under a single name.
21. Pointers are used to store only the ____________ of variables but not values.

Multiple Choice Questions

1. What are the main components of a character set?
   A. Letters and digits B. Blank spaces C. Special symbols D. All of the above
2. Which of the following is a keyword?
   A. void B. goto C. register D. All of the above
3. Which is the correct format of writing #define?
   A. #define pi 3.141 B. #define size 10 C. #define name "APT" D. All of the above
4. What is the range of unsigned char?
   A. 0 to 255 B. 0 to 4255 C. –128 to 127 D. None of the above
5. What is the range of short int?
   A. 0 to 65535 B. –32768 to 32767 C. –128 to 127 D. 0 to 255
6. What is the right way of declaring a constant?
   A. **const int** *size* = 10; B. **const int** *size*; C. **int** *size*; D. None of the above
7. What is the output of the following code?

```
for(m=15;m>7;m-=1)
printf(m);
```

   A. The code is erroneous B. Print numbers from 15 to 7 in reverse order
   C. Print numbers from 15 to 6 in reverse order D. Print numbers from 6 to 15
8. Which of the following is used to represent a null character?
   A. \n B. \0 C. \b D. \f
9. Which of the following is not a valid variable name?
   A. *T_marks* B. *Name* C. *45xy* D. *value*
10. Which of the following operators is used for making comparison between different operands?
    A. Arithmetic operator B. Relational operator C. Logical operator D. Assignment operator
11. Which of the following is a control statement in C?
    A. **While** B. **If else** C. **Break** D. All of the above
12. Which of the following statements is used to make a selection from more than two choices?
    A. **Else if** B. **Nested if else** C. **Switch** D. None of the above
13. Which of the following statements is not an iterative statement?
    A. **While** B. **Continue** C. **Do while** D. **For**
14. Which is the correct form of an array declaration?
    A. **int** *marks*[10]; B. **int** [10]*marks*; C. **int** *marks*[10] D. None of the above
15. Which is the correct form of a string declaration?
    A. **str** *employee*[20]; B. **str** [20]*employee;*
    C. **char** [20]*employee;* D. **char** *employee*[20];
16. Which of the following is a function in C?
    A. **Main** B. **Printf** C. **Scanf** D. None of the above

17. Which of the following keywords is used to declare a structure?

A. **default** B. **struct** C. **structure** D. **static**

18. Which is the correct form of a pointer declaration?

A. **int** *pointer**; B. **int** **pointer*; C. **int** *pointer** D. None of the above

19. Which of the following operators is used as an address operator in C?

A. & B. * C. ++ D. None of the above

20. Which of the following functions is related to file handling in C?

A. **fopen** B. **fclose** C. **fgetc** D. All of the above

21. Which is the correct form to open a file in C:

A. fl = **fopen**("file", "r"); B. **fopen** = fl("file", "r");

C. fl = **fopen**("r", "file"); D. **fopen** = fl("r", file");

22. Which of the following functions is used to read only one character at a time in a C file?

A. **fscanf** B. **fgetc** C. **fgets** D. None of the above

Discussion Questions

1. Give a brief description of the history of C language.
2. Discuss briefly the characteristics of C.
3. What are the advantages and disadvantages of C?
4. What are the various keywords used in C?
5. Explain different data types in C.
6. What is a constant? Explain the constants in C.
7. What is a variable? How are the variables declared in C?
8. What is the significance of & symbol? Illustrate with an example.
9. List the different types of control statements in C.
10. Give the output of the following code:

```
float c = 34.78650;
printf ("%6.2f" , c);
```

11. Write a program in C to find the value of y using the relation $y = x^2 + 2x - 1$.
12. Write a program in C to find the sum and the average of three numbers.
13. Write a program in C to calculate simple interest.
14. Write a program in C to convert the temperature from 0C to 0F.
15. Write a program in C to evaluate the series $S = 1 + 2 * 1 + 3 * 2 + \ldots.. N * N - 1$.
16. Write a program in C to print the factorial of all the numbers from 1 to 15.
17. Write a program in C to generate and print the numbers between 100 and 200 which are divisible by 4 but not by 5.
18. What do you mean by arrays and strings? Explain with the help of an example.
19. Write a C program using functions to find the smallest of the given three numbers.
20. Explain how structures are different from arrays.
21. Describe the concept of pointers with the help of an example.
22. What are the different functions related to file handling in C?

APPENDIX A

MULTIMEDIA

A.1 INTRODUCTION

Multimedia is one of the most commonly used terms in the entertainment industry, which produces various entertainment products such as movies and video games. It is defined as a system, which represents information through various media components, such as music, video, sound, text and images.

Multimedia is of two types, *interactive multimedia* and *non-interactive multimedia*. Interactive multimedia refers to the multimedia, which runs on the basis of the instructions provided by the end user. It consists of the various user interfaces such as command buttons and audio commands that enable an end user to interact with the multimedia application. The interactive multimedia is also known as *non-linear multimedia*. E-learning applications, which include text images and audio, are good examples of interactive multimedia. The non-interactive multimedia does not contain any user interface and runs on the basis of instructions and information stored in the storage medium of computer system. The non-interactive multimedia is generally known as *linear multimedia*. Cartoon films are a very good example of non-interactive multimedia system.

Figure A.1 shows the interactive and the non-interactive multimedia systems.

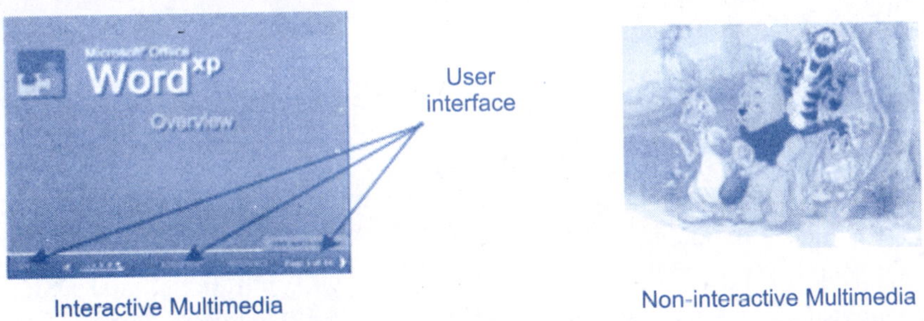

Fig. A.1 Interactive and non-interactive multimedia

A.2 IMPORTANT MULTIMEDIA ISSUES

Whenever we need to develop a multimedia product, which consists of multiple media components, we must take care of the different issues pertaining to these media components, such as text, audio, graphics and video. The issues could be related to the ownership and publication of the multimedia product. The various issues are:

- **Copyright issue** Copyright issue is related to the protection of the ownership of a publishing product. Copyright can be defined as a collection of rights that permits or prohibits the use of the theme of an idea or information. Therefore, copyright concerns the following:

- o Providing rights to an author for reproducing the product.
- o Allowing an author to distribute the copy of the work.
- o Allowing authors to publish their product uniquely.

- **Bandwidth issue** Bandwidth issue is related to the transferring of the multimedia product through a communication channel. It takes into consideration various properties such as frequency, amplitude, data transfer rate, nature of the sending medium, etc. These properties play an important role in the distribution of the multimedia content through a communication medium. These properties help ascertain the speed and accuracy with which a multimedia information would be transferred.
- **Video issue** Video issue concerns the different factors related to the video component of the multimedia product. The file size of the video component, bandwidth and the communication medium used to publish the multimedia are examples of these factors. Whenever we need to develop a multimedia product, we must consider these factors, because it helps in choosing the best bandwidth and storage requirement for digital video. File size of a video component also affects the quality of video used in the multimedia product. A large size video component requires more bandwidth for transmission. Hence, a trade-off needs to be attained between the various properties pertaining to the video component and the available bandwidth. In order to decrease the file size, the following tasks can be performed:
  - o Reducing the size of frame per sample.
  - o Applying compression techniques
  - o Reducing the bit-depth.
- **Sound issue** Sound issue concerns the various properties of the audio component of the multimedia application. A user can access information related to the audio component from the audiofaq directory. The *audiofaq directory* enables the user to select the appropriate frequency, audio file format and sound application formats by providing information related to the sound properties of the multimedia application.

A.3 AUDIO

Audio component produces the audio signals, which make the multimedia application attractive as well as more understandable to the end user. Audio signals include sound alarms and audio instructions in the multimedia application. Whenever audio is to be incorporated into the multimedia application, the developer needs to first record the audio on a storage medium. In order to store the audio signals, a number of digital storage formats are available.

A.3.1 Digital Form of Audio Signal

Originally, audio signals are always in the analog form where the value of an audio signal continuously changes with time. However, when the audio signal is incorporated in a multimedia application, it is converted into digital signal, which uses only two values 0 and 1 at any instant of time. The process by which analog data is converted into digital data is known as *sampling process*. In the sampling process, some samples of voltages are taken from the audio signals at the regular intervals of time.

Quality of sound stored in the form of digital data depends on the number of bits used for a sample and the difference between the time-intervals used to take samples from the audio signals. The files in which digital signals are stored are generally known as *digital audio file*. The digital audio file can be processed like any other binary file in the computer. Computers can playback audio files using audio playback software such as Windows Media player.

A.3.2 File Formats Used to Store Audio

Digital audio is stored in different file formats. These file formats can be categorised into three types:

- **Uncompressed audio** In this type of file format, several combinations of sampling rates can be easily stored in a file. The audio files used to store uncompressed data do not take much time to process the information. However, these file formats occupy a lot of space in the memory.
- **Audio compressed with lossless compression technique** In this type of file format, audio files are compressed with lossless compression algorithms. Lossless compression algorithms are those algorithms, which compress the data without causing any loss of information. Time required to process these file formats is more as compared to the time required to process the uncompressed file formats. The advantage of this file format is that, it uses less space to store files.
- **Audio compressed with lossy compression technique** In this type of file format, data is compressed with lossy compression algorithm. The Lossy compression algorithms are those algorithms, which delete the redundant data while compressing a file. Hence, quality of information stored in these file formats gets affected. These file formats are commonly used to store those audio files, which are embedded in web applications. The small size of these file formats enables the audio files to be easily transmitted over the Internet.

Table A.1 lists the various audio file formats used to store information related to the audio component of a multimedia application.

Table A.1 Various audio file formats

File format	Full name	Use	Extension
WAV	Waveform audio format	To store any combination of sampling rates of the different audio signals having varying size.	.wav
MPEG	Moving Picture Experts Group	To store those audio files, which have to be downloaded from the Internet.	.mp3
WMA	Window Media Audio	To encode and compress digital audio files. This format was introduced by Microsoft	.wma
MIDI	Musical Instrument Digital Interface	To represent different properties such as pitch and volume of the sound produced by the electronic musical components.	.mid
RA	Real Audio	To store the digital audio files that can be directly played using the real player software	.ra

A.3.3 Incorporating Sound in a Multimedia Application

There are certain prerequisites that a computer system must meet before a multimedia application can be created using it. These prerequisites include, sound card, audio media player, device driver, etc. For incorporating audio in a multimedia application, a user has to perform the following steps:

1. Identify the type of sound that has to be incorporated in the multimedia application.
2. Analyze and mark the instances where sound is to be added in a multimedia application.
3. Obtain the audio files in a specific file format on a storage medium.
4. Insert the appropriate commands for playing the audio information in the storyboard or design document of the multimedia application.
5. Play the multimedia application to test the proper integration of sound in the multimedia application.

A.4 MOVIES AND VIDEO

Movies and video are the most important components of a multimedia application. It is preferable to incorporate video elements in a multimedia application because:

- Video elements enable us to include certain sequences, which are not economical to produce with computer animations.
- Video elements enable us to incorporate live lectures, demonstrations and other prerecorded material.

A multimedia application in which multiple video elements are embedded requires a large amount of storage space because movie and video files are generally heavier in size. According to the National Television Standards Committee (NTSC) standards, a video element requires 27 megabytes of storage medium in order to display a video clipping of one second. Hence, a multimedia developer must acquire a storage device with large storage capacity in order to incorporate video elements in a multimedia application.

It is possible to reduce the storage requirements of a video element by means of compression techniques. The various compression techniques used for compressing video files are:

- ***MPEG*** It is one of the most common encoding and compression standard developed by the Moving Picture Experts Group (MPEG). MPEG supports several different standards such as MPEG1, MPEG2, MPEG3, MPEG4, and MPEG7. The video files shared over the Internet are generally stored in MPEG format.
- ***P*64*** It is a compression and encoding technique that is used for transmitting audio and video files over physical transmission media such as fiber optics and coaxial cable. Video and audio data encoded in P*64 format can achieve transfer rates of 4 Mbps.
- ***Indeo*** It is a compression technology that uses Intel-based hardware components for processing image information. While compressing the data, it uses two types of compression techniques, Production Level Video (PLV) and Real Time Video (RTV).

Preparing video element for multimedia While incorporating video elements in a multimedia application, proper care must be taken during shooting and editing of videos. The following are some of the key considerations pertaining to capturing of videos:

- ***Stability of platform*** The surface where the shooting camera is placed should be smooth and flat. This prevents the videos from blurring and shaking affects.

- ***Availability of light*** The light present in the vicinity of the area where video is being shot also affects the quality of the video. A lighting source must be used in order to ensure equal and adequate lighting effect on all the objects.
- ***Blue screen technique*** The quality of a video element is also affected by its background. Multimedia developers frequently use the blue screen technique to manipulate the background of a video element. In this screen, a video is shot in front of a blue plane background. After shooting the video element, a suitable background is edited in to the video element.

A.5 VIRTUAL REALITY AND 3D MODELLING

Virtual reality system is a powerful multimedia environment that is based on the concept of virtual reality. Virtual reality enables the users to attain a virtual identity of their own. With the help of an artificial multimedia environment comprising of sound, animation and video, these virtual identities are realised through moving virtual objects. The artificial environment is actually a simulated environment where users attaining virtual identities interact with each other through different multimedia input devices.

A virtual reality system enables an end user to view a three-dimensional simulated environment. The most common application area of a virtual reality system is video games and flight simulators. Flight simulators are used to train aircraft pilots; it greatly reduces the training cost as well the associated risk.

Virtual reality systems are created with the help of Virtual Reality Modelling Language (VRML). VRML is a computer language that helps create 3D objects and views. VRML uses a special format to store the values that affect the brightness, contrast, colour, size and shape of the objects involved in a scene. A change in the values of these properties depicts the movement of objects as well as changing of a scene.

The various types of virtual reality systems are:

- **Simulation-based virtual reality system** In this system, a simulation of a real environment is created so that the users feel that they are actually present in that environment. A driving simulator is a very good example of this type of virtual reality system. A driving simulator makes the users feel that they are actually driving the vehicle.
- **Desktop-based virtual reality system** In this system, a three-dimensional virtual environment is displayed on the computer screen. The games played on computer are an example of this type of virtual reality system.
- **Projector-based virtual reality system** In this system, the virtual environment is displayed on a projector. The common examples of projector-based virtual reality systems are construction modelling, robot navigation and airplane simulation.

A.5.1 3D Modelling

In a virtual reality system, object movement is represented by the changes occurring in the position, shape and size of the objects. In order to represent the object's movement, developers use various 3D modelling techniques. 3D modelling can be defined as the process of representing an object in the form of wireframe model, which takes into consideration the mathematical properties of an object. The mathematical properties of an object include its dimensions and its distance with respect to a particular point.

The wire frame of an object does not contain any surface elements and the complete object is represented through connecting lines or wires. The wire frame model of the object is also known as 3D model that is developed with the help of special software, such as 3DS Max and Maya. Figure A.2 shows the wire frame model of different objects.

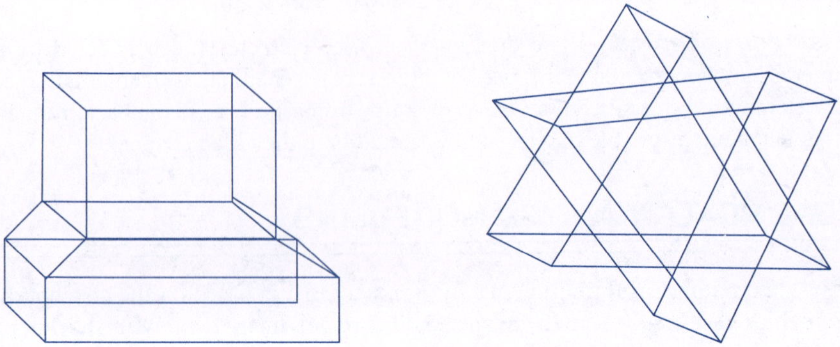

Fig. A.2 Wire frames of different objects

A.6 MULTIMEDIA AND HTML

Multimedia components are included in a Web page or HTML document in order to enhance the interactivity of a Web site. The various multimedia components that can be included in a Web page include images, audio, video, etc. The links that are used to connect to the various multimedia elements in a Web page are called hypermedia. A hypermedia could be an image or text clicking which the corresponding multimedia component gets initiated.

An HTML document is basically divided into two parts, head part and body part. The head part consists of the title of the HTML document whereas the body part contains the text and other elements of the Web page. In an HTML document, everything is specified with the help of tags. To embed multimedia components in a Web page, HTML supports some special tags. Table A.2 lists some of the HTML tags used to insert multimedia elements.

Table A.2 HTML tags used to insert multimedia elements

HTML tag	Multimedia component	Tag syntax
<IMG>	Image	<img src=url_of_image width=image_width height= image_height>
<INSERT>	Video, sound, image, OLE control	<insert data="name_of_video type=" format_of_video> </insert>
<EMBED>	Video and audio	<embed src= "name _of_videofile.extension" width=video_width height= video_height>
<APP> and <APPLET>	Code	<applet code= class file width=applet_width height= applet_height > </applet>
<FONT>	Text	<font size="text_size" color= "text_color" > Text_line </font>

In order to understand how HTML helps developers to insert multimedia components in a Web page, consider the following example where an image is inserted in a Web page using HTML.

```
</title>
</head>
<font color="pink" >
<body bgcolor="purple">
<h1 align="center"> Multimedia images on the Web page</h1>
<font size="6", color="yellow"><b><i>Happiness</b></i> is the key
to success so <b><i>always celebrate</b></i> each moment of your
life <br>
<br>
<img src="disney.jpg" width = "300" height = "400">
</font>
</body>
</html>
```

In this code, the text written between the <body> tags will be displayed on the Web page. The background of the Web page will be displayed in purple color as specified inside the opening <body> tag. The heading written in <h1> tags will be aligned to the center of the Web page and displayed in pink color. The text is formatted using the <font> tags by specifying its attributes such as size and color. The text specified in the <b> tags will be displayed as bold and the text specified in the <i> tags will be displayed as italic on the Web page. The <br> tag is used here to insert a single line break after the text. Here, an <img> tag is used to insert an image on the Web page by specifying its source and attributes such as width and height.

Figure A.3 shows the output of the above HTML code.

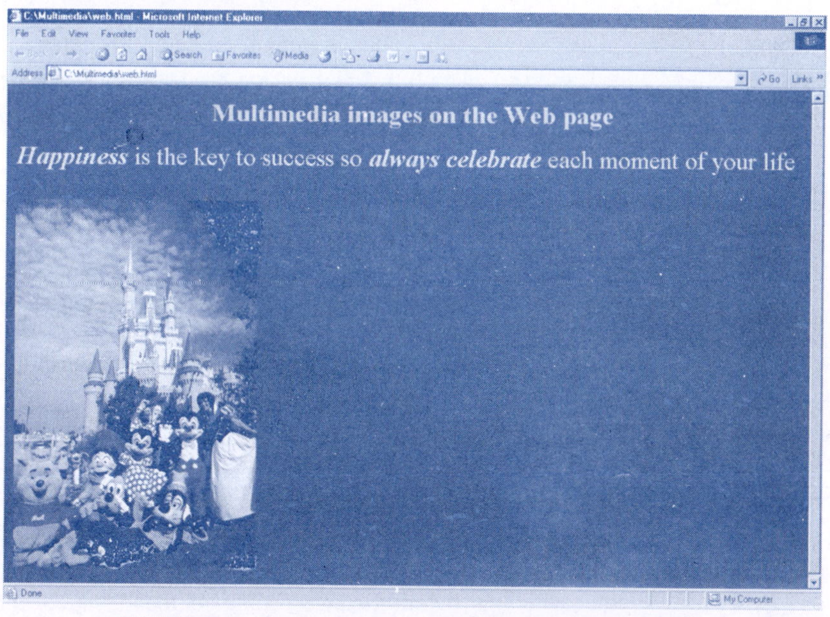

Fig. A.3 A web page containing multimedia image and text

APPENDIX B

COMPUTER GRAPHICS

B.1 INTRODUCTION

Computer graphics is a branch of computer science that deals with the creation and manipulation of visual information on a computer system. It involves the creation of both 2-dimensional (2D) and 3-dimensional (3D) graphics. Graphics can be created on a computer system with the help of special graphics software, such as Macromedia Flash and Corel draw. Computer graphics involves the use of various techniques that are used develop a good quality image of an object. Computer graphics created on the computers can be used to represent surfaces of different shapes and represent the motion in bodies. The images created can also be edited using the same computer programs in which they were created.

The various application areas of computer graphics are:

- **Illustrations** Illustration is used to visually represent a subject or a particular situation in the form of line drawing or painting. There are several graphics software available that allow the users to create illustrations. The simplest of all these software is MS Paint that comes bundled in Microsoft operating systems as a utility software.
- **Designs** Computer-aided Design (CAD) and Computer-aided Modeling (CAM) have revolutionized the way engineering drawings are created these days. Special CAD / CAM software are available that provide a robust user-interface for creating engineering drawings. Some of these software also provide a simulated environment for the user to test their designs.
- **Simulations** Computer graphics are being increasingly used for education and training purposes where the trainees are taught using a simulated environment The simulated environment is rich with graphics and moving pictures that recreate a real-life situation in the best possible manner. One of most common examples of using simulation is a flight simulator, which aids the pilots in running an aircraft in a simulated environment.
- **Animations** Computer graphics are also used for creating animations and cartoon characters that are represented in the form of an animated picture.

B.2 DISPLAY DEVICES

Display device refers to an electronic device, which is used to display the videos and images created using computer programs. In a computer system, the most common display device is a computer monitor. The computer monitor has a specific size, which is determined according to the distance between the two opposite corners of the screen. A display device could be based on different hardware technologies like

Cathode Ray Tube (CRT), Storage tube, Liquid Crystal Display (LCD), Plasma display etc. Nowadays, two display devices, CRT monitor and LCD monitor are the most commonly used display devices.

B.2.1 CRT Monitor

The CRT monitor uses a vacuum tube that controls the movement of electrons in a low-pressure gas atmosphere, to amplify an electrical signal. The CRT mainly consists of a heater, a cathode, an accelerating anode and a focusing anode, which together form an electron gun. The electron gun is enclosed in an evacuated glass envelope. A fluorescent screen is placed in the front of the glass envelope. The cathode produces electrons, when heated by the heater. These electrons get accelerated by the accelerating anode and the focusing anode focuses them towards the screen. These electrons strike at the phosphor coated fluorescent screen, which gets illuminated and forms an image. Figure B.1 shows a CRT display.

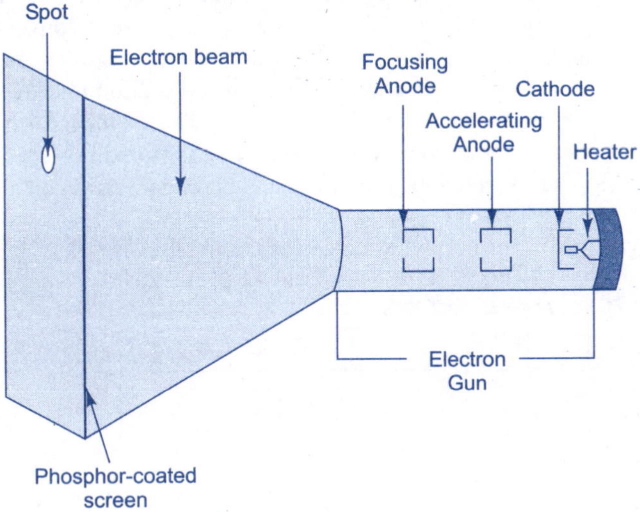

Fig. B.1 The CRT display

B.2.2 LCD Monitor

The LCD monitor uses an LCD device, a thin display device, in which the liquid crystals are placed between the two plates of a glass. The function of this device is to reduce the luminance of the pixels rather than generating it and hence, it consumes less power. The liquid crystals flow in different directions and have the ability to bend a beam of light. In an LCD device, a typical pixel comprises of a number of liquid crystals layered between two transparent electrodes and crossed polarising filters. As the light falls on the liquid crystals, they bend the light and direct them towards the polarising filter. The polarising filter absorbs the light and makes the polariser appear dark, which eventually results in the display of images. Figure B.2 shows an LCD monitor.

Fig. B.2 An LCD monitor

B.3 RASTER SCAN DISPLAY PROCESSING UNIT

In the raster scan display system, an image is displayed by the sweeping of an electron beam at a very fast speed. The electron beam sweeps line-by-line in a particular direction, i.e., from left towards the right of the screen. After reaching the right most position on the first line of the screen, the electron beam returns to the left most position of the next line. This process is again repeated until the electron beam reaches the bottom-right position of the screen. At the bottom-right position of the screen, the electron beam again shifts to the top-left position of the screen. The electron beam becomes blank at this shifting moment.

All the lines on which an electron beam moves are known as the scan lines. The quality of the image displayed on the raster scan device depends on the number of pixels contained in the image. Pixels refer to the smallest unit of an image that is formed by the intersection of the scan lines of the raster scan display device. The process of generating pixels of an image is known as the scan conversion. The number of pixels of an image is dependent on the number of scan lines of the device. A raster scan display device, which has medium-resolution power, contains 480 scan lines and a high-resolution display device contains 1000 scan lines. For displaying all the pixels on the screen, it is necessary to store the information of pixels, i.e., x and y coordinates of each pixel and its colour code. This information is stored in a special memory unit called the frame buffer. Figure B.3(a) and (b) show the scan lines and pixel generation on a raster scan display device.

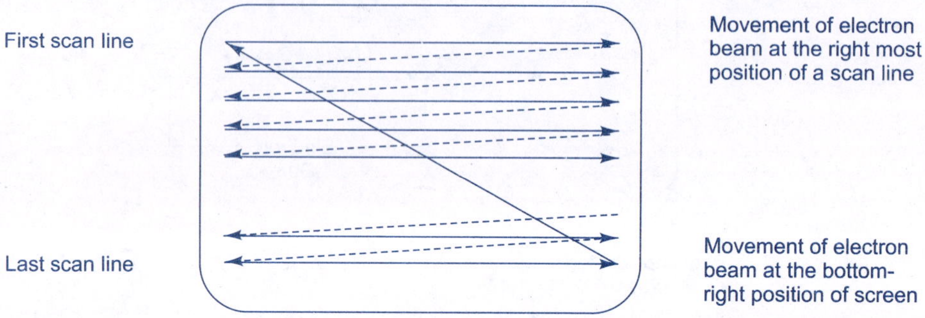

(a) Scan lines in the raster scan display

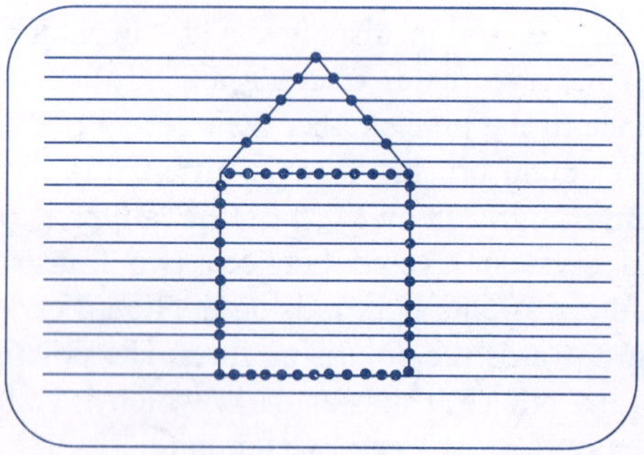

(b) Generation of pixels

Fig. B.3 Scan lines and pixel generation on a raster scan display device

B.4 INPUT DEVICES FOR INTERACTIVE GRAPHICS SYSTEMS

Input devices are used to provide data to the graphics system. Mouse, keyboard, joystick, trackball, etc. are the most commonly used input devices of a graphics system.

All the input devices used in the computer systems are categorised according to the logical functions performed by them. These devices are also known as the logical input devices. The reason behind calling them logical input devices is that the values provided by these input devices are logically generated by the corresponding device software. The various logical functions pertaining to the input devices of graphics system are:

- **Locator function** It provides the coordinate information such as X and Y coordinates of a point on the screen.
- **Pick function** It is used to pick or select an object on the screen.
- **Choice function** It is used to initiate a specific event by specifying a choice. Keyboard is an example of an input device performing choice function.

On the basis of above logical functions, all input devices used in the graphics system, are divided into the following categories:

- Locator
- Picker
- Keyboard

B.4.1 Locator

All the devices, which locate the position of a point, are known as locator devices. Digital tablet is an example of locator devices. A digital tablet consists of a plane surface and a stylus. The plane surface of the digital tablet ranges between 6 × 6 inches to 48 × 72 inches. This plane surface is made up of a grid of connected wires and small microphones and other equipment. Stylus is a small pen type device, which is used to point a position on the tablet. It includes a wire coil, which generates the electro-magnetic signals containing a sequence of electrical pulses. The quality of a locator device is measured according to the different features such as resolution, linearity and size of these devices. Figure B.4 shows a digital tablet containing a stylus.

Fig. B.4 A data tablet

Light pen and touch screen are other examples of the locator devices. A light pen is a pointing device, which includes a light detector at the end. It provides the facility of selecting objects displayed on the screen and drawing on the screen. Figure B.5 shows the image of a light pen.

A touchscreen is a display device, which enables us to interact with a computer system by touching its display screen. Nowadays, touchscreens are being used in multiple devices such as Personal Digital Assistant (PDA) and mobile phones. Figure B.6 shows a touchscreen.

Fig. B.5 A light pen

B.4.2 Picker

Fig. B.6 A touchscreen

All devices, which are used to select, move and drag an object displayed on the display device, are known as *picker devices*. Mouse is the most common example of the picker device. A mouse is a small device, which is used to move a pointer for selecting an item represented on the screen. The pointer enables the user to watch the mouse movement on the screen. A mouse is generally used to click on the elements of Graphical User Interfaces (GUIs) such as buttons, menus and tools. It consists of three components—a left button, a right button and a middle wheel. The left and right buttons are used to select the items on the screen while the wheel is used to scroll the pages displayed on the screen.

The mechanical mouse and the optical mouse are the most commonly used mouse devices. In the mechanical mouse, the pointer movement is done by a ball, which causes rotations in the two wheels attached to the inner part of the mouse. Wheels connected in the inner part of the mouse are used to generate the values of the x and y coordinates of the pointer. In the optical mouse, the movement of pointer is detected by the sensors, which detect the pointer movement by calculating changes in the frequency of light. Figure B.7 shows the different components of a mouse.

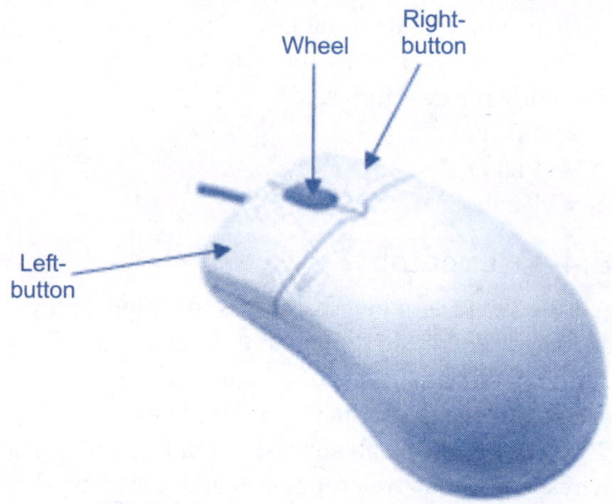

Fig. B.7 The components of a mouse device

Some other examples of picker devices are trackball and joystick. A trackball consists of a ball on the top of the device and the ball movement is used to move a pointer on the screen. When a user moves the ball, different sensors housed in the socket of the ball generate the values for the x and y coordinates. Figure B.8 shows a trackball.

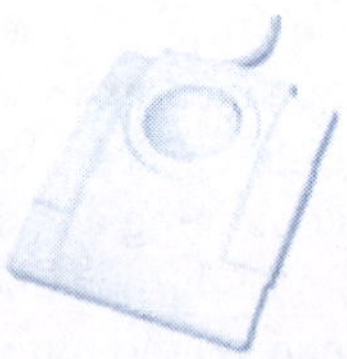

Fig. B.8 A trackball

A joystick is a small input device, which is generally used to move a graphical object in the video games. It consists of a stick, which is attached with a base and some buttons. A joystick can change the angle and direction of the object, which is controlled by it. It is also used in the virtual reality systems such as video games and simulator systems. Figure B.9 shows a joystick.

Fig. B.9 A joystick

B.4.3 Keyboard

Keyboard is the most common device, which is used to enter data into the computer system. It contains different alpha-numeric keys to enter alphabets and numeric data in the computer system. A keyboard provides the character code of a key pressed by the end user to the computer system. A keyboard also consists of the various function keys, which are used as a command interpreter for an operating system. These function keys are labelled with an alphabet 'F'. Figure B.10 shows a keyboard.

Fig. B.10 A keyboard

Some other devices such as joystick and trackball also consist of some function keys, which enable a user to perform specific functions.

B.5 IMAGE ACQUISITION AND STORAGE

Image is one of the most important components of the multimedia system. Obtaining an image in the storage medium is generally known as the image acquisition. A computer graphics system, which processes high-quality images, requires an appropriate technique to obtain image information on the memory unit. During the image acquisition, information related to the images should be obtained in such a manner that no information loss occurs. If the image is not properly acquired in the storage medium, then the user is not able to perform the desired operation on the image.

We can use two types of methods to acquire an image in a computer system, one is scanning of the hardcopy of an image and other one is capturing an image using digital camera.

B.5.1 Acquiring an Image Using Scanner

For scanning the hardcopy of an image, the user has to use a special input device, i.e., scanner. Whenever a user uses a scanner to scan a picture, information related to the picture is directly stored in the computer memory. In other words, scanner generates the binary information of images scanned by it. In order to understand the way in which a scanner generates the binary information of the acquired image, we must have knowledge about the various components, such as lens, mirrors and Charge Coupled Device (CCD) of a scanner. On the basis of tasks performed by these components, all components are grouped into the following units:

- ***Image scanning unit*** It consists of a light beam generator along with mirrors and lens. It is responsible to scan the picture, which is placed over a flat glass surface of the scanner.
- ***Light measuring unit*** It consists of the various CCDs, which are used to deduce the intensity of light reflected by the picture placed over the glass surface. On the basis of the deduced light intensity, the electrical output is generated.
- ***Bits generating unit*** It consists of an electronic circuit, which generates the digital signals or bits corresponding to the image information.

Process to scan an image The complete scanning process is performed in the following steps:

1. The light beam generator produces a thin beam of light, which covers the entire line of the picture placed on the glass surface. This thin beam is generally known as the scan line, which scans the entire picture from top to bottom. When the scan line passes through a character some light is reflected back to the CCDs, which produce electrical values according to the detected light. Intensity of light reflected back to CCDs are dependent on the colours of the characters printed on the picture.
2. CCDs store all the characters and blank spaces present on a line in the form of 0s and 1s. The value of reflected beam generated by CCDs is known as picture element or pixel. In the monochrome pictures, different shades of black and white, i.e., light grey and dark grey can be represented different binary values. Similarly, if a coloured picture is scanned by a scanner, a rotating disk consisting of three filters corresponding to Red, Green and Blue colour is used to detect the colour. According to the colour detected by the disk and the code intensity of reflected light, CCDs generates 24 bits; eight bits for each colour detected by the rotating disk.
3. The motor, which is responsible to move the light beam, determines the total number of scan lines required to scan the length of the complete page. In most of the scanners, length of page is just double of its width.

B.5.2 Image Acquisition with a Digital Camera

A user can also use a digital camera for image acquisition. A digital camera provides the digital form of the image captured by it. Some of the components such as lens and shutter of a digital camera are similar to the conventional camera in which images are captured on a photosensitive film. However, in a digital camera, image is captured by an array of CCDs, which are used to generate the voltage values corresponding to the intensity of light sensed by the CCDs.

Whenever the light is detected by the CCDs, a silicon chip measures the light intensity, which is used to generate the electric charges or voltage. The silicon chip consists of multiple light sensitive diodes. Light sensitive diode is a device, which generates the electrons while a brighter light is incident over it. The amount of electrons generated by these diodes is directly dependent on the brightness of light. The voltage generated by the CCDs is an analog type data which is then converted into the digital format using an Analog to Digital Converter (ADC). This digital format of voltage may provide the complete digital information of an image required by a computer system.

The digital camera image acquisition board helps capture a large image having high resolution at a high speed. A digital camera consists of the following units:

- **Imaging unit** It is responsible to generate images by capturing it with help of CCDs, lens and silicon chip.
- **Receiving unit** It is responsible for collecting the information generated by the CCDs and producing the digital form of an image.
- **Output unit** It is responsible for performing the last task related to the image, i.e., displaying the image or transferring information related to the image to an external device.

Note: *Digital camera also consists of an optical memory or flash memory, which is used to store images while. The storage format used to store images in this memory is JPEG, which is used to store compressed form of image.*

B.6 STORAGE FORMATS FOR PICTURES

A computer graphics system uses different types of storage formats for storing the image information on the storage medium. An image is a combination of a number of pixels, which are arranged in the form of rows and columns, i.e., in the form of a grid on the computer screen. Each pixel in an image has its own brightness, value and colour on which the image representation is dependent.

The size of an image file in which image information is stored depends on the number and colour depth of pixels. This means, if the resolution of an image is high, then the size of image file will be large. Resolution refers to the number of pixels used to display the image on the screen. It can also be affected by the file format used to store the image files. The different file formats help in performing the following activities:

- Generating copies of the stored images
- Providing small size of images in order to transfer over the Internet
- Representing the image with a high resolution

For storing large size images, it is necessary to compress the image and to reduce the size of the image file using compression algorithms. The compression algorithms can be of two types, lossless compression algorithm and lossy compression algorithm. The lossless compression algorithms allow the user to reduce the size of image file without affecting its quality. On the other hand, the lossy algorithm some what affects the visual quality of the image while reducing its size.

There are different types of storage formats, which are used to store the image file. The storage formats used to store image information are categorized on the basis of types of data stored in the image files, i.e., raster formats and vector formats.

B.6.1 Raster Format

In the raster format, the image information is stored in the form of bitmap or pixmap, which refers to a memory organisation used to store the image information. The various raster image formats are:

- **JPEG** JPEG stands for Joints Photographic Expert Group, which is a lossy file format. In the JPEG file format, 24 bits are used to support three colours; red, blue and green. This means 8-bits for each colour. This file format generally produces small size for stored images. The main disadvantage of using this file format is that if an image having the JPEG file format is repeatedly saved and edited, then the quality of the image will be degraded. The files, which use the JPEG format, are saved with the .JPEG extension. All the digital cameras can save an image in the JPEG format.
- **TIFF** TIFF stands for Tagged Image File Format. In this file format, 8 or 16 bits are used to store information related to each colour present in the image. This means, in the TIFF format, red, green and blue colours present in the image are stored as a set of two or three bytes. The image files, which use the TIFF format, are saved with the TIFF extension. The TIFF image file is compressed either with a lossless compression or a lossy compression algorithm. Whenever TIFF is used to save the black and white or gray images, it produces very good quality of the lossless compression. Some of the digital cameras having enhanced features help save an image with in the TIFF format.
- **RAW** It includes all file formats, which are used to store the complete information of an image but can not be directly used to produce images. These file formats are also known as the digital negatives. This file format stores the information, which is minimally processed by the image capturing devices such as digital camera and scanner. The image files stored in the RAW file format can be used by the

bitmap graphics editor, which allows a user to edit, modify or change the image. The files produced by the RAW file format consist of a smaller size than the files produced by the TIFF file format.

- **GIF** GIF stands for Graphics Interchange Format. The image files used in the production of animations and graphics are mostly saved in the GIF format. The GIF format does not support a large variety of colours, i.e., it can only provide 256 colours. It can be used as the lossless compression algorithm for storing those images in which a large area is covered with a single colour and no complex combination of colour is required to represent the image. The GIF format reduces the size of a file by minimising the number of bits required to represent colours in an image. In some cases, when a particular pattern is repeated, then the reduction in size of image is done by replacing repeated patterns with an abbreviation.
- **PNG** PNG stands for Portable Network Graphics, which is used as a lossless storage format. It is the successor of the GIF image format and helps in compressing the file size. The PNG file format supports the storage of true colour images. The PNG format is the most suitable file format for editing pictures and images. The PNG format also enables you to include partial transparency, which helps in fading and anti-aliasing of the image. The PNG format allows you to store a better quality of picture in a small storage area than a GIF format.

B.6.2 Vector Format

The vector storage format stores the geometrical description of images. This information is then rendered using different rendering mechanisms to display the images onto the screen. The various vector image formats are:

- **CGM** CGM stands for Computer Graphics Metafile. It is used to store different graphics objects having two dimensions and three dimensions. In this format, all the graphical objects are represented by different text codes. These text codes are converted into different files containing the binary information, i.e., binary files and other text files. The image file stored in this format can interchange information related to 2D objects without depending on any type of devices, files or software.
- **SVG** SVG stands for Scalable Vector Graphics. It provides a way to create and develop the scriptable and versatile vector format of the various graphical objects used in a web application.
- **SWF** SWF stands for ShockWave Flash and was introduced by Adobe. SWF is used to store information related to vector graphics components. The image files stored in the SWF format can also include information related to animated objects along with the graphical objects.

INDEX

Symbols

A

B

N

O

P

Q

R

S

T

U

V

W

X